THE SPANISH
SOCIALIST PARTY

THE
Spanish Socialist Party

A HISTORY OF FACTIONALISM

Richard Gillespie

CLARENDON PRESS · OXFORD
1989

Oxford University Press, Walton Street, Oxford OX2 6DP
Oxford New York Toronto
Delhi Bombay Calcutta Madras Karachi
Petaling Jaya Singapore Hong Kong Tokyo
Nairobi Dar es Salaam Cape Town
Melbourne Auckland
and associated companies in
Berlin Ibadan

Oxford is a trade mark of Oxford University Press

Published in the United States
by Oxford University Press, New York

British Library Cataloguing in Publication Data
Gillespie, Richard
The Spanish Socialist party: a history
of factionalism.
1. Spain. Political parties. Partido
Socialista Obrero Espanol, to 1986
I. Title
324.246'074
ISBN 0-19-822798-1

Library of Congress Cataloging in Publication Data
Gillespie, Richard, 1952–
The Spanish Socialist party: a history
of factionalism / Richard Gillespie.
Bibliography: p.   Includes index.
1. P.S.O.E. (Political party)—History.   2. Spain—Politics and
government—20th century.   3. Socialism—Spain—History—20th
century.   I. Title.
JN8395.S6G55   1988   324.246'074'09—dc19   88–6617
ISBN 0-19-822798-1

Set by Hope Services
Printed in Great Britain
at the University Printing House, Oxford
by David Stanford
Printer to the University

Preface

Since the 1930s Spain has attracted widespread international interest. Much of this has stemmed from the country's long experience of political polarization and the cultural richness generated by regional diversity. Considerable attention has focused upon the Socialist Party itself, not least because this century-old institution has defied so many of the norms associated with fraternal parties in Northern Europe. During the early decades of this century it embarked upon several revolutionary adventures, and again in the early 1970s it acquired a reputation for being on the far left of the international socialist movement. At other times the party has found itself at the centre of major attempts to develop liberal democracy in Spain. And yet, for all its moderation in the 1980s, today it exhibits some features that belong more to the populist than the social-democratic mould.

Historians have done a lot to elucidate the early life of the Spanish Socialist Workers' Party, the PSOE. Contributions from political scientists have been much more recent. When I began working on the PSOE some six years ago, the experience of the Socialists during the long winter of Francoism was largely uncharted. My main interest lay in the nature of the factionalism that has dominated the party's life at decisive moments in PSOE and Spanish history. However, this subject could only be researched adequately by examining the party more broadly and taking in its strategies, ideological positions, and alliance formulae. The result should thus serve as a general history of the PSOE since 1939 as well as a study in party factionalism, the latter undertaken in the belief that 'the vitality of a movement can be measured much more reliably by its schisms than by its united actions', to quote Michael Waller.

The early 1980s was the ideal time to research the preceding forty years of PSOE politics. By then much of the historical archive material pertaining to the Franco period had been concentrated in Madrid, and most of it was being made available to the public. Moreover, the return to Spain of many exiles in response to post-Franco liberalization provided a unique opportunity to interview some of the Socialists who had been involved in rebuilding the party in Spain and abroad after the Civil War, and who of course were in their final years.

Relatively little has been published on the post-1939 PSOE. This study therefore draws mainly upon primary sources, these including minutes of the meetings and congresses of the expatriate sector of the Socialist organizations, executive reports submitted to assemblies and congresses, correspondence between exiles and clandestine activists in Spain, circulars of the party in exile, a wide range of periodicals produced by Socialists in Spain and abroad, personal archive material provided by political activists, trial papers, short memoirs prepared by veterans for a history project undertaken by the PSOE, recorded interviews stored in research centres, and dozens of personal interviews, many of which were recorded. Of course interviews do not tell the whole story, even when the information imparted is validated by the documentary evidence. Many Socialists were told only what they needed to know about the clandestine organization, for fear of their being arrested and interrogated. And inevitably time plays tricks with human memory. Yet, used cautiously, the interviews cited here have been extremely valuable. Indeed, much of the history of the clandestine PSOE can only be reconstructed from such sources.

The PSOE of the Franco period presents a highly complex picture, one that would be seriously incomplete if one were to ignore the thousands of Socialists who found themselves scattered around the globe after the Civil War. Large concentrations of exiles existed in France, Mexico, and North Africa, and they were highly influential in shaping the party's anti-Franco strategy. Moreover it was the exiles who were in regular contact with the major socialist parties of Europe and who became the main vehicles for the importation of Northern European ways of conducting political and trade union activity. Specially in the case of the second generation of exiles, European experiences and contacts would be organizationally beneficial when the party finally recovered sufficiently to intervene influentially in the post-Franco transition in

Spain. Unfortunately, though they endured some of the adversity that led Socialists in Spain to sink their differences in the 1940s, the exiles proved totally incapable of unity. Early on, each *émigré* concentration developed its own distinct political activity, and even when geographical distances had been overcome each grouping remained riven by controversies surviving from the 1930s.

Even in the interior, Socialist reunification was not to last. Despite a determination there to set aside the factional disputes of the past, unity was undermined from the mid-1950s as challenges to the leadership were presented by Socialists seeking a 'renovation' or renewal of their party. This involved attempts by militants in Spain to regain the leadership of the Socialist movement after it had been assumed by Toulouse-based exiles in 1954. Simultaneously, a process of geographical differentiation affected the party in the interior. While in many parts of Spain the Socialists ceased to possess an organized presence, relatively healthy organizations were maintained in the north.

Finally, on top of all this it is necessary to look beyond the PSOE to a broader Socialist movement that includes a fraternal labour organization, the General Workers' Union (UGT), and the National Federation of Spanish Young Socialists (FNJSE). Since the relationships within this Socialist 'family' have traditionally been extremely close, it is not possible to study the PSOE in isolation.

Although a substantial part of the book is devoted to the Socialists' new role in post-Franco Spain, much coverage has been given to the Franco years. This is justified, in my view, both by the dearth of analytical literature on the PSOE under Franco and by the long-term significance of party developments during that period. For if it can be said that this study has an overriding single argument, it is that the persisting factionalism that hampered Socialist efforts to organize effective opposition to Franco also had a positive side. It was through their internal struggles that the Socialists eventually managed to revise and modernize their outlook and activities, thus enabling the party to play an important part in the processes of democratic transition and consolidation. Unlike its Iberian counterpart, the Spanish Socialist party was not born in Bonn on the eve of regime transformation: the modern PSOE is the product of internal struggles that date back at least to the 1950s (though evidently these have been informed by external influences).

I have started the book with a chapter on the party's development up to 1939. Drawing upon the pertinent literature on the early period, this is intended to provide some basic orientation concerning the traditional values and character of the Spanish Socialist movement. It will become evident that the Socialists who feature here have long, if not always reliable, political memories. I have made mention therefore of the main controversies of the early decades so that later factional rivalry may be comprehended in their light. The core of the book, however, spans the period 1939–82. Early chapters deal with the role of the exiles, the efforts to build and maintain the clandestine organization, and the battles over Socialist renewal. These are followed by a lengthy account of the PSOE's evolution in the 1970s and early 1980s. Finally I provide an overview of the first government headed by Felipe González (1982–6) and mention recent developments in the nature of party factionalism.

Because of the structural complexity of the Spanish Socialist movement, I have included in the appendices an organizational diagram illustrating the main PSOE sectors in 1939–72. Another organigram shows how the party was structured during the Franco period. Further appendices provide a list of the pseudonyms that researchers will encounter in the archive material; details of the various executive committees that existed in Franco's Spain up to 1954, as well the Spain-based component of subsequent executives; diagrams representing the PSOE's parliamentary standing since 1977; and data pertaining to the election performances of the PSOE and UGT over the last decade.

Various people and institutions made this work possible. The Spanish Socialists who kindly allowed me to interview them are too numerous to mention individually here, but their contribution was a major one. Several of them permitted me to return for a second or third interview following further work in the archives. It was through the interviews that I eventually was able to discover the identities behind at least the most important of the *noms de guerre* of the clandestine period. Particularly helpful here were Ramón Rubial, Avelino Pérez, Miguel Peydro, and Manuel Garnacho. Valuable information of this kind also came from correspondence with José Martínez Cobo, Juan Zarrías, and José Martínez de Velasco. I would also like to thank Gabriela Rodríguez and Araceli Herrero for helping me to obtain and arrange some of the interviews. A number of the interviewees subsequently provided me with material from their own personal archives. Here I am indebted to Juan Manuel Kindelán, Manuel Zaguirre, Francisco Bustelo, Eugenio Royo, Manuel Turrión, Alonso Puerta, Francisco Jiménez, and Luis Osorio.

For financial assistance, which enabled me to spend a total of more than two years researching in Spain, I wish to thank St John's College, Oxford, where for four years I held a Junior Research Fellowship in Politics; the University of Newcastle upon Tyne, where most of the book was written following my appointment to a Sir James Knott Research Fellowship; and the former Social Science Research Council, now the Economic and Social Research Council. In the early phase, George Cheyne helped me on my way by generously lending me his large collection of *El Socialista* covering most of the 1960s and 1970s. I wish also to record my appreciation of the encouragement, help, and guidance provided by the staff at the Fundación Pablo Iglesias in Madrid. My various research visits to Spain would have been far less productive had it not been for the advice offered by those in charge of the foundation's library and archives, Aurelio Martín Najera and Antonio González Quintana. Finally, I am grateful to copy-editor David Edmonds for his useful advice and assistance, especially over the references and bibliography.

R.H.C.G.

Warwick
December 1987

Contents

Abbreviations

CC	Comité Central
CD	Comité Director
CE	Comisión Ejecutiva
CEF	Comisión Ejecutiva Federal
CG	Consejo General
CIS	Centro de Investigaciones Sociológicas, Madrid
CN	Comité Nacional
CSA	Comisión Socialista Asturiana
ES	*El Socialista*
FLC	Fundación Largo Caballero, Madrid
FOESSA	Fomento de Estudios Sociales y de Sociología Aplicada, Madrid
FPI	Fundación Pablo Iglesias, Madrid
FSA	Federación Socialista Asturiana
OIDE	Oficina de Información, Documentación y Estudios (PSOE *émigré* service, based in France)
SOMA	Sindicato Minero Asturiano

Note. CE refers to the executive committee of an organization. CD, CG, and CN refer to committees elected by the organizations to supervise the work of these executives between congresses of the organization.

II. ORGANIZATIONS, AGREEMENTS, AND LAWS

i. *Spanish Organizations*

ACR	*Acción Catalana Republicana* (Catalan Republican Action)
ADE	*Alianza Democrática Española* (Spanish Democratic Alliance)
ANFD	*Alianza Nacional de Fuerzas Democráticas* (National Alliance of Democratic Forces)

ANV   *Acción Nacionalista Vasca* (Basque Nationalist Action)

AP   *Alianza Popular* (Popular Alliance)

ASD   *Alianza Social Democrática* (Social Democratic Alliance)

ASE   *Alianza Sindical Española* (Spanish Trade Union Alliance)

ASM   *Agrupación Socialista Madrileña* (Madrid Socialist organization, from 1977 the FSM)

ASO   *Alianza Sindical Obrera* (Workers' Trade Union Alliance)

ASU   *Agrupación Socialista Universitaria* (University Socialist organization)

CCJV   *Círculo Cultural Jaime Vera* (Jaime Vera Cultural Circle)

CCOO   *Comisiones Obreras* (Workers' Commissions)

CCPI   *Círculo Cultural Pablo Iglesias* (Pablo Iglesias Cultural Circle)

CEDA   *Confederación Española de Derechas Autónomas* (Spanish Confederation of Autonomous Rightist Groups)

CEOE   *Confederación Española de Organizaciones Empresariales* (Spanish Confederation of Employers' Organizations)

CIC   *Comité Interior de Coordinación* (Co-ordinating Committee of the Interior)

CNS   *Confederación Nacional de Sindicatos* (National Confederation of Syndicates)

CNT   *Confederación Nacional del Trabajo* (National Labour Confederation)

COS   *Coordinadora de Organizaciones Sindicales* (Co-ordinator of Trade Union Organizations)

CSI   *Conferencia Socialista Ibérica* (Iberian Socialist Conference)

CUD   *canditaturas unitarias y democráticas* (unitarian and democratic election lists)

ERC   *Esquerra Republicana de Catalunya* (Republican Left of Catalonia)

ETA   *Euskadi ta Askatasuna* (Basque Homeland and Liberty)

FELN   *Frente Español de Liberación Nacional* (Spanish National Liberation Front)

FID   *Federación Independiente Demócrata* (Independent Democratic Federation

FLP   *Frente de Liberación Popular* (Popular Liberation Front)

FNJSE   *Federación Nacional de Juventudes Socialistas de España* (National Federation of Spanish Young Socialists)

FNTT   *Federación Nacional de Trabajadores de la Tierra* (National Federation of Landworkers)

FOC   *Front Obrer Català* (Catalan Workers' Front)

FPS   *Federación de Partidos Socialistas* (Federation of Socialist Parties)

FRAP   *Frente Revolucionario Antifascista y Patriótico* (Revolutionary Anti-fascist and Patriotic Front)

FSA   *Federación Socialista Asturiana* (Asturian Socialist Federation)

FSC   *Federación Socialista de Cataluña, Federació Socialista de Catalunya* (Socialist Federation of Catalonia)

FSM   *Federación Socialista Madrileña* (Madrid Socialist Federation)

FST   *Federación Sindical de Trabajadores* (Workers' Trade Union Federation)

FUDE   *Federación Universitaria Democrática Española* (Spanish Democratic University Federation)

GAL   *Grupos Antiterroristas de Liberación* (Antiterrorist Liberation Groups)

HOAC   *Hermandad Obrera de Acción Católica* (Workers' Brotherhood of Catholic Action)

IDC   *Izquierda Demócrata Cristiana* (Christian Democratic Left)

IR   *Izquierda Republicana* (Republican Left)

JARE   *Junta de Auxilio a los Refugiados Españoles* (Council for the Aid of Spanish Refugees)

JEL   *Junta Española de Liberación* (Spanish Liberation Council)

JJSS   *Juventudes Socialistas* (Young Socialists)

JOC   *Juventud Obrera Católica* (Catholic Working Youth)

JSE   *Juventudes Socialistas de España* (Spanish Young Socialists)

JSM   *Juventudes Socialistas Madrileñas* (Madrid Young Socialists)

JSU   *Juventudes Socialistas Unificadas* (Unified Young Socialists)

JSUN   *Junta Suprema de Unión Nacional* (Supreme Council of National Union)

LCR   *Liga Comunista Revolucionaria* (Revolutionary Communist League)

MLE   *Movimiento Libertario Español* (Spanish Libertarian Movement)

MSC   *Moviment Socialista de Catalunya* (Socialist Movement of Catalonia)

NGI   *Nueva Generación Ibérica* (New Iberian Generation)

PASOC   *Partido Acción Socialista* (Socialist Action Party)

PCE   *Partido Comunista de España* (Spanish Communist Party)

PDP   *Partido Demócrata Popular* (Popular Democratic Party)

PNN   *profesores no numerarios* (untenured university teachers)

PNV   *Partido Nacionalista Vasco* (Basque Nationalist Party)

POSI   *Partido Obrero Socialista Internacionalista* (Internationalist Socialist Workers' Party)

POUM   *Partido Obrero de Unificación Marxista* (Workers' Party of Marxist Unification)

PRF   *Partido Republicano Federal* (Federal Republican Party)

PS   *Partido Socialista* (Socialist Party)

PSA   *Partido Socialista de Andalucía* (Socialist Party of Andalucía)

PSC   *Partit Socialista de Catalunya*, *Partit dels Socialistes de Catalunya* (Socialist Party of Catalonia, Party of the Socialists of Catalonia)

PSDE	*Partido Social Democrático Español* (Spanish Social Democratic Party)
PSG	*Partido Socialista Gallego* (Galician Socialist Party)
PSI	*Partido Socialista en el Interior* (Socialist Party in the Interior)
PSOE	*Partido Socialista Obrero Español* (Spanish Socialist Workers' Party)
PSOE(H)	*Partido Socialista Obrero Español* (*sector histórico*) Spanish Socialist Workers' Party (historical sector)
PSOE(R)	*Partido Socialista Obrero Español* (*sector renovado*) Spanish Socialist Workers' Party (renovated sector)
PSP	*Partido Socialista Popular* (Popular Socialist Party)
PSPV	*Partit Socialista del País Valencià* (Socialist Party of the Valencian Country)
PSUC	*Partit Socialista Unificat de Catalunya* (Unified Socialist Party of Catalonia)
RS	*Reconstrucción Socialista* (Socialist Reconstruction)
RSD	*Reforma Social Democrática* (Social Democratic Reform)
SERE	*Servicio de Emigración para Republicanos Españoles* (Evacuation Service for Spanish Republicans)
SEU	*Sindicato Español Universitario* (Spanish University Syndicate)
SOCC	*Solidaritat d'Obrers Catalans Cristians* (Catalan Christian Workers' Solidarity)
SODC	*Secretariado de Ordenación Democrática de Cataluña* (Secretariat for the Democratic Organization of Catalonia)
SOMA	*Sindicato Minero Asturiano* (Asturian Mineworkers' Union)
STV	*Solidaridad de Trabajadores Vascos* (Basque Workers' Solidarity)
UCD	*Unión del Centro Democrático* (Democratic Centre Union)

UDE	*Unión Democrática Española* (Spanish Democratic Union)
UFD	*Unión de Fuerzas Democráticas* (Union of Democratic Forces)
UGT	*Unión General de Trabajadores* (General Workers' Union)
UNE	*Unión Nacional Española* (Spanish National Union)
UR	*Unión Republicana* (Republican Union)
USC	*Unión Socialista de Catalunya* (Socialist Union of Catalonia)
USE	*Unión Socialista Española* (Spanish Socialist Union)
USO	*Unión Sindical Obrera* (Workers' Trade Union)

ii *Spanish Agreements and Laws*

AES	*Acuerdo Económico y Social* (Social and Economic Agreement)
AMI	*Acuerdo-Marco Interconfederal* (agreement between employers' and employees' confederations on framework for collective bargaining)
ANE	*Acuerdo Nacional Sobre el Empleo* (National Employment Agreement)
LOAPA	*Ley Orgánica de Armonización del Proceso Autonómico* (Organic Law to Harmonize the Devolution Process)

iii *Non-Spanish Organizations*

AD	*Acción Democrática* (Democratic Action, Venezuela)
AFL	American Federation of Labor (USA)
CERES	*Centre d'étude, de recherche, et d'éducation socialistes* (Centre of Socialist Studies, Research, and Education, France)
CFDT	*Confédération française démocratique du travail* (French Democratic Labour Confederation)
CGT	*Confédération générale du travail* (General Labour Confederation, France)

COMISCO Spanish acronym for the International Socialist Committee for Conferences of the late 1940s
CIA Central Intelligence Agency (USA)
CIO Congress of Industrial Organizations (USA)
CISL *Confederazione Italiana Syndicati Lavoratori* (Italian Labour Unions' Confederation)
CTAL *Confederación de Trabajadores de América Latina* (Latin American Workers' Confederation)
CTM *Confederación de Trabajadores de México* (Mexican Workers' Confederation)
CUT *Central Unica de Trabajadores* (United Workers' Confederation, Chile)
DGB *Deutscher Gewerkschaftsbund* (German Trade Union Federation, Federal Republic of Germany)
EC European Community
FIOM Spanish acronym for the International Metalworkers' Federation
ICFTU International Confederation of Free Trade Unions
IG Metall *Industrie Gewerkschaft Metall* (West German metalworkers' union)
ITF International Transport Workers' Federation
IUSY International Union of Socialist Youth
IWA International Workingmen's Association
LPYS Labour Party Young Socialists (Great Britain)
MAPAI Israeli Labour Party
NATO North Atlantic Treaty Organization
OCI *Organization communiste internationaliste* (Internationalist Communist Organization, France)
OECD Organization for Economic Co-operation and Development
OTAN Spanish acronym for NATO
PASOK Panhellenic Socialist Movement (Greece)
PFLP Popular Front for the Liberation of Palestine
PRI *Partido Revolucionario Institucional* (Institutional Revolutionary Party, Mexico)
PSF *Parti socialiste français* (French Socialist Party)
SFIO *Section Française de l'Internationale ouvrière* (French Section of the Workers' International)

SPD	*Sozialdemokratische Partei Deutschlands* (Social Democratic Party of Germany, Federal Republic of Germany)
UN	United Nations
WFTU	World Federation of Trade Unions

Notes on Conventions

I. The full titles of official documents of the Socialist Party (PSOE), Socialist labour organization (UGT), and Socialist youth organization (FNJSE) tend to be verbose. For reasons of economy, many of these are shortened in the footnotes. The following Spanish words appear regularly:

Actas	minutes of meetings, assemblies, or congresses
Memoria	report presented by the executive at assemblies and congresses
Circulares	circulars sent by executive committees to members of their organization

To find *actas* and *memorias* in section II of the Bibliography look under the name of the organization in the subsection dealing with the appropriate event. These subsections are headed 'Assemblies and National Meetings', 'Congresses', and (for executive committee minutes) 'Executive Committee'. *Circulares* are to be found under the relevant organization's subsection headed 'Executive Committee'.

II. *El Socialista* is a title that has been used by dozens of socialist periodicals, and *Adelante* by at least two. In preparing this book, the *El Socialista* that was published in Algiers in 1944–7 has not been consulted but papers of the same name produced in Mexico, France, and Spain have. Here the Toulouse-based *El Socialista* produced in 1944–61 by the mainstream PSOE exiles (General Secretary Rodolfo Llopis) is abbreviated simply to *ES*, as are the later versions of the paper that were partly (and later completely) produced in Spain from 1970. Other Toulouse versions are cited similarly as *ES* but with some qualification in parenthesis. Thus the paper produced in France by the Socialist group led by Julia Alvarez is referred to as *ES* (ed. J. Alvarez) and that brought out in 1942–53 by the sector headed by Ramón Lamoneda is cited as *ES* (Mexico). The paper produced by the PSOE (*sector histórico*) is referred to as *ES(H)*.

III. Capitalization for political forces is used to refer just to members of political parties. The Socialists, Communists, and Republicans are members of the PSOE, PCE, and Republican parties. Lower case is used for socialists, communists, and republicans in general.

IV. For the period starting in 1954 the Toulouse-based Socialist organizations are referred to simply as PSOE, UGT, and FNJSE, and not as PSOE in Exile, etc., for in that year the Toulouse-based executives became the leadership for Socialists in Spain too. Congresses held abroad between 1955–75 were styled 'Nth congress held in exile' rather than 'PSOE/UGT/FNJSE in Exile, Nth Congress'.

V. For references to the youth organization of the PSOE I use in the text the fullest abbreviation, FNJSE. The same organization is also known as the FJS, FNJS, JSE, and JJSS.

VI. In the case of Spanish organizations, my general policy has been to use anglicized names and Spanish initials to refer to the main associations whose initials are relatively well known (e.g., the General Workers' Union, UGT); and to use the Spanish name for more obscure organizations not generally known by their initials, or whose names defy precise translation. The initials may be used to obtain Spanish names from the list of abbreviations.

VII. Where necessary to avoid possible confusion, I also use the Spanish names of party committees, such as the Comité Nacional and Comité Director.

VIII. Since political tendencies in Spain are often named after their leaders, I keep to the Spanish names here. The followers of Pablo Iglesias are *pablistas*, supporters of *pablismo*. The names of tendencies appear initially in italic and subsequently in roman print with their first letter capitalized.

IX. All items of the Antonio Amat ('Guridi') correspondence, except when otherwise indicated in the footnote citation, are to be found at PSOE, Correspondence, 'Guridi' file. Similarly, items cited as 'SOMA Archive' will be found listed at UGT, Territorial Organizations.

Spain: regions, provinces, and main cities

1
The Early Years
(1879–1939)

SPANISH Socialism developed under the influence of ideas and practices emanating from the more industrial parts of Europe. In the nineteenth century it was marked most clearly by French influence, both 'Utopian' and 'scientific'. Early in the twentieth century, German Social Democratic ideas also entered the country, though somewhat more surreptitiously, passing first through France before crossing the Pyrenees. The endogenous features of Spanish Socialism did not appear in the realm of ideology and no Spanish Socialist was ever to exert a lasting ideological influence upon the socialist movement outside Spain. Indeed, one of the most powerful socialist intellects, Luis Araquistain, acknowledged the lack of a Spanish theoretical contribution to socialism.[1] Nevertheless, Spanish Socialism did eventually acquire a distinct character of its own. The external influences declined in importance as the Spanish Socialist Workers' Party (PSOE) adapted to the specific circumstances in which it had to operate. Gradually realizing that the establishment of socialism could not be left to the labours of inexorable historical forces, the PSOE became more pragmatic and less dogmatic.

The party that was to play a central role in the political life of the Second Republic of 1931–6, and again in the post-Franco transition from authoritarianism to democracy, was founded more than a century ago. A group of Madrid workers took the initiative in 1879, and nine years later delegates to a national congress established the party more formally. Its immediate antecedents lay in a tiny nucleus within the

---

[1] Luis Araquistain, *El pensamiento español contemporáneo* (Buenos Aires: Losada, 1962), 95–6. The theoretical poverty of the PSOE also has been underlined by Santos Juliá, 'El socialismo español en busca de su historia', *El País* (Madrid), 5 Dec. 1982; and by F. Páez-Camino Arias, 'Tradición y mitos en el socialismo español', *Leviatán* (Madrid), 5 (1981), 73–82.

Spanish section of the International Workingmen's Association (IWA, or First International) that had defended several of Marx's main tenets against his Bakuninist rivals during the early 1870s. Beyond this nucleus only a Utopian socialist tradition had existed, exerting an influence from at least 1835.[2] Étienne Cabet's Icarian communism had found adherents in Catalonia; Charles Fourier's phalansterian Utopia had been embraced by Joaquín de Abreu (1782–1851) and his Cádiz group, before being carried to Madrid with scant success by Fernando Garrido; and Proudhon's federalism was being echoed by the Federal Republicans of Francisco Pi y Margall (briefly President in 1873). After early expeditions to the Americas to found Utopian communities, several of the Utopians had collaborated with liberal, democratic, and progressive forces in Spain, their propaganda blended with that of other republican elements. They were middle-class men whose values were essentially liberal and whose 'socialism' generally could be reduced to advocacy of a republic with a social conscience.[3]

Utopian ideas made little headway among Spain's labouring population, in part because their dissemination was restricted mainly to the relatively brief periods of liberal revolution and political relaxation that existed when *progresistas* rather than *moderados* were in office. Of these two wings of nineteenth-century Spanish liberalism, the radical Progressives differed from the conservative, more oligarchic Moderates through their espousal of popular sovereignty.[4] Although the Progressives never managed to become really dominant, their occasional tenure of office allowed the Utopians' ideas eventually to acquire a certain currency among the men of the International in Spain, and these ideas found some expression in the

[2] One writer has argued that the 17th-cent. Mateo López Bravo was in some respects a Utopian socialist *avant la lettre*. See Henry Mechoulan, *Mateo López Bravo: Un socialista español del siglo XVII* (Madrid: Editora Nacional, 1977).

[3] On the Utopians, see Jordi Maluquer de Motes, *El socialismo en España 1833–1868* (Barcelona: Grijalbo, 1977); Eliseo Aja, *Democracia y socialismo en el siglo XIX español: El pensamiento político de Fernando Garrido* (Madrid: Cuadernos para el Diálogo, 1976); Antonio Elorza (ed.), *Socialismo utópico español: Introducción y antología* (Madrid: Alianza, 1970); Clara E. Lida, *Antecedentes y desarrollo del movimiento obrero español (1835–1888)* (Madrid: Siglo XXI, 1973).

[4] Raymond Carr, *Spain 1808–1975* (Oxford: Clarendon Press, 1982), ch. 5.

programme adopted by the PSOE at its first congress in 1888.[5]

Both the followers of Pi y Margall and the Fourierists were active in the 'Glorious Revolution' against Isabella II in 1868, the last of the liberal revolutions that brought Progressives to power. Subsequently these Utopians concentrated their efforts on the establishment of a federal republic (achieved nominally in 1873) and rejected extremist calls for a 'second revolution'. This moderation on the part of the Federal Republicans led many of their erstwhile followers and allies from the working class to turn to the International, which had reached Spain somewhat belatedly in the wake of the revolution.[6]

The Spanish section of the IWA[7] was dominated from the start by Bakunin, whose emissary Giuseppi Fanelli reached Spain more than two years before a more representative delegate arrived. In 1869 Fanelli established crucial contacts in Barcelona and Madrid. Apparently unwittingly, he distributed to them indiscriminately texts of the International and of the Bakuninist Alliance for Socialist Democracy. The recipients of the new ideas appear not to have detected Bakunin's subterfuge until the Cuban-born Paul Lafargue, Marx's son-in-law, arrived in Madrid in December 1981, having fled the repression that befell the Paris Commune. Fanelli's recruitment of Rafael Farga Pellicer, leader of the 7,000-strong Centro Federal de Sociedades Obreras, gave the Bakuninists a head start over the *karlistas* or *autoritarios* (as Marx's followers were called) in Spain's key nascent industrial region of Barcelona. Yet one cannot accept the view of the early PSOE printer and historian Juan José Morato, who suggested that the outcome would have been substantially different had Marx moved first to exploit the political

[5] Manuel Tuñón de Lara, *El movimiento obrero en la historia de España*, 3 vols. (Madrid and Barcelona: Taurus-Laia, 1977), i, 289; Michel Ralle, 'Acción y utopía en la Primera Internacional española', *Estudios de Historia Social* (Madrid), 8–9 (1979), 75–87; Elorza, 'Los primeros programas del PSOE (1879–1888)', ibid. 143–77.

[6] Maluquer de Motes, 307–9.

[7] On the IWA in Spain see Ralle, 'Acción'; Juan Gómez Casas, *La Primera Internacional en España* (Bilbao: Zero, 1974); Lida *passim*; Rafael Flaquer Montequi, *La clase obrera madrileña y la Primera Internacional (1868–1874)* (Madrid: Cuadernos para el Diálogo, 1977); Anselmo Lorenzo, *El proletariado militante*, 2 vols., 1901, 1923 (Madrid: Alianza, 1974).

opportunity afforded by the 1868 revolution.[8] The success of Bakunin's Alliance was founded also upon the prior penetration in Madrid and Barcelona of the ideas of Fourier and Proudhon, upon the attractiveness of its rhetoric about freedom and equality, with which workers associated with earlier radical republican circles could identify, upon the small-scale nature of production in Barcelona, with which anarchism has been associated historically, and on the strength of anti-political sentiment among workers who were disappointed by the meagre achievements of the revolution and of the First Republic in 1873.[9]

It required the presence of Lafargue in Madrid in 1871–2 for the international polemic between Marx and Bakunin to divide the Spanish section. Under Lafargue's influence and as a result of his communications with the General Council of the International in London, a tiny group was established in the Spanish capital. Later it would be recognized as the first Marxist group to have been organized in the country.[10] It was based upon *La Emancipación*, a Madrid organ of the International that appeared in June 1871 and gradually came to defend an orthodox IWA line of advocating the creation of a working-class party and the conquest of political power by the workers—ideas that to Bakuninist ears suggested authoritarian designs. Editor José Mesa, a printer and former federal republican, became the group's prime mover before having to move to Paris for reasons of employment in the autumn of 1874. Several members of the group, including Mesa and Pablo Iglesias, had served briefly as executive members of the anarchist-dominated Spanish section of the IWA in 1871–2. The fundamental differences only crystallized in June 1872 when Mesa's paper denounced the continuing existence of Bakunin's Alliance despite the latter's

---

[8] Juan José Morato, *El Partido Socialista Obrero*, 1918 (Madrid: Ayuso, 1976), 46.

[9] Jacques Maurice, 'Sobre la penetración del marxismo en España', *Estudios de Historia Social*, 8–9 (1979), 73; Ralle *passim*. Prior to the definitive ban on the International by the restorationist regime early in 1874 Congress had in Nov. 1871 banned the IWA on the grounds of extremism.

[10] On this first Marxist group see Víctor M. Arbeloa (ed.), *Orígenes del Partido Socialista Obrero Español 1873–1880* (Madrid: Zero, 1972); Ralle, '"La Emancipación" y el primer grupo "marxista" español: Rupturas y permanencias', *Estudios de Historia Social*, 8–9 (1979), 93–128.

pledges to disband when it was granted entry into the International in July 1869. When they published the names of Alliance members the nine Marxists were expelled by the Bakuninists, and on 8 July 1872 they established the New Madrid Federation. It was recognized immediately by the General Council in London. By the time the Madrid group set up a rival Federal Council for Spain in January 1873, the Bakuninists had been expelled from the International, leaving the IWA irreparably divided both in Spain and elsewhere.

Neither faction was enthusiastic about the short-lived First Republic set up in February 1873. Carlist revolt in the north killed workers' hopes of seeing the army disbanded and military service ended. Before long the Internationalists were dismissing the regime as a last bulwark of the bourgeoisie against social revolution.[11] Yet both IWA factions were distinctly minority expressions of the working population. Well before General Pavía put an end to the Republic at the end of the year and before the Serrano government's effective ban on the IWA the following January, the 'first Marxist group' already showed signs of the demise it was to suffer in 1874. The New Madrid Federation only held one congress, in May 1873 at Toledo, and just five branches were represented at it. *La Emancipación* collapsed the following month, lacking funds and readers.

What provided the handful of socialists with a minimum of organic coherence over the next few years was the Madrid printers' association, the Asociación del Arte de Imprimir. Composed of 'the best elements among the Madrid printers who occupied the senior positions and were relatively well placed', it was to be 'the cradle' of the PSOE.[12] Founded in November 1871 as little more than a print co-operative, *el Arte*, presided over by Iglesias from May 1874, was transformed into an organization capable of leading strikes, though this resulted in some resignations. It was men from the

---

[11] Gerald Brenan, *The Spanish Labyrinth* (Cambridge: Cambridge University Press, 1943), 151; Miguel Artola, *Partidos y programas políticos 1808–1936*, 2 vols. (Madrid: Aguilar, 1974), i. 320–1; Flaquer Montequi, 129–33; Arbeloa, *Orígenes*, 29–30; C. A. M. Hennessy, *The Federal Republic in Spain* (Oxford: Clarendon Press, 1962).

[12] Morato, *El Partido*, 74; Arbeloa, *Orígenes*, 58.

association who dominated the New Madrid Federation, provided 16 out of the 25 PSOE founders in 1879, staffed the first two national committees of the party, and filled at least three executive positions throughout the period 1879–1925.[13] Moreover, the printers' union became a model for socialist labour organization in Spain and produced some of its most effective early organizers, especially Antonio García Quejido. It represented the labour aristocracy of Madrid, yet one that always had been in the forefront of working-class radicalism.

After the departure of Mesa it was the young printer Pablo Iglesias, a Galician whose childhood had been impoverished and unhappy,[14] who led the small circle of socialists who met informally in Madrid cafés to discuss political matters. Eventually, in 1879 they decided to form a party. The nine Marxists of 1872 had acquired few recruits by this time, but (with one exception) they now possessed the doctrinal commitment and dedication needed to set about the formation of a workers' party. They laid the foundations on 2 May as Madrid celebrated the seventy-first anniversary of its popular uprising against Napoleon.

FROM GUESDISM TO GRADUALISM

During the early decades of its life the PSOE earned itself a reputation for doctrinal intransigence and sectarianism which it was slow to lose in the twentieth century. It fashioned itself in this image in the belief that it was following Marxist prescriptions, though undoubtedly it was responding to domestic circumstances too. The early attitudes and policies of the party therefore must be understood in terms of its understanding of Marxism and the practical problems faced by a group that was seeking to establish and build a workers'

---

[13] Morato, *La cuna de un gigante: Historia de la Asociación General del Arte de Imprimir* (Madrid: José Molina, 1925), 111.

[14] For biographies of Iglesias see Julián Zugazagoitia, *Pablo Iglesias: Una vida heróica*, 1925 (Madrid: Akal, 1976); Morato, *Pablo Iglesias, educador de muchedumbres*, 1931 (Barcelona: Ariel, 1977); Círculo de Amigos de la Historia, *Pablo Iglesias* (Geneva: Editions Ferni, 1976). Biographical sketches of many early Socialists are to be found in Morato, *Líderes del movimiento obrero español 1868–1921* (Madrid: Cuadernos para el Diálogo, 1972).

party in a country where the working class was in its infancy—
still vulnerable, as the Socialists saw it, to ideological
contamination by the Republican parties and bourgeois
society.

For the first hundred years of their history, the Spanish
Socialists were proud of their Marxist tradition. Early on,
when progress was slow and painstaking, it offered them
reassurance and historical sanction. In the 1930s, as they
became a mass party, it offered inspiration when disenchant-
ment with the meagre social achievements of the Second
Republic gave fresh impetus to radicalism. And it continued
to be invoked during the years of political exclusion and
repression that followed under Franco. The appeal of Marxism
in the PSOE was stronger and proved more durable than in
most of its fellow parties of the Second International. This
was hardly surprising, given the Spanish party's political
weakness over long periods of time and the fact that, with
regional variations, capitalism did not inspire widespread
confidence in its capacity to develop Spain until the 1960s.
Apart from two short periods, the PSOE lacked governmental
responsibilities and even the likelihood of office. There was
little inducement therefore to abandon doctrinal positions and
to accept the pragmatic compromises made by power seekers
and holders elsewhere, though there was a growing readiness
to ally tactically with other forces excluded from the political
system.

The early PSOE's acquaintance with Marxism was distinctly
limited and in certain respects the pioneers were guilty of
unwitting misrepresentation. While certain basic Marxist
ideas owe their initial circulation in Spain to the party,
the PSOE's ideological contribution was highly derivative.
Following Paul Lafargue's brief stay in Madrid in 1871–2, the
main supplier of Marxist literature during the PSOE's
formative years was José Mesa.[15] Working in Paris from 1874,
he befriended Jules Guesde and became an editor of his
L'Égalité, a paper that Iglesias received regularly. The PSOE
paper *El Socialista*, launched in 1886, was so meticulously

---

[15] On Mesa see Jean-Louis Guereña, 'Contribución a la biografía de José Mesa: De
"La Emancipación" a "L'Égalité" (1873–1877)', *Estudios de Historia Social*, 8–9
(1979), 129–41; Morato, *Líderes*, 107–22.

imitative of the French paper's successor, *Le Socialiste*, that the Spaniards even tried to use the same fount for headlines. The key doctrinal texts of the PSOE founders came from the pens of Guesde, his colleague Gabriel Deville, and Lafargue; Marx and Engels' famous Manifesto certainly accompanied them, but few Spanish Socialists mastered *Das Kapital* and several major works by Marx were completely unknown to them.[16]

Guesde's publications themselves were based on a partial knowledge of Marxism.[17] In place of Marx's wage theory, he subscribed to Lassalle's 'iron law of wages' (known curiously in Spain as the 'bronze law'), which Marx had attacked in the 'Critique of the Gotha Programme'.[18] The iron law was an assertion that the average wage would be held down at a level barely sufficient to permit the working class to subsist and reproduce. Meaningful trade union gains and social reforms therefore were deemed impossible under capitalism. Indeed, it was thought that the system in the long term condemned workers to increased impoverishment, and that this would drive them necessarily, in resisting economic exploitation, to the creation of a political party and a revolutionary overthrow of the system. Other hallmarks of Guesdism were a reduction of the notion of class struggle to a dichotomic bourgeois-proletarian conflict, a Manichaean presentation of this contest, fierce revolutionary rhetoric, and more than a touch of millenarian promise. In sum, a simplistic and schematic version of Marxism that incorporated a number of pre-Marxist ideas and was weak on dialectics.[19]

[16] Morato, *El Partido*, 78; Pedro Ribas, *La introducción del marxismo en España (1869–1939): Ensayo bibliográfico* (Madrid: De la Torre, 1981), 57–9; A. Elorza, introd. to Pablo Iglesias, *Escritos II* (Madrid: Ayuso, 1975), 15–16.

[17] Engels claimed in a letter to Joseph Bloch that many Guesdists had misunderstood Marxism. See Maurice Moissonnier, 'La estructuración del movimiento obrero en partidos a fines del siglo XIX: Debates doctrinales y experiencias prácticas', *Estudios de Historia Social*, 8–9 (1979), 50.

[18] Karl Marx, 'Critique of the Gotha Programme', 1875, in Marx and Engels, *Selected Works* (London: Lawrence and Wishart, 1968), 315–35; Jules Guesde, 'La ley de los salarios y sus consecuencias', 1878, in Engels, Guesde, and Marx, *Socialismo* (Madrid: Francisco Beltrán, 1930), 69–76. In fact the 'iron law' identified with Lassalle was put forward originally by Johann Karl Robertus. See George Lichtheim, *A Short History of Socialism* (London: Fontana, 1975), 100–1.

[19] On Guesdism see Moissonnier, 56–64; Luis Arranz, 'El guesdismo de Pablo Iglesias en los informes a la Comisión de Reformas Sociales', *Estudios de Historia*

With one important qualification, Guesdism was what passed for Marxist orthodoxy in the eyes of the PSOE founders. However, they did not share Guesde's contempt for trade unionism. The majority of them being members of the printers' association, they had personal experience of some of the benefits to be gained from union action; and before long they would witness strikes and other types of labour struggle playing a crucial role in the growth of Socialist strength in the Basque province of Vizcaya.[20] For a long time the 'iron law' survived on a theoretical plane while being challenged in practice by the Socialists' commitment to trade unionism. The launching of the PSOE as a national party in 1888 was accompanied by the founding of the General Workers' Union (UGT) as a formally autonomous union federation that would function as the PSOE's ally in the labour movement. Its statutes were modelled on those of the printers' federation.

None of the early Socialists used Marxism to produce an original study of the real problems of Spain. For most of them, it remained a series of truths and formulae of universal validity to be propagated as a doctrine and received 'just like children learn the responses to the Catechism', as the philosopher Unamuno sarcastically observed.[21] The clearest early exposition of Marxism in Spain may be found in Dr Jaime Vera's report to the Commission on Social Reform established by Segismundo Moret in 1883.[22] Regarded by the working-class socialist historian Morato as 'the Bible of

Social, 8–9 (1979), 207–14; Claude Willard, *Les Guesdistes: Le mouvement socialiste en France 1893–1905* (Paris: Éditions Sociales, 1965).

[20] M. Tuñón de Lara, 'Sobre la historia del pensamiento socialista entre 1900 y 1931', in Albert Balcells (ed.), *Teoría y práctica del movimiento obrero en España (1900–1936)* (Valencia: Fernando Torres, 1977), 21; Juan Pablo Fusi, *Política obrera en el País Vasco (1880–1923)* (Madrid: Turner, 1975), *passim*.

[21] Quoted in Dolores Gómez Molleda, *El socialismo español y los intelectuales: Cartas de líderes del movimiento obrero a Miguel de Unamuno* (Salamanca: Universidad de Salamanca, 1980), 15.

[22] Jaime Vera, 'Informe de la Agrupación Socialista Madrileña ante la Comisión de Reformas Sociales', 1884, in Juan José Castillo (ed.), *Ciencia y proletariado: Escritos escogidos de Jaime Vera* (Madrid: Cuadernos para el Diálogo, 1973), 81–141. On Vera see too Eusebio Fernández García, *Marxismo y positivismo en el socialismo español* (Madrid: Centro de Estudios Constitucionales, 1981), 117–48; and the chapter by T. Jiménez Araya in A. Elorza (ed.), *Burgueses y proletarios* (Barcelona: Laia, 1973).

the ideas in Spain',[23] this work revealed an uncommon acquaintance with Marxism for an early PSOE member. Yet even in Vera's work one finds the lingering presence of the 'iron law' and traces of positivism. And although he acknowledged his country's economic backwardness, Vera's famous report failed to explore the implications of this for social structure, class alignments, the nature of the revolution required, and other questions considered vital by maximalists in other parts of Europe. To him Spain's underdevelopment just meant that the socialist revolution would come in the distant future. His text, like other less polished offerings from early Socialists, embraced more of a Marxist view of the workings and conditions of capitalism in general than a focus upon Spain's specific pattern of development.

Meanwhile, Pablo Iglesias often wrote as if capitalism already were fully developed in Spain, with social polarization well advanced and the revolution nearby. The main enemy for him was the bourgeoisie; the aristocracy or landed oligarchy merely added a bit of sparkle to a State that was essentially bourgeois.[24] Writing later, Morato presented a somewhat more realistic view of the problems that confronted the nascent party (though one that appreciated only the industrial aspect of capitalist development):

The party was created in a hostile climate, so much so that for many years one could compare it to a plant in a greenhouse. [There was a] general absence of civic customs, a lack of respect for rights, and indifference towards public affairs; a lack of culture, education, and of seriousness; fickleness, ignorance, and servility. The remnants of the [First] International were in the hands of the anarchists, while the Republican parties were strong and had an abundance of truly illustrious and highly able men. The party was born in a country with almost medieval forms of production, where capitalism still really had not taken off and become strong; where there was scarcely a bourgeoisie, only one that could share in the exercise of political power.[25]

However, Morato's own efforts to sketch Spain's economic

[23] Morato, *Líderes*, 352.

[24] Manuel Pérez Ledesma (ed.), *Pensamiento socialista español a comienzos de siglo* (Madrid: Del Centro, 1974), 34.

[25] Morato, *El Partido*, 219–20.

history in the light of Marxism resulted more in an adaption of reality to the historical schema of the *Manifesto* than in a successful application of Marx's method of analysis.[26]

Given the socio-economic and political obstacles recognized by Morato, a Guesdist *classe contre classe* approach[27] was bound to isolate the PSOE politically. While expressing a platonic preference for a republican regime over the restored monarchy, the Socialists none the less adopted a policy of hostility towards the Republicans,[28] the most progressive liberal current, on the grounds that they were the only faction of the 'exploiters' likely to succeed in deceiving workers into providing electoral support. There are several reasons why the PSOE clung to this apparently self-defeating attitude until 1909. First, there was the aforementioned influence of Guesde and his Parti Ouvrier, which had little to say about preferred forms of government (since it was faced with a highly conservative bourgeois republic) and which moreover dismissed the need for alliances in the belief that revolution was imminent. Second, the Republican parties contained a good few employers who, when resisting Socialist trade union demands, seemed no more progressive to their workers than Liberal, Conservative, or Carlist bosses.[29] Third, the Republicans, aware of the PSOE as a competitor for the popular vote, were themselves often hostile towards the Socialists.[30] Their repeated charge that the PSOE was in cahoots with the monarchists was normally baseless, but it was certainly true that Socialist electoral sectarianism made life easier for the dynastic Liberal and Conservative parties as they alternated in power.

Fourth, and perhaps most significantly, there was the proletarian composition of the PSOE. The party's origins lay in the labour movement, and for more than three decades its founders were sufficiently distrustful of intellectuals to debar them from holding positions of leadership. Among the PSOE

[26] Id., *Notas para la historia de los modos de producción en España*, 1897; Tuñón de Lara, 'Sobre la historia', 22.

[27] Jean Jaurès and Jules Guesde, *Les Deux Méthodes: Le Socialisme* (Paris: Les Éditions de la Liberté, 1945), 38–9.

[28] Morato, *El Partido*, 102–5. *El Socialista* (30.4.1886) bemoaned: 'we have been called monarchists, which is as offensive to us as if we had been called republicans.'

[29] Morato, *El Partido*, 78–9, 113.   [30] Vera, 243.

founders, six at most could be considered intellectuals. Of
these only Jaime Vera stayed, and even he absented himself in
1886–90, despairing of the anti-Republican line adopted by
his party. Even the intellectuals of the 'Generation of 1898',
who lamented Spain's national decline, showed little interest
in revolution or the workers' cause, their allegiance being
rather to the middle class or the élite. Alienated by the quite
demanding requirements of PSOE militancy, they also found
the party's ideological rigidity antithetical to their cultural
function in society.[31] Though there were Socialist attempts in
the 1890s to court prestigious names, the party's anti-
Republicanism and working-class orientation discouraged
intellectuals well into the twentieth century.

A further reason for the Socialists' exclusiveness was their
need to assert and maintain a political personality of their own
if they were to survive. The violence of PSOE attacks on the
anarchists and Republicans represented tacit recognition that
for a long while these forces were the main attractions for
Spain's workers. Persisting anarchist popularity left the PSOE
with far less room for manœuvre than socialist parties enjoyed
elsewhere.[32] While the latter could co-operate relatively easily
with liberal parties, Iglesias was well aware that a more
moderate approach by the PSOE would swell anarchist ranks
and leave the party indiscernible from the more progressive
wing of Republicanism.[33] The PSOE had to stand for
something more than democracy plus reforms; it needed a
working-class image and had to offer a vision of a materially
and morally superior social order.

Finally, the nature of the Spanish regime counselled
intransigence, if not the sectarianism to which this was
inextricably bound. The PSOE was excluded from effective
institutional participation under the Restoration monarchy of
the late nineteenth century, installed in 1874 and personified
successively by Alfonso XII and Alfonso XIII. Manipulation
of the electoral system by the dynastic parties, the power of

[31] Donald L. Shaw, *The Generation of 1898 in Spain* (London and Tonbridge:
Ernest Benn, 1975), 12; Gómez Molleda, *El Socialismo*, 13–105.
[32] Miguel Martínez Cuadrado, *Elecciones y partidos políticos de España (1868–
1931)*, 2 vols. (Madrid: Taurus, 1969), ii. 690.
[33] María Teresa Martínez de Sas, *El socialismo y la España oficial: Pablo Iglesias,
diputado a Cortes* (Madrid: Tucar, 1975), 84.

local party caciques, and widespread apathy among the people bred by powerlessness, poverty, and illiteracy, all denied the party the possibility of real progress by parliamentary means, even after universal male suffrage was granted in 1890. The problem was not just that a formally democratic constitution was vitiated by electoral malpractices—there were also plenty of workers who were prepared to sell their votes.[34] Clearly the PSOE could not compete at that level. Moreover, any compromise on basic principles was inadvisable in the absence of complementary policy concessions from the conservative élite. Social and industrial legislation appeared after 1900, but in a country too poor to finance its implementation.[35] And even given Spain's poverty, employers proved exceptionally intransigent, apparently confirming radical beliefs.[36] On numerous occasions the army was used against strikes and protests. The scenario was not one in which reformism and revisionism could flourish.

Other salient features of the PSOE's early ideology were a degree of anticlericalism and quasi-pacifism. The former was most marked in the Basque Socialist paper *Le Lucha de Clases*, founded in 1894, whose disrespectful references to the clergy and flaunting of its atheistic commitment were not simply reflections of the personal preoccupations of its early editors; they were also a mark of the greater influence of Catholicism among the workers of Vizcaya compared with many other parts of Spain, the reaction against this being fuelled by the emergence of the religious Basque Nationalist Party (PNV) in 1894–5.[37] The PSOE as a whole was distinctly less acerbic in its anti-clericalism, and Miguel de Unamuno during his short membership of the party urged that the insistence upon atheism and materialism be dropped altogether.[38] A party of progress, however, had to have some

---

[34] Juan J. Linz, *El sistema de partidos en España* (Madrid: Narcea, 1979), 23–40; Fusi, *Política*, 114–15.

[35] Gerald H. Meaker, *The Revolutionary Left in Spain, 1914–1923* (Stanford, CA: Stanford University Press, 1974), 4.

[36] Referring to Catalonia, Carr (*Spain*, 446) has observed that 'employers get the working classes they deserve'.

[37] Linz, *El Sistema*, 70–1, 123; Fusi, *Política*, 221–30.

[38] Shaw, 44; Gómez Molleda, *El Socialismo*, 31–2; id., *Unamuno socialista* (Madrid: Narcea, 1978). On the young Unamuno see also Fernández García, 149–82.

anticlerical leanings in a country where the Church remained a highly privileged and influential conservative institution, bestowing legitimacy upon its rulers and bridling modernization through its grip on education. Yet while the Basque editor Tomás Meabe tried to make anticlericalism the main platform of *La Lucha* (he was himself a former Catholic), Pablo Iglesias denied that the Church was the main enemy—it was only an auxiliary of the bourgeoisie, to be fought by raising the cultural level of workers and eventually through expropriation.[39]

Campaigns against colonial wars were also launched by the Socialists, who opposed the sending of troops to Cuba in the 1890s and to Morocco a few years later. In the Cuban case, with Spain facing a struggle for independence, the PSOE's prime concern was that workers' blood should not be spilled in a conflict in which their class had no stake. The party did not perceive the Cuban struggle to be one of national liberation, to be supported for that reason. The Socialists' emphasis was upon the need to end a costly war, and only gradually did they come to advocate Cuban independence. For a long time their central demand was that 'either everybody or nobody' should be sent to fight, the idea being that if the sons of the wealthy were prevented from buying their way out of military service, Spain's rulers would soon end the war.[40] This slogan, which was resurrected for campaigns against military intervention in Morocco,[41] showed the PSOE becoming more politically sophisticated: it was beginning to use tactics rather than acting on the basis of first principles.

A somewhat different attitude was adopted in relation to the First World War. Though this was condemned as interimperialist at the outset and a minority in the party stuck to such a line, PSOE sympathy for the Allies soon became clear. An Allied victory was perceived as the best possible outcome for the labour movement on both sides, facilitating an

---

[39] Arbeloa, *Socialismo y anticlericalismo* (Madrid: Taurus, 1973), 158–9; Morato, *El Partido*, 162.

[40] Carlos Serrano, 'El PSOE y la guerra de Cuba (1895–1898)', *Estudios de Historia Social*, 8–9 (1979), 287–310.

[41] It is interesting that the PSOE did not call for immediate Spanish withdrawal from Ceuta and Melilla. See Antonio Padilla Bolívar, *Pablo Iglesias y el parlamentarismo restauracionista* (Barcelona: Planeta, 1976), 178.

extension of democratic liberties throughout Europe.[42] Pro-Allied sympathies in the PSOE also grew as a reflex reaction against the Germanophilism of the conservative élite. Such sentiments became so strong that the party's initial response to the Russian Revolution was shaped above all by consideration of its impact on the Allied war effort. The Socialist reaction to the revolution was originally cool, to say the least, and Brest-Litovsk was considered an act of betrayal.[43] It was not pacifism that prevented the PSOE from advocating Spanish intervention in the war; merely a realistic appraisal of the penury of the country.

Undeniably, the attitude struck by the PSOE towards the Allies was symptomatic of a certain moderation in the outlook of many Socialists, though the party did not go so far as Guesde and accept a ministerial portfolio. This attitude was consistent with a domestic practice of pursuing reformist tactics so long as public liberties were respected, and only resorting to revolutionary tactics when these were threatened. Greater reformism was encouraged by apparently improved prospects of electoral success emerging after the extension of the suffrage in 1890,[44] and by socialist advances in France and Germany, especially the 1.4 million SPD votes in 1890. Though there was a long gap between the first PSOE municipal successes in the 1890s and the first parliamentary triumph in 1910 (made possible by a pact with the Republican Union), elections gradually made the Socialists look beyond the working class for votes, and in doing so they tried to broaden their appeal. Iglesias held that party councillors had to represent the interests of all electors and not merely of their working-class voters.[45]

The liaison agreed with the Republicans in 1909, which lasted a decade before being revived in the 1930s, was

[42] Morato, *El Partido*, 206–7.
[43] The first really positive mention of the Bolshevik revolution did not appear in *El Socialista* until Mar. 1918 (Meaker, 108). See also Tuñón de Lara, 'Sobre la historia', 38.
[44] The electorate grew from 800,000 to 4,800,000 men aged over 25, making it 27% of the total population at a time when the active population was 40% of the total. See Padilla Bolívar, *Iglesias*, 70–1.
[45] Javier Aisa and V. M. Arbeloa, *Historia de la Unión General de Trabajadores: Apuntes sobre el sindicalismo socialista, 1888–1931* (Bilbao: Zero, 1975), 43.

based on pragmatic thinking. It began as a response to the *Semana Trágica*, the Maura-De la Cierva government's brutal repression of workers in Barcelona, which placed at risk the legality and survival of the workers' organizations. Anarchists, Socialists, and Republicans briefly stood together in calling for a general strike. By this time, the diverse Republican forces had united under Salmerón and so constituted a more coherent partner for the Socialists. But above all the PSOE realized that it had reached an electoral threshold beyond which it could not progress alone: it needed an alliance if it were to win parliamentary seats.[46] It may be also that the Socialists reappraised the value of republican co-operation in view of a challenge posed by Catholic unions to their hitherto exclusive representation of the labour movement on official bodies such as the Institute of Social Reform.[47] Alignment with the Republicans was bound to moderate further the PSOE's postures, yet still the party could not become a purely reformist, evolutionary party in a country such as Spain. The political system was open enough to encourage the Socialists to pursue reformist tactics, but too forbidding for many to entertain illusions about a reformist strategy ever leading to socialism.

Pablismo (named after Iglesias) emerged as the compromise, a blend of reformist praxis (which at times seemed revolutionary because of the exclusiveness of the power structure) and verbal radicalism.[48] Eduard Bernstein's revisionism had little direct appeal in Spain; none the less it infiltrated the theoretical arsenal of the PSOE cloaked in the works of the Argentine Juan B. Justo and of the later Deville.[49] It says little for the theoretical sophistication of the PSOE that it failed to recognize revisionism when it saw it. The party lacked a theoretical journal until the appearance of *La Nueva Era* in

[46] Pérez Ledesma, *Pesamiento*, 38. Morato (*El Partido*, 180–1) stresses the very slow growth of the PSOE in the pre-alliance years. Iglesias probably won an election in Bilbao in 1898, but lost the count (Martínez Cuadrado, ii. 604).

[47] Antonio Padilla Bolívar, *El movimiento socialista español* (Barcelona: Planeta, 1977), 131–2.

[48] Meaker, 95–6.

[49] Pérez Ledesma, *Pensamiento*, 42–54; Ribas, *La introducción*, 48–50; id., 'Las relaciones entre el socialismo alemán y el español', *Estudios de Historia Social*, 8–9 (1979), 227–39.

1901–2, and even that mainly published translations.[50] Still, there were distinct limits to the penetration of revisionism, even of Kautskyism, for not many Spanish Socialists prior to the 1930s could envisage social transformation being achieved by parliamentary means. It was working-class industrial struggles, not speeches in the Cortes, that had inspired labour legislation in their country, and the fact that the latter became a dead letter tended to kill hopes that emancipation might be legislated. Pablismo valued universal suffrage for the organizational and propaganda opportunities associated with it. However, the idea that it would take a revolution to bring about socialism (generally defined in economic terms)[51] was never quite dispensed with. While Iglesias did not prepare the PSOE and UGT for revolutionary action, he did contribute importantly to raising the level of political organization and awareness in the labour movement, thereby improving the prospects of effective insurrectional activity.

The character of the PSOE became increasingly hybrid as competing tendencies emerged inside the party. Efforts to maintain party unity, the main concern of the ailing Iglesias prior to his death in 1925, led to a blurring of the party line on fundamental questions. The party congress in 1919 voted in favour of the concept of 'the dictatorship of the proletariat', thus pleasing a pro-Bolshevik faction, yet it decided that this dictatorship could assume diverse forms.[52] While the left looked to the Leninist model, more moderate elements headed by Julián Besteiro followed Kautsky in envisaging proletarian power as something established by free elections, respectful of

[50] For selections and commentary see Pérez Ledesma, *Pensamiento*. On the influence of positivism on the journal see Fernández García, 182–214.

[51] The Declaration of Principles of the PSOE (1888) presented one party aspiration as being 'the transformation of individual and corporate ownership of the instruments of production into collective, social, or common ownership' (Rodolfo Llopis, *Etapas del Partido Socialista Obrero Español* (Toulouse: Editorial Socialista, 1962), 4). In a footnote to his *Comentarios al programa socialista* (1910) (reproduced in Padilla Bolívar, *Iglesias*, 279–300), Iglesias wrote: 'For us Socialism, Collectivism, Collectivist Socialism, and Communism always mean the same thing—an economic system based on social, common, or collective property, and rejecting its individual or corporate appropriation.' Marx too had used the terms 'socialism' and 'communism' interchangeably.

[52] Pierre Vilar, 'El socialismo en España (1917–1945)', in Jacques Droz (ed.), *Historia general del socialismo*, 4 vols. (Barcelona: Destino, 1982), iii. 443.

civil and political liberties, and based on the use of parliament for socialist purposes.[53]

The general trend during the early decades of the twentieth century was towards more pronounced gradualism, especially after the departure of pro-Comintern militants in 1920–1 to form the Spanish Communist Party (PCE). A thoroughly liberal outlook represented by Indalecio Prieto and Fernando de los Ríos saw the future in terms of a gradual conquest of reforms and modernity in alliance with the Republicans. Besteiro and others, while using Marxist terminology, also defended a gradualist position somewhat similar to that of the Russian Mensheviks. Arguing that capitalism had to develop fully before conditions for socialism could mature, the *besteiristas* adopted a two-stage view of the transition to socialism, the first phase of which would be a bourgeois revolution deserving the support of the PSOE, but not requiring its guidance.

Pablismo, however, was something more than a compromise between reform and revolution, for in addition to political postures it offered a moral example for Spanish Socialists to follow. Indeed, some have maintained that Iglesias's moral lifestyle was his essential legacy.[54] Ortega described him as a 'lay saint'.[55] Inveighing against the evils of drink and gambling, defending the family, education, and honour, Iglesias has been depicted clinging to a bourgeois morality that the bourgeoisie itself rarely practised.[56] Yet his values appealed strongly in socialist circles to workers who found moral condemnation of the country's rulers and employers easier to comprehend that an economic analysis of exploitation. Perhaps the morality of the PSOE helped fill a void left by the decline of religion. Certainly the Pablista emphasis upon austerity, sacrifice, devotion to the cause, and industriousness made virtues of necessity for men who were isolated not only from middle-class society but also from the mass of workers. Morato summarized the formidable task facing the PSOE

[53] Massimo Salvadori, *Karl Kautsky* (London: New Left Books, 1979), 12.

[54] Enrique Tierno Galván, 'Pablo Iglesias: Un legado de estilo', in Fundación Pablo Iglesias, *Homenaje a Pablo Iglesias* (Madrid: Editorial Pablo Iglesias, 1979), 179–81.

[55] Martínez de Sas, 127.	[56] Ibid. 321.

pioneers when he described the young Iglesias as the 'editor of a newspaper without readers and president of a party without members in a country without citizens'.[57] As PSOE president, Iglesias personally suffered considerable financial hardship prior to his election to parliament in 1910, and he was incapacitated increasingly by ill health in later life. All of this enhanced the self-sacrificing image of a man thoroughly representative of the early generation of dedicated Socialists.[58]

The pronounced moral stance was a source of strength for the party in periods of adversity, and it was electorally beneficial. Although there were isolated occasions when the PSOE resorted to dubious electoral manœuvres,[59] its general conduct led voters to see Socialist participation in local government as a guard against corruption. Recruitment, too, gained from the ethical image. Many workers joined because of the personal example set by Iglesias and other leaders, rather than in response to the written propaganda.[60] It was a measure of the strength of that example that party veterans a century later would still describe 'the true socialist' in terms of the same values.[61]

Iglesias also left his imprint on the party through his twin obsessions with building the organization and educating the working class. The desire to create and preserve solid structures was understandable in the face of sporadic repression; however, the more that was built, the more there was to lose, and in time extreme caution became a hallmark of Pablismo. Iglesias tried to discipline his followers to advance only one step at a time, and only when the path ahead was firm. Besides organization, education had to be stressed in a country where illiteracy was still high. The PSOE considered itself an educated élite of the working class whose mission was to enlighten the rest.[62] Originally it was based on a labour

---

[57] Morato, *Iglesias*, 88.

[58] Fusi, introd. to Zugazagoitia, *Iglesias*, 26–7.

[59] In general elections in the Basque Country, 1918–23, the PSOE led by Prieto used a tacit understanding with the monarchists and electoral deception. See Fusi, *Política*, 117, 262–3, 386, 482.

[60] Zugazagoitia, *Iglesias*, 28.

[61] Personal interview with Federico Fernández López, Miraflores de la Sierra, 6 Sept. 1982.

[62] Arranz, 211. Indeed, such was the faith placed by the party in the value of education that during the Civil War, in 1937, the PSOE printed a poster depicting a

aristocracy of relatively well-paid and educated printers, whose political zeal and trade union activities on occasions led to dismissal from work. The importance that they attached to education was shared by Jaime Vera, who was drawn to Marxism by its scientific claims and saw the emancipation of workers as requiring not simply education but intelligent activity.[63] Although this pedagogical streak curiously never produced an exceptional level of theoretical debate in the party, it did develop into a tradition of trying to provide members with a basic political education. The party devoted much attention to the *formación*, the training and basic doctrinal preparation of its members, with a view to them eventually occupying positions of responsibility. It demanded a high level of activity and commitment from members, and thus developed as a party of militants rather than as a mass organization with a more relaxed conception of membership.

In the course of time, the party founded by Iglesias acted less according to principles and more in line with a sense of pragmatic opportunism; less ideologically and more politically. The existence of a strong anarcho-syndicalist movement, which gave rise to the National Labour Confederation (CNT) in 1910, forced the Socialists to be constantly aware of working-class sentiments, yet on occasions they seemed to hard-line class warriors to be acting treacherously. Because of their pursuit of electoral respectability, ethical distaste for anarchist violence, and suspicion that workers would only appreciate the inadequacy of spontaneous direct action by suffering punishing defeats, the Socialists boycotted anarchist general strike efforts in 1900, 1902, and 1911. On one occasion they were rebuked even by Second International confrères for their lack of solidarity as hundreds of workers were jailed.[64]

swastika being crushed by a pile of books, and bearing the slogan 'Culture Will Destroy Fascism!'

[63] Castillo, 30, 46–7. Vera wrote that he had been attracted to socialism not sentimentally (as was the case of many Socialists) but 'out of total scientific conviction'; and he described how as a medical student 'on the same dissecting table where I studied anatomy, I read the Communist Manifesto in which society is so well dissected' (ibid. 14).

[64] Vilar, 'El socialismo español de sus orígenes a 1917', in Droz (ed.), ii (1979), 321; Fusi, *Política*, 219; id. *Iglesias* introd., 10–11.

Relations with the CNT improved during the First World War as labour militancy grew in response to inflation. The two labour federations jointly called a general strike at the end of 1916 and the following August the Socialists played a central role in another strike, this time intended as part of a revolutionary bid to bring about political change. However, the apparent boldness of the PSOE and UGT in 1917 did not represent a total throwing of caution to the winds, for earlier that year there had been strong indications that substantial army and middle-class support for a political revolution would be forthcoming.[65] The brutal repression of the general strike gave rise to renewed caution in the Socialist leadership and led some activists to lose all faith in the possibility of liberalizing the Spanish regime. Feeling betrayed by the middle classes, the UGT and CNT subsequently looked seriously at the idea of unification, but it was never achieved. In 1919 extremists imposed a sectarian line on the CNT, giving UGT members just three months to join the rival federation or be declared 'yellow'.[66] This was a period when pragmatic trade union leaders of the CNT were constrained by violent revolutionary anarchists, and could not deliver even when an alliance pact was signed with the UGT in September 1920.[67]

If anything, the UGT pursued a more cautious and reformist path than did the PSOE. Its emphasis was always upon immediate gains. Very quickly it became wary of militant tactics, having inherited much of its prudence from the printers' union. Successive revisions of UGT strike regulations left them so restrictive as to authorize strikes only when success was highly probable. To be made official by 1902, a strike needed to be held at a time of full employment, so that employers could not easily resort to blacklegs; it had to be organized by a union section that had retained as members for at least one year a majority of the workers involved in the dispute; and there had to be a healthy enough strike fund available to sustain strikers for two weeks. Not surprisingly, the vast majority of strikes were unofficial.[68]

[65] On the events of 1917 see Juan Antonio Lacomba, *La crisis española de 1917* (Madrid: Ciencia Nueva, 1970); Meaker, 62–98.
[66] Aisa and Arbeloa, 77–8.   [67] Meaker, 325–36.
[68] Pérez Ledesma, 'La Unión General de Trabajadores: Socialismo y reformismo',

Iglesias invariably counselled workers against making exorbitant demands. Improvements, he felt, should be won gradually, incrementally, for the greater the demand made, the less likely it was to be conceded by employers. The positive strike was the successful strike, even if the material conquest were minor, for success boosted confidence in solidarity and in Socialist leadership; failure destroyed morale, alienated members, and led to reprisals, threatening the survival of organizations so painstakingly built.[69]

The view that strikes were double-edged weapons was inherited by Iglesias's successor in the UGT presidency, Francisco Largo Caballero.[70] In 1923, when the constitutional regime was ended by a military coup and General Primo de Rivera established a dictatorship, Caballero's prime concern was to preserve his organization. The Socialists registered their formal disapproval of Primo's coup, but then allowed material and organizational considerations to outweigh ethical scruples and ideological principles when the dictator made it known that UGT co-operation with his regime might be mutually beneficial.[71] The new regime was inspired by a paternalistic Catholic conservatism that held that the best way of eliminating class conflict and of undermining the appeal of the left was for the State to intervene in society to reconcile the interests of capital and labour. Under the new system the UGT provided labour representatives to sit alongside employers' representatives on factory arbitration boards that formed part of new corporate structures. Caballero himself became labour's member of the Council of State.

During the 1930s anarchists and communists would hark back to this period as one of PSOE-UGT betrayal of the working class. A handful of liberal Socialists headed by Indalecio Prieto were also critical of the involvement with

---

Estudios de Historia Social, 8–9 (1979), 223; id., 'La primera etapa de la Unión General de Trabajadores (1888–1917): Planteamiento sindical y formas de organización', in Balcells (ed.), 113–71.

[69] Pérez Ledesma, 'La primera etapa', 144–6.

[70] Aisa and Arbeloa, 40; Meaker, 275–7.

[71] On this period see José Andrés-Gallego, *El socialismo durante la Dictadura (1923–1930)* (Madrid: Tebas, 1977); Enrique Moral Sandoval, 'El socialismo y la dictadura de Primo de Rivera', in Juliá (ed.), *El socialismo en España* (Madrid: Editorial Pablo Iglesias, 1986).

Primo. Yet in material terms collaboration did produce benefits for the workers. Several pro-labour measures were decreed, and more often than not State representatives voted with the UGT men on arbitration boards in order to resolve industrial disputes.[72] Moreover, by accepting official posts (and only so long as the UGT was permitted to nominate labour's candidates), the Socialist union federation avoided much of the persecution suffered by anarchists and anarcho-syndicalists in the 1920s. A case might also be made for Primo's dictatorship deserving a modicum of left-wing respect for its efforts to modernize the economic infrastructure of the country.[73] What really mattered, though, was whether workers would abandon the Socialists in repudiation of their collaboration. In fact, UGT membership held up and even may have increased.[74] The Socialists ended up in 1930, when the regime fell, with their organizations intact, having been sufficiently responsive to public opinion to end their collaboration a year earlier, in time to avoid public recrimination for it. They broke with the regime as economic deterioration undermined its social support.

On the other hand, CNT activists certainly had a valid point of principle when they condemned Socialist co-operation with a regime that harshly repressed combative sectors of the labour movement. To place the Socialists' overriding concern with the preservation of their precious organizations in context, it should be noted that the CNT, hard hit because of its efforts to resist Primo, rapidly recovered its strength after the regime collapsed.

By the time the Second Republic was established in 1931, most Spanish Socialists could be described as gradualists, despite their tactical resort to insurrectional methods in 1917 and their hesitant involvement in the conspiratorial republican movement of 1930. They were still prepared to take part in a broader coalition favouring a democratic revolution, or to use extreme methods when their own survival seemed at risk.

---

[72] Shlomo Ben-Ami, *Fascism from Above: The Dictatorship of Primo de Rivera in Spain 1923–1930* (Oxford: Clarendon Press, 1983), 282–318.

[73] Ibid. 240–81.

[74] Andrés-Gallego, 151–3; Ben-Ami, *The Origins of the Second Republic in Spain* (Oxford: Oxford University Press, 1978), p. 114 n. 15.

Back in 1908 Iglesias had told a parliamentary commission that if his party were banned the Socialists would resort to terrorism,[75] and the same propensity to fight extremism with extremism was seen again in 1934 when the left felt threatened by the advance of Gil-Robles's movement of the Catholic right. Yet each time that a revolution was attempted, in 1917, 1930, and 1934, the PSOE showed itself to be thoroughly unsuitable for insurgency.[76] On occasions its militants demonstrated an uncommon capacity for struggle, sacrifice, and even revolutionary consciousness, only to end up defeated. Even in July 1936, when they helped thwart Franco's coup attempt and thus obliged him to fight a civil war, their insurgency was spontaneous, reactive, and in part defensive.[77] The problem was that a party that was by now geared to piecemeal progress could not shed its bureaucratic inertia and praxis suddenly when an opportunity for insurrection arose. Neither the organization nor its leaders were prepared or equipped for such eventualities; they were fashioned for legal, non-clandestine, modes of struggle. While in theory the party was highly centralized and disciplined, in practice it was far from being streamlined. Provincial and local sections often went their own way, acting before consulting Madrid.

The prospect of gradual progress coming through social and economic reforms was one welcomed by the vast majority of Socialists in 1931, though there was disagreement over whether the party should enter or merely support governments of the Second Republic. Announced reforms such as land redistribution and the secularizing of education could be welcomed from either a liberal or a Menshevik standpoint. It was to be because the Republic failed to usher in even the limited changes associated with bourgeois revolution that radicalism grew in the PSOE during the next few years.

[75] Quoted in Morato, *Iglesias*, 122.
[76] Ben-Ami, *Origins*, 147–50; Fusi, *Política*, 369–77; Meaker, 84–6, 93; Tuñón de Lara, *El movimiento*, iii. 102–9; Andrés Saborit, *Asturias y sus hombres* (Toulouse: Ediciones UGT-CIOSL, 1964), 228–9.
[77] Hugh Thomas, *The Spanish Civil War* (Harmondsworth: Penguin, 1965), 290–312.

THE PATTERN OF PARTY DEVELOPMENT

The PSOE's early progress was extremely slow, uneven, and precarious, and there were times when its very existence could be doubted. The task of gradually winning adherents (by means of political education, a constant critique of government policies, and the probity of Socialist councillors) was complicated by the close ties that married the PSOE to the fortunes of the UGT. Although the latter recruited non-socialists as well as socialists and never formally pledged its institutional allegiance to the PSOE, its origins, methods, doctrinal outlook, and choice of leaders earned it a lasting reputation as the Socialist union federation.[1] For a long time the roles, and in places the organizational structures, of the PSOE and UGT were not clearly differentiated; socio-economic factors thus intervened to an unusually high degree in influencing the party's development pattern. The party tended to grow when the economic climate was favourable to labour and when Socialist-led workers won strikes; it lost members or stood still in periods of high unemployment and labour defeats. That pattern prevailed until 1930.

Electoral success came first at municipal level in 1891. It took another 19 years and the alliance with the Republicans for the first parliamentary seat to be won—by Iglesias himself. Under the monarchy the greatest number of seats to be gained by the PSOE in an election was 7 out of 409 in 1923, though at 140,000 the party vote was higher in 1918. During the pre-1923 period Socialists and Republicans together never surpassed the achievement of 34 out of 408 seats in 1914.[2] Although elections were rigged by the dynastic parties, it is unlikely that the official results minimized the true level of Socialist voting; electoral management simply rendered the mass of workers too apathetic to vote for the party. It is probable that the PSOE accounted for just one to five per cent of the votes under the manipulated quasi-parliamentary system that was terminated by Primo de Rivera in 1923.[3] At

---

[1] The UGT adopted a clearer socialist identity in 1919. See Andrés-Gallego, 128.
[2] Martínez Cuadrado, ii. 781, 840–7; Artola, i. 515.
[3] Martínez Cuadrado, ii. 863.

the level of party organization, however, the Socialists were laying the foundations for success in the future when more democratic circumstances might be exploited. Membership grew to 58,000 by the start of 1921, but then fell to 21,000 by the end of that year as economic crisis weakened the labour movement and a few thousand members were lost to the nascent Communist Party, mainly in Asturias and Vizcaya.[4] Further losses cut affiliation to approximately 8,000 by the time of Primo's coup, but the fact that the UGT was able to operate under the Dictatorship subsequently buoyed party membership at that level in the mid-1920s, and it eventually began to rise steadily at the end of the decade as the regime lost support.[5]

When the end of the monarchy arrived, finally prompted by the outcome of local elections in April 1931, the PSOE was fast becoming a mass party.[6] Indeed, at the start of the Second Republic, the 'least typically Spanish, the most European of Spanish parties' was the country's only modern organized party.[7] The PSOE grew from almost 17,000 members in mid-1930 to around 90,000 on the eve of the Civil War.[8] While outside parliament it faced major competition for working-class support from the influential CNT, the PSOE was now by far the most electorally important workers' party. Moreover, given the divisions and organizational weakness of the Republican parties, it found itself in the position of being the most crucial buttress of the young Republic. Through the 1931 and 1936 elections the PSOE became the best represented party in the Cortes (though with less than a

---

[4] Tuñón de Lara, *El movimiento*, ii. 333. The PCE itself rapidly lost members in the early 1920s. By 1925 it had only about 500 members and hardly any trade union influence (Meaker, 478).

[5] Llopis, *Etapas*, 7; Tuñón de Lara, *El movimiento*, iii. 39, 47, 56; Manuel Contreras, *El PSOE en la II República: Organización e ideología* (Madrid: Centro de Investigaciones Sociológicas, 1981), 52; Artola, i. 659 n. 331.

[6] After the municipal elections of 1931 the PSOE had 4, 813 councillors (compared with 67 for the PCE and 34,688 for the various Republican parties) (Martínez Cuadrado, ii. 855). The monarchists did marginally better overall, but the anti-dynastic vote was so strong that Alfonso XIII abdicated. The Socialist successes were largely urban.

[7] Linz, *El sistema*, 18, 89; Jean Becarud, quoted in Enrique López Sevilla, *El Partido Socialista Obrero Español en las Cortes Constituyentes de la Segunda República* (Mexico: Ediciones Pablo Iglesias, 1969), 18–19.

[8] Tuñón de Lara, *El movimiento*, iii. 56, 114; Llopis, *Etapas*, 7; Contreras, 91.

quarter of the seats); the achievement of just 61 out of 474 seats in 1933 was poor by comparison, but it represented centre-left disunity and the penalizing of this by the electoral system rather than Socialist electoral decline.[9]

The PSOE's progress was enhanced by that of the UGT which, after struggling with few rewards for a decade, finally began to look secure in the early twentieth century, more than doubling its membership to 32,000 in 1899–1901. By the late 1920s it had grown to 200,000 members; by June 1932 it exceeded the million mark, having managed to rapidly organize a quarter of the country's agricultural labourers.[10] As it grew the UGT was transformed into a bureaucratic organization controlled by full-time officials and based on national industrial federations.[11] Of the 11-man executive elected in 1922, nine members had previously been full-time officers of working-class organizations.[12] The symbiotic relationship with the PSOE, only disrupted seriously in the 1930s when factional conflict produced greater structural differentiation, was seen in the PSOE and UGT leaderships elected in 1928: 14 men occupied the 22 positions on the two executives; 8 men were on both.[13]

Early on, Socialist organizers had their main successes in Madrid and the north, but later the rural regions of Andalucía and Extremadura outgrew the traditional strongholds of Socialist affiliation. From the outset Madrid was the headquarters of the PSOE, and from 1899 of the UGT too. Particularly helpful in assisting growth in the centre was the

---

[9] Llopis, *Etapas*, 6; Linz, *El sistema*, 173–5.

[10] Martínez Cuadrado, ii. 661; Artola, i. 659 n. 331; Tuñón de Lara, *El movimiento*, iii. 115, 120. Spain's population reached 23.5m. by 1930, of whom 8.4m. were economically active (26.5% of them in industry). By 1933 there were 3.5m. workers, including almost 2m. in agriculture and 436,000 in construction (ibid. 9, 69).

[11] The Socialist Enrique de Santiago in his *La UGT ante la revolución* (Madrid, 1932, 141) wrote: 'A good secretary is one who animates the organization. Like secretary, like organization.' Largo Caballero, who became general secretary of the UGT in 1918, apparently was able to choose a number of congress delegates personally (Meaker, 277).

[12] Morato, *La cuna*, 552.

[13] Contreras, 17–20. Prior to 1930 the only significant PSOE-UGT divergence was in relation to the Comintern. In 1920, after the PSOE had voted in principle and conditionally to join the new International, the UGT congress voted to stay in the more conservative Amsterdam International. See Meaker, 268–75.

inauguration of Madrid's Casa del Pueblo in 1908. Such buildings, established by the Socialists throughout Spain as centres for the education of workers and training of militants, also served as social clubs and meeting places, and often housed co-operatives too. Many of the early local unions (*sociedades de resistencia*) affiliated to the UGT after first making use of the Casa del Pueblo, and this was the key to Madrid's rise to pre-eminence in the UGT early this century.[14] In 1907 some 17,000 of the UGT's 30,000 members worked in Madrid, mainly in the craft trades.[15]

Socialist ideas and organization were propagated from Madrid, often by workers who had been blacklisted by employers following strikes in or near the capital. The moves of Antonio García Quejido to Valencia and Barcelona and of the hardened Facundo Perezagua to Bilbao after the printers' strike of 1885 were cases in point.[16] One of the strangest features of the geographical pattern of PSOE development was the long-standing failure to implant socialism as a vital force in Catalonia, Spain's first industrial region. There the Socialists were faced with the prior presence of anarchist influence plus a determined Republican effort to organize working-class support. They then made what turned out to be an unfortunate choice of comrades in the region. Their Barcelona group was based mainly on textile workers who were affiliated to the quite conservative Tres Clases de Vapor union, which from 1886 had responded to economic crises by seeking a common protectionist policy with Catalan employers. This approach alienated the more militant artisans and workers and it strained relations between the Catalan and Madrid Socialists—as did the Madrid decision in 1886 to give the new *El Socialista* an anti-Republican line. The early efforts by the PSOE to build a Catalan federation were disrupted in 1890 when many of the Barcelona Socialists, inspired by the reformist ideas of Paul Brousse and the French Possibilists, broke away to form the

[14] Madrid's Casa del Pueblo began with 102 *sociedades* and 35,000 members (Tuñón de Lara, *El movimiento*, ii. 71, 138). See also Arbeloa, *Las casas del pueblo* (Madrid: Mañana, 1977).

[15] Joseph Harrison, *An Economic History of Modern Spain* (Manchester: Manchester University Press, 1978), 117.

[16] Morato, *El Partido*, 101–2.

honestly-named, if short-lived, Opportunist Socialist Party.[17]

Subsequently, as Catalan nationalism became politically important, the PSOE's centralist image proved a liability in the region. Regarding working-class unity as an indispensable source of strength, and considering that proletarian interests transcended national frontiers, the party showed itself to be deeply suspicious of Catalanism, while remaining somewhat insensitive to the specific problems of Catalan workers. The transfer of the UGT headquarters from Barcelona to Madrid in 1899, though reflecting a shift in the spatial distribution of members, certainly did not help the Socialists in Catalonia. In 1910 only 635 of the UGT's 40,000 members were to be found in Barcelona; by 1915 there were only 209 PSOE members there, compared with concentrations of over 500 in Madrid (1,184), Vizcaya (710), and Oviedo in Asturias (581).[18] In 1918 the PSOE introduced into its programme a commitment to establish a 'republican confederation of Iberian nationalities', but the hostile Castilian attitude towards progressive Catalanists did not disappear.[19]

A Socialist organization existed in Barcelona from 1879 and the Socialist Federation of Catalonia (FSC) was founded in 1903.[20] The federation suffered major dislocation in 1923 when the Socialist Union of Catalonia (USC) was established at its expense and began to cultivate the more radical elements among the Catalanists. As time passed the problem of Catalonia became increasingly apparent to the PSOE yet also more difficult to resolve; for while support for Catalan autonomy was part of the remedy, any such devolution was sure to mean granting power in the region to the party's electoral rivals, at least in the short term. Hence the Socialists' reluctance to accept the Pact of San Sebastián which brought together the pro-republican forces in 1930 and which the PSOE regarded

---

[17] Miguel Izard, *Industrialización y obrerismo: Las Tres Clases de Vapor 1869–1913* (Barcelona: Ariel, 1973), *passim*; Elorza, introd. to Iglesias, *Escritos II* (Madrid: Ayuso, 1985), 25–34; Morato, *El Partido*, 124.

[18] Harrison, 117; Artola, i. 518.

[19] Tuñón de Lara, 'Sobre la historia', 47–9; Luis Gómez Llorente, *Aproximación a la historia del socialismo español (hasta 1921)* (Madrid: Cuadernos para el Diálogo, 1976), 345–7.

[20] For an outline of the history of Catalan Socialism see Partit dels Socialistes de Catalunya (PSC-PSOE), *La unidad de los socialistas de Catalunya* (n.p., 1978).

as conceding too much to the Catalans.[21] Socialist stubbornness over the regional question stymied reunification efforts by the USC and FSC in 1932–3,[22] and finally both the USC and FSC were lost when they allied with other parties to create the Unified Socialist Party of Catalonia (PSUC) in 1936. However, it is far from clear that greater sensitivity by the PSOE to the aspirations of Spain's regions and 'nationalities' would in itself have guaranteed success in Catalonia. The USC, despite meeting this requirement, failed to establish a political space for itself between the party of the Catalanist left, Republican Left of Catalonia (ERC), and the anarcho-syndicalist CNT. By 1933 it had grown only to 3,000 members.[23]

In the mean time success had been achieved in the Basque province of Vizcaya, which underwent a vigorous process of industrialization during the last quarter of the nineteenth century. In 1886 a Socialist *agrupación* was established by Perezagua in Bilbao and the organization then spread to the mining zone, assisted greatly by Socialist leadership of the miners' strike of 1890 and other violent episodes.[24] Recruitment among iron and steel workers in the manufacturing sector only got under way during the First World War. In Vizcaya the Socialists benefited from an absence of pre-existing political and trade union traditions among the workforce. And the fact that local leaders of the organization simultaneously acted as trade union and political leaders and were prepared to place themselves at the head of militant strikers also contributed to making Vizcaya the only place in Spain where Socialists were influencing thousands of workers by the 1890s. Here it was difficult for the PSOE not to oppose the nationalism of the Basque Nationalist Party when it was created in 1895, for one of the salient features of Basque nationalism was its hostility to the large itinerant proletariat; the latter formed at least 65 per cent of the province's iron miners whom the PSOE-UGT sought to represent.[25] The

---

[21] Ben-Ami, *Origins*, 140–4.

[22] Isidre Molas, 'Los socialistas catalanes: La unificación frustrada de 1933', *Leviatán*, 7 (1982), 107–10.

[23] Ibid. 108.

[24] The key source on early Basque Socialism is the classic regional study by Fusi, *Política*. See too Jesús M. Eguiguren, *El PSOE en el País Vasco (1886–1936)* (San Sebastián: Hananburu, 1984). [25] Fusi, *Política*, 50, 81–130.

reactionary nature of the early PNV, which counterposed an idealized agrarian past to the emerging industrial society, no doubt confirmed in many Socialist minds the conviction that regional nationalism *per se* was reactionary.

From Vizcaya the movement was extended to other parts of northern Spain, principally to Asturias whose workers were to earn a reputation for class-consciousness and combativity in future decades. The general strike of 1917 lasted longest in Asturias and the insurrectional movement of 1934 succeeded only there, placing the mining zone in the hands of the workers for a fortnight. Several of the pioneers of Asturian Socialism, notably the 'blind propagandist' Eduardo Varela, had worked earlier in Vizcaya, taken part in the strike of 1890, and come under Perezagua's influence.[26] The first group was created in Gijón in 1891 and the Asturian Socialist Federation (FSA) in 1901. In Asturias, unlike Catalonia, a tradition of good relations with the anarchists developed. It was a reason for the regional success of the revolutionary action in 1934, designed to prevent Gil-Robles' right-wing CEDA party from entering the Lerroux government following the electoral defeat of the centre and left-wing forces the previous year. While the CNT put down roots in the Gijón and La Felguera areas, the Socialists acquired more substantial strongholds in the manufacturing area of Oviedo and in the Nalón coalfield.[27] It was Socialists such as Manuel Llaneza who founded and became the leaders of the Asturian Mineworkers' Union (SOMA) in 1910, and miners who became the main base of Socialist groups, there being little differentiation early on between the PSOE and UGT in the region.[28] In 1911, 80 per cent of UGT members were to be found in Madrid, Vizcaya, and Asturias, the inverted triangle of Spanish Socialism.[29]

A general territorial expansion helped the PSOE to become the only party during the 1930s to field candidates in all parts

---

[26] Indalecio Prieto, 'El propagandista ciego', in Prieto, *De mi vida* (Mexico: Ediciones Oasis, 1965), 211–12; David Ruiz, *El movimiento obrero en Asturias: De la industrialización a la Segunda República* (Oviedo: Amigos de Asturias, 1968), 91–8; id., *Asturias contemporánea (1808–1936)* (Madrid: Siglo XXI, 1975), 25–32; Saborit, *Asturias*, ch. 1.
[27] Ruiz, *Asturias*, 28, 52–4; Adrian Shubert, *Hacia la revolución: Orígenes sociales del movimiento obrero en Asturias, 1860–1934* (Barcelona: Crítica, 1984).
[28] Saborit, *Asturias*, 143. [29] Fusi, *Política*, 317.

of Spain except Catalonia.[30] The most striking change in the original pattern of Socialist development was provided by the penetration of rural areas. Before 1910 the PSOE made little effort to recruit agricultural labourers, and its first agrarian programme was not adopted until 1918. Andalucía, which together with Catalonia was a traditional fiefdom of the anarcho-syndicalists and anarchists, then began to gain greater representation in the party. Andalucía and Extremadura grew from 36 per cent of PSOE membership in 1928 to 45 per cent in 1932, as rural workers joined the UGT's new National Federation of Land Workers (FNTT), encouraged by improvements decreed by Largo Caballero as Labour Minister in 1931–2. The FNTT increased in size from 36,639 members in June 1930 to 392,953 by June 1932, amidst growing agrarian unrest.[31] However, strictly speaking much of the Socialist expansion in the south was UGT development linked to the granting of economic benefits by the Socialist-Republican coalition government of 1931–3. The PSOE won a lot of votes in Andalucía under the Second Republic but it was poorly organized there; this helps explain the republican side's rapid loss of the south-west when the Civil War commenced.[32]

By 1932 the UGT was no longer the tiny organization of craft unions it had been forty years earlier. It had become a mass force whose members were drawn from agriculture (43 per cent), construction (8 per cent), railways (5 per cent), mining (4 per cent), urban transport (3 per cent), and metallurgy (3 per cent). It was still notoriously weak in the Catalan textile industry but now had a rising number of non-industrial workers: bank and commercial employees, teachers, and public functionaries.[33] The social composition of the PSOE early this century cannot be determined with any precision, though some incomplete data exist for Socialist parliamentarians elected in 1931–6. In each of the three elections held under the Second Republic, manual workers

---

[30] Linz, *El sistema*, 88–9.
[31] Ibid. 84–5; Paul Preston, 'The Agrarian War in the South', in id. (ed.), *Revolution and War in Spain 1931–1939* (London: Methuen, 1984).
[32] Linz, *El sistema*, 101.
[33] Fusi, *Política*, 315; Tuñón de Lara, *El movimiento*, iii. 119–20.

constituted the largest single occupational group among elected PSOE deputies, though they were far from providing an absolute majority of the bloc.[34] Some 43.5 per cent of the Socialists elected to the constituent Cortes in 1931 possessed academic degrees.[35]

Intellectuals were slow to move into the PSOE. At the start of the century García Quejido brought out a revisionist theoretical journal, *La Nueva Era*, which might have attracted some intellectuals had it not died an early death, lacking support among party leaders. During its brief life, while not publishing anything particularly original, it at least challenged Guesdist catastrophe theory and the 'iron law of wages' dogma.[36] The party congress of 1915 was the first to be attended by a group of intellectuals, several of whom had been attracted to the party via the New School established by Núñez de Arenas in 1910. The School, a place where socialist intellectuals could use and display their pedagogic talent, was only partially successful. It too encountered resistance from party leaders who felt threatened, rightly suspecting that the School's aim was to transform the PSOE into a theoretically-heterogeneous party similar to the British Labour Party, and thus divert it from its original mission.[37]

Largely as a result of the trade union input provided by the UGT, the party remained theoretically undernourished, concerned mainly with practical and immediate questions. An imaginative approach to socialism was shared only by a handful whom the leadership distrusted. To the dogmatists of working-class origin was added the pragmatism of new middle-class elements such as the journalist Indalecio Prieto. While rejecting the 'workerism' of his arch-rival Perezagua in Bilbao and wanting to attract middle-class voters to the party, Prieto confessed: 'Really I am not a man of doctrine. I am a man of realities.'[38] By the 1930s intellectuals were more prominent in the party, but still much rarer than in the Italian

---

[34] López Sevilla, 39–42; Contreras, 110–12.   [35] López Sevilla, 39.

[36] Pérez Ledesma, *Pensamiento, passim*. Unamuno was dismissive of the journal and said that its poor quality confirmed the absence of theoreticians among the ranks of 'militant socialism' in Spain (Gómez Molleda, *Unamuno*, 70–1).

[37] Ibid. 76–82; Meaker, 14–15; Morato, *El Partido*, 196–7; Tuñón de Lara, *El movimiento*, ii. 122–6, 143.

[38] Prieto, quoted in Fusi, *Política*, 382.

and French socialist movements. At the start of the decade, most were westernizers who saw the party as the most suitable vehicle for democratizing and modernizing Spain.[39] Among them there were original thinkers such as Fernando de los Ríos, later regarded by non-Marxists as an exception to the norm of theoretical poverty in the PSOE.[40] It is significant, however, that the intellectual who rose to the greatest heights in the PSOE and UGT, the philosophy professor Julián Besteiro, did not attack Pablista dogmas.

Other features of the party's early development were the growth of the Socialist press and the creation of women's and youth organizations. By 1903 the total circulation of Socialist weeklies was 35,000, the main organs being *El Socialista* of Madrid, *La Lucha de Clases* of Bilbao, *La Aurora Social* of Oviedo, and *El Obrero Balear* of Palma de Mallorca.[41] *El Socialista* appeared daily for much of the 1913–39 period.

On the question of women, the PSOE had incorporated specific points in its programme right from 1879, but it took the emergence of the Young Socialists (FNJSE) for an organizational initiative to be taken. The largest Grupo Femenino Socialista was probably that of Madrid, founded in 1906. Along with similar groups, its self-appointed tasks were to educate women (in respect of their rights, social duties, and socialism), to build women's organizations, spread socialist ideas, and campaign for legislation on behalf of women and children.[42] Although women constituted a small minority of PSOE members, the party none the less played quite a pioneering role here at a time when politics was practically a male preserve.

The Young Socialists were organized first in Bilbao in 1903 and then launched nationally at their first congress in April 1906. Led by Tomás Meabe, they concentrated their early campaign efforts against militarism, well aware that youth, if not truth, was the first victim of any war. They lacked a

---

[39] Meaker, 14–17, 23.

[40] For a defence of De los Ríos's originality see the introduction by Elías Díaz to Fernando de los Ríos, *El sentido humanista del socialismo* (Madrid: Castalia, 1976), 7–49.

[41] Tuñón de Lara, *El movimiento*, ii. 44.

[42] Mary Nash, 'La problemática de la mujer y el movimiento obrero en España', in Balcells (ed.), 241–79.

specific programme of youth demands and remained quite few in number until the 1930s, but on several occasions they took important initiatives, subverting the party's old ideas and practices. It was the Youth who brought into debate the position of women and the forgotten problems of the countryside, and they had fewer scruples than their elders over co-operating with Republican forces. Within the party there was considerable opposition to the very existence of a youth section, which Iglesias deemed unnecessary, potentially divisive, and dangerously provocative because of the FNJSE's anti-militarism.[43] As in other countries, the youth section caused headaches to the party leadership. During the First World War part of the opposition to the pro-Allied stance of the PSOE majority came from the Youth, and very quickly the latter became much more radical under the influence of Bolshevism and the conditions and insurrectional mood in Spain in 1917. In 1919–21 the FNJSE played a central role in the Communist break with the Socialists, so much so that it took over a decade for a comparable Socialist youth organization to be built.[44] The Young Socialists then quickly grew into a mass organization that became actively involved in the PSOE-UGT internal strife of the 1930s.

TENDENCIES IN THE PSOE

Like other parties of the Second International, the PSOE soon acquired internal currents and tendencies that competed for influence and predominance. From the start there were tensions between dogmatic 'workerists', who in the name of doctrinal purity favoured a policy of working-class isolationism, and more moderate elements who, moved by revisionism, liberalism, or pragmatism, desired an alliance with Republican forces. Organized tendencies that operated as coherent factions at party congresses made their appearance between 1910 and 1920, a decade witnessing not only major national and

[43] On the FNJSE see Antonio González Quintana and Aurelio Martín Najera, *Apuntes para la historia de las Juventudes Socialistas de España* (Madrid: Fundación Pablo Iglesias, 1983), *passim*; Fusi, *Política*, 243–53.

[44] Meaker, 189–279; González and Martín, 37.

international convulsions but also the beginnings of the social diversification of PSOE membership. Spain's post-war revolutionary atmosphere combined with the Bolshevik triumph in Russia to give rise to a *tercerista* tendency which advocated affiliation to the new Third or Communist International and rejected dealings with the Republicans at home. So strong was the radical mood at this time that two party congresses voted in principle for affiliation to the new International, before the Bolshevik 'Twenty-One Conditions' stymied the process.[1] Most Socialists considered themselves to be revolutionaries, but in a party whose years of struggle had demonstrated the value of unity, and in which a sentimental reverence for Iglesias had become permanent, the Leninist insistence upon the expulsion of 'reformist' leaders and the prospect of a schism eventually determined the outcome.[2] In 1921 the PSOE voted by 8,808 to 6,025 votes to support instead the short-lived Vienna International in its attempt to repair the broken unity of the workers' parties. When that failed, it realigned itself with the remnants of the Second International, though it remained supportive of the Russian Revolution and on paper even subscribed to the idea of the dictatorship of the proletariat.[3]

The first major experience of a battle waged between tendencies was a most damaging one and it shaped future attitudes to minority rights in the PSOE. For although the resultant Communist party, the PCE, failed to inherit all the members of the PSOE minority and proved insufficiently troublesome for Primo to bother to ban its paper,[4] the schism itself badly disrupted the Socialist Party's organizational growth. Henceforth Socialists would regard Communists as

---

[1] In 1919 the PSOE voted to join the Comintern if the Second and Third Internationals were unable to unite. The following year the three conditions set by the PSOE for affiliation were: retention of PSOE tactical autonomy; the party's right to doctrinal revision of Third International positions; and a PSOE commitment to work for the international reunification of all socialist forces. Clearly such conditions were incompatible with those of the Leninist International.

[2] Meaker, 362–5.

[3] On this early tendency, strife, and the birth of the Communist Party see ibid. 189–313, 346–455; Gómez Llorente, *Aproximación*, 379–563; Víctor Alba, *The Communist Party in Spain* (New Brunswick, NJ and London: Transaction Press, 1983), 1–63.

[4] Brenan, p. 223 n. 1.

splitters and would be extremely wary of any signs of radicalism among the Young Socialists, the youth section having been prepared to break with its parent party in support of the Comintern. Here there was a degree of hypocrisy, for both Iglesias and his lieutenant Besteiro had warned the Terceristas that the anti-Leninists would not remain in the PSOE if it accepted the Twenty-One Conditions.[5]

What might be termed the historical or classical tendencies of the PSOE developed in the 1920s and 1930s and were to remain a lasting point of reference for disputants within the party. The political issues that separated Socialists from one another were: whether to collaborate with the dictatorship of Primo de Rivera; when to terminate that collaboration; whether to join the revolutionary movement for the establishment of a republic; whether to join Republican parties in coalition governments when the Second Republic was established in 1931; when and under what conditions to break with the Republicans; whether to adopt more revolutionary tactics or retreat into isolationism when the Republic disappointed hopes for reform; again, whether to sit alongside Republicans in coalition governments in 1936; then, during the Civil War, whether to support the Popular Front or seek an alternative united front limited to the workers' organizations; and finally, what attitude to adopt in relation to the Communist Party and its wartime policies. Since detailed historical analyses of Socialist differences over these issues now make up a considerable literature,[6] discussion here will be limited to the character of each tendency.

One common system of characterization presents the 'reformist' tendency headed by Julián Besteiro as being on the right of the party, the 'bolshevist' tendency behind Francisco Largo Caballero as constituting the left, and a 'centrist' tendency led by Indalecio Prieto as being in the middle.

---

[5] Ibid. 223; Meaker, 364.

[6] On the origins of internal party divisions see Preston, 'Los orígenes del cisma socialista 1917–1931', *Cuadernos de Ruedo Ibérico*, 49–50 (1976), 11–40; English version in *Journal of Contemporary History*, 12. 1 (1977), 101–32 and in Preston. *The Coming of the Spanish Civil War* (London and Basingstoke: Macmillan, 1978), 1–25. Other particularly useful sources on tendencies are ibid., ch. 5; Gabriel Morón, *Política de ayer y política de mañana: Los socialistas ante el problema nacional* (Mexico: publ. by the author, 1942); and Contreras *passim*.

However, the simple juxtaposition of right, left, and centre only does justice to the realities of internal party conflict in the years 1934–5. During the 1920s, when it was the only faction opposed to collaboration with Primo, Prieto's group in a sense functioned as the left of the party; and in early 1933, with Largo Caballero still defending Socialist participation in the republican government and with Besteiro critical of this, one might equally regard the former as having been on the right and the latter on the left.[7] Since there was this transposition of the tendencies, some idea of their evolution has to be introduced into any characterization; attempts to reduce internal antagonisms simply to ideological disputes are futile. The fact that these tendencies were labelled often after their leaders, as Besteirista, *caballerista*, and *prietista*, betokens a strong element of personalism and a lack not so much of ideological cohesion as of ideological motivation.

All three tendencies viewed the Second Republic as a bourgeois regime and tended to equate the Republican parties with an ascendant bourgeoisie pursuing a democratic revolution. Anchored to the mechanical vision of historical stages presented in the Communist Manifesto and rigidly adhered to by the Russian Mensheviks, the Socialists misinterpreted what was happening in Spain. The reality was that capitalism had displaced feudalism in their own country a century beforehand and that since then sections of the bourgeoisie had been integrated into the traditional oligarchy.[8] A considerable community of interest now existed between agrarian and urban élites. The Republican parties were bourgeois in that they were pro-capitalist, but more specifically they stood for the elevation of the middle classes through a democratization of the Spanish State, a reduction in the power of the Church, and increased educational opportunities. All three Socialist tendencies erred in basing their strategies on what was thought to have happened in Britain and France in the seventeenth and eighteenth centuries. Certainly, some of the classical tasks of bourgeois revolution had not been performed in Spain, but the renovating ambition of the

[7] This is the view of Ricardo de la Cierva, *La historia perdida del socialismo español* (Madrid: Nacional, 1972), 148.

[8] Preston, *The Coming*, 24–5.

Republican parties was limited largely to political changes. Indeed, their lack of any real interest in land reform was a central factor in Largo Caballero's decision to distance himself from them and attempt to revolutionize the PSOE from mid-1933.

Of the three tendencies, Prieto's was that which worked most determinedly to achieve and then defend the Second Republic.[9] A man of immense natural intelligence who rose from street-seller to wealthy owner of the Bilbao newspaper *El Liberal*, Prieto was more of a liberal than a socialist. In a famous statement of conviction, he declared that he was 'a liberal kind of socialist'; on another occasion he described himself as a 'socialist by sentiment'.[10] Though middle class by birth, he had known poverty during childhood because of the early death of his father, and this mix of circumstance made him the natural proponent of alliance with the Republicans.[11] In the absence of a viable Liberal Party, Prieto sought to steer the PSOE away from its early dogmatic workerist orientation; by attracting able middle-class reformists, he hoped to convert the party into a vehicle for the modernization of Spain. Renowned for his pragmatism and powerful oratory, Prieto's main goal for the foreseeable future was to consolidate the Republic through an alliance with Left Republicans both in parliament and in office.[12] It was in this spirit that he served as Treasury Minister and Minister of Public Works in 1931–3,

---

[9] For an interesting series of centenary appreciations of Prieto see *MOPU*, magazine of the Ministerio de Obras Públicas y Urbanismo, 305 (1983), 5–48.

[10] Prieto, *Discursos fundamentales* (Madrid: Turner, 1975), 45, 294.

[11] Edward Malefakis, introd. to Prieto, *Discursos*, 11–16.

[12] Much earlier Jaime Vera had advocated collaboration with progressive Republicans to rationalize the capitalist system, remove supposed feudal remnants, and establish a bourgeois democracy (Castillo, 9). Prieto stated his argument most clearly at the PSOE congress of 1932, when he declared: 'the tragedy of the Spanish Socialist Party is that, because of the weakness and inadequacies of the Spanish Republican parties . . . the Socialist Party in Spain has had, not to serve the bourgeoisie—which would be pointless—but rather, in order to survive, has had to perform here not only its own party functions but also the liberal and democratic work that in the rest of the world has been done by the bourgeois parties, which have never become a force in the context of Spanish politics.' (PSOE, Thirteenth Congress (1932), *Actas* (Madrid: PSOE, 1934), 392.) Social democrats in the PSOE were still using this quotation to justify their position some 40–50 years later. For example, it appeared (misquoted) in *El Socialista: Especial XXVII Congreso*, 1 (1976), 10–12.

along with two other Socialist ministers, Francisco Largo Caballero and Fernando de los Ríos.

Prieto's acceptance of the use of insurrectional tactics in October 1934 did not indicate a left turn on his part. A widespread fear existed among Socialists that the entry of right-wing CEDA ministers into Lerroux's Radical Party government presaged a fascist offensive against the Republic and its supporters, and Prieto's reluctant endorsement of pre-emptive revolutionary action had eminently defensive intentions, far removed from revolutionary hopes for proletarian dictatorship. He argued that Spain was not ready for socialism, yet he probably had no conception of any future stage at which positive revolutionary action might be acceptable. The defeat of the October Revolution in Asturias and the cruel reprisals that ensued only served to reinforce Prieto's preference for the parliamentary road and to heighten his sensitivity to the dangers of an immoderate left provoking a backlash from the right. In 1936 he helped restore the Republican-Socialist collaboration of 1931–3, and would have been the obvious candidate for premier of the Popular Front government elected in February had it not been for Caballerista opposition to the idea inside his own party. As the PSOE left saw it, Prieto's social democratic ideas were thoroughly Utopian: the economy had declined, the governing classes were as intransigent as ever, and fascism and reaction were threatening a rebellion against liberal institutions.

No less a social democrat in sympathy was Julián Besteiro, who had begun his political activity in the Unión Republicana of Nicolás Salmerón. Though his followers considered him to be a paragon of Marxist orthodoxy,[13] his 'Marxism' was full of positivist and neo-Kantian infiltrations and he openly admired the Fabians and Franklin D. Roosevelt.[14] Besteiro made use

---

[13] See Gabriel Mario de Coca's defence of Besteiro against the 'Leninist' Caballero in Coca, *Anti-Caballero: Una crítica marxista de la bolchevización del Partido Socialista Obrero Español*, 1936 (Madrid: Del Centro, 1975); Andrés Saborit, *Julián Besteiro* (Buenos Aires: Losada, 1967), 264.

[14] Emilio Lamo de Espinosa, *Filosofía y política en Julián Besteiro* (Madrid: Cuadernos para el Diálogo, 1973), 136–72. For Besteiro's main doctrinal statement see his *Marxismo y antimarxismo*, 1935 (Madrid: Júcar, 1980). For a Caballerista

of the lexicon of Marxism and along with many European socialists accepted Kautsky's view that socialism could only come on to the agenda once a bourgeois revolution had been accomplished and capitalism had developed to the full. Having played a leading part in the revolutionary movement of August 1917 and gone to prison for it, he became extremely cautious in outlook and totally boycotted the revolutionary action taken in 1934.

Even before the death of Iglesias in 1925, Besteiro became the leading figure in the PSOE. Over the next decade he was guided by a typically Pablista concern with preserving the Socialist organizations from destruction and contamination. In the 1920s this led him to resist republican conspiracy and to defend the collaboration with Primo, thereby hoping to protect the gains made by the Socialists over the years. The same concern lay behind his 1930s position of advocating Socialist support for, but preferring no PSOE participation in, the governments of the Republic. Besteiro was not indifferent here: he regarded a republican regime as distinctly superior to a monarchy, and he was even persuaded to preside over the republican Cortes during the constituent period. However, he argued persistently for a principle of Socialist non-involvement, fearing that PSOE ministers would become identified with non-socialist governmental measures and thus discredit the party in the eyes of the masses. Better, in his view, to isolate the PSOE as much as possible from the corruption of bourgeois society and, to use Fabra Ribas's phrase, to leave it to the bourgeoisie to furnish the house that the proletariat would occupy later.[15] This analysis was prescient regarding the role that Socialist ministers would play at times in 1931–3 and 1936–7, but it offered no viable way forward, the bourgeoisie in the 1930s being just as conservative as it had been in 1917.[16]

Largo Caballero, in turn, was the leader who most tried to

critique of it cf. Luis Araquistain, *Marxismo y socialismo en España* (Barcelona: Fontemara, 1980), 23–62.

[15] Although this was Besteiro's principle in the 1930s he was prepared to compromise on it at times, accepting Socialist involvement in order not to upset the delicate political balance of the Republic. See his intervention at the party congress in 1932 (*Actas*, 418–20); and Tuñón de Lara, *El movimiento*, iii. 125.

[16] Lamo de Espinosa, 207.

base party activity on working-class and UGT interests, thereby perpetuating the workerist aspect of Pablismo. A master plasterer who like Prieto had lost his father at an early age, he changed from being an archetypal trade union bureaucrat before 1930 into the figurehead of the radicalized wing of the party by 1936, when he was flattered as the 'Spanish Lenin'. Having inherited effective control of the Socialist unions from the ailing Iglesias in 1918, Largo Caballero had defended collaboration and personally served as an official of Primo's regime in the mid-1920s, not only in the interest of UGT survival but also in an attempt to steal a march on the rival CNT. Well attuned to mass moods, he helped end Socialist collaboration towards the end of the decade as working-class militancy was fuelled by economic decline; then, registering the popular enthusiasm for a republican alternative, he belatedly joined the anti-monarchist movement and became Minister of Labour in the Republican-Socialist coalition of 1931–3. The significance of his ministry for labour was ambiguous, for although he was responsible for pro-worker legislation, this was often designed to enhance the influence of the UGT. In 1931 he presided over the UGT May Day demonstration in Madrid while ordering repressions of CNT and Communist activities in Barcelona and Bilbao.[17]

Largo Caballero's subsequent shift to the left in the company of militants wishing to 'bolshevize' the PSOE was primarily a response to workers' discontent with the meagre reform achievements of the new regime—especially the slow implementation of the modest agrarian reform at a time when UGT growth was mainly rural.[18] Those who moved to the left, among them thousands of Youth members, were emboldened by the rapid growth of the Socialist organizations in the early 1930s, and there was also an element of personal chagrin at the way in which Largo's ministerial authority had been flouted at times even by proprietors linked to the Republican parties.[19] The rise of Nazism and Fascism in Europe in the face of inadequate social democratic and trade

[17] Vilar, 'El socialismo 1917–1945', 451.
[18] Malefakis, *Reforma agraria y revolución campesina en la España del siglo XX* (Barcelona: Ariel, 1976), 366–94; Preston, *The Coming*, 19; Brenan, 273–4.
[19] Ibid. 273–4.

union responses provided the international backcloth to the radical advance—'Better Vienna than Berlin' became a slogan of the left, indicating a preference for going down fighting, should this dilemma arise.[20] Radicalism was encouraged further when the right won general elections at home in 1933 when faced with divided opponents; it then proceeded to overturn republican legislation and threatened to attack the Constitution. From the middle of 1933 Largo thus began veering to the left, convinced that the Republicans had exhausted their potential for progressive action. The Socialists, he felt, should break with them, abandon the parliamentary road, and pursue an insurrectional conquest of power by the workers for socialist purposes.[21]

This placed the Caballeristas for a while to the left of the Communists, but their voluntaristic revolutionism soon revealed its limitations in 1935–6. They acted impulsively, without clear perspectives and without a coherent strategy for the seizure of power.[22] Their grasp of Marxism was poor, even in the case of the group of intellectuals led by Luis Araquistain, and in the circumstances this left them open to Stalinist influence. Encouraged by the unconditional entry of the Communist unions into the UGT in 1935, the Caballeristas became over-confident about the Socialists' capacity to 'absorb' the much smaller Communist forces at youth and party levels also.[23] It was hoped that unity with the Communists would strengthen the Socialist left in its bid to

---

[20] Gabriel Jackson, *The Spanish Republic and the Civil War, 1931–1939* (Princeton, NJ: Princeton University Press, 1967), 147.

[21] Largo Caballero's growing radicalism is reflected in his *Discursos a los trabajadores* (Madrid: Gráfica Socialista, 1934).

[22] For a powerful critique of Caballerismo see Juliá, *La izquierda del PSOE (1935–1936)* (Madrid: Siglo XXI, 1977). See also Fernando Claudín, 'La revolución inoportuna (España 1936–1939)', *Cuadernos de Ruedo Ibérico*, 28–9 (1970–1); id. *The Communist Movement* (Harmondsworth: Penguin, 1975), 210–42; Andrés de Blas Guerrero, *El socialismo radical en la II República* (Madrid: Tucar, 1978); Felix Morrow, *Revolution and Counter-Revolution in Spain* (New York: New Park, 1976); Marta Bizcarrondo, *Araquistain y la crisis socialista en la II República*: Leviatán (1934–1936) (Madrid: Siglo XXI, 1975).

[23] There is disagreement over whether Largo Caballero initially approved of the youth unity. For example, Amaro del Rosal (*Historia de la UGT de España 1901–1939*), 2 vols. (Barcelona: Grijalbo, 1977), ii. 621) claims that he supported it, a view disputed by Francisco López Real in 'Largo Caballero nunca quiso la unificación de las Juventudes', *El Socialista*, 3.12.78, 6.

'bolshevize' the PSOE. But 'bolshevization' here meant simply hounding the right-wing Besteiristas out of the party and displacing the Prietistas from the leadership, thus leaving the Caballeristas dominant. In 1936 the Caballeristas gradually lost ground in the PSOE through their incapacity to take political initiatives and their competitive attitude to the vast CNT, whose anarchic ranks contained in Trotsky's view 'the élite of the Spanish proletariat'.[24] Blinded by a faith in their own destiny, the Caballeristas had a weak appreciation of the real balance of forces in Spain and greatly underestimated the threat posed by the right. For much of 1936 they held the view that only total Socialist domination of the government would be worth while: Socialist participation, as advocated by Prieto, would not guarantee the implementation of a programme of change nor the efficient conduct of the war; it would only help the anarchists. Yet since they themselves failed to offer a viable left-wing strategy, the Caballeristas' attitude only served to weaken the embattled republican regime.[25] Many members of this tendency became disillusioned and went over to the PCE, which although less radical at least was dynamic, well-organized, and efficient.[26]

Conflict between the tendencies thus emanated from different appreciations of changing conditions and contrasting attitudes to other political forces. But personality clashes also became bitter in the absence of the movement's undisputed 'grandfather' Pablo Iglesias. The enmity between Prieto and Caballero was particularly corrosive. Largo Caballero was jealous of Prieto's impressive parliamentary performances, resented his indiscipline, and made a lot of his colleague's habit of slipping away to France in moments of danger (1917, 1930, and 1934).[27] The suggestion of cowardice was unfair to a man who was involved in arms smuggling for the revolutionary movement in 1934, but Prieto had earned

[24] Leon Trotsky, *The Spanish Revolution* (*1931–39*) (New York: Pathfinder, 1973), 299.

[25] On one occasion Largo Caballero himself said: 'To tell the proletariat it must fight and then not to prepare it for the struggle is a crime' (quoted by Coca, 96).

[26] Franz Borkenau, *The Spanish Cockpit* (Michigan: Michigan University Press, 1963), 190–2, 285–8; Brenan, 325–6.

[27] Largo Caballero, *Mis recuerdos*, 1954, (2nd edn., Mexico: Ediciones Unidas, 1976), 132–3.

Largo's fury by opportunistically claiming responsibility for this movement from the safety of Paris, at a time when Largo, imprisoned for his leading role in the preparation of the events, was in no position to set the record straight.[28] In turn, Prieto was disdainful of Largo's mental rigidity and intellectual limitations, of his demagoguery and vanity; he was angered by the great popularity acquired by the leader of the left as Largo rose to become a legendary figure in the mid-1930s.

Personalism flourished in the ideologically arid soils of the PSOE, where disputes were never exclusively doctrinal. One might have expected that the growing bureaucracy of the PSOE and UGT, both of which now had substantial paid secretariats, would have tended to depersonalize conflict; instead, combined with organizational growth, it transformed individual differences of opinion into conflicts affecting not just personalities but also the coteries surrounding them, whose fate was linked to the fortunes of their leader. There was an extent to which internal struggles were purely power struggles in which ideas were used as ammunition. This phenomenon had been evident in the PSOE before 1920 in the way in which the Spanish Fabians of the New School, having pitted revisionist ideas against the party oligarchy in 1911–14, became the leading Bolshevik challengers to the leadership in 1919–21.[29] Yet, when all this has been said, and whatever psychological analysis is made of the leading figures, one has to recognize that *personalismo* would not have been nearly so destructive a force had the various personalities not given genuine expression to currents of thought and sentiment in the PSOE and UGT, and in society at large.

During the 1920s the Caballeristas and Besteiristas were dominant in the Socialist movement. Prietismo had little influence until Largo Caballero began to endorse the idea of republican alignment at the end of the decade, but it then became a viable tendency and in a way displaced the Besteiristas as the PSOE right wing in the mid-1930s.[30]

[28] Morón, 29–30.   [29] Meaker, 14–15, 199, 481.

[30] Both factions held that the Republic was as progressive as it could be in the circumstances; they were both Europeanizers, reformists, and opponents of the dictatorship of the proletariat. The Besteiristas gave their tactical support to Prieto

Although the moderate Besteiristas triumphed at the UGT congress of 1932, their authority was quickly undermined by growing social unrest and militancy, so much so that in January 1934 they could not prevent the UGT from committing itself to the idea of pre-emptive revolutionary action to counter the threat of fascism. Defeated, they resigned, leaving the Caballeristas in charge. Meanwhile, in the PSOE the Besteiristas had only a secondary role to play as the Caballerista-Prietista executive elected at the 1932 party congress lost its unity. At the end of 1935 the Caballeristas used a dispute over the relative powers of the party executive and the Socialist parliamentary group as a pretext for resignation from the former, confidently expecting that, since they were now backed by the massive UGT, the Youth,[31] most Socialist deputies, and most of the party branches, including Madrid, the Prietista rump on the executive would not survive. That it did survive was as much a measure of the Caballeristas' incapacity for political offensives as of Prieto's counter-mobilization of his supporters in the north and deft manœuvring to prevent the holding of a party congress.

In the course of the dispute both sides resorted to expulsions and even physical violence against their opponents. Prieto, who was fired upon while touring with the Asturian miners' leaders in 1936, had no compunction about using Assault Guards against the remaining strongholds of Caballerismo a year later.[32] Though Iglesias himself had been intolerant of dissidents,[33] the desire not merely to dominate but to destroy one's rivals was something new to the party. So relentless were the disputes and so appalling the violence that was engulfing Spain that some of the more liberal-minded Socialists retreated

when the Caballeristas claimed the leadership in 1936. Prieto's respect for Besteiro is evident in his *Convulsiones de España: Pequeños detalles de grandes sucesos*, 3 vols. (Mexico: Oasis, 1967–9), iii. 331–7.

[31] On the Youth radicalization see Ricard Viñas, *La formación de las Juventudes Socialistas Unificadas (1934–1936)* (Madrid: Siglo XXI, n.d.); González Quintana and Martín Najera, 45–63.

[32] Burnett Bolloten, *The Spanish Revolution: The Left and the Struggle for Power during the Civil War* (Chapel Hill, NC: University of North Carolina Press, 1979), 27–8; Pierre Broué, *La revolución española (1931–1939)* (Barcelona; Península, 1977), 139.

[33] Morato, *El Partido*, 220–5.

into passivity.[34] Academics such as Besteiro and Fernando de los Ríos (Minister of Justice and Education in 1931–3) were left demoralized when their faith in the power of reason was crushed by events. Neither Besteiro's pseudo-Marxism nor the early influence upon both men of Krausist philosophy, with its belief in the natural harmony of societies, in any way had prepared them for the civil strife of the 1930s.[35] The two men declined to throw themselves into the party battles of 1936–8 or to play leading roles in the conduct of the war.

A fourth Socialist tendency emerged during the Civil War. This was *negrinismo*, named after the eminent physiologist Juan Negrín, the right-wing Socialist who headed the republican governments of 1937–9.[36] The appearance of this tendency mirrored the advance of the PCE after the war had broken out. Very quickly, by exploiting the Socialist and anarchist divisions, and by means of their control over Russian arms supplies, their organizational effectiveness, unscrupulousness, propagandist skill, military proficiency and single-mindedness, the Communists acquired a position of dominance on the republican side. In Socialist ranks Negrinismo denoted recognition and a positive evaluation of the PCE war contribution, plus appreciation of Soviet military supplies in the absence of solidarity from the capitalist democracies of the West. In common with the Prieto tendency, the Republican parties, and the PCE, Negrín believed that the spontaneous social revolution that had greeted Franco's coup attempt in July 1936 needed to be

[34] Preston, *The Coming*, 16; Virgilio Zapatero, *Fernando de los Ríos: Los problemas del socialismo democrático* (Madrid: Cuadernos para el Diálogo, 1974), 105–8, 120.
[35] Lamo de Espinosa *passim*; Zapatero *passim*; De los Ríos, *El sentido humanista*; id., *Escritos sobre democracia y socialismo* (Madrid: Taurus, 1974). De los Ríos posited socialism as an ethical ideal for all mankind and rejected class struggle as a means of achieving it. He none the less disapproved of capitalism (E. Díaz, introd. to *El sentido humanista*, 46).
[36] A. Padilla Bolívar (*El movimiento*, 321–4) sees Negrín along with Ramón González Peña, Luis Jiménez de Asúa, and Julián Zugazagoitia as leading a fourth tendency from January 1936, purely because they at that time issued an appeal for unity based on party democracy and discipline. However, most writers characterize them as having been Prietistas in 1936. On Negrín see Feliciano Páez-Camino Arias, 'Juan Negrín en nuestra historia', *Zona Abierta*, 23 (1980), 129–38; Helen Graham, 'El Partido Socialista en el poder y el gobierno de Juan Negrín', in Juliá (ed.), *Socialismo y guerra civil* (Madrid: Editorial Pablo Iglesias, 1987), 347–80.

suppressed. Otherwise the Popular Front coalition, electorally triumphant in February, would collapse, the war could not be waged professionally, and there could be no hope of any aid being provided by the West. When these forces combined to bring down Largo Caballero's government (of September 1936 to May 1937) and installed Negrín as prime minister, the UGT split. While the Caballeristas within it condemned Negrín and approached the CNT for an alliance, an alternative Negrinista labour executive was created with Communists, Prietistas, and ex-Caballeristas taking part.[37]

To their enemies the Negrinistas were simply stooges of the Communists who had betrayed their own party.[38] Certainly, there were Socialists such as Julio Alvarez del Vayo, head of the general commissariat of the army, who worked zealously in partnership with Soviet agents and local Communists.[39] As for Negrín and most of his associates, however, a more dispassionate and convincing view is that they were essentially pragmatists who in 1937–9 made concessions to the Stalinists because they perceived no other way of winning the war.[40] These concessions included muted complicity in Soviet secret police activities, such as the persecution of the left-wing socialist Workers' Party of Marxist Unification (POUM), which Caballero as prime minister had refused to ban early in 1937.

After the Civil War the memory of this whole factional episode was to leave the PSOE and UGT eternally vigilant for

[37] For sympathetic Negrinista participant accounts of this development see Rosal, *Historia 1901–39*, ii. 645–80; Edmundo Domínguez Aragonés, *Los vencedores de Negrín* (Mexico: Roca, 1976). Rosal (ii. 611) explains his move (in tandem with the PCE) from support for Largo to condemnation of him in terms of the latter having been 'ideologically poisoned' by his advisers early in 1937 and having undergone a dramatic metamorphosis. Javier Tusell (Introd. to Araquistain, *Sobre la guerra civil y en la emigración* (Madrid: Espasa-Calpe, 1983), 48) claims that Largo's faction was still the largest when in Jan. 1938 international mediation led to a partial reunification of the UGT. Bizcarrondo (p. 418) states that by this time Largo had lost control of the UGT, as well as of his press organs and the party's parliamentary group.

[38] Largo Caballero, *Mis recuerdos*, 215. Largo accused the Negrinistas of seeking to have both him and Araquistain shot after May 1937 ('Largo Caballero acusa', *El Socialista* (France), 10.8.46, 1).

[39] Brenan, 308; Carr, *Spain*, 667; Bizcarrondo, 237. On the Soviet role in Spain see Bolloten; Justo Martínez Amutio, *Chantaje a un pueblo* (Madrid: G. del Toro, 1974); ex-Communist Julio Hernández, *Yo fui un ministro de Stalin* (Madrid: G. del Toro, 1974).

[40] Thomas, 535, 666–70, 813; Jackson, 392–412.

the reappearance of tendencies and ever ready to stamp out any signs of incipient organized dissidence. In effect, from the end of 1935 and throughout the war the PSOE had been at least two parties, neither of which functioned properly.[41] In 1936 the Socialists found themselves with the largest bloc of seats in the Cortes, yet because of their divisions they were incapable of taking any constructive political steps in the months leading up to the Civil War. While the Prietistas formally led the party, local Caballerista groups elected a Committee for the Presidency of the PSOE and, together with the Madrid branch of the party, this served as the basis of an alternative authority. And although the Caballerista tendency declined thereafter, hit finally by a ban on propaganda meetings in October 1937, a new dispute between Prieto and the Negrinistas in 1938 ensured that the PSOE remained almost paralysed, weak and fragmented, barely organic. It was not that the PSOE was inherently more fissiparous than the other parties of the Second International. Any socially heterogeneous and politically pluralist mass party with democratic traditions of operation would have been just as vulnerable to disintegration in any comparable period of class struggle and institutional crisis. Nevertheless, the experience paved the way for an era of bans and proscriptions and for a renewed stress upon party centralism and discipline in the PSOE.

Ironically it was the Communists, whom Largo Caballero and Prieto had tried to use against one another (Largo to 'bolshevize' the PSOE, Prieto to help bring down Largo's government) who served to reunify much of the PSOE at the end of the Civil War. The Besteiro tendency had always been anti-Communist and had sharply demarcated Leninism and Stalinism from Marxism. Caballerismo, on the other hand, once radicalized, had been committed to unity with the Communists, hoping in 1934–6 for the establishment of a single Marxist party, a single labour confederation, and even a single International. However, such aspirations were premised upon the notion of a weak 'absorbable' PCE. The Caballerista mood changed in 1936 following the 'unification'[42]

[41] On the splits see Padilla Bolívar, *El movimiento*, 321–78.
[42] In fact the Unified Young Socialists (JSU) was created on the basis of the PSOE

of the Socialist and Communist youth organizations in April and the subsequent defection of Santiago Carrillo and other ex-Caballerista leaders of the new Unified Young Socialists (JSU) to the PCE. Largo may have lost as many as 200,000 young supporters in the process,[43] and he was similarly disappointed when the new Unified Socialist Party of Catalonia (PSUC), to which the Caballeristas had given qualified support, decided to join the Third International.[44] Although the Communists were not alone in the overthrow of his government, their major role in the ousting of Largo, who had belatedly tried to block their takeover of the army, was what his tendency remembered most about the experience. Many of the Caballeristas, especially Luis Araquistain, became visceral anti-Communists as a result.

Finally, Prieto's pragmatic alignment with the Communists, which at one moment led him to accept the idea of a party merger,[45] was weakened gradually in 1937–8. As Defence Minister he (like Largo as premier/War Minister) constantly found his authority disputed when orders to Communist-led military forces conflicted with PCE directives. Although his views on how the war should be fought and social revolution stifled were similar to those of the Communists, this did not prevent him from blaming Moscow for his downfall when he was forced to resign in March 1938. He then became openly critical of the Negrinistas for not resisting the growth of Communist power in the republican camp.[46] In fairness to Negrín, it is hard to see how any government leader in wartime could have tolerated the continued presence of such an inveterate pessimist as Prieto in his Defence Ministry. If Prieto's proverbial pessimism ('defeatism', the Negrinistas and Communists called it) was a realistic reflection of the military

Young Socialists, the FNJSE (Viñas, p. 57; personal interview with Sócrates Gómez, Madrid, 9 Mar. 1982).

[43] Brenan, 308. González Quintana and Martín Najera (pp. 55–7) point to growing Stalinist influence in the FNJSE prior to the creation of the JSU.

[44] Rosal, *Historia 1901–39*, i. 468–9.

[45] Morón, 102–7; Thomas, 535; Guy Hermet, *The Communists in Spain* (Westmead: Saxon House, 1974), 30.

[46] Alba, *Communist Party*, 271–4. For the subsequent Prieto-Negrín exchange of correspondence see Prieto, *Epistolario Prieto y Negrín* (Paris: publ. by the Prietistas, 1939). Prieto also blamed the *sovietistas* for his downfall in his *Entresijos de la guerra de España* (Mexico: PSOE-UGT, 1953), 42.

outlook for the Republic, it none the less was sure to undermine morale, which was crucial to the Negrín strategy of trying to resist Francoism until the outbreak of a world conflict, when support from the Allies might be expected.

By 1939, as the Civil War drew to a close, major sectors of a disorganized PSOE had become anti-Communist. They had seen their leaders treated 'disloyally' by the PCE, had come to appreciate the tremendous subservience of the Stalinists to an external power, and had seen fellow Socialists removed from positions, jailed, and even assassinated as Communist control grew in the republican zones.[47] Some of those who had suffered at the hands of the PCE now wore their anti-Communism as an insignia; others maintained that they were not anti-Communists—rather, the Communists had shown themselves to be implacable anti-Socialists. Either way, the Communists became convenient scapegoats for everything that had gone wrong in the Civil War. The dominant themes became the nefarious intrigues of the PCE and, secondarily, the idea of 'betrayal' by the Western democracies, almost to the exclusion of self-critical analysis.

The way in which the war ended in March 1939 left the Negrinistas with a grievance of their own. The anti-Negrín coup led by Colonel Casado and the setting up of a new authority for the republican side were inspired by the hope that it might be possible to negotiate a dignified surrender with Franco. All the other Socialist tendencies supported this move, regarding further resistance as futile. Besteiro became the civilian leader of Casado's National Council of Defence. Other Socialist members who sat alongside Republicans and CNT representatives were the Besteirista former railway union leader Trifón Gómez, the Caballerista Wenceslao Carrillo, and, in spite of personal misgivings about taking part, the Prietista railway worker Antonio Pérez on behalf of a divided UGT.[48] The Communists and their allies saw the Casado coup and establishment of the Council as acts of treason, though following the failure of armed PCE resistance to the new authority in Madrid, a leader of the party requested

---

[47] Bolloten, 470.
[48] On the UGT attitude to the Council see Thomas, p. 902 n. 1; Rosal, *Historia, 1901–39*, ii. 891–2; Domínguez, 182–5.

membership of it.[49] Great bitterness and mutual recriminations concerning responsibilities for the defeat and its sequel were to dominate the survivors' lives for decades. Though Stalinist activities had helped reunite the greater part of the PSOE in opposition by 1939, it was on a basis that guaranteed the persistence of crippling divisions within the anti-Franco camp.

[49] J. Zugazagoitia, *Historia de la guerra en España* (Buenos Aires: La Vanguardia, 1940), 565; Sócrates Gómez interview. The view that the republican side was not defeated but betrayed appears, for example, in Arthur H. Landis, *Spain: The Unfinished Revolution* (New York: International Publishers, 1972). However, it would appear that prior to the Casado coup Negrín had imparted orders along the lines of 'every man for himself'. See Morón, 156. Sócrates Gómez told me that his father José Gómez Osorio, Civil Governor of Madrid, received such orders on 3 Mar. 1939 for transmission on the 6th, but was arrested by pro-Communist forces on the 5th, the day of Casado's coup. Upon his release on the 12th he found that the manuscript from Negrín had disappeared from his office.

2
Spectators of History:
The Exiles

> We Socialists have known always that we were working
> for future generations
> —Indalecio Prieto[1]

DURING the next 37 years the PSOE co-existed in Spain and abroad. The mainstream 'PSOE in Exile', which was unified by 1946, exhibited most of the time-honoured characteristics of political exiles the world over: the early expectancy that history would reverse itself, as dreams displaced realities; then disappointment, disillusionment, dismay, feelings of impotence, and recriminatory bitterness as the chances of returning home diminished. The Spanish Socialist *émigrés'* main point of reference remained the Spain of the 1930s and an avid interest in the latest news from home proved no effective substitute for experiencing the country's subsequent evolution. *Émigré* attitudes to the Communists and to Francoism soon became antiquated and the generational problems faced by the party were particularly acute. The laws of biology dictated that ageing exiles would find it increasingly difficult to understand and feel empathy with the new generations emerging in Spain; and the loss of so many members of the party's youth movement to the Communists in 1936 greatly compounded the problem.

Yet, for all that, the Socialist emigration was a thoroughly remarkable one. If judged by the regularity of its congresses abroad and all that these implied in terms of membership participation, debate, and controversy, the PSOE in Exile enjoyed the greatest democratic vitality of all the Spanish parties that possessed a presence abroad.[2] Although it lacked

---

[1] 'Mensaje de Indalecio Prieto a nuestro IV Congreso en el Exilio', *Adelante* (Mexico), 22.7.50, 1.
[2] In France the PSOE held 13 ordinary congresses between 1944 and 1974 and an

the potential for internal democracy of a party operating on home ground, and was undermined increasingly by the malaise of demoralization, the exiled wing of the PSOE managed to survive as a functioning party at a time when most other opposition forces were reduced to committees and individuals. This achievement would be recognized in 1951, when the PSOE became the only party composed predominantly of exiles to be admitted with full rights into the reconstituted Socialist International. Moreover, through their regular contact with other member parties, the Socialist exiles kept the issue of Spain alive as a question of solidarity. Their dutiful attendance at international meetings and congresses was responsible for most of the fraternal aid received by Socialists in Spain, woefully inadequate though it was. Of course, the contact with other socialist parties also exposed the PSOE over a good many years to the ideological and organizational influence of the more northern, less radical sections of the International; and in the 1970s this would finally filter through to the party in Spain.

There are several keys to the PSOE's survival in exile. First, as has been seen, it was rather an atypical socialist party. Adversity was no stranger to the Spanish Socialists and the PSOE had always demanded that they be active militants rather than merely nominal members. The level of commitment expected by the party, reinforced by the oft-flouted yet widely subscribed-to norms of party discipline, bestowed cohesion upon at least subgroups of the exiles. Second, the size and social composition of the Socialist emigration was an important factor. It is not known how many Socialist exiles abandoned political activity upon leaving Spain, but it was probably a not very large minority[3] (otherwise, presumably, there would have been major PSOE-UGT campaigns to win these people back). Rather more than 10,000 regrouped

extraordinary congress in 1951. There were also 12 UGT congresses in exile between 1944 and 1973, and 6 FNJSE congresses (including plenums with the powers of congresses) between 1945 and 1975. For PSOE congress documents see Fundación Pablo Iglesias/PSOE, *Congresos del PSOE en el exilio*, 2 vols. (Madrid: Editorial Pablo Iglesias, 1981).

[3] The phenomenon was recognized. See R. Llopis, *Emigración, exilio y perspectivas de mañana* (Mexico and Paris: Ediciones Tribuna, n.d.), 13.

mainstream PSOE and UGT members[4] were sufficient to maintain the structures of a mass party, albeit in skeletal form. Despite a gradual natural decline in membership through deaths, and the political loss of members through breakaways, replenishment was available by the 1960s in the form of the progeny of the original political exiles and newer economic *émigrés*. Third, unlike some political emigrations, the Socialist exodus was by rank-and-file elements as well as intermediate cadres and leaders. Particularly in France, where many exiles became or remained manual workers, there were plenty of members who were content with being ordinary militants and whose tolerance of personal disputes between leaders was limited.

Fourth, there was the concentration of the mass of the *émigré* Socialist organizations' members in just a few areas—in Mexico City and, above all, in southern France, where Spain's proximity was a constant reminder of political obligations. Fifth, international aid (if disappointing when measured against the daunting task of fighting a dictatorship following a devastating defeat in civil war) also helped to preserve the organization. In contrast, a lack of international links placed the Republicans and CNT at a distinct disadvantage and contributed to their long-term political decline. Finally, and perhaps the most crucial key to the durability of the PSOE in Exile, there was the survival of the party in Spain. Even in the darkest hour, when the clandestine organization was reduced to a few hundred activists lacking national co-ordination, its mere existence was a psychological spur to the exiles. Indeed, the more suffering there was in the interior, the greater the psychological pressure there was on the *émigrés* to keep faith with their comrades. And although it was not until the latter years of Francoism that the PSOE in Spain showed clear signs of revival, the resurgence of a more general opposition to Franco, dating from the mid-1950s, periodically

[4] In 1946 the congresses of the mainstream PSOE and UGT in Exile represented 7,727 and 17,155 members respectively. See PSOE in Exile, Second Congress, *Actas taquigráficas*, 235–57, and the *Actas* of the latter, p. 7. In this work, 'mainstream' PSOE and UGT is used to denote the versions of these organizations that have survived to the present day. In the case of the UGT, the Negrinista version was clearly the largest in the mid-1940s, thanks to Communist participation, but this situation did not last.

fed hopes that the regime's days were numbered. It was the prospect of being able to live one's remaining years in Spain that dissuaded so many refugees from trying to start a new life, especially in the alien environment of adjacent France.

SOCIALIST REORGANIZATION AND PERSISTING DISUNITY

Spain's losses through the Civil War included a long-term emigration of at least 300,000 people, in addition to half a million deaths.[5] By far the largest exodus of refugees formed the human stream that flowed into France as Catalonia fell to the Nationalists early in 1939.[6] Others had crossed into France earlier, and about 15,000–20,000 republicans had the good fortune to be picked up and shipped out, mainly to North Africa, as the Civil War ended.[7] While the political refugees received a sympathetic response from the French left, the dominant forces of conservatism in France regarded them with the deepest distrust. Fearing both physical and political contamination, the French authorities treated the mass of refugees appallingly, hoping to persuade them to return to Spain. Over 100,000 did—either prompted by their reception or because they had fled from violence rather than persecution.[8] Among those remaining, some refugees were wealthy or fortunate enough to escape the fate of their compatriots, but tens of thousands suffered the horrors of concentration camps, imprisonment, or labour companies. The beach concentration camps of southern France were established in the interests of national security, not to provide shelter. Koestler found discipline in Le Vernet camp even worse than in Franco's prisons; other victims later claimed that the food, accommodation, and hygiene had been worse than in the German camps. The French had treated German POWs better.[9]

---

[5] Thomas, 926–7.

[6] For a graphic account see Isabel de Palencia, *Smouldering Freedom: The Story of the Spanish Republicans in Exile* (London: Gollancz, 1946), 34–53.

[7] Louis Stein, *Beyond Death and Exile: The Spanish Republicans in France, 1939–1955* (Cambridge, MA: Harvard University Press, 1979), 78–9.

[8] Ibid. 46, 52, 86.   [9] Ibid. 74–5.

The Spanish exile population in France was soon cut by the high death rate in the French camps, the evacuation of refugees to the Americas, Second World War casualties, and natural causes, yet there were still over 100,000 exiles there by 1957 and over half that number by 1968.[10] Mexico, which never formally recognized the Franco regime, received at least 15,000 and probably 20,000–40,000 refugees by the end of the World War.[11] Substantial numbers went to Cuba, the Dominican Republic, Argentina, Chile, and Venezuela, but only Mexico accepted unlimited numbers, partly out of national identification with the republican cause, and also because its rulers saw here an opportunity to benefit from an influx of highly able people of cultural affinity, whose transport and settlement costs would be paid by the republican relief agencies. Most of the best-trained and well-educated Spanish exiles eventually settled in Mexico, unable often for linguistic reasons to find suitable work in France where, in contrast, the demand for skilled and semi-skilled labour was considerable.[12] Meanwhile the refugee population in North Africa rose to over 10,000 republicans, and there were thousands of Spaniards too in the USSR, where admission was limited to Communists.[13] Smaller groups were to be found in capitals such as London and Geneva.

So long as it prevailed, the Socialists were far more respectful of French legality than were the Communists and anarchists. Faced with a ban on refugee political activity, executive members concentrated on refugee relief and journalistic collaboration.[14] The first Socialist refugees to organize themselves effectively were those who reached Mexico, but there were also exile periodicals published in Paris in 1939–40. Leading pro-Negrín trade unionists published the first number of their *Boletín de Información Sindical* there, and six issues of *Norte*, edited by Julián Zugazagoitia, also appeared in the French capital.[15] Both took

---

[10] Vicente Llorens, *La emigración republicana de 1939* (Madrid: Taurus, 1976), 100.

[11] Ibid. 126–7; Patricia W. Fagen, *Exiles and Citizens: Spanish Republicans in Mexico* (Austin, TX: University of Texas, 1973), pp. 38–9 n. 50.

[12] Ibid. 32–3, 38–9.

[13] Llorens, 114–16. Some 3,000 exiles still lived in the USSR by 1967.

[14] Stein, 102–3.   [15] Respectively 1.8.39 and July 1939–Jan. 1940.

an anti-Prieto line and repeatedly condemned the Casado coup and creation of the National Council of Defence as treason. However, the emphases of the two periodicals differed significantly. While defending Negrín even after the PCE withdrew its support for him, the *Boletín* carried a Stalinist interpretation of the Second World War and thus justified the Nazi-Soviet Pact.[16] This was the compromise formula upon which the UGT faction composed largely of Communists and Negrinista Socialists was based. *Norte*, on the other hand, was evidence of the fact that Negrinistas in the PSOE were reasserting their independence of the PCE somewhat more decisively. Even during the Civil War, a pro-Negrín PSOE executive headed by Ramón González Peña and Ramón Lamoneda had established a party youth secretariat to resist the absorption of the Young Socialists by the PCE-manipulated Juventudes Socialistas Unificadas. Now, in exile, they got a congress of the Socialist Youth International, meeting in Lille in July 1939, to expel the JSU for serving the PCE and to recognize the Secretariat as the sole representative of the Spanish Young Socialists. *Norte* expressed approval of this move and was critical of Stalin's pact with Hitler, seen as a betrayal of internationalism.[17]

A few of *Norte*'s collaborators were former or future Prietistas and its criticism of Prieto was more restrained than that of the Negrinista UGT and Communist Party.[18] This suggests that, although the exiles brought their differences out of Spain with them, the fundamental split in the exile community, that separating Negrinistas and Prietistas, only became definitive when France was occupied and Mexico temporarily became the headquarters of republican politics.

Fate played a part in consolidating the division of the Socialist exiles. In March 1939 the failure of Negrín's

[16] '¡Hitler no vencerá!', *Boletín*, 1.6.40, 15–16. Pro-Ally labour leaders were branded 'dogs of the bourgeoisie' (ibid.). The *Boletín* saw the Soviet Union as 'the great proletarian fortress', 'the only country where the proletariat still controls its destiny'; Soviet trade unions were deemed 'schools of revolutionary socialism' (1.11.40, 10–11; 1.5.41, 8; 1.7.41, 9).

[17] 'Las Juventudes Socialistas', *Norte*, 3 (1939), 16; Miguel de Amilibia, '¿Adónde va la URSS?', ibid. 6 (1939–40), 12–13.

[18] *Norte* collaborators included Julián Zugazagoitia (editor), Ramón Lamoneda, José Prat, Matilde de la Torre, Manuel Cordero, Toribio Echeverría, Ramón González Peña, Antonio Huerta, and Gabriel Morón.

representative to turn up at Veracruz in time to meet the *Vita*, a yacht sent from France by the expatriate prime minister, enabled Prieto to take charge of its valuable cargo of jewellery and other precious goods following authorization from President Lázaro Cárdenas. This permitted Prieto in July 1939 to persuade the Permanent Committee of the Cortes at a meeting in Paris to set up a new relief agency, the Council for the Aid of Spanish Refugees (JARE), in opposition to, and challenging the legitimacy of, the exiled Negrín government's Evacuation Service for Spanish Republicans (SERE). Though each agency did more to alleviate refugee distress than their rivals conceded, they also served as important sources of patronage. Thankfulness for any aid received was often translated, at times innocently, into political allegiance.

Both the SERE and the JARE practised favouritism when deciding whom they were to help.[19] Negrín supporters benefited from positive discrimination when passenger lists were drawn up for SERE-chartered ships taking refugees from France to Mexico. On the other hand, detractors of Prieto were later to claim that his control of the JARE split not only the PSOE and UGT but every major organization of exiles.[20] One dissident Socialist even alleged that Prieto's misuse of the funds led him to sabotage the republican institutions in exile for fear that they would investigate his misdeeds as JARE secretary.[21] The accounts that Prieto submitted, first to the Mexican authorities when they took charge of the JARE in November 1942, and then to the Giral administration (the first republican government established in exile) in 1946, were found acceptable, but were not accompanied by documentary evidence concerning the transactions undertaken.[22] The use to

---

[19] Fagen, 34–8.

[20] A. del Rosal, *Historia de la UGT en la Emigración 1939–1950*, 2 vols. (Barcelona: Grijalbo, 1978), i. 90–2; id., *El oro del Banco de España y la historia del Vita* (Barcelona: Grijalbo, 1977); id. '¿Qué pasa con el tesoro del "Vita"?', *Cuadernos para el Diálogo*, 188 (1976), 38–42; interview with Rosal, 21 Apr. 1982. In response to Rosal's attacks on Prieto, *Adelante* (15.10.43, 4) claimed that he had denounced people to the police during the Asturian revolution.

[21] Máximo Muñoz, *Grandeza y tragedia de la emigración republicana española* (Mexico: publ. by the author, 1955), 32.

[22] Rosal, *El oro*, 221; I. Prieto, 'Rendición de cuentas', *Adelante*, 1.12.46, 1; id., 'La historia del Vita', *El Socialista* (Toulouse) [henceforth *ES*], 10.2.55, 1–2; *México*

which JARE funds were put, to develop a Prietista clientele and set up job-creating schemes which made a few exiles in Mexico rather prosperous, thus left doubts which Prieto's enemies sought to exploit.

Those doubts could never be dispelled by documentary evidence. What is clear today, however, now that political passions have cooled, is that the *Vita* affair by no means provoked the crippling divisions among the exiled republicans; it merely reinforced them. Prieto himself was already a wealthy man when the Civil War ended[23] and his life as an exile did not betray any sudden acquisition of greater wealth. Really, the PSOE and the republican camp in general had become polarized irreparably during the Civil War, in reaction to the growing influence of the PCE, and it was this same basic hostility that continued to separate Negrín supporters from his detractors outside Spain during the following decade.

Exacerbating the principal disagreement were differing ideas on how best to work for Franco's removal. Negrín's followers had experienced too much of the effects of the Western democracies' 'non-intervention' policy during the Civil War for them to expect any help against Franco now. They therefore defended a policy emphasizing 'national resistance' to Franco in Spain, though circumstances prevented immediate material support for this from Negrinistas in exile. The Prietistas, on the other hand, claimed that Western doubts about the republican cause had been fundamentally a product of Negrín's supposed subordination to the PCE; hence democratic solidarity might still be forthcoming if the republicans were to regroup independently of the Communists and their former allies. They were encouraged in their beliefs by the signing in August 1941 of the Atlantic Charter, under which Churchill and Roosevelt supported the rights of all peoples to choose the form of government under which they should live.[24] Thus, whereas the Negrinista stance

y la República Española: Antología de documentos 1931–1977 (Mexico: Centro Republicano Español, 1978), 106–12.

[23] M. Muñoz, *Problemas del socialismo español* (Mexico: publ. by the author, 1952), 14.

[24] PSOE, 'El Partido Socialista y la Unión General de Trabajadores fijan su criterio político', *Boletín de Información para Emigrados Socialistas Españoles* (Mexico), 30.9.41, 5.

emphasized resistance in Spain, the Prietistas looked to Western aid for delivery from Franco.

In Mexico, the Prietistas and other anti-Negrinistas organized first and were therefore able to present the pro-Negrín Socialists as 'splitters' when they established a group of their own. Prieto's accumulated prestige, his personal presence in Mexico during most of the years up to his death in 1962, and the power derived from administering JARE funds in 1939–42 made him so influential there that former Besteiristas and Prietistas remained largely indistinguishable in the anti-Negrín sector. Not so the Caballeristas, some of whom had left and others been expelled from this sector by November 1944. From then until July 1945, they brought out their own monthly bulletin, *Cuadernos Socialistas*.[25] The anti-Negrín Socialists established the Círculo Cultural Pablo Iglesias in Mexico City on 21 April 1940 and the Negrinistas the Círculo Cultural Jaime Vera on 21 December 1941. Membership of the former stabilized at around 300 before 1945, making it approximately three times as large as the Jaime Vera group.[26]. In the Mexican capital there were also several hundred Socialists who, without losing their sense of commitment, refused to join either faction in the hope of putting an end to the divisions of the 1930s. Finally, there was a group that established the Federación de Agrupaciones Regionales Socialistas, composed of a few score people who left or were expelled from the Círculo Cultural Pablo Iglesias under the suspicion of favouring regional separatism. This 'Federation' had no equivalent in France and North Africa,[27] its emergence

[25] The rift was caused by a lack of democracy and tolerance in the Prieto-dominated Círculo Cultural Pablo Iglesias (*Adelante*, 15.2.45, 2), whose meetings invariably approved expulsions of dissident members. The stated aim of the Caballerista organ was to promote party unity ('Nuestros propósitos', *Cuadernos Socialistas*, 1 (1944), 2). Its collaborators included Bruno Alonso and Carlos Hernández Zancajo in Mexico, Carlos Baraibar in Chile, Luis Araquistain and Wenceslao Carrillo in England, César Barona and Ildefonso Torregrosa in Algeria, and in France Enrique de Francisco, Rodolfo Llopis, and Pascual Tomás.

[26] *Adelante* (15.4.42, 7) put CC Pablo Iglesias affiliation at 300, that of the CC Jaime Vera at 100, and non-aligned Socialists in Mexico at 500. José Borrás (*Políticas de los exiliados españoles 1944–1950* (Paris: Ruedo Ibérico, 1976), 88–9) put the CCPI at 300 and the CCJV at 100. The CCJV claimed 125 members (*ES*, 16.2.46, 1).

[27] In France some regional committees were set up in the PSOE, but this was to provide a regional dimension to solidarity work, and not to give expression to demands for regional autonomy in Spain.

in Mexico being a sign of the intolerance of the Prietista leadership when it came to regionalist and other dissidence. In exile Prieto refused to countenance the survival of regional groups such as the Comité Central Socialista de Euskadi, which had linked Basque Socialists in Spain. The issue came to a head in mid-1943, when the Pablo Iglesias group voted to withdraw Socialist representatives from the exiled Basque government headed by José Antonio de Aguirre, whose Basque Nationalist Party was now thought by the PSOE to be revealing dangerous separatist tendencies. The Regional Groups attracted mainly Caballeristas, who not only upheld a right to regional autonomy but also emphasized trade union struggle and joint work with the CNT.[28]

While the Círculo Cultural Pablo Iglesias rested its legitimacy upon being the first PSOE group to be organized in Mexico, the Negrinistas based theirs on loyalty to the 'legitimate' executive committees of the PSOE and UGT, meaning those that had existed towards the end of the Civil War in Spain. The credentials of most leading Socialists were questionable, for the vast majority had been elected since the last congresses of the party and union had been held in Spain way back in 1932. Everybody accepted that the national committees of each organization—their highest authorities between congresses —were empowered to fill any vacancies that arose on the executives in the intervals between congresses, but this mechanism only produced disputes when utilized in a time of civil war and with the Socialists fractured into tendencies. Both the Prietistas controlling the PSOE in 1936 and the Caballeristas controlling the UGT in 1937 used partial elections to reinforce their control after first expelling pro-opposition sections that were behind with dues payments.[29] This undermined the legitimacy of executives, as did the way in which the usurping Negrinista executive of the UGT in 1937–9 took advantage of State assistance to dispose of its Caballerista rival—for example, by getting the Post Office to direct all UGT mail to the pro-government faction and by

---

[28] *Adelante*, 15.2.45, 2–3; M. Muñoz, *Tragedia y derroteros de España* (Mexico: publ. by the author, 1952), 55.

[29] Alba, *Communist Party*, 265; Juliá, *La izquierda*, 111–38.

having the Bank of Spain refuse to honour cheques made out to the Caballerista version of the UGT.[30]

In Paris in 1939 the balance of forces among members of the party executive arriving from Spain was unfavourable to Indalecio Prieto.[31] A majority led by president Ramón González Peña and general secretary Ramón Lamoneda defended the idea of maintaining the Negrín government in exile, while Prieto advocated the establishment instead of a junta whose main task would be to alleviate refugee distress. Prieto was able to summon sufficient support from Republicans, Socialists, and Catalanists to get the exiled Permanent Committee of the Cortes to overturn its earlier ratification of the Negrín government, and to create the JARE. Subsequently in Mexico, in one way or another, he was able to win over executive members who in Paris had voted against his manœuvres.[32]

The party executive sent a delegation consisting of Lucio Martínez Gil and Manuel Albar to Mexico, but there they rebelled against the González Peña–Lamoneda leadership. By mid-1940, working with Prieto and Alejandro Otero, they had created the Círculo Cultural Pablo Iglesias and were helping to establish groups in other American countries. The first Negrinista executive member to arrive was González Peña in July 1940, followed by Lamoneda shortly afterwards. On 25 September 1940 Otero, Martínez Gil, and Albar wrote to the Negrinista duo inviting them to a meeting which took place in Albar's home. At it the pro-Prieto faction urged that, since a majority of the executive members were now in Mexico, the party leadership should be established there, replacing the delegation. However, the suspicions of Lamoneda and González Peña were aroused by the fact that the delegation was already using the letterhead of a new executive.[33]

---

[30] Alba, *Communist Party*, 266.

[31] Speech of Manuel Albar at Second Congress of PSOE in Exile (1946), *Actas*, 83.

[32] Ramón Lamoneda, *Ramón Lamoneda, último secretario general del P.S.O.E. elegido en España en 1935: Posiciones políticas—Documentos—Correspondencia* (Mexico: Roca, 1976), 226–38; Domínguez, 273.

[33] The Prietistas in Mexico, moreover, had brought out a *Boletín de Información para Emigrados Socialistas Españoles* in Jan. 1940, which was replaced by *Adelante* in Feb. 1942. For their trade union work they published a *Servicio de Información*

They thus refused to work with the delegation or to accept a Mexico-based executive committee at a time when its establishment would place them in a minority.[34]

Prieto, Otero, Martinez Gil, and Albar then established their own PSOE executive and in October 1941 augmented their forces by holding partial executive elections among just the American sections. These were to fill vacancies left by Francisco Cruz Salido and Ricardo Zabalza, both shot by Franco, and Manuel Cordero, who had died in Buenos Aires in April 1941.[35] It was probably this move that, rather belatedly, jolted the Negrinistas into action.[36] Their decision to create the Círculo Cultural Jaime Vera, taken at a meeting in December 1941, gave the Prietistas a pretext for deeming Lamoneda, González Peña, and Antonio Huerta to be 'outside the discipline' of the PSOE (in effect considering them expelled): for the party rulebook, the *Organización General*, stated that the creation of a new group where one already existed was an act of division, and it gave the party president and general secretary no greater rights than it did other executive members to represent the PSOE. On the other hand, it in no way empowered the party executive to expel dissidents from the PSOE: only the local groups to which members belonged could initiate disciplinary proceedings.[37]

By their actions, then, the leaders of the two major PSOE factions in Mexico had flouted party discipline in the eyes of their rivals and there was nobody in possession of undisputed leadership credentials. Prieto himself had been elected by a properly-constituted party congress in 1932, yet had repeatedly acted as a free agent and against the opinions of the majority of the executive in 1939. And subsequently he had

Sindical from Sept. 1941, which was replaced in 1944 by the *Boletín* of the UGT published in France.

[34] Albar's speech, op. cit. 85–6; PSOE, 'El Partido Socialista y su Comisión Ejecutiva: una invitación, una negativa y unos acuerdos', *Boletín de Información para Emigrados Socialistas Españoles*, 7 (1940), 6–7.

[35] Ibid. 12 (1941), 7; ibid. 13–14 (1941), 8.

[36] The Negrinista Domínguez (p. 273) admitted that the pro-Negrín versions of the PSOE and UGT headed by Lamoneda, González Peña, and Rodríguez Vega did not wage a serious enough battle to dispute anti-Negrinista rights over these organizations.

[37] PSOE, Statutes, *Organización general y modelos* (Madrid: PSOE, ?1926), 12–14, 20–3.

been politically inactive for two years—from the inauguration of the Círculo Cultural Pablo Iglesias in April 1940 until he made a May Day speech in 1942.[38] Nevertheless, the executive on which he was at first just a formal member and later an active participant was supported by Socialist groups in Mexico, Chile, Buenos Aires, Bogotá, La Paz, Montevideo, Caracas, Ciudad Trujillo, Havana, Panama, and New York, as well as by a faction in London.[39] Lamoneda's support in the Americas was largely restricted to Mexico, where his executive's energies were invested in efforts to revive the Popular Front of 1936. Little was done to rebuild the party, even when in mid-1946 Lamoneda and González Peña moved for a while to France.[40]

Of course, these divisions caused no distress to Franco, only to the clandestine opposition when news of them reached Spain. The exiles in Mexico failed to act upon the interior's demands for unity voiced by UGT general secretary José Rodríguez Vega when he got out of Spain and settled in Mexico in early 1943.[41] Although the Círculo Cultural Pablo Iglesias possessed hundreds of members, who were generally better off than their counterparts in other countries, it did not launch a fund to support Socialists in Spain until July 1945.[42] Both the Prieto and the Lamoneda executives posed as the leadership of the entire PSOE, in and out of Spain,[43] yet neither was endorsed by groups in the interior and some *émigrés* such as Wenceslao Carrillo in London refused to join the local organizations of either faction on the grounds that the

[38] I. Prieto, 'Confesiones y rectificaciones', *Adelante*, extraordinary edn., 4.5.42.

[39] 'Don Juan Negrín no representa al Partido Socialista', *Adelante*, 1.8.45, 1.

[40] According to José Sanchis-Banús ('Ramón Lamoneda: El que yo conocí', in Lamoneda, *Posiciones*, 303–18), the main organizer of this sector was Alvarez del Vayo. Lamoneda, though general secretary, was more of a political mentor.

[41] Initially the Prietistas recognized him as UGT general secretary (J. Rodríguez Vega, 'Impresiones de España', *Adelante*, 1.3.43, 2–3); soon afterwards, however, they disavowed him when he sided with the González Peña-Lamoneda sector, having failed in a bid to reunite the UGT. Delegates from the interior, attending a meeting of the CE of the PSOE exiles (*Actas*, 22.3.45), claimed that Rodríguez Vega betrayed his mandate when he reached Mexico.

[42] *Adelante*, 15.7.45, 3.

[43] This was denied by Albar in his speech at the Second Congress of the PSOE in Exile in 1946 (*Actas*, 90), but on several occasions Prieto's speeches were published in the name of the party. For example, PSOE, 'Posición del Partido Socialista frente al problema de España', *Adelante*, 15.11.45, 1.

party and its leaders were in Spain. He had been elected to the party leadership by representatives of provincial federations meeting in Albacete in March 1939, but applied to himself as well as to others the principle that executive mandates expired upon leaving Spain and that leaders should then be replaced by the organization in Spain.[44] Similar views were held widely by Socialists in France and North Africa and were endorsed by the first PSOE congress to be held abroad, in 1944.[45] Against this opinion Lamoneda countered with the argument: Why bother to evacuate from Spain 'hundreds of outstanding leaders' if they are not to be permitted a leading role when abroad? And conversely, how can the interior, operating clandestinely in the midst of blanket repression, either formulate its views collectively or obtain knowledge of the full situation and problems facing the party?[46]

The only way for these disputes to be settled, or begin to be settled, was for the interior to assert its own authority. On 1 June 1945 the executive committee based in Madrid sent a message via Toulouse declaring that the party and its leadership were in Spain, and telling the 'Mexicans' to establish a single organization with a single leadership just for Mexico. Anyone not complying with the order would be expelled automatically. The message expressed 'the indignation of the socialists who fill Spain's prisons and the few who are at liberty' at the failure of the groups in Mexico to establish contact with the interior, and above all at their sterile squabbling, for which the two Mexico-based party executives were blamed equally.[47] Prieto's executive now felt obliged to dissolve itself[48] and to advise the Círculo Cultural Pablo Iglesias and other American sections to subordinate themselves to the more recently created Toulouse-based executive, formed in 1944 and confirmed as the leadership for the exterior by the interior's message of June 1945. Outside Mexico all but the group in Uruguay complied with the

[44] W. Carrillo, speech at PSOE in Exile, Second Congress (1946), *Actas*, 96–107.
[45] Llopis, *Emigración*, 16.
[46] Lamoneda, *Posiciones*, 216.   [47] *Adelante*, 1.9.45, 3.
[48] Only Prieto (elected in 1932), Albar (1936), Otero and Martínez Gil (1938), and Amador Fernández (1941) remained by this time. Anastasio de Gracia and Enrique Puente had resigned and Juan-Simeón Vidarte had been expelled from the CCPI in Nov. 1943 for inviting former King Carol of Romania to a *fiesta* at his home.

Prietista request.[49] Not so the Lamoneda faction, which ignored an invitation from the Círculo Cultural Pablo Iglesias to attend an assembly of all the Spanish Socialists in Mexico, and attempted to cast doubt on the very existence of a party executive in Spain.[50] None the less, over 700 militants attended the meeting on 19 August 1945 that established the Agrupación Socialista Espanōla in Mexico. Presided over by Prieto, its committee, while largely Prietista, included the Caballerista Carlos Hernández Zancajo.[51] Thus, while failing to reunite every Socialist in Mexico, the intervention of the interior at least produced an organizational reunification of the anti-Negrinistas.

In similar fashion, Prietista executives of the UGT and FNJSE were set up in Mexico City, only to be dissolved later in compliance with the voice of the interior. With regard to the UGT, the Negrinistas again based their authority on an executive chosen in Spain, but the presence of Communists within it was anathema to the other version of the UGT. Leaders of the pro-Negrín UGT such as Ramón González Peña (president) and Amaro del Rosal (assistant secretary) were disavowed in May 1940 by a dozen members of the National Committee, ostensibly because the executive's support for the Nazi-Soviet Pact was out of line with rank-and-file opinion.[52] The rebels, who may have represented a majority of national committee members resident in the Americas but were only a minority of the committee that had existed in Spain, organized an assembly of national, regional, and provincial federations which met in Mexico in August 1942. Shortly afterwards their supporters elected an alternative UGT leadership presided over by Prieto supporter Belarmino Tomás, a former leader of the Asturian miners' union.[53] In

[49] Albar, speech at PSOE in Exile, Second Congress (1946), *Actas*, 90.

[50] *ES* (Mexico), Sept. 1945, 7.

[51] *Adelante*, 1.9.45, 4. Following the reorganization the *Memoria* (executive report) presented to the Second PSOE Congress in exile (p. 68) put affiliation in Mexico at: CCPI 780, CCJV 125, and Federation 100, including 7 Basques. It claimed that the unification initiative had brought 100 new members into the CCPI.

[52] *Adelante*, 1.7.43, 3.

[53] On Belarmino Tomás see Saborit, *Asturias*, 122–3. On the UGT dispute, for the Negrinista version see Rosal, *Historia 1939–50*, *passim*, and the *Boletín de Información Sindical*, 1939–55. For the pro-Prieto view, see the *Servicio de Información Sindical*, 1941–4.

due course this was recognized by the Prietista PSOE executive and the Círculo Cultural Pablo Iglesias, as was a new executive committee of the Youth organization elected at an assembly in Mexico City in October 1943 presided over by Julián Lara, with Ovidio Salcedo as general secretary. An extremely tight rein was kept on the revived Youth organization. It pledged unswerving loyalty to the Prietista PSOE executive, a member of which was to attend all executive and national committee meetings and congresses of the FNJSE. The Youth was deprived of political and tactical autonomy; it promised not to make any pacts with other forces without the authorization of the party, 'whose opinions will be supported without question'.[54] In August 1945 this subordination was formally transferred to the executive in the interior, though for most practical purposes this meant to the Toulouse-based Youth federation.

The closely-linked Toulouse executives at first claimed authority only over the PSOE, UGT, and FNJSE in France; then from 1946 over all the exile sections; and only from 1954 did they purport to represent their organizations both in and out of Spain, when conditions there were deemed too hazardous to maintain clandestine executives. The origins of the Toulouse leaderships derive from the liberation of France and, as in Mexico, the anti-Negrín Socialists gained some advantage by organizing first. During the German occupation their policy had been to leave members free to decide whether to join the Maquis and other resistance groups.[55] Some, including Arsenio Jimeno, a Caballerista who had distinguished himself in Socialist struggles in Aragón, did join resistance groups. In 1944 Jimeno became the dynamo of a co-ordinating committee that worked in the Toulouse area to assist and regroup anti-Negrín Socialists, and which organized the first congresses of the PSOE and UGT in France, held in September and November 1944.[56]

[54] *Adelante*, 15.9.43, 3, 15.10.43, 3–4, 15.8.44, 3.
[55] Pascual Tomás, report to First Congress of UGT in Exile (Nov. 1944), *Actas*, 1–2.
[56] Alberto Fernández, 'Las formaciones políticas del exilio', in M. Tuñón de Lara *et al.*, *Guerra y política* (Madrid: Taurus, 1976), 161–2; Borrás, 92. The Comité de Coordinación de Grupos Socialistas was composed of José Aspiazu (president), Arsenio Jimeno (general secretary), Miguel Calzada (treasurer), José Torrente,

This was no mean achievement, for the PCE and its pro-guerrilla alliance, the Spanish National Union (UNE), were highly influential in this region, having made the main Spanish contribution to the French Resistance over the previous two years.[57] Established in France in 1942 and composed of the PCE plus factions of the other republican forces, UNE's strategy was to try to carry the French liberation struggle over into Spain by establishing guerrilla focuses to encourage a national insurrection there at the end of the war. Implicitly denying that the Franco regime had a social base, it claimed that 'all the patriotic sectors, strata, and classes of the country' had an interest in overthrowing him; more to the point, UNE added, 'None of them, whether right or left, rich or poor, can on their own amass sufficient strength to achieve this vital need of our people.'[58] The divide in Spain was characterized by the Communists thus: 'On the one hand, Hitler's agents. On the other, patriots of whatever social origin and political or religious tendency who put the vital interests of the homeland above all others.'[59] In line with its national emphasis, UNE proudly proclaimed the incorporation into its pompously-named Junta Suprema, supposedly directing operations in Spain, of the Popular Catholic Party (ex-CEDA) of Gil-Robles, the Catholic agricultural unions, and even the Spanish Freemasonry.[60] There was more fantasy than fact in such claims—the PCE unscrupulously deemed individual support for the Junta to signify the affiliation of sponsors' organizations. Nevertheless, in 1944 UNE was a real force in southern France and Socialist refugees there had to define themselves in relation to it.

Those who responded positively to UNE's call saw themselves as continuing in the tradition of the Popular Front of

Manuel Palacios, Pablo Careaga, and Cipriano Benavides (PSOE in France, First Congress (1944), *Documentos originales*).

[57] A. Fernández, *Españoles en la Resistencia* (Bilbao: Zero, 1973), *passim*.

[58] *Reconquista de España: Al servicio de la Junta Suprema de Unión Nacional* (Toulouse), 36 (1944), 2.

[59] Manifesto of CC of PCE, 'Para salvar a España: Amplio frente de los patriótas, para evitar que el país sea lanzado a la guerra junto a Hitler, para derribar a Franco y Falange, para llegar a la creación de un Gobierno de Unión Nacional', *España Popular* (Mexico), 25.9.42, 1.

[60] 'El único medio de evitar la guerra en España es la Unión Nacional', *Reconquista de España* (Mexico), 15.2.45, 1.

1936 and of a Socialist-Communist united action agreement of April 1937.[61] They included members of the old Socialist Group of Paris, created in 1911 and based mainly on Spaniards who had been working there for some time.[62] The Group as such was inactive during the Occupation, but militant members including Julio Hernández Ibáñez, a former schoolteacher who had worked in PSOE offices in Toulouse before the outbreak of war, looked upon UNE as a potentially effective organ of combat. During the liberation of Paris, Hernández commanded a group of resisters who occupied the Spanish Embassy to replace the nationalist flag with that of the Republic. Another schoolteacher and prominent Socialist supporter of UNE was the former PSOE deputy Julia Alvarez Resano, who claimed PSOE executive status by virtue of having headed a women's secretariat that functioned in the party during the Civil War. Involved in refugee relief and the arrangement of evacuations to America in 1939, she was betrayed to the authorities and arrested, but escaped to become a *maquisard*.[63] At a UNE conference in Toulouse on 2–5 November 1944, at which homage was paid to Stalin, Roosevelt, Churchill, Tito, De Gaulle, and Chiang Kai-shek, and medals were presented to UNE guerrillas, Hernández and Alvarez were placed on its secretariat, the former as UNE president.

The anti-Negrín Socialists boycotted UNE, exposing it as a Communist rather than a national front. Their fear of PCE absorptive ambitions was fuelled by public Communist declarations about united action being just the first step

---

[61] Lamoneda, *Posiciones*, 51–3, for the text.

[62] In a report dated 23 Nov. 1944 on their meetings with Paris Socialists, Trifón Gómez and Rodolfo Llopis stated that the vast majority of Spanish Socialists in Paris had joined UNE because they were taken in by its claims that the PSOE and UGT were affiliated to it, but that most had been won back since to the mainstream organizations (PSOE in Exile, *Actas* of CE, 30.11.44). This suggests that a spontaneous enthusiasm for left unity still existed in France as late as 1944.

[63] On Hernández see *Adelante*, 1.10.44, 2; Stein, 174–5; and M. Tuñón de Lara, 'Los españoles en la Guerra Mundial', in id. *et al.*, *Guerra y política*, p. 72 n. 12. On Alvarez see *ES* (Mexico), June 1948, 5; *El Socialista Español* (Paris), 9.6.48, 2. Of the 6 female PSOE deputies elected in 1936, 3 became Negrinistas, 2 joined the PCE, and 1 deserted to Franco. See A. del Rosal, 'En recuerdo y homenaje a Ramón Lamoneda', in Lamoneda, *Posiciones*, 23.

towards the creation of a single proletarian party.[64] Moreover, too much blood had been spilled in recent years for the UNE line of reconciliation with the non-Falange sectors that had supported Franco to be generally acceptable to exiles. Nor did the non-UNE Socialists place any faith in the incursions into Spain attempted by Communist guerrillas in 1944—however unpopular Franco was, Spaniards were in no mood or condition for another civil war, nor indeed for any violent solutions.[65] Furthermore, at the time of France's liberation UNE violence and intimidation had been employed against Socialist and CNT militants who opposed its demands for unity. Exploiting to the full its links with the French Communist Party and General Labour Confederation, UNE had used its influence to get rival meetings banned by sympathetic or timorous prefects. There were also cases of UNE gunmen slaying CNT and Socialist militants. After a UNE captain assassinated Auxiliano Benito, a local PSOE committee member, in the suburbs of Toulouse in October 1944, some 6,000 people attended the burial.[66]

It was in this tense atmosphere in the autumn of 1944 that Arsenio Jimeno made an appeal over Radio Toulouse to Socialists to regroup and to send delegates to the constituent congress of the 'PSOE in France'. Isolated PSOE-UGT groups opposed to UNE were now brought into contact with each other and reorganized on an anti-Communist basis. Julia Alvarez and other UNE Socialists were barred at the doors of the congress and then expelled by it without being given a proper hearing.[67] The congress had no statutory authority to exclude the UNE people, just a power based on numbers. It decided to admit only those dissidents who had joined UNE in good faith, those who had believed PCE claims about the PSOE supporting unity, and who were now ready to renounce

[64] Angel Alvarez, 'La acción común de socialistas y comunistas base del Partido Unico', *España Popular*, 28.4.44, 3.

[65] I. Prieto, 'Declaraciones de Indalecio Prieto', *Adelante*, 1.1.45, 1.

[66] The claim that UNE was responsible for 200 murders of anarchists and Socialists (*ES* (Toulouse), 18.7.47, 1) is not credible, but clearly there were several incidents of this nature. See Borrás, 20–3, 91; Llopis, *Emigración*, 15–16; Fernández, 'Las formaciones', 140; PSOE in Exile, *Actas* of CE, 22.10.44.

[67] See the Julia Alvarez (ed.) version of *ES* (Toulouse), 12.10.44, 2. The *Actas* of the congress (pp. 10–11, 49) show that a pro-UNE delegate representing 104 Socialists residing in Ariège did take part in the event.

it. Similar condemnation of UNE was voiced at the UGT exiles' constituent congress in November, where once again Socialist differentiation from the Communists was a priority.

In the mean time initiatives over reorganization had also been taken in Paris, where there had been some very limited activity during the war years. A Provisional Bureau, presided over by the former Besteirista leader of the land workers' union (FNTT), Esteban Martínez Hervás, was set up in opposition to the old Socialist Group of Paris, rejecting its asociations with UNE. Both the Group and the Bureau made efforts to link up with other groups in northern France after the liberation, and they vied with each other for the recognition of the Toulouse leadership. The Bureau managed to obtain use of a headquarters through approaches to the French Socialists, but was then unceremoniously deprived of this base by pro-UNE elements linked to the Group. However, both Parisian factions recognized the validity of the PSOE congress of September 1944; afterwards they accepted the Toulouse party executive's mediation in their dispute.[68] As a result, the Group was recognized and the Bureau Provisional dissolved, although Bureau leader Martínez Hervás was co-opted briefly on to the Toulouse executive. This completed the unification of the anti-Communist PSOE in France in October 1944.

The main strength of the other Socialist faction in France lay in its version of the UGT, though in this it was only a junior partner of the PCE. It held its first plenum in December 1944 and there followed a congress at the end of January 1945 at which the Socialist Enrique de Santiago was elected president. The Communist Luis Cabo Giorla joined him as general secretary when Santiago was re-elected in September.[69] The membership claim of this UGT grew

[68] On the Paris dispute see the Trifón Gómez report, PSOE in Exile, *Actas* of CE, 30.11.44; *ES* (ed. J. Alvarez), 7.12.44; PSOE, Territorial Organizations, Bureau Provisional PSOE (Paris), *Actas*, 1.8.44–5.12.44; PSOE, Correspondence, Bureau Provisional Paris-CE PSOE Toulouse-Grupo Socialista de Paris-Agrupaciones Socialistas de Francia Zona Norte, *Correspondencia*.

[69] 'La UGT en Francia', *Boletín de Información Sindical*, 1.5.45, 11. One indication that the pro-UNE Socialists were no less bureaucratic than their rivals is the way in which Santiago claimed that the dispute over whether the PSOE and UGT belonged to UNE would have been resolved had not the official seals of these organizations been taken to America (*ES* (ed. J. Alvarez), 12.10.44, 2).

from 17,000 to 25,000 between January and September.[70] Even allowing for some inflation here, the UNE-supporting UGT was clearly much stronger than its PSOE counterpart, which late in 1944 set up a provisional executive for France (Enrique de Santiago president, Julia Alvarez secretary), loyal to the PSOE executive headed by Lamoneda in Mexico. The repeated appeals for PSOE and UGT reunification published in the Julia Alvarez version of *El Socialista* were undoubtedly sincere, for in the end it was in the hope of reunification that she helped split her own faction by abandoning UNE in June 1945. It was only at this time that the 'French' followers of Lamoneda became aware of his executive's opposition to UNE and continuing support for the exiled Negrín government—a discovery that catalysed the split. On 7 July 1945 the Socialists who had remained in UNE held a 'congress' of their own in France, but almost simultaneously UNE was dissolved by the PCE as the Communists reverted to an earlier line of republican unity.[71] Economic hardship forced Julia Alvarez to join relatives in Mexico, where she died of a cerebral haemorrhage in May 1948 at the age of 44. Her colleagues in France eventually established a small federation there, organized by former minister Alvarez del Vayo, with Julio Hernández as president and José Sanchis-Banús as secretary.[72]

The other major region of republican exile and hence of *émigré* politics was North Africa. Among the 10,000-plus Spanish refugees there, some 1,320 were paid-up members of the PSOE by the time the Socialist Federation of North Africa held its second congress in February 1945.[73] This followed a year of organizational effort in the wake of the liberation of

---

[70] 'La UGT en Francia', 11; *ES* (Mexico), Oct. 1945, 3; *España Popular*, 8.10.45, 1–2.

[71] *ES* (ed. J. Alvarez), 17.1.45, 3, 18.7.45, 1–2, 4. A few of the pro-Negrín Socialists in France rejected UNE from the start as PCE-dominated and thus not a true union (Lamoneda, *Posiciones*, 317). From Nov. 1944 UNE recognized the Negrín government but called for it to be broadened. A Mexican section of UNE did not appear until June 1945. Lamoneda's faction boycotted it, except for Gabriel Morón who was made a vice-secretary (*España Popular*, 15.6.45). He was also a signatory to a Círculo Cultural Jaime Vera dissidents' document urging a Marxist regeneration of the party: PSOE, Dissident Groups, *Ante la crisis del Partido Socialista Obrero Español* (Mexico, Oct. 1946).

[72] *ES* (Mexico), May 1950, 4.

[73] Llopis, report on visit to North Africa, PSOE in Exile, *Actas* of CE, 1–2.3.45.

North Africa, the first-fruit of which was the publication of a version of *El Socialista* in Algeria, commencing on May Day 1944. Socialists residing in cities stretching from Casablanca to Tunis soon established contact with one another, their work facilitated by the concentration of two-thirds of them in just three places—Oran (447), Casablanca (250), and Algiers (130).[74] The 'North Africans' refused to recognize either the Prieto or Lamoneda executive, and they ignored the Spanish Liberation Junta (JEL), UNE's Prietista rival, for fear that this would imply recognition of the Otero-Albar party executive to which Prieto belonged. There was more empathy in their relations with the Socialists in France. Vizcaíno Vita travelled northwards to Toulouse in September 1944 for the first congress of the 'PSOE in France' and Rodolfo Llopis, elected general secretary at that congress, attended the second congress of the Socialist Federation of North Africa. At the latter event, he persuaded delegates to support the JEL and to affiliate to the Toulouse-based PSOE exile organization, on the grounds that the greater body of Socialist *émigrés* were concentrated in France.[75] A UGT congress held a couple of days later took similar steps, as did a Youth congress in March 1945.

Llopis's Caballerista background was useful in this phase of *émigré* unification, for the secretary of the North African federation in 1944–5, Ildefonso Torregrosa, and other leading militants such as César Barona and Juan Tundidor in Algeria were from the same faction. In general the North African Socialists were of high calibre, having played important roles in the Civil War and then having been evacuated by their organizations when it ended—while most of the refugees in France belonged to the undifferentiated mass that had fled from Catalonia as the nationalist army advanced in 1939.[76] Once in exile, however, geography immediately demoted these senior cadres and before long their representatives became prominent critics of the Toulouse leadership. Part of

[74] Ibid.

[75] Ibid. North Africa's membership was put at 2,000 in Sept. 1944 (PSOE in France, First Congress (1944), 'Documentos originales', 10. By May 1945 the balance was N. Africa 1,500, France 5,526 (PSOE in Exile, Second Congress (1946), *Memoria*, 13).

[76] Llopis report, PSOE in Exile, *Actas* of CE, 1–2.3.45.

their relegation was due to a decision taken by a PSOE plenum in July 1945 to dissolve the North African executive and central plenum altogether, contrary to promises made by Llopis five months earlier.[77]

Negrinistas also made a bid for influence in North Africa. Amaro del Rosal travelled from Mexico to Algiers and Oran in an attempt to drum up support for the González Peña-Rodríguez Vega executive of the UGT. Arriving in January 1945, he was rebuffed by the pre-existing committees of the PSOE, UGT, and even of his own bank employees' union, and had little success with recruitment. According to his opponents, his organizational achievement was limited to a dozen militants who joined a new 'Grupo Jaime Vera de Oran' and a 'pocket UGT';[78] his own claim was that the UGT group in Oran had been established following an assembly of 500 Spanish refugees.[79] Allowing for possible exaggeration on both sides, it seems clear that in North Africa as in France and Mexico, the pro-Negrín and pro-UNE forces were proportionally much larger at UGT than PSOE level as a result of Communist participation in the former. From the late 1940s, as will be seen, the UGT-PSOE ratio in the anti-Communist sector was less than two to one.

With the PSOE, UGT, and FNJSE of North Africa deciding to accept direction from Toulouse in February-March 1945, and Mexico and other American sections following suit in August, the mainstream *émigré* Socialist organizations became unified. Several leading Socialists in North Africa moved to France. The second congress of PSOE exiles held in Toulouse, in the Ancienne Chapelle des Jacobins in May 1946, crowned the process. Some 461 delegates were present, representing 7,727 paid-up members of the PSOE, the largest groups now being in Mexico (689), Oran (409), Paris (402), Toulouse (350), Marseilles (272), Casablanca (262), and Bordeaux (244 members).[80] At that congress the affiliated

---

[77] *Adelante*, 1.9.45, 3.   [78] *Cuadernos Socialistas*, 4.4.45, 3.

[79] *Boletín de Información Sindical*, 1.5.45, 12.

[80] PSOE in Exile, Second Congress (1946), *Actas taquigráficas*, 235–57. At the time of the Fifth Congress in Aug. 1952, of 4,325 members represented 457 were resident in Mexico, 284 in Oran, and 283 in Paris. Some 66.2% of those represented were resident in France, 15.7% in the Americas, 15.6% in Africa, 1.3% in Belgium, 0.8% in London, and 0.3% in Vienna (*Actas*, 5–11). A party census dated 20 Oct.

Socialists all formally became part of a single 'PSOE in Exile' which in theory was just part of the PSOE, based in Spain and led from Madrid.

RELATIONS WITH OTHER FORCES

José Rodríguez Vega was referring to the PSOE's potentially pivotal role when he observed that if the party were disunited, then so would the broader anti-Franco movement.[1] In terms of numbers, organizational capacity, and international links, the PCE had become a formidable rival during the Civil War. However, the PSOE enjoyed the advantage of broader social appeal and, moreover, it was better qualified to play a role in formal and informal alliances. The Socialist Party occupied a unique position, straddling two of the major constituencies that made up the Spanish opposition: the democratic camp and the left (the third constituency being regionalism).[2] Though they went through long periods of great weakness, the Socialists continued to uphold a party tradition that was at least respected by other democratic and left-wing opponents of Francoism, whereas the PCE's democratic credentials would always remain suspect because of its Stalinist past. Given the PSOE's strategically pivotal position, the party's divisions almost inevitably affected adjacent organizations. Like the Socialists, these fractured first in response to events in Spain, then under the influence of events in Paris in 1939 (particularly the creation of the JARE, undermining Negrín's authority), and finally they became polarized in response to Communist Party politics.

Having played a highly controversial role in the Civil War, the PCE did little itself to reunify the republican camp, though the spirit of sacrifice of Communist militants

1953 showed that 3,290 out of the 4,918 PSOE in Exile members were resident in France—66.9% (PSOE in Exile, *Actas* of CE, 22.10.53).

[1] José Rodríguez Vega, 'Impresiones de España', *Adelante*, 1.3.43, 2–3.
[2] For useful overviews in English see Preston, 'The Anti-Francoist Opposition: The Long March to Unity', in id. (ed.), *Spain in Crisis* (Hassocks: Harvester, 1976), 125–56; David Gilmour, *The Transformation of Spain* (London: Quartet, 1985), ch. 5.

earned it the respect of some *émigrés*. The party's continuing subordination to Stalin resulted in an incredibly erratic course involving five separate volte-faces in seven years. It began by trying to ignore the Civil War defeat, then launched into a bout of sectarianism in response to the German-Soviet Pact, and finally, while maintaining a consistent international line, it went through four phases of alternative anti-Franco formulae. The early sectarianism bred isolation and fostered bitter inter-party relations; the war years as a whole gave the PCE an image of inconsistency, opportunism, and untrustworthiness. Despite periodic Communist calls for unity and efforts to build a National Union in 1942–5, critics of the PCE continued to suspect hegemonic designs and interpreted UNE purely as a Soviet move to keep Spain out of the war by courting conservative supporters of neutrality in Spain.[3]

CHRONOLOGY OF THE PCE'S CHANGES OF LINE,
1939–45
(positions noted in bold figures)

1939
March   Collapse of the Republic in Spain. Civil war ends with
             Casado coup, establishment of Defence Council, and
             the military triumph of Franco. PCE [1] declares that
             only a battle has been lost, not the war. Calls for the
             continuation of republican struggle against Franco in
             Spain. Urges Western democracies to end appease-
             ment and to fight fascism.
August   German-Soviet Pact signed.
December   PCE [2] attacks all Socialists (including Negrinistas),
             anarchists, and Republicans as capitulationists and/or
             enemies of unity. Blames them for civil war defeat.
             Declares that the world war is an imperialist war,
             against working-class interests. Opposes Spanish par-
             ticipation. Calls for the abolition of republican insti-
             tutions in exile. Drops republican aims. Calls for the
             creation of a worker-peasant front formed by rank-
             and-file activists; urges the latter to ignore their
             leaders.

[3] *ES* (Mexico), Nov. 1942, 3; Alba, *Communist Party*, 318. The PCE regarded Spanish neutrality as just one aim of UNE. See the manifesto 'Para salvar a España'.

1941
June

Germany attacks USSR. PCE [3] supports British and Soviet war efforts against the Nazis. Begins to prepare members for guerrilla warfare. Now defends the Republican Constitution of 1931 and presents the Negrín government as legitimate. Calls for broad unity including the PSOE (though not Prieto nor Araquistain) around the aim of restoring the Republic. Says the Cortes elected in 1936 and regional governments should function in exile.

1942
March

In Mexico the Spanish Democratic Union (UDE) is formed by the PCE, Catalan Communists (PSUC), and Negrinista factions of the PSOE, UGT, and Republicans.

September

While keeping the same international policy, the PCE [4] withdraws its support for the Cortes, Negrín government, 1931 Constitution, and republican regime. Instead calls for a broad national front of all non-fascist parties to overthrow Franco and the Falange and set up a Government of National Union. Republicans feel betrayed.

November

The Spanish National Union (UNE) is created by the PCE in France. PCE manifesto calls for a Government of National Union and a Constituent Assembly to draft a new constitution.

1943
January

As a result of the PCE volte-face of September 1942, UDE collapses in Mexico and Negrinista Socialists and Republicans abandon the *Hogar Español* in London (set up in October 1941 as a meeting place for all republican groups).

May

Comintern dissolved.

September

UNE supposedly establishes a Supreme Council of National Union (JSUN) in Spain.

November

Socialists and Republicans form the Spanish Liberation Council (JEL) in Mexico. It excludes the PCE, anarchists, and Basque Nationalists.

1944
January

Negrín's *Spanish Newsletter* in London calls the JSUN a fabrication.

October

The National Alliance of Democratic Forces (ANFD) is created by Socialists and Republicans in Spain. Pro-

	Republic; Spain as a Western country; hopes for support from the Allies. JEL Committee in France formed by PSOE, Republicans (IR, UR, PRF), CNT-MLE, and UGT— previously all in the Spanish Democratic Alliance (ADE: also known as the Comité de Relaciones de las Fuerzas Democráticas Españolas).
November	UNE recognizes the Negrín government as legitimate but calls for it to be broadened.

1945

January	PCE [5] calls for the restoration of the Republic and the return of the Negrín government. Sets up a 'unification committee' with Negrinista Socialists.
June	San Francisco Conference plans United Nations. JEL present with observer status. UNE abolished 30 June 1945.
July	UNE dissolution announced in France following the loss of some of its Socialist members. PCE says UNE is superfluous now that the ANFD exists. Hopes to join the latter (succeeds January 1946).
August	First republican government formed in exile by José Giral (IR). Includes JEL forces, excludes PCE (until April 1946) and Negrinistas. Mexican JEL is dissolved.
December	PCE [6]says that, to put an end to the suffering of the Spanish people, it would accept an agreement involving all the national anti-Franco forces on the basis of a plebiscite to decide Spain's future regime. To be organized by a broad national government extending from monarchists to Communists.

Sources. *España Popular*, *UDE*, *El Socialista* (Toulouse/Llopis), *El Socialista* (Mexico/Lamoneda), *Reconquista de España* (Toulouse and Mexico), *Adelante* (Mexico).

Even those Socialists who in principle were in favour of co-operating with the Communists now found it much more difficult in practice. The German-Soviet Pact reduced Negrín, who may have foreseen that it would not last, to silence. *Norte* was sufficiently upset to protest, presenting the pact as evidence that national interests had survived the Russian Revolution, while also pointing to the Soviet Union's lack of socialist democracy.[4] Communist-Negrinista relations were

[4] Miguel de Amilibia, '¿Adónde va la URSS?'

shaken, though not sufficiently to prevent further co-operation following the Nazi attack on the Soviet Union in 1941. The main expression of this reconciliation was the creation in Mexico of the Spanish Democratic Union (UDE). This alliance could last only so long as the PCE recognized the Negrín government and saw, as Lamoneda did, the restoration of the Republic and the revival in exile of its institutions as legitimate and non-negotiable objectives. UNE, regarded by its republican opponents as a proposal to embrace people who had republican blood on their hands, destroyed UDE without achieving its own aim of bridging the gap between a broad left and the non-fascist right. Negrinistas, at least those outside France, saw UNE as a betrayal of those who had given their lives defending the Republic; in their opinion, by refusing to insist on republican legitimacy, UNE had surrendered the opposition's only constitutional weapon without a fight, opening the way for a possible monarchist or military regime.[5] The zig-zag path traced by the PCE led Communists and Negrinistas to coincide once more in 1945, but this time the relationship was strained and the romance brief. Partners again, they shared a republican line and initially also a critical attitude towards the new Giral government-in-exile, regarded as being too narrow (it excluded them). But permanent divergence separated them in December when the PCE, seeing the chances of a republican restoration recede, again appealed to the non-Falange sector that had supported Franco in 1936, and announced that Communists were prepared to leave the question of Spain's future regime to a plebiscite.[6]

The main effect of PCE meandering was to alienate Negrinistas from their own organizations, which lost their *raison d'être* once co-operation with the PCE proved impossible. An unknown number trickled back into the mainstream PSOE and UGT where they were placed on probation for a while before being allowed to stand for office.[7] Anti-Communism was much fiercer in the host sector, which still retained vivid memories of PCE skulduggery in the 1930s. Like the Negrinistas, most of the Socialists who had supported

[5] *ES* (Mexico), Apr. 1944, 1, July 1944, 4.
[6] *España Popular*, 18.12.45, 1–2.
[7] Fagen, 122; Borrás, 100–1; UGT in Exile, *Actas* of CE, 15.2.45.

Largo Caballero, Besteiro, and even Prieto were at this time unwilling to compromise on their republican commitment and were horrified by the idea of extending a hand to the likes of Gil-Robles. What really rankled was the PCE's poaching of so many of their most dynamic militants during the Civil War, and the way in which more recent Communist demands for unity were made against the background of personal attacks on PSOE leaders. Prieto was branded successively 'the Spanish Mikhailovich' and 'the Spanish Papandreou'.[8] Relations were not helped by the fact that a leading Communist, Santiago Carrillo, had not only led the mass organization of Young Socialists into unity with the Young Communists, and many members into the PCE, but had publicly disowned his own father, the Socialist Wenceslao Carrillo, six weeks after the Civil War ended. While announcing 'My love for the Soviet Union and the great Stalin is constantly growing', the future PCE general secretary had dismissed his father as a traitor who had 'betrayed his class': 'you remained on the other side of the trenches'.[9]

Many who agreed with the PCE that Wenceslao Carrillo and the others who had formed the National Council of Defence in March 1939 were traitors, did not regard this as justifying a permanent breach between father and son. The father in question, bitterly upset by the quarrel, none the less managed to nullify any propaganda advantage the Communist Party might have gained from his son's letter. Rather than reply to Santiago, Wenceslao sent his response to the man he believed to have inspired the letter of disavowal: 'Sr. Stalin'. Mocking the Soviet leader as the 'beloved chief of the world proletariat', he pointed to some of the less than glorious aspects of the PCE role in the Civil War and accused Stalin of having enslaved his son spiritually.[10] In some societies the significance of such an episode would have been merely anecdotal and transient; but in the context of Spain, where the family was virtually

[8] *Adelante*, 15.3.45, p. 2. Mikhailovich had been presented as a hero in ibid., 1.11.42, 3.

[9] Letter dated 15 May 1939, first published in *Voz de los Españoles* (Paris), June 1939; reproduced in Alba, *Communist Party*, 303–6.

[10] Wenceslao Carrillo, 'Carta de Wenceslao Carrillo a Stalin como contestación a la que había recibido de su hijo, Santiago Carrillo', 2 July 1939, handwritten copy in 'Amaro Rosal Díaz Materiales'.

sacrosanct, young Carrillo's disavowal provoked outrage and helped perpetuate the anti-Communism of many Socialists for a generation. Even after Santiago Carrillo's eventual departure from the PCE leadership four decades later, aged PSOE veterans would still utter the most appalling oaths whenever his name was mentioned.

Between the Communists and most Socialists there existed mutual suspicion, a sense of having been betrayed by a former partner, and a conviction that the other was the main obstacle to the creation of a viable anti-Franco movement, if not a conscious saboteur of it. Since both parties had grown from the same root, and traditionally had employed the terms socialism and communism interchangeably, the scenario corresponded all too closely to Ignazio Silone's jibe at Togliatti, 'The final struggle will be between the Communists and the ex-Communists'.[11] The classical symptoms of the ex-Communist who becomes an inverted Stalinist were most observable in some of the Caballeristas, who in the mid-1930s for a while had accepted Stalinist positions on the single party and popular front and had worked closely with the PCE. Reactions against this past were often more visceral than intellectual, and some Socialists, notably Luis Araquistain, jettisoned all traces of Marxist influence as they turned against the PCE. Others upheld the Kautskyist line of earlier decades, claiming that twentieth-century events in Russia had nothing to do with Marxist prescriptions. For Wenceslao Carrillo, Russian conditions provided Bolshevism with a justification, but did not make it Marxist.[12] For Arsenio Jimeno 'National-Bolshevism' merely proved Marx's contention that socialism could not be built without the appropriate material base; the Russian Revolution had been the last of the bourgeois revolutions, not the first socialist one.[13]

Prieto's anti-Communism was much more calculating and dispassionate than that of the Caballeristas. The Lamoneda faction accused him of using anti-Communism during the

---

[11] Quoted in Isaac Deutscher's review of *The God That Failed*, reproduced in C. Wright Mills (ed.), *The Marxists* (Harmondsworth: Penguin, 1963), 341–51.

[12] W. Carrillo, 'Ni el socialismo británico ni el comunismo ruso monopolizan las teorías marxistas', in Saborit, *Asturias*, 116–17.

[13] Arsenio Jimeno, *Nuestro ideario: El socialismo* (Toulouse: PSOE, n.d.), 20.

period of the Nazi-Soviet Pact as a device to win British and French support, yet once the pact was broken, he like many other Western democrats praised the USSR. He even went so far as to present it as a socialist model: 'the proletariat has before it, like a lightened beacon, a genuine, totally socialist republic, the Russian Republic . . . [defending] not only the conquests of the proletariat but also the banners of freedom the world over.'[14] When it came to action, however, Prieto's fundamental premise was that, if there were *any* hope of ousting Franco, it lay in a move by the Western allies against him, as the Atlantic Pact of 1941 had seemed to prefigure.[15]

To give the Western democracies an acceptable point of reference in Spanish politics, Prieto established a Socialist-Republican alliance, the Spanish Liberation Council (JEL) in November 1943. Broadly speaking, its components in Mexico—the PSOE, Republican Left, Republican Union, Republican Left of Catalonia, and Republican Catalan Action— had been the mainstays of the Second Republic. Excluded on the grounds of extremism were the PCE, Negrinistas, anarchists, and Basque Nationalists, the latter for unreasonably seeking while in exile to modify Basque constitutional rights.[16] A parallel 'JEL, Committee in France' was established in October of the following year. Significantly, reflecting the more working-class composition of the Socialist emigration to France, the UGT and CNT were included there, the latter because of flourishing co-operation between Caballerista and libertarian militants. Another difference was that, whereas the JEL in Mexico was conceived as an alternative to setting up a republican government in exile, in France the Council was regarded as just a short-term unifying body, to serve only until the Cortes could meet somewhere in exile and endorse a proper government.[17]

[14] *ES* (Mexico), 1.6.42, 3, 6; Prieto, 'Confesiones'. He later claimed that a love of freedom and tolerance, and the imperialist nature of the USSR, were behind his anti-Communism. See id., 'Hitos de mi anticomunismo', *ES*, 25.12.52, 1–2; PSOE in Exile, Third Congress (1948), *Actas*, 168.

[15] See Prieto's speeches, 'Glosa de mi anterior discurso en la Habana', *Adelante*, 1.8.42, 3, 'La libertad es cara en sangre y oro', ibid., 15.3.44, 1–2.

[16] On the JEL in Mexico and for its unity pact see ibid., Dec. 1943–Jan. 1944.

[17] Prieto declarations, ibid., 1.1.45, 1; Llopis speech at congress in North Africa, ibid., 15.4.45, 2; *Cuadernos Socialistas*, 4.4.45, 6–7; PSOE in Exile, *Actas* of CE, 22.10.44.

In Mexico the JEL, presided over by Diego Martínez Barrio and with Prieto as its secretary, met 133 times.[18] It was essentially a body with propagandist and diplomatic functions, not a vehicle of combat like the UNE. Indeed, it discouraged armed struggle in Spain for fear that this would strengthen the hand of extremists.[19] Undoubtedly its greatest triumph came at the San Francisco Conference in April–June 1945 which gave birth to the United Nations. JEL representatives headed by Prieto attended as observers, thanks to an invitation from Roosevelt. They were able to present their case and their labours were finally rewarded when the conference approved a Mexican motion barring entry to the UN to countries whose regimes had been established with the aid of States that had fought against the Allies in the war.[20] It seemed clear from the conference, though, that major Western countries did not see the JEL as a suitable instrument for bringing about change in Spain. Even Prieto, who since 1942 had been proposing a plebiscite as the most viable way of ending the Franco regime, now called reluctantly for a meeting of the Cortes in Mexico to choose a provisional government in exile, hoping that UN members' diplomatic recognition would be transferred from Franco to the latter.[21]

Before dissolving itself, the JEL contributed to the establishment of the Giral government, whose original components were drawn mainly from the JEL. Negrín too helped bring about this development. The Cortes met in Mexico three times, in January, August, and November 1945. On the first occasion, lacking a quorum, it could only pay homage to the 127 deputies of the Cortes of 1936 who had been assassinated, executed, or had died in Spain or abroad since then.[22] On the second occasion Martínez Barrio was elected interim President of the Republic and on the third the Giral government was endorsed by the Cortes. By attending the second session and submitting his resignation to the newly-elected President (either in the interests of unity or because he thought his

[18] Fernández, 'Las formaciones', 145–52.
[19] Fagen, 109–10.   [20] Ibid. 112–13.
[21] Report of Prieto press conference, *Adelante*, 1.7.45, 3.
[22] Of the 99 PSOE deputies elected in 1936, 34 had been shot either during or after the Civil War by the Francoists. For details see *Adelante*, supplement to no. 67, 15.11.44.

government would be asked to continue in office), Negrín had his government's legitimacy over the last six years implicitly recognized,[23] though at the cost of its being replaced by a government that was more concerned with diplomacy than with waging a struggle inside Spain.

While at a political level PSOE relations during these years were best with Republicans of diverse hue, at a trade union level the CNT was the Socialists' natural partner. Although their ideals differed, they were both decidedly anti-Stalinist. There had been a formal reunification of the anarchists with the creation of the Spanish Libertarian Movement (MLE-CNT) in February 1939, but basic differences persisted between purists and those prepared to collaborate with anti-Franco fronts, and these undermined sincere UGT wishes for a partnership. Like the mainstream PSOE, the allied UGT meanwhile regarded relations with the PCE and UNE as out of the question. It rejected proposals made by Rodríguez Vega and others for a Socialist majority to be provided for in the leadership of a reunified UGT.[24] There were no regrets about the implications of this for membership—strength came, as Iglesias had insisted, not from numbers, but from the quality of militants and their moral calibre.[25]

Socialist-CNT co-operation began with clandestine work to help comrades in the prisons and concentration camps of France. Some were saved from German forced-labour camps as a result.[26] Mutual assistance grew as the liberation of France drew near. Joint manifestos appeared, questioning UNE's courtship of the Spanish right. 'Since when have Gil-Robles and Cardinal Segura been anti-fascists?' one such leaflet asked, in response to UNE sponsorship claims.[27] The

---

[23] In 1942 the government composition was: Negrín (President of Government), J. Alvarez del Vayo (Minister of State), Francisco Méndez Aspe (Treasury), José Moix (Labour), Antonio Velao (Public Works), and Vicente Uribe (Agriculture). It maintained 'ambassadors' too.

[24] J. Rodríguez Vega, 'La unificación de la UGT'; UGT, Assemblies, Asamblea de Grupos Departamentales, Aug. 1945, *Actas y acuerdos*, 19. The proposals constituted tacit acknowledgement that Communists and pro-Communists controlled the Negrinista UGT, although the latter differed from the PCE in its attitude to Negrín.

[25] Pascual Tomás at First Congress of UGT in Exile, 1944, *Acta*, 1–4.

[26] Ibid.

[27] PSOE and other organizations, PSOE and CNT, manifesto *Españoles*, Sept.

desire for CNT-UGT unification was strongly expressed at the first congress of the UGT in Exile, held in November 1944. CNT greetings were delivered in person to delegates who went on to vote for the creation of a UGT-CNT liaison committee. There was less enthusiasm for unity in Mexico, though a similar committee existed there as well.

Unfortunately for both movements, the desire for unification was rapidly relegated to dreamland as the CNT lost its coherence and entered upon a long terminal decline.[28] Disputing factions within the MLE-CNT finally became incompatible in 1945 when two leaders became ministers of the Giral government.[29] Dismayed at the plight of its ally, the UGT tried desperately to remain neutral as the purists denounced the collaborators. UGT wartime relations had been maintained with the 'purist' leadership presided over by Germinal Esgleas, whose supporters were dominant in the libertarian movement in France. However, when his executive was disavowed and a new National Committee of the MLE-CNT was set up under the presidency of José E. Leyva, one of the Giral ministers, the UGT in France was obliged by the UGT in Spain to recognize the new committee, the collaborationist sector of the CNT being stronger than the purists inside Spain.[30]

By 1945 the republican forces were not much more united than in 1939, despite passing unitary gestures at the time of the Giral government's formation. The mainstream PSOE and UGT were united in opposition to the Communists but had divided sympathies when it came to other forces. While the Prietistas had an ideological and strategic preference for the Republican parties (their foremost concern being acceptability to Western leaders), the Caballeristas (placing

1944. Gil-Robles's links with UNE have never been proven, but they were believed to exist by many exiles at the time. AP News reported that some of the guerrillas who crossed the Pyrenees into Spain towards the end of 1944 did so shouting *vivas* to him (*Adelante*, 1.11.44, 1).

[28] Borrás (pp. 95, 105, 288) estimates that in France the PCE declined from 15,000–20,000 members in 1944–5 to 10,000–12,000 by 1950, and the PSOE-UGT from 7,000–8,000 to 5,000–6,000 over the same period, while the libertarians lost half their members and those who remained were divided into two main factions.

[29] 'Una incidencia penosa', *ES*, 6.11.45, 1.

[30] UGT in Exile, Second Congress (1946), *Memoria*, 36–42.

greater emphasis upon the issue being decided in Spain) worked for unity and even unification with the CNT, only to be frustrated by factors beyond their control.[31] Both factions, however, believed that some level of international help would be needed to oust Franco, and in order to obtain that aid it was first necessary to establish their organizations' exclusive rights to the initials PSOE and UGT in the eyes of the outside world.

THE BATTLE FOR RECOGNITION

As a result of the general dislocation produced by the Second World War, the battle between Negrinistas and non-Negrinistas to have their credentials accepted by foreign socialist parties and trade unions did not commence until the mid-1940s. However, it was then fought passionately for three years and the outcome naturally helped shape the future character of Spanish Socialism. The Negrinistas eventually lost, but it was only with great reluctance and against a background dominated by the Cold War that fraternal organizations agreed to opt for their rivals. Indeed the initial international pressures were aimed at getting the two main PSOE exile factions to reunite.

Unification was the predominant desire among the French Socialists of the SFIO. After providing a venue for the first congress of the anti-UNE PSOE amidst the disorder of September 1944, the party immediately grew impatient over 'the eternal divisions of the Spanish Socialists', so reminiscent of the 1930s and evident in the efforts of competing groups in Paris to achieve recognition as the true PSOE. Some French Socialists were taken in by UNE's claims to be a real

---

[31] There was also some tension between the Prietista versions of the UGT and PSOE in Mexico. Relations became strained in May 1942 when in a public speech Prieto criticized the excessive power of trade unions *vis-à-vis* the State during the Civil War. In the same speech he described the Asturian revolutionary movement of 1934 as a mistake, regretted the amount of autonomy enjoyed by the Young Socialists in the past, and spoke of the need for private initiative in both large and small enterprises. In response UGT leaders in Mexico presented struggle against the State as part of the class struggle, and rejected Prieto's view that the State could represent national interests. See *Adelante*, May–Aug. 1942.

union, and mistook Socialist opponents of it for incorrigible sectarians belonging to 'some third Socialist Party'.[1] SFIO activists who joined the France-Spain solidarity committees established by UNE in late 1944 and early 1945 recognized Juan Negrín as being still head of the Spanish Republic; since he raised the banners of PSOE reunification himself, the 'other' PSOE led by Rodolfo Llopis appeared divisive in rejecting them. For this reason the mainstream PSOE was not invited by general secretary Daniel Meyer to an SFIO congress in the autumn of 1944, and when the party nevertheless obtained credentials through exploiting its French contacts this only earned the PSOE delegates a lecture on unity from Vincent Auriol when they turned up for the event. Despite this rebuff, the SFIO did join with the Belgian, British, and Italian socialist parties in sending a representative to the second congress of the mainstream PSOE in Exile in May 1946, whereas a few days earlier it had boycotted a 'unity congress' organized by former Negrín minister Julio Alvarez del Vayo.[2]

The duplication of organizations in exile claiming to represent the PSOE served only to confuse European socialists. In 1945 the Czech Socialists invited the Negrinista faction to a party congress purely by mistake![3] No Socialist International existed at this time to mediate in the dispute, though there were plans afoot to relaunch one. Possibly as a result of the activities of Wenceslao Carrillo in London, the Toulouse-based PSOE was the only Spanish party invited by the Labour Party to an international conference in London in March 1945 to discuss a relaunch.[4] During the next two years, similar conferences in Clacton, Paris, Zurich, and Antwerp kept the project alive. Incidentally, they also provided opportunities for the PSOE dispute to be aired.

As hosts of the international conference in Paris in August 1946, the SFIO invited both PSOE factions to attend, but the

---

[1] Report of Trifón Gómez and Llopis to CE, PSOE in Exile, *Actas* of CE, 30.11.44.

[2] Llopis regretted the boycott, for the 'dissident' congress was attended by only 35 delegates claiming to represent 301 members. See PSOE in Exile, Second Congress (1946), *Actas*, 132.

[3] Ibid. 132–3; PSOE in Exile, *Actas* of CE, 25.10.45.

[4] *Cuadernos Socialistas*, 1.5:45, 4.

attempt to reconcile them failed. Negrín insisted that his delegation represented the legitimate party executive headed by González Peña and Lamoneda, and found an echo among delegates with his appeal for unity; Llopis countered that there was only one Spanish party present, plus a handful of dissidents, Llopis, Pascual Tomás, and Emilio Salgado walked out of the conference after presenting their position, saying they were following directives Salgado had brought from the party executive in Madrid. They returned only upon the pleas of Leon Blum and Belgian Socialists, realizing that if they did not do so the Negrinistas would claim the credit for any conference achievements or, alternatively, would blame their rivals if it failed.[5] As late as July 1947 Rodolfo Llopis believed that the SFIO was readier to listen to the 'dissidents' than to his executive, a situation he ascribed to Negrín's facility in diplomacy.[6]

In June 1947 at Zurich, the next international socialist conference approved a French motion advocating PSOE reconciliation and entrusted Louis de Brouckère with the task of bringing the two parties together. In this he was thwarted by the absolute intransigence of the Llopis executive, which completely rejected the view that there were two PSOEs battling for recognition. The Llopis sector simply demanded recognition of the PSOE and its executive in Spain, knowing full well that the latter had by now recognized Toulouse as its external expression, had ordered the expulsion of Lamoneda and company from the party, and had even sent away a Lamoneda emissary. For the Toulouse-based Pablistas, what was at stake was not just a question of party discipline—a moral question, the 'immorality' of their rivals, also stood in the way of reunification.[7] Not afraid to appear petulant, the mainstream PSOE in Exile boycotted congresses of the Italian and Hungarian Socialists because the Negrinistas had been invited also, and it staged another walk-out in August 1947 at

---

[5] PSOE in Exile, Assembly of Delegates (1947), *Acta taquigráfica*, 10–13; ibid., *Actas*, 81–90.

[6] Ibid., *Acta taquigráfica*, 79, 90.

[7] Ibid. 13–17; *ES* (Mexico), Apr. 1946, 1; *ES*, 23.10.45, 1, 16.2.46, 1, 27.7.46, 1. At Zurich the Toulouse-based CE was represented by Antonio Pérez and Wenceslao Carrillo; its rival by Negrín, Lamoneda, Ramón González Peña, Claudina García, and Alejandro Morueta.

an SFIO party congress in Lyons. On the latter occasion, as a Negrinista was about to deliver the fraternal greetings of his organization, Enrique de Francisco stood up and shouted from the floor that the man at the podium was a representative of the 'Communist fifth column' that Moscow was trying to organize in the PSOE![8] Three months later, at the Antwerp conference, De Brouckère had to admit that his mission had failed. With reconciliation out of the question, the permanent executive committee established at the event was mandated to determine the facts of the dispute and then meet in February 1948 to formulate recommendations regarding recognition.

The International Socialist Committee for Conferences (known in the PSOE by its Spanish acronym COMISCO) finally decided in favour of the Llopis faction in February, and then had its decision ratified in June by an international socialist conference in Vienna. The reasons behind the COMISCO verdict are a matter of conjecture. Presided over by De Brouckère and including representatives of the British, French, Italian, Dutch, Polish, Swedish, and Swiss parties, the Committee heard the petitions of Rodolfo Llopis and Antonio Pérez, and then of Lamoneda and Alejandro Morueta, before deciding.[9] In the minds of the victors, the outcome above all represented acceptance of their claims concerning the persisting active presence of the PSOE in Spain. To show foreign socialists that they were not dealing just with *émigrés*, the Llopis executive had used Salgado and Pérez, members who had recently been in the Madrid-based leadership, as conference representatives abroad. To a lesser extent, the rival executive had used Claudina García, a former member of the UGT leadership in Spain, for the same purpose in 1947. However, while the Toulouse-linked PSOE in the interior was undoubtedly rudimentary, there was no sign at all of any Negrinista counterpart in Spain. Moreover, even if the mainstream PSOE at times exaggerated its presence in the interior, its membership in exile was far larger, with 7,727 members in May 1946, in contrast with the 426 in France and Mexico claimed by Lamoneda.[10] Other factors that militated

---

[8] PSOE in Exile, Third Congress (1948), *Memoria*, ch. on 'Relaciones con España', and *Actas*, 14; *ES*, 22.8.47, 4. [9] *ES* (Mexico), Mar. 1948, 1.
[10] PSOE in Exile, Second Congress (1946), *Actas taquigráficas*, 235–57; id.,

against international socialist recognition of the Negrinistas were their creation of a short-lived unification committee with the PCE in January 1945[11] and their advocacy of guerrilla warfare to accompany more traditional mass methods of struggle against Franco.[12] The Negrinistas, then, were only partly right when they attributed the COMISCO decision to a rightward shift among European socialists which had left the embryonic International thoroughly anti-Communist.[13]

COMISCO's adjudication proved to be a turning point, though not in terms of significantly increased material solidarity. Despite the removal of the 'two PSOEs' impediment to giving aid, the latter remained disappointing, even after the creation by the socialist parties of *Entr'aide Socialiste Internationale*. Only its Belgian and Swiss sections functioned, at least in the PSOE's estimation.[14] Undoubtedly, early on it was the Belgian Socialists who did the most for the PSOE. Before long they were joined by the Norwegians and Swedes, links with whom were nurtured by party treasurer Carlos Martínez Parera. From the mid-1950s the West German SPD began to lend support too.[15] Meanwhile, French help for the PSOE was largely infrastructural and British Labour Party backing was for a long time mainly rhetorical and diplomatic, though for a while British trade unions were the main source of UGT aid.[16] The early balance sheet did not reflect creditably on the new Socialist International established at Frankfurt in mid-1951 on foundations laid by COMISCO. By

Third Congress (1948), *Memoria*, ch. on 'Relaciones Internacionales'. Pérez claimed at the Second Congress that there were 4–5 times as many Socialists in the interior (*Actas*, 227), implying that there were between 30,908 and 38,635. *Adelante* (15.8.46, 4) claimed that the PSOE had 20,000 members in Spain. A more realistic figure for active membership was that given to other socialist parties, of 12,000 Spanish Socialists in and outside Spain in 1946 (PSOE, *Circulares* of CE, 5.9.56).

[11] *ES*, 14.7.45, 3.

[12] *ES* (Mexico), July 1948, 1; *ES* (ed. J. Alvarez), 17.5.45, 4.

[13] *ES* (Mexico), Mar. 1948, 1, July 1948, 2. By this time the German SPD had joined the relaunch initiative and the Hungarian, Polish, and Czechoslovak Socialists had left.

[14] Llopis, report on Socialist International congress, in PSOE in Exile, *Actas* of CE, 15–16.10.51, 20.

[15] PSOE in Exile, Assembly of Delegates (1949), *Memoria*, 23; Treasurer's reports in the *memorias* for the CN meeting of the PSOE in Apr. 1954, and for the Eighth Congress of the PSOE in Exile, 1958.

[16] UGT in Exile, Third Congress (1949), *Memoria*, 47–8.

1954 the International had 36 affiliated parties with a total of 10 million members and 64 million voters in the most recent elections. However, as was seen particularly during the Suez crisis (and not least by Llopis), the leading parties of the International tended to put national interests first when it came to action.[17]

Nevertheless, the COMISCO verdict did settle the question of Spanish Socialist representation for 25 years. It thoroughly demoralized the Lamoneda executive,[18] contributing to its disappearance. Together with the failure of España Combatiente, an attempt at a militant republican front to assist active resistance cells in Spain,[19] the COMISCO blow persuaded Lamoneda to return to Mexico in the spring of 1949. After that, he took no major political initiatives, other than an equally unsuccessful attempt in 1951 to persuade dissident Communists to join a new Spanish Socialist Union (USE), based on a programme of democratic socialism.[20]

Negrín too was now showing signs of passivity, interrupted only by semi-independent personal initiatives. Never the dominant figure that Prieto became in the other sector, there were times when Lamoneda and Vayo seemed more Negrinista than Negrín, stressing the legitimacy of the Republic and armed resistance to Franco after Negrín himself

---

[17] PSOE, Assemblies, CD meeting of Aug. 1957, *Actas*, 12.

[18] Personal interview with Rosal, 21 Apr. 1982.

[19] España Combatiente was planned late in 1946, launched in 1947, and held its first congress in Mar. 1948. It failed partly because of the absence of PCE support. Alvarez del Vayo was the only leader to stick to its line of direct action. One of very few exiles ever to go on a mission to Spain (*ES* (Mexico), Sept. 1949, 2, 4), he continued to operate from France and Switzerland after other members of the Lamoneda executive had left for Mexico. In the 1960s he served as president of the Spanish National Liberation Front (FELN), which tried to rebuild a socialist party in the interior while waging an armed struggle against the Franco regime. A spate of FELN bombings in Madrid in the early 1960s was condemned by the PSOE ('La violencia y los valientes', *Le Socialiste* (Paris), 15.8.63, 6). In Jan. 1971 Vayo co-founded the Revolutionary Anti-fascist and Patriotic Front (FRAP). One contradiction in both the España Combatiente and FELN projects was that they were intended to crystallize in broad anti-fascist fronts, but also to regroup revolutionaries who favoured the development of armed struggle. See Vayo's interview with *Tass*, Feb. 1965, in *F.E.L.N.* (n.d.). A few Vayo supporters joined the 'renovated sector of the PSOE after the party split in 1972, but Vayo's own application was rejected because in it he stated that he considered he had never left the PSOE (Fernández, 'Las formaciones', 166–7).

[20] PSOE in Exile, *Actas* of CE, 20.6.51; *ES* (Mexico), 5.1.52, 1.

seemed to have given up the political ghost.[21] Until 1945 Negrín considered himself exempted from any party discipline by his position as head of a coalition government.[22] Three years later, he took advantage of the opportunity derived from the Lamoneda sector's lack of structure and definition to express a latent nationalism (found also, curiously, in his detractor, Luis Araquistain). While the rest of the Spanish opposition favoured the disqualification of Franco's Spain from receiving Marshall aid, hoping for the regime's financial asphyxiation, Negrín in a series of newspaper articles condemned the omission of Spain as a blow to the country rather than to Franco. Marshall aid was in the long-term interests of Spanish development, he argued. A poor and hungry Spain would never be strong enough to oust Franco, and, above all, national interests had to prevail over short-term political considerations.[23] This argument earned the former premier the title 'agent of Wall Street' from the PCE and the epithet 'patented traitor' from the Prietistas.[24] The Lamonedistas themselves hurriedly convoked a congress in Paris and established an official position on the issue similar to that of the rest of the opposition. Negrín then fell silent, accepting but not agreeing with the policy. He engaged little in politics during his remaining years. However, before dying in 1956, he again demonstrated concern for perceived national interests (or for his own posthumous reputation as a statesman) by arranging for the Spanish authorities to receive from his family documentation pertaining to the Republic's shipment of gold to the USSR during the Civil War.[25]

Meanwhile, the UGT battle had taken a different course, with the Negrinistas for a while gaining the upper hand, aided by a new balance of forces in the world labour movement. The map had changed during the Second World War as a result of Anglo-Soviet co-operation from 1941. Common anti-fascist sentiments underlay a new project devised in 1943 to create a

---

[21] See for example *ES* (Mexico), Oct. 1946, 2.
[22] PSOE in Exile, *Actas* of CE, 8.2.45.
[23] *New York Herald Tribune*, 1–2.4.48; *ES* (Mexico), Apr. 1948, 6, June 1948, 2–3; Lamoneda, *Posiciones*, 243–58.
[24] Muñoz, *Tragedia*, 54, 114; *ES*, 9.4.48, 7.
[25] J. Alvarez Sierra and José Gutiérrez-Rave, *Dr. Juan Negrín* (Madrid: Gráficas Yagües, 1966), 101.

true World Federation of Trade Unions (WFTU), though by the time this was launched in 1945 fascism was no longer an overriding preoccupation. During the planning stage of the new International, Spanish Socialists and Communists based in Mexico had far greater freedom to develop contacts than their counterparts in other continents, and the Negrinistas made good use of this opportunity.[26] Their key supporter south of the Río Grande was Vicente Lombardo Toledano, supporter of the JSUN, president of the Communist-influenced Latin American Workers' Confederation (CTAL), and a leading force in the Mexican Workers' Confederation (CTM), at whose headquarters in Mexico City the González Peña-Rodríguez Vega UGT executive was based. Through the CTAL came recognition from confederations of Colombian and Cuban workers, and further support for the Negrinistas came from the *Confédération générale du travail* after the liberation of France.[27]

In February 1945 both UGT executives were represented at the World Workers' Conference that met in London to make plans for the WFTU.[28] Since the American Federation of Labor (AFL, with seven million members) stayed away, objecting to the presence of the Soviet unions and North American Congress of Industrial Organizations (CIO), the event was dominated by the Soviet, CGT, and CTAL delegations, together representing some 35 million workers. Though the two UGT delegations were granted equal status, that composed of Amaro del Rosal, Enrique de Santiago, Antonio Ramos Oliveira, and Luis Espinar was clearly more welcome to the majority than was the team of Trifón Gómez, Pascual Tomás, Wenceslao Carrillo, and Luis Araquistain. Demanding unity, the conference obliged Trifón Gómez to form a single official delegation with Rosal, and, partly

---

[26] In mid-1943 the Negrinista CE was composed of R. González Peña, E. Domínguez, J. Rodríguez Vega, A. del Rosal, F. Pretel, and 5 ordinary members including Daniel Anguiano (*ES* (Mexico), June 1943, 8).

[27] *Boletín de Información Sindical*, 8 (1940), 3; ibid. 9 (1941), 8; ibid. 13 (1945), 5; *ES* (ed. J. Alvarez), 7.12.44; Llopis-Trifón Gómez report in PSOE in Exile, *Actas* of CE, 30.11.44.

[28] For reports see *Adelante*, 1.5.45, 4; *Cuadernos Socialistas*, 4.4.45, 2; *Boletín de Información Sindical*, 13 (1945), 6–8; *Boletín de la UGT*, Mar. 1945, 1–8; PSOE in Exile, *Actas* of CE, 1–2.3.45; UGT in Exile, *Actas* of CE, 1.3.45.

because the latter had been the UGT's most visible international representative in recent years, the Toulouse-based UGT had to suffer the further humiliation of seeing the rival executive— which it deemed 'a blind instrument of the Communist Party'[29]—allocated Spain's seat on the steering committee set up by the conference. Pascual Tomás was made a mere *suplente*, a reserve member. Acceptance of this situation by the Toulouse UGT suggests tacit recognition that the other UGT was larger.[30]

A similar political balance existed in September-October when the WFTU's founding congress was held in Paris. This ratified resolutions of the London conference urging governments to end diplomatic and commercial relations with Franco and to recognize the republican government-in-exile. The Toulouse UGT was pushed into drafting a joint statement with Rosal, but had the consolation of the new International deciding to regard both UGT factions as exile organizations, thus leaving open the question of Spain's representation. Neither faction gained a seat on the executive of the World Federation, grouping over 60 million workers, but before long the Toulouse-based UGT had the satisfaction of receiving exclusive recognition from the UGT in Spain, whose unity had been welded solid by adversity.[31]

The Toulouse-based UGT had deep misgivings about the political orientation of the WFTU and the political dependence of the Soviet trade unions.[32] Before long a row developed when the Toulouse executive claimed that funds raised by the Federation in the name of Spanish solidarity were being sent exclusively to the Communists. Antonio Pérez and Andrés Saborit stormed out of a WFTU secretariat

[29] UGT in Exile, *Actas* of CE, 1.3.45.

[30] The Paris Congress of Sept.–Oct. 1945 based UGT representation on 31,250 members (*Adelante*, 15.10.45, 2). The Toulouse-based UGT affiliated on the basis of 20,000 members, the Negrinistas on the basis of 34,000 (having put their membership at 50,000 in France alone at the London conference). The Toulouse executive suspected that its rival could not afford to pay the WFTU on the basis of 34,000 members and was responsible for the Federation's decision to grant the Spaniards a 50% concession on affiliation fees (PSOE in Exile, *Actas* of CE, 16.10.45).

[31] *ES*, 27.12.46, 1, 3; *Boletín de la UGT*, Dec. 1946, 2.

[32] *Boletín de la UGT*, July 1946, 4–6; UGT in Exile, Assembly of June 1950, *Memoria*, 16.

meeting in mid-1948 because officials refused to provide details of the money received and its destination.[33] Another controversial issue was whether the international industrial federations, such as the transport workers' ITF, whose executive included Trifón Gómez, should remain independent or be subordinated to the Moscow-oriented World Federation. In 1944 the ITF had wanted to maintain relations with both UGT factions in exile; now, however, it played a major role in the break from the WFTU that led to the creation of the International Confederation of Free Trade Unions (ICFTU) at the end of 1949.[34] The Toulouse-based UGT transferred its affiliation similarly, thus bringing its international position into line with its national policy of organizing independently of the Communists.

This move brought the Spaniards some more supportive trade union allies. The fourth congress of the UGT in Exile, held in 1951, was attended by representatives of the ICFTU, AFL, the French *CGT-Force Ouvrière*, West German *Deutscher Gewerkschaftsbund* (DGB), and Italian CISL. *Force Ouvrière*, created in 1947, was the union recommended by the UGT to its members if they wished to join a French union.[35] Several Spanish Socialists were appointed to positions in the international labour movement where they could keep the Spanish issue alive as a solidarity question.[36] All the same, the Western-oriented UGT had to make do for some time with mainly moral and political support from the ICFTU affiliates, among whom 'national interests' so often predominated over internationalism. A stark example of this was the way in which all reference to the UGT was omitted from the opening address at a DGB congress in 1962. The UGT subsequently learnt that the Federal German

[33] *Boletín de la UGT*, July 1946, July 1948–June 1949; UGT in Exile, Assembly of June 1950, *Memoria*, 16; UGT in Exile, Fourth Congress (1951), *Memoria*, 15.

[34] Trifón Gómez report, PSOE in Exile, *Actas* of CE, 28.12.44; *Boletín de la UGT*, Jan. 1949, 7, Jan. 1950, 1.

[35] UGT in Exile, Fourth Congress (1951), *Memoria*, 33; *Boletín de la UGT*, Mar. 1949, 3.

[36] Among them Arsenio Jimeno was appointed head of a *Force Ouvrière* secretariat dealing with Spanish members' applications for work permits in France; Francisco López Real worked for the ICFTU in 1961–78 as head of the Spanish-language section; José Antonio Aguiriano became an ICFTU official in the 1950s; and Antonio Reina worked for the American Federation of Labor in New York.

authorities had persuaded the DGB to be silent on Spain because the country had only 125,000 *gastrarbeiters* and needed 300,000.[37]

Meanwhile, there was no contest between the two factions at the level of youth or women's organizations. The absence of a youth section supporting Lamoneda's PSOE executive facilitated the immediate and untroubled entry of the FNJSE based in Toulouse[38] into the International Union of Socialist Youth (IUSY), founded in Paris in 1946. A fairly strong early commitment to Spain was evident in the admission of the FNJSE general secretary, the accountant Salvador Martínez Dasi, to the IUSY executive, and also in a meeting held by the executive in Toulouse in 1949 to pay tribute to the Spanish Young Socialists.[39] However, that commitment was not maintained, despite the presence of Uruguayan Young Socialist and future Tupamaro founder Raúl Sendic in the IUSY leadership in the mid-1950s. Interest in Spain was difficult to sustain after mid-1947, when the FNJSE general secretary 'Ibarrola' was arrested by the Spanish police. From that moment until early 1952, the Toulouse Youth executive did not receive a single report from the interior and could only fear the worst.[40] Spain lost its place in the leadership at the IUSY conference of October 1957, which reduced the executive from eleven to nine members.[41]

While only one of the PSOE factions had a youth counterpart, neither had a women's section. In the mid-1940s the mainstream PSOE sent delegates to two international socialist women's conferences, but then ceased to do so for financial reasons 'and because of the lack of suitable *compañeras*'.[42] Towards the end of 1953, some 93 per cent of

---

[37] PSOE, *Actas* of CE, 17.11.62.

[38] The Toulouse-based FNJSE held its first congress in Apr. 1945 and by May 1946 had grown from 49 to 122 sections and from 1,500 to 2,500 members in exile, mainly in the 20–5 age-group, according to Martínez Dasi (speech at Second Congress of PSOE in Exile (1946), *Actas taquigráficas*, 15–16).

[39] PSOE in Exile, *Actas* of CE, 12.7.45, 30.6.49.

[40] FNJSE, Correspondence, 'Correspondencia con el Interior 1952/1956', letter of Martínez Dasi to CE of PSOE in Spain, 25 June 1952.

[41] PSOE, *Actas* of CE, 7.11.57.

[42] Llopis's note (ibid., 5.5.51) in which he refers to the party's neglect of women in its international work and the lack of articles by women in *El Socialista*.

the Toulouse-based PSOE in Exile's members were men and 64 per cent of its sections had no women members.[43]

With the benefit of hindsight, one can see that the most decisive battle for recognition was that fought at the level of the socialist parties. In the case of the UGT the Toulouse faction emerged triumphant largely by default. Its rivals were afflicted by their own crippling contradictions, and then reduced to impotence by the PCE decision in 1948 to abandon the UGT (as well as guerrilla warfare) and instead try to infiltrate Franco's official *sindicatos*.[44] Thus, by the 1950s the Toulouse-based Socialist organizations were untroubled by exiled pretenders.

In the course of differentiating themselves, in tandem with allies in other countries, the surviving PSOE and UGT laid themselves open to charges that their intransigent anti-Communism had led them to embrace Western imperialism. For Santiago Carrillo the PSOE's departure from the left wing of international socialism was an unmistakable mark of the nefarious influence of Guy Mollet's SFIO and hence of the US State Department.[45] But of course Western and social-democratic influence provides only a partial explanation of the PSOE's evolution. Carrillo's claim ignored the way in which the German-Soviet Pact, the twists and turns of Stalin's party line, and the fate of socialist parties and trade unions in post-war Eastern Europe affected the outlook of democratic socialists. None the less, there was an undeniable shift to the right by the Spanish Socialist organizations in this period. At its fourth congress in March 1951, the UGT in Exile described itself as 'profoundly anti-Communist', no less opposed to Communist 'tyranny' than to capitalism. And five years later the invasion of Hungary confirmed Spanish

[43] PSOE, *Actas* of CE, 22.10.53.

[44] Joan Estruch Tobella, *El PCE en la clandestinidad 1939–1956* (Madrid: Siglo XXI, 1982), 154. The details of the decline of this sector are not clear, for one symptom of it was the failure of its *Boletín* to appear in 1946–8. *ES*, 18.7.47, 1, and the *Memoria* for the Third Congress of the PSOE in Exile (1948), ch. on 'Relaciones con partidos y organizaciones', reported the expulsion by the PCE from the 'dissident' UGT of socialists belonging to España Combatiente. *ES* (Mexico), Nov. 1948, 3, reported that Rosal had asked for a 'battle station' in the PCE, having attacked his ex-comrades as 'dilettantes'.

[45] Santiago Carrillo, *¿A dónde va el Partido Socialista?* (Mexico: Edns. España Popular, 1959), 29.

Socialist fears about Soviet imperialism posing a threat to European liberty.[46]

It was during the 1950s that theoretical weakness really became evident in the PSOE and UGT. Although POUM veterans such as Julián Gorkín and Joaquín Maurín used the Socialist press to attempt neo-Marxist critiques of Stalinism, the PSOE and UGT merely echoed Western liberal objections. Their traditional anti-capitalism had become diluted during the years of exile. Conflicts with Spanish employers were now but a distant memory, and as exiles the Socialists were too insecure to get involved in militant struggles against French capitalists. In the circumstances, it was almost natural that anti-capitalism should give way to anti-totalitarianism as the main emphasis of the exiled organizations. The totalitarian model may have had serious analytical limitations, tending as it did to subsume some basic differences between Stalinism and Fascism,[47] but it served a triple purpose for the PSOE-UGT: it made it much easier for them to form alliances with most other Spanish anti-Franco organizations than would have been the case had militant anti-capitalism been adhered to; it made the Socialists much more welcome in France than were the Communists, against whom the authorities ordered a crack-down in 1950; and it enabled them in their propaganda and in their minds jointly to anathematize their two immediate adversaries, Franco and the Communists. But convenient and satisfying as it undoubtedly was, the schema proved to be a defective guide for the Spanish Socialists. By any standards, both the Franco regime and the PCE exhibited fewer 'totalitarian' facets as time passed. And the Spanish Socialists' adoption of the totalitarian model encouraged a distinctly negative as well as increasingly anachronistic outlook. The logical corollary of this model was a commitment to liberal democracy, yet the latter alone could never inspire the rank and file in the way that anti-capitalism's corollary of socialism could. Over a period of 30 years, the most repeated refrain at the exiles' congresses was to be 'con los comunistas, nada'

---

[46] *Boletín de la UGT*, Apr.–May 1951, 1, 12; PSOE in Exile, Third Congress (1948), *Actas* 139–40; UGT, Sixth Congress held in exile (1956), *Memoria*, 66.

[47] David Lane, *Politics and Society in the USSR*, 2nd edn. (London: Martin Robertson, 1978), 189–91.

(nothing with the Communists). What the Socialists actually stood *for*, however, was no longer very clear. Alarmed by the advance of the liberal tendency represented by Prieto, Ramón Lamoneda had reacted to the anti-communist attitude with a socialist rejoinder, 'con la burguesía, jamás (never with the bourgeoisie).[48] The PSOE was now in danger of losing its soul.

ATLANTIC DRIFT

The exiled Socialists[1] devoted many long hours to the perfection of formulas designed to facilitate an end to Francoism. Hopes of restoring the Republic survived for more than thirty years, but the intended mechanisms of the restoration were revised periodically. From the outbreak of the world war in 1939 the *émigré* Socialists looked to the Allies for help with ousting Franco. Commencing with an uncompromising position, they gradually 'through a process of elimination' changed their policy on the post-Franco transition, until finally they arrived at a formula thought by Llopis to be that 'most acceptable to the Western world'.[2] However, concessions to Western sensibilities failed to produce determined Western action against Franco. Rather, their main effect was to spark internal battles in the exiled sector of the PSOE, and to encourage Socialists in the interior to look abroad for salvation. A cruel irony of the 1940s was that in large measure it was the democratic procedures of the PSOE's internal life that prevented it from being sufficiently flexible to adapt its position to rapidly changing circumstances and thereby maximize its chances of enlisting the support of the Western democracies. Since each new formulation of the party line required debate and the convocation of a congress, the

[48] R. Lamoneda, *El Partido Socialista en la República Española* (Mexico: Biblioteca de 'El Socialista', 1942), 27.

[1] Henceforth the term 'the Socialists' is used in this chapter to refer to the main expression of the PSOE in Exile (gen. sec. Rodolfo Llopis), for the Negrinista sector lost importance after 1948.

[2] Trifón Gómez's speech, PSOE in Exile, Fourth Congress (1950), *Actas*, 101; Llopis at meeting of CD of PSOE, Aug. 1957, *Actas*, 25.

PSOE constantly found itself responding all too slowly to the few relatively favourable conjunctures that arose.

By concentrating their minds on the fascist aspects of Francoism, and relying upon implacable hostility to Franco from the Western democracies, the Socialists ignored the part played by Franco himself in ensuring the survival of his regime. His moves in the 1940s to weaken the (never dominant) Falange and strengthen the Catholic nationalist character of his regime were dismissed as purely cosmetic changes. His opponents were right when they claimed that Franco was responding to a changing international climate, yet they failed to see that the response was also an early example of the Caudillo's ability cleverly to restructure his regime when necessary, by promoting certain sectors and downgrading others. He was certainly helped by international developments and had enormous armed forces at his disposal, but these factors alone do not explain why he retained power for so long. Besides repression of the opposition and political use of education and the media, Franco's retention of power rested upon his skill in placating, isolating, neutralizing, or delighting the diverse components within his regime. The various 'families' of Francoism—the army, Catholic groups, Falangists, monarchists, and so on—all gained representation in government ministries; Franco's political capacity was seen in the way he maintained the balance, or adjusted it to give greater prominence to certain factions when the political or economic situation changed. In spite of the regime's historical associations, and contrary to the early PSOE presentation of it, Francoism was neither an example of totalitarianism nor of personal rule. It was an authoritarian military-based regime whose political configuration changed over time.[3]

After setting out with an intransigent commitment to a direct restoration of the Republic, from mid-1947 the Socialists were prepared to leave the question of Spain's future regime for the Spanish people to decide by means of an election

---

[3] R. Carr, *Spain 1808–1975* (Oxford: Clarendon Press, 1982), ch. 17; Gilmour, ch. 2; Preston (ed.), *Spain in Crisis*, pt. 1; Fusi, *Franco: Autoritarismo y poder personal* (Madrid: Ediciones El País, 1985); J. J. Linz, 'Spain: An Authoritarian Regime', in E. Allardt and Y. Littunen (eds.), *Cleavages, Ideologies and Party Systems* (Helsinki: Westmarck Society, 1964).

or plebiscite following liberalization. This was the basic alteration made in the PSOE position, but there were also several changes made in the alliance schema pursued by the Socialists. Initially they allied with moderate republican forces in the JEL; then they tried to strengthen the republican alliance by accepting the entry of the PCE and others into the exiled government; next came a policy of allying with all the 'non-totalitarian' forces, which led to negotiations with the monarchists; after that, feeling let down by the monarchists, they became isolationist; and finally, they ended up returning to 'anti-totalitarian' alliance efforts. Early hopes of effective Western supportive action faded after a decade, if not sooner; subsequently, all that most Socialists did was prepare for when Franco was ousted, died, or somehow went away. The PSOE never seriously faced up to the problem of how the Spanish opposition might itself eliminate Franco, although admittedly its chances of success were slim. The Socialists did more waiting upon events than acting upon them, and few of their number, even when dreaming about strategy, contemplated a violent approach. A pacifism rooted in humanism predominated, along with an awareness of the enemy's military might and a rejection of political extremism. At a PSOE congress in Toulouse, a speaker once asked rhetorically, 'How should we get rid of Franco?': when somebody shouted out, 'Kill him!', everybody laughed.[4] The Civil War had cured some Spaniards, at least, of the traditional belief in violent remedies.[5]

Had the exiles realized how long the Franco regime would last, they might have been readier early on to accept a less oppressive right-wing alternative. The reality was, however, that Socialists in and out of Spain had very high hopes that the end of the world war would spell the end of Francoism, as suggested to them by the Atlantic Charter. They therefore opposed the early conspiracies of discontented monarchists, warned of the monarchy's reactionary record, and reminded Spaniards of the pretender Don Juan's efforts to enlist on Franco's side during the Civil War.[6] The JEL represented a

[4] PSOE in Exile, Fourth Congress (1950), *Actas*, 88.
[5] Brenan, 148.
[6] PSOE in France, *Resoluciones y estatutos aprobados en su I Congreso* (1944), 7;

reaffirmation of republican legitimacy; it was essentially a body of moderates who hoped to act in tandem with the victorious Allies at the end of the world war. Its supporters feared that if the Allies lacked a moderate republican point of reference and were faced with a Communist-dominated republican government-in-exile, they would prefer to restore the monarchy.[7] Prieto, the man who persuaded the exiled Socialists to base their strategy on the expectation of Western backing, opposed the creation of governments abroad: in his view they would be cumbersome and expensive instruments of action, likely to frighten off Western governments by recalling the situation a decade earlier when Communist ministers had been appointed for the first time in European history.

When the JEL was only half-recognized by the Allies at the San Francisco Conference of mid-1945, Prieto seemed to change his mind. He called for the Cortes to meet and to set up a provisional government that would aspire to UN recognition, yet even at the moment of the Giral government's ratification by the Cortes he warned that the exiled administration could become an obstacle to solutions attempted inside Spain.[8] Doubts about the Giral government's acceptability to the West grew in March 1946 when the USA, Britain, and France issued their Tripartite Note. This expressed a platonic desire for patriotic liberals in Spain somehow to achieve the peaceful departure of Franco, create a provisional government, restore liberty, and then permit the Spanish people to choose the type of government they wanted.[9] By omission it confirmed the Giral government's lack of recognition by the Western powers, who again ignored its existence when the UN approved a resolution on Spain in December 1946. To the disappointment of Spanish exiles, the resolution did no more than ban Spain from international bodies set up by the UN and recommend that members withdrew their top diplomats from Madrid. By saying that the government that liberalized

Adelante, 15.6.42, 4, 1.7.43, 4, 1.6.44, 1; PSOE in Exile, Second Congress (1946), *Actas*, 68; id., *Actas* of CE, 7.8.45.

[7] Fagen, 110–11.

[8] Prieto's press conference of 20 June 1945, *Adelante*, 1.7.45, 3; Prieto's speech in Cortes, 8 Nov. 1945, ibid., 15.11.45, 1.

[9] ES, 9.3.46, 1, 15.3.46, 1; Centro Republicano, *México*, 169–73.

Spain would gain recognition and economic aid from UN members, it implicitly disavowed Giral, leading Prieto to work for a national government that would organize a plebiscite to determine Spain's future. Under his influence, the PSOE position shifted from 'To Democracy via the Republic' to 'To the Republic via Democracy'.[10]

Since 1942 Prieto had been proposing the holding of a plebiscite under the supervision of a Latin American country. In 1945 he was involved in President Grau San Martín's Cuban initiative, which envisaged that somebody not stained by a repressive past should replace Franco, restore freedom, dissolve the Falange, and then organize a plebiscite on Spain's constitutional future. Among other things, the plan was stymied by Giral's and exiled President Martínez Barrio's insistence upon the Republic's unquestionable legitimacy, and by opposition from the PSOE both in and out of Spain.[11] Prieto himself had to undergo a series of eye operations in New York in 1945–6 and so could not campaign vigorously for his proposal. By the time he succeeded in imposing his formula on the PSOE in mid-1947 at an Assembly of Delegates in Toulouse, Don Juan's attitude towards Franco had become more accommodating, the Cold War was a growing reality, and even Prieto considered it 'almost certain' that his idea had been adopted too late to be successful.[12] Others felt that timing was beside the point; having won a civil war, Franco was hardly likely to surrender to peaceful persuasion, even if it were backed up by Western sanctions.

Prieto's victory was a pyrrhic one, for its main effects were to deepen divisions in the exiled PSOE and to undermine the degree of republican unity that had been achieved by 1945. The catch was always the same: Western leaders stipulated both the unity of the exiles and the emergence of an embryonic national government in Spain as prerequisites for international action, yet each republican attempt to deal with monarchist forces inevitably generated suspicions and divisions among the

[10] R. Llopis, *España espera su hora: Los puntales del régimen de Franco se quiebran* (Toulouse: PSOE, 1958), 43.

[11] Borrás, 112–14; *ES*, 10.9.45, 1, 18.12.45, 1, 25.12.45, 1; *Adelante*, 15.9.46, 1; Prieto at PSOE Assembly of Delegates of 1947, *Actas*, 166–7.

[12] Prieto, PSOE Assembly of Delegates of 1947, *Actas*, 210.

republicans.[13] The Communists, Socialists, and CNT all took their turn in attempting to reach an understanding with the monarchists, only to be suspected by existing allies of preparing to perpetrate a betrayal.

For his plebiscite proposal, Prieto had the backing of the Socialist group in Mexico City, which included most of what remained of the PSOE parliamentary group. The Socialists residing in France were less flexible, though in 1945 they gave tacit encouragement to efforts by Republican politician Miguel Maura to arrange a peaceful change of regime.[14] Their first and second congresses, held in Toulouse in 1944 and 1946, approved resolutions seeking a direct republican restoration. On the second occasion, support for the Giral government, which by then included PCE leader Santiago Carrillo, was not seen as contravening the party line of no relations with the Communists. The PSOE in France ideally wanted the government-in-exile to include all republican forces under a Socialist premier, though not under Negrín; as the 'French' Socialists saw it, the Spanish people had demonstrated their republican preference at the polls in 1936 and during the Civil War, and there was thus no need now for any plebiscite.[15] Differences between Mexico City and Toulouse were exacerbated at the end of 1946 when the Giral government entered into crisis, following the UN resolution and a withdrawal of support by Socialist minisers Enrique de Francisco and Trifón Gómez. Whereas Prieto now wanted to abolish the republican institutions in exile, Llopis and his Toulouse colleagues wanted to reinforce them by forming a Socialist-led government that would work in co-ordination with the democratic forces of the interior.[16] Rejecting the position of the party parliamentary group, the Toulouse-based PSOE and UGT executives gave their blessing when a new government-in-exile, headed by Llopis himself, was created in February 1947.

To win the party over, Prieto personally attended the

[13] Stein, 216.
[14] *Adelante*, 15.4.45, 2; PSOE in France and North Africa, National Plenum of June 1945, *Actas*, 26; PSOE in Exile, Second Congress (1946), *Actas*, 67; id., Third Congress (1948), *Actas*, 154–5.
[15] *ES*, 1.9.45, 1, 10.9.45, 1.   [16] Ibid., 31.1.47, 1.

Assembly of Delegates held in France in July 1947 (having missed the two congresses that preceded it). Following the deaths of Besteiro and Caballero, he was indisputably the most prestigious surviving Socialist *émigré*, and delegates were particularly ready to listen to his proposal now that the West had showed itself unprepared to help the Republic directly. The power of Prieto's oratory and his glacial capacity to reduce all in his path to political debris were seen at their most devastating both here and at the third congress a year later. So determined was he to impose his formula that he got delegates to confer on the Assembly the powers of a congress, thus violating the 'sacred' party statutes. Moreover, he persuaded them to ignore the 'voice of the interior', represented by Antonio Pérez. The veteran tactician applied various forms of pressure to the assembled Socialists: a reminder that he was a sick man, yet had travelled all the way from Mexico in an effort to serve the party; a letter from Socialist *guerrilleros* in the Asturian mountains, asking whether continued resistance was worthwhile (Prieto's subliminal message being 'accept my compromise: we cannot expect our comrades in Spain to make further sacrifices, especially when their struggle is ineffective'); and the bogus claim that the United Nations would be making up its mind about Spain on 16 September, and that for this reason there was insufficient time to consult Madrid before implementing the new policy.[17]

Prieto also won votes by turning anti-Communist feeling against the Llopis government, which contained Vicente Uribe of the PCE. It was one thing to accept Communist participation in a government presided over by the Left Republican Giral, and another for a Socialist prime minister to appoint a Communist. Prieto made out that this was the decisive issue, though really the question of relations with the Communists was a function of a more basic decision: whether to opt for a Western-oriented strategy or concentrate more on gradually building up the opposition's strength in the interior. The allegation of wasteful expenditure by the government-in-exile[18] was another stick used to attack Llopis, whose defeat at the Assembly was so damaging that his government felt

---

[17] PSOE in Exile, Assembly of Delegates of 1947, *Actas*, *passim*.
[18] Ibid. 125–8.

compelled to resign in August. Never again did Spanish Socialists take part in exiled republican governments, though Luis Jiménez de Asúa served as President prior to his death in 1970 in Buenos Aires. What came out of the Assembly was a decision to create a special commission (eventually composed of Prieto, Trifón Gómez, Jiménez de Asúa, and Antonio Pérez) to negotiate with monarchists and republicans alike on the basis of the plebiscite formula. Had it been successful, the commission would have given birth to a Junta, putting the government-in-exile even further into the shade.

This victory had to be confirmed a year later at the third congress of the PSOE in Exile, because Llopis fought a rearguard action questioning the validity of the Assembly decisions. All that this earned the general secretary was a rejection by the Prieto-dominated congress of the executive's report on its work (the *Memoria*).[19] It was the first time in the party's history that this had happened. When it came to electing a new executive, Llopis was re-elected, but henceforth he served in the knowledge that he owed his survival to Prietista munificence and a general concern for party unity. The premium placed upon unity also ensured Prieto the interior's acceptance of his *fait accompli*,[20] though had Spain's message to the Assembly of 1947 arrived on time, events would have taken a different course. Contained in the message from the interior was ratification of the political position agreed in 1946; and as Llopis had pointed out in self-defence, the only aspect of the decisions to which the interior had ever objected was the insistence upon no relations with the Communists.[21] The changing of the PSOE's political position showed that, at most, the notion that the party's leadership was in Spain was a convenient half-truth, useful for winning international socialist recognition and for legitimation of the views of the competing exiled factions whenever they happened to coincide with those of the interior. By 1951, with the interior having sustained heavy casualties and having

[19] PSOE in Exile, Third Congress (1948), *Actas*, 93.

[20] Ibid., *Memoria*, ch. on 'Política del partido', 68.

[21] PSOE in Exile, Assembly of Delegates of 1947, *Actas*, 147, 552–4. The message dated 17 July, for the Assembly on 25–8 July, endorsed recent CE decisions and thus would have helped Llopis resist Prieto's onslaught at the Assembly: but it did not arrive until August.

declined to become a minority of the whole party, executive members in Madrid were recognizing that the effective party leadership was that resident in France.[22] The formal transfer of authority took place three years later (on which more in the next chapter).

Following the Assembly of 1947, the PSOE in Exile's dealings with the monarchists brought it nothing but regret. Under the auspices of Ernest Bevin, Prieto met monarchist leader Gil-Robles in London that October, and there was then a delay of almost a year as lower-level negotiations proceeded and as the Socialists tried in vain to win endorsement of their formula from other republicans. At no stage did either Gil-Robles or the Portugal-based pretender Don Juan agree to the idea that a plebiscite might be held under a transitional government of 'undefined institutional character' (i.e., neither a republican regime nor a monarchy), for this Socialist formula would have meant conceding ground on monarchist legitimacy and the divine right of the pretender to rule. Gil-Robles considered that Britain's desire to see installed a caretaker government of monarchists and moderate republicans indicated a basic ignorance of the polarized realities of contemporary Spain.[23] Though there were differences in the monarchist camp, and some of its negotiators may have acted in good faith, the prevailing line there was one that sought to use Socialist support to lend credibility to a restored monarchy and to restrain the workers' movement from being assertive while the new regime was being consolidated. Delegates of a monarchist alliance eventually signed a pact with Prieto in St Jean-de-Luz in August 1948, under which both parties appeared to agree that Spain's future regime would be left to a free choice of the Spanish people.[24] The pact was immediately vitiated, however, by the news that Don Juan had recently

[22] Trigo Mairal's entry, PSOE in Exile, *Actas* of CE, 12.9.51. Franco also seems to have noticed the shift in the interior-exterior PSOE balance. In Nov. 1951 the party offices in Toulouse were burgled and important documents were seized, though not the most confidential material (which was presumably at the Llopis residence in Albi). The subsequent murder of PSOE member Ciriaco López while in possession of important documents was suspected by Llopis of being a sequel to the burglary. See PSOE in Exile, *Actas* of CE, 12.9.51; id., Fifth Congress (1952), *Actas*, 27.

[23] José María Gil-Robles, *La monarquía por la que yo luché (1941–1954)* (Madrid: Taurus, 1976), 240–1.

[24] For the text see the suppl. to *Adelante*, Oct. 1948; *ES*, 14.10.48, 1.

met Franco on a yacht in the Bay of Biscay to discuss the future of the monarchy; and by additional documents delivered by monarchists to Madrid embassies, 'clarifying' that the proposed plebiscite would take place under a provisionally restored monarchy.

Partly because they were ignorant of the additional document delivered to the embassies,[25] and in part because they still hoped for Western pressures to get Don Juan to challenge Franco, the Socialists did not repudiate the pact until 1952. Only then was there official confirmation of their suspicions about Franco and Don Juan having agreed to restore the monarchy in the person of Juan Carlos at some distant date.[26] Prieto personally recognized his failure at the end of 1950;[27] he resigned his posts and left France for Mexico. Already by 1950 the pretender had made it fairly clear that the monarchy was not something to be subjected to a popular verdict, and that its future was best safeguarded through agreements with Franco, even if that meant accepting Franco as regent and recognizing that he himself would never occupy the Spanish throne.[28] With hindsight, it is easy to ridicule the Socialists' courtship of the monarchists, but at the time there was certainly a logic behind it: if, following a massive civil war defeat, the opposition was itself insufficiently strong to depose Franco in the foreseeable future, the most pragmatic tactic to adopt was to weaken the regime by undermining Francoist support.[29] Nevertheless, the formula's chances of success were meagre, given the undemocratic tradition of the Spanish monarchy, various purges of monarchist generals from the army, and Western hesitation over backing any moves likely to produce instability.

In effect, what the Prietista policy did was isolate the

[25] The Socialists only learnt about this through the publication of Juan Antonio Ansaldo's book, *¿Para qué . . .?* (Buenos Aires: Vasca Ekin, 1951), according to Carlos Martínez Parera (personal interview, Madrid, 12 Nov. 1981) and Llopis, *España*, 48. French radio broadcasts on 10 Nov. 1948 gave the impression that the monarchists had delivered to the embassies just the document that the Socialists were distributing abroad (*ES*, 18.11.48, 1).

[26] *ES*, 17.7.52, 1.

[27] 'Dimisión de Indalecio Prieto', *Adelante*, 27.11.50, 5.

[28] Declarations of Don Juan in *Le Figaro* (Paris), 28.7.50.

[29] Trifón Gómez's speech, PSOE in Exile, Assembly of Delegates of 1947, *Actas*, 182–3.

PSOE from its most natural allies, for only part of the CNT went along with it.[30] As the London delegate Ferrandiz put it at a party congress, to the outside world the party position in 1948–52 seemed to be: 'Republic, yes, but . . . without the Republicans. Monarchy, never, but . . . with the monarchists, yes!'[31] The Socialists had been deceived and effectively neutralized by the monarchists, who in turn received similar treatment from Franco. Equally, the PSOE felt badly betrayed by the Western powers, whose reluctance to act increased as the Cold War grew colder.

Of the three parties to the Tripartite Note of 1946, France was by far the most enthusiastic advocate of concerted action against Franco; she hoped to honour the debt contracted with Spanish anti-fascists during the German occupation. France thus turned a blind eye to guerrilla expeditions from her territory in late 1944, closed the border with Spain in February 1946 (for two years) and urged members of the United Nations to deploy economic sanctions against Franco later the same year.[32] Despite their post-war changes of government, Britain and the United States were far more reluctant to act. In the mid-1940s they contended that external pressures would only strengthen Franco by granting him an external explanation for Spain's penurious state. To intervene unsuccessfully would rekindle the embers of the Civil War, and in them the moderate forces would perish far sooner than the extremists.[33] Moreover, it was beyond the remit of the UN to intervene in Spain unless the regime there began to create international friction. There was also a Western fear that economic sanctions would be ineffective, enabling trade rivals of Britain and the USA to step in and exploit the situation.[34] The Socialist *émigrés* tended to blame the United States most for Western inaction;[35] others have pointed the accusing

[30] *Adelante*, 22.5.50, 5.

[31] PSOE in Exile, Fourth Congress (1950), *Actas*, 87.

[32] Centro Republicano, *México*, 237–8, 250 (Jouhaux interventions); Llopis, *España*, 40–1.

[33] Centro Republicano, *México*, 233, 236–7, 243; Leon Blum's declarations in *Adelante*, 15.5.47, 4.

[34] Centro Republicano, *México*, 146–8, 236–7.

[35] *ES*, 28.11.47, 1, 15.7.48, 1–2, 10.7.52, 2–3; *Adelante*, 27.11.50, 4–5. For US arguments in favour of wartime non-intervention in Spain see Carlton J. H. Hayes, *Wartime Mission in Spain 1942–1945* (New York: Macmillan, 1946).

finger primarily at Britain.[36] Either way, it is clear that neither country was likely to take action without a convincing moderate counter-power to Franco emerging in the interior to establish a provisional government.[37]

Britain's attitude was the most ambiguous of the three and contributed most to the Prieto-guided Socialists' decision to follow the UN 'ray of light' and pursue 'the formula of the great powers'.[38] Declarations by Harold Laski, chairman of the Labour Party, awakened hopes that the Attlee government would take action to restore the Republic.[39] However, while ruling out the monarchy or a military dictatorship as acceptable alternatives to rule by Franco, Labour's delegate to the second congress of the PSOE in Exile, Francis Noel Baker, emphasized Britain's insistence upon a peaceful solution.[40] More worrisome still for the Socialists was the cautious attitude of British Foreign Secretary Ernest Bevin, who at Labour's 1946 party conference opposed economic sanctions and persuaded delegates not to pass a resolution on Spain.[41] With Bevin's views prevailing, the Labour government's policy was one of encouraging Socialists and monarchists in the interior to reach an accord, based on each side abandoning their erstwhile positions on regime legitimacy. The two sides met under his auspices in October 1947, and though Prieto left the Foreign Office 'satisfied and happy' after his conversation with Bevin,[42] real agreement was never reached on Spain's post-Franco transition. Gil-Robles

[36] Madariaga, mentioned in Gil-Robles, 228; and, citing US documents, Angel Viñas, 'La España de Franco: Política exterior', Historia de España 12, *Historia 16* (Madrid), Dec. 1982, 80–92. After a brief visit to Spain in late 1950 Basil Davidson reported that Socialists in the interior felt most let down by Britain: the Labour Party was stronger than the French Socialists and better able to prevail against the USA. See his *Report on Spain* (London: Union of Democratic Control, 1951), 14. However, the *Memoria* for the Third Congress of the UGT in Exile (1949), 47–8, reported that British trade unions were the most important source of UGT aid.

[37] PSOE in Exile, *Actas* of CE, 4.4.46.

[38] Prieto at PSOE in Exile, Assembly of Delegates of 1947, *Actas*, 210; Trifón Gómez's declarations, *ES*, 14.11.47, 1.

[39] *Adelante*, 1.8.45, 1; PSOE in Exile, Second Congress (1946), *Memoria*, 56–60; Stein, 187.

[40] *Adelante*, 1.6.46, 4; *ES*, 3.8.46, 1; PSOE in Exile, Second Congress (1946), *Actas*, 183–4. For the PSOE Trifón Gómez responded to the fraternal delegate's promise of urgent action with the enthusiasm of a drowning man clutching at straws: 'his words sound like celestial music in my ears' (ibid. 189–206).

[41] *Adelante*, 20.7.46, 8.   [42] *ES*, 10.10.47, 1.

left thinking that the Socialists would in the end accept the *fait accompli* of a monarchist restoration, although clearly they could not make such a concession in advance.[43] In fact, despite predictable accusations from the Republicans, there is no evidence that Prieto ever consciously encouraged monarchists to believe that the Socialists would accept Don Juan's return, except through the ballot box.[44] Indeed, the signing of the 'agreement' with the monarchists was delayed for almost a year precisely because the Socialists believed that they had a draft that was respectable enough to win the endorsement of Republican allies.[45]

To win Western support the PSOE defined itself unequivocally in relation to the Cold War. The party's bargaining pitch in the late 1940s was to present Franco as the only obstacle to Spain's integration into a future West European Common Market and NATO, and to the country's receipt of US economic aid.[46] On occasions the logic of their strategy led the Socialists to pose as more reliable anti-Communist allies and guarantors of stability than Franco himself. The PSOE had fought the PCE long before Franco had, Prieto claimed; if Soviet troops reached the Pyrenees, they would arm the Spanish people and thus be welcomed if Franco were still in power.[47] Yet, while trying to allay the doubts and fears of

[43] On the negotiations see Gil-Robles, 131–264 (though it is evident that this 'diary' either was written or revised at a later date); Borrás, 122–37; Alfonso Carlos Saiz Valdivielso, *Indalecio Prieto: Crónica de un corazón* (Barcelona: Planeta, 1984), 249–52; Stein, 181–221; Llopis, *España*, 40–8; Hartmut Heine, *La oposición política al franquismo* (Barcelona: Crítica, 1983), 388–408.

[44] Prieto repeatedly reassured his fellow Socialists on this count. See his letter to Atlee warning against a restoration of the monarchy in *Adelante*, 1.7.43, 1; his speeches at the PSOE Assembly of Delegates, 1947 (*Actas*, 105–6, 217–19), and at the Third Congress of the PSOE in Exile, 1948 (*Actas*, 169); and his message to the Fourth Congress (1950) (*Actas*, 18). See too Gil-Robles, 401–2. In the early 1950s Prieto opposed the acceptance of a monarchical solution by Araquistain and Trifón Gómez, and a year before his death he was still defending the plebiscite idea as being 'as much as we can offer and as much as the United States must accept' (*ES*, 2.3.61, 1–2). Prieto died in Feb. 1962.

[45] Borrás, 130–1; *ES*, 4.11.48, 4.

[46] Prieto's speech in New York, *Adelante*, 15.3.44, 1–2; *Adelante*, 22.5.50, 3; *ES*, 7.4.49, 1; PSOE in Exile, Assembly of Delegates of 1949, *Memoria*, 29–30; PSOE in Exile, Fourth Congress (1950), *Memoria*, *passim*; Ignacio Fernández de Castro, 'Tres años importantes: 1961–1962–1963', *Cuadernos de Ruedo Ibérico* (Paris), 16 (1967–8), 79–97.

[47] Prieto interview, *ES*, 15.7.48, 1–2; id., speech at Second Congress of PSOE in Exile (1948), *Actas*, 168–9; *Adelante*, 22.5.50, 3.

Western leaders, the Socialists were not altogether consistent over the kind of Western support they wanted. In 1944 all that Prieto asked of the West was that it cold-shoulder Franco and not stand in the way of the republicans; a hostile atmosphere would be enough to bring down the regime.[48] The following year, a break in diplomatic relations and recognition of a government established by the Cortes was requested.[49] The second congress of the PSOE in Exile (1946) went further in urging socialist parties to work for governments to terminate both diplomatic and economic relations with Spain.[50] Prieto himself urged a total economic boycott including oil and transport in 1948, while at other times he implied that the regime would die of economic suffocation anyway, so long as Western economic aid were denied it.[51]

Negrín, aware that his potential audience in the West was somewhat smaller, was able to be more consistent. The price of Western assistance, he claimed, would always be too high. For Dr Negrín the need for unity among the republican forces was fundamental. All that he asked of the West was diplomatic recognition of the Republican government—'but first the republicans themselves must recognize it', he warned.[52] He was to be disappointed, for neither his own government nor those of Giral, Llopis, or their successors gained recognition from the authors of the Tripartite Note.

The exiles' desire to enlist Western support is understandable, given that their own short-term prospects of independent success were virtually nil. However, the notion of Western 'betrayal' is a poor explanation of their failure. This 'betrayal' had been foreshadowed in the 1930s by the 'non-intervention' policy of the democracies during the Civil War, which helped the Axis-supported Franco achieve victory. Fearing that the examination of past mistakes might exacerbate internal divisions, the PSOE had failed to learn from that experience,

[48] *Adelante*, 15.3.44, 1–2, 1.6.44, 3, 1.11.44, 1.
[49] *ES*, 5.6.45, 1.　　　　　　　　[50] *Adelante*, 1.6.46, 4.
[51] Ibid., 15.11.46, 3; *ES*, 15.7.48, 1–2; PSOE in Exile, Third Congress (1948), *Actas*, 168.
[52] Juan Negrín, *Informe de D. Juan Negrín a los republicanos españoles* [1 Aug. 1945] (London, 1945), 35; id., *Discurso pronunciado por don Juan Negrín* [3 Sept. 1945] (London: Publicaciones Agrupación Socialista [PSOE] en la Gran Bretaña, 1945), *passim*.

and now new anti-totalitarian ideological influences were once more fuelling illusions about democratic solidarity. If anything, the Socialists were 'betrayed' by their own ideological slackness, which led both themselves and their comrades in the interior to look abroad for solutions. Like Liberals, they based their hopes and expectations on the wartime alignments and dominant political ideologies of Western governments—not on the economic interests that the latter defended. As Prieto recognized after his policy had failed, the PSOE was thwarted by 'capitalist solidarity'.[53] Western disapproval of Spain's political regime was a secondary consideration when compared to that of which political arrangement best served Western economic and strategic interests by at least offering stability and predictability.[54]

In 1950, with the USA and others supporting a Latin American initiative, the UN reversed its recommendations of 1946 with regard to Spain. In 1953 there was the signing of the crucial Francoist pacts with the USA and the Vatican, and in 1955 Spain was admitted to the UN itself.[55] Since this enlargement of the UN also involved the admission of several East European States, even the Soviet Union voted in favour. In fact, a Soviet-Spanish trade agreement had already been signed in June 1954.[56] Now the PSOE's wrath was directed against 'the treachery of Moscow', which the Socialists saw compounded by Soviet-bloc abstention when Spain was admitted to the International Labour Organization the following year.[57] The USSR had never recognized the post-1945 republican governments formed in exile, perhaps because of its reluctance to clarify the accounts pertaining to the depositing of Spanish gold in the Soviet Union to pay for arms during the Civil War; moreover, it had been trading with Franco via certain Arab countries from an early date.[58] The Socialists' well-founded fear was that the new US buttressing

---

[53] PSOE in Exile, Fifth Congress (1952), *Actas*, 102.

[54] Fernández de Castro, 79; Claudín, *Communist Movement*, 236.

[55] A. Viñas, *Los pactos secretos de Franco con Estados Unidos* (Barcelona: Grijalbo, 1981); Centro Republicano, *México, passim.*

[56] *Boletín de la UGT*, July 1954, 5.   [57] *ES*, 22.12.55, 1–2, 19.7.56, 1.

[58] Francisco Giral, 'Actividad de los gobiernos y de los partidos republicanos (1939–1976)', in Tuñón de Lara et al., *Guerra y política*, 179–225; Alba, *Communist Party*, 322.

of the Spanish regime would not only permit its survival but also discredit the idea of 'democracy' among some of Franco's opponents. Having themselves played the Atlantic card, they were left now with a duff hand; the US-Spanish military and economic agreements of 1953 left the PCE with all the trumps.

Combined with the low ebb of resistance inside Spain during the early 1950s, these developments on the international scene had a near-catastrophic impact on PSOE morale. Prieto was not alone in reducing his political activity, convinced that little could be done until Franco died. However, he did recognize that one day Spain would want to 'enter Europe', would thus need to be a democracy, and would find in the PSOE democracy's firmest defender.[59] Party activity dwindled, as did that of the UGT and FNJSE, whose policies had shadowed those of the PSOE.[60] By the time of the fifth congress of the PSOE in Exile (August 1952), the *émigré* sector had lost one-tenth of its membership, mainly through migration to America, as a result of the UN blow. One-fifth of the party's local sections had declined to fewer than the statutory minimum of 7 members.[61] The survival of the exile infrastructure and the holding of regular congresses demanded even greater financial sacrifices from those Socialists who remained.

Of course, throughout the Franco period there was always some sign that the regime was in trouble. This encouraged the Socialists to resist compromise on the monarchy in the early 1940s and suggestions that they take advantage of a rumoured partial liberalization in Spain which some exiles expected to occur following the Franco-US pacts.[62] However, the demoralization caused by the UN reversal was soon reinforced by the Socialists' recognition of their own bankruptcy once the duplicity of the monarchists became obvious. The PSOE

[59] Interview with Francisco Bustelo (Madrid, 26 Apr. 1982), who discussed Spain's future with Prieto in St Jean-de-Luz in 1961; PSOE in Exile, Fifth Congress (1952), *Actas*, 102.

[60] In July 1951 Miguel Calzada was the only member of the CE of the UGT in Exile who was not also on the PSOE executive.

[61] PSOE in Exile, Fifth Congress (1952), *Memoria*, treasurer's report; *Actas*, 24.

[62] The expectation arose prior to the signing of the US pacts with Franco, when US officials asked the Socialists what they might demand in return for economic aid to Franco. See *ES*, 10.12.53, 2.

formally broke the stillborn pact of 1948 only four years later. Subsequently, nothing viable was proposed. Too weak to be effective alone, yet deafened to appeals for unity by past experiences of alliance, the party turned in on itself and for several years concentrated solely upon survival. While paying lip-service to the plebiscite formula, the Socialists ruled out any possibility of long-term alliances[63] and in so doing stymied a unitary initiative taken by the CNT in 1951–3. By allowing no more than 'elbow contact' with other anti-Franco forces,[64] the Socialists opted for a retreat into isolationism, following the path traced by Besteiro two decades earlier. This 'rest cure' condemned the PSOE to years of relative if not absolute passivity.[65]

Appearances proved deceptive here and at times suggested progress. The demoralizing realities of the early 1950s led many Republicans to at last abandon their intransigence over regime legitimacy and to accept the plebiscite formula adopted by the PSOE in 1947. In February 1957 an agreement on this basis was reached in Paris by the Socialists (PSOE and UGT), Republicans (IR and PRF), Catalanists (ERC and MSC), Basques (PNV, ANV, and STV), and Libertarians (CNT).[66] After further negotiations which brought in the Left Christian Democrats (IDC) of the interior, the Union of Democratic Forces (UFD) was established in mid-1961. Soon after, it took in the tiny Grupo de Monárquicos Parlamentarios Constitucionales, but not the main royalist opposition group, Unión Española.[67] However, like previous anti-Communist alliances, the announced UFD failed to produce action; it was just a skeleton upon which the only traces of flesh belonged to the Socialists and IDC.[68]

---

[63] PSOE in Exile, Fifth Congress (1952), *Actas*, 83–125.

[64] *Alianza* (Mexico), Nov. 1953, 1, 3.

[65] Torregrosa's speech, PSOE in Exile, Fifth Congress (1952), *Actas*, 104. The *Memoria* for the Sixth Congress held in exile (1955) describes CNT approaches for unity as a 'unitary offensive'. [66] Text in *ES*, 7.3.57, 1.

[67] Ibid., 29.6.61–10.8.61; *Le Socialiste* (Paris), 22.2.62, 2. *El Socialista* became *Le Socialiste* in Dec. 1961 after a French government crack-down on the *émigré* press. The change just meant that the paper acquired a fictitious French editorial board and published the occasional item in French. There was no shortage of irony here, for the original *El Socialista* had been inspired by Guesde's *Le Socialiste*.

[68] Fagen, 125; PSOE and other organizations, PSOE-UGT, 'Acta reunión conjunta', 15–16 July 1962, 3.

This phase in the PSOE's evolution concluded with the meeting in Munich of Spanish members of the European Movement at the time of the latter's fourth congress in June 1962. Eighty opposition figures from the interior and 36 *émigrés* passed a resolution insisting upon democracy as a precondition for Spain's entry into the EEC. Symbolically the meeting of interior and exile was of momentary importance, uniting as it did republican and monarchist opponents of Franco, but in practice all that it led to were reprisals against those participants who returned to Spain. PSOE leader Rodolfo Llopis was criticized sharply by Arsenio Jimeno for subscribing, ostensibly on behalf of the PSOE, to a joint declaration that renounced the use of violence and failed to say anything about a transitional government of 'undefined institutional status' (thus going far beyond the compromises agreed to by party congresses).[69] Munich was, in the words of one commentator, 'the culmination of the Tripartite Note'.[70] Subsequently, the exiles lost influence.

SHADOWS OF TENDENCIES

When the Spanish Socialists linked up to form the PSOE in Exile at the end of the Second World War, they put behind them the fissiparous 1930s and decided to work in a unified fashion for Spain's liberation. Discussion of the rights and wrongs of past controversies was postponed until the party could hold its next congress in Spain. There were no tendencies in exile; unity prevailed. That is, according to the conventional party wisdom of the post-Franco period.[1] The reality of the matter was rather more complex, for although there were no permanent organized tendencies within the party, the alignments that had crystallized during the 1930s continued to be relevant. As Lenin had shown decades earlier,

---

[69] Ibid. 7–11; Fernández de Castro, 79–86; *Le Socialiste*, 21.6.62, 7–8; A. Jimeno, 'Antecedentes y documentos sobre la reunión de Munich, Junio 1962' (n.p., mimeo).
[70] Fernández de Castro, 85.
[1] Interviews with José Martínez de Velasco, 27 June 1983, and Francisco López Real, 4 June 1984.

a modest periodical could give cohesion and embryonic form to internal currents, thereby furthering factional causes. In the Spanish case, there was *Adelante* to serve the Prietista lobby, campaigning in the mid-1940s against the party position expressed in *El Socialista*. Contemporaneously, *Cuadernos Socialistas* briefly gave expression to a Caballerista current, as did Enrique de Francisco's equally short-lived *Alianza* a decade later. In the internal disagreements, the past weighed heavily on the present and *personalismo* as much as ideological and political differences continued to shape the lines of internal party conflict.

Besteirismo had long been in decline and its loss of identity as an internal faction was completed by its mentor's imprisonment in 1939 and death in captivity a year later. The Besteiristas of the 1930s (such as Trifón Gómez, Andrés Saborit, and Manuel Muiño) became the natural allies of Prieto, who from 1947 dominated the *émigré* sections for two whole decades. Both in origin and persistence, this dominance owed as much to subdivisions within the ranks of Caballerismo as it did to the political talents of Indalecio Prieto. In France, the principal centre of exile politics, Caballeristas (including Rodolfo Llopis, Enrique de Francisco, Pascual Tomás, and Arsenio Jimeno) played the leading roles during the reorganizing phase of 1944–7. Subsequently, however, they underwent a tripartite split, having lost their figurehead in March 1946.

In the final months of his life, Francisco Largo Caballero adopted attitudes that upset some of his followers. During the war he had suffered a long calvary of banishment, harassment, and imprisonment in France until February 1943 when the Gestapo took him to Berlin, whence he became Prisoner No. 69,040 in the Oranienberg concentration camp for the next two years. He spent his time there in the camp infirmary with arterial sclerosis in a leg, and needed months of treatment and convalescence in Berlin and Potsdam before eventually he was well enough to be flown to Paris in mid-September 1945, at the age of 76.[2] In France, despite the lingering memories of his ousting in 1937, Largo adopted a relatively positive

---

[2] *Adelante*, 15.4.43, 4, 15.9.45, 4, 1.6.46, 4; Largo Caballero, *Mis recuerdos*, 251–87; *ES*, 18.5.45, 1; *ES* (Toulouse, small edn. for the interior), Nov. 1945, 4.

attitude towards relations with the Communists: an attitude possibly influenced by the Soviet hospitality he had been afforded following his liberation by Polish troops. He did not advocate immediate co-operation with the PCE, as claimed by Araquistain, but he did recognize a pragmatic need for at least cordiality in inter-party relations; he hoped that gradually these would improve, for working-class unity was for him an imperative.[3] When approached by the PCE regarding co-operation, Largo replied that the creation of a climate of mutual respect was a necessary prerequisite: it was no good the Communists slandering and libelling Socialist leaders one minute and demanding unity with the PSOE the next.[4]

While lacking support among the exiles on this issue, Largo found himself close to Prieto in his pragmatic view that a plebiscite constituted the most viable mechanism for changing the Spanish regime.[5] Gone now was his revolutionary rhetoric of the 1930s. Like Prieto, Largo looked primarily to an international solution to Spain's problem.[6] The use of violence, he still maintained, was legitimate in the face of fascism, but it was not a practical option for Spanish anti-Francoists in the aftermath of a civil war.[7] Largo's final definition of 'the good socialist' indicated a clear preference for evolutionary socialism, though he and most of his followers still remained differentiated from Prieto by their firm opposition to any suggestion of pacts with the monarchists.[8]

Following Largo's death in March 1946, his former supporters lost their cohesion and stressed different aspects of Caballerismo. Luis Araquistain best represented the staunch anti-Communism of the Largo of the late 1930s. He abandoned the Marxism that he had toyed with in earlier years and began to develop a theory according to which the State arose not out of class struggles but out of conflicts between peoples and races; once established, national interests became its motive

---

[3] Araquistain's speech in *Adelante*, 15.11.45, 1–3; Largo Caballero's reply, ibid., 15.1.46, 6; Rosal, *Historia 1901–1939*, ii. 611–12; Largo Caballero, *Mis recuerdos*, 312; Tusell, 85.
[4] Largo Caballero, *Mis recuerdos*, 309–10.
[5] *ES*, 25.1.46, 2.
[6] *Adelante*, 15.1.46, 3–4; 22.2.51, 4.
[7] *ES*, 9.12.45, 1; Prieto's speech in ibid., 25.2.53, 2–3.
[8] *ES*, 9.12.45, 1; Largo Caballero, *Mis recuerdos*, 338.

force.[9] As early as January 1947 Araquistain warned his fellow Socialists against expecting anything from the UN. National interests—not morality—prevailed therein, he argued; thus the only realistic course for the Spanish opposition was to appeal to those national interests rather than to democratic or working-class solidarity.[10] Seeing Western aid as the only hope, Araquistain sought to enlist it by allaying the capitalist powers' fears about future Communist influence in Spain. There could be no question of PSOE relations with the PCE.[11]

Early on Araquistain had little influence, consumed as he seemed to be by personal rancour, and further embittered by the loss of his wife and daughter in quick succession.[12] His position became more acceptable as the *émigrés'* early hopes were destroyed. In 1953 he openly accepted the idea of a monarchist restoration as the only means of ending Francoism. With revolution out of the question, he was counselled by the works of Clausewitz to work for the internal disintegration of the regime. Araquistain's central argument was that Franco owed his survival to fears of Communism both in Spain and abroad; to reduce those fears, the Socialists needed to encourage a strengthening of Spain's international relations, not her isolation. In his view, the PSOE even had to assume the defence of Spain's military and economic agreements with the USA, for if not the great power would abandon any lingering sympathies it felt for Spain's democrats.[13] Araquistain entertained the hope that there would be some political quid pro quo for the Spain-USA agreements of 1953; even if this only amounted to the granting of some limited trade union liberty, similar to that available to the UGT during the 1920s, the opportunity should be seized to return home.[14] Similar sentiments were voiced by Trifón Gómez, who from late 1949, with resistance in Spain declining, began to repeat a phrase he had first used in 1945:

[9] L. Araquistain, 'España ante la idea sociológica del Estado', in id., *El pensamiento*, 97–156. The article first appeared in *ES* in 1953, but many of the ideas were developed earlier.
[10] Id., 'No hay que esperar nada de nadie', *ES*, 17.1.47, 4.
[11] Id., speech in *Adelante*, 15.11.45, 1–3.
[12] *ES*, 18.9.45, 1.   [13] Ibid., 25.2.53, 3–4; 5.3.53, 3–4.
[14] L. Araquistain, 'La UGT y el porvenir de España', *ES*, 26.3.53, 3.

'we shall return to Spain in whatever way possible, not in the manner we desire'.[15]

Such talk was deemed defeatist by the other Caballerista factions. To a lesser degree, they were also anti-Communist, though members such as Rodolfo Llopis had been leading advocates of collaboration in the past.[16] However, Llopis together with Pascual Tomás (general secretary of the UGT in Exile and under-secretary of the presidency under the Llopis government-in-exile of February to August 1947) emphasized a different aspect of Caballerismo, namely the old man's support for a plebiscitary solution to the Spanish question. Here, following political defeat at the hands of Prieto in 1947–8, they went further than Largo Caballero had by accepting the new party line of seeking an agreement with (among others) the monarchists. In strategic terms, this ex-Caballerista sector became Prietista, only disagreeing with Prieto's estimation of when his strategy had failed.[17] Ideologically, however, there remained a distinction. Whereas Prieto had nothing in common with Karl Marx, apart from the affliction of chronic haemorrhoids, and while Prietistas such as Manuel Albar did their best to break with the party's Marxist tradition,[18] Llopis and his circle continued to regard themselves as Marxists. True, their 'Marxism' was a matter of faith, a question of defending a series of ready-made and static conceptions, yet it provided anchorage enough for them to reject the ideas of the Bad Godesberg programme through which the SPD repudiated Marxist influence in 1959.[19]

Llopis was altogether a stronger character than Pascual Tomás and as president of the UGT in Exile he dominated that organization almost as convincingly as he controlled the modest PSOE apparatus. Born in Callosa de Sarría, Alicante, in 1895, the son of a Civil Guard sergeant, Llopis had begun

---

[15] Trifón Gómez speeches in ibid., 5.1.50, 3, 6.8.53, 3–4.
[16] Hermet, 25.
[17] Prieto recognized his failure late in 1950; Llopis and his colleagues did so in 1952.
[18] Manuel Albar, 'Carlos Marx, su doctrina en el tiempo', *Adelante*, 15.3.42. He also urged exiles in Mexico to behave as if they would spend the rest of their lives there ('Pensando en España y la paz', ibid., 1.7.42, 3–4).
[19] Llopis, *Emigración*, 28, 32; and for criticism of Bad Godesberg, *ES*, 24.3.60, 4, 31.3.60, 3–4.

his career as a schoolteacher. He joined the PSOE in 1917, was made Director General of Primary Education when the Republic was proclaimed, became a deputy to the Cortes, and was appointed presidential secretary under the Largo Caballero government of 1936–7. At the end of the Spanish war he managed to get to the French town of Albi, some 35 miles to the north-east of Toulouse, where his children and wife Georgette, a French *lycée* teacher and socialist, were living already. Apart from four years of banishment from Albi during the German occupation of France, this was to be Llopis' residence during his thirty years as general secretary of the PSOE and president of the UGT.[20] Like Iglesias and Largo before him, his influence was enhanced by control over the Socialists' official mail, as well as being maintained through less formal correspondence and possession of much of the documentation. At one executive meeting Llopis made a scene because a colleague had had the audacity to open the party mail; henceforth, the general secretary announced, he would not accept any letters that had been opened by others.[21] Llopis kept a lot of the documents in Albi; when he fell ill, the rest of the party executive could do little in his absence.[22] But most days, even after he had reached the normal age for retirement, a sense of duty and dedication led him to rise at 6 a.m. to catch the train from Albi to go to work in the party offices in Toulouse. He was an extremely methodical man. During meetings he would sit filling his tiny pocket notebook with even tinier notes which would be fed into his master archive when he returned home. Those afforded the rare privilege of admission to the Albi residence sometimes were shown their files, in which all their interventions at meetings were recorded.[23]

The remaining offspring of Caballerismo, the faction that resisted the Prietista overture to the monarchists, was that which stuck most closely to Largo's position of 1945–6. Disadvantaged by geographical dispersion, its chief represen-

---

[20] See the Llopis obituaries in *El País*, international edn., 25.7.83, and *Acción Socialista* (Madrid), 1.8.83, 1–2; information about him also appears in *ES*, 14.2.47, 1.

[21] PSOE in Exile, *Actas* of CE, 25.11.52.

[22] Ibid., 14.10.53.

[23] Interview with Manuel Garnacho, 17 Apr. 1982.

tatives at congresses and assemblies were Wenceslao Carrillo, the former leader of the National Metalworkers' Federation who had deputized for Largo in the UGT leadership in 1936–7, and whose exile took him to London and then Belgium;[24] Arsenio Jimeno, the leading Spanish Socialist personality in Paris; César Barona and Ildefonso Torregrosa, initially based respectively in Algeria and Tunisia; and the Mexico-based Bruno Alonso, General Commissar of the Fleet during the Civil War. Holding a similar position, there was Enrique de Francisco, but he was isolated by a strong sense of self-importance and did not join in the battles over the party position at congresses. He resigned from the presidency of the PSOE in Exile in protest against Prieto's unconstitutional steamrollering at the Assembly of 1947, then moved to Mexico from where he conducted a private propaganda war against the Toulouse officers.

Essentially, the position of this faction was to accept the plebiscite formula as the Socialists' maximum concession, but to reaffirm the party's republican identity and have no truck with the monarchists. The latter in Spain's case were not liberals but 'absolutists or fascists',[25] who had only negotiated with the PSOE in order to neutralize it. Warning too against placing any trust in the 'capitalist governments' of the West, the hard-line Caballeristas called for the establishment of a democratic alliance based primarily on working-class organizations, and looked to labour and socialist allies rather than to great powers for aid.[26] When they spoke of workers' unity, it was eventual UGT-CNT unification that they had in mind, for despite its decline through splits, repression,[27] anachronism, and the weakness of its international links, the CNT for a long time was regarded by the Socialists as the only other effective force in the interior.[28] Only in 1954 did reports

---

[24] On Carrillo see Saborit, *Asturias*, 112–18.

[25] Barona, speech at PSOE in Exile, Fourth Congress (1950), *Actas*, 66–8.

[26] Barona and De Francisco, speeches at PSOE in Exile, Third Congress (1948), *Actas*, 119–25, 148–55; the minority motion on the political position, PSOE in Exile, Fifth Congress (1952), *Actas*, 87–8.

[27] *Alianza*, Aug. 1953, 6, reported that the CNT had lost 15 national committees in the interior during the last 14 years, whereas the more cautious UGT had lost 5 executive committees.

[28] Prieto's speech at PSOE in Exile, Fifth Congress (1952), *Actas*, 96.

from Spain begin to indicate to them that the PCE, assisted by the West's partial rehabilitation of Franco, was gaining ground.[29]

These were the basic subdivisions within the PSOE, which none the less retained a remarkable degree of unity for an exiled party with such slim prospects of success. The Spanish Socialists were held together by their party's traditional stress upon discipline, by their ingrained loyalties to 'the Party', by a need to retain the respect of international allies, and, strategies and tactics apart, by a shared analysis of what was happening in Spain. The claim that the PSOE clung on to a 'fascist' characterization of Franco's Spain and took no cognizance of the regime's evolution is not wholly just.[30] Certainly, a lot of the propaganda sent into the interior did labour the Franco/Hitler/Mussolini comparison well into the 1960s, occasionally leading militants there to dispose of it rather than pass it on to workers among whom they knew the main effect would be derision. However, in the more serious political analyses made by the party, it was appreciated that the Falange was never more than one of several buttresses of the Franco regime; it was never the dominant power, and by the late 1950s it was beyond recovery as the Opus Dei technocrats became more influential.[31] The weakness of the PSOE analysis lay not in an inability to detect the shifting balance of forces within the Franco regime, but rather in its failure to comprehend trends in the Spanish economy. The Socialists repeatedly mistook conjunctural economic problems for structural crises, underestimated the regime's ability to generate growth, and expected that eventually Francoism would bring about economic paralysis.[32] Their analysis naturally led to arguments in favour of waiting for the 'catastrophe' rather than fighting.

A detailed examination of the official records of assemblies and congresses reveals[33] that there was very little conflict within the exiled sector of the PSOE prior to Prieto's *coup de main* at the 1947 Assembly of Delegates. The Caballeristas had an overwhelming superiority in the first party executive elected in 1944, and their dominance was confirmed at the

[29] PSOE, *Actas* of CE, 3.9.54.   [30] e.g. Fernández de Castro, 85.
[31] The best example of the PSOE analysis is Llopis, *España*.
[32] Ibid.   [33] See Appendix B below.

second PSOE congress in 1946, despite the election of the Prietista Manual Albar to a seat. Then came a dramatic shift in the balance of forces, with Prieto's victory being consolidated at the third congress in 1948. From this there emerged an executive dominated by Prietistas (Prieto himself and Amador Fernández), ex-Besteiristas (Saborit, Muiño, and Trifón Gómez, only the latter having been elected previously in exile), and ex-Caballeristas who accepted Prieto's victory (Llopis and Tomás). Of the Caballerista hard-liners only Arsenio Jimeno remained (until 1950); his former colleagues De Francisco and Carrillo were gone, and allies living in countries other than France were excluded by geography.

Before the old lines of battle were well and truly erased, the defeated Caballeristas fought some stubborn rearguard actions and even rallied for periodic counter-attacks. They formed a regular 'opposition' to officialdom at the congresses of the late 1940s and early 1950s (there are references to 'the majority' and 'the minority' in the records).[34] The minority grew as the monarchists flaunted their contempt for the pact signed with the PSOE in 1948, yet even at its peak in 1952 the hard-line Caballerista position received only 40 per cent of the votes. When it came to congress debates, Prieto's oratorical repertoire and the contrasting limitations of his opponents certainly contributed to the outcome. On several occasions Prieto was able to leave delegates with tears in their eyes, predisposed to voting for him for sentimental as much as any other reasons. For instance, when hard pressed by the opposition in 1952 he was not below reminding the assembled Socialists that he had given his whole life to the party, that the congress could well be his last, and so on.[35] No such reserves of sympathy could be drawn upon by the Caballeristas, who often prefaced their congress speeches with admissions that they had little chance of defeating Prieto. At the 1952 congress Jimeno started by confessing that he felt thoroughly intimated by the 'terrible eloquence of *compañero* Prieto'.[36] Prieto's challengers spoke like men who were defeated before they started—who presented their views to remind the party what

[34] PSOE in Exile, Fourth Congress (1950), *Actas*, 83.
[35] PSOE in Exile, Fifth Congress (1952), *Actas*, 124–5.
[36] Ibid. 98.

socialist principles demanded, yet who saw that the situation was pretty hopeless whichever way one viewed it. They functioned as the conscience of the movement, not as its political brain nor as a potential vanguard.

Discontentment over the official position, which must have contributed to a decline in party membership,[37] also found expression in the UGT, where affiliation remained only slightly higher than in the PSOE. Given the unusually strong membership overlap between the two organizations, it is not surprising that the UGT descended to great depths of political subordination at this time. Delivering the UGT's fraternal greetings to the PSOE congress in 1946, Manuel Muiño gave the party *carte blanche*, declaring: 'You are the political expression of the UGT.'[38] However, opposition delegates to the fifth congress of the UGT in Exile (November 1953) represented some 22 per cent of the members; they were strong enough to ensure that this congress, while reaffirming a community of political ideas with the PSOE, reasserted the UGT's independence to express itself politically.[39]

When it came to executive decisions, the only serious debate of the early 1950s was over whether to insist upon total liberalization or accept partial liberty as a precondition for returning to Spain. In this Trifón Gómez, until his death in October 1955, and Luis Araquistain, who died four years later, were the main proponents of exploiting whatever possibilities arose for engaging in legal activity in Spain, it being clear by the 1950s that the early efforts to establish a viable resistance movement in the interior had failed. This attitude was combined with an acceptance of monarchy as the most viable type of regime to succeed Francoism. For these two men, the type of Spain's future regime was secondary to the question of whether it would introduce effective liberty. Against their arguments, Prieto countered that liberty was indivisible; Franco would not offer his opponents a legal opening, such as the right to organize trade unions, for he was well aware that this could be the thin end of a democratic

---

[37] By 1962 paying members had fallen to just below 3,000 (PSOE, *Actas* of CE, 17.5.63).

[38] PSOE in Exile, Second Congress (1946), *Actas*, 27–8.

[39] *ES*, 3.12.53, 10.12.53, 17.12.53, *passim*.

wedge.[40] The debate had an air of artificiality about it: it often seemed that the basic difference was over how much compromise should be publicly accepted in advance, rather than over the extent of acceptable compromise.

Those who wished to compromise more, or more ostentatiously, than Prieto were easily defeated, not least by Franco's intransigence. In the early 1950s, with Spain's immediate future uncertain, varying perspectives were tenable and could be debated, with Prieto taking the line: 'With Franco, never!' and Trifón Gómez replying: 'Against Franco, always, even in Spain if circumstances demand it!'[41] But as De Francisco's *Alianza* observed, once the US-Spanish pacts were signed, Franco had absolutely no need to make concessions to the democratic opposition.[42] Indeed, his continuing vindictiveness provided the strongest disincentive to any thoughts of a pragmatic return to Spain. When Antonio Fabra Ribas went back in 1949, the only generosity shown to him by the authorities was that he was allowed to serve a twelve-year prison sentence at home.[43] No doubt the decision of the sixth congress of the PSOE in 1955 to abolish the party presidency, approved by 57.3 per cent of the members represented, was partly a condemnation of the attitude of its occupant, Trifón Gómez. However, it is also true that the presidency had been ineffective since De Francisco's resignation in 1947: his successor Prieto was often housebound, and too ill to be an active president, and Trifón Gómez's priority was his work for the International Transport Federation, whose Latin American section he took charge of a few months before his death.[44]

Each of the men involved in the controversy over the terms for returning to Spain seemed 'vindicated' in the minds of a later generation of Socialists by the course of the real post-Franco transition: Araquistain and Trifón Gómez through their vision of it involving a restoration of the monarchy and only then a referendum; Prieto in believing that little could be

---

[40] See especially the debate between Araquistain and Prieto at the seventh congress (1958), in Fundación Pablo Iglesias and PSOE, *Congresos del PSOE en el Exilio*, ii. 29–42. For Trifón Gómez see PSOE, *Actas* of CE, 27.6.55.

[41] Trifón Gómez's speech, *ES*, 6.8.53, 3–4.

[42] *Alianza*, Nov. 1953, 1, 3.

[43] *ES*, 6.2.58, 1.   [44] Ibid., 18–25.8.55, *passim*.

done before Franco died. But to the Caballerista veterans of the time both of these perspectives smacked of defeatism. In a sense, history accommodated their pessimistic outlook, but in part this was because defeatism is the ultimate in self-fulfilling prophecies.

There was also a geographical dimension to the internal battles. An early tension existed between France and Mexico as a result of the superior conditions that existed in America and because the 'Mexicans', despite including many ex-parliamentarians, had been ordered to accept the authority of Toulouse (as well as that of Madrid). Mexico remained a dependable fiefdom of Prieto, and in France too, certain sections regularly sided with particular factions. In the mid-1940s the Socialists of Bordeaux and Marseilles advocated relations with the PCE in Spain,[45] as did the PSOE in the interior.[46] Criticism of the Prietista party line in the late 1940s came especially from the groups in Perpignan, Marseilles, Carcassonne, and Narbonne.[47] Opposition to the Toulouse executives persisted above all in Caballerista-influenced Paris. This gave a sharp edge to a recurrent debate about where to base the party headquarters in France, for according to the party rules most if not all members of the party executive had to live in the vicinity. Location affected composition. Toulouse argued that most of the Socialist *émigrés* and their organizations were based in the south, where they benefited from Spain's proximity; Paris stressed the advantages of operating in a capital city, close to France's government and administration, and where its labour organizations were based and international links were centred. Of course Paris offered a far more lively political scene, with regular discussion of new ideas and experiences from home and abroad. There, some of the younger Spanish Socialists for a while flirted with Trotskyism and other revolutionary options. But although the PSOE considered Spain to be an international problem in need of an international solution, the party headquarters were

[45] PSOE in Exile, Second Congress (1946), *Actas*, 165–7. Together they had over 500 members (almost 7% of the members represented at this congress). See the *Actas taquigráficas*, 235–57.

[46] PSOE in Exile, Assembly of Delegates (1947), *Anejos*, 456, letter of 29 July 1946.

[47] PSOE in Exile, *Actas* of CE, 23.3.49.

transferred to Paris only for the two years 1948–50; and even during that short time some executive meetings were held in Toulouse and others in St Jean-de-Luz, where ill health confined party president Prieto.[48] Subsequently Paris retained only the party treasury and the administration of *El Socialista*.

The official PSOE attitude towards tendencies was to see them as damaging and divisive. In 1946 two additional clauses were added to the statutes of the PSOE in Exile. The first allowed for free discussion in the party but permitted no 'permanent groupings of like-minded' Socialists, nor expressions of personal opinions outside it. The second reinforced party discipline by demanding that once official positions were adopted, all members had to defend them.[49] For years these clauses were reproduced in every issue of the Prietista organ *Adelante*. Tendencies were acceptable, this paper maintained, so long as they were mere 'currents of opinion'. However, by saying no to 'systematic opposition' and 'organized discrepancy', *Adelante* showed that its real concern was not so much about organized lobbying for a particular viewpoint as about organized opposition to the party leadership.[50] The memory of intra-party strife in the 1930s and more recent experiences of tendency battles in France and Italy produced majority support for this view in the PSOE. The additional clauses were approved while the Caballeristas were dominant, and no doubt many who voted for them did so in the belief that they might put a rein on Prieto. In fact they were soon reinforcing his dominance. For the minority who became critical of the clauses, discipline was valued only so long as it was based on majority decisions and internal democracy. Rejecting 'barrack discipline', they argued that internal diversity was worth conserving, for it gave the party 'a wealth of shades and multiplies its action, or at least makes it suitable for different kinds of situations'.[51] Yet even while urging the abolition of the two clauses at the fifth congress, the Caballerista minority did not advocate

[48] During this period of ill health Prieto was confined to the Hotel Eskualduna, then moved into the nearby Appartements Florida in the rue Vauban.

[49] PSOE in Exile, Second Congress (1946), *Actas taquigráficas*, 335–40; *ES*, 19.1.50, 1.

[50] 'La unidad del partido', *Adelante*, 1.4.50, 1.

[51] 'La democracia en el partido', *Cuadernos Socialistas*, Dec. 1944, 7.

the establishment of permanently structured tendencies; accepting that the majority had to be allowed to lead the party effectively, their primary concern was with removing rules that prevented minorities from becoming majorities.[52]

It was the demand that some publicity be given to minority views that made the editorial policy of *El Socialista*, the official organ, a matter of considerable controversy. With Saborit as editor in the late 1940s, there was strict enforcement of a ban on polemical articles,[53] especially those written with a knife. His successors Albar and Llopis were also keen to see that contents reflected the party line.[54] A Caballerista attempt in 1952 to remove the ban on tendencies and alter the paper's editorial policy succeeded only in slightly liberalizing the latter. That same year Gabriel Pradal took over as editor and raised the literary quality of the paper while allowing the occasional exchange of opinions. With him in charge, the number of copies produced rose from 5,200 in 1955 to 5,600 in 1958.[55] But still, ordinary members were normally able to air their views in the paper only in the weeks prior to a congress, through the *Tribuna del Congreso* that appeared in *El Socialista* from 1952 to 1958. In 1961 pre-congress polemics were relegated to just one or two internal bulletins.[56]

Most PSOE dissidents found it exceedingly difficult to circulate their views to the party as a whole. Ironically, the principal exception to the rule was Prieto, who himself tolerated no dissent in Mexico and had resorted to regular expulsions of anti-Prietistas from the Círculo Cultural Pablo Iglesias. In November 1945, when the Cortes met in Mexico Prieto had spoken out, putting his personal views as if they were party policy,[57] and he continued to do so on subsequent occasions. On purely technical grounds what he did at the 1947 PSOE Assembly of Delegates was in contempt of the party statutes, as well as flouting the opinion of Socialists in the interior. Moreover, Prieto threatened to terminate his

---

[52] Barona's speech at PSOE in Exile, Fifth Congress (1952), *Actas*, 76.
[53] PSOE in Exile, Fourth Congress (1950), *Actas*, 40–3.
[54] PSOE in Exile, Fifth Congress (1952), *Actas*, 30.
[55] PSOE, Seventh Congress held in exile (1958), *Memoria*, treasurer's report, 4.
[56] PSOE, *Circular*, 29.4.61.
[57] See Largo Caballero's protest, PSOE in Exile, *Actas* of CE, 24.1.46; Trifón Gómez's comment, UGT in Exile, *Actas* of CE, 21.12.45.

prestigious collaboration with the official Socialist organ (which he also supported financially) when on several occasions he was asked to revise contributions that were out of line with party policies. The PSOE congress of 1952 banned personal attacks and sterile polemics from the pages of *El Socialista*, yet threats from Prieto secured the publication of his criticisms of the Socialist International and ICFTU which had been deemed excessively harsh by the party executive. Also published under coercion were a speech, contravening the party line, in which Prieto appealed to Molotov for the USSR to veto Spain's entry into the UN, and a denigratory obituary for Araquistain.[58] Other leading figures on the right were also allowed leeway—including Araquistain himself, who got away with 'going public' with his pro-monarchy arguments,[59] and Trifón Gómez. Meanwhile on the left Enrique de Francisco was suspended for publicly repudiating Toulouse executive claims about the effectiveness of the PSOE in the interior,[60] and lesser lights such as Máximo Muñoz were expelled for personal attacks on Prieto.

Here it is not possible to evaluate the rights and wrongs of specific disciplinary proceedings in the party, but clearly Prieto's own relations with the party did warrant the accusation made by Wenceslao Carrillo that the party operated double standards when moving against dissenters. Those sanctioned

[58] PSOE in Exile, Fifth Congress (1952), 71; PSOE, *Actas* of CE, 21–2.4.54, 5.5.54, 16.11.55, 7.10.59.

[59] Published in *Bohemia* (Havana), 30.6.57, and partially reproduced by the Francoist *El Español*. For the text see PSOE, Comité Director of 1957, *Memoria*, Anejo no. 4.

[60] In September 1949 De Francisco was suspended by the Socialists in Mexico from holding a party position for 2 years, having made declarations to the Ider-Press News Agency when *ES* refused to publish his views (*Adelante*, 1.3.50, 2). He felt that Prieto's behaviour at the 1947 Assembly denoted a return to *caudillismo* (PSOE in Exile, Third Congress (1948), *Memoria*, ch. on 'Política del partido', 66). His offence was to publicize his criticisms and to claim that the CE of the exile sector of the PSOE had lied about the party's strength in Spain. The fourth congress (1950) lifted the suspension because of De Francisco's past services to the party. Later Toulouse learnt but did not publicize the fact that he had been expelled from the party by the CE in Madrid (PSOE in Exile, *Actas* of CE, 4.5.51). It is probable that the clandestine organization had been paralysed by arrests at the time De Francisco made his declarations; but a new executive was formed soon after. For a later polemic between De Francisco and the Toulouse executive see his *Carta a los socialistas de España* (n.p., June 1956) and *Carta a los socialistas españoles* (n.p., Feb. 1957); PSOE, *Circular*, 5.9.56.

immediately pointed to the limitations of PSOE democracy. Mexico City, whose delegates at party congresses could often use a block vote (for 'nominal' voting) based on some 500 members, invariably exercised a defeatist Prietista influence from the 1940s to the 1960s. Yet, as De Francisco pointed out, party activity and attendances in Mexico were far smaller than the paper membership figures suggested. If 100 comrades turned out for a meeting, there was 'a great fiesta'.[61] In Mexico, just 70 supporters pushed through Prieto's motion for the party congress of 1952, and only 83 members attended the meeting at which Muñoz was expelled.[62] The left's claim was that the other Socialists were alienated by official policies, though clearly resignation and old age also accounted for absenteeism, and poor attendances were not confined to Mexico alone.[63] None the less, the truth was that Mexico's delegates to congresses represented only an active minority of the Mexico City group, and yet when votes were taken 'nominally' (and thus delegates had as many votes as there were dues-paying members in their groups), the particularly large number of votes at the disposal of the 'Mexicans' was placed behind the minority-approved position. When in 1952 Prieto defeated the biggest opposition challenge by 2,493 to 1,725 votes, 473 of his votes came from Mexico and over 200 from other parts of Latin America.[64]

Two other circumstances prevented a full flourishing of democracy. One was that members of the party executive mostly had to reside in the same place, whereas party membership was spread over three continents. Thus physically and geographically, if not always ideologically, the Spanish Socialists residing in France were always over-represented in the leadership. The other problem was financial. By the late 1940s, even with levies of the members, the party executive

[61] De Francisco, *Carta . . . espanoles*, 12–13.

[62] Muñoz, *Problemas*, 29; id., *Dos conductas: Indalecio Prieto y yo* (Mexico: publ. by the author, 1952), 7–8.

[63] Another example of this phenomenon is to be found in a congress speech by W. Carrillo: Toulouse had 300 members, yet in the key debate there on the controversial parts of the executive's *memoria* for the fourth congress the vote was 33 to 31, the level of party involvement having declined (PSOE in Exile, Fourth Congress (1950), *Actas*, 99).

[64] Muñoz, *Problemas*, 28–9. In fact, the *Actas* of the Fifth Congress (1952), 5–11, put Mexico's representation at 457 members/votes.

decided that it was no longer possible to pay the full travel costs of North African and American delegates to congresses and assemblies.[65] These areas therefore normally sent, at most, two delegates each to events in Toulouse. These overseas delegates could not possibly represent the diversity of opinion at home as well as larger delegations could. The practice grew of distant or impecunious *agrupaciones* nominating already selected delegates from other parts to represent them too.

In such circumstances it was almost inevitable that a concentration of party power should build up in Toulouse. Following the displacement of the Caballeristas in the late 1940s, there were no dramatic changes in the composition of the party executive for the next two decades. Rather than an oligarchy, what the party leadership became was a clique surrounding the general secretary. So long as he accepted Prieto's overall strategic guidance, the general secretary enjoyed considerable tactical influence. Llopis's control over the party apparatus was enhanced by the abolition of the party presidency and vice-presidency in 1955, and the concurrent reorganization of its highest authority between congresses. Having been the Assembly of Delegates, then the National Committee, this authority (which in theory controlled the party executive) now became the *Comité Director*, whose zonal basis of election made it less representative of the rank and file. Other elements contributing to Llopis's personal influence were his monopoly on the correspondence, his presidency of the UGT, a total dedication to work, and his personal contact with delegates arriving from the interior of Spain for major events or consultations. For security reasons, it was invariably Llopis who spoke at Toulouse congresses in the name of 'those who cannot speak' for themselves, and Llopis too who decided which Spaniards from the interior wearing dark glasses were to be introduced as the authentic representatives of the PSOE in Spain. The formal transfer of executive power from the clandestine organization to Toulouse in 1954 also helped make the general secretary peerless.

[65] PSOE in Exile, *Actas* of CE, 5.4.49, 26–7.2.53.

The personal tragicomedy of Rodolfo Llopis derived from the fact that his influence grew as the residual force of his party dwindled. On occasions he behaved as if he *were* the party, particularly at Munich in 1962. The phenomenon was a very human one, a product of the tremendous personal sacrifices made by Llopis over the years. There were few rewards to be had; even representation of the PSOE at international conferences was an arduous business, for the party generally could only afford rail fares. Moreover, because of the parlous financial state of the party, remunerated positions were limited in 1948 to just three of the executive members and two party workers, while the youth section lost its subsidy.[66] The salaries paid by the party often lagged a bit behind the Parisian metalworkers' wage scales upon which they were based from 1958.[67]

Nevertheless, while acknowledging the personal sacrifices made by Llopis and the old guard, one must recognize also that their period of preserving the party in exile was one that saw a distinctly conservative mentality develop: one that was suspicious of all proposals for change and any demand for greater dynamism. The veterans' readiness to remove determined dissenters gave the PSOE the appearance of coherence for many years, but a price had to be paid for this. Coherence was achieved at the expense of the party's ability to respond to fresh thinking and proposals inspired by developments in Spain. In the name of unity, the party executive often acted as a tendency itself, lobbying for its ideas via the party press in the run-up to congresses and ensuring that only the like-minded would attain positions of authority or be able to retain them. In the long term, inflexible attitudes brought internal tensions to the point of dividing the party, and the basis of that split would inevitably be personalized as a result of the preceding accumulation of individual control over the party by its general secretary. The Toulouse-based clique of veterans helped preserve the party in its darkest hour, but later became an obstacle to its recovery in Spain.

[66] Ibid., 22.5.48.
[67] PSOE, *Actas* of CE, 16.11.62.

3
Men Without Names:
The PSOE in Spain
1939–1970

FOLLOWING defeat in the Civil War, the Socialists' rebuilding of their party in Spain was essentially an act of self-defence. Its most immediate aims were to save the lives of the imprisoned and the persecuted and to lend succour to at least some of the families of Franco's Socialist victims. The regime's vindictiveness, which went well beyond its determination to eliminate the leaders and cadres of the defeated forces, claimed perhaps 200,000 lives during Franco's first five years in power.[1] Thousands of Socialists were among those executed, the most eminent being party executive members José Gómez Osorio, Ricardo Zabalza, and Carlos Rubiera, and the writers Julián Zugazagoitia and Francisco Cruz Salido, these last two captured in France with the aid of the Gestapo and then returned to Madrid to be shot. Many others, including Julián Besteiro, died in prison or were physically wrecked by the privations and iron discipline of prison life or the inhuman demands of labour companies. A schoolteacher from Badajoz who served five years in prison commented later on his state when released: 'I was as old then from suffering and hunger as I am today.'[2] Outside, such men found a more widespread adversity, that of a nation facing a decade of hunger and epidemics. It would not be until 1950 that Spain would be restored to the economic level of 1936. Even professional people, State officials, and the police went hungry.[3] But for those who had defended the Republic the situation was even

---

[1] Official figures issued in 1944 put the number of political executions at 192,684. Stanley Payne (*Falange* (Stanford, CA: Stanford University Press, 1961), 242) sees this as greatly inflated; Edouard de Blaye (*Franco and the Politics of Spain* (Harmondsworth: Penguin, 1976), 129) puts the figure at 250,000.

[2] Personal interview with Mario Tanco, Madrid, 22 May 1984.

[3] Heine, *La oposición*, 41–50.

worse. Stigmatized as 'Reds' (*rojos*), their families suffered discrimination at school and in the labour market. Besides that, they remained under surveillance, having to report to the police at least monthly; their travel was restricted and their homes were subjected to regular police searches. For some this situation lasted until the late 1950s.[4] In these circumstances many former members of Socialist organizations kept their heads down, having decided upon release from prison that they had done their duty and now had to rebuild their lives. None the less, several thousand Socialists were resolved to continue the struggle, regardless of the hazards.

The history of the clandestine PSOE passed through various phases. Long months of grim despair were broken only by brief spells of hope. Frustratingly slow organizational growth alternated with almost total collapse. There was first a phase of reorganizing in the concentration camps and prisons in 1939–40; then a gradual shift towards reorganizing outside as prisoners were released. A lot of the younger prisoners and those considered mere 'prisoners of war' were released in 1940. Some of the more 'dangerous' prisoners had their death sentences commuted to thirty years' imprisonment around the same time, and were then granted 'conditional liberty' in 1944, their sentences still hanging over them in case of fresh arrest. From 1944–5 there were attempts by six successive Madrid-based party executive committees to build a clandestine and deliberately skeletal party organization in much of Spain. Each executive in turn fell victim to police raids and their inevitable sequel of interrogation, beatings, threats, information; then surveillance followed by more raids. After this period, the *émigré* executive in Toulouse assumed the leadership of the entire party, attempting in 1954–8 to control and reorganize the interior by means of an authorized envoy and separate links with each province or region where there were signs of Socialist activity. Widespread police raids in November 1958 eliminated many of the gains of the mid-1950s and put an end to the first efforts by militants in the interior to recover control over the party. After a recovery retarded by further key arrests in 1960, there was a gradual strengthening

[4] Interviews with María Lacrampe, Julia Vigre, and Isabel Ponce, Madrid, 12 June 1984.

of the party in the 1960s, accompanied by new demands that the positions of leadership should be returned to the activists of the interior.

Only very approximately can the numbers involved be estimated.[5] In 1944–5 the conjuncture of most prisoners having been released and the widespread expectation of Franco's downfall, aroused by Allied advances, momentarily led the Socialists to relax their stringent entry criteria and even contemplate a transition from a cadre to a mass organization. For a few months, between 3,000 and 6,000 militants were involved in party activity. But just as international events had fed enthusiasm, so too did they generate a sense of complete demoralization and powerlessness in 1946 when it was seen that effective Western action against Franco would not be forthcoming. Throughout the opposition the level of involvement declined, hit too by improvements in the efficiency of the regime's repressive forces. By the mid-1940s these were becoming much more adept at rooting out guerrilla resisters and infiltrating anti-Franco organizations. And with each national executive committee of the PSOE that fell, the authorities were able to round up dozens of provincial activists and to destroy inter-Socialist communications for long periods on end.

Although the Socialists again deliberately limited their ambitions to the building of a cadre organization from the late 1940s, they were none the less decidedly weak in terms of the number of regularly active members. Between 1946 and 1974 it is improbable that the party ever had more than 2,000 such *militantes* at any one time.[6] Given that even that figure slumped periodically in response to mass arrests and organizational deficiencies, and that affiliation was concentrated mainly in just two provinces of the north, it is not surprising that to most ordinary Spaniards the PSOE came to be thought of as, if anything, little more than a collection of exiles—as

[5] The estimates vary greatly. Antonio Pérez implied at the second congress of the PSOE in Exile in 1946 that there were over 30,000 Socialists organized in Spain (*Actas*, 277), whereas another leading activist, Ramón Hernández, later put active involvement in 1944–5 at 2,000–3,000 (interview, Madrid, 23 Aug. 1982).

[6] Here I am in agreement with the estimates made by Benjamin Welles (*Spain: The Gentle Anarchy* (New York: Praeger, 1965), 200) and by Miguel Boyer, who was politically active in the capital in the early 1960s (interview, Madrid, 2 Mar. 1982).

men who may have helped make history but who now were decidedly part of it.

'THE SOCIALIST FAMILY'

At the end of the Civil War an anti-Negrín party executive presided over by José Gómez Osorio was elected by national committee members still in Spain to replace Negrinista PSOE leaders who had left the country. Vacancies on the national committee were filled also, though the precise circumstances of these renovations are not clear.[7] Most of the new leaders, who supported the establishment of Colonel Casado's National Council of Defence, were unable to leave Spain when the defeat overtook them. Along with other republicans, they made their way to the port of Alicante where capture by Italian Legionnaires and Spanish Falangists, rather than sea-borne escape, was to be the fate of more than 20,000. Since the local jails were already full, the captives were herded into the Los Almendros concentration camp on the slopes leading up to Santa Bárbara prison, before being transferred to the more secure Campo de Albatera. Thereafter, those who were not picked out by parties of itinerant Falangists bent on vengeance were redistributed gradually throughout Spain, some to be shot, others to be returned to their place of origin where local judges had issued warrants.[8] Even the survivors often spent months with summarily-dictated death sentences hanging over them before learning that these had been commuted to thirty years' imprisonment. None of the prisoners, deemed 'rebels' by the victors, in fact served such a long term; indeed, by 1945 the great majority had been conditionally released, as Franco attempted to shed some of the fascist trimmings of his regime to appease the West.

---

[7] There is confusion as to whether the meeting took place in Mar. or Apr., or whether there were two meetings. For references to them by participants cf. W. Carrillo's speech at the second congress of the PSOE in Exile (1946), *Actas*, 96–107; Ramón Hernández, 'Conferencia, Juventudes Socialistas del Departamento del Sena', Paris, 7.10.56, 4; Federico Fernández López, 'Apuntes para la historia del PSOE', 1976, 1; id., 'Apunte histórico. El Partido Socialista', 1981, 4; Francisco López Real, 'La celda 72 de Sevilla', *ES*, 24.12.78.

[8] Llopis, *Emigración*, 3–4.

In Franco's prisons the Socialists immediately organized themselves for survival. There were no spectacular escapes: early attempts to break out of Seville Prison were punished with exemplary executions in full view of the prison populace.[9] Virtually all the Socialist inmates seem to have held on to organization and comradeship as lifelines and defences against insanity. Ironically, unity and communication among them were facilitated by chronic overcrowding. In 1940 in Málaga Prison some inmates were obliged to sleep on the patio regardless of weather conditions because a prison built for 600 was packed by 6,000.[10] Meanwhile the women's prison of Ventas in Madrid, which had been built by Victoria Kent as a model institution, had up to twelve people crowded into cells designed for one. Against a background of executions, which extended even to minors who had been members of the JSU, the Socialist women in Ventas ran discussion groups, organized a nursery for inmates' children, and tried to educate the illiterate.[11] In many places Socialists constituted a large proportion of the prison population. Often they linked up into groups of five, as at the Puerto de Santa María prison (Cádiz), where half of the 6,000 prisoners were organized as Socialists, according to their leader Ramón Rubial. Before long an information network existed to link the prisons. Sometimes with the connivance of a sympathetic prison official, messages were sent in the care of relatives and loved ones, or with transferred prisoners obliged to do *turismo penitenciario*.[12]

Once the basic prison organization was in place and the immediate threat of execution had receded, more ambitious activities were undertaken in some places. A form of prison dues was collected: 25 *céntimos* here, a day's bread there, cardboard coupons elsewhere, used primarily to provide

[9] PSOE, Historical Project, memoir of María-Jesús Alfonso Fernández Torres (mimeo, no title, 1976), 2.

[10] Interview with party veteran Antonio García Duarte, Madrid, 6 June 1984.

[11] Interviews with Lacrampe, Vigre, and Ponce. See Valentina Fernández Vargas, *La resistencia interior en la España de Franco* (Madrid: Istmo, 1981), 87–8, and Ángeles García-Madrid, *Requiem por la libertad* (Madrid: publ. by the author, 1982), *passim*, on the horrors of the women's prisons.

[12] Taped interviews by Carlos Cruz with Rubial, Luis Fernández, and Félix García Fanjul, c. 1976; personal interview with Rubial, Madrid, 29 Apr. 1982; Rubial interviews in *Cuadernos para el Diálogo*, 261 (1978), 21, and in *ES* suppl., 6.5.79, ii; López Real interview in *ES*, 17.6.79, 14–15.

comrades languishing in the prison infirmary with food.[13] Particularly in Yeserías (Madrid), Socialist prisoners also worked with some success on the administrative staff, exploiting inefficiency, sympathy, and casual attitudes wherever these were to be found. Given the opportunity to perform tasks that gave them access to prison offices, some inmates were able to falsify and fabricate documents and thereby secure the release of prisoners. Some sentences were 'shortened'; other inmates gained their release on spuriously documented 'medical grounds' as new decrees were issued to reduce the prison population. In December 1945 Luis Fernández obtained his conditional liberty on the pretext that he had tuberculosis, only to discover later that his fiction was a fact.[14] Occasionally a prison typewriter was used or prison directors were fed extra forms to sign by inmates 'assisting' them. Hard-boiled eggs served as rubber stamps. Certain prison officials became more accommodating as the Allied victory drew near: seeking an insurance policy against a change of regime, they turned a blind eye to infringements of regulations. Thus occasionally prisoners gained access to newspapers or might be allowed to overhear the BBC News; they would then relay what they had learnt by means of the clandestine, single-issue, hand-written editions of *El Socialista* which they produced. Another organ, *Redemción*, reached several prisons from its base in Madrid. Meanwhile some beautifully crafted editions of the youth paper *Renovación* appeared in the prison of Alicante in 1946, testimony to an almost religious devotion to the socialist cause. One, commemorating the death of Largo Caballero, had a splendid coloured cover depicting a coffin draped with the red banner of the PSOE, UGT, and FNJSE; it bore the legend: 'Socialists do not die. [Like seeds] they are sown.'[15]

Of the PSOE executive members chosen at the end of the Civil War, only a minority were able to leave Spain. At least three others were shot by Franco[16] and of the rest only two

---

[13] García Duarte, Rubial, and Luis Fernández interviews.

[14] Federico Fernández's memoirs; Luis Fernández interview.

[15] *Renovación* (Alicante prison edition), 6, 1.4.46.

[16] Gómez Osorio, Zabalza, and Rubiera were shot. For further details see Appendix C below.

survived prison and went on to participate in the clandestine organization (Juan Gómez Egido and youth representative Sócrates Gómez). Retrospective disputes over which was the first clandestine anti-Franco force to be organized are of less relevance than consideration of how much activity each could manage at any particular time. The PSOE could legitimately claim a minimal clandestine activity beyond the prisons by late 1940—later than the CNT but before the PCE[17]—yet this only began to bear fruit visibly in 1942–3. The early 1940s saw efforts to reorganize the 'Socialist Family': to relaunch the party, union, and youth without structural differentiation as PSOE, UGT, and FNJSE. This enterprise was familial in more senses than one, for not only did the resurgent movement regard Pablo Iglesias as its *abuelo* (grandfather); its survival owed something to genuine kinship as well. In February 1940, on the eve of their execution, the PSOE president, José Gómez Osorio (formerly Governor of Madrid) and Ricardo Zabalza (leader of the land workers' federation) entrusted to the former's son, FNJSE president Sócrates Gómez, the task of reorganizing the movement. Though the son was himself still a prisoner, the party leaders understood that a youth team had the best chances of surviving to fulfil their mandate. Ratified by other imprisoned executive members, the idea was implemented with the creation of an organizing committee, the Comisión Gestora Nacional, led by Gómez and incorporating Mario Fernández Rico, Julio Méndez López, Cecilio Macho, and Julián Lapiedra.[18]

Both in Madrid and in the provinces, the tasks of reorganization fell overwhelmingly to young Caballerista militants whose dynamism could be harnessed thanks to the relatively light terms of imprisonment they actually served. Officials rarely suspected that youth leaders of such tender years could have played the important political and military roles they did during the 1930s. Moreover, Caballerista

[17] See Alba, *Communist Party*, 315; on the CNT, J. M. Molina, *El movimiento clandestino en España 1939–1949* (Mexico: Editores Mexicanos Unidos, 1976), 41–87.

[18] Sócrates' brother Bienvenido was also an active Socialist. Their mother received a 30-year prison sentence for 'encouraging' their father in his political activities (interview with S. Gómez, Madrid, 9 Mar. 1982). See too his interview in Julia Navarro, *El desafío socialista* (Madrid: Maisal, 1977), 24–43.

prominence was enhanced by the fact that the Negrinistas and Prietistas who had been in the front line in 1937–9 were now in exile or were keeping their heads down.[19] Many young militants, such as Federico Fernández López (who replaced Méndez in September), were released in 1940 and subsequently the youth team went through two phases. In its first couple of years, lacking resources and infrastructure, it could do little more than improve communications between the prisons, and between prison interiors and militants outside, while beginning to organize a small group of redundant lawyers to advise prisoners' families. Only during the second phase, in 1942–4, did the team begin to look more like a party leadership than a relief agency. Indeed, around 1942, to appear more authoritative, it began to present itself alternatively as a national party executive or as the Madrid provincial leadership. Vacancies brought about by arrests, including the second detention of Sócrates Gómez in 1942–3, were filled by Ramón Hernández, Paco Domingo, Mariano Redondo, and Ramón López Pintor. In these dark days nobody fought over the leading positions, for the only certainty in the minds of the clandestine militants was that sooner or later they would be caught and would suffer. Leading comrades were still likely to be shot or, like Cecilio Macho, left half dead by their prison experience.[20]

The youthful clandestine team needed a basic propaganda apparatus if it was to succeed. This was obtained from the British Embassy in Madrid whose propaganda section provided a Roneo duplicating machine and a small subvention of 3,000 pesetas a month, in return for the Socialists' production of wartime 'leaflets for freedom' and insertion of war news in their *Servicio de Información Socialista* bulletin. This contact was developed through a certain comrade Legorburu who was married to the daughter of a veteran Socialist and worked at the embassy. The young activists passed on information to the British about a Flying Fortress

---

[19] Personal interviews with S. Gómez and R. Hernández; Hernández, 'Conferencia', 5; Heine, *La oposición*, 244; V. Alba, *Historia de la resistencia antifranquista (1939–1955)* (Barcelona: Planeta, 1978), 28–9.

[20] Fernández López's memoirs, *passim*, and personal interview with him, Miraflores de la Sierra, 6 Sept. 1982; Hernández, 'Conferencia', *passim*.

that had come down in Gandía, whose engines were then destroyed by secret service agents before they could be transported to workshops in Toledo; they revealed the location of a Gestapo radio station code-named 'Quijote', which was also destroyed; and they secretly photographed people entering and leaving Gestapo headquarters in Madrid, thereby uncovering the identity of a double agent who was later assassinated in a chalet by the road to Burgos. It was the British Embassy that spirited UGT general secretary Rodríguez Vega out of Spain in 1943, after the Socialists had used subterfuge and good fortune to secure his release from prison and had hidden him for several months in Madrid. The authorities had not realized who their prisoner was.[21]

According to a later account, the young Socialists deceived the embassy by producing only very small quantities of the war propaganda.[22] This may have been so, but any guilt associated with the collaboration was not evident at the time. As Rodríguez Vega told a mass audience when he arrived in Mexico, the embassy leaflets were exceedingly popular; they were read more than any newspapers, he claimed. Although the US Ambassador had declared that the victory of the Allies would not affect the Spanish regime, neither the Francoists nor the opposition believed it.[23] The Socialists' own initial characterization of the regime as fascist encouraged them to believe that Franco could not survive a defeat of the Axis powers—that he could not simply curb Falange influence and somehow prevent Spain from being decisively embargoed by the democratic victors. Many Socialist militants faced the firing squads with their spirits buoyed by the conviction that Allied advances meant that their own cause was about to triumph too. In one of his last letters before execution early in 1943, Pedro Fernández Sánchez Carrasco paid tribute to the USA, Russia, England, China, Canada, and the other allies: 'Their victory is ours . . . Long live the triumph of the Allied Nations! Long live Spain and its Workers' Revolution!'[24]

---

[21] See the Fernández López and Hernández sources cited in n. 20 above.

[22] Personal interview with R. Hernández.

[23] J. Rodríguez Vega, *El régimen de Franco* (Toulouse, 1943), 18–19; id., 'Impresiones'.

[24] PSOE, Historical Project, 'Testimonios de la resistencia antifranquista'.

Meanwhile the youth team continued to offer what assistance it could to prisoners and their families, helped Socialists who had to hide,[25] published underground propaganda, built an organization in the capital, introduced a degree of specialization into the 'Family', developed Madrid's contacts with the provinces, established an alliance with the CNT and Republican parties, and got in touch with anti-Franco guerrilla groups. Beginning with a May Day edition in 1943, 6 duplicated issues of *El Socialista* were produced over the next two years,[26] plus 3 issues of *Renovación* in 1944. Through the efforts of the young organizers, the cadre structure in Madrid grew by the end of 1944 to embrace some 300 militants, in addition to a women's group that included Julia Vigre, María Lacrampe, and Isabel Ponce. The Comisión Gestora Nacional may not have had sufficient authority really to lead the provincial groups but it did assist in their recovery. Using a direct delivery packet agency and personal visits to build links with provincial groups, the youth team was eventually in touch with about 27 provincial federations and more than 100 local groups. Travel was facilitated by military carnets and safe-conduct passes obtained from military sympathizers. But it was in Madrid that the Gestora's work was most effective, and with growth came structural differentiation. The Madrid Young Socialists were organized in 1943, as was a UGT team headed successively by Antonio Pérez and Gerardo Ibáñez.[27] Whereas some separation of the youth work was logical, the simultaneous relaunch of the UGT was not such a straightforward move, given that mass work was still virtually impossible. Most likely, the Socialists restored the UGT initials simply because the PCE had started issuing propaganda in the name of the union. In practice, however, this was not a major step; the UGT would only acquire a degree of real separation from the PSOE in the 1950s, with the organization

[25] Most activists who were persecuted hid for a short period, then left Spain or resumed activity, but some stayed in hiding for most of their adult lives. See R. Fraser, *In Hiding: The Life of Manuel Cortes* (London: Allen Lane, 1972), about a Socialist mayor of the 1930s who only emerged from hiding in 1969 following Franco's amnesty to civil war 'offenders'.

[26] Either 1,000 or 2,000 duplicated copies of *ES* were produced, according to the varying figures in Fernández López's two memoirs.

[27] Fernández López's memoirs, *passim*.

of a series of embryonic labour federations, yet until the early 1970s the two bodies would remain virtually identical at the level of leadership and of some provincial organizations.[28]

The young militants also showed the way when it came to alliances. Having felt betrayed in 1936 by the 'desertion' of Santiago Carrillo and other Socialist JSU leaders to the PCE, and having struggled from May 1937 to reorganize the FNJSE on an independent basis in the face of JSU hostility, they were now in no hurry to embrace the young Communists. Strategically the young Socialists could see the need for left unity. However, they felt there could be no meaningful relationship with the Communists while the PCE was persisting with its fiction about the two youth organizations still being 'unified' in the JSU, and so long as the Communists were attempting a national union with the right. Even the Civil Guard was joining the Unión Nacional, the young Socialists joked.[29] Although there were some Socialists who still identified with the JSU experience,[30] the Socialist youth leadership preferred to co-operate with the libertarians and Republicans. With them it established an Anti-Fascist Youth Alliance in 1943, a year before the adult organizations of the three partners set up the National Alliance of Democratic Forces (ANFD). This preference in no way betokened a lack of combativeness among the youth leadership. Simultaneously it established contact with the Socialist guerrillas led by José Mata in Asturias, with a short-lived group led by the *Manco de la Pesquera* in the Sierra de Cuenca, and with the guerrillas headed by the Republican Adolfo Lucas Regullón in the Toledo mountains. Mariano Redondo also had some contact with the Galician guerrillas and after a visit to Granada in

[28] UGT, History, 'UGT 1940–1972, treinta y dos años de lucha clandestina'. For focuses on the UGT see César Tcach and Carmen Reyes, *Clandestinidad y exilio: Reorganización del sindicato socialista 1939–1953* (Madrid: Editorial Pablo Iglesias, 1986); Abdón Mateos López, 'Sindicalismo socialista y movimiento obrero durante la dictadura franquista (1939–1976)', in Juliá (ed.), *El socialismo*, 191–211.

[29] Personal interviews with S. Gómez and R. Hernández. Relations with the PCE were impaired also by Socialist suspicions that the Communists were responsible for Sócrates Gómez's second arrest. In fact the betrayal was perpetrated by a police agent with a PCE carnet, according to Gómez.

[30] For example, Antonio García Duarte wanted to organize the youth in Málaga Prison on a JSU basis, so much so that when the party committee there vetoed the idea, he refused to organize it on an FNJSE basis (personal interview).

1943 he developed good relations with the Quero brothers, notwithstanding their CNT affiliation. In March 1945 Redondo and Manolo Juarranz had to flee to France to escape capture: documents supplied by them were discovered on the body of the fourth Quero after he was gunned down by the police. They left France with Rafael Robledo, the first envoy sent by the Socialists of the interior to establish a link with Toulouse.[31] A message and some propaganda sent by Arsenio Jimeno that same month was the first consignment of aid that the interior received from the exiles.[32] But by this time the PSOE had established a proper party executive in Madrid.

STRATEGIC UNITY, TACTICAL DISUNITY

Upon his release from prison in April 1944, Juan Gómez Egido, a former Madrid councillor and treasurer of the building workers' federation in the capital, decided to take charge of the PSOE. He had been appointed to its executive in 1939 and his seniority now enabled him to persuade Vicente Valls Anglés, Antonio San Miguel, Francisco de Toro, and Antonio Pérez—all experienced PSOE and UGT veterans who had occupied prominent public posts in Madrid during the 1930s—to join him on what became known as the 'first' executive committee in the interior.[1] In fact it was only the 'first' executive to be recognized by the Toulouse-based exiles, whose establishment of the title denoted considerable *émigré* influence long before the exiles' leadership took control of the whole party in 1954. At the same time a new provincial executive (including Enrique Melero and José Díaz Méndez) was created for Madrid, and the Youth leadership became structurally differentiated from the party executive. In future, the PSOE and FNJSE executive committees occasionally would meet jointly and at least one Youth representative would attend party executive meetings, but now a separate

---

[31] PSOE in Exile, *Actas* of CE, 22.3.45; UGT in Exile, *Actas* of CE, 15.3.45, 29.3.45.

[32] PSOE in Exile, Second Congress (1946), *Memoria*, 72; Fernández López's memoirs, *passim*.

[1] This new committee was formed probably over a period of time. The Fernández López memoirs variously date it June and Sept. 1944.

FNJSE executive was established. Presided over by Sócrates Gómez, it also included Mariano Redondo, Francisco Domingo, Ramón Hernández, Federico Fernández López, Mario Fernández Rico, and Ramón López Pintor. It was more genuinely independent of the PSOE than was the UGT, in spite of the fiction that Antonio Pérez was the UGT representative on the party executive.[2]

A shared adversity served to discourage a prolongation of the factional disputes of the 1930s. Aware that disunity would imperil the very existence of the party, the Socialists moved quickly to exclude anyone who tried to impose a sectarian line. Beyond any differences, the prevailing philosophy was that all were Socialists, and even Marxists in the mould of Pablo Iglesias, whose example during the early 'heroic' years they now sought to follow. Nobody, in Madrid at least,[3] discussed the respective merits of Caballero, Prieto, and Besteiro, nor defended the government of Negrín. It was not that ideological unity was restored; rather that the schisms of the past had lacked ideological depth and that the bloodshed and hardship of more recent years had formed such a terrible new enveloping reality that it had deadened all passions for factionalism.

Nor was there any controversy in Madrid regarding the alliances that the party should build. Here there was not the visceral anti-communism associated with exiles such as Luis Araquistain. Certainly a profound distrust of the PCE had persisted, fed in recent years by the signing of the Nazi-Soviet pact (which led to fights between Socialists and Communists in Franco's prisons) and by PCE attempts to attract monarchist right-wingers into their National Union.[4] In the early 1940s the great majority of Socialists were adamant that there could

---

[2] Fernández López's memoirs; Hernández, 'Conferencia'; interviews with Fernández López and Hernández. The FNJSE was represented on the CE of the PSOE at different times by Francisco Domingo, Mariano Redondo, Ramón Hernández, and Sócrates Gómez.

[3] In the Asturian mountains, however, guerrilla leaders did continue with such a discussion, without it undermining unity. Arístides Llaneza Jove argued that Prieto, the monied owner of *El Liberal* of Bilbao, was virtually a Republican, not a Socialist with any spirit of sacrifice (SOMA Archive, Box A.LIX, letter of Llaneza to José Mata Castro, 2 July 1955). *Note*: SOMA material is listed in the Bibliography at UGT, Territorial Organizations.

[4] Fernández López and S. Gómez interviews.

be no concord with those who had helped Franco to power,[5] yet in Spain they were equally aware that the left and labour movements had to be united if opposition to Franco were to be effective. Thus, when they established the National Alliance of Democratic Forces with the Republicans and libertarian CNT in mid-1944,[6] the possibility of PCE entry was considered and left open. The terms set by the PSOE for PCE admission were a declaration that the National Union was defunct, and public recognition of the demise of the Unified Young Socialists, conditions that had been satisfied by the end of 1945 when the ANFD's expansion was agreed upon, one year after the arrest of its founders.[7]

Anti-communism was the one feature of the second congress of the PSOE *émigrés* to which the Socialists of the interior objected.[8] However, left-wing unity through the broader ANFD did not last, nor did it have important practical consequences. Relations were impaired by the effects of the Cold War, which had thoroughly polarized the Spanish opposition by the late 1940s, and by allegations that the PCE had put to sectarian use money raised abroad in solidarity with the Vizcaya strike of May 1947. When the ANFD was reorganized in September 1948, the PCE was not invited to participate.[9] In the mean time far better relations developed between the other ANFD partners. Their association had its limitations, for whereas the Republicans lacked activists, the much more committed CNT continued to be afflicted by its perennial internal tensions between men of violent deeds and those of a more moderate disposition. Emotionally the Socialists were at one with many of the libertarians, and this proximity was expressed by a joint UGT-CNT manifesto issued in November 1944.[10] But even when the desire for workers' unity was at its strongest, political obstacles stood in its path. Paradoxically, in view of its prominent combative

---

[5] *ES* (Madrid), 2 (1944), 1–2.

[6] On the origins of the ANFD see Heine, *La oposición*, 244–51.

[7] *ES* (Madrid), Dec. 1945; PSOE in Exile, Second Congress (1946), *Memoria*. 77.

[8] PSOE in Exile, Assembly of Delegates of 1947, *Anejos*, 456; SOMA Archive, Box A.LIX, letter of José Mata to José Barreiro, Dec. 1945, criticizing the exiles for their opposition to a single opposition front including the PCE.

[9] *Adelante*, 1.8.48, 4.

[10] Molina, 101–3; suppl. to *Adelante*, 15.11.44; *ES*, 19.9.47, 2.

role in the guerrilla resistance of the 1940s, the CNT was to the right of the Socialists when it came to thinking about a post-Franco transition. Having suffered from State repression under the Second Republic, the CNT lacked the republican fetishism of the PSOE; long before the Socialists, the libertarians argued that the class of regime that one lived under was of less importance than the degree of effective liberty that it afforded the working class. Seeing the removal of Franco as its priority, albeit as the first step in a revolutionary process, the CNT from early on was much more amenable than the PSOE to the idea of a monarchist restoration which a plebiscite would merely legitimate (or, in theory, repudiate) after the event.[11]

Until 1948 the Socialists in general had a much stronger practical attachment to republican forms of government, as was reflected in the slogan 'Neither a referendum nor a plebiscite! Republican legality!'[12] They regarded the ANFD as an embryonic anti-fascist union and they hoped to lead it in the direction of republican goals, which for them were virtually synonymous with political democracy.[13] Although they did not reject the possibility of violent action (and indeed, on occasions a role for guerrilla warfare was recognized), the ideal scenario for the Socialists was a peaceful transition, with Franco's departure secured by some combination of a passive (as opposed to 'active') general strike, manifestations of opposition unity, guarantees that public order would be kept and no retribution exacted for right-wing crimes, and a determined Western economic boycott and political ostracism of Franco.[14] While presenting its programme as Marxist, the PSOE's analysis of fascism was in fact essentially liberal. The party regarded the Iberian regimes as incompatible with the triumphant Allies and was convinced that democratic capitalism would be impelled to move against the 'rearguard' of European fascism. To succeed Franco, the Socialists were prepared to accept a provisional government that enjoyed

[11] PSOE in Exile, *Actas* of CE, 24.1.46; Heine, *La oposición*, 246–7.
[12] *ES* (Toulouse mini-edn. for interior), Nov. 1945, 1.
[13] *ES* (Madrid), 2 (1944), 1–2.
[14] PSOE in Exile, Second Congress (1946), *Memoria*, 77–80.

public confidence and would organize local and then national elections.[15]

Contrary to the *émigré* case, the overall strategy did not create party divisions in the interior, despite significant compromises on it as Franco became stronger. Initially the Socialists refused to have any direct dealings with the monarchist right, though like their ANFD partners they made it clear to interlocutors from other parties that no obstacles would be placed by the PSOE in the way of a *golpe de estado*, so long as it was understood that free elections would be held within the following 12 months.[16] While the ANFD was in contact with monarchists, the PSOE's only direct military relations at first were with Republican officers purged at the end of the Civil War, who were now in indirect communication with the main military candidate for an anti-Franco rebellion, General Aranda.[17] There was more wishful thinking than hard calculation in the conspiracies of the mid-1940s, for by then Aranda no longer had men under his command and many of the opposition's military contacts were no longer even in uniform. However, the ANFD was too weak to undertake an offensive of its own; it could do little more than prepare for 'the moment' when the regime would fall.[18] Both the Socialists of the interior and the *émigrés* recognized that. Those active in Spain were distinctly slower to abandon the defence of republican legitimacy publicly, but eventually they shifted far more abruptly than the exiles when the need for greater compromise with the right was deemed necessary. Once the *fait accompli* of a policy of formal alliance with the monarchists had been presented to them by Prieto in 1947–8, the Socialists of the interior were quick to accept the monarchist interpretation of the Pact of St Jean-de-Luz and thus accept that a 'provisional' restoration of the monarchy

[15] May Day manifesto, *ES* (Madrid), May 1944, 1.

[16] Fernández López interview.

[17] Interview with Félix Fuentes, Miraflores de la Sierra, 6 Sept. 1982. On the military relations of the ANFD see Heine, *La oposición*, 351–68. On Aranda see Antonio Marquina Barrio, 'Conspiración contra Franco', *Historia 16*, 72 (1982), 15–30. The *Actas* of the PSOE in Exile, 26.5.49, show that the *émigré* leaders saw the Socialist-monarchist pact as involving Socialist activity to isolate the regime, then monarchist moves to oust Franco.

[18] *ES* (Madrid), 2 (1944), 1.

should precede any plebiscite on Spain's future regime.[19] By this time the PSOE had lost its first two executive committees through police action in Madrid and the opposition in general was much weaker than two years earlier. Not only the PSOE but the whole ANFD, when briefly refloated in 1948, became more moderate, unequivocally ruling out violent methods whereas four years earlier the party had retained an option on armed struggle. The new emphasis was upon the need to cultivate a 'climate of tolerance' and 'national concord'. The ANFD, originally designed as a broad republican anti-fascist alliance, now tried to accommodate the sensibilities of Western Liberals by calling for 'Neither Franco nor Communism! Democracy!'[20]

To this extent, the Socialists in Spain were united; not so when it came to tactics. Organizational separation of the PSOE and FNJSE aggravated generational tensions which found expression in tactical disagreements. The veterans now responsible for the party were far more cautious spirits than the Young Socialists who had supported Caballero, though some of the old guard had been Caballeristas too. Permanently distrustful of youth following the JSU episode and loath to take further risks after several years of incarceration, the old men put a brake on some of the activities that the preceding youth team had struggled to make possible. Complaints were made about the Youth once again beginning to act as a party within a party.[21] Since most of the Socialist propaganda apparatus was in FNJSE hands and most of the articles were written by young militants, the conflict took the form of the party executive curbing the appearance of *El Socialista* and *Renovación*. Taking their aspiration for a diplomatic solution involving the Western democracies to its logical conclusion, the veterans strove to suppress anything that might resurrect the spectre of the 'red threat' in Allied eyes. Thus the content of propaganda became a contentious issue, as did its financing. Notwithstanding their illusions concerning the West, the veterans feared that the younger activists had jeopardized the

---

[19] See the *memorias* for the congresses and assemblies of the PSOE in Exile, 1949–52. The ANFD endorsed the pact (*ES*, 30.9.48, 1).
[20] Cf. *El Socialista: En un lugar de España*, Dec. 1945; *Adelante*, 1.8.48, 4.
[21] Hernández, 'Conferencia', 8.

ethical standing of the PSOE through their dealings with the British Embassy; they had placed the party at the service of British Intelligence. This was a charge that the Young Socialists could not entirely refute, but they were quick to defend their pragmatic collaboration on the grounds that, in the absence of external socialist aid, it was the only means of acquiring the necessary propaganda equipment.[22]

In the minds of the FNJSE leaders, the veterans were not doing enough to organize the party and develop a cadre of activists. To them the old men seemed too content to live off political capital accumulated in the past, and to spend their time conspiring and appending the PSOE-UGT initials to anti-Franco documents. A more sacrificial style of leadership was seen by the Youth as the only approach whereby the party could recover for itself a leading role in workers' struggles. The Youth executive shared the gradualist perspective that the veterans held of the anti-Franco struggle, but while the party leaders adopted an *ad hoc* approach to party activity the Youth leaders demanded a proper plan of activity, with clear objectives and proper co-ordination.[23] Moreover, there was generational tension with regard to violence. While accepting that Franco could not be deposed by popular insurrection, the Young Socialists none the less were keen to experiment with guerrilla action, and maintained that this would provide Allied governments with a justification to move against Franco. The logic behind this thinking was dubious, yet the FNJSE endorsement of armed action at least betokened a combative spirit. And not only did the Youth establish contact with the main Socialist guerrilla units outside the capital; it also took steps to organize 'city Maquis groups' in Madrid, inspired by the news that the guerrillas who had infiltrated Spain from France in late 1944 had left behind arms caches in Pamplona and other places before retreating. Several such groups were

---

[22] Details of the PSOE-FNJSE dispute come from ibid. 5–10, the Fernández López memoirs, and interviews with Hernández and Fernández López. When interviewed, S. Gómez did not recall the dispute. He may have been unaware of it because of imprisonment and the fact that police vigilance at his home often prevented him from attending meetings. At times, the dispute was bitter: on one occasion Mariano Redondo pulled out a pistol (Hernández interview).

[23] Hernández and Fernández López interviews.

being organized when the party leadership stepped in to veto the plan.[24]

The Socialist Party's shunning of armed struggle was entirely in line with its long-standing values of humanism and serenity. Socialist guerrilla activity existed in several parts of Spain, but nowhere was it the result of a PSOE executive decision. In Asturias it came about in October 1937 when, with the fall of the province to Franco, several thousand republican fighters took to the mountains both to survive and to oblige the enemy to maintain a substantial rearguard. The numbers greatly declined in 1939 and in January of that year there was the first of several attempts to evacuate guerrillas: 800 attempted to get out by sea, only to suffer 57 losses in unexpected clashes with the enemy.[25] The Socialists had an early preponderance in the Asturian guerrilla movement, but for several years they struggled alongside PCE and CNT *resistentes* without any sectarian trouble. Initially they all rejected the Nazi-Soviet Pact and only from about 1943, according to the main Socialist account, did the Communists there start to defend their own party line, relayed to them by PCE envoys arriving from France.[26] In September 1939 the Asturian Socialist leaders Mata and Flórez raided the San Vicente mine, which had been owned by the miners' union until confiscated by Franco. There were other raids, too, occasional 'acts of justice' against officials responsible for atrocities,[27] and successful extortion demands that brought in revenue from local mayors and army officers. Kidnappings were abandoned after they claimed their first innocent victim. Bullets were purchased indirectly from hungry members of the Civil Guard. But from its origins in 1937 until October 1948 when a boat chartered by Indalecio Prieto brought 26 Socialist guerrillas plus one CNT and two Communist fighters

[24] Fernández López, 'Apuntes', 6–7.
[25] Eduardo Pons Prades, *Guerrillas españolas 1936–1960* (Barcelona: Planeta, 1977), 178.
[26] José Mata, 'De la resistencia en Asturias', n.d.
[27] Juan Falechosa Vázquez was assassinated on 9 May 1948 for his part in the Pozu Funeres massacre, but other Socialists 'disappeared' as a result: PSOE in Exile, Assembly of Delegates of 1949, *Memoria*, 33–7; letter of CE of Federación Socialista Asturiana to CE of PSOE in Exile, 13 Aug. 1948.

out via Luanco, the struggle in Asturias was essentially defensive.[28]

The same is true of the León guerrilla movement, some of whose Socialist members (like *comandante* César Ríos) had come from their Asturian homeland in 1942 to develop links, and later would leave Spain with Mata's men. The 'Guerrilla Federation of León and Galicia' was created that year and is a further example of unofficial Socialist collaboration with other anti-Franco forces including PCE guerrillas. It was formed before the creation of the National Union's so-called Supreme Council (JSUN) and subsequently backed the Union in the interests of national co-ordination and to appear to form part of a viable rebel army. In 1945, however, a guerrilla congress voted to disaffiliate the federation from UNE after the PSOE's non-involvement nationally had become known. When the federation proclaimed its support for the ANFD in 1946, this produced a regional Communist-Socialist rift.[29]

As in Madrid, militants in León worked with the British in order to obtain resources. César Ríos was a personal friend of a road engineer named David Easton whose farm in the province had been requisitioned by fascists in 1936. It was Easton who provided the federation with its first typewriter and duplicator, which it employed to produce *El Guerrillero* from 1943. He also brought the guerrillas a radio, introduced them to a JSUN contact, and acted as a messenger using the protection afforded by a job as courier between Britain's consulates in the north-west of Spain. In turn the guerrillas organized an escape line for unfortunate Allied pilots and prisoners of war.[30]

This Socialist guerrilla involvement was on a fairly small scale. After 1939 Mata at times had as few as 15 men with

---

[28] 'We never thought we were going to defeat an army', Mata explained later (Pons Prades, 181). When the Comité Nacional of the PSOE met in Sept. 1945 it praised the guerrillas but recommended that they remain on the defensive, conserving their ammunition and just operating enough to survive (PSOE in Exile, Second Congress, *Memoria*, 82). For general sources see 'José Mata' memoir; Mata, 'De la resistencia'; *Cambio 16* (Madrid), 8.11.76, 26.12.76; *Cuadernos para el Diálogo*, 183 (1976); PSOE, Territorial Organizations, *Circular* 15 of the Federación Socialista Asturiana, Nov. 1948. The Communist Party also abandoned guerrilla warfare in 1948.

[29] The main sources on the León guerrilla group are the papers of César Ríos, and Heine, *A guerrilla antifranquista en Galicia* (Vigo: Xerais de Galicia, 1982).

[30] Heine (*A guerrilla*, 47) suggests that Easton was an agent of British Intelligence.

him in the Asturian mountains, though on occasions the number swelled to 100; in León province, following a reorganization in 1944, Ríos commanded about 40 guerrillas, plus sympathizers.[31] An escalation of repression in Asturias and the proven futility of armed resistance in each place led to guerrilla evacuations in 1947–8. A year later, consulted about whether a group of Socialists should stay any longer with Communist guerrillas in the Sierra Pandilla, the *émigré* executive in Toulouse told the last contingent to leave.[32] Though the Asturian fighters described themselves as 'soldiers of the Party', none of the Socialist guerrillas received any material aid from the PSOE in exile or in Madrid; and much of the money levied by the Asturian guerrillas went not into the means of warfare but to the relief of Socialist prisoners and their families.[33] Occasionally, party leaders would cite the Asturian guerrillas (though not the others) as an example of heroism and sacrifice, to raise morale; simultaneously, with Prieto in the forefront, they were seeking ways of ending guerrilla warfare as soon as they possibly could.

Apart from humanitarian considerations and fears about alienating potential allies to their right, the Socialists' attitudes to guerrilla warfare were informed by the sheer futility of it. There seemed little prospect of moving from armed resistance and self-defence to a situation where the resisters would be able to seize the initiative. By 1948 Franco had some 900,000 men under arms, more than two-thirds of them in his army.[34] Pitted against them, the various communist, libertarian, and socialist guerrillas found it well nigh impossible to recruit as their casualties mounted; mostly they were former Civil War participants who, once gone, could not be replaced. Of course, no military odds in themselves rule out the possibility of guerrilla success; what made these count so much in the Spain of the 1940s was the exhaustion of the civilian population, denying as it did a combative periphery and recruitment prospects to the guerrilla forces. There was also some truth in

[31] Pons Prades, 184; Heine, *A guerrilla*, 109–10.
[32] PSOE in Exile, *Actas* of CE, 18.5.49.
[33] SOMA Archive, Box A.LIX, letter of Mata to Barreiro, Dec. 1945; Mata, 'De la resistencia'.
[34] *ES* (26.12.47, 1) gives the following numbers: Army, 670,000; Air Force and Navy, 30,000; Guardia Civil and Policia Armada, 200,000.

the lament of Young Socialists languishing in Alicante prison: 'Spanish fascism has inoculated unconscious youth with the bellicose nationalist virus that serves as a defence of capitalist interests.'[35] By now socialization under Francoism was having an effect, though perhaps it was less crucial than the political constraint imposed by the desperate economic hardship, which made the loss of a job potentially fatal.[36]

Rather than being healed by compromise, the tactical rift between the party and its youth section was overtaken by arrests early in 1945.[37] After this the FNJSE, already depleted by its JSU and Civil War losses, found it extremely difficult to find new organizers and to recruit among the young generation of the 1940s. In 1947, when the youth organization was destroyed by further arrests, any possibility of a Madrid-based PSOE executive employing more energetic or violent tactics disappeared. Later on, party accounts of the clandestine period would recall party victims of Francoism while ignoring those who held a more combative attitude. They would remember the 22 Asturian Socialists who were detained and tortured and later thrown down a mine-shaft called Pozu Funeres, where they were finished off with petrol and dynamite in 1948.[38] They would pay tribute also to Tomás Centeno, the PSOE president who died under police interrogation in 1953, and to men such as Emilio Salgado, Eduardo Villegas, and Ramón Rubial who spent long years in prison.[39] But references to socialist involvement in guerrilla activity would be restricted to the Asturian example, and men of action such as Antonio Amat would be mentioned but rarely. Moreover, Socialists who put up armed resistance when cornered by the regime's forces would be totally forgotten: members such as Antonio Donoso, who exacted a high price for his life when the police raided his home

---

[35] *Renovación* (Alicante prison edn.), 16.2.46, 4.

[36] Max Gallo, *Spain Under Franco* (London: Allen and Unwin, 1973), 169–70.

[37] Hernández, 'Conferencia', 10–11.

[38] On this see Saborit, *Asturias*, 233–7; *Adelante*, 1.10.48, 1.

[39] At his trial Villegas had the courage to turn to the public and salute the widow of executed party president José Gómez Osorio. Later he used the prolonged hunger strike as a form of political protest. See PSOE in Exile, Third Congress (1948), *Actas*, 13; *ES*, 17.7.58, 1.

containing the PSOE propaganda apparatus for Madrid, and Andalusian veterans Antonio Recio and José Pérez.[40]

This was no oversight: the PSOE had always shied away from the image of the gunman, which it associated with the anarchist *pistolero* or *vengador*. The Socialists identified more with the persecuted than with fighters; they venerated the martyr, not the avenger. Their preference was for peaceful collective action, and even when that was not possible, with their enemy at its most brutal, the Socialists still attempted to set an example of morality, civility, and humanity. At the same time, the cautionary attitude against fruitless sacrifice of human life was of course a sign that old men were in charge of the party. So too was the pronounced sentimentalism that characterized the party in Spain, seen in its annual ritual of commemorating the death of Iglesias by depositing flowers on his tomb in Madrid's Civil Cemetery.[41] In his final letters written just hours before he was executed in February 1940, Ricardo Zabalza instructed his wife to annually adorn the tomb in this fashion, while to his son Abel he wrote urging that he honour his father's memory, not by seeking vengeance, but by holding high the torch of liberty.[42]

The Socialists' early characterization of Francoism as Spanish fascism also encouraged a certain fatalism and lack of activity that was seen clearly by the late 1940s. The disappointing stance adopted by the United Nations in December 1946 strengthened the theoretical argument in favour of a new opposition strategy being tested, but by sowing demoralization the UN vote simultaneously deprived the PSOE and the opposition in general of sufficient public backing to challenge Franco inside Spain with any prospect of short-term success. Once the wafer-thin chance of a diplomatic solution had passed, all that most Socialist veterans could offer was a defence of party traditions and ideas for future generations to inherit, an attitude that left them unreceptive to new developments in socialist thought. Many of them turned inwards, making the welfare of their families a

---

[40] *ES*, 23.6.45, 2; Fernández López, 'Apunte histórico', 13–14; *Boletín de la UGT*, Dec. 1949, Apr. 1950.

[41] e.g., see *Boletín de la UGT*, Jan. 1947.

[42] See Llopis's speech, *Adelante*, 15.7.45, 2.

central concern and reducing political activity to periodic conversations with old and trusted comrades and the occasional passing on of propaganda to fellow Socialists. Sustained efforts to build and extend the party organization were restricted largely to the north of the country. In Madrid, Andalucía, and elsewhere, concern with self-preservation, one's family, and one's job ruled out hazardous activity for most Socialists.

This was perfectly natural in the appalling conditions in which the Socialists found themselves. They were extremely isolated, and so many veterans had already been in prison and thus were known to the police. Yet such attitudes were bound to create problems later, from the late 1950s, when a new working class began to take action while in vast areas of Spain the PSOE and UGT remained invisible. Perhaps the PSOE, so hidebound by tradition, was rather too ready to dismiss the possibility of encouraging a judicious use of direct action in combination with the resurgence of mass opposition. One feature of modern Spanish history that the PSOE ignored was the manner in which major defeats of strikes and revolts, when marked by heroic resistance to authority, had been transformed into moral victories that had helped the left to advance.[43] Even those Socialists who considered the Asturian insurrection of 1934 to have been a mistake, with the benefit of hindsight recognized that it had revived the PSOE's prestige among the working class after it had suffered as a result of governmental collaboration with Republicans in 1931–3.[44] Clearly nothing on that scale could be contemplated during the early years of Francoism, but even modest forms of direct action would at least have publicized the clandestine presence of the party. As it was, the PSOE in most parts of Spain became highly introverted, when not moribund, for a period of two whole decades.

THE QUASI-CLANDESTINE ORGANIZATION

Survival and the capacity to struggle in Franco's Spain demanded that the Socialists adopt far greater security

---

[43] Brenan, 221.   [44] Barreiro, quoted in Saborit, *Asturias*, 228–9.

measures than they had known at any time in their history. Yet though the outlawed activists took precautions and reorganized the party to make it cellular, the PSOE in the interior was never truly clandestine. Many activists adopted *noms de guerre* and letters from Madrid to Toulouse occasionally bore the signature 'men without names',[1] but the truth is that none of the leading figures were totally unknown to the authorities, even if their precise roles were unclear. Men such as Gómez Egido, Eduardo Villegas, Antonio Trigo, Emilio Salgado, Sócrates Gómez, and Tomás Centeno Sierra occupied key positions in the underground organization almost immediately after their release from prisons where they had spent years paying for political prominence in the 1930s. They were therefore subject to periodic surveillance and were hardly ideal candidates for their new roles. Under other circumstances, far from being entrusted with the fortunes of a party, such men would have been given a wide berth by their former comrades; they would have been regarded as *quemados*, as individuals disqualified from playing leading roles precisely because they were known to the police. But for the PSOE at this time there was no apparent alternative.

For one thing, the party was undergoing a grave generational crisis following its telling losses, both political and mortal, during the Civil War. At the same time, virtually no new people were being recruited to the organization. While ordinary citizens were all too aware of the dreadful consequences of enrolling in opposition forces, the PSOE itself was fearful of infiltration; only briefly, at the end of 1945, did it begin to consider expanding beyond its basic cadre. After the early rounds of arrests virtually no young militants emerged to offer themselves for national responsibilities. By 1947 the youth federation had collapsed everywhere apart from the Basque Country. Experienced party leaders recently released from prison had great limitations as organizers of anything clandestine, but at least they had demonstrated great loyalty to the party and now trustworthiness was at a premium. It was these Socialists who, out of a sense of duty, agreed to take responsibility for a party that, anyway, had traditionally

[1] *ES*, 27.1.49, 1–3.

regarded experience and maturity as the most essential qualities of its leaders.

A preference for staying out of prison, moral objections to violence, and a typical PSOE concern with preserving the party organization in the hope of being able to use it to influence future events when circumstances became more propitious—all these factors made the party hyper-cautious in the late 1940s, and they possibly explain why the Socialists suffered rather fewer upsets than the PCE and CNT during that decade. Yet even the prudent Socialists could not build an impregnable structure. Over a period of eight years, from 1945 to 1953, the party suffered the destruction through police action of six executive committees based in Madrid, these being headed successively by Juan Gómez Egido, Eduardo Villegas, Miguel Angel Martínez, Antonio Trigo Mairal, Antonio Hernández Vizcaíno, and Tomás Centeno Sierra.[2] In theory, infiltrated police agents such as Luis Alfaro[3] were unlikely to do much damage so long as they remained outside the executive, for the provincial structures of the party were subdivided into cells of four or five militants, only one of whom would be in touch with delegates from other cells. But there could not be absolute 'compartmentalization': all parts of the classical pyramidal structure of the clandestine organization had to be linked at least minimally. Thus a local arrest followed by a chain of interrogation and further arrests could in the end lead to the fall of an executive. None the less, the PSOE was compartmentalized to a fair degree; indeed, in the case of Centeno's downfall in February 1953, it is thought that members of the Madrid provincial organization, which suffered the initial raids, might well have been able to forewarn the party president of his betrayal and impending capture if only they had been able to discover his identity.[4] Moreover, during long periods of time the apex and base of the PSOE pyramid were disconnected by force of circumstance; this undermined the party's effectiveness but enhanced its

---

[2] See Appendix C below.

[3] Fernando Jáuregui and Pedro Vega, *Crónica del antifranquismo*, 3 vols. (Barcelona: Argos Vergara, 1983–4), i. 35.

[4] Interview with Máximo Rodríguez, member of the Centeno CE, Madrid, 28 July 1982.

chances of survival. Only very rarely in the early years was there a meeting of the Comité Nacional (CN, the committee formed by the direct representatives of the provincial organizations and which in theory controlled the party executive, the Comisión Ejecutiva). There was no meeting between 1939 and 16 September 1945, when delegates from 40 provinces met to discuss, among other matters, relations with the PCE.[5] The CN met again on 18 April 1946, this time in a Protestant church, to ratify the composition of the renovated party executive and the PCE's entry into the ANFD, but then seven years elapsed before sufficient national co-ordination was restored for it to meet again.[6]

How then did the damaging *caídas* (downfalls) of executives come about? In two cases (Gómez Egido and Trigo), disaster approached via PSOE allies. When police raided the home of Republican leader Régulo Martínez in December 1944, they found the unexpected gift of an original copy of the ANFD founding document complete with signatures; and in July 1949 Trigo's arrest was a sequel to the interrogation of CNT ally Antonio Castaños, general secretary of his organization's sixteenth National Committee to be formed since 1939.[7] An element of carelessness, and perhaps too a bureaucratic compulsion formally to commit party matters to paper, was evident in the first case and again in that of the Vizcaíno executive, whose downfall followed the arrest in March 1952 of party envoy Patricio Cruz while in possession of lists naming national and provincial leaders.[8] Meanwhile, Villegas was a victim of the duplicity of a false ally working at the US

---

[5] *ES*, 30.10.45, 1; PSOE in Exile, Second Congress (1946), *Memoria*, 76.

[6] Luis Fernández, interview by Carlos Cruz, on the meeting in 1946. The next meeting was mentioned in the *Actas* of the CE of the PSOE in Exile, 27.7.53. Several months later (ibid., 17.2.54) José María Fernández claimed to have held a CN meeting at which Galicia, Andalucía, Aragón, and Extremadura were represented. No such federations functioned in 1954, though four men from these regions, by then resident in Madrid, may have met with Fernández and encouraged him to continue acting as provisional general secretary of the PSOE and UGT.

[7] Hernández, 'Conferencia', 9; Molina, 247–8; PSOE in Exile, *Circular*, Aug. 1949.

[8] Llopis to 'Guridi', 28 June 1954. *Note*: Except where otherwise indicated, the correspondence of Antonio Amat ('Guridi') is all to be found in PSOE, Correspondence, 'Guridi' file.

Embassy in Madrid, who betrayed him after promising help with propaganda and a diplomatic car to transport the PSOE president to the northern frontier, *en route* to the second congress of the PSOE in Exile. The car was stopped by police on the outskirts of the capital and its passenger, who had already made two trips to Toulouse, was arrested back in the city. He was not to regain his freedom until the end of 1960.[9]

Behind the *caídas* there was also an important element of human frailty which led many detainees to impart information and a few to collaborate actively with the police. Whatever their political hue, most detainees told the police something: if beatings or torture did not break their resistance, the threat of violence to their loved ones occasionally did. Often a war of wits would ensue, with the prisoner seeking to leave the interrogator satisfied with relatively trivial information, and perhaps to mislead him as to the party's structure and the status of different activists.[10] Even after the official executions of Socialists had ceased around 1943, a failure to satisfy interrogators could still prove fatal, as the death in police custody of Centeno illustrated in 1953. Very few Socialists fully co-operated with their captors, yet those few sufficed to wreak terrible destruction. Most damaging of all was the defection of Miguel Angel Martínez who, after being arrested in 1946, was released by the authorities to serve as their eyes and ears observing PSOE and ANFD activity. He seems to have managed to take in the succeeding party president Antonio Trigo and other activists in Madrid, where two provincial committees fell as a result in the late 1940s.[11] Another sad memory for the PSOE concerns the executive member Rafael González Gil. Following his arrest early in 1953, his collaboration helped bring about the police capture of members of the Madrid committee, several organizers of

---

[9] Luis Fernández, interview by C. Cruz; Heine, *La oposición*, 360; Jáuregui and Vega, i. 35–7; PSOE in Exile, Fifth Congress (1952), *Actas*, 45.

[10] Personal interview with F. Fernández López.

[11] F. Almendros Morcillo *et al.*, *El sindicalismo de clase en España (1939–1977)* (Barcelona: Península, 1978), 125–6; Heine, *La oposición*, 360–1; Fernández López, 'Apunte histórico', 15; *ES* (Mexico), Nov. 1948, 3; 'Piriri' to Llopis, Jan. 1962; Vigre, Ponce, and Lacrampe interviews. It was Martínez who presented the *émigré* leaders with the interior's view on the establishment of the Llopis government-in-exile (PSOE in Exile, Fourth Congress (1950), *Actas* 110).

an embryonic national rail union, and Centeno himself.[12]

A breach of security at the top or the arrest of an *enlace* (a courier linking interior and exterior, Madrid and the provinces) could cause not only the downfall of a national executive but also that of the Madrid committee and several other provincial committees. And just as damaging as the return of Socialists to prison was the widespread distrust that such events sowed. Very quickly a psychosis typical of clandestine movements developed, with provincial activists beginning to mistrust Madrid executives and any leader fortunate enough to evade arrest in police raids immediately being suspected of betraying the latest victims.[13] Since national executives scarcely managed to help the provincial federations before they fell themselves, various provincial groups (especially in Asturias) began to consider that links with Madrid only brought them danger. Viewed from the provinces, such links meant less anonymity, less security, and no material advantage. It was probably true then, as Llopis claimed, that there was some support inside Spain for the idea of the *émigré* executive taking control of the whole party, as occurred in April 1954.[14] However, as exile leaders had recognized earlier when ignoring points of view dispatched from Spain, there was absolutely no way of Toulouse knowing which views were representative of activists in the interior. The verdict on them was given invariably by the general secretary himself.

Rodolfo Llopis always invoked security reasons for limiting the information made available to other members of his Toulouse-based party executive. However, it is known that just two communications from Spain formed the immediate pretext in 1954 for Toulouse disavowing putative new national executive committees that were announced in Madrid following

---

[12] Interview with M. Rodríguez; Jáuregui and Vega, i. 147–50; UGT in Exile, *Actas* of CE, 24.4.54.

[13] See Llopis's speech, *ES*, 18–25.8.55, 3–4.

[14] Ibid., where Llopis refers to a letter from the interior dated 8 Apr. 1954 which said there was no need for two CEs; it was all the same if the CE were based in 'Madrid, Aranjuez, or London', so long as it exercised control over the whole organization. At the CE of the PSOE in Exile meeting on 12 Sept. 1951 (*Actas*), Trigo said the interior recognized that effective leadership was now based abroad. The message of the interior to the party congress of 1952 recognized that the *émigrés* were by then the main body of the party (PSOE in Exile, *Actas* of CE, 12.8.52).

the death of Centeno.[15] These included a report from Antonio Amat, who since 1952 had been entrusted by the exiles with clandestine missions in the interior. The real motives behind the transfer of control were probably threefold.

First, there was an undeniable need to restore order and improve security in the Spanish section of the party. Amidst the general confusion that had accompanied the discovery of Hernández Vizcaíno's executive early in 1952, two new leaderships had been formed simultaneously. Differing in their attitudes towards a restoration of the monarchy and the spending of party funds, one was selected by party veteran and lifelong Prieto admirer Teodomiro Menéndez, while the other was organized by the survivors of the preceding executive, Tomás Centeno and Máximo Rodríguez.[16] The downfall of the Centeno executive (the party's sixth in the interior) a year later did not simplify matters, for José María Fernández quickly established an executive that disputed its rival's authority. Menéndez, whose life had been spared in 1939 in recognition of his role five years earlier in saving right-wingers from revolutionary violence in Asturias, was by now well into his seventies.[17] He was still strong enough to organize relief aid for prisoners and their families but was hardly the man to rebuild a clandestine party, and in fact he favoured direction from Toulouse. No greater confidence was inspired by Fernández, who claimed to be in touch with various party federations that Amat later found to be fictitious.[18] Neither man sent proper reports on his activity to Toulouse, and the letters from Menéndez contained little more than gossip and offensive references to other Socialists.[19] Since neither of these executives was attempting to reorganize the party, there

[15] At this time Teodomiro Menéndez urged the exiles to take control of the party, and the decision was taken after *émigré* leaders heard a report by Amat on his visits to Madrid, Barcelona, and the Basque Country. See UGT in Exile, *Actas* of CE, 23.4.54; PSOE in Exile, *Actas* of CE, 21–2.4.54.

[16] Initially this took the form of the party's Madrid provincial committee refusing to recognize the Madrid-based CE (C. Martínez Parera interview, 12 Nov. 1981), but it seems that very quickly the former committee also began to present itself as a CE (PSOE in Exile, *Actas* of CE, 30.12.52).

[17] On Menéndez see Saborit, *Asturias*, 99–118; the obituary in *ES(H)*, 1.9.78, 5.

[18] UGT, *Actas* of CE, 23.4.54; 'Guridi' to CE, 13.2.54, 10.10.54.

[19] UGT, *Actas* of CE, 16.7.54, 3.9.54; PSOE, Correspondence, 'Piriri' file; CE to 'Guridi', 18.3.54.

was a strong argument for making Toulouse the centre of party activity, linked directly with the various provincial federations.

Just as persuasive, at least in Toulouse, was the second argument, that with six party executives having fallen and the opposition now virtually crushed in Spain, a transfer of control to the *émigré* executive was essential to guarantee survival. The party inside Spain had declined far more rapidly than had the PSOE in Exile, and at least since the late 1940s the exiles had formed a majority of active party members. *Emigré* acceptance of the principle that those who took the risks should lead soon became conditional upon the rider that leaders should seek to reflect the views of the whole party, both in and out of Spain; then, in 1952–4, there arose a growing questioning of just how representative the executive committees in the interior were.[20]

However, this questioning was linked to a third and most important reason why the exiles wanted to take charge of the PSOE: to restore cohesion to its political line. Since 1948 interior and exterior had disagreed over the potential of the Pact of St Jean-de-Luz.[21] Executives in Madrid had tended to interpret it as meaning that a plebiscite on Spain's future regime would be held following a provisional restoration of the monarchy. For them, the democratic logic behind the *émigré* formula of neither republic nor monarchy until the people themselves could pronounce was impeccable but impractical. Therefore the negotiations conducted by Prieto and Trifón Gómez in the Socialist-monarchist steering committee that met abroad were undermined by the Madrid-based Socialists' participation in a Co-ordinating Committee of the Interior (CIC). While formally declaring its support for the pact, the CIC spent its time urging Don Juan to make a bid for power.

In these circumstances, relations between Socialist leaders in Madrid and Toulouse declined so drastically that from mid-1949 there were eight months during which long breaks in

[20] For example, Prieto in 1946 was urging support for the interior, even when comrades there were deemed by *émigrés* to be making mistakes (*Adelante*, 15.11.46, 3); but by 1952 he was casting doubt in public as to how representative the Madrid-based party executive was (*ES*, 10.7.52, 2–3).

[21] PSOE in Exile, Fourth Congress (1950), *Memoria*, ch. 3.

communication, along with dissimulation and mistrust, almost split the PSOE. *Emigré* doubts about the representativeness of the Madrid executives appeared to be substantiated early in 1950. On that occasion, just a few arrests and a partial renovation of the party executive committee brought the interior back into line with the Toulouse way of thinking.[22] However, this was not to last, and a readiness to go along with monarchist manœuvres persisted in the interior. Rather than become committed constitutional monarchists, the Socialists of the interior tended towards *accidentalismo*: that is, they regarded the type of regime as no longer paramount, and encouraged any move that might undermine Franco and permit a return to legal or semi-legal forms of activity. A second reconciliation between interior and exterior was reached at the fifth congress of the PSOE in Exile (1952), at which the interior dropped its acceptance of monarchist restoration and the *émigrés* their a priori pledge to campaign on behalf of a republic in the event of a plebiscite.[23] Yet throughout the 1950s the interior remained decidedly more open than did the exiles to the monarchist option, even in the case of militant students belonging to the Agrupación Socialista Universitaria.

Admittedly, this third motive is a matter of conjecture, but it is strongly suggested both by the background to the transfer of control and by the manner in which it took place. Although the attendance of José María Fernández at an executive meeting in Toulouse on 24 April 1954 was expected, the executive committees of the PSOE and UGT in Exile decided to assume control of the interior at meetings on 21–2 April, rather than wait to consult him. Moreover, the minutes indicate that firm decisions were taken at the earlier meetings although the participants were well aware that a meeting of the *émigrés*' Comité Nacional, statutorily the PSOE's highest authority in between congresses, was scheduled for 24–5 April.[24] This meeting duly endorsed the transfer after hearing a report

[22] Prieto speech at PSOE in Exile, Fifth Congress (1952), *Actas*, 120.

[23] Ibid. *passim*. Reconciliation between interior and exiles was helped in the early 1950s by the destruction of the CIC (presided over by Aranda) through police action (*ES*, 27.2.58, p. 2).

[24] UGT in Exile, *Actas* of CE, 12.2.54, 24.4.54; PSOE in Exile, *Actas* of CE, 21–2.4.54.

by Llopis on the state of the party in Spain.[25] Following his mentor Prieto, the general secretary had now mastered the art of the *fait accompli*.

This move underlined the fact that there was no effective structural difference between the PSOE and UGT in the interior:[26] basically it was still a single organization whose leadership was transferred abroad. Regardless of whether leaders in Madrid had been putting out propaganda in the name of the PSOE or UGT, it was the same people who had been trying to reorganize the party and establish a few embryonic UGT federations—such as the national rail union, whose activists fell with Centeno. Certainly by this time the clandestine structure was extremely weak and its voice incoherent. Apart from the internal divisions, there were still a considerable number of Socialists in prison—some 400 members, according to figures received by the *émigré* UGT executive in 1953.[27] The transfer of leadership to Toulouse made the executive more politically as well as geographically remote from Spain, but at least it ensured a continuity and direction that had been lacking. Moreover, the exiles deserve some credit for certain initiatives in the 1950s that were designed to enable the PSOE to compete more effectively with the PCE for influence. With its leadership based in Prague from 1950, the Communist Party had a far superior 'apparatus' to that of the PSOE. Regular radio propaganda beamed into Spain from abroad, more expensively-produced printed propaganda, full-time party organizers in Spain—these were the great advantages enjoyed by the PCE.[28] The Communists were also to benefit from the West's partial rehabilitation of Franco during the 1950s and the regime's propensity to characterize diverse opposition activists and activities, including those of the PSOE, as communist.[29]

---

[25] PSOE, Assemblies, *Actas* of CN, 24–5.4.54, 12–14.

[26] See the speech by 'Rafael' (Antonio Pérez) at the PSOE in Exile, Second Congress (1946), *Actas*, 107–11.

[27] UGT in Exile, *Actas* of CE, 13.11.53. Earlier, the *Memoria* presented to the PSOE Assembly of Delegates in May 1949 had put the number at thousands of prisoners, including 1,223 in Burgos alone (p. 33), but that estimate may have been on the high side or, more likely, it may have been dated by the time it was published.

[28] Alba, *Communist Party*, 327–8. For a dissenting view see Borrás, 105.

[29] Lacrampe, Ponce, and Vigre interviews. One exception was the Centeno case,

Commencing in 1944, the PSOE *émigrés* made repeated efforts to arrange for broadcasts to Spain from a West European State, only to encounter insurmountable official obstacles. However, in 1953 prospects improved as a result of a thaw in PSOE-Yugoslav relations. Back in 1948 the Socialist press had styled Tito the 'communist dictator of Yugoslavia', a 'vengeful, cruel, fanatical, intolerant nationalist' heading an 'abominable' regime.[30] Since then, though, Belgrade's political distance from Moscow had increased, as had the Yugoslav need for new allies. Thus Llopis was invited to a meal hosted by the Yugoslav ambassador in Paris; not long afterwards, he was on a flight to Belgrade accompanied by Martínez Dasi. The two men returned home well pleased by their free visit which included a meeting with Tito that lasted over an hour.[31] While Trifón Gómez saw the new link as repugnant, given the restrictions on social democratic activity in Yugoslavia, the majority of his colleagues now recalled the role of Tito and other Yugoslavs as internationalist volunteers in the Spanish Civil War; they also pointed to Yugoslavia's determined opposition to Franco in the United Nations, and claimed that the new link would tend to encourage democratic experimentation in Yugoslavia.[32] The visit resulted in the broadcasting in Spanish from Belgrade of propaganda material supplied by the PSOE, which in 1955 set up a specialized Office for Information, Documentation, and Studies (OIDE), originally staffed by Martínez Dasi. However, the romance with the Yugoslavs was brief: by 1956 Belgrade radio was using little of the material supplied by OIDE; Yugoslavia had voted for Spain's entry into the UN and had softened its anti-Franco line, ostensibly in the interests of peaceful coexistence.[33]

when the official press described the detainees as 'a gang of outlaws, swindlers, and forgers' (*Arriba*, 28.2.53).

[30] *ES*, 1.7.48, 8.7.48.

[31] PSOE in Exile, *Actas* of CE, 5.8.53, 30.9.53, 18.11.53; PSOE, Sixth Congress held in exile (1955), *Memoria*, ch. 3.

[32] PSOE in Exile, *Circular*, Oct. 1953; id., Assemblies, *Actas* of CN of PSOE, 24–5.4.54, 10–11; Prieto speech in *ES*, 12.5.55, 3–4; PSOE, *Actas* of CE, 27.6.55.

[33] PSOE, *Actas* of CE, 13.9.55; *Actas* of CD, 7.8.56, 15. The PCE benefited from much greater radio support. According to Welles (p. 215) in 1960–1 the Communist bloc broadcast a total of 116 hours per week to Spain, including 53½ hours from the Prague-based *Radio España Independiente*, the voice of the exiled PCE.

The main enduring hope of external aid now lay with the PSOE-UGT's labour allies in the ICFTU. Fearing that the PCE would exploit the loss of Socialist influence in the Spanish labour movement (though Communist success only became clear to the outside world a few years later),[34] the Brussels-based International made an effort to revive the UGT presence in Spain in 1957. Following a meeting in April of the PSOE-UGT executives with ICFTU leaders Jacob Oldembroek and Walter Schevenels, the head of the International's Latin American department Hermes Horne went on a tour of inspection of the interior in November.[35] He left Spain quite impressed by the state of the PSOE, which Antonio Amat had been rebuilding since 1954, but he found little evidence of a UGT presence.[36] Presumably Horne was expecting to find differentiated structures there, as there were in exile. Nevertheless, he recommended to the ICFTU that it finance UGT organizers, increase the level of aid and propaganda help, and designate a member of the International's secretariat to concern himself with Spanish matters on a daily basis. To avoid suspicion, and because their style of activity was really only semi-clandestine, the Socialists used this opportunity to finance the work of six part-time, rather than full-time, regional organizers (*activistas*) whom Amat had already persuaded to do such work for the PSOE-UGT. Subsidies were also made available for the work of a co-ordinator (originally Amat himself) and a propaganda organizer. The ICFTU furthermore provided six Roneo duplicating machines worth $2,400. Most of these were captured within the year, leaving the main effect of the Brussels aid an organizational rather than a propaganda one.[37]

Not all Socialists welcomed this transnational assistance. Opposition to it was voiced by Arsenio Jimeno, the main

---

[34] The PSOE executive noted the growing success of Communist propaganda in 1954, but felt that this had not helped the PCE to grow as a party (*Actas* of CE, 3.9.54). Heine (*La oposición*, 472–3) is probably correct in his affirmation that by 1959 the PCE still had no more than a maximum of 2,000 militants in Spain, though it would soon grow larger as a result of its work in the Comisiones Obreras during the 1960s.

[35] UGT, *Actas* of CE, 15.4.57, 6.12.57.

[36] Ibid., 10.1.58; UGT, Assemblies, *Actas* of CG, 13.8.58.

[37] UGT, *Actas* of CE, 10.1.58. Horne did try to make arrangements for radio broadcasts, but could not find a government that was sympathetic to the idea.

standard-bearer of neutralism in the PSOE-UGT, who feared for his organizations' autonomy. To him, the way in which the ICFTU had made an inspection, drafted a report, formulated proposals, and then had them generally accepted by the Spaniards, was tantamount to 'trade union colonialism'.[38] Before long dissidents such as José Cardona were also lamenting outside influence and portraying the ICFTU as a conduit whereby nefarious US imperialist interests were served.[39] They were able to point to the strong presence of US and West German unions in the International and to the PSOE leadership's growing readiness to accept neo-capitalist solutions to Spain's problems. Conspiracy theories gained in popularity among such dissidents. For the majority of Socialists, however, aid was welcome from whichever quarter it came. They grew more accommodating and pragmatic as their period abroad lengthened and as their chances of ever returning to Spain receded.

THE GEOGRAPHY OF SOCIALISM

By no means did the outlawed PSOE manage to maintain a national presence during these years. Throughout the Franco period the party strongholds, such as they were, were situated in Asturias and in the Basque province of Vizcaya. A lesser presence was maintained in Madrid and Valencia, while in Barcelona, Zaragoza, Guipúzcoa, Santander, and a few isolated *pueblos* of Andalucía PSOE groups were even weaker. In much of Old and New Castile the party's representation was limited to dispersed individuals, and there was no organization at all in Galicia, Extremadura, and large areas of Catalonia and Andalucía. Thus the strongest centres of activity were in the north, followed by the capital and east coast; from the late 1940s to the late 1960s the PSOE amounted to little or nothing in the north-west, north-east, west, and south.

[38] UGT, *Actas* of CE, 14.2.58. See too the *Actas* of the CN meeting of the PSOE, 24–5.4.54, 19–20, for Araquistain's attack on Jimeno's defence of Spain's independence from the two blocs.
[39] José Cardona, 'El guiñol sindical en el tablado de la CIA', *Cuadernos de Ruedo Ibérico*, 8 (1966), 111–16.

Of course, there were repeated efforts to develop a national organization, but these neared success only in the mid-1940s, when there were surviving groups to build upon, and during the final months of Franco's life. The various Madrid-based executives were generally too hard pressed at the centre to link up with the periphery, and when they did the connection often proved more harmful than beneficial: little aid could be bestowed from Madrid, yet security diminished. There was greater security all round from 1954, with Toulouse serving as the communications nexus for the whole party. Antonio Amat, who had already begun to perform missions in the interior for the *émigré* leaders,[1] now became the protagonist of efforts to extend the organization into new areas. Under his auspices various organizational zones were designated. Each had a centre (where there was already some activity) plus target areas with whose organization these centres were entrusted. Thus Asturias was charged with extending the organization to Santander, Galicia, and León; Madrid was to try to organize Guadalajara, Ciudad Real, and other parts of New Castile; Málaga was to be the base for Andalucía, from where it was hoped eventually to extend into Extremadura; Vizcaya would organize the other provinces of Guipúzcoa and Alava; Barcelona would eventually tackle other parts of Catalonia; Valencia was to be the centre for other parts of the Levant; Aragón would attempt to organize Soria and Logroño; and Burgos would be responsible for activating Navarra and Valladolid.[2] Although the plan was sensible in conception, it made no allowances for the marked unevenness in the potential of the various 'centres'. The reality of the mid-1950s was that in the cases of Burgos and Aragón, the PSOE had only one reliable militant in each place.[3]

This organizational approach was severely disrupted by police raids in September and November 1958 when about

---

[1] The regular use of such envoys by the early 1950s was a sign of growing *émigré* misgivings about the CE in Madrid. Amat agreed to do such work at the party congress of 1952, or soon afterwards. A notable predecessor was 'Javier' (Agustín Mendía).

[2] 'Guridi' to CE, 2 June 1954, 20 Apr., 12 July 1955, 9 Apr. 1957; CE to 'Guridi', 8 June 1955. Occasionally Basque Socialists attempted to organize the semi-Basque province of Navarra too (PSOE, *Actas* of CE, 1.12.54).

[3] 'Guridi' to CE, 13 Feb. 54, 18 Sept. 54.

100 Socialists were detained, including Amat. The gradual renewal of co-ordination among the clandestine groups brought about by Amat in the mid-1950s now gave way to another phase of extreme decentralization, with each major group in the interior being linked only to Toulouse.[4] Possessing a strong historical sense of being custodians of the party and all that it stood for, the *émigré* leaders were extremely wary of local political initiatives taken in the interior. There were political as well as security reasons for Toulouse preferring a decentralized structure in Spain. However, it would be unjust to say that control of the party was the *émigrés'* only ambition. Whenever growth seemed possible and mere survival was not at risk, the exiles recognized that a degree of co-ordination in the interior was imperative if the groups there were to work efficiently. As the interior gradually became stronger, a co-ordinating committee was authorized in 1963,[5] though by now Toulouse's main lieutenant in Spain was Ramón Rubial, a loyal and cautious Basque who could be relied upon to discourage any challenges to the party leadership. By late 1965 this Comité de Coordinación had 10 members, they being an extension of the *activistas* envisaged in the ICFTU plan of the late 1950s. The committee served to co-ordinate regional activity and to provide for territorial representation in the interior. Only Galicia and Extremadura remained outside the network.[6] Meanwhile, as a result of pressures from groups in Spain, a number of seats on the Toulouse-based party executive were left for the Socialists of the interior to fill. At first there were two seats (from 1958), then three (1962–4), then five (1964–5), then three (1965–7), then seven (1967–70), and finally the interior acquired a majority with nine seats early in 1971.[7] These executive members based in the interior formed what was called the Comisión Permanente, which as it grew became an embryonic Comisión Ejecutiva just as the Comité de Coordinación effectively became a Comité Nacional.

The level of PSOE organization in the different parts of

---

[4] PSOE, *Actas* of CE, 12.10.60.   [5] Ibid., 8.2.63, 12.6.63.

[6] PSOE and other organizations, PSOE-UGT, Comisión de los asuntos de España, *Actas*, 11–12.11.65.

[7] For details of membership see Appendix C below.

Spain was affected by four major factors. Undoubtedly the most important was tradition: the party (in places presenting itself as the UGT) did best in the north where roots had been established in the late nineteenth century and strong organizations had grown since. Qualifying this factor was a second one, namely that the maintenance of the traditional presence proved least difficult where there was a strong sense of community or proletarian concentration, as existed among Asturian coal-miners and among the metalworkers engaged in shipbuilding and other activities on the left bank of Bilbao's Nervión estuary in Vizcaya. In other parts of Spain, apart from a relative absence of these factors, there were other causes of weakness. One of them, related to repression, was that Socialists who previously had occupied leading positions in small towns (especially in the south and south-west) tended to move after being released from prison in the 1940s. Often they were drawn by the greater anonymity of Madrid or Barcelona. Either they were banished from their home provinces (as was Antonio García Duarte from Málaga) or they were too well known in their *pueblos* to obtain employment and avoid recriminations by the right (for example Mario Tanco and Lázaro Movilla, who moved from Extremadura to Madrid).[8] Finally, in several places there were extremely unproductive personal rivalries, such as those between Urbano Orad de la Torre and Alfonso Fernández Torres in Seville, between Lucila Fernández and Juan García in Barcelona, and between various people in Madrid and in Valencia.[9] This problem never affected the Basque Country and only touched Asturias briefly in the mid-1960s. It may have been a contingent factor, though there are some indications of there being greater *protagonismo*, or leadership ambition, in areas where PSOE activists included a large middle-class component.

[8] Personal interviews with Antonio García Duarte and Mario Tanco; and with Lázaro Movilla, Madrid, 11 June 1984.
[9] See the *Actas* of the PSOE and UGT executives, and PSOE, Correspondence, 'Guridi' file, *passim*.

The Basque Country

Although regional studies of the PSOE under Francoism are only just beginning to appear, the general situation in each place can be gleaned from executive committee minutes, correspondence, memoirs, and interviews. From such sources it is clear that during the Franco period Vizcaya (and particularly Bilbao) played the most significant role in the party's survival and recovery, even if there were periods when the Asturian organization was held up as the example for other provincial federations to follow.[1] Vizcaya not only had tradition and proletarian concentration to fall back upon but also, thanks to Basque Nationalist Party support for the Republic, it lacked a vengeful civilian right wing bent upon persecuting the vanquished or collaborating in repression ordered by Madrid. Moreover, given the party's enduring strength in the north and the existence of the *émigré* concentrations in southern France, Bilbao occupied a key strategic location for the purposes of the PSOE. It was an obvious distribution centre for propaganda, correspondence, and money smuggled in from France, especially during the years 1954–72 when the leadership was based in Toulouse. Bilbao did much to extend the organization to the northern half of Spain, and its links with Madrid, maintained early on by the shirt-maker Manuel Garrido Díaz and the Gondra brothers, were better than those of any other provincial city.[2] Yet there was another side to this picture: with the exception of the years during which Amat served as a genuine national organizer in the interior, success in the north often meant neglect of the south.

There were three other reasons why Vizcaya should play host to the strongest Socialist organization. For one, a lot of political prisoners were sent by Franco to workplaces on the left bank of the Nervión estuary, and many of these highly politicized workers remained there after completing their

---

[1] This was also the view of Sergio Vilar when he undertook a study of the Spanish opposition in 1967. See his book *La Oposición a la dictadura: Protagonistas de la España democrática* (Barcelona: Aymá, 1976), 680.

[2] Fernández López, 'Apunte histórico', 10. Even so, at one time the Basques went for a year without any contact with Madrid (PSOE in Exile, *Actas* of CE, 24.4.50).

sentences.[3] Ramón Rubial was one of the main figures here. After commencing a long prison career in June 1939 in the Puerto de Santa María, and continuing it in Aranjuez, in 1944 he was sent to work at Babcock Wilcox of Bilbao. There he helped to rebuild the organization until his activity was discovered a year later.[4] Secondly, Vizcaya was one of few places where Socialists cultivated more of a UGT than a PSOE image, as they had in their pioneering days.[5] Though the organization was structurally undifferentiated, with the only difference between the Comité Central Socialista de Euskadi and the Comité Central de la UGT de Euskadi being a matter of rubber stamps, the Vizcayan Socialists realized that the UGT initials had a broader appeal in this industrial area. Very few of the leaders here were middle-class socialists; rather they conformed to the *obrerista* traditions of the provincial party and recruited among fellow workers, especially those in the Naval shipyards at Sestao (later renamed Astilleros Españoles) and at Babcock. When ICFTU official Hermes Horne toured Spain in 1957 it was only in Bilbao that he managed to find a Socialist with whom he could discuss trade union issues and who had a lot of working-class contacts.[6] Thirdly, although for the first two decades the Vizcayan organization was led by experienced activists (such as Rubial, Nicolás Redondo Blanco, José Macua, Fermín Oñate Santamaría and Eulogio Urréjola[7]), the veterans here, unlike senior Socialists in many parts of Spain, recognized

[3] José Manuel Arija, *Nicolás Redondo: Perfil humano y político* (Madrid: Cambio 16, 1977), 15.

[4] On Rubial see *Cuadernos para el Diálogo*, 261 (1978), 21. The first clandestine committee in Rubial's native Erandio was also based on former prisoners (*ES*, 26.2.78, 14–15).

[5] Jáuregui and Vega, ii. 328; Rubial, taped interview. On the PSOE in the Basque Country see also the taped interviews by Carlos Cruz with Félix García Fanjul, José García Maillo, and Giordano García Blanco.

[6] UGT, *Actas* of CE, 10.1.58. Presumably this reference was to Rubial, who had been released from prison in Aug. 1956 and who from 1959 played the role of Toulouse's main coordinator in the area. He adopted the pseudonym 'Gil' and later, as a widely respected veteran, was referred to as 'Pablo', an almost sacred name in the party of Iglesias.

[7] Redondo was the father of Nicolás Redondo Urbieta who became the leader of the UGT in the early 1970s. In 1958 he was treated so badly in a Basque police station that he threw himself over the side of a staircase when on the third floor, breaking many bones (*ES*, 10.6.48, 4; Arija, 22). Urréjola was a Bilbao solicitor who died shortly after attending the seventh party congress held in exile (1958).

that the PSOE's future lay with the youth. It was necessary to sow seeds now in order to reap a harvest later.[8] During the 1950s the Basque Country was the only region of Spain to possess even a suggestion of a Young Socialist organization. However, even here it proved impossible to recruit at a time when young people of all social classes appeared to be in a political coma, and in the absence of material support from the youth International, IUSY.[9] None the less, the basis existed for a slight revival of the FNJSE here in the 1960s, when relatively young militants such as Nicolás Redondo (jun.) and fellow fitter Eduardo López were also encouraged to take on important responsibilities in the UGT-PSOE.[10]

Vizcaya was the scene of the first mass industrial stoppages under Franco. Isolated strikes in 1946 and early 1947 were followed by an attempt at a more general strike, triggered by a lock-out ordered by the Governor in response to May Day protests. Although the strike, which was most effective in Bilbao, was also supported by the CNT, the Basque Nationalists, and the Communists (all present with the Socialists on a Resistance Council representing the Basque government-in-exile), it seems to have been the PSOE-UGT that proposed the action.[11] By this time the Socialists had recovered from losses sustained in 1945, had reorganized especially around Bilbao, and were producing underground issues of *La Lucha de Clases*.[12] However, the strike was more

[8] See PSOE, *Actas* of CE, 29–30.1.66 for details of a meeting of the interior and exterior leaders at which Rubial and Redondo jun. explained their emphasis on the recruitment of youth.

[9] FNJSE, Correspondence, letters from the Juventudes Socialistas de Euzkadi to S. Martínez Dasi, 5 Mar., 27 May 1954; Martínez Dasi to Federación de Juventudes Socialistas de Euzkadi, 30 Dec. 1954. Youth groups existed in Vizcaya and Alava (*ES*, suplemento elecciones, June 1977).

[10] See the Martínez Dasi memo to Llopis, P. Tomás, and T. Gómez, 6 July 1954 (FNJSE, Correspondence, 'Correspondencia con el Interior 1952/1956'), about the importance of getting young Basques to attend a PSOE summer school held in Biarritz, where they could meet activists from other parts of Spain. These were organized mainly by the FNJSE, beginning in 1952. See too 'Txiki' Benegas, *Euskadi: Sin la paz nada es posible* (Barcelona: Argos Vergara, 1984), 45–7; José Maravall, *Dictatorship and Political Dissent: Workers and Students in Franco's Spain* (London: Tavistock, 1978), 78–9.

[11] On the strike see Llibert Ferri, Jordi Muixí, and Eduardo Sanjuán, *Las huelgas contra Franco* (Barcelona: Planeta, 1978), 94–130; *Adelante*, 15.5.47, 3; PSOE in Exile, Third Congress (1948), *Memoria*, ch. 5.

[12] Rubial, taped interview.

of a swan-song of traditional trade unionism than the prototype for labour opposition to Franco.[13] It was followed by a wave of repression that forced Socialist leaders such as Juan Iglesias to flee to France and led to the detention of many others.[14] At the same time, relations with the PCE were broken off as the Communists were expelled from the Basque government, accused of retaining a lot of the money raised abroad in the name of solidarity with the strike.[15] This, combined with CNT decline in the 1950s, left the Basque Nationalists as the main regional allies of the Socialists for the rest of the Franco period.[16]

Losses in Vizcaya were never catastrophic, for from the early 1940s until the early 1970s there was stricter compartmentalism here than was practised in other parts of Spain. Cells of five were established whose representatives were known only to general delegates of the Comité Central Socialista de Euskadi (which was operating by 1945).[17] The chain of arrests initiated by a single loss was limited structurally to 25 activists. Perhaps for this reason, reorganization proved possible after key figures were arrested in 1945, 1947, the early 1950s,[18] 1958, 1960, and the late 1960s. Several of the men who played significant roles until they were arrested in the late 1940s—Macua, Gregorio Illoro, and the welder Eduardo Marauri—were still (or again) prominent in the late 1950s, not only building the Vizcaya federation but also transporting propaganda, money, and letters to Asturias, Zaragoza, and Madrid.[19] The 1950s was a relatively lean

[13] Ferri *et al.*, 128–30.

[14] García Blanco, interview by C. Cruz; José María Benegas and Valentín Díaz (eds.), *Partido Socialista de Euskadi PSOE* (San Sebastián: Haranburu, 1977), 97.

[15] Rubial, interview by C. Cruz.

[16] Basque envoy Carlos Fermín Gondra reported to the *émigrés'* party executive on 21 June 1945 that there were good relations with all opposition forces except the PCE (*Actas*). His brother Cecilio Gondra was also an important Basque link-man in the 1940s. See also Rubial's taped interview with C. Cruz; PSOE, *Actas* of CE, 15.2.61; PSOE and other organizations, PSOE-UGT, *Actas* of CD/CG, 15–16.7.62, 5.

[17] Personal interview with Rubial, Madrid, 29 Apr. 1982.

[18] PSOE in Exile, *Actas* of CE, 21.3.52, 13.6.52: a new Basque executive was set up after the arrest of leaders and flight of C. Gondra (on whom see ibid., 23.7.52, 25.11.52). Detentions in March 1953 again included the leaders and followed the downfall of Centeno's CE in Madrid.

[19] Macua, the Basque Country 'activist' (*permanente*), went into exile in Sept. 1960 (PSOE, *Actas* of CE, 12.10.60). For details of this activity see the trial papers of

decade for the federation but it still remained one of the two most impressive in Spain.[20] In the 1960s, as a measure of its consolidation and growth, Vizcaya became one of the earliest federations to collect dues,[21] and this enabled provincial leaders to assess the numerical strength of their organization more precisely. A Basque delegation to an executive meeting in Toulouse in 1961 included one militant who was in charge of 150 Socialists and another who led 'a considerable number'.[22] By 1966 some 700 members were reported to be paying dues in the Basque Country, principally in Bilbao.[23]

Vizcaya's strength was seen too in its being the only province of Spain where the Socialists' trade union strategy prospered at all, although even here it collapsed after 1970. An agreement was reached among *émigrés* in France to launch a Spanish Trade Union Alliance (ASE) in 1960,[24] embracing the UGT, CNT, and (in the Basque Country) the nationalist STV. However, internal divisions in these organizations and the decline or disappearance of the main components in many parts of Spain made the Alliance virtually impossible to build in the interior.[25] ASE groups were established in three places in the Basque Country, involving just UGT and STV people (CNT veterans refused to take part).[26] There were little more

Illoro *et al.*, PSOE, Trial Papers, 'Sumario 273–61'. Both Marauri and Illoro worked at La Naval, where Marauri recruited the young Redondo, an apprentice fitter, to the FNJSE and UGT in 1945 (Arija, 14–16). In Aug. 1960 some 30 Socialists including Redondo and Asturian leaders Herminio Alvarez Iglesias and Avelino Pérez were arrested, but only Illoro and Macua received prison sentences (for illegal propaganda). The trial revealed substantial sub-national co-ordination in northern Spain. See too PSOE, *Circular*, 9.1.61; *Le Socialiste*, 21.12.61, 6. Redondo was arrested 13 times between 1951 and 1973 (PSOE, Congresses, file marked 'XXVII Congreso. Datos Biográficos Comité Nacional').

[20] Amat reported to Llopis (2 June 1954) that Vizcaya was the only Basque province that was organized. In the interior, only the Asturian and Vizcayan federations were working well (UGT, *Actas* of CE, 17.6.54).

[21] Rubial, taped interview.

[22] PSOE, *Actas* of CE, 15.2.61.   [23] Ibid., 29–30.1.66.

[24] The Alianza was established on 25 Feb. 1960 by the UGT, STV, and CNT National Sub-Committee (but not the International Committee of the CNT). CNT divisions left it stillborn. However, following reunification of the CNT in Nov. 1960, ASE was re-established after a meeting between the UGT, STV, and CNT on 12 May 1961, a pact being signed on the 23rd (*ES*, 17.3.60, 1, 17.11.60, 1, 1.6.61, 1, 10.8.61, 1–2).

[25] PSOE, *Actas* of CE, 29–30.1.66.

[26] Ibid., 15.2.61; PSOE and other organizations, PSOE-UGT, *Actas* of CD/CG, 15–16.7.62, 5.

than symbolic alliances in Catalonia and Asturias, and elsewhere ASE did not exist at all.[27] Following UGT promotion of a strike at La Naval in 1962, in solidarity with striking Asturian miners, ASE achieved its greatest success in 1964 when it led protests against the cost of living, calling strikes in May and October.[28] The Alliance may have become a dead letter subsequently,[29] but its initials were used by the UGT when it convoked a Bilbao demonstration in support of the long strike at Laminación de Bandas of Echevarri in April 1967, and again when calling strikes against a new labour law early in 1969, when 6,000 workers went on strike in Bilbao.[30]

Throughout this period the UGT advocated an independent trade union strategy, rejecting participation in elections to the official *sindicatos*—theoretically corporative bodies involving employers and employees alike—on the grounds that this would lend credibility to unrepresentative State-controlled institutions that were a negation of class struggle. Of course, one consequence of participation would have been to expose the UGT's own weakness and the greater force in places of either the Workers' Commissions (CCOO) or new trade unions such as the Workers' Trade Union (USO). Workers' commissions had been set up spontaneously in the late 1950s and early 1960s to represent workers involved in industrial disputes. Many of the representatives placed on the commissions by their workmates were communists, and their selection combined with a deliberate PCE bid for control enabled the

---

[27] UGT, *Circular*, 24.11.62; PSOE and other organizations, PSOE-UGT, *Actas* of CD/CG, 20–1.7.63.

[28] *Le Socialiste*, 7.5.64, 1, 28.5.64, 1–2, 22.10.64, 1.

[29] F. Almendros Morcillo *et al.*, 128.

[30] *Le Socialiste*, 13.4.67, 1–2, 4.5.67, 1, 6.2.69, 1, 20.2.69, 1–2. The question of who effectively led such events is something that only a detailed regional study might answer. Because of police vigilance established labour leaders often could not lead strikes and protests directly, and there was a strong 'wildcat' element in these workers' struggles anyway. None the less, it is widely recognized that there was at least important UGT involvement in the events mentioned here. Along with the organizational growth of the UGT, these interventions help explain the large number of arrests of Basque Socialists in the late 1960s, sometimes followed by banishment to the remote inhospitable area of Cáceres province known as Las Hurdes. For details see *Le Socialiste*, 1967–9; Arija, 22–32; Maravall, *Dictatorship*, 78–9; SOMA Archive, Box A.LVII, FNJSE, *Hoja informativa*, 27.5.67. In 1967 a total of 243 Socialists were arrested to prevent a May Day demonstration in Bilbao (*Le Socialiste*, 4.5.67, 1).

Communists by the mid-1960s to dominate these bodies, with CCOO becoming a parallel organization to the 'vertical' *sindicatos*. The PCE had been implementing its policy of infiltrating the *sindicatos* since the early 1950s, but the tactic only gained the Communists a mass audience when they were able to use the workers' commissions to camouflage their candidates in syndical elections.

In contrast, the UGT tried to set up independent factory committees and officially shunned any contact with the *sindicatos*. Success was achieved only in Vizcaya.[31] Committees were established at La Naval, Babcock Wilcox, and in some smaller companies.[32] La Naval's was the first. It was formed in 1968 when 94 per cent of the work-force elected a co-ordinating committee of some 80 workers, which in turn chose a factory committee of 15 (eight from the UGT, the rest Basque nationalists and independents). At first recognized by management, the committee was shortly afterwards arrested while preparing for wage negotiations, though it was released on bail following a protest strike by 5,000 workers. A second committee there was a more clandestine body on which the UGT and Workers' Commissions had a majority, but by 1970 these committees had failed everywhere.[33] Repression was a greater problem for activists outside the official *sindicato* structure. Over 60 PSOE-UGT militants were arrested in 1969.[34] Yet even without police action it would have been difficult for the UGT's appeals for class unity to prosper in the circumstances, for each labour faction (including the UGT) had a highly politicized strategy. While the UGT remained structurally undifferentiated from the PSOE (until 1972 when the PSOE split but the UGT did not), the Communists sought to involve all factory committees in their CCOO project and the revolutionary left tried to translate labour militancy into new Leninist parties.[35]

---

[31] Ibid., 20.2.69, 1–2.   [32] Almendros Morcillo *et al.*, 129.

[33] This account is based on Arija, 29–32. However, in a personal interview (Madrid, 11 June 1984) Redondo stated that there was some PCE representation in the first factory committee too. Such collaboration went against PSOE-UGT policy; the interior was adopting a flexible approach in the interests of securing united labour action.   [34] Arija, 32.

[35] For the aims of Communist labour strategy see Hermandad Obrera de Acción Católica, *CCOO. en sus documentos 1958–1976* (Madrid: HOAC, 1977); Julián

Of the remaining Basque provinces, Alava was where the PSOE was least in evidence. Like Navarra it shared neither Vizcaya's experience of early industrialization nor the liberal republican tradition that was to be found in parts of Guipúzcoa.[36] After 1952 Alava was put on the Socialist map by the activities of Amat, 'the lion of Vitoria', though his was essentially a national co-ordinating role during the 1950s; only after spending two and a half years in prison followed by three years of house arrest in 1958–64 did he play more of a role in the province, serving for a while as the UGT 'activist' there.[37] The key man in Alava during the 1950s was Amat's brother-in-law José Antonio Aguiriano. For several years he led the Basque Young Socialists and UGT in Alava, before being sent by the Socialists to Brussels to work at the ICFTU headquarters. What was supposed to be a six-month training visit became a permanent job because of police raids towards the end of 1958 which claimed Amat among their victims.[38] Nevertheless, a small organization survived in the province and in August 1967 the three main Basque provinces of Spain were all represented, for the first time together, at a meeting of the PSOE Comité Director in France. By this time a further group had been organized in the Navarra capital of Pamplona, but the semi-Basque province was not represented at the meeting.[39]

As for Guipúzcoa, it was reorganized by prisoners in 1942, mainly in Eibar and San Sebastián.[40] José Elcerreca and

Ariza, *Comisiones Obreras* (Madrid: Mañana, 1976); Maravall, *Dictatorship*, 29–34; Sebastian Balfour, 'The Origins of Comisiones Obreras', *Spanish Studies*, 6 (1984), 21–33. On USO see José María Zufiaur, *Unión Sindical Obrera* (Madrid: Mañana, 1976); Hermandad Obrera de Acción Católica, *USO en sus documentos 1960–1975* (Madrid: HOAC, 1976). USO suffered a split in 1970 caused by militants influenced by the events in France in May 1968 who returned to Spain with the idea of transforming USO into a vanguard party (interviews with Eugenio Royo, 15 June 1984; Agapito Ramos, 23 May 1984; Manuel Zaguirre, 13 June 1984; José María Zufiaur, 13 June 1984; Enrique Barón, 1 June 1984).

[36] Eguiguren, 24–34.
[37] PSOE, Trial Papers, Sumario 10,960, 'Conclusiones de fiscal'; personal interview with Rubial. Amat was released from prison into house arrest in May 1961 and the trial of those arrested in late 1958 did not take place until Feb. 1964.
[38] *ES*, suplemento elecciones, June 1977, 6; ibid., 25.6.78, 12.
[39] PSOE, *Actas* of CE, 29–30.1.66; id., Assemblies, *Actas* of CD, 9–10.8.67.
[40] PSOE, Territorial Organizations, Basque Country, 'La lucha clandestina de la UGT y el PSOE. Guipúzcoa: 1942–1976'.

Benigno Bascarán were the key men in the early years. After fighting in the French Resistance and being put in a concentration camp, Bascarán returned to Eibar to build the clandestine organization; after becoming provincial president of the party, he acquired public renown as Eibar's undertaker.[41] Guipúzcoa was hit by arrests in 1944 and again in 1950 when the provincial committee based in San Sebastián was put out of action and 33 Socialists were detained. There then followed several years of inactivity before Amat persuaded the painter Celestino Corcuera to reorganize the city group in 1954.[42] Amat's recruitment of a small circle of San Sebastián intellectuals to the PSOE in 1957 was potentially of great qualitative importance. The group included Luis Martín-Santos, who from 1951 was head of the San Sebastián Psychiatric Hospital, fellow psychiatrist Vicente Urcola, and the lawyer Joaquín Pradera. These men had already been in contact with other socialists including the scientist Miguel Sánchez-Mazas and the aspiring diplomat Vicente Girbau of the Agrupación Socialista Universitaria in Madrid.[43] Amat had great expectations of the two psychiatrists, whom he found enthusiastic, hard-working, and likely to attract other intellectuals to a party that had been notably lacking in this department. Martín-Santos was an abundantly gifted recruit, a polymath who first made his name as an eminent surgeon, then distinguished himself in psychiatry, and finally displayed his literary genius with the publication of the neo-realist *Tiempo de silencio*, one of the most influential novels to appear in post-war Spain.[44]

Early in 1958 Martín-Santos and Urcola settled in a frontier town and began to smuggle propaganda and duplicating machines for the party from Biarritz to San Sebastián.[45] After the PSOE congress of 1958 the Socialists of the interior chose

[41] Ibid.; *El País*, 14.5.84.
[42] 'Guridi' to CE, 2.6.54; PSOE, Trial Papers, Sumario 10,960, 'Conclusiones de fiscal'.
[43] 'Guridi' to CE, 12 Oct. 1957; CE to 'Guridi', 21 Oct. 1957; PSOE, Trial Papers, Sumario 10,960, 'Conclusiones de fiscal'.
[44] 'Guridi' to CE, 8 Nov. 1957; L. Martín-Santos, *Tiempo de silencio* (Barcelona: Seix Barral, 1961).
[45] *What is Happening in Spain? The Problem of Spanish Socialism* (Madrid, 1959), p. 117 n. 3; PSOE, Trial Papers, Sumario 10,960, 'Conclusiones de fiscal'.

Martín-Santos along with Rubial as their representatives on the party executive. However, the former was never able to fulfil his new role properly. Following the congress, there were police raids in San Sebastián and seven militants were arrested including Martín-Santos, Urcola, and Corcuera.[46] After spending four months in Carabanchel prison before being re-arrested in May 1959, Martín-Santos decided in June 1960 that he had become far too conspicuous to remain on the executive. He resigned his place, but remained active in the party until his life ended tragically after a car crash near Vitoria in January 1964, when he was still only 39 years old.[47]

In the same year the lawyer Enrique Múgica, a former PCE militant who had known Amat in Burgos Prison, switched his allegiances to the PSOE. He soon became a leading organizer in northern Spain, along with Rubial, Redondo, López, and others. Múgica joined the party's Comisión Permanente in 1967.[48] However, the Guipúzcoa federation to which he belonged, and which had been linked to Vizcaya by means of an inter-provincial committee in the 1950s, suffered decline in the 1960s because of the predominance of inactive veterans.[49] As late as 1971–2, when José María Benegas joined, Guipúzcoa was based overwhelmingly on veterans and lacked youth. The main group was in Eibar though there were a few Socialists in San Sebastián and Irún. Overall the situation in Guipúzcoa as in Alava was that the provincial federation was in need of rebuilding.[50]

---

[46] *ES*, 9.10.58, 1, 28.5.59, 1; *Le Socialiste*, 6.2.64, 1–2; 'Guridi' to CE, 20 Oct. 1958. For details of the sentences see *Le Socialiste*, 20.2.64, 1, 5.3.64, 1, 3.

[47] PSOE, *Actas* of CE, 15.7.60. There are obvious comparisons to be drawn between Martín-Santos and Albert Camus in relation to their literary style, interest in existentialism, political views, North African birth, and the manner of their deaths. In Jan. 1964 Martín-Santos had not recovered fully from the early death of his wife. See his appearance in Jorge Semprún, *El desvanecimiento* (Barcelona: Planeta, 1979), 186–8; and the tributes to him in *Kantil* (San Sebastián), 3 (1977), and *ES*, 4.9.77, 23.

[48] On Múgica see Jáuregui and Vega, ii. 134–5; *ES*, 25.9.77, 14–15; Alvaro Santamaría, *Enrique Múgica: Perfil humano y político* (Madrid: Cambio 16, 1977), especially 24–8. Múgica broke with the PCE, which he regarded as dishonest, and with Leninism, seen as a denial of liberty, to become a leading social-democratic influence in the PSOE.

[49] PSOE and other organizations, PSOE-UGT, *Actas* of CD/CG, 3.7.66.

[50] Benegas, 45.

Catalonia

The 'national question' proved a good deal less troublesome to Socialists in the Basque Country than it did in Catalonia. Many of the industrial workers on the left bank of the Nervión were of non-Basque origin and like the Redondo family did not speak Basque.[1] Before the 1970s there were no significant local parties of the left to compete with the PSOE in the Basque region, unlike Catalonia which had felt the force of left-wing nationalism in the 1930s. None the less, within the PSOE there was some tension between Basques, and between Basques and non-Basques. This could be seen in 1956 when a World Basque Congress was held. The attitude of the Llopis leadership was that Basque and Catalan nationalism were 'damaging and inopportune': they complicated the task of building anti-Franco alliances and made potential right-wing opponents of Franco refrain from acting for fear that the unity of Spain might be jeopardized.[2] Acceptance of the autonomy statutes of the 1930s was the maximum concession that the Toulouse executives were prepared to make to the peripheral nationalists, and even this at times seemed too much for Prieto. In 1958, when the Socialists of the interior urged support for a federal Spain, with a view to winning over separatist militants, he replied that the Basque and Catalan statutes were the reason why so many Socialists were in exile.[3] Preferring to devolve power to municipal authorities, Prieto boycotted the Basque congress, as did the party executive which claimed that a draft congress resolution went beyond existing juridical entitlements.[4] This attitude proved unacceptable to the Comité Central Socialista de Euskadi which the executive allowed to function in Spain and France (in France to analyse the specific problems of the region and to promote regional PSOE solidarity). The committee not only attended the congress but voted for a Basque nationalist resolution, to the annoyance of all the PSOE leaders except

[1] Arija, 11.
[2] PSOE, *Actas* of CE, 1.6.56.
[3] PSOE, Assemblies, *Actas* of CD, 11–12.8.58, 30. On Prieto's attitude see also Saborit in *Le Socialiste*, 1.3.62.
[4] Prieto, *Esbozo de un programa de socialización en España* (Toulouse: PSOE, 1946); PSOE, *Actas* of CE, 5.9.56, 14.11.56.

the Basque Paulino Gómez, who was also a member of the Basque government-in-exile.[5]

This antipathy to peripheral nationalisms did not damage the PSOE noticeably in the Basque Country, but it was harmful in Catalonia where nationalist alternatives of the left had some popular appeal. Here repeated efforts to base the PSOE on workers from other parts of Spain, especially Basques,[6] proved no adequate substitute for a more imaginative approach to native Catalans. Eventually, rhetorical concessions to Catalanism had to be made. In 1964 the ninth PSOE congress to be held in France passed a resolution on Iberian nationalities, specifically with reorganization of the Socialist Federation of Catalonia (FSC) in view; and at the following congress the political resolution spoke of a 'Republican Confederation of Iberian Nationalities' as being a Socialist goal.[7] Just how much sincerity there was in this formula, and in a Llopis speech about the need for a federation of Iberian socialist parties, was shown by the way the PSOE executive ignored several Portuguese approaches for co-operation. These overtures dated from 1955 when the Portuguese Labour Party proposed a merger of the two parties and the elaboration of a plan for an Iberian revolution. Llopis issued a joint document with Mario Soares of Portuguese Socialist Action during a Socialist International congress in 1969, but there was no effective Iberian collaboration before the 1970s.[8]

In Catalonia the favoured PSOE tactic of disdainfully ignoring rival parties just would not work; unless it was prepared to co-operate with the Catalanist left, the party ran the risk of being unrepresented in the region. This was not

[5] PSOE in Exile, Third Congress (1948), *Memoria*, ch. 1, pp. 5–6; PSOE, *Actas* of CE, 14.11.56, 7.12.56; id., Assemblies, *Actas* of CD, 7.8.56, 21–2.

[6] Rubial, interviewed by C. Cruz; PSOE, *Actas* of CE, 7.11.56; 'Guridi' to CE, 9 Apr. 1957. By 1957 a group of Basques was working with Juan García, a bricklayer, who was the principal FSC figure from the mid-1940s until his death in a car crash in July 1967.

[7] PSOE, *Actas* of CE, 9.10.64; *Le Socialiste*, 24.8.67, 1–2. The formula was first approved in 1918.

[8] PSOE, *Actas* of CE, 25.5.55; ibid., 11.6.69; PSOE, Assemblies, Comité Director, June 1969: 'Nota informativa que de sus actividades presenta la Comisión Ejecutiva al Comité Director del Partido, que se reunirá el 14 de junio de 1969', 13–14.

always so. During the 1940s the PSOE had considerable support, at least in Barcelona. Despite some falling-off after 1946, membership still ran into hundreds. Around 1947 the Catalan Young Socialists had some 250 militants, more than before the Civil War.[9] Yet even early on, there were signs of future trouble. The FSC was based largely on people who had gone to Catalonia to flee from repression or had been banished from their home province.[10] Coming from all over Spain and perhaps seeing their migration as temporary, they organized on the basis of their province of origin. This was a much less firm foundation than the non-native bedrock in the Basque Country, because those who migrated to Catalonia were new arrivals with little sensitivity to Catalan issues and feelings. Moreover, deep personal and possibly political divisions were sown in the mid-1940s when the *émigrés'* executive in France proceeded to reorganize the FSC, putting in charge Juan García, a man who had moved from Madrid and was distinctly wary of Catalanism.[11] In so doing, the exiles created a long-standing animosity between García and Lucila Fernández, the women who had done most to rebuild the federation in the early 1940s.[12]

It is likely that the internal division also had something to do with the founding in Toulouse in January 1945 of the Socialist Movement of Catalonia (MSC). Formed by ex-members of Catalan left parties of the 1930s—the POUM, PSUC, and possibly the USC—the MSC was inspired by a libertarian socialist philosophy and advocated a federal framework for Spain, ruling out any possibility of subordination

---

[9] García Duarte interview. After moving from Málaga to Barcelona in 1943, he became a member of the regional executive of the PSOE-UGT. Some 90–100 people attended a Socialist youth congress on the outskirts of Barcelona around 1947, which confirmed him as general secretary of the Catalan Young Socialists. He led them until having to flee to France in 1949. See too *ES*, 25.5.79, 28.

[10] García Duarte interview.

[11] 'Guridi' to CE, Aug. 1956.

[12] Partit dels Socialistes de Catalunya (PSC-PSOE), *La unidad de los socialistas de Cataluña*, 11. The clash lasted for over a decade. See 'Guridi' to CE, 13 Feb. 1954; PSOE, *Actas* of CE, 13.6.57, in which Fernández is referred to as 'La Amazona', an appellation that the all-male PSOE leadership reserved for women whom they found troublesome (later Josefina Arrillaga). Notwithstanding this attitude, efforts were made to develop Socialist women's groups in the late 1960s, at least in the Basque Country (PSOE, *Actas* of CE, 25.5.70).

to a Madrid-based political party.[13] Its driving force Josep Pallach was a former POUM militant who had organized a resistance group against the Germans in France before returning secretly to Spain in 1942; he was captured in 1944, escaped two years later, and then worked for the MSC from France, remaining there until the late 1960s.[14] In the 1950s the MSC became a much more viable force than the FSC,[15] but for this reason it was hit all the harder during the police round-up of Socialists in late 1958. One third of the 51 arrests that led to charges took place in Barcelona, and of these all but two involved members of the Movement.[16] The MSC never fully recovered from this set-back, which was compounded in August 1966 when it suffered a split over relations with the PCE. While a majority in the interior led by Joan Reventós and Josep María Obiols wanted to build a broad anti-Franco front, Pallach along with Amedeu Cuito and others established the Reagrupament Socialista i Democràtic de Catalunya, which favoured a narrower alliance and negotiations with elements of the regime that were open to change.[17]

From the 1940s PSOE activity in Catalonia placed great emphasis upon trying to revive the UGT in the region, a project that led to collaboration with the POUM from 1945 and with the MSC from 1950.[18] However, co-operation proved difficult given the attitudes of the PSOE *émigrés* as reflected in Barcelona by Juan García. The non-negotiable position of Toulouse was that there could only be one socialist party in Catalonia, namely the PSOE.[19] Thus the party

---

[13] Partit dels Socialistes de Catalunya, *La unidad*, 13; *Endavant* (Mexico, Distrito Federal), 1 (1946), 1–2, 14–20; PSOE in Exile, *Actas* of CE, 14.3.46; Vilar, 255–7.

[14] On Pallach see *ES*, 15.1.77, 10; *ES(H)*, 15.3.77, 4, 15.3.77, 2; *Exprés Español* (Frankfurt), Feb. 1976, 14–18. For the MSC outlook see Josep Pallach, 'El socialisme i els problemes de les nacionalitats hispániques' and 'El problema de l'estat espanyol', *Endavant* (France), Feb. 1959, Feb.-Mar. 1964. [15] 'Guridi' to CE, 24 June 1956.

[16] *What is Happening*, 124–7; *Endavant* (France), Dec. 1958. A majority of the 17 were middle class and they included four lawyers. The MSC had been hit by arrests already in 1953.

[17] Jáuregui and Vega, ii. 172–6; PSC-PSOE, *La unidad*, 16–17. On Reventós and Obiols see *ES*, 13.12.77, 28.1.79, 13–19.7.83; *El País*, international edn., 30.4.84; Vilar, 253–64. Reventós came from a wealthy family and was active in a Christian Democratic group before joining the MSC in 1947.

[18] Almendros Morcillo *et al.*, 126–7; PSC-PSOE, *La unidad*, 11.

[19] This is what Llopis told MSC leaders including Pallach and Ramón Porqueras in 1956 (PSOE, *Actas* of CE, 6.7.56). On Porqueras cf. UGT, *Actas* of CE, 22.12.55.

repeatedly vetoed attempts by the MSC to gain admission to the Socialist International, seeing these as acts of 'aggression'.[20] The real issue here was who was to be the interlocutor and recipient of aid *vis-à-vis* the international labour and socialist organizations.[21] The successful retention by the PSOE-UGT of its monopoly on Spanish socialism did not weaken *émigré* feelings of resentment towards the MSC, viewed as a movement living off the funds of the UGT without accepting PSOE-UGT discipline.[22] For its part, the MSC was prepared to encourage its members to join the UGT, but was openly critical of the *españolista* orientation of the PSOE and resisted any suggesstion that it should become a disciplined PSOE agency in a region where the Catalanists clearly enjoyed numerical superiority.[23]

In 1951 Toulouse decided that its Catalan federation was solidly re-established and reunited, only to see provincial leaderships successively arrested in 1952 and 1953 following the detention of Patricio Cruz and the downfall of the Centeno executive.[24] Effective rebuilding depended on liaison with the MSC and a new approach to the region. Already there had been some MSC-FSC collaboration as a result of an agreement reached in 1950, which a year later had led to a modest joint intervention in an economically-inspired strike in Barcelona.[25] Following the arrests of 1952–3 co-operation really began to flourish, thanks largely to the personal initiative of Amat.[26] While other PSOE leaders continued to regard 'Catalanist feeling' as a problem and seemed content to rely upon a non-Catalan regional base for the party, Amat told his executive bluntly that if they wanted a party in Catalonia, they would need MSC people; and if the trade union 'activist' for Catalonia envisaged in the Horne report was to achieve

---

[20] PSOE in Exile, *Actas* of CE, 20.6.51; PSOE, *Circular*, 31.7.59.
[21] UGT, *Actas* of CE, 28.9.53.
[22] PSOE, Assemblies, *Actas* of CD, Aug. 1959, 39.
[23] PSOE, *Actas* of CE, 5.9.56; id., *Circular*, 31.7.59.
[24] PSOE in Exile, *Actas* of CE, 13–14.6.51, 22.9.51, 21.3.52, 25.3.53; PSOE, Correspondence, 'Guridi' file, Llopis to 'Guridi', 28 June 1954.
[25] Almendros Morcillo *et al.*, 126; Ferri *et al.*, 161.
[26] Rubial, interviewed by C. Cruz.

anything, he would have to 'be Catalan, speak Catalan, and think Catalan'.[27]

A visit by Amat to Barcelona in April 1954 led to a strengthening of FSC-MSC collaboration.[28] To reorganize the region, Amat contacted Juan García and an old associate, Salvador Clop Urpi; through them he met Miguel Casablanca Juanico, reorganizer of the MSC in the late 1940s, and fellow MSC leader Joan Reventós.[29] While formally recognizing García as the party representative in Catalonia, Amat provided the MSC with a duplicating machine and invited its representatives to attend PSOE-UGT national meetings as members of the UGT Regional Secretariat of Catalonia.[30] To him they were young, active, intelligent, and 'preponderant' in the region.[31] While García worked primarily with a group of Basques in Barcelona, the Catalanists found a few recruits among the metallurgical enterprises of Barcelona, and even developed a group in the *Policia Armada*![32] They had much more respect for Amat, who urged the PSOE to publish something in Catalan, than for *émigrés* whose congress resolutions so often ignored the Catalan question.[33] For their part, the exiles feared that Amat was relying exclusively on the MSC in Catalonia, or was accepting the FSC's subordination to it.[34] At one point, the UGT executive broke off relations with the MSC for participating in a dissident meeting in Perpignan to discuss the possibility of channelling aid from the Metalworkers' International directly to Catalonia,

[27] PSOE, *Actas* of CE, 24.3.54, 20.6.56, 7.11.56; 'Guridi' to CE, 27.12.55; UGT, *Actas* of CE, 30.5.58.

[28] Amat's impression was that the POUM had the strongest opposition organization there. The FSC and MSC had 'very little strength' though the latter included 'very good people', two of whom were already in the UGT ('Guridi' to CE, 13 Feb., 2 June 1954; UGT, *Actas* of CE, 17.6.54). The FSC did have some Catalan members (PSOE, *Actas* of CE, 24.3.54).

[29] PSOE, *Actas* of CE, 21–2.4.54, 30.11.54; UGT, *Actas* of CE, 28.9.53; PSOE, Trial Papers, Sumario 10,960, 'Conclusiones de fiscal'. Clop was a Barcelona pastrycook, Casablanca a wood merchant (*Le Socialiste*, 5.3.64, 3).

[30] PSOE, *Actas* of CE, 13.6.57; 'Guridi' to CE, 9.4.57; PSOE, Trial Papers, Sumario 10,960, 'Conclusiones de fiscal'; PSC-PSOE, *La unidad*, 11. Four Catalans attended a plenum arranged by Amat in Apr. 1957; Reventós attended a CG meeting in Aug. 1957 and the CD and congress of the PSOE in Toulouse in Aug. 1958.

[31] 'Guridi' to CE, 18 Sept. 1954, 24 June 1956.

[32] Ibid., Apr. 1957.

[33] Ibid., 18 Sept. 1954; PSOE, *Actas* of CE, 28.9.55.

[34] CE to 'Guridi', 1 June, 24 Dec. 1956.

bypassing Toulouse.[35] Though the link was repaired for a while, relations deteriorated further following the arrest of Amat and most members of the old UGT Catalan Secretariat towards the end of 1958. Younger elements, many of them students, took charge of the secretariat and, while remaining interested in the UGT as a source of finance for the MSC, they refused to echo Toulouse's calls to boycott the Communist attempt at a general strike in June 1959 or to build the Spanish Trade Union Alliance when it was announced in 1960. In opposition to ASE, and together with the CNT in Catalonia and the Catalan Christian Workers' Solidarity (SOCC), they formed the Workers' Trade Union Alliance (ASO) in October 1962.[36]

This forced a radical reorganization of the region upon the weakened PSOE-UGT, but by financing *activistas* both for party and union work a number of industrial contacts were established. A new Federaçio Socialista de Catalunya was launched in 1967 and a Catalan paper was produced.[37] The slow resurgence was based on young new militants, notably Valentín Antón ('Emilio'), a metalworker born in Valencia in 1941 who joined the PSOE-UGT in 1960, and Josep María Triginer, an industrial engineer from Lérida, born in 1943, who came across the Young Socialists in 1962, joined them in 1968, and subsequently became a member of the FNJSE executive and leader of the FSC.[38] Yet for all their labours, Catalonia continued to be a relatively weak region for PSOE activism. During the next decade the FSC would look to convergence with the MSC's descendants as the only way of

[35] UGT, *Actas* of CE, 25.4.58. In the PSOE executive Barreiro proposed a similar break unless the MSC accepted an ultimatum to affiliate to the party. Llopis prudently counselled against such a rash move so long as the FSC remained weak (PSOE, *Actas* of CE, 9.4.58).

[36] UGT, Assemblies, *Actas* of CG, 10–11.8.59; id., *Circular*, 24.11.62; Jáuregui and Vega, ii. 172–6. The CE of the PSOE, *Actas*, 13.8.69, reported continuing bad relations with both of the ex-MSC factions.

[37] PSOE, *Actas* of CE, 7.4.59, 21.10.59, 16.11.59, 26.7.61, 3.12.62, 6.12.62; untitled document submitted by federations of the interior to the CD and congress, Aug. 1967 (with PSOE, Executive Committee, *Circulares*, 1964–7); *Le Socialiste*, 23.1.69, 2. *L'Opinió Socialista*, a duplicated part-Catalan, part-Spanish FSC organ, appeared first in May 1968.

[38] *La Opinión Socialista* (Barcelona), 5 (1977); PSOE, *Actas* of CE, 29–30.1.66; *ES*, 13.12.77, 6, 23.7.78, 14–15.

overcoming the party's centralist image and becoming a real force in the region.

Asturias and its neighbours

In spite of its rebel traditions, Asturias did not witness major strikes until the late 1950s, significantly later than Vizcaya (1947) and Barcelona (1951). One explanation for this is that the mining and metallurgy enterprises here benefited from Franco's early autarkic policies, with their workers receiving relatively high wages and gaining exemption from military service.[1] However, the advantages of employment in basic industries were not exclusive to Asturias. Equally important explanations of labour passivity there were first, the high level of repression as the regime attempted to punish Asturias for its past and to wipe out its prolonged guerrilla resistance, and second, the insecurity caused by an abundant labour supply as migration from other parts of Spain was encouraged by the authorities.[2] Economic militancy grew in the late 1950s after the autarkic economic model had run into crisis and as local industries suffered from a lack of modernization which eventually obliged the State to take them over.[3] During the bitter strikes of the late 1950s, the first workers' commissions were formed here by rank-and-file miners, with the sympathy of some local priests and the active involvement of Catholic workers' organizations. Socialists too figured among their early participants, but later they withdrew as the PCE gradually managed to impose the Communist strategy upon them.[4] The strike movement was exhausted by the end of 1964, though it revived in 1969.

The Asturian Socialist Federation (FSA) was reorganized by Socialist guerrillas, who later transferred the leadership to

[1] Ruiz, *Asturias*, 129.

[2] Ibid. 128–31; Pons Prades, 178; Faustino Miguélez, *La lucha de los mineros asturianos bajo el franquismo* (Barcelona: Laia, 1976), 89–91.

[3] Ruiz, *Asturias*, 129–30; Ramón Bulnes, 'Asturias frente a su reconversión industrial', *Cuadernos de Ruedo Ibérico*, 4 (1965–6), 37–53.

[4] Interview with Avelino Pérez, Madrid, 27 Apr. 1982; PSOE, *Actas* of CE, 23.5.62. On the evolution of the CCOO, see Balfour; Sheelagh Ellwood, 'The Working Class under the Franco Regime', in Preston (ed.), *Spain in Crisis*, 157–82; 'El año X de las Comisiones Obreras: Historia y análisis de un proceso de degradación política', *Cuadernos de Ruedo Ibérico*, 31–2 (1971), 53–67.

civilians as they were released from prison.[5] With much reorganizing still to do, a committee of six was designated early in 1943, headed by Florentino Zápico, who also served as the FSC representative on the Comité Nacional of the PSOE. By the mid-1940s, the federation was publicizing its existence by producing a paper called *Valor*. It responded to news of a forthcoming visit by Franco by distributing leaflets that warned: 'Only fascists should attend a fascist rally.'[6] The Asturian Socialists divided their province into 20 organizational zones, of which 17 were represented when the FSA held a plenum in Oviedo in August 1946.[7] Such an event may suggest less security consciousness than existed in Vizcaya, but it also reflected the momentary optimism of the mid-1940s. Zápico presided over the FSA until April 1946, when police learnt of the identities of the provincial committee members; they fled to France. By late 1946 two committees had fallen, and a third lasted only until May-June 1947.[8] Meanwhile, efforts were made to resuscitate the miners' union SOMA, if at first only symbolically. Reorganized in March 1946, the leading positions of president and secretary were filled by the *guerrilleros* José Mata and Manuel F. Flórez, though representatives of three sub-regional committees (for Langreo, San Martín, and Mieres) were also included on the executive.[9] Early on, there can have been little or no FSA-SOMA differentiation, for what organization there was had its heart and body among the miners of the Nalón valley.[10]

When repression was stepped up in 1947–8, the thirty or so surviving guerrillas once more safeguarded the FSA's

[5] PSOE, Territorial Organizations, FSA former executive, 'Informe absolutamente reservado a la CE de la Unión General de Trabajadores en el Exilio', France, Nov. 1948; Juan Antonio Sacaluga, *La resistencia socialista en Asturias 1937–1962*, ch. 3. (Madrid: Editorial Pablo Iglesias, 1986.)

[6] PSOE, Territorial Organizations, Comisión Socialista Asturiana (CSA), *Circulares*, Sept. and Nov. 1946; Heine, *La oposición*, 331.

[7] SOMA Archive, Box A.LIX, letter of Zápico to Barreiro, 6 Sept. 1946.

[8] CSA, *Circulares*, Sept. and Nov. 1946; *Memoria* presented by executive to zonal groups of FSA for plenum on 17 July 1948, in CSA, *Circular* 14 (Sept. 1948). *Valor* ceased to appear after the typewriter and duplicator used to produce it were lost in the same police raids. Among leaders who reached France were Zápico, Bernardo Díaz, Silvino García, and Wenceslao Fernández.

[9] SOMA Archive, Box A.LVIII, 'Acta de la reorganización del Sindicato Minero Asturiano', Mieres, 23.3.46.

[10] SOMA Archive, Box A.LIX, Mata to Barreiro, 25 July 1946.

continuity. Having in the interim kept in touch by sending delegates to FSA executive meetings and plenums, and having helped to establish a UGT Provincial Secretariat early in 1947, the 'committee of the mountains' led by Mata and Flórez consulted zonal delegates and then assumed the leadership of the FSA in order to take pressure off their 'free' (i.e. civilian) comrades in mid-1947.[11] The transfer did not much affect the federation's life. Even with the executive committee meeting in the mountains and increasingly hard-pressed by Francoist forces, it none the less meticulously took minutes of its proceedings, sent copies of them to Toulouse, and apologized profusely when the minutes did not bear the official rubber stamp of the federation.[12] Similarly, its relations with the PCE and CNT in the mountains matched parallel attempts at collaboration with these forces in the provincial branch of the ANFD. Both the 'free' men and the *comité del monte* were to give the latter alliance a negative post-mortem report: in Asturias, they claimed, it had been undermined by Communist sectarianism, treachery, and irresponsibility, in spite of the participation of the 'loyal and courageous' CNT.[13]

During 1948 the enemy drag-net tightened around the guerrillas, leaving evacuation or death as their only prospects. Regime surveillance of suspected couriers increased while assassinations of known FSA and SOMA militants served to terrorize and demoralize guerrilla sympathizers. Between March and May, 22 Socialist miners were rounded up by special brigades, to be massacred at Pozu Funeres on 21 May 1948. Other killings followed, taking the death toll to at least 25 before the remaining 26 Socialist guerrillas were brought out in October.[14] The FSA survived this exodus, but the

[11] PSOE, Historical Project, 'El PSOE bajo el franquismo', 'Tamayo' (= 'Yo Mata', José Mata Castro) to CSA, 12 Aug. 1948, in CSA, *Circular*, Sept. 1948; PSOE, Territorial Organizations, Asturias, FSA former executive, 'Informe'.

[12] Ibid.; PSOE, Historical Project, 'El PSOE bajo el franquismo', FSA provincial executive report to Toulouse, 12.8.48.

[13] SOMA Archive, Box A.LIX, Zápico to Barreiro, 6.9.46; PSOE, Territorial Organizations, Asturias, FSA former executive, 'Informe'.

[14] *Adelante*, 1.10.48, 1 for FSA and SOMA report to British diplomatic officials; PSOE, Territorial Organizations, FSA, *Circular* 15 (Nov. 1948); *ES*, 8.7.48, 28.10.48. Another three activists were assassinated by the brigades operating in the mining zones in 1951 (PSOE in Exile, *Actas* of CE, 11.4.51; *Boletín de la UGT*, April-May 1951, 7).

guerrilla episode left its mark on the provincial organization. The prolongation of resistance and fierce repression in Asturias help explain why Socialist trade union organization was attempted somewhat later here than in Vizcaya, and why it had scant success early on. Although many of the guerrillas were former mineworkers themselves and could act as an armed unit, they could hardly present themselves as a credible trade union cadre, isolated as they were from the work centres. Various gestures to trade unionism were made, but in organizational terms these amounted to very little before the 1950s, and there was only a clear shift of emphasis from PSOE to UGT after Hermes Horne visited Asturias in 1957 and recommended ICFTU funding for a UGT 'activist' in the province.[15]

Another feature of Asturian Socialism was a very deep distrust of Madrid-based national executives following the 'Miguel Angel Martínez raids' of 1947: the provincial organization often preferred no link at all with the capital. Distrust and a certain insularity may also explain why, following Zápico's departure, no Asturian played a major role at national level until Agustín González joined the Comisión Permanente in 1967.[16] During the 1960s the Asturians showed themselves to be unreceptive to the idea of outsiders coming in from France to consolidate PSOE-UGT federations, as occurred in Catalonia and other places.[17]

In the early 1950s, with rebel activity in the mountains having been crushed generally, the Socialists were able to use an easing of the police presence to rebuild their organization. Within a few years they recovered well. Although no youth organization existed before the 1960s, the adult organization,

---

[15] Ferri *et al.*, 136; UGT, *Actas* of CE, 6.12.57, 10.1.58.

[16] UGT in Exile, *Actas* of CE, 13.11.53; PSOE in Exile, *Actas* of CE, 20.10.49, 23.7.52, 30.12.52, 24.3.54. Aragón and Santander similarly complained of a lack of assistance from Madrid in 1949 and tried to get Toulouse to send aid directly from France (ibid., 2.5.49). No Asturians went on to Amat's 5-man central committee set up in 1957, but two (from Sama de Langreo and Oviedo) did attend a national meeting that he organized ('Guridi' to CE, 9 Apr. 1957). The trade union 'activist' (*permanente*) in Asturias, Manuel Martín Rueda, attended meetings of the Comité de Coordinación from the mid-1960s (PSOE and other organizations, PSOE-UGT-FNJSE, *Actas* of the Comisión de los asuntos de España, 11–12.11.65).

[17] A. Pérez interview.

which fused its PSOE and UGT leaderships around 1955,[18] became for a while the most impressive in Spain. After a visit to the province early in 1954, Amat observed that a basis of strength existed already. In mid-1955 he returned from a further visit extolling the excellent spirit, serious attitude, and good working methods of the Asturians: 'If only all the regions were like that!'[19] Juan Iglesias, who took charge of the French side of the Toulouse-Bilbao link in the late 1940s, also considered the Asturian comrades to be 'excellent'.[20] In 1957–8 the FSA seems to have had 600 militants, more than any other provincial federation.[21] The heart of the organization lay in the Langreo coalfield, whereas the cities of Oviedo and Gijón were weak spots. As was traditional in Asturias, the PSOE failed to attract intellectuals. The organized Socialists were pre-eminently miners, and occasional attempts were made from here to launch a national mineworkers' union. In mid-1954, a SOMA congress attended by 11 provincial sections decided to attempt this, but it was not to be until late 1972 that a real national federation was finally established, based on SOMA and the UGT mining 'federations' of Ciudad Real, Huelva, and León.[22]

Already, though, there were signs that the FSA foundations were not as solid as Amat had thought. Above all, the Socialists had to recognize that many young miners were joining the PCE in preference to the PSOE. It was largely the sons of Socialist miners who joined their fathers' organizations, and when they did they found many veterans to be distrustful of young newcomers.[23] Moreover, Asturias was not to enjoy a lasting leadership core like that which facilitated organizational progress in Vizcaya. In May 1956 Asturias lost

[18] Ibid.; FNJSE, Correspondence, 'Correspondencia con el Interior', clandestine FSA to FSA in Exile, Nov. 1954.
[19] 'Guridi' to CE, 13 Feb. 1954, 21 June 1955.
[20] PSOE, Correspondence, 'Guridi' file, letter of 'Plácido' (Juan Iglesias) to Pascual (Tomás), 22 July 1958.
[21] A. Pérez interview; PSOE, *Actas* of CE, 11.9.57.
[22] 'Guridi' to CE, 2.6.54; A. Pérez interview; UGT, *Actas* of CE, 16.7.54; SOMA Archive, Box A.LVIII, 'Acta de constitución de la Federación Nacional de Industria de la Minería', 21.10.72.
[23] 'Guridi' to CE, 2 June 1954; *ES*, 10.4.58, 1. A. Pérez told me that he was one of the few youths who 'managed' to join the PSOE in the mid-1950s, in the face of veteran hostility.

an outstanding activist, Vicente Requena, who earlier had organized the embryo of a transport federation in Madrid. Before slashing his wrists (for unknown reasons) he had become the 'soul' of the party in Asturias and its main internal link-man. His replacement Cándido Jiménez died only a year after taking on the responsibility.[24] Then, in 1958–64, Asturias suffered from far too frequent arrests, some of them part of the national round-up of late 1958, the others in response to miners' strikes. Some 18 militants were detained in 1958, of whom half were committed for trial. FSA president Rufino Montes Suárez was forced to flee the country that year and those arrested included leading figures such as Jenaro Fernández López, whom Amat had used as his main contact in Oviedo.[25] A younger leadership formed by the miners Herminio Alvarez Iglesias, Avelino Pérez, and Prudencio Magdalena Velasco began to function in 1959, chiefly reproducing and distributing UGT propaganda in the mining areas.[26] Lacking the resources of the Communists, the Socialist 'apparatus' here consisted of no more than a wooden duplicating device made by Pérez, and a rather conspicuous Vespa scooter from which leaflets were scattered in working-class centres. This team fell into police hands in August 1960, and heavier losses were to come in 1962 when Pérez was forced to escape to France to avoid re-imprisonment. He reported there that some 200 workers had been 'victimized' for their involvement in the miners' strike of that year.[27]

Socialist involvement in the strikes of 1962–4 (which were another spur to the adoption of a UGT image) was proclaimed by the party, acknowledged by its rivals, and punished by the regime. Some of the miners accused by the courts of being strike leaders were also charged with PSOE-UGT membership (though they were acquitted).[28] However, the Asturian Socialists were not strengthened by their role in the

[24] 'Guridi' to CE, 20 May 1956, 12 Oct. 1957.
[25] A. Pérez interview; *What is Happening*, 124–7; PSOE, *Actas* of CE, 28.5.58; PSOE, Trial Papers, Sumario 10,960, 'Conclusiones de fiscal'; *Le Socialiste*, 5.3.64, 1, 3.
[26] PSOE, Assemblies, *Actas* of CD of Aug. 1959; id., Trial Papers, 'Sumario 273–61'; *Le Socialiste*, 21.12.61, 6.
[27] PSOE, Trial Papers, 'Sumario 273–61'; A. Pérez interview; PSOE, *Actas* of CE, 13.6.62, 12.9.62.					[28] *Le Socialiste*, 9.1.64, 7–8.

strikes, and general labour demoralization only offers a partial explanation of why this was so. While the strikes helped to maintain UGT prestige, the Socialists were far from becoming the undisputed vanguard of the provincial labour movement. One problem was that from the 1950s Asturian Socialism had not been producing the natural working-class leaders it had in the past; there was nobody here with the same authority among workers as the Socialist leaders in Vizcaya. From the mid-1950s the leadership had included figures in Oviedo such as the industrialist Jenaro Fernández and the insurance agent Vicente Fernández Iglesias.[29] True, by the 1960s the federation's social composition was becoming generally somewhat less working class, with proportionally fewer miners and more teachers; but while a more middle-class leadership facilitated extension beyond the coal-fields it did not enhance the UGT's competitiveness when it came to bidding for miners' support.[30] This problem was compounded by a deliberate policy of putting young inexperienced militants in the front line during disputes, the idea being to train them in the struggle and not to risk activists who had been detained before.[31]

By the mid-1960s the Asturian Socialists possessed a sizeable organization, but one which was relatively inactive. A rather too rosy impression of its true strength was provided in 1966 by a report stating that it had distributed some 600–700 membership cards to both SOMA and a metalworkers' union, for members' dues to be entered.[32] The true picture, which emerged from a meeting of the UGT Provincial Secretariat in September 1967, attended by 40 zonal delegates, was of many members and sympathizers but little activity. Repression was certainly a factor: at least 20 Asturian Socialists were arrested that year, among them an emerging leader, Emilio Barbón.[33] However, the greater problem that

---

[29] A. Pérez interview; *What is Happening*, 125–7.

[30] Ibid.; PSOE, Trial Papers, 'Sumario 273–61'. Asturian envoy Antonio Ruiz reported on the existence of groups in Mieres, Sama de Langreo, Oviedo, Gijón, and Avilés (PSOE, *Actas* of CE, 10.4.62).   [31] PSOE, *Actas* of CE, 23.5.62.

[32] Ibid., 29–30.1.66. Union dues were collected but no fixed amount was set. A monthly periodical *Adelante* was being produced by this time.

[33] SOMA Archive, Box A.LX, UGT Provincial Secretariat meeting, *Actas*, 17.9.67; ibid., CSA, *Circular*, Nov. 1967.

prevented the Socialists (by now organized simply on a UGT basis) from being active throughout the province was generational conflict. After veterans had allowed the organization to decline for several years, a new inexperienced leadership was established in mid-1967. This UGT Provincial Secretariat was faced with the need to reorganize at PSOE and FNJSE level, and to get SOMA to function—tasks that were not made easier by a boycott of the Secretariat by inactive veterans, who allegedly slandered its members and accused its president ('Alfredo') of being a police agent.[34] Meanwhile, collaboration was entered into at provincial level with USO for interventions in the sporadic miners' strikes of 1969, the CNT by now having ceased to be a force in Asturias.[35] From having begun the Franco period with a PSOE emphasis and later having developed more of a UGT approach, or at least appearance, the Asturian Socialists finally came full circle early in 1970 when a new FSA executive committee was chosen to work for unity. A new phase of steadier growth ensued.[36]

Partly because it had had so many problems of its own to resolve, the Asturian Federation failed in the mission entrusted to it in the mid-1950s to extend the clandestine structure to León and Galicia.[37] Occasional exploratory visits for talks with scattered contacts produced nothing in organizational terms. Traditionally the left as a whole had been weak here in the north-west, which had been in Franco's hands right from 1936. The Socialists' presence in the region in the early 1940s was constituted mainly by guerrillas, several of them Asturian in origin. These rebels raised the party banners in the north-west but took them with them when they left in 1947.[38] Although at times it seemed as if Galicia were about to be added to the Socialist map, this was always as a

---

[34] SOMA Archive, Box A.LXI, UGT Vice-Sec. to 'Pablo' (R. Rubial), 23 Feb. 1968; ibid., *Actas* of provincial committee of UGT, 25.8.68. The PSOE leaders (*Actas* of CE, 19.7.67) attributed the problem to personality clashes.

[35] PSOE, *Actas* of CE, 27.8.63, 6; *Le Socialiste*, 8.5.69, 3.

[36] PSOE, *Actas* of CE, 7.2.70.

[37] 'Guridi' to CE, 9.4.57, 20.10.58.

[38] PSOE, *Actas* of CE, 1.4.54. On Galicia see H. Heine, *A guerrilla*; id., 'La evolución política en Galicia (1939–1975)', *Cuadernos de Ruedo Ibérico*, 51–3 (1976), 21–49.

result of outside initiatives.[39] Galicia had no representative at national party meetings and no 'activist' was sent to work there. Even as late as 1973, when Francisco Bustelo went there to take up a post at the University of Santiago, the PSOE in the north-west was 'virtually non-existent'.[40]

Santander was a different matter. After Amat had found some recruits there in 1955, the Asturians did manage to implant a small organization in this northern city.[41] And although Santander itself did not give rise to a large organization, its trade union 'activist' Basilio Rodríguez performed sterling services for the party by extending it to Old Castile.[42] During the 1960s, with Santander as the zonal base of operations, already well co-ordinated with Asturias and Bilbao,[43] Rodríguez oversaw the creation of three small provincial federations in Valladolid, Salamanca, and Burgos, which were first represented together at a Comité Director meeting in August 1967. No progress was made in the other provinces of Old Castile.[44]

Aragón

In Aragón there was virtually no organized body of Socialists outside Zaragoza, but in that city the PSOE had a relatively

[39] PSOE, *Actas* of CE, 7.11.56, 27.8.63, 20.12.67; 'Guridi' to CE, 2.6.54, 21.6.55; UGT, *Actas* of CE, 7.11.58.

[40] PSOE, *Actas* of CE, 16.11.59, 28.9.63; personal interview with Francisco Bustelo, 26 Apr. 1982.

[41] PSOE, *Actas* of CE, 1.4.55, 25.5.55; 'Guridi' to CE, 2 June 1954; CE to 'Guridi', 8 June 1955; 'Guridi' and Comité Central Socialista de Euskadi to Prieto, 1 Apr. 1957; UGT, *Actas* of CE, 6.12.57; PSOE, Assemblies, *Actas* of CD, 11–12.8.58.

[42] Jáuregui and Vega, i. 213; PSOE and other organizations, PSOE-UGT-FNJSE, Comisión de los asuntos de España, *Actas*, 24.7.63, 11–12.11.65. Rodríguez was Old Castile's representative on the Comité de Coordinación.

[43] As seen in 1960, when Socialists of the north including José Pérez Andrés and Santos Alonso Cañas of Santander were arrested. See *Le Socialiste*, 21.12.61, 6; PSOE, Trial Papers, 'Sumario 273–61'. Santander was affected again by arrests in 1968 (*Le Socialiste*, 26.12.68, 1).

[44] PSOE, *Actas* of CE, 29–30.1.66; PSOE and other organizations, PSOE-UGT, *Actas* of CD/CG of 25 Feb. 1967; PSOE, Assemblies, *Actas* of CD, 9–10.8.67. From 1954 at least, the PSOE had contact with an important militant in Burgos, Manuel Cantos Solís, who brought in a few others; but its organization as a group dates from the 1960s. See 'Guridi' to CE, 2 June, 18 Sept. 1954, 1, 9 Apr., 8 Nov. 1957. In 1954 the Socialists had 20 prisoners in Burgos compared with 397 classified as Communists (UGT, *Actas* of CE, 17.6.54).

durable organization. This was built in 1942–6, following a visit by San Sebastián comrades the previous year. Although historically this had been a weak area for the PSOE, dominated as it was by the CNT, several hundred Socialists had been reorganized by the mid-1940s, as was reflected in the 1,000-copy print-run of the local fortnightly issues of *El Socialista*, *UGT*, and *Vida Nueva*.[1] Again, this was a place where support was forthcoming from the British consul; indeed he lost his job as a result. Zaragoza's decline owed a lot to police action: a few arrests in 1947, then over 40 more in February 1948 when the leadership and party apparatus fell. This forced the federation to re-employ leaders who had been detained in 1947 and who since then had enjoyed only 'conditional liberty'. It may well be the case also that militants were lost to the PCE, for this was one of the few parts of Spain where the PSOE enthusiastically took part in the Communist-led National Union.[2]

After rising again to 50 or 60 militants, Zaragoza's organization declined notably in the early 1950s. When Amat visited the city in 1954 he found that nearly all the contact names he had been given were of 'pro-Soviet' elements; rather than a federation, he found there just one 'good' comrade ('Ibor').[3] In what remained of the decade the Zaragoza group was gradually rebuilt. Despite the lack of an 'activist' for Aragón, it began to be represented at national party meetings in the mid-1960s.[4] However, no branch of the Spanish Trade Union Alliance came into being here—a sign that UGT weakness, and not always the non-availability of

---

[1] PSOE, Territorial Organizations, Zaragoza, Federación Provincial de Zaragoza, 'Informe sobre la situación del PSOE en la posguerra', 1976. Dues of 1 pta. were levied and according to this source the UGT collected 950 ptas., the PSOE 650 ptas., and the FNJSE 400 ptas. (each had a committee). Of course some militants may have paid more than the minimum. Heine (*La oposición*, 332) puts the number of active Socialists here at 300 in 1943.

[2] PSOE, Territorial Organizations, Zaragoza, FPZ 'Informe'; *ES*, 5.3.59, 4 (report on the trial of 32 of the Zaragoza Socialists arrested in 1948).

[3] PSOE, Territorial Organizations, Zaragoza, FPZ 'Informe'; 'Guridi' to CE, 13 Feb. 1954.

[4] 'Guridi' to CE, 12 Oct. 1957; PSOE, Assemblies, *Actas* of CD, Aug. 1959, Aug. 1967; PSOE, *Actas* of CE, 16.11.59, 28.9.63, 29–30.1.66; PSOE and other organizations, PSOE-UGT-FNJSE, Comisión de los asuntos de España, *Actas*, 12.11.63, 11–12.11.65.

CNT partners, was a fundamental reason for the Alliance's failure.[5]

The Levant

Further south, Valencia was another province of strong CNT tradition where there was a failure to establish the Alliance, in spite of a surviving UGTpresence. Reorganization in Valencia began in 1944, when Socialists including the former Albacete Civil Governor and Caballerista Justo Martínez Amutio were released from prison. An important role was played too by Antonio Cuadra, who after spending the years 1939–43 in hiding, went to Valencia with false papers to gain employment as a metalworker; he reorganized the party in Turia, became president of the Valencian provincial federation, suffered imprisonment in 1948–52, and later presided over the Santander group.[1] The loss of an entire UGT committee in May 1945 and further arrests in the early 1950s may help explain why Valencia was one of the weakest organizations early on.[2]

Amat established a link between the *émigré* party executive and Valencia early in 1954 and from then on he looked to his contacts there to organize in other parts of the Levant. He found the Valencian Socialists to be weaker than both the anarchists and the Republicans. In contrast with the situation elsewhere, they all seemed to want to be leaders.[3] By the end of 1955, however, greater unity had been nurtured and the organization strengthened. The Levant was divided into 10 districts and some 23 embryonic union federations were set up. This raised Amat's hopes of there being solidarity action here (along with Asturias) in support of a Bilbao strike the following year, but these were dashed completely. Vizcaya remained the only province where Socialists occasionally could mobilize workers for short strikes and protests in

[5] PSOE and other organizations, PSOE-UGT, *Actas* of CD/CG, 20–1.7.63, 157; PSOE, *Actas* of CE, 13.6.52, 29–30.1.66.
[1] PSOE, *Actas* of CE, 13.6.52; Martínez Amutio, op. cit.; Almendros Morcillo *et al.*, 126; *ES*, 15–21.6.83; *ES(H)*, 1.4.81.
[2] Almendros Morcillo *et al.*, 126; PSOE, *Actas* of CE, 11.6.52; Llopis to 'Guridi', 28 June 1954.
[3] PSOE, *Actas* of CE, 12.1.55; 'Guridi' to CE, 13 Feb., 2 June 1954.

support of struggling workers in other provinces. In Valencia the primary Socialist activity was one of looking after comrades who were in prison.[4]

Only mildly affected by the raids of the late 1950s, the Valencian federation for a long time could report little in the way of activity, even when it became represented more regularly on national party organs and provided an executive member (Agustín Soriano) in the mid-1960s.[5] But by then some growth was occurring in Alicante (where the UGT gained as a result of a CNT schism) and in Murcia, and by the end of the decade Valencia itself was becoming slightly more active as some exiles returned to Spain and as veterans resumed their political involvement.[6]

Andalucía and Extremadura

In spite of an impressive spread of UGT influence in the south during the 1930s, Socialist support here had been poorly rooted and dependent upon the State patronage of Andalusian workers that had existed under PSOE ministers. Thus in both Andalucía and Extremadura the outlawed PSOE-UGT suffered from a weak organizational starting-point. The greater part of these two regions had been controlled by rebel forces since early in the Civil War, and when it was over many left-wing militants abandoned the south in search of the anonymity afforded by big cities. Another source of party weakness in the south were the personal animosities to be found in Seville, for this city became a regional reorganizing centre for the PSOE in the mid-1940s (not least because several of the most prominent Andalusian Socialists were incarcerated together in the city). In Seville considerable disruption was caused by leadership rivalry between the former provincial leader of the PSOE in Jaén, Alfonso Fernández Torres, and a former lieutenant-colonel in the

---

[4] 'Guridi' to CE, 2 June 1954, 27 Dec. 1955, 2 May 1956; UGT, *Actas* of CE, 17.6.54. In 1955 there were 15 Socialist prisoners in Valencia.

[5] *What is Happening*, 126; *ES*, 28.5.59; 'Guridi' to CE, 19 Dec.1957; PSOE and other organizations, PSOE-UGT-FNJSE, Comisión de los asuntos de España, *Actas*, 11–12.11.65; PSOE, *Actas* of CE, 29–30.1.66.

[6] PSOE, *Actas* of CE, 1–3.12.64, 29–30.1.66; Almendros Morcillo *et al.*, 130.

Republican Army, Urbano Orad de la Torre.[7] Each man had his own coterie of followers, neither of them organized properly as a PSOE *agrupación* (branch) or as a cell. Both men's professional careers, as lawyer and as soldier, had been ruined by the military defeat; both had death sentences hanging over their heads (and Fernández's father was executed) until reprieves were eventually granted. Their experiences left them extremely cautious when subsequently they were urged by their party to undertake tasks of reorganization.

Andalucía's efforts to rebuild in the 1940s were based on 'the old militants',[2] those whom one could trust; when these veterans' capacity for struggle waned, it would not be until the 1960s that a new team of dynamic youths would begin to take the initiative. A further reason for Socialist organizational weakness in the south, particularly in the period after 1954, was the geographical distance of this region from the party headquarters in Toulouse, which for example meant that *El Socialista* would be at least a month old by the time it arrived. Poor communications also help to explain the strength of internal party dissidence in the south, represented by the Seville veterans and by Francisco Román Díaz in Málaga, who during the 1950s and 1960s repeatedly defied external direction of the party. For all these reasons, steady PSOE progress was not evident in Andalucía until the early 1970s, nor in Extremadura (doomed by executive decision to develop there only in the event of Andalusian success) until the mid-1970s. Together these regions formed one-third of the land surface of Spain, and the long distances between individual party supporters or incipient nuclei made rebuilding more difficult than elsewhere. Nevertheless, the Communists managed to organize there as the CNT gradually lost its traditional hold on the south.[3] The reputation for Andalusian strength which the PSOE gained later was less a reflection on the level of Socialist anti-Franco activity there, than upon the

---

[1] On Fernández see *ES*, 22.5.77, 22, 24.12.78, 1, 6; on Orad see Vilar, 315–18. Fernández was born in 1907, Urbano in 1904.

[2] PSOE, Historical Project, 'El PSOE bajo el franquismo', memoir of María Jesús Alfonso Fernández Torres (1976), 5.

[3] Hermet, 117; UGT, *Actas* of CE, 7.11.58.

Andalusian origins of the new party leaders who dominated the national leadership from 1974.

Besides Seville, there seem to have been some rebuilding efforts in the mid-1940s in Jaén, Málaga, Granada, Almería, and Córdoba, but the fruits of this activity had withered by the end of the decade. The flight from Spain of regional general secretary Francisco López Real at the end of 1947 marked the start of a long period of Andalusian inactivity, apart from the periodic reunions of nostalgic veterans.[4] When Antonio Amat visited the region in 1954, Andalucía was virtually devoid of Socialist activity. After years of isolation from the Madrid and Toulouse executives, there were no more than handfuls of veterans in Seville, Jaén, and Granada. Meeting Fernández in Seville, Amat found him 'apathetic in the extreme', reluctant to distribute propaganda and claiming that nothing could be done.[5] For this reason, Málaga became the regional headquarters for Amat's rebuilding efforts, though he hoped later to subdivide Andalucía into western and eastern zones, with Seville as the base for the west. In Málaga, Francisco Román became Amat's delegate and from 1955 he attempted to connect and inject dynamism into the other three Andalusian groups. By late 1956 links existed with a further group in Córdoba, and two years later there were signs of Seville becoming more active. In October 1958 an Andalusian plenum of provincial representatives was held in an attempt to reconcile the two Sevillian cliques, but Amat's imprisonment and the brief detention shortly afterwards of the two Sevillian antagonists by the police seem to have stymied the initiative.[6]

---

[4] PSOE, Historical Project, Fernández Torres memoir, 5; Heine, *La oposición*, 331; *ES*, 17.6.79. 'Curro' López Real was general secretary of all three Socialist organizations (PSOE, UGT, and FNJSE) in Andalucía because so few people were prepared to accept positions. He left Spain after Socialists in Almería were tortured and identified him to the police as the regional leader (personal interview, 4 June 1984).

[5] PSOE, *Actas* of CE, 30.11.54, 9.3.55; Llopis to 'Guridi', 28 June 1954; 'Guridi' to CE, 10 Oct. 1954.

[6] 'Guridi' to CE, 1 Mar., 20 Apr., 12 July, 2 Aug. 1955, 7 May, 12 Dec. 1956, 9 Apr., 19 May 1957, 2 Jan., 20 Oct. 1958; PSOE, Assemblies, *Actas* of CD, 11–12.8.58, 9. Román, an administrator born in 1914, also played a major role nationally, especially while Amat was co-ordinator. He was secretary of the 5-man central committee established at a national meeting in Oct. 1957 (PSOE, *Actas* of CE, 30.11.57, 24.2.58).

The pattern of isolated nuclei persisted well into the 1960s in Andalucía, while total amorphousness remained the fate of Extremadura. However, some slow progress was made in the south, especially after Román became the UGT *activista* for Andalucía. The regional 'take-off' point came in 1967 when a visit by 'Félix', on behalf of the party executive, laid the basis for an Andalusian federation. His tour resulted in new groups being formed in several provinces. Six of the eight Andalusian provinces were by now organized, and Jaén and Córdoba took only a few more months to reactivate. All eight provinces of Andalucía were represented, for the first time together, at a meeting of the PSOE Comité Director in August 1967. Extremadura continued to be unrepresented, a region where there were Socialists but no groups.[7]

In the reorganization of Andalucía the part played by Sevillians was somewhat less important than later versions have suggested. Although Alfonso Fernández was to side with Llopis in a gesture of generational solidarity when the PSOE split in 1972, both he and Urbano Orad were regarded by Toulouse as trouble-makers during the 1960s. Orad signed a dissident letter to the ICFTU in 1964, appealing for aid to be sent directly to the interior, bypassing Toulouse; and Fernández was equally rebellious. He joined the executive for a brief spell in 1965, as secretary of the interior's Comisión Permanente, but his uncooperative attitude helped condemn the latter to a short life—as did, supposedly, the geographical dispersion of its members.[8] Toulouse blamed Seville for the weak state of the party in Andalucía. In February 1967 the leadership went to the extreme of deeming the Seville

[7] PSOE, *Actas* of CE, 13.6.52, 7.6.67; id., Assemblies, *Actas* of CD, Aug. 1967.

[8] SOMA Archive, Box A.LIX, letter of 18 Feb. 1964 from 11 Socialists of the interior to Omer Becu of the ICFTU, contained in letter from Pascual Tomás to Arcadio Martínez Fernández, 20 Apr. 1964; letter from Juan Zarrías, member of the same Comisión Permanente, to the author, 4 Oct. 1982; PSOE, *Actas* of CE, 29–30.1.66; PSOE and other organizations, PSOE-UGT-FNJSE, Comisión de los asuntos de España, *Actas*, 11–12.11.65. With the exception of Rubial, whose Bilbao base facilitated the link with Toulouse, the next Comisión Permanente was composed of Madrid Socialists: Emilio Agüero and Antonio Sierra. At this time the PSOE decided to give Andalucía two places on the Comité de Coordinación on account of the region's size. Román started to represent the eastern part and Antonio Martín Rueda (brother of the Asturian 'activist' Manuel Martín Rueda) covered the western part.

organization to be dissolved and decided to rebuild it from scratch. Though some observers would reduce the problem to the personal animosity that existed between Llopis and Fernández, it is worth noting that this move against the Sevillian veterans was supported by the first meeting of the Comité Director in France at which representatives of the federations of the interior were in the majority. By now both interior and exterior were fed up with the repeated manifestations of Seville's personalized dissidence and the group's failure to send representatives to major meetings.[9]

The rebuilding of the Sevillian organization came finally through the local efforts of a handful of young militants. Around 1962, Alfonso Fernández Malo (son of the Sevillian veteran) and Alfonso Guerra had begun to organize a Young Socialist group, which before long had recruited Luis Yáñez, Felipe González, Guillermo Galeote, and a few others. The newcomers were young students who early on concentrated on recruiting faculty colleagues and trying to win young workers too; then, from the middle of the decade, as they graduated to join professions such as law and medicine, the young Socialists joined the provincial committee of the PSOE and began to organize in the name of the party. Inevitably, they rowed with the old men, who resisted the assembling of even a rudimentary propaganda apparatus on the grounds that the police discovery of their *vietnamita*, their crude home-made duplicating machine, would jeopardize the organization's existence. Yet while they increasingly bypassed the veterans, the younger Socialists retained immense respect and affection for these elders who had spent long years in prison for their beliefs and had introduced some of the youngsters to socialism. In the latter part of the 1960s, the younger Sevillians also visited other Andalusian centres, such as Huelva, Cádiz, Málaga, and Granada, where contacts were established. Through this activity an incipient Andalusian federation emerged in the early 1970s.[10]

[9] PSOE, *Actas* of CE, 29–30.1.66; id., Assemblies, *Actas* of CD, 9–10.8.67; PSOE and other organizations, PSOE-UGT, *Actas* of CD/CG, 25.2.67.

[10] Interview with Luis Yáñez, Madrid, 1 June 1984. On this period in Seville see Eduardo Chamorro, *Felipe González: Un hombre a la espera* (Barcelona: Planeta, 1980), *passim*; Miguel Fernández-Braso, *Conversaciones con Alfonso Guerra* (Barcelona: Planeta, 1983), 51–60; 'Señor Presidente', *Diario 16* (Madrid), 2.12.82.

Felipe González attended his first meeting of the FNJSE's Comité Nacional in 1965 and of the PSOE's in 1969. The *émigrés* found these younger militants to be more active and co-operative than the Andalusian veterans, and thus the quarantine of Seville was lifted in 1969.[11] However, there continued to be a distinctive Sevillian approach to politics. Although they impressed the Socialists of the north by being dynamic, mobile, and articulate, the new Sevillian team led by Guerra and González sowed doubts in some minds by its refusal to organize an Andalusian UGT federation, or even to use these initials. As the young Sevillians saw it, the Workers' Commissions had become predominant in labour struggles in the south, and they therefore urged Socialists to affiliate to and strengthen the Commissions, even though by now these were Communist-led.[12] None the less, the political prestige of the Sevillian nucleus soon began to grow among Andalusian workers, for the legal practice where González worked was one that specialized in labour law and tried to assist working-class clients. Quite often, the latter would become useful political contacts.

Madrid and New Castile

Finally, there was a rather more sizeable Socialist organization in Madrid, though one that was distinctly inferior to those of the north. Even in the mid-1940s, when it reached its numerical peak for the period 1939–74, the organization in Spain's capital involved just over 300 militants. In other words, it was no larger than the PSOE in Zaragoza.[1] Naturally, State vigilance was most pervasive here and the Madrid Socialist organization (ASM) lost committees in police raids at least as regularly as the early national executives were destroyed. But repression alone does not explain

[11] PSOE, *Actas* of CE, 11.6.69, 3.1.70; PSOE and other organizations, PSOE-UGT-FNJSE, 'Comisión Permanente 1965/1969', 'Perez' (Peydro) to Armentia, 23 June 1969.
[12] Interviews with Manuel Garnacho, Madrid, 13 Sept. 1982, and L. Yáñez; Jáuregui and Vega, ii, 336.
[1] PSOE, Territorial Organizations, Zaragoza, FPZ 'Informe'; Fernández Lopez, 'Apunte histórico', 9.

Madrid's weakness, for even when relatively untroubled by arrests after 1954 the ASM as such was not particularly active. Although young militants were the architects of party re-organization in Madrid, veterans inherited control of the organization when the early front-liners were arrested. In the 1950s, with some exceptions, veteran predominance in the official ASM spelled inactivity or at least little activity that involved risks.[2] Then in the 1960s, when a new generation of activists began to want more party activity, their demands at first served only to kindle internal conflicts that distracted the party from the anti-Franco struggle, and were a forerunner of things to come in the PSOE as a whole. The social composition of the PSOE in Madrid was strongly middle class,[3] a fact that militated in favour of leadership rivalry and ideological discord. Thus, for most of the period after 1945 the Madrid Socialists were introspective, when not inactive, and they did nothing to extend their organization from the city to the province of Madrid, nor to expand into New Castile as the schema of reorganization demanded.[4]

Successive police raids and the general decline in anti-Franco morale and action left the ASM exceedingly weak by the early 1950s. Reports reaching the *émigré* UGT executive indicated that several embryonic federations were working well (rail, building, wood, metallurgy, communications), but not in Madrid.[5] The only sign of a Socialist working-class presence in the capital was provided by the party's leading role alongside monarchists in the bakers' strike of May 1951. It resulted in 50 arrests, many of the detainees being PSOE veterans who were accused of paying dues to a subversive organization.[6] The problem in the capital was that the few workers who stuck with the PSOE were ageing, hyper-

---

[2] Interviews in Madrid with Antonio Villar Massó, 28 June 1983, Miguel Boyer, and Antonio Diez Yagüe, 25 June 1983; 'Guridi'-CE correspondence, 1954–8, *passim*.

[3] Ibid.; interviews with José Antonio Muñoz Atienza, Madrid, 25 June 1983, and Pablo Castellano, Madrid, 20 July 1982; Pablo Lizcano, *La generación del 56: La Universidad contra Franco* (Barcelona: Grijalbo, 1981), 256–7.

[4] Castellano interview.

[5] UGT, *Actas* of CE, 13.11.53, 12.2.54, 23.6.54, 7.11.56; PSOE, *Actas* of CE, 12.11.54, 12.1.55, 8.2.55; 'Guridi' to CE, 1 Aug. 1956.

[6] *ES*, 24.5.51, 4, 14.6.51, 1, 16.8.51, 4; PSOE in Exile, *Actas* of CE, 13.6.52. The bakers' union was again one of the best-organized Madrid unions at the end of the

cautious, and distrustful of young people. Some veterans had been affected permanently by the JSU desertion of the 1930s; for others, the mistrust of youth reflected either the PSOE's traditional esteem of seniority and experience, or doubts about the origins and sincerity of any youths who became socialists during the 1950s. For it was students who were in the vanguard of anti-Franco rebellion in this decade, and almost the entire university population was of bourgeois extraction. Several outstanding members of the new left were even of Falangist or monarchist parentage. Most of them became radicals at university, where the obligation to join the Falange syndicate, the SEU, and the authoritarian and dogmatic nature of higher education led them to struggle for democratization and liberalization, in some cases by revolutionary means. Their attitudes and concerns were substantially different from those of the typical Socialist veteran, who feared that any youths brought up under Francoism could not escape contamination. Moreover, there was obviously a considerable intellectual gulf between the two groups.

Once raids and arrests had removed the more dynamic members of the ASM from activity, the representative posts were left in the veteran hands of Teodomiro Menéndez, who was the party's main interlocutor with the monarchists, and Juan Gómez Egido, who was released from prison in 1954 and became the UGT 'activist' in Madrid in 1958. The latter, a painter, organized the infiltration of Francoist *sindicatos* in the mid-1950s, acting upon Amat's suggestion, but ASM activity as such barely existed at this time, while the PCE was beginning to show signs of strength.[7] Though the PSOE mood began to change at the end of the decade, when lawyers Rodolfo Vázquez and Miguel Peydro joined and Antonio Diez Yagüe and Manuel Gómez Ovejero were brought in from the New Iberian Generation (NGI),[8] for much of the decade total

Franco period, when it was under the revolutionary-socialist leadership of Agapito Recio de la Peña, on whom see *ES*(H), 15.6.80, 4.

[7] 'Guridi' to CE, 2 June 1954, 1 Mar., 20 Apr. 1955, 15 Feb. 1957, 4 May 1958; Llopis to 'Guridi', 28 June 1954; UGT, *Actas* of CE, 29.1.54.

[8] In 1957 Peydro returned from exile in Morocco despite opposition from the Toulouse leadership, which saw the move as too dangerous (UGT, *Actas* of CE, 26.7.57). Vázquez joined the PSOE-UGT in 1958 and went on to their provincial committees in 1964. The NGI pair were recruited by Amat in 1959. Since the mid-

demoralization and the need of individual sympathizers to earn a living left the ASM a mere skeleton. There were still several dozen Socialists who were prepared to receive the party paper and to meet periodically as a symbolic reaffirmation of political solidarity, but having known the hardship of prison life, in many cases, and often being responsible for the livelihood of a family, they abstained from building the party.

Nevertheless, there was socialist involvement in protests and strikes in the capital. It was mainly provided by two independent groups, though with the encouragement of Amat. First, there was a group led by Antonio Villar Massó, a law student who served as secretary of the SEU in Madrid's law faculty before turning to socialism. A trip to Paris in the early 1950s enabled him to contact Arsenio Jimeno and arrange to receive propaganda from abroad. Paris, rather than Toulouse, subsequently formed the principal French connection for the new sector represented by Villar.[9] Upon graduation Villar went to work in the legal firm of the liberal monarchist Antonio Garrigues, formerly Spanish ambassador in Washington and noted for his good relations with the US Embassy and multinationals; but the young socialist retained his university links by simultaneously serving as an assistant lecturer in law at Madrid University. By 1958 Villar had brought together some 40 political associates, of whom the most regular participants in *El Socialista* discussion groups at his home were his wife, fellow lawyers José Federico de Carvajal, Antonio Sempere, and Josefina Arrillaga, and the journalists Juan Antonio Matesanz and José Antonio Muñoz Atienza. It was through Villar that the Socialists acquired a degree of influence in Madrid University prior to the student

1950s the NGI had issued a bulletin called *Libertad* and had sent reports on Spain to Victoria Kent's New York magazine *Ibérica* (Diez Yagüe interview). On the NGI see Comisión Internacional de Juristas, *El imperio de la ley en España* (Geneva: Comisión Internacional de Juristas, 1962), 114–45.

[9] Interviews with José Federico de Carvajal, 23 Apr. 1982, and Villar Massó. Villar put his affiliation date for the PSOE at 1951 (interview; SOMA Archive, Box A.LX, letter of Villar to Carlos Martínez Cobo, 11 Jan. 1963). But what seems to be an account of his approach to the party in Paris appears in PSOE in Exile, *Actas* of CE, 7.4.53.

protests at the start of 1956, though unlike the Communists they had no proper organization there.[10]

During his first visit to Madrid on an official party mission, Amat found that the veteran circle surrounding Teodomiro Menéndez was squandering the aid it was receiving from France. He was delighted therefore when he found a Madrid group that was working with enthusiasm and seemed ready to accept party discipline.[11] It was this Villar group that in 1958 established an embryonic UGT Lawyers' Federation, headed by Carvajal, which took up the defence of political prisoners and, significantly, became the main symbol of the UGT in Madrid.[12] Lawyers had far greater possibilities than other mortals for trouble-free activism. They were articulate, their work and income gave them the necessary opportunities to travel freely and meet with regime opponents, and their social class and professional status made the regime reluctant to take action against them. Though Villar was among the Socialists who were rounded up towards the end of 1958, he was released on health grounds before the end of the year, while Carvajal escaped imprisonment entirely. Subsequently, Villar's role became more marginal: Amat was in prison, the police were more vigilant, and the Toulouse-based leaders were wary of his readiness to bypass them and work directly with Jimeno in Paris and *amatistas* at home.[13]

The other active socialist group in Madrid in 1956–60 was

[10] *ES*, 27.11.58, 1, 3; *New York Post*, 8.1.59; Jáuregui and Vega, i. 153–4. Another Socialist who started in Falangist circles was the scientist Miguel Sánchez-Mazas. Welles (p. 202) credits the PSOE with the student protests of Feb. 1956 but does not support his claim with evidence. On the events see Lizcano *passim*; Roberto Mesa (ed.), *Jaraneros y alborotadores* (Madrid: Universidad Complutense, 1982).

[11] 'Guridi' to CE, 13 Feb. 1954, 15 Feb. 1957, 11 June 1958. Martínez Parera (interview) also considered that Menéndez was misusing party funds.

[12] PSOE, Correspondence, 'Guridi' file, 'Plácido' to Pascual (Tomás), 22 July 1958. By 1960 this secretariat had problems (PSOE, *Actas* of CE, 20.4.60, 26.10.60).

[13] *Le Socialiste*, 1.11.62, 1–2. Reventós, also from a wealthy background, was similarly released on health grounds. One *émigré* complaint was that Villar held back from the Toulouse CE the details of his group's membership (interview with José Martínez de Velasco, Madrid, 27 June 1983). For some, the doubts were confirmed when Villar became a Freemason in 1972 and then Gran Maestro of the Gran Oriente Español in 1975. He left the PSOE at the time of Franco's death, explaining that he no longer considered himself indispensable to the party; he complained about the PSOE's persisting anti-monarchist sentiments (especially its ridiculing of Prince Juan Carlos); and decided that his own task was to reorganize the Freemasonry, which Franco had suppressed (Villar interview).

the University Socialist organization (ASU), whose links with the PSOE Amat also handled. ASU members had great respect for Amat, the man of action, and they identified with Spain's socialist tradition, as embodied in the PSOE and represented symbolically by the exiled leaders. But the socialist students were not prepared to subordinate themselves to the party executive in Toulouse, which they regarded as out of touch with Spain's problems and under the social-democratic influence of Guy Mollet. Feeling more at one with the left-wing socialism of Pietro Nenni and with the humanistic strain within Marxism, they none the less sought some kind of loose association with the PSOE.[14] Ironically, they approached the Socialists in the belief that the party could offer them a solid link with the working class; little did they know that by now the PSOE in Madrid lacked a proletarian base, and that they would have to visit the north to meet Socialist workers such as Ramón Rubial and Avelino Pérez.[15] ASU never had more than several dozen members, principally in Madrid, and its activities were disrupted regularly by arrests and the transience of student activism. Still, by establishing the Spanish Democratic University Federation (FUDE) to mobilize students on a broad democratic basis, they did manage (along with the Communists and the new Catholic left) to give student protest some direction in the late 1950s.[16]

This work continued in the first half of the 1960s, despite a decision to dissolve ASU in March 1961.[17] Not wanting to surrender ideological and organizational autonomy by affiliating to the PSOE,[18] the third 'generation' of ASU activists agreed on a compromise with the party: they would organize the Madrid Young Socialists (JSM) in the hope that

[14] Interviews with Juan Manuel Kindelán, Madrid, 26 Mar. 1982, M. Boyer, and F. Bustelo, 26 Apr. 1982.

[15] Kindelán interview; Lizcano, 256–7. The loss of working-class support was noted in 'Guridi' to CE, 11 June 1958.

[16] The major source on ASU is Lizcano, 174–99, 249–54. Predating ASU, in 1954 there were Young Socialist groups in the Medical Faculty at Valladolid and in the Law Faculties of Zaragoza and Madrid ('Guridi' to CE, 21.8.54).

[17] FNJSE, Assemblies, 'Informe de la CE al Consejo General', Oct. 1965, which reported that the Madrid Young Socialists were no longer active.

[18] ASU, Iª Conferencia Inter-regional (1960), *Actas*. The conference was attended by 9 delegates from Madrid and 1 from Valencia.

this group would become the corner-stone of a revived FNJSE at national level, the Youth having been absent since 1947. But from the start, the JSM's activity remained moored to its student bedrock, limiting its development. It was in the University of Madrid that the JSM had its only audience. When Luis Gómez Llorente addressed it in 1962, publicly to denounce SEU control of the student movement, the result was several months in prison for himself, Miguel Boyer, and Miguel Angel Martínez.[19] The JSM withstood these losses and brought in new cadres, including a Trotskyist group close to José Luis Abellán, but the core remained essentially a group of like-minded friends who had been educated together in the relatively liberal atmosphere of the Liceo Francés.[20]

From the late 1950s the overall Madrid picture was composed of two sectors, old and new, veteran and youth. There was no automatic identification between these sectors and their counterparts abroad. Early on, Madrid veterans such as Menéndez were regarded by Toulouse as unreliable, as a result of the pro-monarchist views that they shared with the more youthful sector in the interior. Moreover, until 1958, when he associated himself with demands for a new PSOE orientation, Antonio Villar was regarded by many as the metropolitan lieutenant of Rodolfo Llopis.[21] But the old/new dichotomy did tend to translate into passivity and activity, and the problem for the Toulouse executives was that from the late 1950s all the younger, more active people in Madrid, both in ASU and the Villar group, were completely identified with calls for a party 'renovation'. As early as 1958 Toulouse recognized that it had no properly organized group in the capital: it just had semi-autonomous groups which, although

---

[19] PSOE, *Actas* of CE, 15.2.61, 22.3.61; Lizcano, 254–61; *Le Socialiste*, 15.2.62, 4, 22.2.62, 2, 1.3.62, 8, 5.7.62, 1. Martínez was the son of the man of the same name who was expelled from the PSOE for informing in the late 1940s. In Apr. 1967 the son sent the party CE four documents that were said to prove that the allegations against his father had been untrue. The CE accepted his explanations (*Actas*, 3.5.67) but Madrid Socialists continued to regard the father as a traitor.

[20] Lizcano, 253, 260–1. This was the first case of Trotskyist involvement in the FNJSE, though Young Socialists collaborated with Trotskyists in Catalonia in the late 1940s and in Paris during the 1960s (García Duarte interview; Ildefonso Gómez ('Raul') interview, 15 June 1983).

[21] Bustelo interview (1982); SOMA Archive, Box A.LX, Villar to Carlos Martínez, 11 Jan. 1963.

increasingly dissident in their views, were able to go and speak to the foreign press in the name of the PSOE because of the inactivity of so many of the veterans.[22]

As part of its effort to achieve the desired blend of activity and discipline in Madrid, the party executive tried to find a suitable local delegate. In 1959–60 the executive looked to Miguel Peydro to do this job, but he proved unsatisfactory because of the opposition to him from the young radicals and from Josefina Arrillaga, Amat's lawyer and ardent admirer. She felt that her client, using herself as intermediary, could run the PSOE in Spain from a headquarters in Carabanchel Prison. For more than two years after Amat's incarceration, disputes over who really represented the party prevented negotiations taking place with other anti-Franco forces in the interior.[23] Eventually Toulouse got its loyal servant in Bilbao, Ramón Rubial, to visit Madrid and place authority in the hands of a trusted veteran. Following a trip at the end of 1961, Emilio Agüero became co-ordinator of the Madrid groups and was made responsible also for relations with other forces.[24]

PSOE politics in Madrid nevertheless remained a labyrinth of diverse currents and tendencies, even if to the public the party image (to the very limited extent that it had one) tended to be that presented by the veterans. The confusion that reigned is exemplified best by the case of Professor Enrique Tierno Galván's brief association with the ASM in the early 1960s. Tierno and his university group had been involved in public opposition to the regime for a decade, and for tactical reasons had agitated alongside the liberal monarchists of the Unión Española on behalf of the monarchy's restoration.[25] They were admitted to the ASM in December 1962 by a new committee presided over by Menéndez and including Peydro and Villar. This seems to have been named by the local

[22] CE to 'Guridi', 21 May 1958; PSOE, Assemblies, *Actas* of CD, 12–16.8.59; *Actas* of CE, 26.10.60.

[23] PSOE, *Actas* of CE, 7.4.59, 15.6.60, 26.10.60, 15.2.61, 12.9.62; 'Guridi' to CE, 11 June 1958.   [24] PSOE, *Actas* of CE, 31.1.62, 13.7.62.

[25] On Tierno's political development see Elías Díaz, *Pensamiento español en la era de Franco (1939–1975)* (Madrid: Tecnos, 1983), 75–8, 95–9, 126–9; E. Tierno Galván, *España y el socialismo* (Madrid: Tucar, 1976); id., *Cabos sueltos* (Barcelona: Bruguera, 1981); Partido Socialista en el Interior, *El Socialista en el Interior* (Madrid, 1971); *Le Nouveau Socialiste* (Oct. 1972–Nov. 1976); *Gaceta Socialista* (Mar. 1977–Apr. 1978).

representatives of Toulouse, Agüero, and the ASM secretary, Juan Zarrías. However, Llopis from afar opposed this affiliation and used Zarrías to deliver a notice terminating it. Ostensibly the general secretary had doubts about Tierno's 'monarchism', but behind these there may have lain a former schoolteacher's fear of being intellectually overshadowed by a university professor.[26] Moreover, by now Toulouse no longer regarded Villar as dependable. Not only had he participated in *amatista* efforts to restore control of the party to the interior, he had also attended the Munich meeting to reject Francoist Spain's membership of the EEC in 1962, thus creating confusion as to who really was representing the PSOE at the event—Villar or Llopis.

After Villar and Menéndez had resigned over the general secretary's intervention in the affairs of Madrid, Llopis achieved what presumably he had been seeking: to oblige Tierno to make a slightly humiliating pilgrimage to Toulouse to obtain the benediction of the party leader. This gained Tierno admission to the ASM in the eyes of Toulouse, but it provoked the resignation from the Madrid committee of Federico Fernández López, who protested that the procedure violated the party's statutes. Finally, in May 1965 Tierno was expelled from the ASM by a local committee that included Gómez Egido, Peydro, Zarrías, Mario Tanco, and Lázaro Movilla. His offence was to have acted as if he were the party leader in Spain and to have made unauthorized public statements abroad which *Le Figaro* presented as declarations by the leader of Spanish Socialism.[27] From 1968 Tierno's circle would pose as the 'Socialist Party in the Interior' (PSI), though in truth it remained a Madrid intellectual group and only began to build a party structure following its transformation into the Popular Socialist Party (PSP) in 1974.[28]

---

[26] SOMA Archive, Box A.LX, Villar to Carlos Martínez, 11 Jan. 1963; Villar interview; and, for Llopis' version of the events, Chamorro, 223–38. Tierno did not clarify the episode in *Cabos sueltos*. In a personal interview (Madrid, 22 Mar. 1982) he claimed that the PSOE had not understood his work with the monarchists.

[27] F. Fernández López interview; Chamorro, 223–38; Jáuregui and Vega, ii. 233–5.

[28] Fernando Morán interview, Madrid, 21 July 1982; Tierno Galván interview; *Triunfo*, 29.5.76, 14–16.

Throughout the 1960s, while loyalist veterans remained numerically predominant among Madrid's Socialists, defiance of Toulouse persisted stubbornly among the few dozen, mainly younger, members who were truly active.[29] Any co-operation with other anti-Franco forces could hardly be hoped for when it was absent from the metropolitan PSOE itself. With the Socialists now lacking a labour following here, and with the CNT not organized as such either, the Spanish Trade Union Alliance was doomed to failure in Madrid, though there was an attempt to base it locally on an agreement between the UGT and the Workers' Trade Union Federation (FST).[30] Neither did the UFD political alliance, for which Toulouse had negotiated hard and long, materialize in Madrid. As usual, the PSOE was quick to point to divisions affecting their prospective partners—in this case the Christian Democrats—but in the end the Socialists had to acknowledge that their own Madrid militants showed little interest in this projected alliance, either because they were absorbed in the routine of propaganda tasks, or because they saw that by now no effective anti-Franco alliance could be formed on an anti-Communist basis, with the PCE and Workers' Commissions excluded.[31]

Until the Young Socialists revived in the early 1970s, no mass work was done among workers and students, in spite of ⁺he growth in student numbers and appearance of major new industrial enterprises in the province during the 1960s. By the end of the decade there were fewer than 100 active members in Madrid. Their labour influence was significant only among the bakers and their student presence was restricted to the solitary Enrique Moral. Moreover, there was very little co-ordination between the northern, southern, eastern, and western circles into which the capital was reorganized in the mid-1960s.[32]

[29] PSOE, *Actas* of CE, 10.8.66; PSOE and other organizations, PSOE-UGT, *Actas* of CD/CG, 25.2.67. At least half the active Socialists in Madrid signed a dissident document that was sent to Toulouse.

[30] PSOE, *Actas* of CE, 29–30.1.66.

[31] Ibid., 15.5.66; PSOE and other organizations, *Actas* of CD/CG, 25.2.67; PSOE, *Circular*, 5.1.67; Hermet, 117. Propaganda work was the main activity in Madrid (UGT, *Actas* of CE, 10.1.58; Jáuregui and Vega, ii. 329; interviews with Luis Novo (22 July 1982), Diez Yagüe, Miguel Peydro (21 Apr. 1982), Castellano, and Muñoz Atienza). A local bulletin, *Eco Socialista*, was produced during the 1960s, and later *Tribuna Socialista*.

[32] Lacrampe, Ponce, and Vigre interviews; PSOE, *Actas* of CE, 29–30.1.66,

Although from the late 1950s there was always a current in Madrid seeking to 'renovate' the PSOE, its success did not come until shortly before Llopis suffered defeat in the party at large. Early on, the obstacle was that many would-be renovators were students and hence only organized on a short-term basis. Also of relevance was the fact that the sector loyal to Llopis did contain some active Socialists (such as the propaganda organizer Félix Bárcena), as well as many more who could be mobilized when congress delegates were to be selected. Furthermore, year after year of manœuvring and struggling against Llopis, let alone Franco, produced a growing frustration that led even some of the more dynamic elements to neglect political activity and concentrate for years on career development. Some found themselves 'expelled' by Madrid committees encouraged by Llopis: Villar and Carvajal for attending a monarchist banquet, Boyer for arranging with the Communists a delegation to attend a conference in Yugoslavia.[33] Only in the late 1960s, with Madrid lawyer Pablo Castellano becoming the main spokesman for the 'new' sector and veteran Eduardo Villegas finally encouraging a break with the Toulouse officials, did the *renovadores* begin to pose a coherent alternative to the pro-Llopis sector. The veteran sector presided over by Gómez Egido remained numerically superior, but now, at the turn of the decade, Madrid's dissidents at last began to build the party independently of any external discipline.

Overall, then, the PSOE presence in Franco's Spain was geographically uneven and displayed different characteristics in the various areas in which it was to be found. In no part of Spain did a significant 'left opposition' emerge to challenge party orthodoxy. Reformist attitudes were securely entrenched in the northern proletarian areas which remained the strong-

10.8.66; Castellano interview; Jáuregui and Vega, ii. 233, 326–8. Francisco Jiménez Gutiérrez (interview, Madrid, 27 June 1984) put Madrid affiliation at about 40 in 1968; Ildefonso Gómez (interview) stated that there were about 100 members when he joined in the early 1970s.

[33] Boyer nominated Villar and Diez Yagüe as the Socialists to join Ignacio Gallego of the PCE in a 'Spanish Anti-Fascist Alliance' delegation for the Yugoslav conference. On the expulsions see PSOE and other organizations, PSOE-UGT, *Actas* of CD/CG, 3.7.66, 25.2.67; PSOE, Assemblies, *Notas* of CD, July 1966; id., *Actas* of CE, 10.8.66, 9.11.66, 17.12.66, 24.9.69; id., *Circulares*, 28.7.66, 8.3.67.

holds of the illegal party. More revolutionary attitudes were voiced from time to time by the young university bloods of Madrid, but their relative autonomy from Toulouse precluded any effective attempt to transform the party from within. Meanwhile, any shift by the PSOE in a social-democratic direction was barred by the intransigence and authoritarianism of the regime.

The PSOE's level of activity depended a lot on local group initiatives. Where the party was organized, these initiatives tended to be parochial or at most provincial, involving intervention in a nearby strike or protest. Propaganda work— the distribution of *El Socialista* and in places the production of a modest clandestine bulletin—was the lowest common denominator of party activism. Persistent recruitment and organizational efforts were confined largely to the north. Only from the mid-1960s, following two very difficult decades, did the PSOE begin to revive on anything like a national scale. At this time the payment of dues became a far more general phenomenon, the interior's attendance at meetings and congresses in France became more representative of the active groups, the Comisión Permanente grew to form a large minority of the seats on the party executive, and the Comité de Coordinación expanded steadily as new provincial groups began to take part in national deliberations. Yet geographical disparities in the PSOE presence in the interior remained pronounced and became a factor in internal party disputes. Most immediately, Madrid's poor performance in the late 1960s, in contrast to the Socialists' advances in Asturias and Vizcaya, led to the capital's representation on the Comisión Permanente being reduced from two out of seven members in 1967 to one out of nine in 1970: a national decision that spurred Madrid into revolt. But by this time a broader mood of rebellion against the party executive was also gathering strength. As the party in the interior reached into new provinces and began to co-ordinate its activities within Spain, more and more Socialists began to question the need for the party leadership to be based abroad. Those who wished to 'renovate' the PSOE were becoming dominant among the active members. To make the party reflect this new reality, they now had to surmount opposition from the old guard.

4

Renovation

IN common with other doctrinal parties, the PSOE has been always reluctant to deny its past. Indeed, it has taken pride in tracing its heritage directly back to the pioneering days of Pablo Iglesias a century ago. Until the late 1970s, at least, it stressed the historical continuities while denying any basic changes of direction: renovation or renewal there may have been, but no drastic new departures. And even in the post-Franco years, when gradually Marxism was played down, any suggestion that the party had become social democratic remained anathema to all but a few party members. The PSOE had known too much adversity and made too many sacrifices for its traditional beliefs to be dismissed lightly.

This claim to historical consistency was shared by both of the PSOE tendencies that competed for control of the party in 1954–74 and that came to be known as the *renovadores* and the *históricos*. The demands of the renovators were themselves remarkably constant. They stood for a greater effort to promote Socialist activity in Spain; the return of substantial, and later on total, authority to leaders of the party in the interior; an updating of the party's outlook to take account of Spain's dramatic economic growth of the 1960s;[1] and following from this, the elaboration of a new party programme and system of alliances to attract new recruits to the party and contribute to the more effective co-ordination of anti-Franco activity. As a matter of principle, neither faction wished to renounce Marxism or class struggle, nor did they seek to split the party. Many renovators in fact had great respect for the 'historical' figures of the party who, in turn, at times claimed to favour a renovation of the party's membership, leadership, and ideology. Even Rodolfo Llopis, who did more than anyone to resist the

---

[1] On the development of the Spanish economy see Sima Lieberman, *The Contemporary Spanish Economy: A Historical Perspective* (London: Allen and Unwin, 1982).

triumph of the *renovadores*, recognized from exile that the world was changing: capitalism had been made more stable by State intervention and planning, while Spanish society had evolved. New generations, demanding change, had to be accommodated by the PSOE. The general secretary hoped that by presenting the 'eternal ideas' in modern language, the party could appeal to newly emergent middle-sector groups without impairing its traditional role as the main political expression of the working class.[2] As late as 1967, most PSOE members were holding on to this basic philosophy: 'Socialism is of essence dynamic and bears within it the necessary and adequate means of its own renovation. Thus our slogan today, as always, is *Continuity and Renovation*, or in other words *Renovation without Self-Negation*.'[3]

Compromise between the two tendencies none the less proved impossible in the long term. In retrospect, they had more in common with each other than they recognized— particularly their shared antipathy towards the Communist Party—but generational antagonism and an accompanying power struggle were too strong for unity to prevail. For, in spite of some acknowledgement of the modernization occurring under Franco, the basic attitudes of the old guard were rooted in the 1930s and were felt to have been confirmed by the Cold War, while those of more recent generations (and of veterans who were 'young in spirit') related more directly to the realities of the Spain of the late 1950s to early 1970s. Existing accounts of the renovation struggle tend to ignore the early unsuccessful bids for change, yet the truth is that the basic demands for renovation were articulated well before many of the successful renovators became involved in political activity. The renovation of the PSOE has to be understood as a process rather than an event, and before it finally triumphed in the party it swept powerfully through the youth section and UGT, with decisive implications for the struggle in the PSOE itself.

[2] Llopis, *Emigración*, 26–8; id., *Etapas*, 10–11.
[3] PSOE, Tenth Congress held in exile (1967), *Fidelidad a las ideas y lealtad al Partido* (Socialist International, 1967), 5.

ANTONIO AMAT AND THE REASSERTION
OF THE INTERIOR

It has already been seen that for years successful opposition to the dominant Prieto-Llopis axis in the PSOE was thwarted by, among other factors, the disunity that existed between oppositionists in Spain and abroad over the idea of monarchy as a formula for the post-Franco transition. While opposition tendencies in the exiled section mainly upheld an uncompromising republican formula, critics of the party line residing in the interior (including, ironically, several pre-1954 party executive committees) advocated acceptance of monarchy as a way out of liberal Spain's impasse, while entertaining no illusions about it offering a solution to the country's social problems. The early renovators, who began to press their demands for change in the mid-1950s, failed largely because they found few allies in the *émigré* camp.

If one rejects the claims of José María Fernández, whose short-lived calls for renovation were motivated seemingly by his being frustrated in an attempt to become general secretary when Toulouse took charge of the party in 1954,[4] the man most deserving of the distinction of being the precursor of renovation in the interior was Antonio Amat. Though he voiced the shared feelings of several of the more active Socialists in the interior, and never encouraged a personality cult, the struggle that developed did become quite personalized and some viewed it as a battle between *amatistas* and *llopistas*.[5]

Antonio María Sebastián Amat Maíz was born in Vitoria in 1919, the son of a captain in the merchant navy. Having been educated by the Marians, he too went to sea, before leaving to study medicine at Valladolid. Just before completing these studies, he transferred to study law at the University of Madrid. This provided him with a professional qualification, but he was never to pursue a legal career. When German forces withdrew from the frontier region of the Pyrenees in 1944, Amat made an unsuccessful attempt to reach France to

---

[4] PSOE, *Actas* of CE, 8.2.55.
[5] PSOE, Correspondence, 'Piriri' file, 'Piriri' to Llopis, 14 Dec. 1961.

join the Resistance, only to be arrested in Lequetio and sentenced to 20 years' imprisonment. He served six years of the sentence before being released. Amat is said to have spent the years 1951–2 in hiding, following participation in the first major strike of the period in Madrid. In 1952 he joined the PSOE in Vitoria and made the first of many clandestine trips to France to establish better links with the exiles. Early in 1954, or perhaps earlier, he began to perform the role of *enlace* for the *émigré* leaders, which involved taking into Spain propaganda, correspondence, and money for the dispersed groups of active Socialists.[6]

Amat's activities soon brought him more trouble with the authorities. In 1953 he was arrested during a strike and spent six months in Huesca prison followed by a similar period of banishment to Madrid. In 1954, just as he was beginning to perform the most vital national role for his party, he returned to Vitoria with orders to present himself at a police station every Sunday. He remained in 'vigilated liberty' for several months, though none the less travelled to other provinces on party business.[7] Following a further arrest in 1955, which led only to police questioning about Socialist-monarchist negotiations in Madrid, Toulouse decided that its man in the interior was *quemado* and had to be replaced.[8] However, despite an executive decision to this effect, Amat had become virtually impossible to replace. In practice he was allowed to continue as chief courier, a job he rapidly transformed into that of chief organizer. A fourth clash with officials occurred in July 1958 when he was detained by French Customs personnel and released only after the intervention of SFIO deputy Joseph Parat.[9] Then, finally, in November of the same year Amat was arrested in a café in Madrid's Plaza de Bilbao. This time his imprisonment lasted until May 1961 and was

---

[6] Vilar, 178–81; PSOE, Trial Papers, Sumario 446/58, 'El pleito contra los socialistas españoles', 14 Feb. 1964, report sent to the *Neue Zürcher Zeitung*; ibid., 'Sentencia'.

[7] Vilar, 180; UGT, *Actas* of CE, 12.1.55.

[8] PSOE, *Actas* of CE, 8.2.55, 18.2.55. There was indeed contact at this time to discuss a plan to hold a student protest outside the residence of Prince Juan Carlos. Amat promised 200 Socialist demonstrators for every 25 monarchists, knowing that the monarchists could mobilize only a few sympathizers for direct action.

[9] UGT, *Actas* of CE, 4.7.58.

followed by three years of confinement to the family home at Postas, 34–2°, Vitoria.

A single man from a supportive and quite wealthy family, Amat was much more free to travel than most Socialists. He was the archetypal man of action: dynamic, thoroughly dedicated to the party, courageous, and charming. He also possessed a good sense of humour and a great capacity to enjoy life. The active Socialists of the period all warmed to this attractive Basque whom they found energetic, honest, and deeply humane, always readier to make excuses for others than to criticize them. Because he himself took such risks and clearly was achieving things in the mid-1950s, he had a motivating effect on Socialists in several parts of Spain.[10] Naturally he had his defects also, and two of them had implications for the clandestine PSOE. On occasion he could be absurdly careless for a man who had become the *de facto* co-ordinator of the PSOE in the interior. He continued to operate when in 'vigilated liberty' in 1955, and it would seem that he had been followed by the police for many weeks prior to his final arrest in 1958.[11] Apparently, the police knew that he was a leading activist, but were unaware of his precise role until they netted dozens of activists towards the end of that year; they knew that the number-one Socialist in the interior was a certain 'Guridi', but only discovered that this was Amat's *nom de guerre* that fateful November.[12] Of course, Amat's simply allowing himself to be followed enabled the authorities to develop a more complete picture of the PSOE network.

Amat's other weakness lay in the theoretical department. Among most Socialists theoretical weakness would not have been remarked upon; after all it was the party norm. But

[10] Personal interviews with Diez Yagüe, Villar, Muñoz Atienza, Redondo, Bustelo, Kindelán, and Carvajal; Juan M. Kindelán, 'Cuarenta años de vacaciones', *ES*, 3.2.80; 'Salud compañero Antonio Amat, un luchador', *Punto y Hora*, 158 (1980), 15–18. In the latter (p. 18) it is claimed that Amat visited Cuba and Czechoslovakia, but this may have been after his final term of imprisonment.

[11] UGT, *Actas* of CE, 12.1.55; PSOE, Correspondence, 'Piriri' file, 'Piriri' to Llopis, 14 Dec. 1961.

[12] Welles, 203; Villar interview. For months detainees had been interrogated concerning the identity of 'Guridi', a name possibly derived from the composer of *Diez melodías vascas*. Amat's identity was unknown even to most of the Toulouse-based leaders.

through his dynamism and personal attractiveness Amat became a highly influential figure in the interior and one whom the *émigrés* grudgingly had to allow a degree of autonomy in deciding the party attitude to local protest activity. Untempered by theoretical guidance, Amat's abundant vivacity and commitment to struggle led him into a voluntarism whose benefits at times were dubious. *Amatismo* was a necessary antidote to the lethargy affecting much of the PSOE, but on occasion Amat came close to promoting action for action's sake. Though he never went quite that far, he did alarm some Socialists through his rather cavalier responses to their ethical scruples. While they held the traditional party view that the organization's survival depended on its discipline and moral authority, and not on its numbers, the essence of Amatismo was that the PSOE would disappear unless it were fully involved in mass struggles.[13] To this end he keenly entered into joint activity with groups such as the Moviment Socialista de Catalunya and the Agrupación Socialista Universitaria, about which the exiles had severe reservations. For the *émigrés*, the problem with these groups lay in their independence.

Several of the activities encouraged by Amat were thought to be dangerously opportunist by the ageing leaders in Toulouse. For one thing, without pushing such activity, Amat was atypical in indulging the local initiatives of Socialists who had managed to gain positions within the State-controlled corporative structures of the *sindicatos verticales*. In Burgos, for example, Manuel Cantos Solís attained one of the top provincial syndicate posts with a view to influencing workers, only to lose it overnight and be thrown in jail when he decided that the moment had come to speak out against the regime.[14] Although the Toulouse executives did not try to reverse any cases of syndicate infiltration that they learnt of, the *émigré* leadership thoroughly disapproved of a tactic that they saw as hazardous and unproductive, and likely only to legitimize the

[13] 'Guridi' to CE, 8 Nov. 1957; CE to 'Guridi', 20 Nov. 1957.
[14] On Burgos see 'Guridi' to CE, 2 June, 18 Sept. 1954, 1 Apr. 1957. The construction syndicate in Madrid was infiltrated as well ('Guridi' to CE, 1 Mar. 1955) and such efforts were paralleled by orders to student supporters in Valladolid, Zaragoza, and Madrid to occupy positions in the SEU ('Guridi' to CE, 26 Aug. 1954).

regime's structures in workers' minds.[15] The reality was, though, that in places camouflaged opposition candidates could be elected in syndicate elections, and Amat was ready to use any means of contact with the work-force. In 1957 the Socialists as usual boycotted these elections in most places and were pleased to see abstention reach 82 per cent in the mining zones of Asturias; but in Santander and the Basque Country local groups covertly fielded candidates who were elected.[16]

A clearer case of opportunism occurred one year earlier, during the Madrid student revolt in February. To protect PSOE activists and exploit the growth of dissidence and splits within the Falange, Amat and other Socialists went into one Madrid demonstration to the chant of 'Viva la Falange pura!'—a ruse that earned one comrade a thump in the face from a student who was opposed to all wings of the Falange.[17] On other occasions, to encourage an exacerbation of monarchist–Falange conflict, Socialists in the capital produced pro-monarchist leaflets, and even attacked a bookshop where a monarchist book was on display, hoping that the Falange would be blamed.[18] Amat's agitprop stunts were restricted to Madrid and were characterized by increasingly militant tactics. During the public-transport boycott in Madrid in 1957, amid general discontent over the cost of living, he organized flying pickets who whistled and threw stones at vehicles, then disappeared in cars manned by taxi-driver comrades.[19]

Behind these actions there was at least as much frustration as design. The cautionary words of the *émigrés*, who for 20 years had been relying on economic disasters, diplomatic initiatives, and paper agreements to make the regime collapse, fell upon deaf ears. They feared that such 'provocations' would lead to a crack-down that would undermine the recent organizational progress. But by now active members in the interior had heard enough from the *émigrés* about what should happen following the downfall of Franco: as Amat lamented, 'nobody presents or proposes a viable means of promoting or

[15] PSOE, *Actas* of CE, 8.2.55.
[16] Ibid., 30.10.57; 'Guridi' to CE, 12 Oct. 1957.
[17] 'Guridi' to 'Piriri', 13 Feb. 1956.
[18] 'Guridi' to CE, 20 Mar. 1957.   [19] 'Guridi' to CE, 15 Feb. 1957.

accelerating that fall, forgetting that that is and must be the immediate objective'; 'Our *principal* objective must be the overthrow of the Franco regime; it is *secondary* to theorize about the legality of the kind of regime that must succeed Franco.'[20] Amat was in favour of making one last effort to unite the opposition around acceptance of a monarchist way out of Francoism, and then to see if Don Juan would take a stand. However, he was not at all optimistic that such an appeal would bear fruit; thus simultaneously he strove to build an organization capable of intervening in protests, and to plan a more spectacular and even violent Socialist campaign of activity.[21] From 1954 he repeatedly passed on to Toulouse requests from the interior for *antibióticos* and *medicinas*, code-names for arms.[22] Although superficially the two tactics were contradictory (for serious armed opposition to Franco would surely rally his monarchist dissidents), Amat's position obeyed a single logic: the need to use force to oust Franco. 'Fascism can only be destroyed by force; if we do not have that force, we must find it elsewhere', Amat wrote. Any means were valid if they produced the departure of Franco. 'Let us be realists and opportunists', he urged his executive; 'the purity of our Cause will clean the dirtiness from the road.'[23]

By the late 1950s it was apparent to men as different as Amat and Prieto that Don Juan was too financially dependent upon Franco and too weak to be of use to the opposition; but whereas Prieto concluded that the demise of Francoism had to be left to the inexorable laws of biology, Amat refused to accept that the Caudillo's departure could not be hastened by political struggle.[24] The leading Socialist in the interior never fully articulated an alternative strategy, but his unanswered call for arms went beyond rhetorical bravado. He acquired a weapon himself (entrusting it to Villar); and more signifi-

---

[20] 'Guridi' to CE, 20 Mar., 8 Nov. 1957.

[21] 'Guridi' to CE, 12 Oct. 1957. In the late 1950s monarchism became more popular among conservatives; it was seen as offering a more flexible alternative regime, better equipped than Francoism to prevent a social explosion. Influenced by the emergence of mass protest, the Catholic Church also began to distance itself from Franco (Payne, 250).

[22] 'Guridi' to CE, 2 June 1954, 8 Nov., 19 Dec. 1957, 20 Oct. 1958.

[23] 'Guridi' to CE, 8 Nov. 1957.

[24] 'Guridi' to CE, 12 Oct. 1957; Bustelo interview, 26 Apr. 1982.

cantly, a plenum arranged by Amat in March 1957 approved a Vizcaya proposal to set up action groups to exploit any incidents provoked by the Falangists. Although the plan was more modest than that of Alvarez del Vayo for an urban guerrilla campaign in the 1960s, Amat's idea was for such groups to operate separately from party structures (like Vayo's FELN) and thus not endanger the PSOE.[25] Little had been achieved here by the time of Amat's downfall. He was probably too humane to seriously contemplate attacks on regime personnel. On the other hand, he saw no reason why violence against property should not be used to show the USA that Franco's Spain was not a secure location for American bases.[26] But to keep his line on violence in perspective it must be emphasized that for Amat, the urgent necessity was for more *action*, of diverse kinds.[27] As with Pablo Iglesias, violence for Amat was a last resort to be tried when all else had failed and the PSOE was isolated. Of course, this made its success highly unlikely.

Amat's ideas were shaped by the practical experiences of activists in the interior. Like Villar, he initially earned himself a place in the good books of Rodolfo Llopis; only later did he join the growing flock of black sheep. An early letter from Toulouse to 'Guridi' praised his 'tact, intelligence, and love for the ideas' (of socialism).[28] Yet very quickly Amat began to question some established party practices. He criticized the anti-communist preoccupation of party propaganda and called for sharper criticism of Washington. Among opponents of Franco the Spanish-American military pact of 1953 had encouraged considerable pro-communist feeling, Amat maintained; to persist with Toulouse's negative propaganda would give the PCE opportunities to attack the PSOE, and would make the Socialists appear to be opposed to working-class unity.[29] 'North America is the object of hate for the Spanish anti-fascist; and we feel we should not be negative but instead

[25] Villar interview; 'Guridi' report on meeting of 10 Mar. 1957 (PSOE, Correspondence, 'Guridi' file). Terrorism was condemned in *Le Socialiste*, 15.8.63, 6.
[26] 'Guridi' to CE, 19 Dec. 1957.
[27] Ibid., 8 Nov. 1957.
[28] CE to 'Guridi', 18 Mar. 1954.
[29] 'Guridi' to CE, 2 June 1954, 21 June, Sept. 1955.

point to the advantages of Socialism', Amat wrote.[30] While not proposing an alliance with the PCE, Amat pointed to the need for Socialist-Communist contact in the interests of organizing effective opposition activity. From Toulouse, however, a policy of isolating the PCE was the perennial response of the *émigré* leadership: in their view, contact with the PCE would simply enable Moscow's agents once more to sow division in the ranks of the PSOE and would enable Francoism, both at home and abroad, to present Spain's options as being 'Franco or Communism'.[31]

Ideally, Toulouse wanted Amat to function as a messenger who would merely deliver things to the interior and bring back written reports and receipts from the provincial groups (the receipts were needed for international donors to show that their solidarity was not merely feeding a bureaucracy in Toulouse). But because of his ability and personality and the reticence of groups in the interior when asked to submit reports, Toulouse rightly feared from the start that Amat would become the mentor and interpreter of the PSOE in the interior.[32] Not only did Amat provide the *émigrés* with the only written reports on interior activity worthy of that name, he also took independent initiatives to co-ordinate PSOE and opposition activity. He organized party plenums that resulted in October 1957 in the establishment of a Socialist Central Committee composed of a Basque (Amat), an Andalusian (Román), and members from Catalonia, Madrid, and ASU; and he also engaged in negotiations designed to produce a co-ordinating committee or 'assembly' of opposition forces that would urge Don Juan to come out against Franco.[33]

These initiatives set off more than one warning bell in the pre-revolutionary church, more recently a cinema, that housed the party headquarters in Toulouse. Just as worrying as the establishment of the Socialist CC was its composition.

---

[30] 'Guridi' to CE, 11 June 1958.

[31] 'Guridi' to CE, 7, 20 May 1956; CE to 'Guridi', 8 Dec. 1955, 11 Apr. 1956.

[32] PSOE, Assemblies, *Actas* of CN, 24–5.4.54; id., *Actas* of CE, 21–2.4.54, 3.9.54, 8.2.55; UGT, *Actas* of CE, 3.9.54. The prosecutor at Amat's trial in 1964 described him as the 'soul, motor, and nerve' of the organization (PSOE, Trial Papers, Sumario 446/58, 'El pleito').

[33] PSOE, *Actas* of CE, 21.11.57, 30.11.57, 24.2.58; 'Guridi' and Comité Central Socialista de Euzkadi to Prieto, 1 Apr. 1957; 'Guridi' to CE, 9 Apr., 9 Dec. 1957.

The mistaken exiles feared that the Moviment had been allocated the Catalan place on the CC, and they were implacably opposed to the admission of a youth group such as ASU, which moreover gave access to the party's secrets to a body that rejected party discipline.[34] The knowledge that ASU had been infiltrated in 1956 by Communist students reinforced residual *émigré* fears about youth serving once more as a trojan horse in the PSOE. Only recently, splits in the Argentine and Uruguayan socialist parties had been catalysed by the challenge of youth radicalism. Equally unpalatable to the *émigrés* were Amat's efforts to form a co-ordinating committee and even an Anti-Francoist National Front. To them he seemed to have been seduced by the 'all together' idea exploited by the PCE. Even if such a front helped to restore the monarchy, Toulouse feared that this would mean years of dictatorship, for which the PSOE would be blamed; and if it did not, then the question of launching into armed struggle was not something that they felt should be decided on the basis of a response from Don Juan. Undoubtedly, all these fears and doubts were magnified by the *émigrés'* experiences in the 1930s, which left them too prejudiced to be moved by the mature and efficient manner in which ASU dealt with its infiltration problem.[35]

When letters of persuasion failed to move the Toulouse veterans, Amat and other activists began to apply more pressure. Although the plenum on 10 March 1957 (attended by representatives of Asturias, Santander, Málaga, Catalonia, Madrid, and the Basque Country) endorsed the *émigrés'* unitary Paris agreements of that year, to lend them more authority, it was felt quite generally in the interior that monarchy provided the most viable formula for removing Franco.[36] A document expressing this view was forwarded to Toulouse in June and unanimously rejected by the party executive. When it was ratified by a second plenum held in Bilbao in October, it was again rejected unanimously by the *émigrés*.[37] In the meantime, the PSOE Comité Director had

---

[34] CE to 'Guridi', 3 Jan. 1958.
[35] Lizcano, 184–9; 'Guridi' to CE, 19 May 1957; PSOE, *Actas* of CE, 17.5.57.
[36] PSOE, *Actas* of CE, 13.6.57, 11.9.57.
[37] Ibid., 13.6.57, 21.11.57; 'Guridi' to CE, 8 Nov., 19 Dec. 1957.

met in August and Amat, Román, and Reventós had travelled
to France to present the document and again argue the case for
giving support to the monarchy on a transitional and
conditional basis. While the *émigrés* were determined that the
PSOE should not be used again by the monarchists as in 1948,
the delegates from the interior complained about being used
by Toulouse as propaganda agents while their views were
being ignored.[38] Much of 1957 and 1958 were consumed by
interior–exterior disagreements which prevented either faction
from achieving anything meaningful *vis-à-vis* other opposition
forces. The exiles were able to quash the idea of a co-
ordinating committee of opposition forces in Spain, on the
grounds that this would be a 'permanent alliance' and thus
contrary to established party policy;[39] but they could not
persuade the interior to work energetically for the fanciful
émigré formula embodied in the Paris agreements, which
reflected what Ridruejo termed their 'inflexible democratic
puritanism'.[40] At the end of 1957 relations deteriorated
sharply when, for the first time, it seemed that Socialists in the
interior were attempting to develop an independent link with
the PSOE-UGT's international allies. During Hermes Horne's
visit to Spain, Andalusian Socialists travelled to Madrid to
present him with a copy of the dissident document of 1957,
described as the views of the interior.[41]

Moves such as this were countered by Toulouse with
immediate approaches to the Brussels headquarters of the
ICFTU, where sympathetic responses were assured by
Pascual Tomás's presence on the International's executive.
Dissident Socialists travelling from Spain to Brussels would
be welcomed by Francisco López Real, head of the ICFTU
Spanish-language translation section, and sometimes they
were received by officials, but the International's line continued
to be that all relations with the PSOE and UGT had to pass
through the hands of the Toulouse-based executives. Plans to
follow up the dissident document with a deputation from the
interior were shelved as soon as Toulouse told Amat that it
was not to go ahead.[42] On this occasion momentary discipline

---

[38] PSOE, Assemblies, *Actas* of CD, Aug. 1957, 22–37.
[39] PSOE, *Actas* of CE, 24.2.58.   [40] CE to 'Guridi', 23 May 1958.
[41] PSOE, *Actas* of CE, 28.2.58.   [42] Ibid.

was restored, but that left interior activists all the more determined to air their views at the seventh congress in exile of the PSOE in August 1958.

The delegation headed by Amat and Román was persuaded on security grounds to address only the Comité Director which met on the eve of the congress. The document they presented began with an analysis of recent developments in Spain.[43] The regime had won more international acceptance but had lost internal support, it was argued; its deflationary measures had provoked popular protest, and a new political opposition had emerged composed of ex-Falange elements, middle-class intellectual circles, and Christian Democrats. Falange influence had declined as Opus Dei technocrats had gained key governmental posts. PCE activity had increased and in some respects had overtaken that of the PSOE. The army was disillusioned but would not challenge Franco unless the bourgeoisie and Church did. Whereas the Church was still pro-Franco, the document continued, there was now significant bourgeois opposition to the regime coming from ex-Francoists who wanted an end to dictatorship, providing that a stable monarchy could be installed. And although public opinion was still pro-republican, it was ready to accept a monarchist transition if this introduced the freedom to opt later for a new republic.

On the basis of this analysis, the Socialists of the interior advocated agreements with the new opposition groups to form a democratic bloc, tactically supportive of the monarchy. Co-operation with the PCE was proposed also, though the Communists were recognized as being rivals whose appeal to workers had to be bettered by the PSOE. The Socialists had to offer something more than their competitors, by producing positive propaganda for democratic socialism and being at least as active as the PCE. It was also necessary, in the words of the document, to 'kill any suspicion among the Spanish proletariat of there being a softening or *embourgeoisement* of the PSOE'. Anti-communism was deemed an attitude that played into the hands of Franco and the US State Department, while discouraging the working class. 'Now, like it or not, we

---

[43] 'Para el acta C.D.' (PSOE, Correspondence, 'Guridi' file).

are aligned shoulder to shoulder with the Communist workers by a single prime objective: to destroy the Dictatorship. After that, we shall see who shoots whom.'[44]

Other demands were that the PSOE should pay more attention to the new generation of socialists in Spain and also seek to win over separatist militants by drawing up a new programme embodying plans for a federal Spain. The *émigrés* were urged to concede to the interior two places on its 11-man executive, to be filled by activists who would enjoy some room for manœuvre within the overall context of congress policy decisions.

Probably the least acceptable suggestion in *émigré* ears was that, in case repression rendered a campaign of peaceful protests impossible, the party congress should grant the executive discretionary powers to adopt a new line of struggle. The interior's espousal of violence as a last resort, ill-defined as it was, must have alarmed the old men of Toulouse, especially the document's declaration that it was a 'scandal' that in 20 years of repression no leading Francoist had been executed. Not that Amat and his colleagues ignored the disadvantages of violence:[45] they acknowledged that it would alarm the bourgeoisie and the PSOE's foreign allies,[46] but felt that the international situation could get no worse and that violent activity was at least preferable to inactivity. 'The blood of martyrs is never wasted,' their document affirmed; 'at least it sows the seeds of future heroism.' Of course, one can speculate at length about the possible effects of a violent campaign. What one can say more definitely is that this was hardly the most diplomatic moment to raise a contingency plan of this sort.[47] Amat and his fellow activists did not want to have to await a further congress if their immediate plan were to fail. But merely by mentioning a more violent reserve

[44] Ibid.

[45] At an international trade union conference in Brussels in Oct. 1961, the British and Finnish delegates abstained rather than vote on a declaration on Spain, because of UGT insistence on a phrase about not renouncing any means of struggle (PSOE and other organizations, PSOE-UGT, *Actas* of CD/CG, July 1962, 5). *Le Socialiste*, (26.6.69, 1–2, 3.7.69, 1) claimed that a more revolutionary Socialist strategy would meet with US opposition. It cited a report in the *International Herald Tribune* (16.6.69) on US participation in joint military manœuvres in Spain designed to suppress an imaginary revolution against Franco.

[46] 'Para el acta C.D.'   [47] Ibid.

plan, they lost any chance of the immediate plan being considered on its merits.

Of its set of demands, the interior secured only the desired representation on the party executive. The *émigré* Comité Director remained dogmatically opposed to any dealings with the PCE and argued that the Spanish monarchy was still a 'traditional' and not a 'constitutional' one. Araquistain, the only exile there who was sympathetic to the monarchist formula, was just as strongly opposed to links with the PCE. A realignment of this kind would simply alienate the PSOE's foreign allies. To Daniel Díaz, meanwhile, the document of the interior suggested that the party in Spain had been infiltrated by Communists; it could have been written by Khrushchev, he declared. Prieto, who despite the precarious state of his health had travelled from Mexico for the meeting and congress, cast doubt on how representative of the interior the document was, while Llopis, failing to capture the new mood of militancy in Spain, rejected any contemplation of violence with the argument that Spanish people were tired of civil war. To no avail Amat and Román stressed that their attitude to the monarchy was purely pragmatic, claimed that there was a popular demand for united opposition to the regime, and denied that their goals went so far as a pact with the PCE and a total transfer of the executive back to Spain.[48]

Following total defeat in the Comité Director, the delegates from the interior were unable to argue their case in the congress itself. Afterwards, Amatista efforts to co-ordinate activity in Spain were increased: a 12-person council based on provincial and regional representation was chosen, together with three senior advisers to assist the two executive members representing the interior.[49] A further clash was prevented by the major police raids and arrests of late 1958, Amat being among the detainees. Though it has been suggested that he was betrayed by *émigré* leaders desperately seeking to retain control over the party, he himself soon dismissed such suspicions. If he had been betrayed to the police, Amat wrote, it was by the Madrid 'activist' whom he himself had appointed, whom he had begun to suspect but had done

[48] PSOE, Assemblies, *Actas* of CD, 11–12.8.58.
[49] 'Guridi' to CE, 20 Oct. 1958.

nothing about. At the same time, Amat acknowledged that he personally had been careless, having failed to notice his police followers and being caught in the possession of addressed correspondence.[50]

Arrests and imprisonment thus put a halt to the first renovating efforts made in the interior. For the next few years Amat was able only to take indirect initiatives as a result of his imprisonment and subsequent home confinement (occasionally evaded). A document not very different to that of 1958 was delivered to the next party congress, held at Puteaux in August 1961, by Young Socialists Luis Gómez Llorente and Miguel Angel Martínez. Inspired by Amat and drafted by Gómez Llorente and the sociologist Angel de Lucas, the heretical document was defended at the congress by Gómez but then violently attacked by Jimeno, who on this occasion sided with Llopis and Prieto. The distance between interior and exterior was seen in the vote: with the interior having a voice but no voting delegates, the document obtained just seven votes.[51] It is worth noting, however, that by now at least one moderate *émigré* leader, Luis Jiménez de Asúa, was concluding that moderation had been useless: neither the USA nor the UK would help the democratic opposition.[52] An equivalent intervention to that of Gómez Llorente in 1961 was made by Frankfurt delegate Manuel Fernández Montesinos at the UGT congress a year later. Criticizing the *émigré* leadership for believing that a '*revolución de salón*, remotely-controlled from Paris, Munich, or Washington' could bring freedom to Spain and the return of a strong UGT, he called for the clandestine return of the executive to the interior and insisted: 'Franco can be thrown out by strikes, demonstrations in the streets, massive protests, not by Gil-Robles or Ridruejo with their salon- and coffee-house politics . . .'. Montesinos warned that if the UGT did not promote strikes in the

---

[50] Welles, 203; *Le Socialiste*, 30.12.65, 7; PSOE, *Actas* of CE, 7.4.59, 26.7.61; UGT, *Actas* of CE, 30.12.58; PSOE, Assemblies, *Actas* of CD, Aug. 1959; PSOE, Correspondence, 'Amat' file, Amat to CE, 10 Nov. 1961. The Madrid activist was Manuel González Méndez, a Galician who ran a car parts business in the Plaza del Campillo; he apparently went off to Switzerland with a girl-friend when Amat was released from prison.

[51] PSOE, Actas of CE, 26.7.61; *ES*, 14.9.61, 1; Lizcano, 256–9.

[52] *ES*, 5.10.61, 3.

interior, foreign trade unions would begin to ignore Toulouse when it came to disbursing aid. But his appeal was unsuccessful, despite claims that support for his views existed in Albacete, Alicante, Barcelona, Castellón, Madrid, Málaga, Seville, and Valencia (which was of course unquantifiable).[53] From this moment on, the Toulouse leadership prepared congresses with far greater care, encouraging its supporters in Spain to send delegations to speak in the name of the interior. At the next party congress, in 1964, at which a peaceful, national (rather than class) solution was approved, the so-called 'message from the interior' echoed the main preoccupation of the Toulouse gerontocracy: 'Nada con el comunismo'—no dealings with the Communists, nor with any forces to the left of the PSOE. For Llopis, they were all 'in the East'.[54]

The executive was able to defeat the early challenges relatively easily because of the pro-monarchism of the interior and widespread *émigré* antipathy both to this and to the PCE. In the light of the Communist penetration of ASU, it was not too difficult to sow suspicions about would-be renovators having become *comunistoides*. Llopis was notorious for slandering those whom he felt had betrayed his trust, and he was extremely adept at turning activists in the interior against each other by telling them stories about one another. He managed to instil in Socialist minds all sorts of doubts about Amat by publicizing claims that he had collaborated with the police when detained, had spent a lot of time fraternizing with Communist inmates in Carabanchel Prison, and subsequently had taken to drink.[55] Many minds were poisoned in this way, for in a police state few militants were going to take any risks

[53] UGT, Dissident Groups, 'Exposición de Montesinos en nombre de UGT Frankfurt', Eighth Congress of UGT held in exile (1962).

[54] *Le Socialiste*, 27.8.64, 4.

[55] In the end Amat did drink heavily, possibly because of the effect upon him of the Llopis rumour machine, and the great pressures to which he had submitted himself. The strain of clandestine leadership led him to resign momentarily from his position in Apr. 1957, exhausted by 'that continuous lie; one moment you are a doctor who lives in Bayonne, the next a lawyer from Santander or a modest employee in a Toulouse store' ('Guridi' to CEs, 9 Apr. 1957). Amat was treated badly by the PSOE under Llopis and received no recognition for his services even after the party underwent its renovation in 1972. He committed suicide in December 1979, knowing that he had cancer.

with doubtful contacts. Llopis was at his most ruthless in discouraging 'usurpers' in the interior early in 1964. When a group of socialists including Villar, Bienvenido Gómez, and Urbano Orad de la Torre wrote to the ICFTU urging that it lend direct support to a UGT executive to be established in Spain, Llopis exposed them to imprisonment by circulating the names of the signatories, despite an express decision of his executive to the contrary.[56]

What is perhaps surprising is that so many frustrated renovators remained loyal to the PSOE-UGT in the circumstances. Not all of them did. In particular, former members of ASU, which had never been incorporated formally into the PSOE, were ready to bypass Toulouse even though several of them joined the party when forced by police persecution to leave Spain. The earliest case was that of Miguel Sánchez-Mazas, who publicly exchanged perspectives with Indalecio Prieto through the pages of *Adelante* in 1958.[57] It was quite an amicable dialogue. Sánchez-Mazas, who was about to follow former ASU colleague Vicente Girbau and join the PSOE, argued that the growing concentration of capital in Spain meant that Franco's fall had to come via a revolution that would be simultaneously social and liberal. He wrote of the PSOE's need to appeal to the growing middle classes as well as to workers, of the need to unite the party's veterans and its university supporters, of the desirability of a National Democratic Front, and of the urgent need to change *El Socialista*'s contents, to focus more upon Spanish rather than exile events. While appearing to agree with the young socialist on the dual nature of the Spanish revolution, Prieto emphasized the importance of a pro-Western foreign policy and, most significantly, he issued almost a warning to incoming graduates: 'We have had some extraordinary university men in our ranks, such as Jaime Vera, Julián Besteiro, and Fernando de los Ríos. Their chief virtue consisted in their education and culture;

---

[56] PSOE-UGT, *Circular* 27 (1964); SOMA Archive, Box A.LIX, Pascual Tomás to Arcadio Martínez Fernández, 20 Apr. 1964; PSOE, *Actas* of CE, 30 June 1964. One of the signatories was not a PSOE-UGT member. Antonio García López led a small group called the Frente Unido de los Socialistas de España. Later he formed the Partido Socialista Democrático Español.

[57] Prieto and Sánchez-Mazas, 'Cruce de ideas Miguel Sánchez-Mazas e Indalecio Prieto', *Adelante*, Nov.–Dec. 1958, 3–4; reprinted in *ES*, 15.1.59, 3–4.

their chief contribution consisted in understanding what was meant by party discipline and adapting themselves to it.'[58] Very quickly this traditional disdain for theoretical innovation and insistence upon discipline and conformity proved too much for the young intellectuals. Equally, one can sympathize with the party veterans when confronted with talented but clearly inexperienced and often imprudent young enthusiasts. One can imagine how the veterans felt when Francisco Bustelo was admitted to the Comité Director meeting of August 1958 to discuss PSOE-ASU relations, and promptly declared that it was a great honour to be allowed to address the 'old symbols' of the PSOE.[59] They must have felt like mummies in a museum. But again, on this occasion the main demand made of the potential recruits was the acceptance of party discipline; there was little encouragement of Socialist activism.

In the face of such attitudes the young university men took independent initiatives almost from the start of their PSOE collaboration. The first incident was a meeting in April 1958 in Perpignan organized by Sánchez-Mazas with help from the International Metalworkers' Federation, for which the Spaniard had already written a report on the economic situation in Spain.[60] Apparently the meeting was called to establish a united metalworkers' committee formed by individual CNT, UGT, STV, and MSC members to channel aid from the federation to metalworkers in the Basque Country and Catalonia.[61] The feeling both of old oppositionists such as Wenceslao Carrillo (who though too ill to attend supported the meeting)[62] and of the younger Socialists Sánchez-Mazas and Girbau was that not enough was being done by the UGT inside Spain. In the international labour movement only the metalworkers' federation actively supported independent initiatives over the next few years. It was led by relatively left-wing socialists who were wary of socialist parties that when in

---

[58] Prieto had said this first at the party congress of 1958. See *What is Happening*, 119; *ES*, 28.8.58, 1–4.

[59] PSOE, Assemblies, *Actas* of CD, 11–12.8.58, 26.

[60] M. Sánchez-Mazas, *Informe sobre las causas económicas de la crisis social española* (Geneva: International Metalworkers' Federation, 1957).

[61] UGT, Actas of CE, 11.4.58; id., Seventh Congress held in exile (1959), *Memoria*, 29.

[62] Id., Assemblies, *Actas* of CG, 13.8.58, 30–4.

office tended to neglect trade unions. The federation was disturbed by allegations made by Sánchez-Mazas that half its aid was being dissipated in the Toulouse bureaucracies (probably an exaggeration); moreover, it feared that UGT inactivity would leave the Communist Party with no effective rival to represent the principles of socialist trade unionism in Spain.[63] By reacting sharply to news of the meeting and organizing a boycott together with the CNT executive, the Toulouse veterans managed to sabotage the event and even elicit disclaimers from Charles Levinson, a secretary of the federation. Subsequently, the latter was instructed by the ICFTU to send its aid via Brussels.[64] The episode showed just how proprietorial the UGT/PSOE leaders were, for notwithstanding the enormous need for aid in the aftermath of strikes and lock-outs in Spain, the meeting was branded by Llopis as 'a manœuvre of the worst kind', through which the federation had interfered in matters over which the Spanish Socialist executives had exclusive competence.[65]

In spite of UGT and ICFTU rebukes to the Geneva-based metalworkers' federation, whose general secretary was the Swiss Adolph Graedel, it continued to sponsor moves to bypass Toulouse. With the UGT possessing no organization among metalworkers in Spain, the federation began to assume responsibilities itself, hoping to build a union that would embrace most metalworkers, contrary to the traditional partisan model of Spanish trade unionism. Actively involved in this plan were Francisco Bustelo, who temporarily left the PSOE after the congress of 1961, having decided that the party was irrevocably reformist and pro-Western,[66] and Manuel Fernández Montesinos, who was now working in Frankfurt as an official of the massive West German metal-

[63] Ibid. 35–7; UGT, Dissident Groups 'Informe de F.B. a la UGT del Interior', 8.6.62.
[64] UGT, *Actas* of CE, 23.5.58. Before working in Geneva Levinson had worked for the American CIO (ibid., 8.1.54). [65] Ibid., 25.4.58.
[66] Bustelo, 'Por que me he dado de baja en el Partido y la Unión' (1.2.62), explaining his resignation of 1 Nov. 1961. Earlier, he along with Kindelán and Girbau had resigned their party responsibilities in protest against the CE's boycott of the unsuccessful Communist attempt at a general strike in July 1959 (ASU, Iª Conferencia Inter-regional, *Actas*). While the leadership was determined to keep the PCE isolated, some Socialists in the interior supported the strike call (PSOE, *Actas* of CE, 21.5.59).

workers' union, IG Metall. Around 1962 the German union, representing 1.8 million workers, decided to give DM 100,000 to Spanish strikers. Amid pleas from Bustelo, Montesinos, and Carvajal to send the money directly to the interior, it was passed on to Graedel's federation, which was itself ready to donate $10,000 to bring the total to $40,000 (2 million pesetas). While not wishing to provoke an ICFTU reaction as it had in 1958, the federation believed the UGT to be inactive in Spain; influenced by the Horne report, its leaders regarded the Toulouse-controlled forces in the interior as mainly politicized PSOE militants, not UGT trade unionists. Graedel, it seems, urged the dissidents to appeal to Toulouse for a share of the official aid, and then authorized payment to them when evidence was produced to show how Llopis was starving the rebellious groups of aid. The dissidents' argument, that Toulouse did not want to see an effective organization develop in Spain because it would escape the veterans' control, seemed persuasive.[67]

Simultaneously, the dissident groups in Spain began to talk about constructing new union federations, whose prospective builders were visited by the political architects, Bustelo and Montesinos, in June 1962. Vitoria was designated the centre of a proclaimed Northern Federation, while Madrid was chosen as the headquarters of a Centre Federation to be organized by Arrillaga, Villar, and Carvajal. Alicante was selected as the basis for a Levant Federation, and Málaga, the home of Francisco Román, was decided upon as the centre for Andalucía. Really, the visitors had only a series of sympathetic contacts in these places and the talk of embryonic federations was aimed mainly at attracting external funding.[68] In Alicante the visitors found UGT veteran Justo Martínez Amutio receptive to their plans. However, in the Basque Country, while seeing the need for greater activity and for aid to be channelled directly to the interior, neither Amat nor Martín-Santos was prepared to defy Toulouse, at least not without the sanction of Ramón Rubial.[69]

[67] 'Informe de F.B.'
[68] UGT, Dissident Groups, 'Rapport de l'UGT d'intérieur à la FIOM' from the 'federations' of Alava, Andalucía, Centre, and Levant, 20–30.6.62.
[69] Bustelo interview, 26 Apr. 1982.

Unable to organize an effective UGT breakaway in the interior, the travellers broke radically with the official Spanish organizations in October 1962 by helping to establish the Workers' Trade Union Alliance (ASO). Although initially, as a ruse, it was claimed that ASO was merely the expression in the interior of the *émigré*-sponsored Spanish Trade Union Alliance (ASE) and enjoyed UGT and CNT approval, ASO's objective was to develop into a single broad Spanish trade union confederation, independent of political parties and doctrines.[70] As ASO's founders saw it, the traditional trade unions were moribund, the Spanish people were wary of politics, and there was an obvious need for working-class unity, though they sought to exclude the PCE. Tactically ASO was prepared to participate in the regime-sponsored syndicate elections as a means of obtaining information, building unity, and fielding 'genuine' working-class candidates. The UGT's objection that this stance helped give the regime a quasi-liberal face had some substance. ASO's dealings with the official syndicate structure in Madrid in the mid-1960s were inspired by, and possibly fed, the illusion that the authorities might legalize genuinely autonomous unions.[71]

ASO was the medium for the first West German attempts at gaining influence in Spain. Sponsorship came from IG Metall and the Friedrich Ebert Foundation linked to the SPD.[72] German aid formed the bulk of the International Metalworkers' Federation support for ASO and was facilitated by the trade union positions held by the Spaniards Montesinos in Frankfurt and fellow ASO promoter Carlos Pardo in Geneva. While the foundation organized a number of ASO meetings, the federation's aid reached a total of 20 million pesetas (about $400,000) by the end of 1965.[73] Yet in spite of this backing,

[70] Alianza Sindical Obrera, 'Alianza Sindical Obrera Nacional', Oct. 1962, founding document; ASO, *A.S.O.: Nuestras raíces* (Ediciones Iberia, ? 1966); *A.S.O.* bulletin, 1963–7.

[71] SOMA Archive, Box A.LX, 'Reunión oficiosa, Paris, 13 Marzo 1966'; Tierno Galván, *Cabos*, 302–7. Arrillaga had already been to see Solís, the Secretary-Minister of the Falange, early in 1960, to appeal for Amat's release (PSOE, *Actas* of CE, 30.3.60).

[72] Tierno Galván, *Cabos*, 304; José Calviño interview, 8 Sept. 1982; Cardona, 'El guiñol'.

[73] PSOE and other organizations, PSOE-UGT, *Actas* of CD/CG, 25.2.67; PSOE, Executive Committee, *Actas*, PSOE-UGT-FNJSE, 'Reunión Interior-Exterior 29–

ASO never really grew. In Spain its only significant group was in Barcelona, where in time it helped to split the MSC. Other forces abstained from joining because of loyalty to exile-based executives, objections to dependence on the West Germans (seen by some Socialists as conduits of even less desirable United States influence), or worries about the way in which ASO tried to negotiate with Spanish officials and seemed to enjoy a degree of official protection (though some of its militants were arrested).[74]

There were various dissident meetings to discuss ASO and other projects designed to out-manœuvre Toulouse. After the Perpignan meeting of 1958 *émigré* leaders were alarmed by accounts of ASO meetings in Metz, Paris, and Châtelineau, and of two visits of ASO delegations to Brussels to appeal to the ICFTU for support.[75] Toulouse retained control, not only because of the good relations it had developed over the years with European labour leaders, including ICFTU general secretary Omer Becu, but also because the dissident camp itself was deeply divided. Following the near-total rejection of the Amatista alternative at the PSOE congress of 1961, several former renovators gave up all hope of being able to reform the PSOE and UGT from within; they decided that the groups in the interior that were demanding change were too weak to persuade international sponsors to transfer their backing from Toulouse.[76] Possibly because of the situation in the metal-workers' International, they opted initially for the building of an independent trade union movement (ASO) rather than a new socialist party. The Socialists most committed to this project were Bustelo, Montesinos, and Pardo abroad, and Villar, Carvajal, Arrillaga, and Calviño in the interior,[77] the involvement of the last four being influenced probably by the party's industrial weakness in the capital.

30.1.66'. At the same time the SPD was offering finance to the PSOE to hold seminars in Germany and to produce pamphlets (PSOE, *Actas* of CE, 14.1.66).

[74] Tierno Galván, *Cabos*, 304–5; *Le Socialiste*, 14.7.66, 1; PSOE, *Circular*, 28.7.66; PSOE and other organizations, PSOE-UGT, *Actas* of CD/CG, 25.2.67. The trial was attended by SPD deputy Hans Matthöfer (*A.S.O.* bulletin, Jan. 1967). ASO was defunct by 1967.

[75] PSOE, *Actas* of CE, 17.11.62, 17.7.63, 19.7.63; PSOE and other organizations, PSOE-UGT, *Actas* of CD/CG, 20–1.7.63; UGT, *Circular*, 24.11.62.

[76] 'Informe de F.B.'

[77] PSOE and other organizations, PSOE-UGT, *Actas* of CD/CG, 20–1.7.63.

On the other hand, there were Socialists who were deeply concerned about the lack of dynamic leadership in the PSOE-UGT but who remained loyal to the party, either for sentimental reasons or because they appreciated that, given its traditional role and international connections, the PSOE would continue to occupy whatever openings there were for democratic socialism in Spain. When Bustelo went to Spain in 1962, offering money from European metalworkers to prominent socialists whom he hoped might be prepared to break with Toulouse, he found that the Basques were unwilling to sanction a breakaway. Amutio also seems to have had his reservations; he refused to accept money and even persuaded Villar to return some, though he did continue to collaborate with ASO.[78] It is also known that Asturian Socialists rejected money sent by their comrades in Châtelineau because it had not come through the official channels.[79] The division of the dissidents was seen at a meeting in Spain in December 1962 at which Villar and some Catalan Socialists urged the establishment of an executive in the interior while Amat and Román voted against.[80]

Thus the various challenges posed to Toulouse by those it saw as 'trouble-makers' (ASO), 'greenhorns' (ASU, Madrid Young Socialists), and 'usurpers' (the Tierno Galván and García López groups)[81] did not succeed initially. Whether or not they felt the time had come to return control to the interior, those seeking a new approach to socialist struggle in Spain were defeated by a mixture of Llopista manœuvres, their own internal differences, and continuing support for Llopis in the Socialist International, ICFTU, and PSOE-UGT, including significant numerical support in Spain. Toulouse could rely upon the support of veterans such as Juan García in Barcelona and Gómez Egido and Emilio Agüero in Madrid. More importantly, its control rested for a long time on the insularity of the Asturian Socialists and the loyalty of Vizcaya, as personified by Ramón Rubial, whose adherence to

---

[78] Ibid.; Bustelo interview, 26 Apr. 1982.

[79] PSOE and other organizations, PSOE-UGT-FNJSE, Comisión de los asuntos de España, *Actas*, 10.7.63.

[80] PSOE, *Actas* of CE, 19.12.62, 22.6.63.

[81] PSOE-UGT, *Circular*, Jan. 1963.

party discipline earned him the epithet 'the viceroy' from Madrid dissidents.[82]

The early efforts at renovation were defeated, but at a substantial cost. While Llopista dominance suited many veterans and the inactive members, it provided nothing but frustration for the younger and intellectual sectors of the PSOE. To them, Toulouse with its enshrined principle 'without discipline, no organization is possible'[83] seemed more assiduous in policing the party than in promoting the struggle against Franco. A lot of young militants scaled down their activity after repeatedly coming up against the obstructionism of Toulouse, or were isolated by reorganizational manœuvres. In contrast to Amat, who shortly before his downfall had devised a plan to relaunch the FNJSE,[84] the *émigré* leadership saw youth as a source of problems rather than as the key to the future. Little wonder then that Spain's capital was devoid of Young Socialists in the second half of the 1960s.

Equally, the successful clamp-downs on dissent prevented the party from developing theoretically, as it should have done following the influx of graduates in the late 1950s. Llopis and his colleagues welcomed their arrival and even commissioned studies of Spanish conditions from them, but the new recruits quickly discovered that their theoretical contributions were only welcome when they fell within established norms. No airing of dissenting views was tolerated beyond the party, least of all within earshot of the PSOE's international interlocutors. In the process considerable talent was wasted and no theoretician of the party's renovation emerged. Certainly Luis Martín-Santos had all the literary and intellectual skills required for this role. His knowledge of Marxism was far superior to that of the average Socialist, for he was well versed in German philosophy and had read *Das Kapital* and *Anti-Dühring* in the original. He was a critical Marxist for

[82] Diez Yagüe interview. The Toulouse veterans regularly expressed their appreciation of Rubial's loyalty, discipline, honesty, modesty, and prudence (PSOE, *Actas* of CE, 12.10.60, 15.2.61, 12.6.63). In 1967 the Comité de Coordinación (PSOE and other organizations, PSOE-UGT-FNJSE, Comisión Permanente file, *Acta*, 15.10.67) chose him to be the party president, but at first he refused the post.
[83] SOMA Archive, Box A.LIX, Pascual Tomás to Arcadio Martínez Fernández, 20 Apr. 1964.
[84] PSOE, *Actas* of CE, 9.4.58.

whom the Communist bloc held no appeal, especially after the publication of Djilas's *New Class*. His admiration for Rosa Luxemburg contrasted with a rejection of Leninism and all dogma. Both here and in other postures, he anticipated attitudes that were to become far more prevalent among Spanish Socialists a decade or so later. While identifying with Marxism's vision of transforming society in order to liberate man, Martín-Santos regarded the PCE's view of society as archaic. His own social milieu was middle class and he was well aware that the PSOE would need to find support there in the future. Like the party leaders of the late 1970s, he was much concerned about the 'image' that the PSOE should project.[85] But literary priorities and a premature death prevented Martín-Santos from becoming the theoretician of the PSOE renovation. The formulation of dissenting views thus remained a collective phenomenon arising from the practical problems encountered by Socialist militants in Spain.

PHASE ONE: THE YOUTH RENOVATION

It was fitting that an organization whose newspaper bore the name *Renovación* should become the vanguard of the movement to transform the PSOE and UGT. During the 1960s this role was fulfilled by the FNJSE, which returned its executive to Spain before the senior organizations, and agitated for similar changes to be made in the socialist movement as a whole. Not that the youth organization was strong in the interior. It had survived through the darkest hours only in Vizcaya, and even there without autonomy from the PSOE-UGT; only in the mid-1960s did the Basque Young Socialists regain an independent provincial committee, after a decade of apparently being without one.[1] By that time small new groups had been organized in Valencia, Barcelona, Zaragoza, Seville

---

[85] Muñoz Atienza interview; Andrés Sorel, 'Martín-Santos: El novelista y el hombre', *ES*, 4.9.77; Semprún, 187.

[1] FNJSE, Correspondence, 'JSE: Correspondencia con la CE del PSOE 1951/67', 'Al Consejo General', 14.10.64; Benegas and Díaz, 100.

and Asturias,[2] while in the capital the youth federation maintained a precarious existence, still based on students. The Madrid Young Socialists (JSM) continued in the ASU tradition and in the early 1960s earned Toulouse's distrust by working alongside Communist students in the Spanish Democratic University Federation (FUDE).[3] They were hit by arrests including those of Angel de Lucas and Prudencio García in 1963, and then as one of the most indisciplined units of the movement consumed most of their energies in battles with Miguel Peydro and other party leaders in the capital. Particularly here and in Seville, renovating impulses existed in the Youth, but for the greater part of the 1960s these groups were isolated. Curiously, the main battleground of the youth renovation lay abroad, where one might have expected control by the *émigré* veterans to be most secure. However, during the 1960s the FNJSE in exile developed some very stimulating lines of communication with active Socialists in Spain, both through its involvement with Spaniards working abroad and through the practice of sending members into Spain on missions and to settle. As the most dynamic section of the movement, the Youth was at once the most responsive and the most sympathetic to the stirrings for change that were growing in the interior.

In exile the FNJSE had been saved from extinction by the PSOE and UGT early in 1954, when a small subsidy was restored to a youth section that was too small to support itself.[4] During the early 1960s it benefited occasionally from the arrival from Spain of persecuted young militants, notably Avelino Pérez[5] and Miguel Angel Martínez. However, by now most of the Youth leaders were sons and daughters of Socialist exiles. By the time they reached the youth executive, they tended to be well into their twenties and several even exceeded

---

[2] FNJSE, Correspondence, 'JSE: Correspondencia con la CE del PSOE 1951/67', 'Al Consejo General', 14.10.64; PSOE, *Actas* of CE, 19.9.63.

[3] PSOE and other organizations, PSOE-UGT, *Actas* of CD/CG, 15–16.7.62, 12–13; id., PSOE-UGT-FNJSE, Comisión de los asuntos de España, *Actas*, 11–12.11.65.

[4] FNJSE, Congresses, *I Pleno Ampliado de la Federación* (*con facultades de Congreso*) (1954), 46–7.

[5] Pérez told me that he chose to work mainly in the Youth because the leaders of the PSOE-UGT 'annoyed me too much' (interview, 27 Apr. 1982).

the 35-year age-limit. Yet despite their maturity, there was a considerable generational gulf, exacerbated by the events of the 1930s, between these young people and PSOE and UGT leaders who were now in their sixties. The veterans could see that organizational survival depended on youth recruitment; they wanted to possess a youth section, just like the other parties of the Socialist International, and they knew they could not be unresponsive to news that their Communist rivals were trying to re-establish a youth organization in the interior.[6] But painful memories persisted of the damage wreaked by the party's youth section in the early 1920s and mid-1930s, leaving the veterans ever vigilant against any repetition of such events.

The FNJSE revival began in the early 1960s under the general secretaryship of Carlos Martínez Cobo, whose brother José was another driving force on the youth executive. It was under their auspices that the first steps were taken to establish a co-ordinating committee of the youth groups in Spain (as existed in the PSOE) and to give such groups representation on the federation's General Council, which met periodically in France. Most importantly, the brothers began to send young militants into Spain to visit and assist groups operating there, while simultaneously they tried to organize among Spain's economic *émigrés* in Europe.[7] In 1963 Manuel Simón, who had been born to exiled parents in France and spent his childhood in the mining zone of Belgium, agreed to move to Hamburg to work for the three Socialist organizations among Spanish *gastarbeiter*s. Such dedication by a handful of Young Socialists rapidly produced organizational growth. Meeting in May 1964, the General Council heard that this work had given rise to 16 new sections in two years, especially in Belgium, Holland, and Germany, while the circulation of *Renovación* had jumped from 1,800 copies every two months to a monthly figure of 5,500.[8]

A new mood of confidence and ambition began to take hold

---

[6] *Mundo Obrero*, Nov. 1961; FNJSE, Congresses, V Pleno (1963), *Memoria*, 54.

[7] See FNJSE, Correspondence, 'JSE . . . 1951/67', 'Al Consejo General', in which it is reported that 8 comrades had visited groups in the interior since the previous May.

[8] *Le Socialiste*, 18.6.64, 2; interview with Manuel Simón, 22 Feb. 1982.

of the FNJSE which, while reaffirming its loyalty to the PSOE, clearly was disappointed that no Young Socialists had been put on to the executive at the party congress of 1964.[9] That event, at which Llopis marshalled his delegates from Spain so effectively, led some youths to have doubts about the 'myth' of the interior; they began to wonder just how representative those men in dark glasses were—men who never spoke at the congress rostrum, yet who enabled Llopis to go unchallenged whenever he claimed emotively: 'I speak in the name of those who have no voice.'[10]

The turning-point in party-youth relations came in April 1965 when a new FNJSE executive was chosen, headed by Manuel Garnacho as general secretary and also including Simón, Pérez, and Martínez.[11] This new team had a mandate to work for the return of the federation's executive to Spain, beginning with a phase of 'shared leadership'. This was translated into practice with the incorporation from the interior of Eduardo López ('Lalo') of Vizcaya as president, Carlos Corcuera of San Sebastián as treasurer for Spain, and Triginer of Barcelona as the man responsible for extending the clandestine organization.[12] Garnacho's executive, unlike that of Llopis, sent young militants such as Carlos Revilla, Sebastián Gallardo, and María Luisa Fernández back to fortify the Socialist organizations in Spain. Just as important, it continued the work among the economic exiles. When Garnacho reported on such work to the UGT congress of 1965, he was hoping that the senior organizations would want to follow the youth example. After all, this was the first congress attended by a significant number of economic *émigrés* and the Youth leader could boast that the FNJSE was responsible for their presence, while suggesting that these new delegates were better able to reflect the current sentiments of the interior than were the political *émigrés*. But instead of impressing the veterans, Garnacho's intervention merely raised their hackles. The Llopis generation had made efforts

[9] *Le Socialiste*, 18.6.64, 2; FNJSE, Correspondence, 'JSE . . . 1951/67', 'Al Consejo General'.
[10] Simón interview, 22 Feb. 1982.
[11] *Le Socialiste*, 6.5.65, 1, 13.5.65, 6–8.
[12] Simón interview, 22 Feb. 1982; M. Garnacho interview, 17 Apr. 1982.

to distribute propaganda among Spaniards emigrating to France for employment reasons in the late 1940s, but it had done little to organize them. Now, the predominant veteran attitude (or excuse) was that the newer *émigrés* were dangerous: they had been born or socialized in Franco's Spain and thus posed an ideological or a security threat to the Socialist organizations.[13]

In spite of the mounting tension that strained party-youth relations, the Young Socialists retained much respect for the veterans; however anachronistic they had become, their example of service to the party was impeccable. Twenty-five years after Franco's victory they remained thoroughly dedicated to the PSOE and made tremendous sacrifices for it, week after week, year after year. The affection that Young Socialists felt for the old-timers was expressed after the death in September 1965 of Gabriel Pradal, the long-standing editor of *El Socialista*. As a tribute to a 'true socialist', the FNJSE published a volume of the veteran's ironic 'Pericles García' column.[14] This restored the standing of the Youth to such an extent that Garnacho was chosen as Pradal's replacement on the UGT executive, and thus attended the meetings of all three executives (that of the PSOE ex officio). Meanwhile the FNJSE executive established the planned co-ordinating committee in the interior in July 1965; it began to function in April 1966.[15] With the aid of their Swedish comrades, the Young Socialists now began to bring out local *Renovación* bulletins in Asturias, Vizcaya, and Madrid, though the appearance of the latter was held up by Peydro because of its controversial contents.[16]

[13] Ibid.

[14] G. Pradal, *Comentarios de Pericles García* (Toulouse: Edns. Renovación, 1967); PSOE, *Actas* of CE, 13.11.65. The prologue by Jiménez de Asúa was seen by the Youth as an indication of this prestigious exile's recognition of their work (Garnacho interview, 17.4.82).

[15] FNJSE, Circulars, 'Circulares 1961/67', *Carta-Circular* 29 (July 1966). This Comité de Coordinación had the same function as that of the PSOE-UGT.

[16] PSOE, *Actas* of CE, 10.8.66. The Madrid youth group called for participation in *sindicato* elections, defying the orthodox policy of the CE of the FNJSE, which in the end had to get members from Asturias and the Basque Country to go to Madrid to run a boycott campaign. The Madrid Young Socialists even refused to provide them with accommodation, but the problem disappeared shortly afterwards when a new committee was formed in the capital (Garnacho interview, 17 Apr. 1982).

By mid-1966 the balance of FNJSE affiliation was 65 per cent economic *émigré* against 35 per cent political *émigré*, and some 25 per cent of the youth militants were female. Most members were also in the UGT (65 per cent) and a growing proportion (24 per cent) belonged to the PSOE. Madrid was the federation's most obvious weak spot.[17] Through developing stronger interior-exterior links and stepping up the level of FNJSE activity, Garnacho's team hoped to capitalize upon what seemed to be growing radicalism among the youth of Spain. A study of youth attitudes conducted in 1967, while not a precise indicator, encouraged the Young Socialists in their work, for it suggested that 42 per cent of Spanish youth favoured socialist economic forms (against 15 per cent for State capitalism and 36 per cent for free enterprise) and that 61 per cent were in favour of pluralist democracy.[18] To work effectively, more resources were needed and the most obvious source was the IUSY, on whose executive the FNJSE had recently regained its seat. More international support had been pledged in late 1963 and this was most forthcoming from the IUSY's stronger sections in Norway, Austria, and Germany.[19] But by 1966 the Spaniards were sure that their

[17] PSOE, Assemblies, Comité Director, July 1966, 'Notas de la reunión celebrada por el Comité Director del PSOE el día 4 de Julio de 1966 en Bayona'. The PSOE itself had 259 female members at this time (ibid.), and they were dispersed. This made it very difficult for the Secretariado Femenino established in 1964–5 to function well. Its objectives were to encourage women to become more active in the PSOE, to recruit among the *émigré* population, advise the PSOE executive on women's problems, set up women's groups based on members and sympathizers, and to take part in international Socialist Women's events. Headed by the Paris-based Carmen García de Robledo, it (like the FNJSE) sent envoys to the interior, and groups were established in Vizcaya and Guipúzcoa. The number of women members and sympathizers outside Spain grew to 400 by 1970. But faced with a limited recruitment pool and the indifference or hostility of many male Socialists, women's groups only got off the ground in Paris, Toulouse, and Mexico City. The secretariat was abolished in 1970, at which time the PSOE had 235 female members and the FNJSE 72. Many Socialists opposed the idea of a women's section on the grounds that it was too reminiscent of the Falange structure, or that it implied unequal treatment. (Interview with Carmen García Bloise, 7 Apr. 1982; *Le Socialiste*, 3.9.64, 5; PSOE, *Actas* of CE, 16–17.2.65; PSOE, Eleventh Congress held in exile (1970), *Memoria*, 'Anexos'; PSOE, Secretariats, Secretariado Femenino, *Memoria*, 1969).

[18] *Le Socialiste*, 1.6.67, 3, reprinting a study by José Félix Tezanos and Rafael Domínguez that was first published in *Cuadernos para el Diálogo*, special issue on 'La Universidad', 1967, 96–9.

[19] PSOE and other organizations, PSOE-UGT-FNJSE, Comisión de los asuntos de España, *Actas*, 25.10.63; PSOE, *Actas* of CE, 26.2.64; Simón interview, 22 Feb. 1982.

allies still did not understand just how difficult clandestine activity was. They therefore decided that the IUSY executive had to visit Spain.

Agreement on such an 'operation' was reached at the end of an IUSY congress in Vienna in May 1966 and around the same time an IUSY delegation held a preparatory meeting in Spain with FNJSE representatives.[20] As usual, though, the party veterans saw only the risks involved in what was being planned: it could lead to raids and arrests and thus jeopardize the whole organization. The party executive's grudging assent came only after the Youth had enlisted the support of Ramón Rubial, and after Garnacho had agreed to give Llopis a letter acknowledging that, if anything went wrong, it was the exclusive responsibility of the FNJSE.[21] Happily, everything went well for the meeting on 3–5 February 1967, despite the evident problems involved in holding a secret three-day meeting of almost 50 people including distinctive Japanese, Malaysian, Mauritian, and Scandinavian IUSY leaders as well as delegates from various parts of Spain and members of the FNJSE executive. Each morning and evening the foreign visitors had to be smuggled to and from hotels in Bilbao, while during the day the assembly took place in a semi-ruined house by a cemetery at Portugalete, which the local young socialists had transformed into a bunker for the event. This was an impressive feat of organization and a considerable publicity coup, for as soon as they reached home the IUSY leaders called press conferences to report on the visit. The operation generated increased IUSY interest in Spain; duplicators and typewriters now began to arrive regularly, especially from Scandinavia. The event had reassured the foreign participants, showing the FNJSE to be united, and interior and exterior to be working in harmony. Word of the event also percolated through the European socialist parties, tending to make even the PSOE executive seem dynamic! Thus, momentarily the Youth returned to the good books of the party leadership; for a while Garnacho and his colleagues were 'good chaps'.[22]

[20] *Le Socialiste*, 16.6.66, 1, 6, 16.2.67, 1–2.
[21] Garnacho interview, 17 Apr. 1982.
[22] Ibid.; *Le Socialiste*, 16.2.67, 1–2; Jáuregui and Vega, ii. 232; PSOE, *Actas* of CE, 18.2.67.

The point of no return in these relations was reached after the Youth's third congress in exile in May 1967. Whereas the PSOE and UGT congresses were still *émigré* affairs at which the interior would be represented but not participate, the FNJSE allowed delegates from the interior to intervene in the debates and to vote with equal rights. This did not affect the outcome of the congress, for criticism of the PSOE was voiced by nearly all the delegates, but it did set a worrying precedent for the party and UGT leaders: delegations from the interior were hard to control and it was impossible to verify how many members they represented. However, in an effort to avoid a frontal clash, the congress decided not to pass any resolutions critical of the PSOE; instead it mandated the executive to express to the party 'the uneasiness and worries that exist in some youth sections'.[23]

The first opportunity to do this came in August 1967 at the PSOE's tenth congress in exile, for which the FNJSE had urged members to get themselves elected as delegates.[24] As usual, Paris was strongly critical of the party executive's performance and even the Toulouse delegate Máximo Rodríguez was partially critical. Present for Grenoble, Manuel Garnacho joined in the censure and spoke out strongly in favour of the kinds of innovations made by the Youth. However, this was the prelude to an easy victory for Llopis. After rallying delegates with a tirade against elements seeking to remove 'Obrero' (Worker) from the PSOE name ('Our party must be increasingly socialist, working class, and Spanish'),[25] he managed to get virtually the whole congress, including people from the interior, howling at the Grenoble delegate. 'You can apply that in the Youth!' Nicolás Redondo thundered at him, not to be appeased when Garnacho replied that they were doing so and with quite pleasing results. Only one delegate voted against the party executive's performance, while seven abstained. The young delegates were hammered, and the FNJSE was left in such bad odour that for the first time ever it

---

[23] *Le Socialiste*, 1.6.67, 1–2; Garnacho interview, 17 Apr. 1982; Simón interview, 22 Feb. 1982.

[24] FNJSE, Circulars, 'Circulares 1961/67', *Carta-Circular* 11 (n.d. [mid-1967]). It also reported that 3 members of the youth Comité de Coordinación had been jailed or banished from their home towns in Spain.

[25] *Le Socialiste*, 24.8.67, 4.

was refused permission to deliver its fraternal greetings to the congress. Recalling the JSU desertions of the mid-1930s, veterans began to refer to Garnacho as 'Santiagín' and 'Carrillo No. 2'.[26]

In October Garnacho duly submitted a document summarizing the Youth grievances, as was his congress mandate. After describing the growth of the FNJSE in Spain and abroad, this document gave expression to frustrated activism. The now dynamic youth federation was unable to serve as the 'nursery' of the PSOE, it complained, because Young Socialists were given a cool reception in the party and kept coming up against 'inertia'. The document urged the party to become much more active in mass working-class struggles in Spain, and to make such involvement the centre of its strategy. Alluding to the Union of Democratic Forces, it dismissed the value of party alliances with bourgeois or phantom organizations, and instead called for co-operation (though no alliance) with other working-class forces, including the PCE.[27] Inevitably, though not deservedly, such FNJSE talk provoked veteran memories of the JSU, and Llopis exploited this reserve of prejudice to the full. As astute as ever, he made no attempt to defend the UFD from criticism. With the Socialists' Christian Democratic allies now disastrously divided, Llopis no doubt shared fellow veteran Manuel Muiño's opinion that the Union was a 'cadaver'.[28] So after ostentatiously taking the trouble to 'consult' 'Pablo' (Rubial) before replying to the document, he tried to redefine the controversy in a way calculated to maximize veteran solidarity. Accusing the FNJSE of proposing an alliance (albeit for concrete actions) with the Communists, he reminded the Youth of its duty to defend party policy, and claimed that the federation had become far too concerned with PSOE and UGT matters at the expense of youth issues. In his view, the practice of Young Socialists also joining the party had created an anomalous situation: two carnets, two disciplines.[29]

[26] Garnacho interview, 17 Apr. 1982.
[27] FNJSE, Correspondence, 'Documento de JSE al PSOE (Octubre 1967) y polémica posterior'.
[28] PSOE, *Circular* 10 (5 Jan. 1967); PSOE, *Actas* of CE, 25.10.69.
[29] FNJSE, Correspondence, 'Documento de JSE . . .'; PSOE, *Actas* of CE, 13.9.67.

There was some validity in the claim that the youth section was beginning to operate as a party. For decades its structures had been similar to those of the PSOE,[30] and now it was addressing itself to grand strategy and thinking for itself. But even at this late stage, with Llopis on the offensive, the Youth leaders were doing all they could to avoid splitting the PSOE, and certainly they were not guilty of any subservience to the PCE. Llopis's questioning of the *doble militancia* of Young Socialists was in fact a red herring. While never a common practice, it had always been possible for Young Socialists to be members of the PSOE, and Prieto for one had taken advantage of this in his youth.

The argument was left to be resolved in the presence of senior Socialists from Spain who were coming to France for a meeting of the party's Comité Director in June 1969. Shortly before the meeting, which took place in Bayonne, FNJSE leaders approached Rubial and offered to resign or even dissolve the federation if this greatly respected Basque Socialist deemed such measures necessary to avoid a party schism. This show of party patriotism reduced the Bilbao veteran to tears. His advice was for the Youth to absorb all the criticisms and insults that were thrown at them, but to continue with their activities. At the party-youth meeting that followed, this was what the Youth Socialist did, registering the veteran counter-attack stoically.[31] Immediately afterwards, however, came the Comité Director meeting, at which they found the general secretary of the PSOE once more railing against them. The FNJSE had been urged by the IUSY to take up an invitation to go and study self-management schemes in Yugoslavia; it had referred the matter to the PSOE, knowing that the party, now strictly applying its 'no relations with the Communists' principle, had refused to attend a Yugoslav

---

[30] The PSOE, UGT, and FNJSE each had local groups (*agrupaciones* or *secciones*) which would elect a committee and send delegates to periodic congresses at which a Comisión Ejecutiva would be elected. There would also be a committee to control the latter, this being the Consejo General in the UGT and FNJSE and the Comité Director in the PSOE. Theoretically an organ based on territorial representation (the equivalent of the traditional Comité Nacional), the controlling committee in fact tended to be elected in exile by congresses or plenums because of the shortage of money available for postal ballots. Like the PSOE-UGT, the FNJSE meanwhile had a Comité de Coordinación in Spain, parallel to the CG/CD abroad.

[31] Garnacho interview, 17 Apr. 1982.

party congress in March.[32] But to the surprise of the Young Socialists, they found Llopis denouncing them to the Comité Director, and claiming that he had learnt of the planned visit from unofficial sources! Garnacho responded by expressing envy at the general secretary's capacity 'to distort the truth without turning red'.[33] Llopis took this as a personal insult and relations rapidly deteriorated—to such an extent that, although the IUSY called off the Yugoslav visit, the FNJSE sent Manuel Simón to attend a seminar organized by the Romanian Young Communists in Bucharest, notwithstanding a party ban.[34]

By now, any hope of real reconciliation was gone and in practice the FNJSE made full use of its autonomy. The party fought a rearguard action by sending José Martínez de Velasco to a Comité Nacional meeting of the federation in August, to argue against transferring the Youth executive back to Spain,[35] but his only achievement was to get the decision deferred until the fourth congress of the FNJSE at the end of March 1970. That congress, attended by 47 direct delegations from Spain, Belgium, Germany, Sweden, Switzerland, and France, representing some 244 members abroad and 361 in Spain, unanimously approved a motion proposed by Vizcaya, Barcelona, Seville, and Madrid, under which the leadership of the youth organization was returned to Spain.[36] The PSOE executive condemned this move as 'an adventure'. Though it initially rejected a proposal to suspend its financial subsidy of the Youth, within months the payments were terminated.[37] It was too late to make much difference. By now the FNJSE was organized in 15 provinces of Spain.[38] Its old executive resigned, its mandate fulfilled. Only Manuel Simón remained as an external member of the new leadership that was drawn

[32] Ibid.; PSOE, Assemblies, Comité Director, June 1969, 'Nota informativa' of CE, 13–14. The PSOE took umbrage when the Yugoslav ambassador in France expressed surprise at the PSOE's lack of relations with the PCE after the latter had articulated a 'correct' line on Czechoslovakia.

[33] Garnacho interview, 17 Apr. 1982.

[34] PSOE, *Actas* of CE, 11.6.69, 24.9.69.

[35] Ibid., 13.8.69.

[36] *Porvenir* (Paris FNJSE bulletin), May 1970.

[37] PSOE, *Actas* of CE, 25.4.70; id., Executive Committee, Circulars, *Carta-Circular*, 4.3.71.

[38] Jáuregui and Vega, ii. 334.

overwhelmingly from the interior and selected by the federation's Comité de Coordinación in Spain.

Although each part of the 'socialist family' underwent its own process of renovation, crowned with the successive FNJSE, UGT, and PSOE congresses of 1970, 1971, and 1972, what occurred in each organization naturally affected the others. The determination of the Youth to carry through its plans in 1970 set an important example for the parent bodies. While having no great effect on the strength of opposition to Franco, it at least showed that Socialist struggle could be approached in a different manner without dire consequences. Moreover, those who organized the Youth renovation went on to play outstanding roles in the battles to renovate the UGT and PSOE.

The key turning-point in the overall process was the UGT's eleventh congress in exile in August 1971, for it was here that the major bodies of Socialists both within and outside Spain finally agreed upon the need to return control of their organization to the interior. After this, the writing was on the wall for Llopis and his supporters. Winners and losers alike were conscious that many of the participants in the UGT battle would be present a year later to determine the outcome of the next PSOE congress. Only marginally larger than the party, its membership almost exclusively Socialist, the UGT provided a rough indicator of trends in the party itself. What happened in the UGT between 1968 and 1971 was therefore absolutely crucial for future developments in the PSOE. It is well worth dwelling on the UGT process, for it revealed the nature of the renovation in its true light. Later on, journalistic accounts of it would focus upon the personal rise in the party of Felipe González, confirmed in 1974 at the PSOE congress at Suresnes. Many party members thus came to confuse the renovation process with the growing dominance of the Sevillian Socialists in the PSOE leadership from 1972.[1] But

---

[1] In May 1985 a professional spokesman for the Socialist government, Miguel Ángel Molinero, lost a bet that the party congress at Suresnes took place in 1972

what the UGT phase of the process shows quite clearly is, first, that the renovating initiative came more from the exterior than from the interior; second, that apart from active exiles, the main push for renewal came from the large northern federations of Asturias and (eventually) Vizcaya— not from the Sevillians (who, as noted earlier, could see little point in trying to revive the UGT); and third, that although a generational clash was central to the whole process, a number of influential veterans did side crucially with the renovators in the end. Thus it is incorrect to see the renovation process as simply a matter of interior challenging exterior or of young against old. And equally it is important to separate the process of renovation from the ensuing jockeying for predominance within the new leadership.[2]

Unease within the UGT grew as a result of its tenth congress in exile, held in August 1968. In that year the health of Pascual Tomás, general secretary since 1944, had deteriorated to such an extent that he was no longer able to attend to his work at the union offices. Yet in spite of chronic heart disease, and for purely sentimental reasons, he was re-elected by the congress. This was a tactical blunder on the part of the old guard, because although Tomás's position was unassailable, his re-election left the key post in the UGT unmanned. An opportunity was lost to vest legitimate authority in a more vigorous replacement. Moreover, the tenth congress ended without resolving a contradiction of its own making: when the moment arrived to elect an executive committee, the delegates also elected a Consejo General (thereby guaranteeing that this control body would have a similar outlook to that of the executive); but later in the congress, when statutory reform came up for discussion, it was decided that the Consejo had to be elected on the basis of the geographical zones where UGT members were resident.[3] Thus, a congress that the old guard had no trouble in managing generated increased disgruntlement.

rather than 1974 (*El País*, international edn., 20.5.85). This confusion was common among the newer members of the PSOE interviewed by the author in 1982–4.

[2] This argument is developed at greater length in my 'The Clandestine PSOE, 1939–75', *Spanish Studies*, 6 (1984), 34–47.

[3] *Le Socialiste*, 15.8.68, 1–6; UGT, Eleventh Congress held in exile (1971), *Memoria*, 19–28; id., *Circular* 12 (1 Sept. 1969), 4.

Further antagonism grew out of post-congressional attempts by Llopis and company to deal with these problems. To legitimize the Consejo General that had been elected but then implicitly disavowed by the congress, the UGT executive organized an internal referendum. This validated (though only just) the procedure whereby congresses were to elect the Consejo General. The outcome would have been different had not the vote of the Mexican section (440 members) arrived late. Around the same time, Pascual Tomás was persuaded to resign by fellow veterans now worried about the leadership vacuum. Llopis managed to secure the top UGT post for former vice-secretary Manuel Muiño, but only by resorting to a questionable procedure. Balloting was restricted to the Consejo General, leaving out members of the Comisión Permanente and Comité de Coordinación in Spain; and when this was challenged by Garnacho and others, Llopis simply invited them to stand against Muiño themselves (and thus make it seem that their objections were motivated by personal ambition). In this way Muiño became general secretary of the UGT with the votes of only 10 members of the 25-strong Consejo General.[4]

These manœuvres were in the minds of four UGT leaders who resigned from the executive in 1969. Among them, Paulino Barrabés, who had joined the three Socialist organizations in 1944, was a relative youngster, but accompanying him were the veterans José Barreiro, Antonio García Duarte, and Arsenio Jimeno. Apart from these specific grievances, they had reached the conclusion that the hour had come to gradually return the power of initiative to the interior. Although in a minority on the executive, their departures were of the utmost symbolic significance among Socialists. Above all, they showed that the criticism levelled against the Llopis clique could not be dismissed as a problem of juvenile impatience. And certainly they provoked a lot of debate. Arsenio Jimeno, of course, had been the main head of the French-based opposition to Llopis for many a year; he had

[4] SOMA Archive, Box A.LIX, Barreiro to CE of UGT, 5 June 1969; Garnacho interview, 13 Sept. 1982; UGT, Eleventh Congress held in exile (1971), *Memoria*, 19–28; SOMA Archive, Box A.LVII, coverless UGT bulletin [1971]; UGT, *Circular* 12 (1 Sept. 1969).

fought a succession of good battles against the general
secretary of the PSOE but had always ended up compromising,
unable to carry the challenge through to victory.[5] Behind him
he had the solid support of Paris, where Socialist *émigrés*
traditionally had favoured a greater say for the interior and
had wanted the exterior's responsibilities to be entrusted to an
executive based in the French capital, which they felt was
rather more responsive to developments in Spain than was
Toulouse. José Barreiro, on the other hand, rebelled against
Llopis only late in life. A teacher in Asturias who had been
obliged to go down the mines to earn a living in France,
Barreiro had been a dependable member of the *émigré*
executive since the 1940s, while Jimeno had been tolerated
mainly only at the level of the Consejo General. By the late
1960s, however, Barreiro had decided that his movement had
only two options: 'to renovate itself or die'.[6]

The problem was generational in that the veterans who now
took a stand were echoing the concerns and demands of the
Youth. But the crux of the matter was how the UGT was to
operate: were its command posts to remain in distant
Toulouse, for security reasons, or be transported to the scene
of struggle? Posed less explicitly, a further question was
whether the UGT should remain so closely bound to the
PSOE that it accepted all the party's alliances, or should it
assert sufficient political autonomy to be able to collaborate
with any other labour organization, including the Workers'
Commissions? In other words, was the UGT to be a political
shadow of the PSOE, or take its own political initiatives?

In their resignation letters of mid-1969, the UGT dissidents
expressed worries about a growing bureaucratic sterility. The
union executive was old and hidebound, yet seemed capable of
surviving with the aid of loyal part-time organizational workers
in Spain. Critics of the leadership feared that the UGT was
losing its credibility in the international labour movement,
symptoms of this being the International Metalworkers'
Federation's earlier support to ASO and its more recent
acceptance of USO as a Spanish affiliate. By resigning,
Barreiro, Jimeno, Barrabés, and García Duarte hoped to jolt

---

[5] López Real interview, *ES*, 17.6.79, 14–15; Garnacho interview, 17 Apr. 1982.
[6] Avelino Pérez interview.

influential veterans out of their apparent lethargy and complacency. They were trying to make others see the need to bring younger, more energetic militants urgently into the leadership, to give the interior an increasingly determining part in running the UGT, to launch a more dynamic and imaginative propaganda effort, and to permit co-operation with other organizations that were seeking to practise trade unionism. It was totally unrealistic, the four men felt, to continue behaving as if the UGT and CNT were still the main union alternatives in Spain, as the documents of the last congress had suggested.[7]

Although unable to attend the Consejo General meeting on 12–13 July 1969 at which the resignations were presented, Barreiro sent a letter saying that the UGT had failed to 'win the new generations' because of its 'work and propaganda formulas'.[8] As for the three critics present at the meeting, they were very nearly persuaded to withdraw their resignations. They began to vacillate when faced with appeals from the Basque leaders Rubial and Redondo. It was a scene in which veteran embraced veteran, with tears in eyes, and even a hard man like Jimeno faltered. Had it not been for Barreiro's absence, the resignations might have been withdrawn. But when on the verge of changing their minds, his three colleagues felt obliged to consult him by phone at his home in Marénac. It was Barreiro's firmness that determined the outcome: 'Do what you want,' he said; 'my resignation stands.' In his view, the matter could be postponed no longer. Out of solidarity his three colleagues then confirmed their resignations from the executive, whereupon several sympathizers resigned from the Consejo General.[9]

Barreiro's stand was crucial, for not only was he a highly respected veteran but also a leading Asturian Socialist whose

---

[7] UGT, Tenth Congress held in exile (1968), *Memoria*, 52; Simón interview, 22 Feb. 1982; Barreiro to CE of UGT, 5 June 1969; SOMA Archive, Box A.LVII, open letter of Barreiro, Jimeno, and Barrabés to CE of UGT, 14 July 1969; UGT, *Circular* 12 (1 Sept. 1969); id., Eleventh Congress (1971), 'Materiales diversos', 'Réplica obligada de los compañeros José Barreiro, Paulino Barrabés, Arsenio Jimeno', Jan. 1970; UGT, Eleventh Congress held in exile (1971), *Memoria*, 19–28; SOMA Archive, Box A.LVII, coverless UGT bulletin of 1969; ibid., Box A.LIX, 'Carta del Compañero José Barreiro', 7 July 1969; Paulino Barrabés interview, 27 June 1984; García Duarte interview.

[8] 'Carta del Compañero José Barreiro'.   [9] García Duarte interview.

attitude would greatly influence his fellow Asturians and help
shape the position adopted by the large Asturian federation at
the next congress of the UGT.[10] The main obstacle to change
was not so much the Toulouse veterans as the prudent
Basques inside Spain whom those veterans could cite as the
authentic 'voice of the interior'. Besides Rubial and Redondo
in Vizcaya, Enrique Múgica in San Sebastián was at this stage
still opposed to the idea of transferring authority to the
interior, fearing that this would mean a transfer of PSOE and
UGT leaders to Franco's jails. By now, however, Francoist
repression had eased considerably and Socialists arrested for
'illicit association' or 'illegal propaganda' were seldom sentenced
to more than six months' imprisonment. The Basque Socialists
themselves were rather slow to react to the limited relaxation
of repression in the 1960s; they thus had to be pressured by
the renovators if they were now to assume the responsibility of
leadership.[11]

The resignations of 1969 served as the catalyst of a process
leading to a triumph for the *renovadores* in August 1971 at a
UGT congress in Toulouse held in the Sala Léon Jouhaux
belonging to Force Ouvrière. Some 2,739 exiles were represented at the congress, and the representation of the
interior and of the economic *émigrés* was stronger than ever
before.[12] Already, the report that the executive had to present
to the congress had been circulated to delegates and it was
abundantly clear from this that veteran thinking had changed
very little since the 1950s. With emphasis it boldly stated:
'reality has shown that our having organized the UGT abroad,
with legal status in France, has been, is, *and will continue to
be the fundamental basis of the UGT's existence and survival,
and will go on being so as long as we are unable to operate
freely in Spain.*' Encouraged by the fact that Vizcaya had
submitted a motion saying it would be 'suicidal' to transfer the
bulk of the executive to Spain,[13] the old guard arrived at the

[10] Avelino Pérez interview.
[11] García Duarte interview; Simón interview, 22 Feb. 1982; Castellano interview,
20 July 1982.
[12] Simón interview, 22 Feb. 1982; UGT, 'Confederal XI° Congreso'.
[13] UGT, Eleventh Congress held in exile (1971), *Memoria*, 13, 220–1, and
'Materiales diversos'. Similar motions to that of Vizcaya came from Mexico,
Santander, Burgos, Caracas, and Aragón, while the return of the CE to Spain was

congress in a relatively confident mood. Immediately, however, its candidates for officials to staff the platform of the congress were defeated by a list headed by Paulino Barrabés and composed of young renovators from the exile sections. It is important to record that a majority of the exile sections voted for this opposition slate,[14] since afterwards, and for the first time since 1939, the UGT delegations from the interior spoke and voted with full and equal rights in the congress, and the old guard would claim that it had been defeated by votes from the interior whose representativeness could not be verified. When the old executive raised this objection on the first morning of the congress, thereby questioning the probity of delegates who had travelled from the interior, they sowed tremendous ill-feeling among the militants who were taking the risks in Spain. In the end, a delegate from Asturias silenced the executive's argument by issuing the following challenge: 'If anyone wants to count the votes of Asturias, let him come and be a militant in Asturias, and not stay in Brussels or Toulouse!'[15]

Llopis, as president of the UGT, did not have the central role at the congress. His speech, scheduled for the first morning, was dropped because of the lengthy wrangles over the accreditation of delegates. It fell to the new general secretary Manuel Muiño to defend his executive's record, as outlined in its report (the *memoria*). Here the absence of Pascual Tomás made itself felt, for he had possessed a rare ability to move a congress, which Muiño decidedly lacked. When confronted by critics, Tomás would recall memories of past battles and former glories, using his command of words and a sentimental appeal that would leave the whole congress weeping and in no mood for a battle.[16] Muiño, however, was

---

proposed by Asturias, Catalonia, Paris, Guipúzcoa, Seville, and many of the newer exile sections, especially in Germany. In all, in the 'Statutes and Organization' section, 24 of the 32 motions presented to the congress favoured the return of the CE to the interior.

[14] M. Simón interview, 7 Sept. 1982; Garnacho interview, 13 Sept. 1982; Castellano interview; Barrabés interview; UGT, Eleventh Congress held in exile (1971), *Actas*.

[15] Simón interview, 7 Sept. 1982. There were delegates from Spain who were not yet *renovadores*, but who voted against the CE, feeling that it had shown contempt for the interior earlier in the congress.

[16] Garnacho interview, 13 Sept. 1982. The health of Tomás continued to decline

far more brusque and offhand; he faced his opponents head-on, without any subtlety. He simply stated that while the UGT of course was 'in Spain', its apparatus had to remain abroad. His speech was followed by a barrage of criticism that had been prepared in advance by the younger Socialist exiles. The Martínez Cobo brothers, Garnacho, Barreiro, Salgado, Jimeno, and others attacked an executive report that, in the words of Barreiro, was 'a report of self-satisfaction'.[17] They tore into the outgoing executive for failing to carry out congress decisions, for its neglect of the training of militants, for the way in which the Consejo General had been elected, and for the general lack of UGT dynamism which had allowed alternative trade unions to emerge in Spain. After an ineffectual response to his ambushers by Muiño, the report was rejected by the congress, with both interior and exterior delegates voting.[18]

This defeat deprived the Llopistas of the nerve to present candidates for the new executive which, it was decided, was to be composed of nine members from the interior and five from exile. Reacting against the way in which the old guard had come to see themselves as personifying the UGT and as absolutely essential to its survival, the congress now suppressed the posts of president and general secretary and instead adopted what purported to be a 'collegiate' model of leadership.[19] None the less, the new UGT team possessed a *primus inter pares* in the form of the political secretary Nicolás Redondo. A lot of Basques had changed their views on the renovation actually during the congress (from which Ramón Rubial was absent). The prestigious Basque exile Juan Iglesias, for many years responsible for the French side of the link with the interior, voted with the old guard on the first day but then, after talks with Basques from the interior and other delegates, voted with the renovators on the second. Other Basque exiles, of whom there were many among the delegates,

---

and he returned to his family's home in Valencia shortly before dying at the age of 78 in May 1972 (*Le Socialiste*, 18.5.72), 1–2.

[17] UGT, Eleventh Congress held in exile (1971), *Actas* of 2nd session.

[18] Ibid.; UGT, *Circular* 1 (1 Sept. 1971). Of the members represented in this vote, 53.4% rejected the *memoria*, 29.4% voted for it, and 17.2% abstained.

[19] Redondo interview.

followed suit.[20] Thus it was finally with Basque backing that the decisions were taken to return control of the UGT to the interior and to seek an alliance with all the forces of the political and trade union opposition to Franco. The strongest resistance to the changes was put up by the delegation from Mexico, though it is interesting to note that many of the *renovadores* in the exile camp joined the 'Mexicans' in abstaining from the executive election, feeling that it was unfair that the interior should be able to vote for the exile-based seats on the executive while only the interior chose the Spanish-based members. For the Mexico delegation, the main argument was that the new UGT alliance policy contradicted the congress's proclaimed identification with PSOE policies, for the latter included the party's rejection of any relations with communists.[21]

The sequel to the congress was unspectacular. There was no sudden strengthening of the UGT in the interior, nor any dramatic announcement of new alliances, though informal relations with the Communists in Spain now gave way to co-participation in broad opposition co-ordinating groups.[22] There was no change of heart on the issue of participating in *sindicato* elections, which was just as well given that the regime's days were numbered; it was now essential to offer an example of democratic trade unionism.[23] In Spain the UGT was still extremely weak. Using its Vizcayan stronghold as a basis, it had just established a National Metalworkers' Federation but had little else at national level. Many Socialists now acknowledged that, for years and in most of Spain,

[20] Garnacho interview, 13 Sept. 1982; Castellano interview.

[21] UGT, Eleventh Congress held in exile (1971), *Actas* and CE election papers; id., Twelfth Congress held in exile (1973), *Memoria*, 7–30; SOMA Archive, Box A.LVII, UGT, Sección de México, Distrito Federal, *Circular*, 13 Sept. 1971; ibid., Box A.LIX, V. Salazar to A. Jimeno, 3 Dec. 1971. In 1973 an executive of 9 : 5 was elected by the whole congress of the UGT (UGT, *Circular* 1 (10 Sept. 1973)).

[22] SOMA Archive, Box A.LIX, Jimeno to Salazar, 24 Nov. 1971; PSOE, Twelfth Congress held in exile (1972), *Memoria* issued by Llopis faction, ch. 3.

[23] Maravall, *Dictatorship*, 170; Simón interview, 7 Sept. 1982; Garnacho interview, 13 Sept. 1982. The Socialist attitude was that the *sindicatos verticales* would have a role in the post-Franco transition only if the Communists gave them one. The Socialists' independence of the *sindicato* structures, in Garnacho's view, helped to prevent Spain from experiencing what happened in Portugal after 1974, when the Communist Party reaped the full benefits of a former strategy of infiltration in the absence of a socialist alternative.

propaganda had substituted for organization in UGT activity.
If Socialist trade unionism was to have a future, it was
imperative to 'move on from a testimonial phase to a policy of
being present' in workplaces in the many areas where the
UGT was at best a memory.[24]

What had taken place in Toulouse had not been a conflict of
ideology. Although the congress reaffirmed the *'clasista* and
revolutionary traditions of the UGT',[25] the interior had not
yet felt the pressures of radicalism that were to come shortly
from the Youth. Above all, the clash was about flexibility,
both mental and tactical, and its outcome left the UGT
distinctly better equipped to revive rapidly after the departure
of Franco, if not before. As Jimeno wrote to Víctor Salazar,
the leading opponent of renovation, based in Mexico, the
congress had helped to prevent 'the death by decomposition of
the UGT'.[26] And it had done so without dividing the organization. The UGT sections in Mexico City, Caracas, and Albi
boycotted the new executive but no alternative was formed.[27]
Caught off-guard at the congress, the old leaders had suffered
such a visible defeat that they found it morally impossible to
lead an immediate break-away. Moreover, they trusted that
this was all an aberration, and hoped the following year to
regain ground at the forthcoming congress of the PSOE, and
then use the party as a springboard to recuperate the UGT.[28]
This illusion would not last long, for by now the process of
renovation was virtually irreversible.

PHASE THREE: THE PSOE SCHISM OF 1972

In August 1970, at the eleventh congress of the PSOE to be
held outside Spain, the renovators finally broke through at the
level of the party. Despite stubborn resistance on the part of

---

[24] UGT, Eleventh Congress held in exile (1971), 'Informe de la gestión de la
Comisión Ejecutiva en el interior', June 1971.
[25] UGT, Twelfth Congress held in exile (1973), *Memoria*, 13.
[26] Letter of 24 Nov. 1971.
[27] UGT, Twelfth Congress held in exile (1973), *Memoria*, 49–53.
[28] Simón interviews, 22 Feb., 7 Sept. 1982; Garnacho interview, 13 Sept. 1982.
Only about five years later was a rival UGT attempted, but it failed to get off the
ground (interview with José Prat, Madrid, 19 June 1984).

the main Toulouse-based leaders, substantially increased powers were granted to the part of the executive based in Spain. This breakthrough helped set in motion events leading to another congress two years later at which a thorough renovation was sanctioned, but in the process the party split into two: the PSOE *renovado*, or PSOE(R), and the PSOE *histórico*, or PSOE(H). As in the 1940s, the existence of two rival parties, each claiming to be the country's traditional Socialist party, awakened renewed international socialist interest in Spain; once more the PSOE's foreign allies would play an important role in adjudicating the issue. The international outcome would prove decisive, for since no socialist force in Spain was strong enough to convincingly assert its pre-eminence in a field now disputed by four major contenders and dozens of acronyms, future voters would be greatly influenced by which sector the major European socialist parties looked upon as their Spanish counterpart. It was important to lay claim to the precious 'P.S.O.E.' initials for historical reasons, and international socialist recognition was the quickest means of legitimating such a claim. Later it could be ratified in an election.

Sociological explanations of the party renovation process are of rather limited value. It is an oversimplification to portray it in terms of new middle-class professional elements emerging to challenge the hold on the PSOE of hitherto dominant working-class veterans. Certainly, this was the period when politically talented graduates who had just joined the legal and medical professions were beginning to play leading roles in the PSOE, both in certain regions and at national level; and almost invariably they took the side of the renovators. It was only at the end of the 1960s that University of Seville graduates such as Felipe González and Alfonso Guerra and the doctors Luis Yáñez and Guillermo Galeote began to break through the long-lasting political quarantine of Andalucía imposed by Llopis, and gain participation in the PSOE's decision-making bodies.[1] Shortly afterwards came the numerically small but significant transfer of former Left Christian Democrats to the PSOE in Madrid; these lawyers and

[1] Yáñez interview; PSOE and other organizations, PSOE-UGT-FNJSE, Comisión Permanente, *Acta no. 3*, 26.5.69; PSOE, *Actas* of CE, 3.1.70.

university lecturers, among whom Gregorio Peces-Barba was
the best known, had earlier engaged in Christian-Marxist
dialogue through the pages of the magazine *Cuadernos para el
Diálogo*.[2] Meanwhile, in the Basque city of San Sebastián, the
recruitment of a number of young lawyers including José
Antonio Maturana and José María ('Txiki') Benegas also
helped to increase the party's social diversity.[3] But while such
developments denoted a new trend in the pattern of party
affiliation, these relatively new young professionals lacked the
political weight to carry through a party renovation themselves.
No matter how politically active they were, they none the less
constituted a minority of the PSOE in Spain around 1970;[4] to
achieve anything, they relied decisively on an alliance with the
younger Socialists of the political and economic *émigré*
sectors, as well as the backing of several prestigious veterans
based in France. And these renovators residing abroad were
overwhelmingly working class.

Thus the political tendency that favoured renovation was
socially diverse. So too was the tendency headed by Llopis,
which besides worker elements contained quite a few school-
teachers whose careers had been ruined by the advent of
Francoism, and even more lawyers, in Madrid and elsewhere.
Although one cannot examine the composition of each
tendency in any detail, it seems clear that age was a more
crucial differential factor than was social class. While the older
tendency had experience enough to appreciate just how
unscrupulous communist parties could be, the generally
younger and less experienced tendency had the virtue of being
more sensitive to the contemporary circumstances and possibilities for action that existed in Spain. Neither of them
possessed an independent organization, or attempted to build
a 'party within the party'; rather, their coherence as tendencies
rested upon newspapers, caucus meetings, and the fact that
from 1970 the differences corresponded to a large extent to the
division between the interior and exterior parts of the PSOE
executive.

[2] See *Cambio 16* (Madrid), 8.7.85, on the 'sons' of Joaquín Ruiz-Giménez.
[3] Benegas, 43–8.
[4] Castellano interview; Peydro interview; I. Gómez interview; Jiménez Gutiérrez
interview.

By this time many Socialists had come to recognize that the PSOE had not taken sufficient advantage of the changes that had occurred in Spanish society since the late 1950s. Spain in the 1960s had the most rapidly expanding economy in Western Europe, stabilization having been achieved by the development of tourism, the foreign exchange earned by the economic *émigrés*, and foreign investment.[5] This progress undermined long-standing Socialist hopes and convictions that Francoism would end in an economic disaster. Moreover, with economic growth came a changing social structure that presented problems for the traditional workers' party. In 1970 one sociological survey found that half of Spain's 33-million population was now 'lower middle class', the 'lower class' having contracted to 29 per cent. Just as challenging for the PSOE was the rejuvenation of Spanish society. Almost 65 per cent of the population now was under the age of 40.[6] Survey findings suggested, moreover, that decades of Francoism had made far less of an impact through indoctrination, or a less durable one, than those who identified it with Fascism had imagined. A FOESSA study in 1971 found that in a free election the left (Communists and Socialists) would obtain 41 per cent of the vote, Christian Democrats a further 40 per cent, Liberals 13 per cent, and Social Democrats 4 per cent.[7] In addition, there was some evidence to sustain the belief that although the Socialists had allowed their Communist rivals to attain prime position in the ranks of the active opposition, this ranking would be reversed as soon as democratic elections were held. Among Spanish students, at least, one survey suggested that the PCE would gain only about two per cent of the votes.[8] The relevance of such data lies less in its reliability, or degree thereof, than in the fact that it was reproduced in the PSOE press, providing particular comfort to the less vigorous members. Those whom the renovators accused of complacency did not necessarily believe that it would be enough 'to unfurl a socialist flag from the Casas del Pueblo for the workers to go

---

[5] Harrison 149–70.
[6] *Le Socialiste*, 28.5.70, 3, citing a study by the Fomento de Estudios Sociales y de Sociología Aplicada (FOESSA); ibid., 15.10.70.
[7] Data reproduced in Landis, 407.
[8] *Le Socialiste*, 3.12.70, 3, reproducing survey results from *Le Peuple* (Brussels), 29.10.70.

and affiliate *en masse*[9] when Franco died. Their lack of
energy often derived, if not simply from old age, then from an
inhibiting caution that came from years of developing a
strategy dependent on bourgeois co-operation and Western
sympathy.

Although the old guard's critics themselves would be careful
to keep the renovated party some distance from the PCE, they
were aware that the challenge presented by the Communists
had to be met sooner rather than later by the PSOE becoming
much more active in places of work and study throughout
Spain and thus posing a more convincing left-wing alternative
to the PCE. To achieve this the party needed a more modern
image, a more methodical approach to intervening in mass
struggles, and more credible propaganda than that which
emanated from Toulouse. As late as 1967 *Le Socialiste* was
carrying cartoons by Emilio Juan depicting starving workers.[10]
But this was no longer the hungry Spain of the 1940s and
activists in the interior were beginning to discard the Toulouse
material and rely more on local socialist bulletins. They
wanted to see a regular clandestine *El Socialista* with more
commentary on the latest political news and events.[11] Among
the active minority in Spain there was a growing conviction
that the PSOE could only be energized if both its leadership
and propaganda base returned to the interior.

This view found qualified support at the eleventh congress
in 1970. The executive's report that was circulated before the
event showed that opposition to the existing policies was
expected. Crises in the Italian and French socialist parties
were cited there as examples of what would happen if
discipline were lax and organized tendencies or clubs were
allowed to flourish.[12] Resolutions submitted to the congress
by Llopista 'federations' such as Santander, Burgos, and
Alicante stressed the need for the party to remain united, and
for roughly the same balance between interior and exterior to

[9] E. Múgica, quoted in Santamaría, 31.
[10] *Le Socialiste*, several issues, early 1967.
[11] PSOE, *Actas* of CE, 9.11.66.
[12] PSOE, Eleventh Congress held in exile (1970), *Memoria*, ch. on international
relations, 7–11. See too PSOE, *Circular* 15 (3 June 1969); id., *Circular* 7 (Mar.–Apr.
1971).

be maintained on the party executive.[13] Most of the motions on this matter favoured a continuation of 'shared leadership'. However, some sections, including Seville, represented for the first time ever at a party congress abroad (by labour lawyer Felipe González), urged that the executive be returned to the interior. Such a demand could not prosper in the absence of support from the prudent Basques, but when it came to a compromise at the congress the three Basque federations of Alava, Vizcaya, and Guipúzcoa along with Asturias, Barcelona, and Madrid joined the Sevillians in co-sponsoring a single motion. This called for the executive members based in Spain to be granted autonomous decision-making powers (within the confines of established party policy) for matters pertaining to the interior, and an equal share in the international representation of the party.[14] Notwithstanding Llopis's arguments against it, delegates representing some three-quarters of the party's *émigré* members supported the change in a vote restricted as usual to the exile sections.[15] This was a major defeat for the general secretary. His executive's report had been approved by a comfortable majority and nobody challenged his re-election when the moment came. Concerned with maximizing support, González and others wisely did not attack him. Yet with the benefit of hindsight one can see that this was when Llopis began to lose control of the party. Henceforth the interior as well as the exiles would be represented directly at international socialist events and would have the opportunity of putting the views of Socialists in Spain to foreign socialist parties.

The resolutions submitted to this congress are of interest because they show how political differences were beginning to grow in the party. Typically, Mexico defended a social-democratic line involving an alliance with liberal democratic parties. Foreshadowing the way in which the PSOE's Marxist tradition in later years would be undermined more by dilution than negation, the 'Mexicans' presented the congress with

[13] PSOE, 'XI Congreso. Ponencias, Proposiciones de las Federaciones, Carpeta del delegado y Tarjetas'.
[14] Ibid.
[15] Felipe González, 'Entrevista a Felipe González', *Leviatán*, II época, 1 (1978), 19–20; Chamorro, 74.

drafts for a new Declaration of Principles and party Programme that put 'religious and humanitarian principles' on a par with the 'scientific methodology of Marxism', both being seen as useful in the struggle for socialism.[16] Asturias and Seville, meanwhile, were urging a reaffirmation of the PSOE's Marxist traditions, with Asturias also calling for a position of independence *vis-à-vis* the world power blocs, and Seville arguing that party alliances should be restricted to revolutionary working-class forces. Catalonia, for its part, was the standard-bearer of regional interests, offering the vision of a future federation of Iberian nationalities and requesting autonomy within the party on Catalan questions.[17]

Thus, in addition to the already well-established dispute over renovation, there were signs here of the left–right and centre–periphery cleavages that would become more evident in the party in the 1970s. For the moment, unanimous support could be gained by a fairly standard political resolution—one that still saw the PSOE as representing the working class, but which defined the class broadly enough to include peasants, industrial workers, and intellectuals 'conscious of their growing proletarianization'; and which combined an economic pro-gramme envisaging widespread nationalization and socializ-ation with an immediate political goal of establishing re-presentative democracy in Spain.[18]

Shortly after the congress, on 1 November 1970, the Comité de Coordinación met with the interior's members on the outgoing party executive to select a new Comisión Permanente (the part of the leadership residing in Spain). Presided over by Antonio Amat, this meeting took the controversial decision to increase the Permanente's size from seven to nine members, of whom only one (Basilio Rodríguez of Santander) regarded the renovation efforts as premature. Since the eleventh party congress had elected only seven members of the new executive (those who were to be based in Toulouse), this shifted the interior–exterior balance dramati-

---

[16] PSOE, Eleventh Congress held in exile, *Propuesta de la Agrupación Socialista Española en México al XI Congreso del PSOE*, 9. This printed pamphlet, contrasting with the poorly typed motions submitted by other party sections to the congress, is an indication of the financial strength of the Mexican section.

[17] PSOE, Eleventh Congress held in exile, 'Ponencias, Proposiciones'.

[18] *Le Socialiste*, 27.8.70, 1.

cally, and greatly alarmed Llopis and his supporters. One of them, Ildefonso Torregrosa—who had become editor of *Le Socialiste* after replacing Pradal on the party executive in January 1966—even voted to reject the enlargement, but there was little that could be done without splitting the party.[19] Ironically, after the tenth congress in 1967 Llopis had written to the Permanente acknowledging its right to decide the number of its members, where they were to reside, and the distribution of their work.[20] But in fact the enlargement of the interior's representation, seen now by the Llopistas as a *coup de main*, was not decisive, for two members of the exile part of the new executive (Juan Iglesias and Julio Fernández) would back the forthcoming challenge of the renovators, giving the latter a total of 10 votes at leadership level to the Llopistas' six.

The same Comité de Coordinación meeting was responsible for a further important decision, proposed by Guipúzcoa, to alter the geographical composition of the Comisión Permanente. For the last three years Madrid and the Basque Country had accounted for two places, and Asturias, Andalucía, and Catalonia one place each.[21] Madrid's representation could be defended on the grounds of it being the centre of Spanish politics, and possessing quite a large paper membership, but it was clearly over-represented in relation to its level of activity. If the latter were taken as the criterion, the geographical spread of the new Permanente chosen in November 1970 was fairer: two places each went to Vizcaya and Asturias and one each to Guipúzcoa, Andalucía, Santander, Catalonia, and Madrid.[22] Of the 14 federations represented at the meeting, 10 favoured Madrid's relegation to a single place, and only the small federations of Valladolid, Burgos, and Santander echoed

[19] Martínez de Velasco interview; Manuel Murillo Carrasco, *PSOE* (*Sector Histórico*) (Bilbao: Albia, 1977), 43. At party level, it was not until 1972 that the Llopis faction denounced the move as betraying a desire to 'dominate' the party (PSOE, *Circular* 16, (17 July 1972)).

[20] PSOE and other organizations, PSOE-UGT-FNJSE, Comisión Permanente, Llopis to Comisión Permanente, 24 Aug. 1967.

[21] PSOE and other organizations, PSOE-UGT-FNJSE, Comisión Permanente, PSOE-UGT, *Acta* of Comité de Coordinación meeting, 15.?10.67. The Andalusian member of the executive was the lawyer Antonio Ramos, who had been chosen by the executive to organize the region.

[22] PSOE, *Circular* 16 (17 July 1972).

Madrid's protest.[23] This brought to a head a conflict between Madrid and the Permanente that had been brewing for three years, and which emanated from more deeply rooted antagonism between Madrid and the provinces and between Madrid's 'old' and 'new' sectors.

Relations between Madrid and the Permanente had deteriorated after the party congress of 1967, with one of the metropolitan group's nominations for the national body being rejected by the Permanente in December. Instead of accepting Mario Tanco as a member, the Permanente had opted for the man nominated by Madrid as Tanco's *suplente* (reserve member), Cristóbal Cáliz, and had made him its secretary.[24] This the Madrid committee had refused to accept, with the result that the formation of the new Permanente had been delayed for nine months.[25] And even after that, Madrid continued to defy the executive body in the interior. The Permanente meanwhile rejected attempts by Cáliz to resign (in the interests of harmony) and pointed to the incompatibility of Miguel Peydro's simultaneous membership of the Permanente and the Madrid committee.[26] Mixed in with personal rivalries, what was involved here was a determination by members of the Permanente to bring into being a more dynamic committee in Madrid. To this end, from 1969 Enrique Múgica made a number of visits to the capital to intrigue with youngish renovators, such as Miguel Boyer and Carlos Revilla, who rejected the official Madrid leadership presided over by Gómez Egido or had been expelled by it. A delegation from the 'old' sector was accepted at the eleventh congress of the PSOE in exile in 1970, in preference to a rival delegate who turned up armed with a document signed by 42 party members in Madrid; but it was told even by the Toulouse

---

[23] 'Informe sobre gestión de la Comisión Ejecutiva residente en el Interior', in PSOE, Twelfth Congress held in exile (1972), *Memoria*, ch. on Spain. See too Jáuregui and Vega, ii. 337.

[24] PSOE, *Actas* of CE, 5.7.68; PSOE and other organizations, PSOE-UGT-FNJSE, Comisión Permanente, Llopis to Comisión Permanente, 6 Jan. 1969; ibid., 'Masín' (Cristóbal Cáliz) report to C. Permanente, May 1969.

[25] PSOE, Assemblies, Comité Director, 'Nota Informativa' of CE, 31.7.68.

[26] PSOE, *Actas* of CE, 21.9.68, 11.6.69; PSOE and other organizations, PSOE-UGT-FNJSE, Comisión Permanente, 'Masín' to C. Permanente, 3 May 1969; ibid., Comisión Permanente, *Acta no. 3*, 26.5.69; ibid., 'Masín' to 'Moncho', 17 Nov. 1969.

veterans that the metropolitan committee needed changing.[27] After the congress, when Madrid made its defiance of the Permanente explicit by refusing to take part until the capital regained two seats on it, the renovators seized the initiative. In December the new Permanente established a steering committee to prepare for the election of a new Madrid committee, and within months this duly took place. In the final years of his life, the veteran Eduardo Villegas rallied to the renovators' cause and presided over the transition in Madrid.[28] The new committee named the lawyer Pablo Castellano—a former libertarian who had arrived in the PSOE in 1966—as its representative on the Permanente, thereby further weakening Llopis's influence in the party executive.[29]

Similar developments took place in Alicante, Seville, and (possibly) in Valladolid[30] before the party as a whole split. Faced with rivalry between 'old' and 'new' groups in these places, or with veterans resisting the authority of the Permanente, the latter intervened to help renovators form alternative committees which it then recognized officially. Llopis and his colleagues in Toulouse went along with this procedure, having themselves in the past clashed with certain veteran local officials, thereafter regarded as trouble-makers, while other old-timers did not meet even Toulouse's relaxed standards of 'activity'. For a while, there then co-existed two committees and two local socialist bulletins in a number of places, but gradually the renovators came to be seen as the main PSOE representatives, simply because they were more active. By 1970 these activists in Madrid numbered no more

[27] PSOE, Twelfth Congress held in exile (1972), *Memoria*, ch. on Spain; id., *Actas* of CE, 25.4.70; PSOE and other organizations, PSOE-UGT-FNJSE, Comisión Permanente, 'Masín' to 'Pablo', 21 Nov. 1969. On Revilla see *ES*, 4.6.78, 21.

[28] PSOE and other organizations, PSOE-UGT-FNJSE, Comisión Permanente, 'Masín' to 'Moncho', 17 Nov. 1969; PSOE, Twelfth Congress held in exile, 'Informe . . . Ejecutiva residente en el Interior'. Villegas died on 8 Mar. 1971. For tributes see *Tribuna Socialista*, Mar. and Aug. 1971, and *Le Socialiste*, 18.3.71, 1, 25.3.71, 1–2.

[29] The new committee was recognized by the party executive on 4 July after reconciliation efforts had failed (PSOE, Twelfth Congress held in exile, *Memoria*, ch. 4).

[30] PSOE and other organizations, PSOE-UGT-FNJSE, Comisión Permanente, *Acta no. 3*, 26.5.69; ibid., 'Masín' to 'Moncho', 17 Nov. 1969; Miguel Peydro Caro, *Las escisiones del PSOE* (Barcelona: Plaza y Janes, 1980), 140; PSOE, *Actas* of CE, 25.3.70.

than one hundred and in Seville probably no more than a score; they were only a minority of the Socialists who possessed membership cards.[31] Yet, between congresses at least, this put them at no political disadvantage in relation to the majority, since the latter more closely resembled a secret society of war veterans than a clandestine party of the left. The veterans were altogether more timid, having known Francoism in its more repressive earlier periods. They did little more than circulate the party press internally and meet in each other's houses. Illustrative of the difference in mentality was the way that Madrid delegates Miguel Peydro and Francisco Jiménez limited themselves to attending the small Comité Director meeting prior to the congress of 1970, whereas 28-year-old Felipe González did what young Gómez Llorente had done nine years earlier and addressed the congress itself.[32] The young González set many delegates talking as they left the event, having heard—often for the first time—a dynamic delegate from the interior put to them, in powerful but dispassionate oratory, without demagogy, a serious present-ation and incisive analysis of the real situation existing in Spain. The young Sevillian addressed himself to the present and the future, not to the past.[33]

After this congress and its sequel of the Permanente unilaterally increasing its size, the executive members in Spain and abroad managed to co-operate for a year, but their outlooks became increasingly divergent. One indication of this was provided when Nixon visited Spain in late 1970: the Toulouse executives' denunciation of the event spoke about the US-Spanish pacts of 1953 and the sell-out by the democracies to Franco, while the interior's condemnation of the visit referred to much more recent cases of US imperialist aggression, especially in South-East Asia.[34] The trade union triumph of the renovators at the UGT congress of August 1971 encouraged them to seize the initiative in the party too.

[31] One young Madrid militant claimed that although the 'historical' sector was larger in this period, it was so well 'hidden' that he did not know of its existence until a partial reunification was achieved in 1976. He then learnt that this rival sector included a group in Vallecas that was the only one in Madrid province to have been organized permanently since the mid-1940s. (I. Gómez interview.)

[32] Jiménez Gutiérrez interview.

[33] Simón interview, 22 Feb. 1972.   [34] *Le Socialiste*, 15.10.70, 1.

Following the UGT event, at which the majority of the delegates had been under 45 and had not participated in the Civil War,[35] a new executive took charge, formed basically by the members of the PSOE executive who lived in the interior. It was mandated to seek the unity of all the anti-Franco forces, without restricting such unity to 'democratic' (i.e. non-Communist) forces, as had been stipulated, according to one reading, in the political resolution of the previous PSOE congress.[36] The new UGT leadership managed to commit the party to this broad-alliance initiative at a plenary meeting (interior and exterior) of the Comité Director in December 1971.

A literal interpretation of the deepening schism would suggest that this clash over alliance formulae, and particularly over relations with the Communists, was the crux of the matter. Llopis and his supporters looked for allies to their right, to the various Christian Democratic factions and the former Falangist, Dionisio Ridruejo.[37] They had been prepared to tolerate informal PSOE/UGT relations with the PCE and Workers' Commissions in the interior, for example in the Basque Country, but they were well aware that their interlocutors to the right had just rejected dealings with the Communists.[38] Word that PSOE leaders in the interior had sent a representative to attend a meeting in May 1971 of the 'Mesa Democrática'—a new opposition forum promoted by the PCE—greatly alarmed them.[39] The renovators, meanwhile, looked to both their left and right for allies. They were not opposed in principle to agreements with Christian Democrats, but pointed out that the latter only had a real following in the Basque Country and Catalonia.[40] Dealings with the Communists and the eventual formation of an opposition bloc were deemed necessary if there were to be an

---

[35] *Tribuna Socialista*, Aug. 1971.

[36] The resolution stated that the PSOE would call on all political parties and trade unions whose immediate aim was democracy, to establish a representative co-ordinating body. See Fundación Pablo Iglesias and PSOE, ii. 157.

[37] PSOE and other organizations, PSOE-UGT-FNJSE, Comisión Permanente, Llopis to C. Permanente, 6 Jan. 1969.

[38] PSOE, *Circular* 16 (17 July 1972).

[39] PSOE, *Circular* 10 (2 Nov. 1971).

[40] Felipe (González's) speech, *Le Socialiste*, 5.10.72.

effective struggle against the regime. No matter how the renovators argued their case, though, Llopis suspected them of moving towards a pact with the PCE that would divide Franco's democratic opponents and enable the Communists to damage or manipulate the PSOE. It was not just a question of how badly Communists had behaved towards Spanish Socialists in the past, he maintained; the issue of relations with the Communists itself threatened to divide the PSOE, as it had the Italian Socialists twice in recent years.[41]

On the other hand, neither at the time nor afterwards was there any real evidence of the renovators seeking a solid alliance of the traditional parties of the left; all they were advocating was co-participation in a broad opposition bloc. Socialists in the interior already had co-operated with PCE militants in some of the protests against the Burgos trials of Basque nationalists in 1970;[42] there also had been conversations with the PCE about Catalonia, leading to both parties (among others) signing a document issued by the 'Asamblea de Catalunya';[43] and both parties took part in the Mesa Democrática. Yet the status of these relations was best indicated by the renovators themselves, when they looked back on the PSOE schism at the end of 1972. Both sides in the party dispute, they affirmed, saw the PCE as totalitarian and the PSOE as democratic; both sides regarded the PCE as dogmatic and their own party as standing for a scientific but self-critical Marxism. The only difference between them, it was argued, was that the renovators recognized, while their opponents ignored, the reality of the Communists' preeminent role in the struggle against Franco.[44]

More fundamentally involved in this dispute were the demands of one sector for the rejuvenation of the PSOE and the resistance to them of veterans who had preserved the Socialist organizations through all adversities and who now were deeply reluctant to relinquish their control over them. The old men of Toulouse had come to 'personalize the PSOE and UGT in themselves'.[45] That is why Llopis had so much

[41] PSOE, *Circular* 7 (Mar.–Apr. 1971), 6.
[42] PSOE, *Circular* 6 (Jan.–Feb. 1971), 1.
[43] PSOE, Executive Committee, Comisión Reorganizadora, *Circular*, 4.10.72.
[44] *Le Socialiste*, 28.12.72, 4–5.   [45] Garnacho interview, 17 Apr. 1982.

archive material at his home in Albi; he virtually saw himself as the party. On one occasion, he declared that if he ceased to be general secretary the Socialist International's recognition of the PSOE would disappear. The basic feeling of the old guard in Toulouse was that the party was in danger, and had to be saved from the young. However, Llopis was still wily enough to exaggerate the predisposition of his detractors to collaborate with the PCE. He knew very well that an appeal to anti-Communist sentiment was his best means of rallying the faithful and deflecting criticism of the party press and of his sector of the executive.[46] From February 1972 the anti-Communist content of *Le Socialiste* grew into a barrage, and the views of the renovators only gained an airing here through the 'Tribuna del Congreso' that appeared for four pre-congressional months in 1972. But from mid-1970 the interior also had a paper, albeit an extremely irregular one that was denied a financial subsidy by Toulouse[47], and from late 1970 Felipe González and the Seville group were allocated responsibility for its contents. This latest version of *El Socialista* was much more Marxist in appearance than its exile counterpart, which reached the north of Spain but was found much more rarely in other parts of the country.

Chronologically, the split developed in the following manner. In May 1971 the executive members in the interior alarmed those in exile by attending a meeting called by the Communist-led Workers' Commissions to establish the Mesa Democrática. Though this particular initiative proved abortive, the fears that it aroused in some veterans led them to revert to intransigence. However, the old line of 'no relations with the Communists'[48] received a further set-back at the UGT

[46] The appeal to anti-Communism rallied several old Caballeristas who had opposed Llopis's abandonment of republican intransigence in the 1940s. It was still a key issue for those who blamed the PCE for Largo Caballero's fall from office in 1937. Probably too there was an element of generational solidarity both here and in the case of Alfonso Fernández of Seville, who had been an implacable opponent of Llopis in the past. Examples of old Caballeristas who now defended Llopis were Ildefonso Torregrosa and César Barona (see *Le Socialiste*, 17.2.72, 4). Their arguments were still left-wing: Poland had supplied strike-breaking coal in 1962 during the miners' struggles in Asturias; the Communists were not democratic and not communist; the Communists had always divided the working class.

[47] PSOE, Executive Committee, *Circulares*, 1970–2, Interior ('Juan') to CE, 17 June 1972.

[48] This was the established policy but in practice there had been flexibility in its

congress in August and yet another on 11 December when the Comité Director gave the PSOE's endorsement to the UGT line: participation in the Mesa Democrática in the hope of forming a common bloc against the regime, without maintaining bilateral relations with the Communist Party.[49] Nine members left the meeting before this decision was taken. Becoming desperate, the old guard now resorted to the statute book, remembering that party sections technically had a right to approve or reject decisions taken by the Comité Director. By March 1972 an internal referendum had been held, organized by the general secretary, who subsequently announced that 32 sections, including Mexico and representing 683 members, had rejected the Comité's resolution, while only 15 sections, including Toulouse and Paris and representing 480 members, had endorsed it.[50] This result infuriated the renovators, for not only were 1,312 votes from the interior not counted[51] (presumably on the grounds that affiliation there was unverifiable), but even the results from the exile sections looked highly suspect. Using the data that had been used for the accreditation of delegates and determination of their voting power at the last party congress, the renovators calculated that the 32 sections opposing the Comité Director decision represented 619 members while the 15 sections confirming it had 698.[52]

Relations between the majority of executive members in the interior and the majority of those based in France deteriorated sharply. They reached breaking-point after Alfonso Guerra published a deliberate provocation in May 1972: an article in which he wrote that in the socialist camp, 'within the sphere of action, some "act" at the level of thought, discussing, proposing, and manœuvring; and others "act" at the level of physical struggle, that of action in the workplace and in the

implementation. It was resurrected and reasserted officially by Llopis in PSOE, *Circular* 16 (17 July 1972).

[49] PSOE, *Circular* 13 (26 Jan. 1972).

[50] PSOE, *Circular* 14 (15 Mar. 1972).

[51] PSOE, Thirteenth Congress held in exile (Oct. 1974), *Memoria*, ch. 3 on organization.

[52] These figures appear in handwriting on a copy of *Circular* 14 at the FPI. A similar calculation, 608 to 688, appeared in a special Twelfth Congress issue of *Acción Socialista* (internal bulletin of the PSOE in Paris), 1972.

streets'. The question of relations with other forces, he added, was a smoke-screen that 'hides the real basis of the differences'. Socialists had a dual struggle ahead of them; there was one against the capitalist system, but there was also 'the struggle against certain structures of their own organization that threaten to sterilize their activity'.[53] Receiving this as 'a serious collective insult', designed to poison the political atmosphere, the executive members based in Toulouse demanded an apology; when this was not instantly forthcoming, in mid-June they declared their 'incompatibility' with the executive members in the interior.[54]

Meanwhile a related dispute had been brewing over the kind of congress that was necessary to resolve the party controversy. In December 1972 an extraordinary congress had been convoked by the executive for the following February, but just two days later a further executive meeting decided to replace this with an ordinary party congress in April. The attraction of an extraordinary congress to Llopis was that it would focus solely on relations with the Communists, would involve no executive election, and would set back the next ordinary congress by one year, giving him more time to prepare a counter-offensive. The aforementioned referendum, for those who regarded it as legitimate, authorized him to postpone the twelfth congress of the party in exile until the second half of 1972.[55] However, a majority of his party executive was pressing hard for an earlier date. To stonewall them, Llopis insisted that only he, as general secretary, could convoke a congress, and that to do so in the circumstances would formalize the split. Under the statutes, the convocation of congresses was certainly the responsibility of the general secretary, but the latter had no right to defy executive decisions such as that mandating him to convoke the twelfth congress in exile for 1–3 April 1972.[56] When by mid-April Llopis had done nothing, and when efforts to persuade him to act had failed, the majority of his executive met in Bayonne and themselves decided to hold the congress on 13–15 August.

[53] 'Los enfoques de la praxis', *ES*, May 1972.
[54] PSOE, *Circular* 15 (28 June 1972); ibid., 16 (17 July 1972).
[55] PSOE, *Circular* 14 (15 Mar. 1972).
[56] PSOE, *Circular* 12 (21 Dec. 1971).

The old guard branded that congress 'illegal' and 'seditious'; to them it was the 'congress of the split and of ambitions'. They tried to get it banned by the French authorities, boycotted it when it went ahead, and then held their own 'Twelfth Congress' in exile in December 1972.[57]

Nevertheless, the August congress of the *renovadores* was a considerable success. Numerous recent visits by Spanish-based members of the executive to party sections and foreign socialist parties, to publicize the renovators' version of the dispute, now paid off. The congress was attended by delegates from 49 sections of the *émigré* sector, claiming 1,187 members (65 per cent of the exiles), and from 11 regional federations of the interior, claiming (possibly with some inflation) 2,216 members.[58] Most of the major European socialist parties were present at the congress and for the first time in ages their representatives did not merely deliver fraternal greetings, but worked hard with delegates to examine ways of increasing material solidarity.[59] Moreover, the French Socialist Party (PSF) delegate, Bernard Montanier, was there also as an observer for the Socialist International. He was able to see that it was a serious congress, lent extra authority by the presence (for the first time at such an event) of Ramón Rubial, the undisputed patriarch of the Spanish Socialist movement. Mimicking Llopis, Arsenio Jimeno pointed out that Rubial was not exactly 'an ambitious youth who wants to take over the party to hand it over to who knows whom'.[60] Nor was Juan Iglesias, who presided over the congress of a party he had joined in 1929. And just as influential in persuading the observer from the International to write a sympathetic report was the way that delegations made repeated efforts to get Rodolfo Llopis to take part. It was a bizarre scene: as the congress opened, Llopis was seated in the party offices on the

[57] For the Llopista version of the split see PSOE, *Circulares* 14–19 (1972); Peydro Caro, *passim*; Murillo Carrasco, 41–8; *Le Socialiste*, 2.11.72, 6; *Le Nouveau Socialiste*, 1 (1972), 1–2, ibid., 8–9 (1972), 2–3.

[58] *Le Socialiste*, 21.9.72, 1–3. The claim here that 99% of the members in Spain were represented at the congress in August is clearly an exaggeration.

[59] For reports see *Le Socialiste*, 21.9.72, 5.10.72, 19.10.72, 2.11.72, *passim*.

[60] Ibid., 21.9.72, 6. It is significant that in the C. Permanente dispute with the old committee in Madrid, Rubial was the only member of the Permanente recognized by the Madrileños (PSOE and other organizations, PSOE-UGT-FNJSE, Comisión Permanente, 'Masín' to 'Moncho', 17 Nov. 1969).

floor above the conference hall, attending to business, but he stubbornly refused to recognize that what was going on down below was a congress of the PSOE, since he, the general secretary, had not convoked it! Joining his boycott of the event, according to the report reaching the International, were some 764 other exile members, including the majority of the large section in Mexico and many small sections in France.[61] Unfortunately for them, the French Socialists had recently undergone a kind of renovation themselves. Since the PSOE was lodged at headquarters of the French party's federations in Paris and Toulouse, and also depended on PSF co-operation to get *Le Socialiste* produced, the renovators were able to take charge of the party infrastructure relatively easily after the congress.

The August 1972 congress was the first such party event at which the interior voted, and with Alava, Asturias, Catalonia, Córdoba, Guipúzcoa, Madrid, Seville, Valencia, Vizcaya, and Elche, along with *émigré* sections such as Paris, Toulouse, and Zurich, having submitted resolutions urging renovation,[62] the outcome was never in doubt. Reacting against the degree of personal power accumulated by Llopis over the years, the congress abolished the post of general secretary and a new collegiate form of leadership was adopted, with specific responsibilities for each member. Only five exiles—renovators Jimeno, Iglesias, López Real, Carmen García, and Fernando Gutiérrez—were on the new executive, a majority (nine) of whom were to be based in Spain and chosen, for security reasons, by a restored Comité Nacional. The latter replaced the Comité Director in an ostensible reassertion of rank-and-file control over the executive, the intermediate organ's powers having been eroded gradually, the renovators claimed, by years of 'cunning *caciquismo*' on the part of the 77-year-old Llopis.[63]

No individual dominated this congress. The keynote speeches came from interior leaders Castellano, Múgica,

---

[61] PSOE, Twelfth Congress held in exile, 'Informe del representante de la I.S. y del P.S.F. en el XII° Congreso del P.S.O.E.', 4.9.72; Simón interview, 22 Feb. 1982.

[62] PSOE, Twelfth Congress held in exile (Aug. 1972), *Memoria*, ch. 7.

[63] *Le Socialiste*, 21. 9.72, 1–2.

González, and Redondo, and were marked by a concern with practical problems. González cautioned against triumphalism, reminding delegates that, although anti-Franco struggles had increased in recent years, repression had hardened in response. The regime was not on its last legs, he warned, and the idea of it collapsing through economic catastrophe was at odds with the economic growth of the 1960s. A bourgeois economic revolution had occurred, contrary to expectations that this could happen only alongside political democratization. The need to be more realistic was González's main message and it was echoed by Múgica's argument that the PSOE needed to be a national as well as a class party.[64]

The twelfth congress resolutions emphasized the importance of organizing the working class, but they also revealed a growing awareness of the need to entertain and respect regionally-based nationalist sentiments. Bourgeois democracy was valued as a way of improving the conditions for working-class struggles in pursuit of power for the class and a radical transformation of society from capitalism to socialism. In seeking to achieve these objectives, the executive was granted great discretionary powers to negotiate agreements with forces sharing the PSOE's immediate aims.[65] However, it was made clear that neither subordination to bourgeois projects nor a firm alliance with the PCE commanded support in the renovated party. The PSOE was now beginning to acquire a new face. It was not yet particularly more radical than in the past, though some shift of mood was announced perhaps by the special greetings sent from the congress to the Chilean Socialist Party, supporting 'its experience of revolutionary struggle'.[66] For Nicolás Redondo, the congress had recovered the Pablista and Marxist traditions of the PSOE and prevented its decline into opportunist deviations and enchantment by bourgeois ideals, but he warned of a new danger now of it falling into leftist dogmatic deviations characteristic of groups lacking a working-class base.[67]

When Llopis and his supporters went ahead and organized their own congress in December, foreign socialist parties

[64] Ibid. 4–6.   [65] Ibid.; 1 Fundación Pablo Iglesias and PSOE, ii. 204.
[66] *Le Socialiste*, 21.9.72, 8.
[67] 'Juan', 'Práctica socialista', ibid., 19.10.72, 1–2.

characterized the situation as a split: not, as each contender for their recognition claimed, a question of there being one true PSOE plus a group of dissidents. Condemned by the renovators' congress, Llopis and his colleagues were able to reorganize their supporters and bring out *Le Nouveau Socialiste* with the financial aid of wealthy Socialists in Mexico. Traditionally, the 'Mexicans' had been influential because they controlled a lot of votes, travelled 14,000 kilometres to congresses in Toulouse, and were relatively well off. Both at this time and four years later the roles played by Víctor Salazar, formerly Prieto's secretary, and his affluent partner Ovidio Salcedo were viewed by many Socialists as undermining efforts at PSOE reconciliation, although formally they spoke the language of reunification. There have been several hints that something rather more than solidarity with Llopis was afoot here.[68]

The 'historical' sector of the PSOE, which gave equal representation to interior and exterior when electing its executive and national committee in December, tried to belittle the 'renovated' sector by referring to the relatively small number of exile sections represented at the August congress (49 out of the total of 132) rather than the relatively large number of members accounted for by them. Only 10 out of the 16 official federations in Spain had been represented, it claimed, not to mention a group of autonomous 'federations' that protested that they had not been invited.[69] Of course, such mathematics tended to put Vizcaya, with some 500 militants, on a par with Llopis's Albi, with a handful. Aware

[68] Interview with Simón, 22 Feb. 1982, who said the two Socialists from Mexico 'had other ambitions'; SOMA Archive, Box A.LIX, letter of Barreiro to Arcadio Martínez, 2 Jan. 1974, blaming Salazar and Salcedo for the split; Barreiro to Arcadio Martínez, 20 Feb. 1974, alleging that the PSOE(H) was financed by Mexico 'not exclusively from the pockets of the *nouveaux riches* but from another source, about which it would be indiscreet to speak'. Of possible relevance here is the fact that, prior to moving to Madrid in the mid-1970s to establish a local branch of the Friedrich Ebert Stiftung in Spain, Dieter Koniecki, once a president of the Liberal Youth in Berlin, worked for a time in Mexico seeking to influence progressive parties through the SPD-sponsored foundation (Alonso Puerta interview, 17 June 1983). On the congress of the *históricos*, see *Le Nouveau Socialiste*, 8–9 (1972), 1–3; ibid., 10 (1972), 1–3.
[69] PSOE, *Circular* 18 (19 Aug. 1972). According to the PSOE(R) half the 132 exile sections were really only paper organizations (PSOE, CN of 17–18.3.73, *Memoria* presented by CE, 11).

that the August event in fact had been rather more than a 'mini-congress', the 'historical' leaders of the PSOE now appreciated the need for reinforcements if they were to pose a credible alternative to the renovators. These they tried to bring in from two sources. In July 1971, having been disavowed by the PSOE executive, the old Madrid committee had called a meeting of similarly disgruntled veterans from various parts of Spain. This meeting had established a provisional national committee (which in fact was identical to the old Madrid committee presided over by Juan Gómez Egido) and had decided to seek a partnership with Tierno Galván's Socialist Party of the Interior (PSI). For this act of subversion, these dissident 'federations' had been expelled from the PSOE, yet had continued to maintain informal relations with Llopista members of the executive in Toulouse.[70] Seventeen such 'federations' complained of not having been 'invited' to the congress of August 1972 and subsequently they affiliated to the PSOE(H).[71] Described by José Barreiro as mainly a 'philatelic' association, with many stamps but little projection in Spanish society, this group of 'federations' constituted no real threat to the PSOE(R). They were not very adventurous and their leadership was poor.[72]

More formidable as a potential reinforcement of the Llopis sector was the PSI, not because it had any influence among Spanish workers but because of the backing it received from the West German Social Democratic Party (SPD). Along with guests from the Belgian and French socialist parties, Tierno as PSI leader attended the *histórico* 'Twelfth Congress' in December 1972. He pronounced it the only 'authentic' congress of the PSOE, expressed a will to unite, and finally signed a unification agreement with the PSOE(H) in May 1973.[73]

---

[70] *Tribuna Socialista*, May 1972. As early as 27 May 1972 Peydro and Lázaro Movilla of the old Madrid committee were spotted with a colleague of Llopis in Hendaye railway station (PSOE, Executive Committee, *Circulares*, interior ('Juan') to CE, 17 June 1972).

[71] PSOE, *Circular* 16 (17 July 1972); SOMA Archive, Box A.LX, 'Declaración' of provincial federations of Burgos, Salamanca, Valladolid, Madrid, Málaga, Alicante, Jáen, Granada, Almería, and Seville, Nov. 1971.

[72] 'Hervás' (Castellano) speech, *Le Socialiste*, 5.10.72; Jiménez Gutiérrez interview.

[73] *Le Nouveau Socialiste*, 21.12.72, 28.12.72; Peydro Caro, 150–7; Peydro interview; Manuel Turrión interview, 29 May 1984.

Thus, by the end of 1972 the panorama of Spanish Socialism had become extremely complex: two organizations were claiming to be the PSOE; Tierno's group presented itself as a further party, as a 'Socialist Party in the Interior' (insinuating that the PSOE had become an *émigré* association after the Civil War, and that the renovators were just *muchachos*, inexperienced youths); and a fourth sector was constituted by a growing number of regional socialist parties, including the long-standing expressions of Catalan Socialism and more recent creations in Galicia and Valencia.[74] Upon finding that reconciliation between the two PSOE sectors was impossible, the Socialist International felt obliged to choose which of the two to support, and it also had to respond to a petition from the PSI for observer status.

Having sent observers to both PSOE congresses in 1972, the Bureau of the International established a special commission to examine the claims of the two parties. With Austrian socialist Bruno Pittermann as its president and Rodney Balcomb as secretary, and members drawn from the Italian Socialists and Social Democrats, the British Labour Party, Chilean Radicals, and French Socialists, the commission listened to the case presented by each leadership in January 1973.[75] It then took a whole year before the Bureau decided, on 6 January 1974, that the congress of August 1972 had been 'proper, legitimate, and legal'.[76] There were no votes for the *históricos*, though the Belgian Socialist on the Bureau abstained because of a long-lasting friendship with Llopis.[77] The latter felt especially betrayed by the French Socialists, after 30 years of solidarity.[78] Llopis had won a similar battle for international recognition a quarter of a century earlier. Now worn out, he could not repeat his success. Ideologically, his faction might have seemed the more attractive to the

[74] See Castellano's survey of the socialist movement in Spain at the congress of Aug. 1972 (*Le Socialiste*, 5.10.72).
[75] PSOE, Assemblies, CN of 17–18.3.73, *Memoria*, 24–5; 'Informe' of PSOE(R) to special commission of Socialist International, 9 Jan. 1973 (ibid. 30–6).
[76] PSOE, Thirteenth Congress held in exile (1974), *Memoria*, ch. on international relations; *ES*, Jan. 1974.
[77] López Real interview; id., interview in *ES*, 17.6.79, 14–15.
[78] Supposedly presenting the executive report at the second *histórico* congress in 1974, an ailing Llopis in fact filled his speech with recrimination against those by whom he felt let down. See *Le Nouveau Socialiste*, 59 (1974), 3–5.

International. It stood firmly for Western alignment and anti-Communism, whereas its rivals sounded more Marxist, supported the EEC more critically (as a capitalist organization that had made little progress towards a federal Europe, but which provided a useful source of pressure for political change in Spain),[79] and advocated Spanish neutralism *vis-à-vis* the world power blocs. But if the renovators had some 'untamed' elements in their ranks, they also had moderates in their leadership such as the social democrats Múgica and Castellano and the practical trade unionist Redondo. PSOE(R)–PSOE(H) differences could not be reduced simply to a left–right option.

The fact that the Socialist International had been renovated itself since the 1940s, with many old colleagues of Llopis having departed, also helps to explain the Bureau's verdict. A new socialist party, the PSF, had been established in France in 1969 and at its unity congress in June 1971 the positions defended by François Mitterand had triumphed narrowly over those of Savary and Mollet.[80] Above all, though, the International opted for the sector that it thought had a much more active presence in Spain. The PSOE had not maintained its international standing over the years simply because Llopis was an assiduous attender of foreign socialist-party congresses; its prestige had come from the maintenance of a clandestine presence in Spain, which was something that neither the Greek nor the Portuguese socialists could boast. The PSOE(R) lobbied hard in various countries to win external support, but probably the most decisive factor in its success were the visits to Spain by Italian socialists and Michael Foot during 1973.[81] They were able to see that where there was Socialist activity in the interior, the PSOE(R) was normally responsible for it. There was no reason to expect any reversal of this situation given the elderly nature of the PSOE(H). It may be the case also that foreign socialists lost patience with the *histórico* insistence that the only issue at stake was relations with the

---

[79] *Le Socialiste*, 21.9.72, 5 (González's speech at Twelfth Congress in exile).

[80] PSOE, Twelfth Congress in exile (1972), *Memoria*, ch. on international relations, pp. 8–9.

[81] PSOE, Thirteenth Congress in exile (Oct. 1974), *Memoria*, ch. on international relations; Castellano interview. Llopis attributed the *histórico* defeat to the Labour Party as well as the French Socialists (*Le Nouveau Socialiste*, 59 (1974), 3–5).

Communists.[82] Their position must have sounded extremely negative and any credibility that they had enjoyed must have vanished when they began to circulate a document in which adversaries Castellano, Villar, Carvajal, and Simón were accused of being infiltrated police agents.[83] Early on, support for the PSOE(R) was evident in the British, French, Italian, and Nordic parties, and eventually the SPD adopted a fairly positive attitude too.

It was probably because the outcome was already signalled that Tierno's PSI pulled out of its unification with the party of Llopis towards the end of 1973, thus finally sealing the fate of the *históricos*. The marriage of convenience between Tierno and some of the Socialists who had expelled him from the PSOE just eight years earlier never inspired confidence. Unification documents were signed and were ratified by the PSI leadership, but then they became meaningless in the face of a quarrel over control of the unified party. While the PSOE(H) argued that both parties should send delegates to a unification congress according to their numbers of members, and leave it to the congress to elect an executive, the smaller PSI demanded a guarantee of parity in the leadership. When that was not conceded, the PSI sections refused to endorse the merger (as was required by the pact).[84]

Thus socialism in Spain still had four main expressions by the start of 1974: the renovated PSOE under a collective leadership and recognized by the Socialist International, though supported only symbolically by it; the PSOE(H), still led by the aged Llopis and strongest, apart from Mexico, in Madrid, Alicante, and Seville;[85] Tierno's PSI, which within months would become the Popular Socialist Party (PSP) and begin to organize more seriously as a party; and the regional socialist groups and parties, which gradually were beginning

[82] J. Martínez de Velasco, a leading *histórico*, told the International that this was the only issue (interview, 27 June 1983).

[83] Garnacho interview, 17 Apr. 1982; Castellano interview; Chamorro, *González*, 108. For the document see 'Avante' (Madrid), Informativo 12, n.d. (? June 1979). Castellano identified Tierno's colleague Raúl Morodo as the author of the document, which of course did not enhance the credibility of the PSI either. Its application to the International for observer status was rejected in Mar. 1974.

[84] Peydro interview; Turrión interview. See too Peydro Caro, 151–7; Tierno Galván, *Cabos*, 428–34.

[85] Turrión interview.

to form an alliance among themselves on the basis of a shared antipathy to control from Madrid and 'Spanish' dominance. It would require a further three to four years for the panorama to be simplified and for the modern PSOE to establish its clear pre-eminence.

A NEW LEADERSHIP EMERGES

No spectacular progress was made by the party in Spain during the two years that followed the renovation congress and that led up to the thirteenth congress of the PSOE in exile, held in the Parisian socialist-controlled municipality of Suresnes in October 1974. Rather, this was a period of consolidation for the renovated party, during which organizational growth was insufficient even to make up for the losses occasioned by the split of 1972. In addition to Llopis supporters, these losses included a small number of people who refused to take sides and who instead worked for reunification.

Away from their traditional strongholds, the Socialists did not manage immediately to increase their intervention in the mass struggles against the regime, which had persisted since the late 1960s. In large measure, their lack-lustre performance can be attributed to the dislocation involved in the transfer of control over party operations back to the interior, and to the need to work out a new *modus operandi* for the activists in Spain and those exiles who were still involved in the production (as opposed to the writing) of the party paper. But there were also important personal and political tensions within the new collegiate leadership and these too encouraged a continuation of PSOE introversion in 1972–4. In the process of resolving them, the balance of power in the party shifted from north to south as an Andalusian-based leadership emerged, forging alliances and making enemies as its influence grew.

According to the figures issued by the renovated PSOE, the split of 1972 (seen as a 'break-away') represented a total loss of between 30 and 35 per cent of the party membership—mostly outside Spain, but also in Madrid and the provinces. This was hardly compensated by the growth of the PSOE(R) from

3,403 members in August 1972 to 3,586 by October 1974. Over the same period the affiliation level in the exile sector fell from 1,187 to 1,038, while that for the interior rose from 2,216 to 2,548.[1] Of course, the number of paying members who were represented at congresses does not tell the whole story. The *memoria* produced for the Suresnes congress suggested that exile membership was as high as 1,500 and reported that eight new federations had been established in Spain.[2] It should be taken into account that the party was impecunious and could afford no full-time organizers. Clearly, though, at a time when demand for change was growing in Spanish society, the PSOE had scarcely begun to channel it; the party was still at a stage of extending its basic organizational structures and resolving its internal contradictions.

Within the collective leadership Pablo Castellano quickly became a *primus inter pares*. Reasonably competent in French, able to read English, and enjoying the financial independence that facilitated travel and absence from work, this lawyer who had been born in May 1934 was allocated the responsibility for the party's international affairs.[3] The fact that, like him, most other opposition forces were based in Madrid also enhanced his standing within the executive. Many Socialist meetings took place in Castellano's legal offices and he became the person whom people wanting to contact the PSOE automatically approached. To that extent he was the public image of the PSOE. However, political tensions, primarily manifested in expressions of Sevillian dissatisfaction, soon became apparent in the collegiate executive. Just a month after the congress of August 1972, the young men from the south were already up in arms about an interview given by Castellano to *Criba*, a magazine close to the PSI. In this, the Socialist representative emphasized democratic liberties as being his party's immediate concern; he stated that the PSOE

[1] PSOE, Thirteenth Congress held in exile (Oct. 1974), *Memoria*, ch. 3. In the absence of strict verification procedures for affiliation, it is possible that one or two federations exaggerated their membership, but if they did that in 1974 they may have done so also in 1972. It would seem safe to assume that at least the pattern—of very slow growth—is reliable here. PCE affiliation had been estimated by the CIA at 5,000 in 1968 (Hermet, 116).
[2] PSOE, Thirteenth Congress held in exile, *Memoria*, ch. 3.
[3] Castellano interview.

was open to anyone who accepted the party's discipline and statutes, even ex-Falangists; and he seemed favourable to the existence of limited-liability companies. These statements were branded 'social democratic' by the Sevillian group, which demanded Castellano's removal from the party executive.[4] His defence was accepted by the leaders of the larger northern federations, leaving González and Guerra powerless to enforce their demand, but Sevillian attacks on Castellano did not cease. At this stage the tension was mainly ideological; the Sevillian offensive was that of one of the more radical federations against a leader who seemed far too conciliatory towards the enemy. Andalusian lawyer Rafael Escuredo, though himself a moderate social democrat, left the PSOE for two years when the Sevillian demand was rejected by the party executive.[5]

Not long after, further conflict flared up over the content of *El Socialista*, which was replacing *Le Socialiste* as the central organ of the PSOE. Felipe González had joined the party executive in 1970. Two years later he had become Secretario de Formación, encharged with members' training and political education, while his political partner Alfonso Guerra went on to the executive as press secretary. The party paper was written by the Sevillian group headed by Guerra and González and then sent to Arsenio Jimeno in Paris to be published. This arrangement never worked well; too many dominant personalities were involved, and political differences surfaced too. As a fellow member of the executive, Jimeno considered that he enjoyed co-responsibility with the Sevillians for the content of *El Socialista* and therefore he proceeded to edit the Seville material when it contradicted traditional PSOE policies.[6] An article virtually defending the idea of the dictatorship of the proletariat was blocked, as was another defending the PLO and opposing the existence of the state of Israel.[7] In the past, the PSOE had defended Israel because of the party's international links with Israeli socialists and

---

[4] Chamorro, *González*, 107.

[5] Yáñez interview. It may also be that Escuredo's personality clash with González, later much more evident, was a factor. In Oct. 1968 the two men had established a joint labour-lawyers' practice with Antonio Gutiérrez in Seville.

[6] Ibid. [7] Chamorro, *González*, 106.

Franco's Arab friendships. Now the Sevillians were attempting to put forward 'a Marxist analysis of the Arab–Israeli problem'. When executive member Enrique Múgica Herzog reacted against this, he was accused of Zionism by the *El Socialista* team.[8] Contemporaneously, there was some Sevillian criticism of the way that Múgica and Castellano were handling the party's relations with other forces.[9] The details of this whole episode are obscure but at least the battle-lines are clear: it was virtually the Sevillians versus the rest. Jimeno's editorial decisions were seen in Seville as pure censorship and tampering. González tried to get the executive to accept as a principle that all material sent from the interior was sacrosanct.[10] But again the Sevillians failed to obtain a majority in support of their position. Guerra resigned in December 1972, possibly in protest (he was not explicit at the time); González and the rest of the seven-person editorial staff did likewise in April 1973, leaving Castellano to pick up the pieces and add responsibility for the party press to his existing international and representational tasks.[11]

Seville's criticisms of the executive became harsher from the spring of 1973. González and Guerra did a lot of travelling around Spain at this time, not just to build the party but also to canvass support for their opinions. In the view of the main target of their criticisms, Castellano, they had embarked upon an 'assault on power' in the PSOE; they were organizing secretly behind his back and were not afraid to use slanders

---

[8] *Andalucía Socialista*, 94 (1973), 7–8. When the Middle East conflict worsened in 1967 the PSOE sent a telegram of support to the Israeli Labour Party (MAPAI) (PSOE, *Actas* of CE, 7.6.67). See Múgica's two-part defence of Israel, 'Israel, encrucijada de la izquierda', in *Cuadernos para el Diálogo*, 68–9 (1969), and the interview in *ES* (25.9.77, 14–15) for his general outlook. In the Young Socialists, Manuel Simón abandoned his executive post to enlist as a volunteer in the Israeli aid office. He received a temporary suspension as international secretary for this unauthorized act, though the FNJSE's position on the conflict was one of 'sympathy and total solidarity with the Israeli people', Israel being seen as 'a people in arms, attacked by more than 10 Arab countries' (FNJSE, Executive Committee, 'Circulares, 1961/67', *Carta-circular* 4 (6 June 1967), 9 (June 1967), 11 (n.d.)). There were fraternal delegates from Israel at the PSOE congresses of 1967, 1970, and Aug. 1972.

[9] Yáñez interview.

[10] Ibid.

[11] PSOE, Thirteenth Congress held in exile (Oct. 1974), *Memoria*, ch. 4 on press and propaganda; *Andalucía Socialista*, 94 (1973), 6–7.

against him, just as the PSOE(R)'s competitors had.[12]
Eventually Castellano resigned from the executive just a
fortnight before the congress in Suresnes, stating that he was
not prepared to play the Sevillian game (and maybe hoping
through his resignation to avoid criticism in the congress of his
own performance on the executive).

It is difficult to determine whether the Seville group went to
Suresnes with the intention of becoming dominant in the
leadership, but certainly they wanted to increase their
influence and to secure an executive that would be more
sympathetic to the Sevillian outlook. The travels of the
southerners had begun in Andalucía in the 1960s, and in 1970
González had become known in Asturias when he visited the
north collecting money for strikers in Seville. Now, however,
the Sevillians were even encouraging Trotskyists to send
delegates to Suresnes to oust the social democrats from the
party leadership.[13] On the other hand, when it came to the
election of a new executive, the Sevillians along with the rest
initially supported Nicolás Redondo for the position of PSOE
leader. For, as predicted by the Llopis clique,[14] the collegiate
approach did not last; a 'First Secretary' was deemed
necessary, the argument presented by the Sevillians being that
with the PSOE still illegal, its initials could not be used easily
in public, whereas a personality could speak for the party and
be projected as its public image.[15] Redondo, affectionately
called 'Nico' by his fellow activists, was the most prestigious
and uncontested socialist leader at this time. Already the key
man in the UGT, he had been sacked the previous year by
Astilleros Españoles of Bilbao following his arrest in a strike,
notwithstanding 31 years of service at this naval shipyard.[16]
But he regarded himself more as a trade unionist than a
future politician and no amount of persuasion from his fellow
Basques could get him to accept a nomination for First

---

[12] Castellano interview.   [13] García Duarte interview.
[14] PSOE, *Circular* 19 (25 Aug. 1972).
[15] González's interview in *ES: Especial XXVII Congreso*, 1 (5 Dec. 1976), 3–4;
M. A. Aguilar and E. Chamorro, *Felipe González: Perfil humano y político* (Madrid:
Cambio 16, 1977), 138.
[16] *ES*, 27.9.73, 1. Since 14 June 1973 *El Socialista* had been published in
Brussels with the aid of the Belgian Socialists, though all the copy was still being
supplied by the interior.

Secretary. Only when he declined it did Luis Yáñez, head of the Seville delegation, put forward the candidature of Felipe González.[17]

The battle for the leadership that ensued, taking the form of wheeling and dealing behind the scenes as the congress progressed, illustrated many of the antagonisms that existed in the party. Only after a lot of coming and going did the Basques and Andalusians finally reach agreement on a common list of candidates for the executive. Its triumph would be derided by Pablo Castellano as the consummation of a 'Pact of the Nervión with the Betis' (referring to Basque and Sevillian rivers), but subsequent talk by him on this *Pacto del Betis* was largely an a posteriori reconstruction of the battle which revealed more about Castellano's sense of humour than about the event.

Once Redondo had excluded himself from the running, the two senior candidates seemed to be Enrique Múgica of Guipúzcoa and Madrid's Castellano. However, the former was unacceptable to many because of his Communist past, his current social-democratic or Prietista views, and his evident sympathies for Israel, while Castellano's reputation had been affected by all the shortcomings of the outgoing executive. None the less, the Sevillian proposal of Felipe González initially created quite an uproar, causing the negotiations to be adjourned. The story of these negotiations (in which the intermediaries were Antonio García Duarte, Máximo Rodríguez, and Carlos Martínez Cobo) reveals considerable antipathy between the Basques and Sevillians up to this moment. The intermediaries were quite favourable to the 32-year-old González, as were several exile sections, Catalonia, Asturias, and the whole of Andalucía; but at first the Basques resisted the idea. After some persuasion, they were prepared to accept González in the team but not Guerra, who was altogether a more abrasive character and seemed to them a dangerous radical. The moderate, ponderous Basques wanted Castellano to remain in the executive and they also insisted upon the presence of their own Múgica and Iglesias. All these men were

[17] The account of these negotiations is based on the Yáñez and García Duarte interviews and Yáñez's account in Alfonso Guerra (ed.), *Felipe González: De Suresnes a la Moncloa* (Madrid: Novatex, 1984), 73.

initially unacceptable to the Sevillians, who denied that the three were socialists and feared that even a limited Basque participation would become a channel for conservative pressures upon the leadership. Moreover, González insisted on the inclusion of Guerra. The negotiations were so protracted that the PSOE almost ended the congress without an executive. In the end, though, the Basques through Redondo were persuaded to accept the Sevillians, and Guerra was persuaded to tolerate Iglesias, Castellano, and Múgica.[18]

Or so it seemed. Upon learning of the composition of the list, and gaining word about who had tried to veto whom in the negotiations, several members of the new team tried to pull out just as the congress was closing. Castellano and Bustelo had never agreed to join a list headed by González, Iglesias did not want to accept a nomination that was controversial, and Guerra had second thoughts. Only the need for unity and a common desire not to damage the PSOE led them to accept their election to an executive in which there were now five Basques (Redondo, Múgica, Iglesias, Benegas, and Eduardo López), three Andalusians (first secretary González plus Guerra, editor of *El Socialista* and press and information secretary, and Galeote, propaganda secretary), two Madrileños (Castellano and Bustelo) who considered Madrid to be under-represented,[19] and one Asturian (Agustín González).

The most obvious loser in all this was Madrid, whose poor reputation in the party was reflected in its virtual exclusion from the negotiations. Disdain for Madrid stemmed from its weakness and from the *centralismo*, whether real or imagined, that Socialists in some regions criticized. From the capital would come allegations that one or two of the dominant federations, particularly Guipúzcoa, had inflated their membership claims to increase their voting power at the congress.[20]

---

[18] Ibid.   [19] F. Bustelo interview, 25 June 1984.

[20] Castellano interview; I. Gómez interview. According to the affiliation figures accepted at the Congress of Suresnes in 1974, eight federations had more than 100 members: Asturias 525, Guipúzcoa 510, Vizcaya 492, Alicante 200, Seville 151, Madrid 135, Alava 126, Catalonia 109 (Guerra, *González*, 75). Allowing for growth in the early 1970s, all these figures are credible except for that of Guipúzcoa, for which there is no evidence of anywhere near such a large Socialist presence. Inflation of affiliation figures was easy to do since dues were only 100 ptas. a month and heads

However, the Madrid Socialists also recognized that their decline in the party hierarchy and the rise of the Sevillians had a further explanation: while the team of González and Guerra may have been small, it was at least united, knew what it wanted, and worked vigorously in pursuit of its objectives. Madrid meanwhile was deeply divided: at least three tendencies and even more subcurrents existed. A meeting of the PSOE in Madrid was more like a 'co-ordinating committee of political parties' than a party affair.[21] Time was consumed in internal debate, leaving the party incapable of influencing the world outside. Madrid could hardly compete effectively for influence in the party while it was itself rowing about the leadership of Castellano (who, moreover, still being a bit of an anarchist, was not interested in building a 'team' to promote his personal cause). At Suresnes Madrid was uninfluential not only because the metropolitan organization was weak, with only 135 paid-up members; it was also because there was no way in which it could present a rosier picture. If any member of the Madrid delegation had tried to make out that the capital now had a thriving organization, and thus was entitled to a lot of votes, some other member of the same delegation would have derided the claim, turning it to sectarian advantage.[22]

It took several more months before a homogenous leadership emerged and the position of the Sevillians was consolidated with Basque support. Greater coherence was secured through the resignations of Castellano in April 1975 and Bustelo in January 1976 (these men being replaced respectively by the Sevillian Luis Yáñez and González supporter Luis Gómez Llorente). Continuing as international relations secretary in 1974–5, Castellano had clashed with the first secretary, who now liked to handle the PSOE's foreign links and international work personally, and did so without reference to Castellano.[23]

of congress delegations only had to come up with the money from the previous 3 months to justify their affiliation claims. To justify 510 members would have involved the payment of only 153,000 ptas.

[21] Puerta interview, 17 June 1983; I. Gómez interview.

[22] Fundación Pablo Iglesias and PSOE, ii. 219; I. Gómez interview; Aurelio Martín interview, 12 Feb. 1984. The Madrid delegation was Francisco Rodríguez, Enrique Moral, Pedro García, Justo Fernández, Cayetano Hernández, Aurelio Martín, and Alejandro Cercas. It had three left-wingers, three right-wingers, and a centrist. It abstained in the executive election when faced with the slate headed by Felipe González.   [23] Castellano interview.

The latter did not get on personally with the Sevillians and rivalry grew because González was slow to move from the south to Madrid, and so for a while it often still fell to Castellano and Bustelo to represent the party at joint opposition meetings.[24] Much of the Madrid opposition still regarded Castellano as the PSOE leader. When González eventually reached the capital in the spring of 1975, the party establishment there was distinctly inhospitable if not hostile. Rather than attempt to win them over, the first secretary built his own 'apparatus' there; aided by Miguel Boyer, he totally bypassed many of the Madrid Socialists.[25] Further ill-feeling arose from the PSOE leadership's rapid loss of interest in the holding of an Iberian Socialist Conference that Castellano had helped to plan.[26] The prospect of a genuine federation of socialist parties was frustrated by a firm PSOE conviction that its own hegemony was both possible and desirable. Finally, criticism was voiced by the Madrid executives of the style and methods of the Sevillian leadership, which tended to exclude rather than placate critics. Bustelo got into trouble for expressing his views on the leadership at a dinner attended by a few dozen comrades in December 1975. When Luis Novo raised this lapse of discipline at a Comité Nacional meeting the following month, Alfonso Guerra successfully proposed a motion that members of the executive should not voice any differences externally. Feeling that a right to free expression was being curbed, Bustelo resigned. Later he complained about being denied the possibility of explaining his reasons at the following party congress.[27]

For their part, the Sevillians and those supporting them had a powerful argument: the party was weak and would grow stronger only if it could speak with one voice. A loss of individual licence was the price to be paid for effective leadership. And certainly with Felipe González a more dynamic and single-minded executive began to emerge.[28] His

[24] Bustelo interview, 25 June 1984.

[25] Puerta interview, 17 June 1983; Luis Osorio interview, 20 Aug. 1982.

[26] Chamorro, 121.

[27] Castellano interview; Bustelo interview, 25 June 1984. The latter with 3,382 votes had topped the poll in the executive election at Suresnes. González came second with 3,259 votes (data from Bustelo and in Guerra, *González*, 77).

[28] On González several interviews, providing a variety of personal experiences,

political talents were acknowledged even by his critics. The young Sevillian was extremely articulate; he used popular language and could 'connect' with people. He also possessed a rare ability to grasp a situation, to simplify an issue, or to present a synthesis of information in a reasoned and convincing manner. Moreover, he was not without charisma: he stood out in a group and drew attention at meetings. To Socialists who met him then, he seemed to possess the values of modesty and honesty traditionally appreciated by the party, and he also had a great natural intelligence. His commitment to the party was evidently total and it had grown out of radical socialist convictions. At the same time, though, he stressed the need for realism, let all aspects of reality (as he saw it) guide his actions, and often told fellow activists that they were being too ideological. González formed an ideal political partnership with Alfonso Guerra, a man who had trained as an industrial engineer but who was far more interested in the arts.[29] While González was calmer and more personable, Guerra provided the cutting edge of the duo: he was a 'political Robespierre'.[30] While Felipe was perfect raw material for media stardom, Alfonso was a meticulous organizer, much more important behind the scenes and in the apparatus than on congress platforms.

The combination of the two, supported above all by the Andalusian and Basque federations, brought a greater decisiveness to the party leadership. But with it came a certain intolerance and a cliquish desire to be all-powerful in the party. González himself was never keen on listening to criticism. It was almost as if he considered himself a providential leader and saw those who disagreed with him as opponents of what needed to be done. In his mind, other Socialists either saw things as he did, or they simply did not

proved useful, in particular those with López Real, Puerta, Yáñez, Simón, and Bustelo. See also the books by Chamorro; Guerra, *González*; F. González, *Socialismo es libertad* (Barcelona: Galba, 1978), with 'Notas para una biografía' by Antonio Guerra; F. González, *Un estilo ético*, conversations with Víctor Márquez Reviriego (Barcelona: Argos Vergara, 1982).

[29] On Guerra see Fernández-Braso; interview, 'Alfonso Guerra entre la dureza y la ternura', *ES*, 11.9.77, 12–13.

[30] The description comes from Alonso Puerta.

see them. Opposition was neither rewarded nor forgotten.[31] Like Llopis, he preferred to have 'yes-men' around him; unlike Llopis, he insisted upon talent as well as loyalty. Thus his leadership was more coherent than the collegiate experiment preceding it, precisely because it was exclusive. The Sevillians forced activists to align themselves either for or against them. And of course those who fell by the wayside as the Sevillians advanced were not content with this new state of affairs. Their rearguard action against the drift of events now led the PSOE's internal life to acquire new lines of differentiation which replaced the previous divide between *renovadores* and *históricos*.

---

[31] Naturally, criticism of the Sevillians' style of leadership has come principally from its victims, whether they lost internal political battles or were expelled from the party (interviews with Castellano, Bustelo, Puerta, Osorio, and I. Gómez).

5

Socialism in Transition
1974–1982

As the Franco regime entered its dying phases, the PSOE was still in the process of reorganization and reassertion. Spanish Socialism had recently acquired an international reputation for being on the far left of the Socialist International. This image of the PSOE owed much to the gathering atmosphere of political and economic crisis that hung over Spain, as well as to the renovated party's rhetorical radicalism and that special aura that surrounds any clandestine force. Yet during the decade in which Spain negotiated the hazardous road from authoritarianism to representative democracy,[1] the Spanish party underwent a quite dramatic shift that took it well over to the right of the International, only cushioned from a polar position by the Portuguese Socialists of Mario Soares. This remarkable 'transition within a transition'[2] was somewhat more fundamental than the national process, for the latter involved an evolutionary institutional change, achieved only through the political survival of authoritarian élites, while the party transition involved the virtual elimination or transformation of most of the features and figures that had given the PSOE its Iberian firebrand image. If the party that formed a government in 1982, not long after celebrating its centenary, was recognizable to outsiders as that which had renovated itself a decade earlier, this was mainly because the image of the party leader had become synonymous with the party initials.

Later on, this shift to the right by the PSOE, simplistically

---

[1] On the Spanish transition see especially Gilmour; P. Preston, *The Triumph of Democracy in Spain* (London: Methuen, 1986). For bibliographical guidance see Andrés de Blas Guerrero, 'La transición democrática en España como objeto de estudio: Una nota bibliográfica', and José A. Gómez Yáñez, 'Bibliografía básica sobre la transición democrática en España', in *Sistema*, 68–9 (1985), 141–8, 149–73, a special issue on the transition.

[2] On this theme see Donald Share, 'Two Transitions: Democratization and the Evolution of the Spanish Socialist Left', *West European Politics*, 8. 1 (1985), 82–103.

characterized by some as a move from Marxism to social democracy, seemed to have had a certain inevitability about it, owing not least to the electoral success with which the process was crowned. Certainly, the rightward move corresponded to a view broadly held among Spanish democrats that a national across-class compromise was vital in the middle and late 1970s to secure a successful regime transition. The circumstances in which Francoism ended were not such that its opponents could determine Spain's future exclusively. Moreover, the various experiences of regained legal status, growing access to commercial media, increasing institutional participation, party growth, internal and external encouragement to act 'responsibly', and the logic of electoralism, all encouraged the PSOE to be less doctrinaire and more pragmatic. European socialist parties, originally founded to represent the industrial working class, by now aspired to become 'catch-all' parties,[3] though to differing degrees. This ambition was to be found in Spain as elsewhere, here involving not just ideological revision but also a change in the model of party organization. From being a party of militants, who in theory at least were expected to be disciplined, thoroughly committed, active, and schooled in the theory and practice of socialism, the PSOE went a long way towards an alternative electoralist model in which the role of the militant was relegated and party leaders sought direct communication with an electoral clientele by means of the mass media and marketing techniques.

These basic changes were not embarked upon by a united party. Rather, they came about in the midst of the greatest internal controversies experienced by the PSOE since the 1930s. Battles were fought, leaving winners and losers; a mass of new recruits arrived to reinforce the antagonists, while other forces were driven from the field of battle or left of their own accord. Ostensibly, the principal struggle was ideological and the sparring at two congresses in 1979 over 'marxismo, sí, marxismo, no' brought comparisons with the SPD's Bad Godesberg congress and the Labour Party dispute over Clause IV. Yet while the party did show an uncharacteristic degree of

[3] Beate Kohler, *Political Forces in Spain, Greece and Portugal* (London: Butterworth, 1982), 37.

interest in ideology during the 1970s,[4] the so-called theoretical debate on Marxism was pretty superficial. Behind it was a fundamental conflict over the future political constituency of the PSOE. Was it to remain a party of the radical left, gradually seeking to convince a majority of Spaniards that its cause was worthy of support, or was it to trim its ideological sails and accommodate the views currently deemed to be held by a centre-left majority of the electorate? But mixed in with this basic controversy were clashes of personality and the thinly concealed frustrations and aspirations of past and would-be future party leaders. Along with the evident left–right tensions, there were occasional signs too of the 'periphery' rebelling against the 'centre', with Socialists in the regions resisting control by Madrid. And all of this internal conflict naturally had implications for party organization. As the various disputes were resolved, many of those lacking or losing power and influence agitated for an extension or the retention of party democracy, while many of those enjoying or expecting office stressed the electoral importance of appearing united and coherent, and thus the need for strict party discipline. In fact, the key changes for the PSOE in that watershed year of 1979 were not the ideological reformulations that the congresses of May and September seemed to be all about, but rather amendments to the party's statutes that weakened the influence of the rank and file and of dissenting minorities. Once this battle had been won, the outcome of the conflict would prove difficult to reverse.

STEERING TO THE RIGHT

It was not just the PSOE that moderated its demands and accepted a consensual approach as the post-Franco transition got under way. The conciliatory mood was evident in each of the main sectors of the labour movement. Both the Communist-led Workers' Commissions and the self-management socialists of USO toned down the rhetoric of class struggle and helped work for the successful establishment of liberal

---

[4] Even so, efforts to produce a doctrinal periodical were extremely short-lived. See *Yunque*, 1 (1974).

democracy. The revolutionary left, meanwhile, saw recent gains among students and young workers eroded; by the late 1970s its influence was restricted largely to the Basque Country. As for the PSOE and UGT, it is perhaps useful to chart the main phases in their rightward course, before examining in greater detail the reasons behind it and the internal disputes it provoked.

The Congress of Suresnes, October 1974

This was the event mistakenly regarded as the PSOE 'congress of the renovation' by many new recruits for whom it was their first party congress. Held in the 'Albert Thomas' hall in Suresnes, the thirteenth congress of the PSOE in exile officially sanctioned a strategy aimed at producing a *ruptura democrática* in Spain.[1] This meant a dismantlement of the Francoist state root and branch and rejection of any moves to merely reform it, such as the current inherited scheme of Franco's last prime minister, Arias Navarro, to legalize certain political 'associations', but not parties, within the framework of the official Movimiento.[2] By 1974 it was clear to the PSOE that the life of the regime, like that of Franco, was drawing to an end, its final doom sealed by ETA's assassination of Arias Navarro's predecessor Admiral Carrero Blanco in December 1973.[3] Implicitly, in its references to a future 'constituent period',[4] the PSOE officially held on to the old party schema of a provisional government of no specific regime type restoring liberties and calling elections in which Spain's future regime could be decided. During that period the PSOE would campaign for its preferred system of government, rather than seek to impose one by force. Its preference was for a Federal Republic of Nationalities that would reflect Spain's diversity yet maintain working-class unity. The Congress of Suresnes defended the right of each Iberian 'nationality' freely to choose its relationship with 'the rest of the peoples forming the

[1] Initially called for in *ES*, 28 (1974), 1–2.
[2] See the interview with F. González in *El Correo de Andalucía* (Seville), 19.10.74.
[3] Editorial in *ES*, 28 (1974), 1–2; El País, *Golpe mortal: Asesinato de Carrero y agonía del franquismo* (Madrid: El País, 1983).
[4] *ES*, 29 (1974), *passim*.

Spanish state'.[5] This ambiguity was doubtless deliberate: presenting Spain's nationalities as part of the same State while promising them rights to self-determination offered hope to those who insisted that Basques and Catalans be allowed the option of independence, as well as to those who just wanted them to have a say in their form of future autonomy.

The political resolution of the congress noted that Francoism had ceased to be the best political system for the bourgeoisie. This is what made multi-class alliances and the idea of a *ruptura* feasible. The PSOE declared itself ready to ally with other classes and political forces in the pursuit of liberty, but a certain radicalism was expressed in a stated preference for partners 'of the left' and in the limitation of the new party executive's mandate, in this regard, to making agreements that would last only until democratic liberties were restored. After that, an extraordinary congress was to decide whether these alliances were to be extended or terminated.[6] All this implied that the struggle for socialism would commence very shortly after the restoration of democracy. At the level of strategy, then, the PSOE prepared itself to make a contribution to the liberalization of Spain, but was alert to the danger of being used by the new democrats of the right. Its own approach was described as one of 'seeking liberties from a class perspective', these liberties being valued primarily for their utility in facilitating the achievement of a socialist democracy. In that sense, it was claimed, the *ruptura democrática* would be revolutionary.[7]

Here the PSOE presented itself as being to the left of the Communist Party, which earlier in the year had established an opposition platform, the Junta Democrática, along with the monarchist Calvo Serer, parties of the left, and Carlists.[8] The

---

[5] Ibid. 6; Fundación Pablo Iglesias and PSOE, ii. 222–3.

[6] Ibid. 222. [7] *ES*, 33 (1975), 1.

[8] On the PCE see Jonathan Story, 'El pacto para la libertad: The Spanish Communist Party', in P. Filo della Torre *et al.* (eds.), *Eurocommunism: Myth or Reality?* (Harmondsworth: Penguin, 1979), 149–88; P. Preston, 'The PCE in the Struggle for Democracy in Spain', in Howard Machin (ed.), *National Communism in Western Europe: A Third Way for Socialism?* (London: Methuen, 1983), 154–79; Eusebio Mujal-León, 'Spain: The PCE and the Post-Franco Era', in David E. Albright (ed.), *Communism and Political Systems in Western Europe* (Boulder, CO: Westview, 1979); and David S. Bell, 'The Spanish Communist Party in the Transition', in id. (ed.), *Democratic Politics in Spain* (London: Pinter, 1983).

PSOE's traditional anti-monarchism and past experiences of Don Juan de Borbón, on whose behalf the Junta initially offered itself, led the party to boycott the Communist initiative.[9] The Socialists dismissed the democratic potential of both Don Juan and of his son Juan Carlos, but there was an element of demagogy in the PSOE leaders' rejection of the Junta for serving bourgeois interests and in their insistence that the working class had to be the 'protagonist' of the anti-Franco struggle.[10] Here, no doubt, they were echoing the sentiments of most of their militants, but they must have understood that the so-called 'bourgeois opposition' would not ally with them on the basis of workers' leadership (if they would, why the two-stage approach?).

Behind the alliance tactics of the PSOE there also lay a fear of subordination to the PCE. Aware that the Communists had greater strength in terms of militants, the Socialists were wary of any alliances that the PCE was likely to dominate by virtue of the discipline and dedication of its cadres. PSOE fears were greatest at the level of the labour movement, where Socialists warned of the possibility that the Workers' Commissions could emerge to lead a single post-Franco labour confederation based on the old syndicate structure. But given that the UGT was still weak or non-existent in most parts of Spain, the PSOE also needed to differentiate itself from the PCE and its strategy at a political level. This it did by resisting any alliance formula that was based on PCE prompting rather than opposition negotiation, and by criticizing the Communists' readiness to compromise with the right to the extent of accepting a monarchist future. There was no danger of the Socialists being swept aside by a PCE initiative here. The PSOE knew only too well that successful attempts to build a democratic alternative to Francoism would involve approaches to itself, 'not just because of its existing strength but because of its potential strength'.[11]

None the less, the PSOE's radicalism was not simply tactical. The Sevillian group that became largely dominant at Suresnes was decidedly to the left of the Basque and Madrid

---

[9] It was rejected for being too conciliatory and too centralist (*Andalucía Socialista*, 103 (1974), 5–6).

[10] *ES*, Dec. 1974, 2, 5.   [11] Ibid.

Socialists, and the mood of the delegates was mostly combative, especially when positions on international matters were being defined. Pro-Palestinian feeling was so strong that Enrique Múgica had to work very hard in the international *ponencia*[12] to ensure that its motion to the plenum of the congress would defend Israel's right to exist, as well as recognize the national identity of the Palestinian people. And though François Mitterand along with SPD, Swedish, and Yugoslav fraternal delegates attended the event, it was the left-wing Chilean Socialist leader Carlos Altamirano who received the most emotional reception—*vivas* were shouted, clenched fists were raised, eyes became tearful. However, unlike the other party congresses in exile, this one was attended by a lot of 'observers' from Spain. Although the latter had no statutory rights, many political discussions took place between delegates and observers and, according to one delegate,[13] these tended to make delegates ignore the mandates decided for them by their local *agrupaciones* and to accept more moderate or at least ambiguous policy resolutions when it came to voting.

Unity moves, 1975–6

While sniping at the Junta Democrática from the left, the PSOE could see the danger of isolating itself at a time when mass sentiments ran in the opposite direction. Yet for all their statements, Socialist leaders showed no practical interest in building unity on the left. Revolutionary groups briefly flourished in this period, but still provided no adequate alternative to Communist involvement for those seriously interested in left unity. Dissuasion from reaching a *rapprochement* with the PCE was provided by the counsel of the SPD,

[12] *Ponencia* refers here to the workshop discussions that are central to PSOE congresses. Each workshop (working committee composed of delegates who have signed up to participate) deals with a major area of policy; following discussion of the motions submitted to the congress, a resolution (also called a *ponencia*) is adopted; more often than not, it is subsequently approved when the congress reconvenes in full session, though of course it may be amended there, or alternatively a *voto particular* (a minority motion coming from a member or members of the workshop) can be chosen in preference to the majority resolution. The most important discussions and decisions usually take place in the *ponencias* and in behind-the-scenes political trading.
[13] Aurelio Martín, a member of the Madrid delegation (interview).

the existence of powerful regime reformists, and fears of an army reaction against anything reminiscent of the Civil War era. Admittedly, on paper the PCE now looked a more suitable partner than in the past, having dissociated itself increasingly from Soviet alignment since the late 1960s. However, the PSOE remained extremely wary of it. González himself seems to have become deeply distrustful of Communists as a result of the attempts by the more clearly Stalinist Portuguese party to gain power by exploiting political-military tensions in 1975.[1] Equally, PSOE tacticians were worried about the prospect of a conciliatory PCE, similar to the Italian party, occupying a major social-democratic 'political space' in Spain, and, at both political and trade union levels, of the major 'anti-fascist' resistance force becoming the main left movement in a more liberal polity, again as in Italy.[2] Thus the PSOE had to differentiate itself from the PCE, and it did so by reflecting the sentiments of its own militants and denouncing PCE opportunism.

When the Socialists themselves reached an alliance agreement in mid-1975 (one year after the Communists), the breadth of their front was not substantially narrower than that of the Junta Democrática. Their alternative to the Junta, the Plataforma de Convergencia Democrática, included sixteen parties and trade union organizations, stretching from Carlists on the right to unorthodox Communists on the left, but the main partners of the Socialists were the left Christian Democrats of Joaquín Ruíz Giménez.[3] The Plataforma was established, not so much to compete with the Junta, but rather to enable the PSOE to negotiate a common opposition front without the terms being set by the Communists. Contact between the two fronts was established in September 1975 and it led to a merger with the formation of Coordinación Democrática (the *Platajunta*) in March 1976.[4]

By this time the PSOE leadership had decided that Spain's transition to democracy was unlikely to come about through a

---

[1] Guerra, *González*, 158. For Carrillo's supposed Eurocommunism see S. Carrillo, *Eurocommunism and the State* (London: Lawrence and Wishart, 1977) and id. (with R. Debray and M. Gallo), *Dialogue on Spain* (London: Lawrence and Wishart, 1977).
[2] Puerta interview, 17 June 1982.   [3] *ES*, June, July 1975, *passim*.
[4] Ibid., 48 (1975), 3; ibid., 60 (1976), 1; *Triunfo*, 3.4.76.

clear *ruptura*. Indeed, from the start Coordinación Democrática used such terms as *ruptura negociada* and *ruptura pactada*.[5] The alliance served as a symbol of opposition unity and as a body for negotiations with regime reformists, but only its left-wing components were able to channel popular pressures on the regime for change, in the form of strikes and protests. By 1975 at the latest, along with the other main opposition parties, it is highly likely that the PSOE had held informal discussions with regime figures who were prepared to entertain some post-Franco changes.[6] And just as the encouragement of reformists within the old regime to facilitate real change became a PSOE concern, so its attitude to the monarchy was modified. When Juan Carlos had been chosen by Franco as his successor as head of State, the Socialists had seen this as heralding 'the monarchy of the *Movimiento*'. They had written off the prince as a 'puppet' and had insisted that the monarchy could not be democratic.[7] The PCE also had misgivings about Juan Carlos, because of his Francoist education, and for that reason it backed Don Juan, hoping he might block his son's succession.[8] When Franco died, at long last,[9] in November 1975, the Socialists' immediate feeling was that Juan Carlos would not help bring freedom to Spain. Shortly afterwards, however, they did mention that as a possibility and began to tone down their republicanism.[10]

Until genuine reforms were on offer, the Socialists had everything to gain from total intransigence, at least in their public discourse. When Juan Carlos received Chile's dictator, the Socialist press attacked the new monarch: 'Juan Carlos cannot show a different face to that of Pinochet.'[11] Yet the PSOE attitude was not rigidly uncompromising; it merely demanded that members of the regime who were seeking to project a new image actually took decisive steps towards the dismantlement of the regime. These only got under way in

---

[5] P. Castellano, *Informe a la Agrupación Socialista Madrileña* (publ. by the author, Oct. 1976), 3.

[6] Puerta interview, 17 June 1982.

[7] PSOE, *Actas* of CE, 13.8.69; *ES*, Dec. 1972, 3, 5.

[8] Chamorro, *González*, 118–20.

[9] The *ES* banner headline read: 'AT LAST! HE HAS DIED!' (supplement to no. 51 (Nov. 1975)).

[10] Ibid., 51 (1975), 1; ibid., 52 (1975), 1.   [11] Ibid., 53 (1975), 2.

mid-1976, when Adolfo Suárez was appointed by the new king to replace the discredited Arias Navarro. The Socialists regarded this as an intelligent appointment, there being no person better qualified than Suárez (former general secretary of the Movimiento) to dismantle Francoism if he were so minded.[12] When announced, his political reform measures disappointed them, however, for they fell far short of the ideal *ruptura*, whether negotiated or not.[13] Various safeguards for the right were built into them. None the less, even the Socialists recognized that a qualitative shift in Spanish politics had occurred in mid-1976, and any lingering thoughts of holding out for a true *ruptura* vanished towards the end of the year when people largely ignored PSOE and PCE calls for a boycott of the referendum on the Suárez reforms. In spite of the absence of political freedom objected to by the left, over 77 per cent of those entitled to vote did so, and of these some 94 per cent endorsed the reform plan.[14]

The political transformation of Spain in these years was more a case of gradual yet profound reform than of *ruptura negociada*. However, it is a misrepresentation of the reality to portray the PSOE as having supported a regime transition merely agreed between a series of élites on a collaborative basis.[15] For besides all the compromises made by the PSOE and PCE leaders, the latter did resort to mass pressure to ensure that purely cosmetic reforms would prove unworkable. They gave their full support to workers' protests against declining economic conditions in 1976, while being careful to rule out any essays in insurrectionism. Early in the year 'active' strikes in the north of the country helped to undermine the Arias government, as did a general strike in response to a wage freeze and the threat to employment in November.[16] This latter event was the main achievement of the Co-ordinator of Trade Union Organizations (COS), created by the Workers' Commissions, UGT, and USO in July. From its

---

[12] Ibid., 66 (1976), 1.   [13] Ibid., 67 (1976), 1–2.

[14] See Raymond Carr and Juan Pablo Fusi, *Spain: Dictatorship to Democracy* (London: Allen and Unwin, 1979), 225.

[15] This is the contention of Diego Armario, *El triángulo: El PSOE durante la transición* (Valencia: Fernando Torres, 1981).

[16] Carr and Fusi, 210; Story, 173–5. During the general strike some 93 UGT members were arrested (UGT, Thirty-First Congress, 1976, *Memoria*).

origins, the days of the COS were numbered, for while the Workers' Commissions and USO regarded it as an embryonic single labour confederation, the UGT was determined to limit its remit to that of promoting united workers' action, without any lasting organizational implications.[17] If the Socialists were associated more closely with the Communists here than at the political level, it had a lot to do with rank-and-file pressures for unity. Dissident UGT militants had participated in 'unitarian and democratic election lists' (CUD) for the *sindicato* elections of 1975, which had been officially boycotted by their organization, and the UGT bank employees' federation in Madrid had been dissolved and reorganized by the national leadership because of its indiscipline.[18] Moreover, it is significant that the announcement of the COS at national level was preceded months earlier by the establishment of a similar *coordinadora* to resist a wage freeze in Vitoria, scene of the most violent battles between workers and police.[19]

Within the COS, however, the UGT continued to defend what it regarded as the standard West European model of trade unionism. To secure the dismantlement of the *sindicato* structure (the CNS) and thus prevent it being 'inherited' by a Communist-led labour grouping, the UGT urged the clandestine unions to withdraw the militants they had succeeded in having elected in *sindicato* elections; when the Comisiones and USO refused to do this, the UGT left the COS in March 1977, ensuring its collapse.[20] The perpetuation of a labour movement divided along political lines, seen by the UGT as a situation of 'trade union pluralism', was thus facilitated. The Socialist union's assertion of independence at this time carried with it little risk of self-damage. Not only did the UGT have strong international links, but it could also expect to grow as a result both of legality and the PSOE's performance in the general election of June 1977; and perhaps too it had foreseen that reinforcement would come from a divided USO.[21]

[17] UGT, Thirty-First Congress, *Memoria*, 11; Unión General de Trabajadores, *UGT XXX Congreso* (Madrid: Akal, 1976), 90.

[18] UGT, Thirteenth Congress (1976), *Memoria*, 6, 21; Almendros Morcillo *et al.*, 129.

[19] *ES*, 59 (1976), 1; Story, 175.

[20] UGT, Thirty-First Congress (1978), *Memoria*.

[21] Manuel Zaguirre interview, 13 June 1984.

A further way in which the PSOE sought to improve its position was by unifying Spain's socialist movement. With the backing of the Socialist International, it undertook a unitary initiative known as the Iberian Socialist Conference, which was designed to build the PSOE in competition with Tierno Galván's new Popular Socialist Party (PSP) and the Communists. The Conference met first in Paris in June 1974, with new Galician and Valencian socialist parties represented (the PSG and PSPV) as well as the PSOE, USO, the Catalan Moviment and its social-democratic splinter, the SODC. A second meeting arranged by the SPD took place the following September.[22] At first, the PSOE represented by Pablo Castellano made major efforts to find common ground with the socialist groups of the Spanish periphery, it being worried about its weakness in Catalonia and virtual non-existence in Galicia. The party not only recognized the plurinational character of Spain, but even discussed the possibility of a federal approach to socialist organization, with existing PSOE federations merging into 'national' socialist parties in regions where the latter were significant.[23] The main stumbling-block was provided by trade union considerations, for both the UGT and USO had Spanish horizons. And while USO stood for union autonomy and regarded the UGT as a 'transmission belt' of the PSOE, the UGT sought to incorporate but not compromise with USO.[24]

There was a distinct change in the PSOE attitude once the Congress of Suresnes had chosen a new party leadership. Paradoxically, although the new, more left-wing, Sevillian-led executive was ideologically closer to many of the party's interlocutors in the Iberian Socialist Conference,[25] the PSOE line on unity hardened. Encouraged by the international recognition it was receiving now from fellow European socialist parties, the González team insisted that unification had to be based on the renovated PSOE, rather than on fusion. As USO veteran Eugenio Royo saw it, the Conference

[22] Enrique Barón, *Federación de Partidos Socialistas* (Madrid: Mañana, 1976), 13.

[23] Ibid. 14.

[24] Ibid. 15; Agapito Ramos interview, 23 May 1984; Enrique Barón interview, 1 June 1984; Zaguirre interview; Eugenio Royo interview, 15 June 1984.

[25] Ramos interview; Barón interview.

participants now divided into those who wished to 'restore' Socialism in Spain and those who wanted to 'reconstruct' it on a new basis.[26] His own group, Socialist Reconstruction, established at the end of 1974, wanted to see a socialist movement that would reflect Spain's national diversity and accept USO's conception of autonomous (though not apolitical) trade unionism and self-management.[27] After the PSOE withdrew from the Conference project in April 1975,[28] the remaining groups developed their own version of unification by entering processes of 'socialist convergence' with other groups in their regions, leading to the creation of Socialist Convergence in Madrid and Catalonia. Eventually, in March 1976, the various parties and groups announced the formation of a Federation of Socialist Parties, the FPS.[29]

In late 1975 Tierno Galván's PSP had combined with a series of small, scattered socialist groups to form a Socialist Confederation of the Spanish State.[30] Subsequently, members of the FPS regarded both the PSOE and PSP as essentially

[26] Zaguirre interview; Royo interview.

[27] See Unión Sindical Obrera, '10 Puntos básicos a discutir para Reconstrucción Socialista', Dec. 1974.

[28] The PSOE pulled out after the CSI meeting had recognized the 'plurinational nature' of the Spanish State and its regional dimension, and had decided to have majority voting (Reconstrucción Socialista, 'Propuesta de declaración de la Conferencia Socialista Ibérica', 27.4.75). Moreover, the PSOE's temporary allies had called for the party to dissolve its federations in those 'nationalities' where a 'nationalist' or 'regionalist' socialist party existed; and to hand over its international representation and treasury to the CSI (*ES*, 61 (1976), 2). The PSOE would go no further than unity in action.

[29] *Triunfo*, 687 (1976), 18; ibid., 700 (1976), 8–9. By mid-1976, under a collective leadership including Barón, Reventós, Alejandro Rojas Marcos, Royo, and Joan Garcés (a university lecturer who had worked for Allende's Popular Unity in Chile), the FPS was composed of Convergencia Socialista groups in Andalucía, Aragón, Catalonia, and Madrid; Reconstrucción Socialista groups in Asturias and Murcia; Eusko Sozialistak in the Basque Country; the Partido Autonomista de Canarias, the Partido Socialista Galego, PS de les Illes, and PS del País Valencià. The RS groups in Madrid and Catalonia by now formed part of broader *Convergencia* processes there.

[30] *Triunfo*, 676 (1976), 74; ibid., 689 (1976), 22–3. The Confederation presided over by Tierno was composed of the Alianza Socialista de Andalucía, Alianza Socialista de Castilla, Democracia Socialista de Asturias, the Federación Independiente Demócrata, Movimiento Socialista de las Baleares, Partido Autonomista Socialista de Canarias, PS de Aragón, and PSP. It broke up after the launch of the Coordinación Democrática in Mar. 1976. While the PSP backed this new opposition front, the rest of the Confederation took the view that 'regional' and 'national' unity had to precede unity at the level of the Spanish left. These groups subsequently joined the FPS in July 1976.

sucursalista parties of Madrid,[31] seeking dependent 'branches' in the provinces but resistant to any suggestion of an equitable federation, and even to genuine federalism within their own parties. However, the FPS project, whose strongest backers were the Catalan and Madrid sections,[32] failed to reach fruition. Events moved far too fast for what it required—a slow process of linking and co-ordinating 'national' and regional socialist groups and parties. Almost as soon as it was born, the Federation had to adapt to the realities of forthcoming elections. Financial considerations and pragmatic alignments then became more urgent and polemics within the socialist camp something of a luxury.[33]

Presenting Socialism

In 1975 the PSOE began to project a new image, borrowing from the Swedish Social Democrats the symbol of the sun rising over the party initials, and making 'Socialism is Liberty!' its central slogan.[1] The language of the party press, while full of Marxist concepts, presented ideas that were more reformist than revolutionary. In February it declared that though the Franco regime was in crisis, capitalism was not; there could be no revolutionary solution, for the balance of forces was unfavourable to the working class. Two months later, as Spain continued to suffer from the effects of the first oil crisis, the PSOE decided that there was now a crisis of the capitalist system, and it would mean growing unemployment; yet instead of taking up a more revolutionary stance in response, the party urged only that the sacrifices imposed by the economic situation be shared equitably.[2] The PSOE message to a politically anxious public was not exactly new,[3] but the latest emphases and packaging made it seem so. While

[31] *Triunfo*, 699 (1976), 18.

[32] The Madrid component was made up of Reconstrucción Socialista, the Federación Independiente Demócrata, and a group of untenured university teachers including Joaquín Leguina (the PNNs); these three sectors formed Convergencia Socialista de Madrid. In Catalonia, militants from the MSC also entered a Convergencia Socialista and this gave rise to the founding of the Socialist Party of Catalonia, the PSC (Congrés).

[33] Royo interview.   [1] *ES*, 43 (1975), 8.

[2] Ibid., 33 (1975), 1; ibid., 37–8 (1975), 1.

[3] One can find the slogan 'Socialism is Liberty', in fact, in *ES*, 12.4.1895.

trading upon its historical reputation for honesty and integrity, the party presented itself as 'young, modern, the axis of the Spanish political process: the Party that offers the most guarantees of a radical transformation of society, respecting liberty and pluralism, and basing its action on a scientific interpretation of reality by following the dialectical method';[4] in other words, a synthesis of Liberalism and Marxian socialism.

By 1976, while still outlawed, the PSOE was able to operate with less fear of sanctions. The holding of opposition rallies and even congresses became possible for the non-Communist forces, though in March the shooting of striking workers by police in Vitoria and in November the wave of arrests during the general strike reinforced left-wing convictions that a class war was still being fought. In February the renovated PSOE held a public rally of 10,000 people in Seville and a homage to Manuel Llaneza attended by 4,000 Socialists in the Asturian civil cemetery of Mieres; in mid-August some 8,000 people went to a meeting of the Asturian Socialist Federation in Gijón.[5] Attempts to hold the PSOE's twenty-seventh congress led to a government ban in November, but a party threat to hold the event as its fourteenth congress in exile, and thereby show the outside world that Spain remained Francoist, led to permission being granted for it to be held in Madrid in December 1976.[6]

Earlier in the year, in April, the Socialists had been able to publicize their ideas by means of a UGT congress, the organization's thirtieth. Held in Madrid's Biarritz Hotel, the event prefigured the forthcoming party congress. UGT leaders were well aware that it was a dubious distinction to be allowed to hold the first major democratic event by a government of Francoist origin, but they believed that it was necessary to force the issue of 'legality' thereby, and they were able to vitiate the stigma of authorization by having representatives of the Workers' Commissions, USO, the CNT,

[4] Ibid., 50 (1975), 1.
[5] Ibid., 57 (1976), 1, 4, 7; ibid., 69 (1976), 4–5. The year before, over 1,000 Socialists had gone to the civil cemetery of Madrid on May Day to pay their respects to Pablo Iglesias. There were almost 100 arrests, though the PSOE leaders by now enjoyed impunity (Guerra, *González*, 86).
[6] *ES*, 74 (1976), 8.

and Basque and Catalan unions to participate in the closing ceremony.[7] This first socialist congress to be held in Spain for 44 years was significant for a number of reasons. In more than a symbolic sense, it was the moment when the interior and exterior were reunited, and quite remarkably they found they had much in common, notwithstanding the preponderance of 25- to 30-year-olds among the 400 delegates.[8] Secondly, although the Basque and Asturian delegations from the north remained dominant, the UGT's rapid numerical growth in Andalucía over the past year was seen at the congress. Still not much larger than the PSOE, the UGT's 6,500 militants at this time came mainly from the Basque Country (21 per cent, including Vizcaya 684 and Guipúzcoa 674), France (12 per cent), Andalucía (11 per cent, including Seville 275), Asturias (9 per cent, 625 militants), Madrid (9 per cent, 606 militants) and Catalonia (6 per cent, 400 militants). Two-thirds of the members were based in Spain.[9]

Thirdly, the congress was organizationally significant for it established a model of sectoral *federaciones* and territorially-based *uniones* which combined the need to be present in each industry with the desire for national solidarity among the membership. In fact, 12 sectoral federations already existed, by far the strongest of which was in the metallurgical sector; most of the others still had to be built, as quickly as possible.[10] As they grew, an informal distinction would emerge in UGT ranks between the traditional 'militant' (implying activism) and the less active 'member'; moreover, differentiation between the PSOE and UGT memberships would become really marked for the first time since the 1930s.[11] Another decision of the congress, taken partly as a gesture to those who were attracted by USO's rejection of Madrid centralism, was to transform the Comité Nacional into a Comité Federal, but no real moves in the direction of UGT internal federalism were taken before an extraordinary congress was held in July

[7] Redondo interview; *Triunfo*, 691 (1976), 6–7, 12–13.

[8] Simón interview, 7 Sept. 1982; *Triunfo* 691 (1976), 12–13.

[9] Unión General de Trabajadores, 33; *Triunfo*, 691 (1976), 13; Almendros Morcillo *et al.*, 138–9.

[10] UGT, Thirteenth Congress (numbered thus originally when it seemed it would have to be held abroad), Apr. 1976, *Memoria*, 21; *Triunfo*, 691 (1976), 13.

[11] Garnacho interview, 17 Apr. 1982.

1977.[12] Moves to strengthen UGT autonomy by making its officers ineligible for party or political office were defeated. Realizing that its own recovery would benefit from the PSOE's electoral potential, Nicolás Redondo presented the UGT as the party's union counterpart, and Felipe González delivered a major speech.[13]

Fourthly, in a move that had clear implications for left unity, the UGT rejected proposals to join other forces in the establishment of a mooted new labour confederation for all Spanish workers; instead it presented the latter with its own model of trade unionism, and to legitimate it as the 'European' socialist option it had on hand an array of foreign supporters—ICFTU leaders Otto Kersten and Omer Becu, West German SPD minister Hans Matthöfer, delegations from the Chilean CUT and French CFDT, and so on.

Finally, the congress was the Socialists' first major opportunity to put forward their decidedly ambivalent political message, at once reformist and revolutionary. They wanted it both ways. In the words of the re-elected leader, the UGT stood for 'class and democratic trade unionism, in which all workers have a battle station, without discrimination', but also for 'revolutionary trade unionism that advances towards a socialist society with self-management'.[14] In the report presented by the outgoing executive, the factory committees that the UGT was establishing were described as 'future expressions of proletarian democracy and the origins of authentic socialist self-management of the economy'; yet the linking of democratic and socialist struggles that this implied was qualified by an immediate emphasis on the recovery of freedom and especially of trade union rights.[15] Rather less equivocal was the congress address of the PSOE First Secretary. Admitting that his message would come as a 'jug of cold water' to many delegates, González urged the UGT to be realistic, and said that this was what politics was all about. One was no more revolutionary for using revolutionary language, he declared; liberty had to be recovered first, socialism would come later.

[12] *ES*, 7.8.77, 9.
[13] Unión General de Trabajadores, 14.
[14] Redondo (ibid. 89).
[15] Ibid.; UGT, Thirteenth Congress (Apr. 1976), *Memoria*, 6.

To pretend otherwise was pure demagogy.[16] Days later, on 22 April he described the PSOE as methodologically but not ideologically Marxist, it being open to everyone 'from non-Leninist Marxism to genuine social democracy that is not just a mask for liberalism'. Here the party leader was welcoming gradualists so long as they subscribed to an ultimate goal of socialism. Within a month, however, the more militant side of his image was refurbished by means of a five-hour meeting with Fidel Castro in Havana, which reportedly produced a broadening of the areas of agreement between the 'two revolutionary parties'.[17]

Between the UGT congress and the PSOE set-piece at the end of the year, the other socialist options each had their turn. Professor Tierno Galván's Popular Socialist Party was the first left-wing party to hold an authorized congress, on 5–6 June. Already by then the party had differentiated itself from the PSOE (at least for the initiated) through Tierno calling for an electoral alliance and a common programme of the left; González then rejected the proposal by declaring that a left government with 51 per cent of the votes behind it could not survive in Spain.[18] The alliance idea had only limited success, given the PSOE's lack of interest and the PSP's limitations as seen by socialists of the periphery. Tierno's party recognized the right to national self-determination within Spain and proposed the creation of a Chamber of nationalities and regions, but it refused to allow the latter any veto in Spanish decision-making.[19] PSP progress was hampered by its lack of a trade union counterpart, its labour link being with the Communist-led Workers' Commissions. Moreover, the party was barely organized: during the Franco period, membership amounted to just a few hundred, mainly *madrileños*, and there were no membership cards before 1976.[20] Just as important is the fact that it lacked international socialist support. At his party's so-called third congress (effectively its first), general

[16] Unión General de Trabajadores, 43–6.
[17] *Triunfo*, 692 (1976), 20; *ES*, 65 (1976), 2.
[18] Tierno in *Triunfo*, 676 (1976), 22–3; González's Seville press conference, 30 Jan. 1976 (*ES*, 57 (1976), 5).
[19] Report on Third Congress of PSP, *Triunfo*, 698 (1976), 10–11; ibid., 701 (1976), 33–7.
[20] Morán interview.

secretary Raúl Morodo praised the leaders of Mexico and Venezuela in the presence of fraternal delegates from Libya, Yugoslavia, the Arab Socialist Union, the Mexican Institutional Revolutionary Party (PRI), and Venezuelan social democrats.[21] Financially, the PSP had found patrons to compensate for the withdrawal of West German support from Tierno and Morodo's previous grouping,[22] but none of the new allies was likely to convince Spanish voters that the Popular Socialist Party was the Spanish Socialist Party. Rather, it seemed all too obviously a target for the projection of international influence by the newly-rich oil exporters of the Third World.

A lack of international socialist support was also a problem for the Federation of Socialist Parties (FPS) which was presented to the public in July. Making a virtue of necessity, the FPS claimed that the PSOE was paying more attention to external than internal links; it decried that party's alleged dependency on the SPD, and dismissed the Socialist International as bourgeois and reformist.[23] In December 1976 the Federation joined forces with the PSP, Labour Party of Malta, and Arab Socialist Union of Libya to host a conference of socialist parties of the Mediterranean region, held in Barcelona. The desire voiced there by Joan Garcés to move the centre of socialist politics to the Mediterranean differentiated this sector somewhat from 'official' socialism, though the alternative offered was not easy to assimilate.[24] Even with the presentation of a Mediterranean image, however, the panorama was not entirely clear, for the PSOE was the Spanish participant in two conferences of Southern European socialist parties in January 1976 and May 1977, organized under the auspices of François Mitterand.[25] Ostensibly held to study the specific problems encountered by Mediterranean affiliates of the Socialist International (such as the presence of strong communist parties, underdevelopment, and a politically active

---

[21] *Triunfo*, 698 (1976), 10–11; Partido Socialista Popular, *III Congreso del PSP* (Madrid: Tucar, 1976), 58. Of similar content is id., *Por un socialismo responsable: El P.S.P. ante el futuro español* (Madrid: Tucar, 1977).

[22] Chamorro, *González*, 79.

[23] José Barrionuevo Peña, 'Algunas cuestiones en torno a la unidad', *Cuadernos para el Diálogo*, 149–50 (1976), 34–6; Ramos interview.

[24] *Cuadernos para el Diálogo*, 188 (1976), 126–7.

[25] For reports see *ES*, 25.2.76; *Cuadernos para el Diálogo*, 211 (1977), 18–20.

military), these displays of 'Mediterranean Socialism' must be seen also as a bid by Mitterand to challenge West German dominance in the International, an attempt that failed chiefly because of successful SPD courtship of the Iberian parties.

The ever-extending list of FPS affiliates, which besides parties with a genuine regional base (such as the Andalusian Socialist Party, created in July[26]) included many groups that were parties in ambition only, must have suggested something of a rag-bag to many politically-conscious Spaniards. Its own organizational secretary later acknowledged that the FPS had never functioned properly as a federation of socialist parties; there simply was not time for the process to mature.[27] Moreover, some of the promoters of the Federation in Madrid, within the Socialist Reconstruction group, had been arguing in favour of unification with the PSOE since 1974, following the election of the González executive.[28] Throughout 1976 the PSOE leader had made repeated efforts to undercut the appeal of alternative socialist formations. Democracy, González insisted as late as February, was not just a question of voting every four or five years; the Socialist version of it also offered workers' control in the workplace within the context of a federal republic.[29] Then in April, speaking in Barcelona, the Socialist leader indicated that his party was willing to modify its structures; on major strategic matters it would still want to be able to take decisions for the whole of Spain, but on regional issues, or rather issues of 'nationality', it was prepared to cede full autonomy to component federations in regions where peripheral nationalisms were strong.[30] The offer was to reinforce federalism within the PSOE, not to enter into a new federation of socialist parties. Charges of 'centralism', of being a party of Madrid, were rejected repeatedly.[31] In the meantime the PSOE had enjoyed good relations with the Catalan affiliate of the FPS since the

---

[26] *Triunfo*, 705 (1976), 6–7; ibid., 708 (1976), 6–8. The PSOE boycotted its creation, saying that it had increased the dispersion of socialist forces, and that its analysis of the 'centralist' parties failed to isolate the real enemies of the Andalusian people.
[27] Royo interview.
[28] Ramos interview.
[29] *ES*, 57 (1976), 1.
[30] Ibid., 61–2 (1976), 3.   [31] *Triunfo*, 708 (1976), 6–8.

time of the Iberian Socialist Conference.[32] By the end of 1976
the virtual defection from the FPS of the Catalan Socialists led
by Reventós and a small majority of the Madrid contingent led
by Enrique Barón in response to PSOE unity overtures had
undermined this socialist sector greatly.

A further victim of transfers of members to the renovated
PSOE was the *sector histórico*. By the time the PSOE(H) held
its version of the party's twenty-seventh congress in Madrid in
October 1976, it had lost four executive members including
the president, Alfonso Fernández, whose reunification efforts
were endorsed by part of the rank and file. Membership was
claimed to be 6,000 in September, and this figure included 900
newcomers.[33] As the congress revealed, however, the party's
largest concentrations were in Mexico (15 delegates) and
Toulouse (17).[34] Despite the effective retirement of Llopis
through ill health in 1974, the 'historical' sector had been
plagued by clashes between interior and exterior.[35] In 1976,
still devoid of international support, it became desperate for
allies. In the eyes of left-wing socialists it now sullied its
reputation by joining forces with social democrats who earlier
had followed Dionisio Ridruejo's evolution away from the
Falange. In October the PSOE(H) signed an electoral pact
with the Spanish Social Democratic Party (PSDE), which
rejected Marxism and whose leader Antonio García López had
been booed and whistled by delegates at the Congress of
Suresnes. When the resultant Social Democratic Alliance
(ASD) was expanded to take in former *falangista* Cantarero
del Castillo's Social Democratic Reform (RSD) in December,
the alliance claimed 70,000 members, seven times more than
the renovated PSOE![36] (How much support it really enjoyed
would be shown by the general election of June 1977, when
the alliance failed to win a single seat in the Cortes.) Socialist
veterans were alienated by what for them was a repugnant

[32] González's interviews in *ES*, 32 (1975), 3–4, and 39 (1975), 4–6; Partit dels
Socialistes de Catalunya, 12.
[33] *Le Nouveau Socialiste*, 102 (1976), 5.
[34] Ibid., 104 (1976), 2.
[35] PSOE(H), Twenty-Seventh Congress (Oct. 1976), *Memoria*: this led to a
leadership reshuffle in Feb. 1975 when the 'Mexicans' Víctor Salazar and Ovidio
Salcedo were elected general secretary and vice-president.
[36] *ES(H)*, 2 (1977), 1; 6 (1977), 3.

alliance with dubious social democrats, and by a persisting negative emphasis on anti-communism insisted upon by the 'Mexicans'. If it had a political message, the PSOE(H) lacked the financial and physical resources to put it across. If it had an image, it was that of a relic from the past. When the election campaign began in spring 1977, the veterans in Castellón would have to pay a lad a few pesetas to put up their posters simply because they were too ancient to perform such tasks themselves.[37]

In contrast the renovated PSOE displayed far more vigour, and its claim to a seven-fold increase in numbers since Suresnes[38] was more or less credible. At its twenty-seventh congress, held in Madrid's Hotel Meliá early in December, the delegates represented some 9,141 members, including 1,377 in Andalucía, 1,280 in the Basque Country, 1,239 in Valencia, 903 in Asturias, 837 in Madrid, and 1,408 abroad.[39] Andalucía's recent rapid growth was again in evidence. None the less, to put the PSOE performance in perspective the 8,000 or so militants the party now possessed in Spain[40] should be compared with the 3,500 membership of the far-left Revolutionary Communist League, founded just six years earlier.[41] In the student movement in the mid-1970s the PSOE not only had fewer militants than the PCE, but less even than the Trotskyists and Maoists.[42]

The twenty-seventh congress was a triumph for the Socialists' international work, the key to which was sponsorship by Willy Brandt. With him vouching for the Sevillian-led party, a broader range of International Socialist support was forthcoming. In most cases, it was expressed not in financial aid but in the public endorsement of the PSOE by the big names of European socialism who were present at the congress.[43] Brandt himself, Olof Palme (both men speaking in

[37] Martínez de Velasco interview.
[38] *ES*, 73 (1976), 6.
[39] PSOE, Twenty-Ninth Congress (1981), *Memoria, Informe de Gestión*, i. 73–5.
[40] See too Jorge de Esteban and Luis López Guerra, *Los partidos políticos en la España actual* (Barcelona: Planeta, 1982), 116.
[41] FLP-FOC militants created it and ETA(IV) people joined in 1973 (*Triunfo*, 713 (1976), 15).
[42] Interview with a former member of the Agrupación Socialista Universitaria (no relation to the ASU of 20 years earlier), 29 July 1982.
[43] Yáñez interview.

Spanish), Mitterand, Pietro Nenni, and Michael Foot all attended the *fiesta*, as did representatives of Cuba and Romania, though the most emotional welcomes were reserved by delegates for the guests from the Chilean Socialist Party and Polisario.[44]

It being essentially a celebration and a publicity exercise, the PSOE leaders strove to present the public with an apparently united party. In doing so, they accepted criticisms and went along with left-wing motions that must surely have troubled their sense of realism. This was the first and last congress of the clandestine party; it lacked the moderating influence of long-standing exiles desperate to return to Spain and of the kind of recruit that would be forthcoming only when the party became legal and could offer political careers to loyal members. In the view of Felipe González, the twenty-seventh congress reflected the great 'ideological accumulation' that had built up during the clandestine struggle; there had been no point in discussing practical policy issues under Franco, when the conditions of struggle naturally engendered a hard rhetoric of class war. Political ideas became dogmas with the greatest of ease so long as the party remained illegal and isolated, unable to present its views to a broad public, and with no need to justify them in the face of intelligent criticism. Yet it was not just clandestinity that was responsible for the radicalism. Also important was the economic background: a crisis considered by socialists on the left of several European parties to be a structural crisis of capitalism. Moreover, there was the violent atmosphere that continued to surround strikes and labour protests for at least a year after Franco's death, and there was also the impact of the Chilean defeat. From the start of the Allende period, the PSOE had identified very strongly with the left-wing Chilean Socialists. Now many Spanish Socialists shared the analysis put to their party congress by Carlos Altamirano: while declaring that in the end the Chilean experiment in democratic socialism had been frustrated by a stronger enemy (US imperialism), the exiled Chilean politician acknowledged that his socialist party had been too ready to see Chile's political institutions as liberal, its bourgeoisie as

[44] *ES*: *Especial XXVII Congreso*, 1 (1976), 16.

give her a dreamy look as she is in love with Tom Fowle, one of Mr Austen's pupils. I'm not sure how I should draw someone in love, so I hope I have it right.

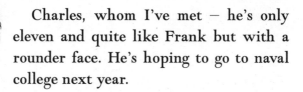

Frank — a year older than Jane (the same age as me) and a midshipman — I did my best with Frank's collar, but Jane had to sketch it for me. I don't think I have ever seen a midshipman, though I have seen a captain and I'm sure I could sketch a captain's uniform.

Charles, whom I've met — he's only eleven and quite like Frank but with a rounder face. He's hoping to go to naval college next year.

I told Jane I thought she was very lucky to have five brothers.

Jane laughed. 'Five . . . well.' There was something odd about her expression and a sort of dryness in her voice.

I just turned back to the page where I have drawn Captain Thomas Williams. My journal opened automatically at that page and I could see that the corner of the page was a bit dog-eared. I don't think Jane saw . . .

Sunday, 6 March 1791

Jane's brother Frank came in to see me today. He is on shore leave from his ship, where he is a midshipman. He looked quite like the picture that I had drawn of him, but his hair was even curlier. He is my age and the nearest in the family to Jane.

He was quite like Jane, very chatty and very funny. He just came into my room, sat on the bed and asked me how I was and then started doing imitations of the first lieutenant, who was a silly numbskull according to Frank, and of the captain, who was as old as the hills. Frank stumped around the room to show us what the captain was like on deck when a wind was blowing and how once he stumbled when his legs got tangled in a sail and he lay stretched out on the deck until the mate pulled him to his feet. Frank found that very funny, but said that all the sailors had to pretend not to notice in case they would be flogged for insubordination. Then Frank did a good imitation of the captain lying stretched out on the floor, thrashing about with his legs, trying to dislodge the heavy sail.

'And the helmsman at the wheel was staring out to sea like this.' And Frank blew his cheeks out and tightened his lips so much that the cords on his very brown neck stood out. His face was very brown too, I noticed, and he had nice dark eyes.

'It's a hard life,' he said, but I thought he looked well on it, and very cheerful.

'Not as hard as school,' said Jane promptly. 'We were starved there.'

'Bet you didn't have to eat ship's biscuit,' said Frank, his mouth filled with a slice of cake his mother had sent up to tempt my appetite.

'We had worse! Tell him, Jenny!'

'Fish heads for dinner,' I said. 'And fish tails.'

'And it smelt bad!'

'Tell him about the stinking fish of Southampton, Jane,' I said. I was enjoying Frank's visit. It seems strange, but I have hardly ever spoken to a boy before except my brother, Edward-John.

'Well, Mrs Cawley was reading out from a book where a woman is giving advice to her daughter . . .'

'And she was reading it in a very deep, solemn tone of voice.' I put this in so that Frank could imagine the scene.

'And then she came to this bit — it was priceless . . . She said, *"Belinda, beware the dissipations of London, the idle luxuries of Bath and—"'*

'Let me tell! Frank, listen to this . . . and then Jane said, very quickly, just when Mrs Cawley paused to take a breath, she said: *"And beware the stinking fish of Southampton."* All the girls started to laugh so much that Mrs Cawley sent Jane out of the room.'

'If she were on a ship, she would be flogged with a cat-o'-nine-tails,' said Frank.

I don't think he found Jane's joke as funny as I did. Perhaps boys like broad jokes like people slipping and falling and girls think jokes in word form are funnier.

Frank didn't seem to want to hear any more stories from our school. He produced a pack of cards from his pocket. 'Let's have a game of pontoon,' he said.

I had to tell him that I didn't know how to play. My brother, Edward-John, regards cards as an instrument of the devil. I couldn't help laughing when I imagined his face and Augusta's if they saw me sitting up in bed, my nightcap thrown on the floor, not just playing cards but playing for money!

Neither Jane nor I had any money, but Frank lent us some pennies to bet on our cards. It was nice of him, but he won it all back from us bit by bit. I felt almost well again; it was such fun pretending to have good cards, laying our bets, shouting for another card to be twisted and groaning in agony when we got to more than twenty-one. Jane even got down on her knees and held up her hands in prayer for a nice small card – I wonder what Edward-John would have said to that! He would have thought it blasphemy. And then she screamed in agony so loudly when a ten of clubs turned up that Mrs Austen came in and said it was time for me to go to sleep.

But Frank charmed her until she borrowed some

pennies from him and had a game where she had such lucky cards and ended up laying them all out, one by one, in a five-card trick.

And then she refused to give Frank back his money and told him it served him right for playing cards on a Sunday.

'Dear madam,' said Jane sweetly, 'why did you not remind us if you remembered that it was Sunday? La, I do declare that the day had slipped my memory. Perhaps you should give those ill-gotten gains back to Frank, since they were won on a sacred day like today.'

'Take care that you are not so sharp that you will cut yourself, Miss Jane! Men don't like girls that are too witty. You don't want to be an old maid, do you? Now off you go, Frank. These two girls need to go to sleep.' Mrs Austen's good humour had vanished. As usual, Jane had rubbed her up the wrong way. From what I have seen, Charles and Frank seem to get on well with their mother, and so does Cassandra, but Jane and she are always arguing, and I have to admit that some of it is Jane's fault.

Monday, 7 March 1791

Up to now I had been having all my meals upstairs so that I didn't get cold in the draughty corridors and stairway, but today Mrs Austen said I could come down to join everyone for dinner. The dining parlour was full when Jane and I came in.

I must write down what it looked like, though I hardly saw it in the first few minutes, as I was too embarrassed to look around.

It was a big room, with no carpet, not even rugs: just a wooden floor, marked by the boys' boots. Augusta would have thought it very meanly furnished. A large table made from scratched and battered oak, rather than the modern mahogany, occupied most of the space. Instead of pieces of light, delicate Sheraton furniture tastefully arranged against modern striped wallpaper, as in my brother's house, here there was just a vast, old-fashioned oaken sideboard, with its shelves, cubby-holes and drawers, covering one of the panelled walls.

At the top of the table was Mr Austen, busily slic-ing meat. Beside him Mrs Austen was putting the meat on plates and adding vegetables and gravy. As she filled each plate, Cassandra carried them, one by one, to the boys, who were sitting on the far side. I hadn't met any of the pupils yet, except Charles, Jane's brother, but they all smiled kindly at me. It looked like a lot of boys and I felt my cheeks becom-ing quite hot.

'Sit between me and Tom Fowle, Jenny.' Mr Austen gave me a kind smile as I sat down. I noticed that Cassandra gave me a rather sour look. I remembered Jane telling me that her sister was in love with this Tom Fowle, so perhaps Cassandra didn't like me taking the place beside him. Perhaps she normally sat there between her father and her beloved. When she had finished handing out the plates, she went down to the bottom of the table beside Charles, her eleven-year-old brother. She looked annoyed and I felt rather awkward.

'Are you hungry, Jenny?' asked Mr Austen, and I told him that I was starving. Both Mr and Mrs Austen were very pleased at that and Mr Austen insisted on putting an extra slice of boiled mutton and roly-poly pudding on my plate to fatten me up.

It was while I was trying to munch my way through all of this that Cassandra, from the bottom of the table, suddenly said, 'Jenny, how did you get the letter to Mama about Jane's illness? Mrs Cawley couldn't understand how she had heard. Indeed, she said that she had forbidden you to write.'

I choked on a piece of mutton and spent the next few minutes coughing while Jane thumped me on the back and Frank brought me a glass of water from the carafe on the sideboard. I kept the coughing up a bit longer than I needed to; I was hoping that everyone would forget about Cassandra's question, but when I took my final sip of water I looked around the table and everyone, even the schoolboys, seemed to be waiting for my answer. I realized that the subject had been discussed before – probably while I was ill – and now they wanted an answer. I couldn't say that Becky had done it; that might get her into trouble. What could I say? My mind was a blank.

'She tossed it out of the window to a charitable lady who was passing by,' said Jane quickly. She patted me on the back like a solicitous mother and said in a worried way, 'Don't try to talk, Jenny. You'll bring on the coughing fit again and that won't be good for you in your condition.'

All the boys began to laugh then and Mrs Austen scolded them for bad manners at table, and Gilbert East, who is a baronet's son and a great favourite with Mrs Austen, said something cheeky and she rapped his knuckles with a spoon. And then one of the boys proposed that everyone should find a word to rhyme with the word 'rose'. Various suggestions were made and then Mrs Austen, on the spot, made up a long poem beginning with the lines:

This morning I woke from a quiet repose,
I first rubb'd my eyes, and I next blew my nose;
With my stockings and shoes I then covered my toes,

All the boys were proposing various words, like 'froze' and 'clothes', and there was such noise and confusion that everyone forgot about me.

'By the way, Jenny, how *did* you get that letter to Mama on the night that I was so ill? Charles told me that it had been sent by the midnight mail; he was the one that collected the letters that day.' Jane hardly waited for the door to be closed behind us when we went up to our room after dinner before she started to cross-question me.

My heart was hammering. I stared at Jane. I had almost forgotten about that night and the danger I had been in, but now it had all come flooding back into my mind.

'Go on; tell me. I won't tell a soul. I promise you.'

I looked at Jane doubtfully, but then nodded. Surely I could trust her.

And so I told her the whole story of that night, about the sailors and about the man with the sword and about Captain Thomas Williams.

Jane listened to me with her mouth open and she didn't say a word until I finished.

'That is the most romantic thing I ever heard,' she said. 'It's as good as anything that Mrs Charlotte Smith wrote; it's even as good as *Ethelinde, the Recluse of the Lake*. What did he look like?'

I told her all about how handsome he was, about his black hair and brown eyes and his lovely smile and high cheekbones and broad shoulders, and then I showed her the picture that I had drawn.

Jane was very interested in this and she said that

she was going to turn the story of me and Captain Williams into a wonderful romance when she had finished writing *Love and Friendship*. She says that when I talk about Captain Thomas Williams my voice sounds like Cassandra's when she talks about Tom Fowle, which can't possibly be true.

I asked her how many stories she has written and she said, 'A few,' then pulled out the bottom drawer of her chest and I saw that it was absolutely stuffed with pieces of paper that were filled up with Jane's fine handwriting.

'What about this?' she asked, tossing me half a sheet. 'I never finished that but I could write something like it for you. I could just change 'Sir Williams' to 'Captain Williams'. You can stick that in your journal if you like – I've already copied it into my notebook and left a blank page so that I can finish it some time.'

After staying at the Village for a few days longer, Sir Williams went to stay in a freind's house in Surry. Mr Brudenell had a beautiful Neice with whom Sir Williams soon fell in love. But Miss Arundel was cruel; she preferred a Mr Stanhope. Sir Williams shot Mr Stanhope. The lady then had no further reason to refuse him and they were to be married on the 27th of October. However . . .

I read it with Jane reading over my shoulder, but she didn't seem too pleased with it when she had finished.

'I've changed my mind — throw it away; I wrote that when I was only about thirteen,' she said disdainfully. 'I'd make a much better story of it now.'

'No, I'd like to have it,' I said. I thought I would prefer to have that than to have a story about myself and Captain Williams. Deep down, I suppose I was feeling that I'd prefer to make up my own stories about him.

And then Jane copied some more of her present story into her notebook and I wrote a letter to Edward-John and Augusta. I had just finished it when Jane suddenly said, 'You'll have to marry this Captain Williams, Jenny. That would be just so romantic.'

I laughed at that. 'Jane,' I said to her, 'it would be best if Captain Williams and I never saw each other again. He could ruin my reputation forever with one incautious word.'

'Well,' said Jane, 'I don't suppose we'll go to Southampton again so you should be safe.'

Tuesday, 8 March 1791

I had such fun today. I've just said this to Jane and she said I should write it all down quickly before I forget it. That is what she does. When she thinks of an idea for a story – even if it is the middle of the night – she flies over to her desk and scribbles it down on a piece of paper. Afterwards she reads through it again and if she likes it she copies it into her notebook.

This morning Frank came in just after I had had my breakfast but before I had dressed. I got a bit of a shock when he just banged on the door and then came flying in. The curtains were drawn back from the bed so all I could do was pull up the blankets very close to my chin and try not to blush. I can't get used to being in a house where boys are running around all the time. Soon there will be even more because Henry and James, who are at Oxford University, are expected for the weekend, and Edward, Jane's brother who was adopted by rich relations in Kent, will be coming back from his visit to Europe.

Frank is very nice and most amusing. He and Jane and I were playing cards again yesterday evening, using buttons for money this time. It was great fun as Frank kept trying to cheat and Jane kept tut-tutting and saying things like: 'He is but sixteen years old, but already he has embarked upon a life of crime. His parents brought him up from an early age to have

no principles. I fear that he will end by being transported to Australia as a convict.'

Frank looks a bit like Jane, with his dark curly
hair and dark eyes – and even at the end of the winter he is very suntanned. He has Jane's rosy cheeks
also, and now they were glowing with excitement.
He came right up and sat on my bed.

'The hunt's meeting at Deane Gate Inn this morning, Jenny. Do you want to come and see us off? Jane
is coming.'

I hesitated and told him I wasn't sure. Though I
had been getting up each day after breakfast, my legs
were still a little weak. 'How far
away is it?'

'Not far and it's a lovely day.'
Frank jerked the blind so suddenly that it flew up and the
knob on the end of the cord
pinged sharply against the
window.

It was a lovely day.
The poplar tree outside
my window had some
tiny green buds on it and
the sun lit the branches
so that they shone gold.
There was a flock of star-
lings whirling merrily
around under a pale blue

sky. Suddenly I felt a lot better and I thought I would love to go out and see the hunt set off. Frank looked very pleased when I told him.

'Good! Get up quickly.' He still hung around, looking out of the window at the woods beyond, as if he thought I would just slip out of bed and dress while he had his back turned. I coughed. I felt very embarrassed.

'Oh, I'll get out of your way so that you can dress.'

Once he was gone, the door slamming behind him and his feet drumming on the wooden staircase, I got out of bed. The water in the pitcher was cold, but I poured some into the basin on the washstand and had a quick wash, drying myself in front of the fire. I put on two petticoats, a flannel one over my chemise and then my linen one, and I pulled on a pair of new woollen stockings, which went right up to my knees and made me feel nice and cosy. Then I got out my blue muslin gown from the clothes press. It had been washed and ironed, I think, because it was quite clean around the hem. The last time that I had worn it was in Southampton on that terrible night and I remembered noticing a streak of mud on the bottom of the skirt when I hung it up.

Jane and Charles were just coming in the front door when I got to the bottom of the stairs.

'Oh, Jenny, you're coming to see the hunt — that's good.'

'Mama, Jenny is coming to see the hunt go off.' Charles had a high voice that penetrated the whole house.

Mrs Austen popped out from the preserves room, where she and Cassandra were labelling jars of pick-led spring onions.

'It's too far,' she said decidedly. 'You're not strong enough yet, Jenny. That hill is steep.'

'She could go on Frank's old pony,' said Jane.

I felt terrified at the idea because I can't ride, and I said as much.

Frank had joined us by then. 'Anyone can ride,' he said confidently. 'We'll put you on old Squirrel's back – she was my first pony. I'll lead it. Don't worry, Jenny, you'll be fine.'

I asked him why the pony was called Squirrel. To be honest, I was just trying to delay. In one way it was rather fun to go out with all the boys and to have Frank, who was quite handsome, lead me on the pony's back. On the other hand, I was terrified that I might fall off or do something silly.

'I was the one that called the pony "Squirrel's Pony" because Frank used to look like a squirrel on its back – it was far too big for him. He did look funny, perched up there,' said Mrs Austen over her shoulder as she turned to replace the stopper in the big jar of vinegar. 'He saved up all the money that he could earn scaring crows. Then he got a nice tip from a rich cousin and he went straight out and bought the pony when he was only seven years old. I made his first hunting coat out of my red wool wedding dress.' Mrs Austen was smiling good-humouredly at the memory. It's funny how much fonder of the boys she is than of Jane, I thought. She always seemed to be a bit irritated by Jane.

I made a little curtsy to Mrs Austen and said that I would go, if she allowed me. Suddenly I really did want to try to ride, even if Frank was going to lead me. Surely I could manage to sit on a pony's back and be led.

'What happens if she feels faint?' Mr Austen had appeared from his study, following out the older boys, and he looked worried.

'She'll be all right.' Mrs Austen was tired of the subject; she wanted us all to go and allow her to get on with preserving her onions.

'I feel faint; it's the fumes of this vinegar. I wish I could get out in the fresh air for a half-hour.' Cassandra was pouting, standing there with a big apron over her oldest gown and looking as if she wished that she could go too. Her eyes went to Tom Fowle and then she looked away. He was looking at her and both of their faces turned slightly pink. I saw Mrs Austen's eyes go irritably from Cassandra to Tom. But then Jane jumped in between her mother and her sister, her hands clasped and an imploring expression on her face.

'Oh, Cassandra, don't faint whatever you do!'

Jane was pretending to sound alarmed. 'Beware of fainting fits; in my story *Love and Friendship*, Sophia dies after a fainting fit. Her dying words were to her friend, saying, *"Dearest Laura, beware of swoons. Run mad as often as you choose, but do not faint."*'

Even Mrs Austen chuckled at that, and Mr Austen threw back his head and laughed. He rubbed his hand over Jane's dark curls. 'What a little genius this girl is,' he said fondly. 'I love her stories. They are so clever, so humorous. It's a pity she's a girl. What do you think, Frank? Do you think that your sister could beat you at Latin if she were a boy?'

'I don't like Latin,' said Frank. He didn't look a bit worried or jealous of Jane, he just sounded impatient. 'Mathematics is the only subject that is useful to me at sea. That's what they study at the naval college. Come on, Jenny, let's go.'

What fun I am having at Steventon, I was thinking as we all went up the hill together. There was Jane on Frank's pony, teasing Tom Fowle about Cassandra, and Gilbert, with Charles sitting in front of him, pretending that his horse would fall down on the road from Charles's weight. The other students were splashing mud from the puddles over each other. I thought of Bristol and of myself and Augusta sitting in the parlour sewing, or she reading aloud while I was drawing, and it all seemed very dull. And now I was going to see a hunt!

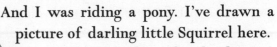

And I was riding a pony. I've drawn a picture of darling little Squirrel here.

We were almost late by the time we arrived at Deane and the space in front of the inn was crowded by red-coated riders and dozens of tail-wagging dogs, yelping with excitement.

'Quick, give me my pony!' In his hurry Frank let go of the reins of my pony while he grabbed his own from Jane and they both went over to talk to a boy who was sitting on a grey pony. I got a fright to find myself on my own, but nothing happened.

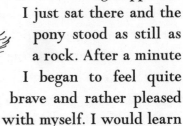

I just sat there and the pony stood as still as a rock. After a minute I began to feel quite brave and rather pleased with myself. I would learn to ride, I planned. Perhaps Frank would teach me, although of course Squirrel was far too small for me; my feet almost touched the ground. Still, it would be fun, I thought, and then I saw one of the red-coated gentlemen smiling at me. I smiled back before thinking and then I blushed. The gentleman didn't look away. I heard him say to the man next to him, 'Who's that pretty girl?' Then I did look away quickly and I didn't hear the reply, but when I looked back I saw that he

was still looking at me.
He smiled even more,
and then took off his
hat and half raised
his whip in a salute to
me. It was lucky that my
sister-in-law wasn't there.
She would have considered
it all very unladylike. The
man had a very handsome
horse though, a big black stal-
lion, and he had a hunting horn in his hand
so he must have been someone important in the hunt.
I wish my picture showed quite how splendid he
looked – I'm never satisfied with my drawings. I
showed it to Jane, who is writing away at her desk,
and she liked it, but I don't think I've made him
handsome enough.

'I wish I was allowed to go hunting,' said Charles
sadly as they all moved away, shouting and laughing.
They were a wonderful sight in the spring sunshine,
I thought, and I wasn't surprised that Charles was
upset not to be going too.

'You know that Squirrel is too old for hunting,'
said Jane. 'She'd drop down dead if you tried to gallop her or jump with her. You'll have to have a new
pony, and you know that Father can't afford to buy
you one.'

I told him he could ride her back home though, if

he liked, because it was downhill all the way to the house and I could easily walk that distance.

Charles was very grateful — he is such a nice boy. When he is happy, his grin seems to go from ear to ear.

As Jane and I walked slowly down the hill together I told her how lucky I thought she was to have brothers like Frank and Charles.

'And Henry,' said Jane. 'He'll be back at the weekend. Henry's my favourite brother. He's splendid; wait until you see him! Alethea Bigg told me that she is madly in love with him.'

I asked Jane to describe Henry again as I gazed over the fields in what I hoped was a nonchalant way. I wondered what Henry would think of me. Life was getting very exciting with all these young men around.

'He's very good-looking — tall and dark-haired,' Jane told me. 'Don't you remember? I told you that when you drew that picture of him.'

'Frank is different to the way I imagined him though. Is Henry as fine-looking as Frank?' I pretended to be looking at something in the hedge so that she wouldn't see me blush.

'Much, much better-looking.' Jane sounded quite scornful. 'And much, much taller. Frank's only a boy; Henry is a man. He's nineteen now. He's a year older than Cassandra. Why, you haven't fallen in love with Frank, have you? Why are you blushing?'

'No, of course I haven't fallen in love with Frank,'

I said indignantly, but I knew I was still blushing. I wish I didn't blush so easily. It's so silly. I remembered that gentleman at the hunt looking at me and I could feel my cheeks getting even warmer. I wondered whether he admired me. I wished that I was not so short and that I had a better nose.

I tried to distract Jane by asking her about the boy on the grey pony, and it worked.

'Oh, that's Tom Chute; I'm madly in love with him.' She didn't blush though, so I think it was just a joke.

Wednesday, 9 March 1791

Today was another good day. The weather was fine and sunny, but very frosty. Mr Austen and his students were working hard to make up for the loss to their studies from the day's hunting, so Jane and I went for a walk by ourselves.

It felt odd to be able to put on our bonnets and cloaks and just stroll out of the front door without saying a word to anyone. Back home, in Bristol, my mother never used to allow me out by myself, not even to a shop a few doors away from our house. She always had to accompany me, and as we had no gentleman in the house we could never go out once it became dark. And of course Augusta was so prim and proper that she didn't walk out without Edward-John or a servant to accompany her once evening came.

But here at Steventon, in the country, it was different. It was so lovely to be able to pick primroses and watch the birds building their nests. As we went down the laneway towards the church I told Jane how much I admired her house, especially the casement windows. I think they are much nicer than sash windows.

'It's a terrible old ruin of a place.' Jane had to make everything very dramatic. The house could have done with a coat of paint, inside as well as out, but it certainly wasn't a ruin.

'Why are we going to church?' I was surprised at Jane. On Sunday she had begged her mother to allow her to stay at home with me when the others went to church; when I had thanked her, she just told me that church bored her.

'Aha,' said Jane mysteriously. 'I am on the track of something.'

She didn't say any more until we reached the churchyard. Just next to the church door there was a huge yew tree. It looked immensely old — half its branches were broken off and its trunk was as big as a small tower.

'It's hollow inside.' Jane led me around the back and put her hand in. When she took it out she held a sheet of paper, sealed with a blob of sealing wax. She held it out to me.

'Guess who,' she said, pushing it under my nose.

It wasn't difficult. 'Tom Fowle,' I guessed. It was in a large bold hand, written on paper that looked torn from a notebook.

'I suspected this.' Jane was giggling. 'Every morning Cassandra writes a letter and then she makes some excuse to go to the church or to the village,  but she always goes down here. She and Tom Fowle are using this hollow tree as a letter box.'

I was a bit puzzled. I asked Jane why they didn't just hand them to each other – they must meet twenty times every day. Mr Austen's pupils live as if they are part of the family. We meet them at every meal and they are in the parlour every night, playing chess or cards, singing, dancing, or joking and laughing.

'My mother doesn't approve,' said Jane. 'It would be different if it were Gilbert. He's the son of a baronet. Tom has three older brothers; he'll be penniless. He wants to be a clergyman, but it will be years and years before he even has a parish. My father has a parish and a farm but we are still very poor. And Cassandra will have no money. There is no money for any of us. The boys will have to make their own way, but Cassandra and I can't go in the navy, or become clergymen, so we will have to marry money.' Jane sounded indifferent, but I could see how she kicked viciously at a clod of earth while she said, in the sort of high, scolding voice that sounded just like Mrs Austen, *Affection is desirable; money is essential.* And then her voice changed again, back to the usual joking tone. 'Shall we play a trick on them? Write something of our own and put it into the hollow tree instead?'

'Put the letter back.' I felt uneasy. Cassandra was the least friendly member of the Austen family. I didn't know whether it was that she thought I was a nuisance, or whether she didn't like me very much, but she seemed to look at me in a slightly sour way. I didn't want her to know that I had been spying on her.

'Let's go into the church then.' Jane tossed the letter back as if she was bored with the whole matter.

The church at Steventon was very old, much smaller and older than the churches at Bristol. There was no one there.

'Come on,' said Jane, seizing me by the hand. 'I know where Father keeps the forms for calling the banns. I love the idea of banns, don't you? You see, it might be that some wicked baronet is leading some poor innocent girl astray, pretending to be a young bachelor when really he has a mad wife locked away in the attic of his house. If they call the banns the chances are that one of the neighbours will jump up and say, "I know that Sir John Berkley and he is married to my first cousin." And then a ghastly pallor will come over Sir John's evil face and he will dash from the church, jump on his horse and ride away, while the gentle girl, Emma, will faint away into the arms of her cousin, who has secretly loved her for many years.' Jane, as usual, had to turn it all into a story while she was fishing out some pieces of printed paper from a cupboard in the vestry. I wondered what her father would say if he found her meddling with church property, but then I thought he would probably just laugh. He was very indulgent to Jane. She was, I guessed, his favourite in the family.

'Who do you want to marry?' she asked.

I told her that I didn't know, because I don't really know any gentlemen.

'I think I'll marry Tom Chute.' Already Jane had picked up a quill from a selection lying on the table, dipped it into the inkpot and begun to fill out the form.

The Form of an Entry of Publication of Banns

The Banns of Marriage
between . .Thomas Chute of the Vyne. . . . . .
And . . .Jane. Austen of Steventon . . . . .

were duly published in this Church for the first time,

on Sunday . . .Thirteenth . . . .
Day of . . . . .March. . . . .
in the Year of .Ninety-one. . . . .

I was going to ask who Tom Chute was, but I remembered that he was the boy on the grey pony who was teasing and joking with her outside the inn before the hunt. Then I asked what Jane knew about him and his family – I felt quite grown-up when I said that. It was true though. You couldn't just marry a man because he made good jokes.

'He lives at the big house called the Vyne. It's not too far from here. It's on the way to Basingstoke.'

'Have you known him for a long time? My mama always said that you should know a gentleman for at least a year before you allow him to pay addresses to you.' I said this jokingly. I was beginning to be able to mention my mother without tears coming to my eyes. I seemed to be living in such a different world now, a world of noise and jokes and boys flying around laughing and talking.

'No, I only met him a few months ago. He will soon come into a large estate and the Vyne. We will probably dine there one evening, so you will see for yourself.'

'How old is he?'

'He's sixteen, just a bit older than me.'

I wasn't sure that you could really come into a large estate when you were only sixteen, but Jane always has an answer for everything.

'Yes, of course you can . . . oh, well, it's his eldest brother really, but he's sickly and cross so Tom will inherit when William dies. I can't stand William. He's always trying to make mock of me. Luckily he lacks the wit to do it with any sense.'

'What does William look like?'

'You saw him yesterday, at Deane. Do you remember the man on the black stallion, the one holding the horn?'

I was glad that it was quite dark in the little vestry so that she wouldn't see me blushing. Then I started to laugh. I told Jane that I didn't think he looked sickly or cross and that I would marry him and then I'd be the one with the big house and the large estate. I told her she could come and stay with me and I'd find her a young man to marry.

'In possession of a large fortune, I hope,' said Jane primly, as I seized the quill and began to fill in another banns form – like this:

The Form of an Entry of Publication of Banns

The Banns of Marriage
between *William Chute of the Vyne*
And *Jenny Cooper of Steventon*

were duly published in this Church for the first time,
on Sunday *Thirteenth*
Day of *March*
in the Year of *Ninety-one*

'What about Captain Williams though? Dear, dear, dear, Jenny, what a sad flirt you are – going from one young man to another.' Jane made her voice sound just like Mrs Cawley at the school.

I told her immediately that I didn't even want to think about Captain Williams because he could ruin my reputation forever. Jane nodded wisely and said, 'Very true!' twice.

I would do my best not to think of Captain Williams – not even when I was in bed at night, I decided as we went home, slipping and sliding on the frozen puddles of the lane.

After dinner all the boys decided to have a game of cricket. The ground was hard with frost but the sun was still warm and Mrs Austen said that I could go out if I wrapped up warmly.

'You can bowl, Jane.' To my surprise John Warren handed her the ball. I had thought that we would just be watching, but Frank was sending me up to the top of the field with instructions to throw the ball to Jane if it came anywhere near to me.

Tom Fowle was first to bat and I saw Cassandra come out and stand where she could see him and smile shyly at him. I felt quite sorry for her, though she wasn't very friendly to me.

I was so interested in watching the
two of them that it was only when
everyone started shrieking 'Jenny!'
that I realized that the ball was
actually at my feet.

Frank, the captain of our team, was very nice to
me. He said that I probably wasn't well yet, so he
sent Charles up to help me in my part of the field.

We had almost finished the game and Tom Fowle
was fielding when Frank hit the ball a tremendous
whack so it went right over towards a row of poplars
on the far side of the field. One
minute we could see Tom running
after the ball, and the next there
was no sign of him. It was Cassandra
who realized first that something was
wrong. She gave a shriek of 'Tom!' and then she set
off running across the field. Jane and I followed and the
others came behind. Tom Fowle was stretched out on
the ground, his head pouring blood, and the colour
was completely drained from his normally healthy-
looking face. His eyes were shut.

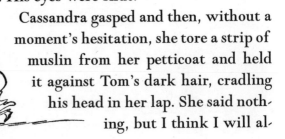

Cassandra gasped and then, without a
moment's hesitation, she tore a strip of
muslin from her petticoat and held
it against Tom's dark hair, cradling
his head in her lap. She said nothing, but I think I will al-

ways remember what she looked like in those few minutes before Mr Austen came running up and Tom opened his eyes.

'Slipped on a piece of ice,' said Gilbert nonchalantly. 'You all right, Tom, old son?'

'Cassandra, get up off that wet grass,' scolded Mrs Austen as she came puffing up the field. By this stage Tom had sat up, but Mrs Austen's eyes went immediately to Cassandra's torn petticoat, to the blood-stained strip of muslin around Tom's head and to her daughter's stricken face. Cassandra didn't even glance at her mother. All her attention was on Tom, and her whole soul was in her eyes as she tenderly stroked his hand. It was true love, Jane and I agreed afterwards — no one, remarked Jane wisely, would ruin a good petticoat for a man unless they loved him.

It's bedtime now and I should be asleep, but I can't sleep. My candle was blown out about an hour ago by Mrs Austen when she came in to say goodnight. I just lay tossing and turning for half an hour. Jane was asleep so I could think my own thoughts. At the moment everything in my mind seemed to be about falling in love and getting married. I was thinking of Cassandra and Tom Fowle and how she had looked when she thought he was injured. I thought about the two of them a lot, of the way they kept looking at each other – during meals, when they passed each other on the stairs, when they danced together in the evenings. And then I thought of the handsome William Chute, sitting on his black stallion with the hunting horn in his hand. It's the first time, really, that I seriously thought about falling in love.

In the end I got out of bed and came to sit by the fire with my journal on my knee. There is enough light from the fire to write by. So I've written down the bit about Cassandra and about the fun that Jane and I had in the church, filling out the forms for calling the banns.

But in a few years this will all be very serious for us.

I will have to find a husband.

And it will have to be a rich husband, if Mrs Austen is right.

After all, my mother was much poorer than Jane's

father, who is rector of a parish and has a large farm. I know that she only left fifty pounds a year for my maintenance. Edward-John won't want to give me anything when I marry — even if he did, Augusta wouldn't allow him.

I will have no fortune, so who will marry me?

Jane was telling me about a girl who lived near to one of her cousins. This girl was aged barely sixteen when she ran away with an army captain. According to Jane, she was attracted by the soldier's red coat! When her relations caught up with her, the couple had already been living together as man and wife so there was nothing to be done except to get them married as soon as possible.

I just can't imagine!

Thursday, 10 March 1791

It's nice sharing a bedroom with Jane. Cassandra and Jane used to share it, but now Cassandra has her own bedroom as James has left home. I like sharing with Jane; it is good fun to be able to chat together. We stayed awake so late last night, talking and joking – and even after that I had got out of bed and written in my journal – so this morning we both woke up late, and had barely enough time to wash our faces and just smooth our hair before running down to breakfast.

After breakfast I asked Jane to come and help me to brush my hair and said I would do hers for her after that. My mother always said that to have nice hair you had to give it one hundred strokes of the brush twice every day.

When we got to our bedroom, Jane started doing an imitation of her mother scolding the butcher.

'*I really cannot think, Mr Baxter, that you can know what you're talking about. How anyone could pretend to be a butcher and sell those pieces of scrap meat for gigot chops, I declare to goodness, I just do not know. These were no more gigot chops than I am a donkey. Do I look like a donkey, Mr Baxter?*'

I asked Jane why she did not like her mama. There is something about the way she imitates her mother that makes me feel a little uncomfortable.

'She's not my mother,' said Jane, and her voice was all sort of hissy and low. 'My real mother has been imprisoned in a lonely castle hundreds of miles away. She's been locked up there since I was born. That woman's just my stepmother.'

'What?!' I said, and I must have screamed it because Jane put her hand over my mouth.

'Shh,' she said mysteriously. 'Terrible things can happen in this house. Haven't you read Mrs Parson's book *The Mysterious Warning*? Did you hear that creak last night at midnight? And those footsteps coming slowly up the stairs? Did you hear a dripping sound?'

In a way I found it funny, but in another way I felt uncomfortable. It wasn't really like one of Jane's weird stories where you can tell that, inside, she is finding it all just as funny as you are. Jane actually sounded bitter when she spoke of her mother. I tried to think of something to divert her.

I reminded Jane that since her mother is my aunt — and my mother's sister — then she couldn't possibly be Jane's stepmother. As if my mother would have kept that piece of family news from me! I said all of this in a joking tone of voice. I hoped that she would laugh, but she didn't. She just kept on brushing my hair until she had finished the hundred strokes.

'Ah, mothers don't very often tell their daughters the truth.' Jane's voice sounded sort of hollow. I twisted round again and saw that she was laughing now and I laughed too, with relief. I brushed her hair and then there was the sound of the kitchen door opening.

'Jane, Jenny, come and do your drawing lesson!' Mrs Austen sounded impatient, so we rushed down. She was standing tapping her foot in the parlour. She had promised my brother and sister-in-law that we would do some lessons every day, but really the poor woman had hardly any time for us. She had to look after the pupils' meals and clothing, see to the dairy and the butter making, the vegetables and the baking, and supervise the servants and the monthly washwoman. In reality, she did not have the time to tutor us also. She tried to get Cassandra to take over our education, but Jane argued so much that Cassandra had refused to have anything to do with teaching us. Now Mrs Austen just told us to draw a farm and then she left the room.

I did my best, but Jane did her worst, on purpose. Mrs Austen was not pleased when she came flying in half an hour later. We hadn't done much as we had been discussing Tom and William Chute.

'Jane, your cow looks like a pig and your ducks look like hens,' she scolded. 'You can just sit there and rub it out and do it again and again until you show some improvement. I declare, I'm quite ashamed of you! Now what is that Betty Dawkins doing with those sheets? I declare to the Lord, she is trailing them on the yard. She must be the worst washerwoman I've ever had.'

And then she went running out of the door, and when we looked out of the window we saw her flying across the yard with her pattens clicking on the muddy cobbles.

I went on with my cow, shading it very carefully. Jane's mama scared me a little. My own mother never used to scold like that all the time. Still, I liked Mrs Austen much better than I liked Augusta, and she was a very busy woman, so it was not surprising that she found Jane a bit of a trial. My mother only had me to look after – not a whole household of about twenty people.

I tried to keep my mind on my drawing and keep the thoughts of my mother out of my head. It worked best like that, I found.

'Look, Jenny!' Jane had been rubbing out, but she had made her cow look worse – now it looked like a real pig with a curly tail and a lot of little piglets in a long line behind it. There was a balloon coming out of one piglet's mouth and it said, *'Mother's cross.'*

'You'd better rub that out,' I said, but Jane is stubborn.

'No, I won't,' she said. 'I think that piglet looks like a little cherub. I'll give him wings.'

And then Mrs Austen came in, red-faced and very cross, and when she saw the drawing she got crosser than ever.

'Jenny, you go up to your room and read a book until I call you. Jane, come with me. I am going to speak to your father about you.'

Jane came in just as I was drawing a picture of Tom Chute. She looked quite normal and she hadn't been crying, so I didn't think that her father was too annoyed with her.

'That's pretty good,' she said, examining the picture. 'Give me your pencil.'

I handed over the pencil and she put whiskers on Tom's face. 'Imagine kissing a man with whiskers,' she said, and we both giggled. I was glad that I hadn't drawn the picture of William yet. I wouldn't have liked that to be spoiled.

'Anyway, the rain has stopped now and I have to go and draw a picture of our house,' said Jane. 'That's the punishment that my father gave me. *I suppose even Jane can draw a house.*' She imitated her mother's high, scolding voice exactly.

I said that I would help her as I didn't want her to get into any more trouble; when Jane is in that sort of mood she gets more and more sarcastic and I get worried about what she might do or say next.

There was no sign of Mrs Austen when we went out and stood in the carriage sweep, so I took the drawing pad from Jane. It would be easier to do the picture myself.

'Four diamond-paned windows downstairs and a door with a porch in front of it in the middle, and five windows upstairs and then three garret windows in the roof,' said Jane, peering over my shoulder. 'Don't forget the two sets of chimneys on each side of the roof. Hurry up; don't fuss. I want to go and do something more interesting.'

I wished that she would leave me alone because she was making me nervous, but I didn't want to suggest that she should go and feed the hens and leave me in peace to finish drawing the house. If Mrs Austen came out now I could hand the drawing quickly to Jane, but if she was not there then I would be in trouble too, and I hate being scolded.

As I shaded the eight-paned windows I asked Jane if she minded being scolded.

'No, why should I? They're all so stupid. I just make up jokes when my mother is scolding me, and then I mimic her to the boys. It's lucky that the boys are here. They are such fun. I like Tom Fowle the best. Last year he pulled me down the three flights of stairs on a tablecloth.'

'I thought you liked Tom Chute.' I determined that no one would pull me down the stairs on a tablecloth. I could understand my mother pitying Mrs Austen. The boys are quite noisy and they do make a lot of work in the house, running in and out in muddy boots. This is a very different school to Mrs Cawley's Seminary for Young Ladies. I suppose the Austens and my brother thought they were sending us to a place that would be like another home for us, because they imagined it would be like Steventon.

'Oh, I'm going to marry Tom Chute and I'll leave Tom Fowle for Cassandra,' said Jane carelessly. 'Why don't you draw one of the casement windows open and Mama shouting out of it at someone? That's the way our house is usually. Give me the pencil and I'll draw her.'

'No, don't, you'll spoil it.' I turned away from her and began to mark in the roof tiles. I hated to rush a drawing, but Jane was in a wild mood and I thought I'd better get it finished quickly. I needn't make it too good; Jane was much cleverer than me, but I was better at drawing.

'You do the front door,' I said, handing the board to her when I had finished the roof. The drawing looked quite nice and I hated to have it spoiled, but I thought it was better that she should be doing something. Any minute now she would get bored and would be off climbing a tree or something. And then her mother would look out of the window and be furious. Jane was funny. One minute she was talking about love and marriage, and the next she was behaving like some sort of boy.

I told Jane not to forget to put nine windows in the top half of the door, trying to sound bossy.

Jane had finished the door in one minute and then went flying into her father's study to give the drawing to him. The sun was coming out so I went to fetch my bonnet. My mother always told me that I should keep the sun off my face or my complexion would get brown.

'Let's go down to the village,' said Jane as soon as she came out. 'We won't need to wear pattens because the ground is hard with all the frost. I hate wet, dull springs, don't you? And I really hate wearing pattens.'

I agreed with her. I certainly dislike wearing pattens too. I hate the way your foot is up so high and your ankle twists.

The road to the village was still nice and dry. Our feet stayed clean and I didn't get any mud on my petticoat. It was a lovely afternoon, with the hedges ornamented with tiny snow-white buds of blackthorn and curling strands of bright green woodbine and the ditches lined with white and yellow daffodils. I've drawn them here in my journal. They would make a lovely picture in watercolours.

Steventon village is a poor sort of place. I suppose there are about thirty cottages there and they all look a bit dirty and wretched. Jane seemed to know most people and even teased a girl called Bet about seeing her with Mr Austen's bailiff.

And then a boy came up to us. I didn't know how old he was, but he was strange-looking. He was very small, as small as an eleven-year-old perhaps, but his face was older. He looked very odd as he came shambling up to us making a strange noise in the back of his throat, just like a cock crowing, with his left hand jerking around as if he had no control over it. I got a terrible fright and jumped back, but he kept coming. He was making for Jane. I was very scared. It looked as if he was going to attack her. And then he sort of threw himself at her. I looked all around, seeking help, but no one seemed to be taking any notice. Two women were drawing water from a well, another was herding her ducks to the pond and Bet, the girl that Jane had joked with, was picking up a little boy who had fallen over.

But Jane didn't seem worried. She was laughing. And then she put her arms round him. She kissed him. 'George,' she kept saying. 'What's the matter, George? Look, here's Jenny come to see you.'

And then she turned around. I was still scared, but I tried not to show it.

'I'm pleased to meet you, George,' I said primly.

'Jenny is your cousin, George,' said Jane, and the boy made his strange crowing noises.

I didn't know what to think. How could this boy be my cousin? My mother had only one sister – Jane's mother – and only one brother who had no children, and my father came from a different part of the country.

Jane had her arm around the boy. She was looking into his face lovingly and then she turned and looked at me. She wore an odd, defiant expression.

'George is my brother, Jenny,' she said quietly.

I'm not sure what I said or how I looked. I remember stammering something stupid like, 'Pleased to meet you, George,' again, but my mind was in a whirl. How could this boy be Jane's brother? I had never heard of him, and he didn't live at Jane's house.

And then I began to feel a bit ashamed of myself, standing there so stiffly and awkwardly. I saw George look at me and I hoped that he could not read my thoughts. Jane was talking to him as though he were a small child, so, on the impulse of a moment, I bent down and picked three tiny wild daffodils and handed them to him.

I think he was a bit puzzled by them, turning them round and round in his hand.

I was glad that I had done it though, because Jane smiled with that lovely smile she has when she is pleased, and then George smiled and then he handed the flowers to Jane and she smelt them and then he smelt them and sneezed, and Jane laughed at the expression on his face and then he laughed and I laughed too.

And the three of us just stood there in the evening sunshine until the girl Bet came up and took George by the hand and led him away, telling him it was time for his supper, and Jane and I were left together.

What could I say?

Even now I am not sure what would have been the right thing to say.

You see, dear journal, I didn't want to hurt Jane's feelings. A thousand questions jumped into my mind, but I didn't want to say anything like, 'How on earth could George be your brother?' or, 'Why is he not living in your house?' or, 'Why has his name never been mentioned?'

Jane said nothing, just stood there looking at me with an odd expression on her face. In the end I just said — and I said it as carelessly as I could, just as though I were talking about Charles or Frank — 'Isn't it funny the way that boys never appreciate flowers?'

And then we both laughed again and Jane said, 'Race you back to the gates.' And we both ran in the frosty air until we were breathless.

When we stopped, Jane slipped her hand inside my arm. I didn't say anything for a moment, but then I asked her whether she wanted to talk about George, but she just shook her head so I didn't say any more.

When we came back from seeing George, Tom Chute was here, chatting with Frank about shooting the crows that were robbing the seed corn from his father's farm. He called out a cheerful greeting to

Jane and she teased him about his coat; I gathered it was a new one, but Jane was pretending that he had robbed a scarecrow for it. I went on ahead of her into the house – I was still a bit shy of all the joking and teasing that went on between Jane and the neighbouring boys.

Mrs Austen was in the hall and she had an invitation card in her hand and a smile on her face, but she waited until Jane came in before showing us the card.

'The Chutes are having a supper dance at the Vyne on Saturday.' She looked quite excited. Mrs Austen loved a dance. When we rolled up the carpet in the evening and the boys danced with Cassandra, Jane and myself, she played the piano, but sometimes Cassandra took over and her mother partnered with someone like Gilbert East or Tom Fowle, looking as if she was really enjoying herself. I must say that for her age she danced in a very sprightly fashion.

'A supper dance!' I could hardly breathe with excitement. Mrs Austen smiled at the look on my face and Jane took hold of both my hands and whirled me round the hall until we were both dizzy.

Friday, 11 March 1791

Something very exciting happened today. Just before supper Jane was looking out of the window and she gave a shriek.

'A donkey! Oh, a lovely donkey! Frank's got a donkey!'

'What?!' Mr Austen got out of his chair. 'He hasn't broken the knees of his new pony!'

'No, he's riding the pony. He's just leading the donkey.' Jane rushed out and I went with her and the rest of the family followed.

'It's for Jenny,' Frank said when he dismounted. 'William Chute gave it to me. He said that Jenny could learn to ride on a donkey. He said that . . .' Here Frank frowned a bit, but then said gruffly, 'He said, "She's a bit shy and nervous, that pretty little cousin of yours. She'll be better with a donkey until she gets a bit of confidence."'

I blushed, but no one took any notice. They were too busy inspecting the donkey, stroking him, looking at his feet, passing hands down his back and estimating how old he was by looking at his teeth. Mrs Austen gave me a sharp, appraising sort of glance – rather like the way that everyone was appraising the donkey, I thought – but no one else seemed to find it strange that a young man should send a present like that to a girl he hardly knows.

* * *

After supper when Jane and I were clearing away the plates Mrs Austen came in, closing the door behind her with a firm bang. Jane raised her eyebrows and said, 'Uh-oh,' under her breath.

'Jenny dear, it was very kind of William Chute to send you a donkey, and I suppose you may keep it, but in general it's not a good idea for a young girl to accept presents from a young man who is not related to her, unless, of course, they are engaged to be married.' Mrs Austen's speech came out in her usual rush of words.

I felt my cheeks turning scarlet with embarrassment.

'A donkey!' said Jane contemptuously. 'Who cares about a donkey? It's not as if he sent her an Arabian mare. Donkeys are two a penny around here.'

'Now, Jane,' said Mrs Austen crossly, 'don't be ridiculous. I'm talking about the propriety of accepting a present from a young man. Young girls like you two have to be immensely careful of your reputation. Nothing scares off a good matrimonial proposal like rumours about a girl being fast.' She lowered her voice to a hissing whisper. 'Men talk together in card rooms and drinking places about girls like that.'

I told her that I didn't mind giving it back. I could hear my voice shaking. Her words made me wonder what she would say if she knew I had walked alone at night with a strange young man through the streets of Southampton. I could even feel my ears burning as I thought of how he had looked at me so gently with his beautiful brown eyes and how he took my hand and tucked it through his arm. Would Captain Thomas Williams talk about me in card rooms and drinking places?

Mrs Austen was looking at me so piercingly that I was afraid that she could read my thoughts. I could feel tears welling up in my eyes.

'You're upsetting Jenny,' said Jane. 'Anyway, if you send the donkey back you make a big fuss of the whole thing.'

Mrs Austen turned her attention from me to Jane. She took a deep breath and I thought she was furiously angry, but then she surprised me by saying, 'I suppose that might be true. Well, I'll get Mr Austen to write a note to William Chute thanking him for the donkey and saying that the two girls will enjoy it. In that way it will divert attention from Jenny. Don't be upset, dear. I have to tell you these things since your poor mother is not here to do it – it's just for your own good. You know it is important for you, as well as for Jane and Cassandra, to get a good offer of marriage.'

And then she was gone, whirling from the room, and we could hear her shouting to the kitchen maid about cleaning out the fire in the breakfast parlour.

'Anyway, she's going to get a bit of a shock about Cassandra,' said Jane, her lips curling in amusement. 'Guess what, Miss Goody-Two-Shoes Cassandra has a little looking glass in her cabinet that I've seen her kissing.

What's the betting that Tom Fowle gave it to her?'

I dried my eyes and laughed. 'And I kissed the donkey earlier. Don't tell your mother that!'

Tonight Jane told me about George.

I had been waiting since yesterday for her to tell me, but I didn't want to push her.

And this was the way our conversation went. It was like a play. It was beginning to get dark, but I didn't light my candle. Jane sat on the window seat — one of those windows that I drew yesterday. As she spoke she played with the catch and sometimes opened and closed the window softly, like someone idly swinging a door. I sat on the bed and watched her face. I could see her because there was still some light, but she couldn't see my face because I was in the shadows.

'You see,' said Jane, 'George was born like that. He was born with something wrong with him.'

I watched the way her mouth tightened and her eyes filled with tears.

'Go on, say something,' she said fiercely.

I couldn't think what to say, and in the end I just asked her why it was such a secret.

'Because my mother is ashamed of him, that's why.' Jane's voice hissed like it does when she is reading out a story about a villain. And then when I said nothing she said impatiently, 'Well, go on, ask me why my mother is ashamed of George.'

I could guess why, but I asked the question all the same.

'Because she cares about money more than anything else! She wants all the boys to be rich and famous and she wants Cassandra and me to marry men with big estates. At least she has hopes for Cassandra — she's pretty and accomplished. If only she can keep her from marrying Tom Fowle, Cassandra might make a splendid match. I don't think she has much hope for me. If I can't even draw a cow, she can hardly say that I am accomplished, can she? And I'm not very pretty either, am I? My cheeks are too red and my mouth is too small.'

I told Jane I thought she was very pretty and that she has a much better nose than I have, but she wasn't listening to me. Her cheeks were bright red now, and her eyes were glittering. I felt like crying. I didn't know what to do.

'How old is George?' I asked. 'Is he younger than you?'

Jane shook her head. 'No, he's older than Henry and older than Edward — wonderful Edward who managed to get a rich cousin to adopt him. That's one of us off our mother's hands.' She was nearly spitting out the words. 'Now she doesn't have to bother about Edward and she can boast about him. That makes her forget that one of her children is deformed and can't speak or read or write. She tells everyone that she has five boys and two girls. I think that she even manages to convince herself of that sometimes.'

'Is that why you pretended she was your step-mother?' I felt very sorry for Jane. Sometimes I feel as if she is older than me, but now she seemed like a little sister who was upset because she was hurt. I went across, sat beside her on the window seat, put my arms around her and gave her a hug.

'I wish she *were* my stepmother.' Jane's voice was choked, as if she wanted to cry but was not allowing herself. She pulled away from me and stood with her back turned. Her voice was hoarse and choked when she said, 'If she were my stepmother, it wouldn't matter that I hate her.'

'But George is definitely your brother, your real brother?' I tried to sound sort of casual, but I had to know the truth. For a moment I wondered if this was just one of Jane's stories. Perhaps she had seen this poor unfortunate in the village and had made up the tale because she was sorry for him.

'Of course he's my brother. I've got six brothers, not five.'

And then Jane ran from the room and slammed the door. I heard her running down the stairs. I guessed that she was going into the privy at the back of the house and that she would lock herself in there until she finished crying.

And I've written all this in my journal. Now I'm going to lock it and I am going to hang the key around my neck.

Saturday, 12 March 1791

Today was a day that I am never going to forget in my life. I have never had a day like it. It all started at breakfast time, when Mr Austen looked up from his book and asked, 'Who's going to walk up to Deane Gate Inn to meet James and Henry from the Newbury coach?'

'I'm going riding with Harry Digweed,' said Frank.

'What about you, Jane and Jenny? Will you go?'

'Yes, let's, shall we, Jenny?' Jane sounded enthusiastic. I was glad to see that she looked herself this morning. I nodded happily. It was very exciting meeting people off the stagecoach. I even enjoyed going with Jane to collect the letters from Deane Gate Inn.

'I'll come too then,' said Frank, suddenly changing his mind. 'Harry won't mind what time I arrive. His mother can never get him out of bed in the morning.'

'And me,' said Charles.

'You'd better wash your face first,' said Jane smartly.

'Dear, dear, look who's talking,' said Mrs Austen, but she was smiling as she said it. She was in a very good mood. She was excited that James — her favourite son, according to Jane — was coming for a visit. She hadn't seen him for months. I gathered that James studied very hard, unlike Henry, who, apparently, liked to amuse himself and to attend every ball in the neighbourhood.

The coach was late, so we needn't have hurried. When it arrived we saw James and Henry sitting up in front beside the driver. They were glad to get down and to walk with us. They said they were frozen as they had set off in the early morning, but they were both in very good spirits. I had a good look at them so that I could compare their likenesses with the pictures in my journal.

And this is what they look like. They are both quite tall and they both had greatcoats, which they took off and slung over their bags as they walked along. James has the small thin nose and pale skin of his father and he has blond hair — I don't know the colour of Mr Austen's hair because he is always wearing a wig. Henry is quite like Jane in appearance, dark-haired and dark-eyed. Both were dressed in the same way, in well-fitting white trousers, a blue coat with a stand-up velvet collar, and a white shirt with a

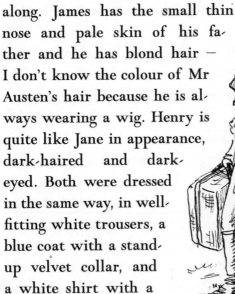

high stock tied round the neck in a loose bow. They both wore their own hair and they wore it quite long, almost touching their shoulders. I've tried to do a picture here of them and I think it's quite good.

Henry gave Jane a great hug when he descended. She is obviously his favourite. Jane was so excited to see him and straight away started to tell him about all of her latest stories. James wasn't so interested in her. I thought I liked Henry better than James. He was very friendly to me and paid me some compliments, telling me how well I looked and that he liked my cloak and that the blue bonnet suited me.

'I've decided on a play for our end-of-team taster production, Frank,' said James, as we all went at a brisk pace down the hill. 'It's Sheridan's *The Rivals*. There are parts for everybody in it and I've written a prologue and an epilogue. I've been in touch with Cousin Eliza and she has promised to be Mrs Malaprop.'

'She will be excellent, won't she, Frank?' Henry had an amused grin. I thought he was probably like Jane in his sense of humour as well as in appearance. 'No one can be as funny as Eliza.'

'And Cassandra will be Lydia.'

'Then you'll have to have Tom Fowle as Captain Jack Absolute,' said Henry with a little of his mother's decisiveness. 'Tom's not much of an actor, bless him, but he will play the part of a lover of Lydia very well indeed.'

So everyone knows the secret about Tom Fowle and Cassandra, I thought. It was highly unlikely that Mrs Austen didn't know it also.

'What about me and Jenny?' asked Jane. James was definitely not Jane's favourite brother, I thought. Her voice was quite sharp.

'Well, I'd forgotten about Jenny, but I thought you might be the maid,' said James carelessly. Even though he is quite handsome, I didn't think he was as nice as Henry.

'Who's going to act the part of Julia, then?' Jane sounded quite pert and James clicked his tongue disapprovingly at her.

'Don't say that Father has allowed you to read *The Rivals*,' he said with a stern look. 'I must say that I think he should supervise your reading. There are parts that are quite shocking. I've cut them out of our production.' He sounded so prim when he said that, and Jane made such a comical face, that I found it hard to hold in a fit of the giggles.

'Dear, dear,' said Henry with a wink at Jane. 'She's got a point though, James. Who is going to be Julia?'

I was looking at Henry with interest because I remembered Jane saying that he was her favourite brother. She was right – he was very handsome – taller than William Chute, although he was years younger. He saw me looking at him and gave me a very wide smile and a quick wink. I looked away quickly; I could feel one of my embarrassing blushes coming on.

'I thought of Frank.' James gave his young brother a sidelong glance. 'He could wear one of mother's old gowns.'

'Well, you can think again.' Frank sounded quite alarmed. 'My voice is broken now.' He was so upset that his voice rose and cracked and he turned very red. James looked dubiously at him and I had to bite my lip to stop myself from laughing. There was no way that Frank, with his breaking voice and moustache fluff around his upper lip, could pass for a girl.

'Perhaps Charles then. And I will be Sir Anthony Absolute, the wealthy baronet.' James smiled to him-self; his good humour had come back. He seemed to fancy the part of a baronet.

'What about Jenny for the part of Julia? Wouldn't she be lovely?' enquired Henry. 'Are you good at faint-ing, Jenny?'

I said that I wasn't. I remember that I almost shouted it. Or perhaps it was more like a squeak. I definitely didn't want to act in a play and I didn't think that I would be able to faint. I said that they should let Jane be Julia and I would be the maid.

'No, Jenny will be perfect as Julia,' said Henry. 'I'm going to be Faulkland and I am madly in love with you. Don't worry, Jenny. I'll help you to learn your words. We'll make a great pair.'

I didn't say any more after that. I liked the idea of

Henry helping me to learn my part in the play. And I quite liked the idea of him pretending to be in love with me.

'What do I have to say as the maid?' demanded Jane.

'Not much,' said James. He was frowning. I felt a bit uncomfortable. I think that he didn't like all his arrangements being upset.

'I'll make some more up then. I'll make up something funny. The maid could be made very amusing,' said Jane.

'And I don't mind being a servant or something,' offered Frank.

'In fact, you'll do anything as long as you don't have to wear a dress; it wouldn't do for the sailors on board the good ship *Perseverance* to find out about that,' joked Henry.

'By the way, Frank,' said James carelessly, 'I was down in Southampton with the two Portsmouths, Newton and Coulson, and they took me on board one of *Perseverance*'s sister ships, I think it was the *Bonaventure*. The captain gave us dinner, and I must say I thought it was a very smart, well-run ship.'

'What's his name?' asked Frank. He was always intensely interested in anything to do with the navy. He was always talking to me about it. That must be where I had heard the name *Bonaventure* – it seemed familiar to me.

'Oh . . .' James snapped his fingers with the air of

a man who has a lot to think of. 'One of those ordinary names: Thompson – Jameson – Williamson – no, it was Williams, Captain Thomas Williams. Come to think of it, I almost forgot' – he turned to me and I could feel the palms of my hands icy with cold sweat – 'yes, he knows Jenny – at least, when I told him that I lived at Steventon, he asked me whether I had a cousin called Jenny Cooper.'

It was amazing that he couldn't hear the thumping of my heart – that they could not all hear it. The beats sounded so loud to me that I even expected the mare and foal who were cropping the grass in the field over the hedge to lift their heads and stare at me.

'How many guns had she, James?' I began to be able to breathe a little again when Frank asked that question. I clutched Jane's hand, and when she squeezed mine back I knew that she understood the danger I was in.

'I don't know – I never looked.' James sounded bored with the whole subject, but he was still half looking over his shoulder as if waiting for me to say something. I stared fixedly at the star-like shape of a tiny golden celandine on the opposite side of the road. Jane let go of my hand and moved up next to her eldest brother. I dug my nails into the soft part below my thumbs while I listened to her.

97

'James, I don't want to be just a maid. Why can't I be Mrs Malaprop? I could do it just as well as Eliza. Why do you have to be the one giving the orders all the time? Why can't we all choose our favourite parts?' Jane had a very petulant tone and now no one was looking at me.

'Well, you can't, and that's that! The trouble with you, Jane, is that you always think that you can get your own way. I agree with Mother. It's time that you started to behave like a young lady, not a spoiled child. Aren't you supposed to be in school or something?'

'My dear man, I'm too busy with my writing for things like school,' said Jane primly. 'I am just about to embark on writing a play in three acts, which I shall dedicate to you, James, and I hope that it will make you ashamed of your ill-temper to such a talented person as myself.'

Even James had to laugh at that, and then Henry took his arm and began asking his advice about a new horse that he was going to buy from John Portal, one of the neighbours. James, of course, had plenty of advice to give, and Jane and I gradually got further and further and further to the rear of them as we lingered to pick some primroses.

'Oh, Jane,' I said, when we went up to our bedroom to wash our hands, 'what will I do? Do you think that Captain Williams has told James all about me?'

'No, I don't think so.' Jane dried her hands on the

towel by the fire and tipped the water into a pail below the washstand. She looked quite calm when she turned round and I began to feel a little better. 'No, I'm certain that he didn't. James would have looked quite different. He's a very fussy, pernickety sort of man, but he didn't even seem very interested. If he had heard anything like that he would have been on to Mama instantly with a big, long, pompous letter and when he met you he would have looked at you like this.' And Jane tilted her nose in the air and looked down it with such a self-important and haughty manner that I had to smile.

I smoothed out the soft petals of the primroses and shut them between the leaves of an old book, and began to feel hopeful that Thomas had not told James how we met, and I asked Jane if she agreed.

'Thomas!' teased Jane. 'Oh, so he's Thomas! Don't you know that it is considered very fast for a young lady to use the first name of a young man? My dear creature, you quite make me blush!'

Jane could always make me laugh, but I pleaded with her to tell me what to say if James asked me about Thomas in front of his parents. I couldn't imagine Mrs Austen being diverted by Frank's questions about gun ports.

'You could say, "La, my dear cousin, my acquaintance is with admirals, vice-admirals, rear admirals, all kinds of admirals, but as for the inferior ranks I know little: post-captains may be very good sorts of men, but to tell you the truth, I don't know one from the other.""

She made me giggle, but I begged her to think of something that would be believed by her mother. I was feeling much better though. It did look as if Thomas had said nothing about meeting me at midnight. I promised myself that I would have a look at his portrait in my journal and see whether I could make him even more handsome. I would stick the primroses into my journal once they were pressed and I would think of him every time that I looked at them.

'Or you could just open your eyes very wide and say, "I'm not sure, Aunt. Perhaps he was one of Augusta's visitors." Don't worry about blushing – you often do blush when my mother asks you a question. Now let's go down and see if there's any toast left. I'm hungry again after the walk.'

As soon as James and Henry had had breakfast, we all went out into the barn where the play was going to take place. I could see that they had set plays there before because there were some pieces of old furniture, carefully covered over with straw, and a pair of old curtains were in a box at the back. Henry started to paint the scenery on big pieces of board, and Jane and I were set to work sweeping the stage while Charles and Tom Fowle put out some benches for the audience.

'I've got some small parts for the Terry children and for the Digweed boys,' said James.

'Just so that their parents will come to watch your play,' said Jane. 'That should build up the audience numbers – otherwise we might just have our dear parents and no one else.' I thought that was quite funny and I giggled, and then I was sorry because I thought James looked cross.

'Why don't you read the play to us while we're working, James,' said Henry, starting to paint a blue sky across the top of the board. The lime wash wasn't quite dry, but he worked some white into clouds and it made the blue sort of hazy and the sky looked very realistic. I told him that I thought it was very clever and he gave me a lovely smile and told me that the play was set in Bath so he was going to do two sets of scenery, one outside the houses in the Crescent and one drawing-room scene.

'Well, this is Jenny's bit.' James gave me a fright. I didn't know that I would be called upon to say any-thing so soon. I had a feeling that James wanted me to be useless so that he could cast someone else. My mouth was dry and I could say nothing. He frowned a bit and then he said the words again and looked at me impatiently. Henry repeated them in a very high-pitched voice and that made everyone laugh so I relaxed a bit and repeated the sentence.

Then James read Jane's bit. It was just, '*Yes, madam.*' Jane didn't like that and she put in a funny bit about hiding the book that I had been reading and getting out a boring book by Dr Johnson instead.

'Oh, why not,' said Henry when James objected. 'It's quite amusing.' So Jane went on putting in funny bits and by the end of a quarter of an hour her part was bigger than mine.

'Now you must say this in a very weak tone of voice, Jenny,' ordered James. 'Say, "*I think that I am about to faint.*"'

I repeated the words but they didn't satisfy James. 'Your voice must be weak but clear,' he objected. 'You'll never be heard in the back row if you speak like that.'

'We haven't got a back row,' shouted Charles, 'and we're not having one either, because I'm going out now. I promised to help John Bond with marking the new lambs.'

'Try it again, Jenny,' said Henry, busily putting the finishing touches to a stately house.

I tried again, but I knew by the frown on James's face that he didn't think much of it.

'Now, Jane, you say, "*Oh, my dear mistress has fainted.*"'

'That's boring,' objected Jane. 'In any case, the audience can see – even the back row, if there's going to be one – can see that she's fainted. Why should I say that? It isn't interesting or funny, and it doesn't tell anything new.'

And then she clasped her hands together and shrieked, '"*Oh, my dear mistress, don't faint to that side; that's not your best side. Faint to the right and*

*then you will be in a good position when the gentle-
men come in."* That's better, isn't it, Jenny? Go on —
say your bit again.'

I said it, and it did sound much better this time,
probably because I was trying not to laugh and that
made my voice sound all quavery and when Jane said
her lines then I collapsed in a heap, as elegantly as I
could, but making sure that I was on my right side,
and Henry clapped, sending a shower of green paint
spots over his scenery.

Today was a very busy day. Now it is night-time and
Jane and I have brushed each other's hair and we
are here in our bedroom; Jane is on the bed with her
writing desk balanced on her knee, reading from a
book and scribbling on a piece of paper, and I am
sitting at the washstand, writing in my journal. We
have two candles in our room now. Jane asked her father whether we could and he immediately said yes,
so Jane fetched another one with-
out asking her mother.

'We need two because I like to
read and Jenny likes to write in
her journal or draw,' she said to
her father. I felt very nervous because I think that my aunt, Mrs
Austen, is someone who has
rules, and that one of her
rules is one candle for each

bedroom. But Jane is right; we do need two candles.

'What are you reading?' I asked.

'It's a book about teaching people who can't hear and can't talk how to spell out letters using their fingers,' she said briefly. 'I found it in Father's library. Look, it has pictures of how you make the shapes of the letters with your fingers and thumb. I was thinking that if I could teach George his letters, he could talk on his fingers. You see, I have tried and tried to teach him to talk, but he doesn't seem able to learn.'

I said I thought that if he learned his letters, then he could learn to read also – more to please her than anything else. I'm not sure that George, from what I have seen of him, would be able to read. I told Jane that I would help her teach him.

Jane's face lit up and she gave me a big smile. 'Shall we start tomorrow?'

I came across to her bed and peered over her shoulder.

'The A looks a bit like an apple with a stalk standing up,' I said. 'We can start with that. We'll bring him an apple so that he knows what it's all about.'

I was just going to put this journal away when I remembered that Mr Austen, when he heard about it, told me that I should write down my thoughts as well as the day's events.

Let me see . . .

I suppose I'm thinking that it must have been sad

for Mr and Mrs Austen to have a child like George, someone who will never grow into a man like James or Henry. And how Mrs Austen is so fond of James, and Mr Austen is so fond of Henry. I wonder . . . are they extra fond because they are comparing these two, who are so handsome and clever, with poor George? I wonder too if they ever feel sorry for George. He doesn't seem very well looked after down in the village. I think he just shambles about all day. When I saw him he was not properly washed and his hair wasn't combed. If he were well cared for, he would have a look of Charles. He has lovely eyes, and when he saw Jane, they lit up.

And then I start to think about Henry. He is very nice. He paid me a lot of attention today. He admired my hair and how blonde it is. He praised my blue eyes and told me that they reminded him of sapphires. He told me that I am the perfect height, and that he doesn't like girls who are too tall. When we rolled back the carpet in the evening and Mrs Austen played some tunes for country dances, Henry was my partner for all of them and Jane teased me about him.

He looks so very handsome, with his black hair tied behind with a black velvet ribbon and his hazel eyes smiling at me, that I would love to draw a proper picture of him. From the first moment that he arrived, he has paid me attention.

'Isn't Jenny looking so much better?' That was the

first thing he said to his mother when we arrived back from Deane Gate Inn.

'You were raving with fever when he saw you the last time.' Jane made it sound very dramatic. 'He was the one that carried you into the house. And he knelt by your bed and sobbed, "My own dear love, don't you know me?"'

I felt myself getting as red as if I still had a fever, but Henry just laughed and pulled Jane's dark curls. 'Jenny was beautiful even then,' he joked, and then both he and James went into the parlour to have some breakfast and we all followed to talk to them.

'How's the romance getting on in *Jack and Alice*?' enquired Henry, while James told his mother all about Oxford. 'You know about Jane's novel, I suppose,' he said to me. He probably just said it to include me, because everyone knows about Jane's stories.

'Well, Alice proposed to Charles and was rejected,' said Jane thoughtfully. 'Wait a minute and I'll read you a bit.' She dashed across to her little portable writing desk that her father gave to her for her fifteenth birthday. She took out her notebook and read aloud in a very dramatic way:

'However, I was determined to make an end to the matter and therefore wrote him a very kind love letter, offering him with great tenderness my hand and heart. To this he returned an angry refusal, but thinking it might be rather the effect of his modesty than anything else, I wrote again offering my undying affection.'

Henry was laughing and I giggled also. Jane was very good at imitating the style of the romances that she loved to read. I wondered what Henry would think of my journal and then I felt myself blush, despite myself. I wish I could learn not to blush. I am always doing it.

Jane has just asked me what I was writing and when I told her it was about reading out to Henry about Alice, she tossed me over a piece of paper.

'Here, you can stick that in your journal,' she said.

I read it through and raised my eyebrows. I told her I didn't think that James would like the dedication. I believe he will think Jane is laughing at him, mentioning his two plays like that.

The Visit
A comedy in 2 acts
Dedication:
To James Austen Esq.

Sir,

The following Drama, which I humbly recommend to your Protection and Patronage, tho' inferior to those celebrated Comedies called 'The School for Jealousy' & 'The Travelled Man', will I hope afford some amusement to so respectable a scholar as yourself, which was the end in veiw when it was first composed by your Humble Servant the Author.

'Well, Henry liked the dedication that I wrote for him. He said that he would pay me a hundred guineas.' And Jane tossed me another piece of scrap paper.

I asked her whether Henry did pay her a hundred guineas, but I laughed as I asked it and she just laughed as well. From what I've heard of Henry and his spendthrift habits he probably couldn't spare a hundred pennies.

To Henry Thomas Austen Esq.

Sir

I am now availing myself of the Liberty you have frequently honoured me with of dedicating one of my Novels to you. That it is unfinished, I greive, yet fear that from me, it will always remain so, that as far as it is carried, it should be so trifling and so unworthy of you, is another concern to

Your obliged Humble Servant,
The Author.

Messrs Demand & Co. - please to pay the demand of Miss Jane Austen Spinster the sum of one hundred guineas on account of your Humble Servant.

H.T. Austen

105.0.0 pounds

Sunday, 13 March 1791

Yesterday was a wonderful day – the day of the supper dance.

Let me see what I can remember about the Vyne. The house is very big and old-fashioned. Mr Austen told me that that sort of building with the timber beams showing is called Tudor.

The house was full of guests. The Lefroys and Portals and Terrys and Digweeds were there, as well as the Chutes, of course.

When we went to take off our wraps and cloaks in Mrs Chute's bedroom there were three sisters there and Jane introduced them to me. Their name was Bigg and Catherine was the same age as Cassandra, Elizabeth the same age as me, and Alethea the same age as Jane. All of them were dressed very fashionably in gowns of fine soft silk with a sheen. I've drawn a picture of the three of them here.

Catherine

Elizabeth

Alethea

'Jane!' screamed Alethea when we came in. 'I so wanted to see you. What's this I hear about you nearly dying at boarding school?'

'I was carried out of there unconscious,' said Jane dramatically. 'And so was Jenny. We were left for dead.'

'I knew that!' Alethea's eyes were sparkling with excitement. 'I kept asking Papa to bring me over to see you. I know all about it. Wait until you hear!'

'What?' asked Jane. I could see that she was excited. I almost felt a little jealous. It was obvious that Alethea and Jane were great friends. I took a few steps back and waited.

'Have you heard what happened after you left?' Elizabeth took part in the story.

'It was a scandal,' said Catherine to Cassandra. 'Mrs Cawley didn't want anyone to know, but then girl after girl took the fever and parents started rushing down to Southampton and removing their daughters by post-chaise.'

'Maria Bertram wrote to Catherine,' said Alethea.

I said nothing. I remembered Maria and Julia and the insults that they heaped upon me. I remembered their sneers at my poor education and their peals of laughter when I couldn't put together the jigsaw of the countries of Europe and how they had jeered at my lack of artistic knowledge.

'Well, Maria wrote and told us everything,' said Elizabeth, 'and apparently Mrs Cawley had to close the school. Maria and Julia go to a very good school in Bath now.'

'I like your new gowns,' said Cassandra politely to Catherine. She obviously didn't want to spend the evening talking about boarding schools.

'We shouldn't be wearing them really,' said Catherine, 'because they are intended for the Basingstoke Assembly Rooms ball next fortnight.'

'But we begged and begged and in the end Mama said that we could as long as we made very sure to spill nothing,' said Elizabeth primly.

Alethea was whispering something in Jane's ear. I could just hear the words, 'Mama . . . Catherine . . .' And then something about William Chute and then both Jane and Alethea collapsed into fits of giggles and I could see Jane whisper something back in Alethea's ear. Under all the giggles I could only make out one word and that was 'Cassandra'.

'They're made from sarsenet, you see,' Elizabeth was saying, glancing down at the glossy material.

'And they won't wash,' added Catherine.

'So don't you dare make me laugh when we're at supper, Jane,' threatened Alethea. I think she is the one that Jane likes the best. I liked her too as she seemed to be more fun than her sisters, even though I felt a little jealous that I was not part of the whispering and giggling.

'The Biggs must be very rich to be able to afford silk for their girls,' I whispered to Jane as we went out to the hall to greet Mrs Chute and her sons.

'I don't care for the colours too much though,' Jane whispered back with a shrug, and I agreed with her. Catherine had a very bright purple, Elizabeth a strange shade of green and Alethea wore blue — but a very dark blue.

'Muslin is nice when it's new,' said Catherine with a slightly disdainful glance at my gown.

I felt embarrassed. My best gown is more than two years old. It still fits me because I haven't grown at all in that time, but it has been in the washtub so often that it has a washed-out, limp appearance.

'William Chute is here tonight,' whispered Elizabeth to Jane. 'He's just back from a visit to London. I declare he gets handsomer and handsomer. They say that he doesn't care for balls, only for hunting.'

'I prefer Tom,' said Jane bluntly. 'Cassandra can have William.'

Cassandra gave her a condescending smile and moved away to talk to Catherine. She wasn't listening to Miss Bigg though. Her attention was on the door, and in a moment it was opened and Mr Austen and the boys came in. Cassandra moved towards them, and Tom Fowle's face lit up with a big smile. I saw Mrs Austen's eyes go suspiciously to the two of them, but Jane was by her side in a moment.

'Mama, can't we have some new gowns? These old

muslins are as limp as a piece of lettuce, and mine's far too short,' whispered Jane in her mother's ear. 'Look at the way Elizabeth Bigg keeps twirling to show off the twill weave.' Jane's whisper was very loud, and Mrs Austen frowned at her as we went up to curtsy to Mrs Chute.

There were only three of the Chute family – as well as Mrs Chute, I mean. Our host was William Chute, the man who sent me a donkey; he's the eldest son, the squire. Jane keeps saying that he will die soon because he's sickly and cross and then Tom Chute will be the heir to the estate and she will marry him.

However, I think that's just Jane having fun. William certainly didn't look sickly or cross. He gave me a great welcome and smiled at me when I thanked him for the pretty little donkey, but mostly he just chatted away to Henry and Frank about hunting and about the rumour that a couple of highwaymen were hiding out in the woods outside Steventon. They seemed very excited about that and talked about getting up a party to get rid of these menaces to the stagecoaches.

As well as William, there are Mary, who is older even than Cassandra, and Tom. At seventeen, he's the youngest of the family.

Tom is great fun. I'm not surprised that Jane likes him so well. All during the supper before the dance Mrs Austen and Mrs Chute were having a whispered conversation and Tom and Jane were imitating them, nodding their heads and pinching their lips and saying things like, *'I would never have believed it'*, *'And after all I did for her!'* and *'. . . in my own kitchen, too.'*

'What's the joke, Jenny?' Henry gave me a fright. Mrs Austen stopped whispering and turned round to look at me. Tom and Jane looked like a pair of owls, staring at me with round, serious eyes, and that made me want to giggle even more, especially as I overheard Jane saying to Tom, *'Dear child — she has not been out in such exalted society as this before. She is very young.'*

'She's thinking of how she's going to play the piano for us in a minute,' said William.

'I — I don't play the piano,' I stammered, feeling quite alarmed, although I thought it pleasant of him to try to get me out of an embarrassing moment.

'Let's start the dance,' said Henry. He looked across at me and smiled. I thought that no one in the world could smile like Henry. The smile starts at his mouth and lights up his whole face and then spreads to his bright hazel eyes, which become very soft and dreamy. His gaze lingered on me for a moment and then he turned his smile on to his mother and asked her to play the first dance. Apparently there was a servant in the kitchen with a fiddle who would play the rest of the tunes.

And then, while Mrs Austen was exclaiming about

how out-of-practice she was, Henry whispered across the table. 'You'd like to dance, Jenny, wouldn't you?'

Henry is very good at getting his own way. In a minute, we were all in the long drawing room, where the furniture had been moved to the sides and the floor waxed to a high shine. I'm not sure how I managed to get from the dining room to the drawing room; I was so excited at the idea of dancing, especially with Henry. My legs felt weak, almost as though I were ill again. Henry took my hand, his skin feeling cool to my hot palm, and led me in and then went over to talk to his mother. There were two servants there with fiddles, but Mrs Austen, looking quite good-humoured, sat down at the piano.

'Dance this one with me, Jenny,' said Henry. He held out his hand and I took it. I couldn't believe that he asked me first – before any of the Bigg girls or Mary Chute or anyone. My cheeks were bright red, I know – I could even feel the lobes of my ears glowing. Jane was chatting to Tom Chute as if he were Charles or Frank and she didn't blush at all. She mustn't care anything for him, I thought.

I had three dances with Henry, one with Frank, one with William Chute and then another one with Henry. Jane danced two dances with Harry Digweed, but after that she went back to Tom Chute and they danced together for most of the rest of the evening. Whenever I overheard them they were going on with their game of pretending to be two gossipy old ladies, saying things like, '*Did you ever know such a thing?*' and '*Wait till I tell you what she said*' every time they met and crossed hands in the dance.

'Are you coming to the ball at the Assembly Rooms at Basingstoke Saturday fortnight?' William asked me when I was dancing with him.

I told him that would be up to Mr and Mrs Austen and then he said something rather nice.

'Oh, Henry will make sure that you come! He told me that he was going, and I don't think that he will want to go if you are not there to dance with him. Henry always wants to dance with the prettiest girl in the room.'

I wondered if he was just being polite, or if he really did think that. I looked up at him doubtfully. Perhaps he was just joking. In my mind was always the memory of my sister-in-law, Augusta, saying to one of her friends, 'Jenny is such a thoroughly unattractive girl, no manner, no style. I declare it embarrasses me to take her out with me. Only my duty to Edward-John persuades me to sacrifice my own comfort.'

'Don't you believe me?' asked William as I looked at him uncertainly. 'Prettiest girl in the room — you'll be the belle of the ball at Basingstoke!'

I must remember to tell Jane that I don't think William is cross and sickly at all. I think he is very nice.

After that I danced with Henry again for the last dance of the evening. I couldn't think of anything to say. I wasn't good at dancing and talking at the same time like Jane did with Tom Chute. Henry didn't say anything either, just smiled at me and pressed my hands gently when we were doing the two-hand turn. I was glad that I didn't have to talk. I was too busy looking at his face. There was something about the way that he looked at me with a half-smile that made my heart thump very fast. From time to time I thought of saying something to break the tension, but I didn't. We stood up opposite Tom Fowle and Cassandra and they didn't say anything either, just gazed into each other's eyes. It was very romantic.

What does Henry think about me? I was wondering about that all the way home in the coach. I thought that he liked me, but I knew that his mother would not approve of his paying attention to me. I was afraid that she might think I was fast if I encouraged him. Earlier in the evening when William Chute brought me back to her after our dance, she had patted me on the arm approvingly and told me that I was looking very well. But all the time as the coach bumped and jolted its way down the road towards Overton and then turned down the narrow laneway from Deane to Steventon, she hardly said a word to me.

All through the journey I kept wishing that I weren't always worrying and being anxious about things. I wish I were more like Jane and just looking for fun all the time. She never seems to care when her mother's in a bad mood — she just laughs and jokes and takes no notice.

And then . . .

When the coach arrived back at Steventon parsonage, Frank and Charles jumped out from the seat at the back. Henry handed out his mother and Tom Fowle handed out Cassandra. They went up the steps side by side while Jane jumped out, taking no notice of Henry, and ran up after Cassandra.

And then, after the others had gone into the house, Henry put out his two arms and lifted me down.

And he held me close for a moment and then he kissed me very quickly.

Not on the hand.

On the cheek.

I don't think that I have ever been so close to a man before. Men smell so different.

I wished that I could stay outside in the starlit garden, just stand quietly by myself and think about everything that happened this evening — think about dancing with Henry — think about Henry kissing me — think about what William Chute said about my being the prettiest girl in the room, even prettier than the fashionably dressed Bigg girls — think about dancing with . . .

Think about Henry . . .

I couldn't though. I had to walk ahead of Henry and go through the porch and into the best parlour.

As soon as we came into the room I thought Mrs Austen looked at me rather critically. I quickly moved away from Henry and went over beside Jane, who was telling her father all about the evening.

'Did you have a good time, Jenny dear?' Mr Austen was so kind to me always.

I told him that I had.

'Not too tired?'

I exclaimed that I could have danced twenty dances more without getting tired, and I think I must have said it very loudly, because everyone looked over at me.

'She was looking very well tonight.' Mrs Austen came across and joined us. 'William Chute paid her a lot of attention. He told his mother that she was the prettiest girl he had seen for a long time.'

'He was only being polite.' I had a quick look at Henry to see if he was jealous of William Chute, but he didn't seem to be interested. And then I felt embarrassed that I had looked at him. I hoped that he hadn't noticed, and I felt my cheeks burn. I knew it was stupid to be always blushing like this, but Mrs Austen didn't seem to be annoyed. She was looking at me in a pleased sort of way. Actually she made me feel quite uncomfortable as her eyes moved up and down. I wished that I were a bit taller.

'This child needs a new gown,' she said eventually.

'What do you say, Mr Austen? Perhaps all of the girls need new gowns. Jane's is too short and Cassandra's has faded and Jenny's—'

'Of course, my dear. Whatever you think best.'

Jane was beside me now, squeezing my hand. I squeezed back. I knew what she was going to say.

'Mama, could we all go to the Basingstoke Assembly Rooms? There's a ball in two weeks' time. The Bigg girls are going and the Chutes. Oh, please say that we may – please, please, please, please!'

'What do you think, Mr Austen?' I knew that Jane had won when Mrs Austen made a pretence of consulting her husband. She is always the one who makes the decisions. She wouldn't have asked him unless she had made up her mind.

'Well, my dear, I would certainly enjoy a game of cards with some of my old friends. The Harwoods should be there and Hugh Digweed and the Portals – we'll make a whist table or two, I dare say.' Mr Austen beamed his gentle smile at Jane's excited face.

'Well, in that case, Mr Austen, perhaps we will hire the coach and go to Basingstoke for the ball.' Mrs Austen did her best to sound like an obedient wife.

Jane and I threw our arms around each other. We were both laughing with excitement. It was a great feeling. I'd never felt so happy in all my life.

'And the new gowns?' enquired Jane. 'Could they be made by a dressmaker?'

'We'll see,' said Mrs Austen, and she gave a broad smile.

'Oh, Mama!' For a moment I thought Jane was going to kiss her mother – she never seems to do this – but she just gave her a lovely wide smile and Mrs Austen smiled back and tugged at one of Jane's dark curls just as Mr Austen did sometimes.

'My mother thinks that William Chute has fallen in love with you,' said Jane as soon as we were safely in our bedroom.

I told her not to be silly, but she put on a very wise, elderly look and told me that he would be a very good match for me.

'Think of the property,' she said solemnly. 'A fine house, a great estate – do you think that you could fall in love with him?'

I giggled, but then I stopped and thought about it. William Chute was very nice but . . .

'Well, what would you say if he proposed to you?' enquired Jane. Her head was on one side and she was looking at me the way you look at someone when you want to capture their likeness to draw a picture of them.

I told her I wasn't sure, and she nodded briskly. 'My dear Jenny, that answers the question. If a lady doubts whether she should accept a man, then she certainly should not do so.'

I was glad that she hadn't asked me whether I

would accept Henry if he asked me. I'm not sure that I would have told her the truth. My feelings for Henry are very private. And I'm not yet sure what they are, exactly!

There is one more thing that I must write.

When I saw Jane and her mother looking at each other in such a friendly way, I felt a terrible sort of pain. I suppose it was jealousy. I miss my mother so much. My feelings and my sorrow got hidden while I was with Edward-John and Augusta. They were so critical of my mother that I never wanted to talk about her. I even stopped myself thinking of her, but now, suddenly, I miss her terribly. For a moment I almost hated Jane for having a mother and father while I have neither.

There was something else that I thought also.

I realized that I had always been feeling guilty when I was staying with Edward-John and Augusta — guilty that I didn't do or say the right thing, guilty that I was a nuisance to them.

But now I have stopped feeling guilty.

They should have been nicer to me, I decided. I did my best not to be a nuisance. I tried hard to please them both. Despite what Augusta whispered to her friends, I probably wasn't an expense to them, since Edward-John had charge of my income from Mama's estate.

I know a bit more about money and what things

cost these days as Mrs Austen is always adding up her accounts in a loud voice and calling Frank to help her. The sum of fifty pounds a year should have more than covered my food and laundry and no one ever thought to buy me new clothes. If Mrs Austen can run a large house and feed her big family on not much more than four hundred pounds a year (Jane told me that is what Mr Austen gets from his position as rector and his farm and the school), then Augusta and Edward-John could not have been out of pocket on my account.

Now I shall lock up my journal and go to bed and dream of the ball at Basingstoke.

And Henry will be there . . .

Monday, 14 March 1791

The Austens' cousin, Cousin Eliza, arrived from Basingstoke this morning just after we finished breakfast. She is going to stay a week, she said.

'I shouldn't have come; I have a hundred things to do, but I couldn't resist a play,' she declared, leaping out of the post-chaise and waving her hands around. She has a strong French accent, though she was born in India and has lived half her life in England. Her hat, with its feather, looked quite French, I thought, and she kissed everyone on two cheeks – she even kissed Jane on two cheeks and then a third time. 'Jane,' she cried in a very foreign way, '*mon chou chou*, how you have grown! And Henry, my cherub, la, I declare you are a man now, Henry.' And then she was off on another round of kissing. Even I got kissed and my curls patted. Apparently she is a countess; Henry, for fun, keeps calling her *Madame la Comtesse*. Her husband is a French nobleman. She shed tears when she spoke of him, because he is over in France and as she said herself in her French accent: 'These are revolutionary times.' And she rolled the letter *r* so that it sounded as though there were six *rs* at the beginning of *revolutionary*. Even the king and queen of France are in danger, apparently. Eliza shed a tear for them too, dabbing at her eyes with a beautiful, lace-trimmed handkerchief.

handkerchief lace-trim

And then a minute later, she was whispering behind her hand with Henry, telling some story which sounded very scandalous – I overheard words like 'her bedroom' and 'he was hiding in the closet!' I saw Jane move her chair a little nearer – so as to pick up details for her novels, I suppose.

We had great fun today practising for the play. James's friend John Portal was the villain, Sir Lucius O'Trigger, an Irish baronet; he had to carry me in his arms when he was abducting me. I was very embarrassed in the beginning, but he made a joke of it, pretending that I was too heavy – although he carried me very easily, as he is very tall and strong. Henry shouted out, 'Lucky man!' when Mr Portal said that about my being heavy, and James got annoyed with both of them. No one took any notice though, and Henry winked at me. I do think that Henry likes me. I'm glad that Cousin Eliza is going back to London next week. Henry isn't paying me nearly as much attention as he did yesterday. I'm not as good at flirting as she is. Cassandra says that it is abominable that a married lady should flirt in the way that Eliza does, but Jane said that she has to keep in practise as her husband is across the sea in France.

'Don't be silly, child,' said Cassandra with a superior air. 'Women don't flirt with their husbands.'

'And that's why married women have to have lovers, I suppose,' said Jane. She sounded thoughtful and her face was very serious, but I could see that she was trying to shock Cassandra, who is very prim and proper.

I wish I could flirt. I would love to say witty things to Henry and have him laugh the way that he does with Cousin Eliza. I'm just not good enough at making jokes, or else I am too shy.

Cousin Eliza is a born actress. Even after breakfast this morning, when you would think she would be tired after her long journey from London, she was doing a minuet with Henry around the sitting room, declaring that 'He is the very pineapple of politeness,' and slipping slightly on the polished wood, and the sunlight streaming in through the two casement windows behind her made her look as if she were

127

on a stage. It was like a play that I once saw at Bristol. I made up my mind that I would try to be like Eliza – sophisticated, clever and amusing, the sort of person that would attract men. Of course, she was brought up in India and then France so I might not be able to be as stylish and elegant as she is. Jane and I had a talk about it in our bedroom. We tried waving our hands around and introducing a few words of French into English sentences. And then we practised walking the way that Eliza walks, sort of sweeping around. Of course she had a train, even on her walking gown – it looked so elegant with her stylish spencer fitting so tightly around her bosom and her large hat with a feather in it. I have never seen a hat like that before.

'Men fall at her feet all over Europe,' Jane said with an air that impressed me very much, but then she spoiled it by adding, 'even my father,' and that made us both giggle.

We both pinned our wrappers to the shoulders of our gowns and stuck a couple of new quills in our hair. Then we tried sweeping up and down the bedroom saying, 'la' and *'chérie'* to each other. We both decided that a train certainly made you feel much more elegant – especially as we had to keep our noses in the air in order to prevent the quills falling out of our hair.

And then Jane whispered to me that she had seen Eliza kissing Henry — on the lips too! And that the kiss lasted for ages!

I thought of how I would feel if Henry kissed me like that; I felt quite jealous of Eliza but I didn't want to show it, so when I saw Jane looking at me I said that Eliza had a way of pursing up her lips and perhaps that was what made Henry do it, and Jane nodded wisely. 'That's the secret of sophistication,' she said. 'You must always look as if you are ready to kiss a man once you are alone.'

'What about a girl's reputation though?'

'Perhaps it's better to get married first,' said Jane thoughtfully. 'If you were a sophisticated widow with plenty of money left you by your husband, then you could do what you wanted.'

Monday afternoon, 14 March 1791

Mrs Austen was in very good humour this afternoon. About twelve o'clock, when I began my usual chore of dusting and polishing the sideboard, rubbing up the brass handles on the many drawers and trying to work around the books and papers and cricket balls and spinning tops and an old doll belonging to either Jane or Cassandra and all the other items that littered the shelves and cubbyholes of that huge piece of wall furniture, she stopped me.

'Never mind about that now, dear,' she said. 'Jane, leave the kettle – it can do without a polish for once. Go upstairs and put on your bonnets and cloaks, the two of you; we're going shopping at Overton.'

'We're getting new gowns!' exclaimed Jane.

Mrs Austen nodded. 'Make haste,' she said. 'We should go in the next few minutes. Where is Cassandra? We'll miss the coach. I declare she takes longer over those hens every day.'

'Here I am, Mama.' Cassandra came in with pink cheeks and the three of us went clattering upstairs to get ready.

'Such excitement!' exclaimed Eliza, coming out of her room and smiling with amusement. 'Ah, at your age there is nothing so exciting as a new gown!'

'Are you coming, Eliza?' asked Jane.

'*Chérie*, I would love to, but I am only here for a

few days and I feel that I owe it to your brother to give all of my energies to the play.'

'She's a great performer,' said Jane, grinning as I closed the door of our bedroom behind us. 'She sounds just like a classical actress wedded to her art. I bet she just wants to flirt with Henry.'

'Or James,' I said.

'Or both,' said Jane. And we giggled, but I kept thinking that I hoped Eliza would flirt with James, not Henry.

Overton is a small town compared with Bristol, but still it holds all the shops necessary to the people who live in the countryside around. There are five grocers, two butchers, four tailors, seven shoemakers, one hairdresser, two breeches makers, a clockmaker and two millinery and haberdashery shops. As soon as we had got down from the coach and Mrs Austen had expressed a hope to the coachman that there would be clean, dry straw for our feet to rest on when we returned, we went straight to Ford's, the biggest shop in the town.

'You've come just at the right moment, ma'am,' said Mrs Ford when Mrs Austen explained our errand. 'I've just got the prettiest selection of muslins, new in from Bristol.' She bustled off and was back in a moment with her arms laden with a rainbow of stuff, all lovely pale colours: lavenders, yellows, pinks, blues and delicate greens.

'I was thinking of pink for all three,' said Mrs Austen bluntly. 'It would save money.'

Cassandra made a face, and I took my eyes reluctantly from a sky blue. I love blue, and my mother always told me it suited me best of all.

'Why do Jane and Jenny have to have pink?' Cassandra sounded quite upset. 'If we are all dressed the same, it will make me look about fifteen. You know pink suits me best, but I don't want us to look like triplets.' She picked up a pink and gazed at it longingly.

'That's a lovely colour, Miss Austen,' said Mrs Ford. 'That's a true shell pink. It will go very well with your complexion and your grey eyes.' She took her eyes from Cassandra and glanced from Jane with her dark hair and her dark eyes to me with my blonde curls and blue eyes.

'This would look good on Miss Jane,' she said, picking up a primrose-yellow muslin and holding it against Jane, turning her around to see her reflection in the large cheval looking glass that stood on the floor next to the counter.

'I like that much better than the pink,' said Jane with conviction. 'I'm sick of pink.'

'Well, don't have a new gown then,' said Mrs Austen drily. 'Wear your old one.'

'How can I?' Jane clasped her hands dramatically. 'Dearest Mama, you know that I look like a half-grown pullet in that.'

I could see that Mrs Ford was trying hard to keep a smile off her face, and one of the young assistants in the background was giggling. I kept my lips tightly pressed together and did my best not to smile at the thought of Jane like one of those lanky half-grown chickens that struts around the farmyard with its long legs and small body.

'Well, we'll take seven yards of that pink,' said Mrs Austen, 'but, Jane and Jenny, you'll have to agree on a colour.'

I immediately said that I didn't mind the yellow, though my eyes were still on that lovely blue. It was like the sky on a fine winter's day.

Mrs Ford held up the yellow doubtfully against me and then shook her head. 'Not her colour,' she said decisively. 'That makes her look far too pale.'

'Well, let's have blue for the two of them,' said Mrs Austen. 'You don't mind, Jane, do you?'

Jane shook her head, but she still looked longingly at the primrose-coloured muslin. Mrs Ford did not bother holding up the blue against her. Anyone could see that it wasn't her colour.

'It's a pity they are not more alike in colouring, ma'am,' she said to Mrs Austen. 'You're right, of course. If you can get something to suit both, you'll save at least a yard on the making up. Wait a moment – I've got an idea. Where did I put those sprigged muslins?'

'They're in the back room, under the tamboured muslins, Mrs Ford,' called one of the girls, going after the flying figure of her employer.

Mrs Ford didn't run back though. She walked slowly and carefully, bearing a brown-paper parcel reverently in her arms.

'There you are, Mrs Austen, ma'am. This came from London yesterday.' Slowly and gently she stripped off the folds of brown paper.

And there on the counter was lying the most lovely stuff for a gown that I had ever seen in all my life. The cloth was so beautiful, of the finest cotton, and woven so softly, that it looked just like Indian muslin. It was whiter than any snow could be and the tiny sprigs were not of a colour but were silver. Mrs Ford picked it up, and as she moved it on to her arm the light from the oil lamp caught it and made it sparkle.

'It's just like frost on snow,' I said eventually, and Mrs Austen gave me a pleased grin.

'See how it will suit both of them, ma'am.' Mrs Ford held it up to Jane. 'Look, it makes the dark hair and eyes look even darker, and isn't it lovely with those rosy cheeks?'

And then she held it against me and I looked at myself in the mirror and all the young lady assistants crowded around smiling and whispering praise. I looked at myself and felt that I looked like something from the land of dreams. Only a princess could have a gown as beautiful as this one.

'We'll take twelve yards,' said Mrs Austen decidedly.

After dinner, Jane and I slipped out down to the village. Jane had managed to put a basket under her shawl and in the basket she had a nice ripe apple from the orchard at Steventon. I had done a drawing of an apple and I had written the letter A beside it. I had also copied the finger shape of the sign language from Mr Austen's book.

George was pleased to see us. He snatched the apple from Jane immediately and started to eat it in huge chunks. I was quite shocked – I didn't expect him to have good table manners, but it seemed almost as if he were starving. He even ate the core of the apple and the little stalk on the top.

Then we showed the picture and the sign for apple, but it wasn't a success. He just kept poking in Jane's basket to see whether she had another one hidden there.

'Tomorrow we'll just show him the apple and then we'll keep it until he makes the sign,' I said to Jane as we walked back from the village. 'He'll soon get the idea.'

* * *

It was so funny today when we were passing the shrubbery — we were walking on the gravel sweep and we were not talking; I think we were both thinking about George — when we suddenly heard a sound — someone saying, 'Shh!' very quietly. Jane looked at me with a grin and put her finger to her lips. We both walked on until we came to a laurel bush, and then Jane ducked behind the large green leaves and I followed her. We stood there very silently for a moment.

'They're gone.' It was Cassandra's voice.

Jane put her finger to her lips again and began to steal deeper into the shrubbery. I followed her, trying not to laugh. We passed a few more evergreen bushes and then stopped. In the centre of the clearing was a huge rhododendron bush. It was a very old one and the branches with their peeling bark splayed out sideways, just a couple of feet above the ground. The bush was covered with small fat flower buds, their tips just showing purple, but deep within the leaves was a flash of pink. Hardly daring to breathe, we came a little closer and there, right in the centre, were Tom Fowle and Cassandra. They had made a little nest with heaps of old sacks and a couple of cushions. They were just lying there, not kissing, not touching, just lying there side by side looking at each other. I tapped Jane on the shoulder and turned and started to go back. Somehow

I couldn't bear to disturb them. They looked so in love with each other.

'Don't tell,' I said to Jane when we were going in through the door.

'Of course I won't.'

But during supper, once Mrs Austen had gone out, Jane couldn't resist saying to her father, 'Papa, Jenny and I have been thinking about doing some nature study – perhaps starting off with trees and bushes. Do you think that is a good idea?'

Mr Austen, of course, did, and went into a long explanation about deciduous trees and evergreens – he recommended books and he even told us we would find some excellent examples of evergreens in the shrubbery.

Jane nodded thoughtfully and said, 'That's just what I was thinking myself today. Like rhododendrons, for instance.'

It was good luck that Mrs Austen was out of the room because Tom Fowle went bright red and Cassandra blushed a rosy pink. It was funny, because she kept trying to shoot Jane angry glances, but then she would look at Tom and her face would get all soft again. I'm beginning to like Cassandra. I hope things work out for her.

Tonight Jane was busy with her notebook while I was doing my journal. I had just finished writing all of this when she said, 'Look at this. You can stick it in your journal. I might use it in a story some time.'

Mrs George Austen
The Parsonage,
Steventon.

Dear Madam,
　　　　　We are married and gone.
　　　　　　　　Tom and Cassandra Fowle.

Her Highness Madam Austen, having read
this letter which, of course, sufficiently explained
the whole affair, flew into a violent Passion and
having spent an agreeable half an hour calling them
all the shocking Names her rage could suggest to
her, sent after them 300 men with orders not to
return without their bodies whether dead or alive,
intending that if they should be brought in the latter
condition, to have them put to death in some torture-
like manner, after a few years' confinement.

Tuesday, 15 March 1791

We had just finished breakfast and Jane and I were airing our bedroom when the dressmaker, or mantua maker, as Cassandra grandly called her, came around. We saw her on the sweep when we looked out of our bedroom window. She was a small woman with a pale face and rounded shoulders and she was carrying a flat basket in her hand.

Jane and I were downstairs before she reached the front door.

'Miss Jane Austen,' she said, dropping a curtsy. 'Miss Cooper,' she said to me, and then as Cassandra came out of the dining room, she dropped another curtsy and murmured, 'Miss Austen.'

'Come in, Mrs Tuckley, come into the best parlour. Mrs Austen is there.' Cassandra was very grand today. I don't think that she has quite forgiven Jane and me for spying on her and Tom Fowle in the rhododendrons yesterday – she wouldn't speak to us for the rest of the day.

'She should thank us,' Jane had said this morning when we were brushing our hair. 'If we don't tease them, he might never declare his intentions to Papa.' She lowered her voice and hissed, 'He might abduct her by midnight in a post-coach and then she would be ruined.'

The idea of decent, kind, shy Tom Fowle abducting

the very virtuous Cassandra had made us both laugh so much that Mrs Austen tapped on the ceiling of the parlour below and told us to hurry down.

'I've just brought some patterns today, ma'am,' said Mrs Tuckley. 'I thought that the young ladies could choose the styles that they like and then I could make sure that you had enough material and I could start work first thing tomorrow. I should have the gowns ready for a week on Saturday with no trouble, because my niece is coming to help me tomorrow and she is a good, fast worker.'

'The young ladies can do their share also,' said Mrs Austen firmly.

Jane made a face, probably only because she is in the middle of her novel *Love & Freindship* (as she spells it). Jane is very accomplished with her needle, better than I am.

'Let's see the patterns,' she said, lifting the cover off the basket.

'Jane!' reproved Mrs Austen.

'We have seven yards of pink muslin for me and twelve yards of white muslin for the two young girls to share between them,' said Cassandra to Mrs Tuckley in a very matronly manner.

'Two young girls and one elderly one,' whispered Jane to me, and we both had a giggle at that. I stopped first because I feared it wasn't very polite to Mrs Austen when she was going to such a lot of trouble for us.

'These are the paper patterns that I made from the Misses Biggs' new gowns,' said Mrs Tuckley, bringing out some large shapes of brown paper from her basket. 'These ones are from Miss Bigg's gown, these are from Miss Elizabeth's gown and these from Miss Alethea's gown.' While she was talking to us she was able to sort out the patterns in a moment although they all looked the same to me.

Cassandra didn't look too pleased at that. 'Catherine Bigg will be at the Assembly Hall's ball at Basingstoke; I don't want to look the same as her.' I could see that Mrs Tuckley was looking a bit worried so I picked out some black silk ribbon from her basket.

'If this was to be plaited across the top of the bosom it would look very unusual and different and it would go well with the pink,' I said, and Cassandra even smiled at me.

'You are very artistic, Jenny,' she said approvingly.

Mrs Tuckley looked relieved. 'I'll slot it in and out of the muslin, Miss Austen.'

Cassandra nodded graciously. She liked the very polite way that Mrs Tuckley talked to her and the way that Mrs Tuckley was always so careful to give her, as eldest girl in the family, the title of Miss Austen while Jane was just Miss Jane. Cassandra will probably make a very good mistress of a house when she and Tom Fowle get married.

'Here's Elizabeth's pattern for you, Jenny – she's about your size.'

As soon as Jane handed it to me, I couldn't help giving a cry of delight. 'Oh, it's got a train on it!'

'They've all got trains.' Mrs Tuckley was looking at Mrs Austen a bit nervously. Mrs Austen had pursed her lips and was looking disapproving. 'Don't worry about that, ma'am. The young ladies will be able to help each other to pin them up before they start dancing so the material won't get spoiled.' She was talking very quickly now. No doubt she was anxious to use these patterns, as they would save her quite some work. I was anxious too. I had never had a gown with a train before, but I could just imagine how fine I would look as it flowed behind me when I walked down the long passageway at the Assembly Rooms that Jane had told me about. Perhaps Henry would hand me out of the coach, which was to be hired for the evening, and we would walk in together, the tips of my fingers just resting on his arm, perhaps with a blue ribbon holding back my curls – if I can get my hair to stay in curl – and the train whispering along the ground behind me.

Now I must write about George. Today was a success. We fed him the apple slice by slice, and each time we made him make the sign with his fingers. In the beginning we had to position his fingers, but once he got the idea that he would only get the apple if he made the sign, he did it himself. Bet came along while we were teaching him and she asked what we were doing. Jane told her that we were teaching George to read and she just laughed and went away.

I said to Jane that I thought Bet was unkind, but Jane shook her head and told me that Bet could not read herself and probably thought it was a very hard thing to do.

'She's just jealous perhaps,' I said when we were walking home, but Jane wouldn't agree. That's the nice thing about Jane. Once she gives her friendship she won't let anyone say a word against a friend, and Bet was a friend of hers.

'Bet and I were brought up together until I was three years old,' she said. 'She's my foster-sister.'

I was amazed at that and she nodded. 'Yes,' she said. 'My mother left us all down in the village until we could walk and talk and dress and feed ourselves. She only took us back when we wouldn't be a nuis-ance to her.'

She didn't say anything for a while. Then she added, very sadly, 'And George never learned to do anything, so he was just left down in the village.'

Wednesday, 16 March 1791

'Jenny, this is something that I've had for you for a long time. I took them from your poor mother's jewellery box before *Madam* (Mrs Austen always called Augusta *Madam*) could take them for herself.' As usual, Mrs Austen was in a rush. She took a box from her reticule, handed it to me, put down her teacup, finished her pound cake in two bites, pushed open the breakfast-room door and in a moment was outside shouting orders to the gardener to be sure to get more potatoes planted today than he managed to do yesterday.

The breakfast room was very quiet after she left, Mr Austen sipping his tea and reading a poem by Cowper, Henry frowning over a piece of paper from his pocket with some figures on it and Jane scribbling in her notebook. Cassandra had gone to feed the hens and all of the other boys had gone into the school-room. Cousin Eliza was having breakfast in bed as she did most mornings.

I opened the box very slowly. It was a beautiful box, made of thin sandalwood covered in blue silk. I had often admired it on my mother's dressing table.

But I had never seen it opened before. It had always stayed locked.

The box was full of pale blue glass beads. They glistened in the light of the pale winter sun that came through the breakfast-room window. I couldn't stop myself giving a cry of delight. Everyone looked at me with surprise. There was a piece of paper on the top of the box with the words 'Beads from my wedding gown for Jenny's first ball gown' written on it. I've stuck it in here as I don't ever want to lose it.

Beads from my Wedding Gown for Jenny's first ball gown.

I felt very sad for a moment after I put the note down; no doubt my mother had kept these glass beads from her wedding gown in memory of my father.

'What's the matter, Jenny?' asked Jane.

I couldn't speak, but I handed her the piece of yellowed paper. She glanced at it quickly and Henry looked over her shoulder.

'What colour is your gown, Jenny?' Henry put away his figures and looked at me kindly.

I told him about the white sprigged muslin, almost whispering the words because I was just thinking how beautiful the gown would look if the beads were sewn all over it. I would have to talk to Mrs Tuckley about it.

Jane and I rushed upstairs to fetch our work baskets, and as we came out of our bedroom again we saw something strange. Henry was going upstairs very quietly, making no noise on the wooden boards, and we saw him turn the handle of Eliza's door and slip inside without even knocking. Jane looked at me and raised her eyebrows and I did the same back, but I didn't know what to think. We tiptoed downstairs, and as we passed Eliza's room we could hear them both laughing and joking.

I've decided that I don't really like Cousin Eliza very much. I think she is a shallow, insincere sort of person. I don't believe that she cares for Henry. I think that she is just leading him on.

It's night-time and Jane and I are in our bedroom. We should be in bed, but we are both writing, she in her notebook and I in my journal. I have just finished writing about the gowns and I am trying to think of something else to write in order to fill up the page. Jane is writing very fast. I think she is very clever. She is almost a year younger than I am, but she can write much more quickly.

I'll ask Jane to read out what she's writing so I can finish my page . . .

She says she has finished copying and has tossed the piece of paper to me. Here it is:

It may now be proper to return to the Hero of this Novel, the brother of Alice, of whom I believe I have scarcely ever had occasion to speak; which may perhaps be partly owing to his unfortunate tendency to alcohol, which so completely deprived him of the use of those faculties Nature had endowed him with, that he never did anything worth mentioning. His Death happened a short time after Lucy's departure & was the natural Consequence of this heavy drinking.

When he died, his sister became the sole inheritress of a very large fortune, which as it gave her fresh Hopes of rendering herself acceptable as a wife to Charles Adams, could not fail of being most pleasing to her – & as the effect was joyful, the cause could scarcely be lamented, so she did not mourn her brother.

I read it through and laughed, but then I asked Jane how she could write about things like love and marriage when she had never been in love.

'I've never been drunk either,' she said, 'but I can write very well about that.'

I told Jane that for all I knew she was drunk every night before I came here, and that it was a good job I was such a good moral influence on her, and she laughed.

Then I asked if she would ever write a love story with Eliza as the heroine.

147

'Oh, Eliza is not in love,' said Jane impatiently. 'She just flirts. That's different. Flirting is great fun. What about you? You're in love with Henry, aren't you? I know by the way you blush.'

I said that I thought Henry was in love with Eliza, but Jane just laughed at me.

'He's just flirting too,' she said. 'Henry is a terrible flirt; everyone knows that. There's a difference between flirting and being in love. Real love is what Cassandra feels for Tom Fowle.'

I wish Eliza would go back to London. I'm sure Jane's right and that Henry is just flirting with her – but I wish she would go.

Oh, and I forgot, we taught George the sign for the letter *B* today. He learned it by having bits of bun.

Thursday, 17 March 1791

One of Augusta's many letters arrived this morning. Mrs Austen passed it to Eliza with a grin, and Eliza read out bits of it with great spirit and soon she had the whole table rocking with laughter, as she skimmed down and picked out the choicest snippets in her wonderful French accent.

'*My dearest husband — He really is engaged from morning to night — There is no end of peoples coming to him, on some pretence or other — The magistrates, and overseers, and churchwardens, are always wanting his opinion. They seem not able to do any thing without him. "Upon my word, Mr C.," I often say, "rather you than I — I do not know what would become of my drawings and my piano, if I had half so many people calling on me" — Bad enough as it is, for I absolutely neglect them both to an unpardonable degree — I believe I have not played a bar this fortnight — But I have so many calls on my time — Mrs John Colwell, herself, called on me yesterday. "Mrs Cooper," she said, "you are such a good charitable person — I declare to goodness that I actually saw you speak to one of those poor creatures that came to hear your husband preach"— pray tell Mr Austen that Mr Cooper means to pay him the compliment of posting the book of his sermons to him . . .*'

'Well, that's very kind . . .' Mr Austen sounded a little taken aback.

I told him that I thought his sermons were better than my Edward-John's — I wanted to reassure him because he is always so nice to me.

'Still, to have a published volume of his sermons! And such a young man too! There's writing ability in your family, my dear.' He gave a nod at his wife, who preened herself; she is good at writing funny poems, I must say.

'Jane will be the writer of this family,' said Henry, and Jane looked very pleased.

After dinner Jane asked Susan if she could have a tiny slice of cake. She had been making her-self useful in the kitchen and complimenting the cook on the dinner so I wasn't surprised when the cake tin was opened and a slice given to her. I had already prepared my drawings so we went straight down to the village.

There was no sign of George anywhere around. He wasn't near the pump, nor hanging around out-side the inn. We went to Nanny Littleworth's house, but she hadn't seen him for a while.

And then we found him on the lane to the church. He was lying on the ground, on his side, and he was twitching. There was still enough light to see how his eyes rolled in his head and how his lips were cov-ered with froth. He was having a fit. But it wasn't the sort of fit that Augusta would have; this was a real fit. I had never seen anyone have a fit before and it seemed terrible.

I think I will always remember how Jane dropped to her knees beside him and cried over him as if it were the end of the world. I couldn't stop crying myself. And then Mrs Littleworth came along and told us both to go home immediately. Bet was with her, and it was Bet who lifted up Jane and walked us to the gate of the parsonage.

'He'll be fine tomorrow, he'll be fine,' she kept saying in her country voice. 'He doesn't mind. He's used to it and we're used to it. Now, go home the pair of you, and for God's sake don't say a word to your mother about this. Promise me, Miss Jane, and you, Miss Jenny, nothing must be said, or it will be trouble for my mother.'

Jane and I cried the whole way up to the house, and now I am crying again.

I must stop crying or else I will just start thinking about my mother's death and Jane will notice. I've told her that I don't like talking about it and she doesn't ask me any questions, but I think it upsets her when she thinks I am unhappy. Even though she and her mother fight from time to time, I think that she finds it a terrible thing to imagine being someone like me with no family – I can't count Edward-John, as I don't believe that he cares anything for me. We hardly knew each other before he married and came back to Bristol, as he lived in Berkshire.

And now I'm going to try to stop worrying about this by thinking about the ball at Basingstoke Assembly Rooms.

The gowns are progressing very well. They've been cut out and the side seams have been sewn so that now we have an idea of how beautiful they will look. Mrs Tuckley pinned them around us today, and tomorrow she will sew the seams in the bodices so that they will fit us snugly. I just can't wait. Every time that I think about dancing in the Assembly Rooms in less than a fortnight I feel little thrills running up and down me. I think it will be the most wonderful night of my life. Even Cassandra is excited. She goes around singing to herself and exchanging small, secret smiles with Tom Fowle. Jane and I think that being in love must be very good for the complexion; Cassandra looks very nice these days, with lovely pink lips and pink cheeks – even her hair seems to curl more beautifully.

Friday, 18 March 1791

This morning at breakfast Henry had a little parcel beside him.

'What's that, Henry?' asked Jane as soon as she saw it.

'Curiosity,' teased Henry. 'Just something that I bought at the mercer's shop yesterday when I was escorting Cousin Eliza to Overton.' I saw him give a quick, joking look at Eliza who was at the breakfast table for once, pouring out the coffee she insists on having for breakfast. She blew him a kiss, and Mrs Austen scowled, though Mr Austen just laughed.

'A pair of gloves,' guessed Jane, but Henry shook his head.

'He's got six pairs of gloves already,' said Gilbert East.

'A cravat then,' persisted Jane.

'And he's got a drawer full of them,' said Tom Fowle's brother William.

'In any case, I am hoping that Jane will make me a cravat if there is a square of muslin left over from her gown,' said Henry. He didn't really need another cravat, I guessed. He was always beautifully dressed, and this morning he was wearing a snowy white one knotted under his chin in the latest style.

'I will if you show me what you've got there.' Jane kept on pestering him until he undid the twine and took out two beautiful bandeau-style ribbons.

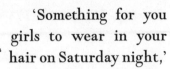

'Something for you
girls to wear in your
hair on Saturday night,'
he said. 'There's a pink one for you, Cassandra, that
should match your gown.'

'Oh, thank you, Henry.' Cassandra rushed over
and admired herself in the looking glass.

'And the red one for Jane — matches her rosy
cheeks.' Henry pinched Jane's cheek. She wriggled
away, but she was pleased with the bandeau. It was
made from silk, like Cassandra's.

Cassandra was still admiring herself. She had a
quick look at Tom Fowle and a smile passed between
them. I think Tom really loves her. There is a look
of adoration in his eyes. I made a promise to myself
not to laugh at them any more, no matter what jokes
Jane makes. I feel very sorry for the two of them and
hope that Mrs Austen will allow them to get engaged.
I'm sure Mr Austen won't mind. He seems to like Tom
Fowle very much.

'And this is for Jenny, to match her beautiful blue
eyes.' I was so busy looking from Mr Austen to Tom
Fowle that I got a shock when Henry opened the parcel a little more and slid out a gorgeous bandeau made
from the deepest and softest blue velvet. I couldn't
say anything; I loved it so much.

'Let me put it on.' In a moment Henry had it
around my head and had pulled one of my curls forward. He placed one hand on my shoulder while he

was arranging my hair and I could feel myself tremble. I wished that we were alone and that the whole of the breakfast table wasn't staring at us. He was so close to me that I could feel a warmth coming from him and could see that his dark eyes had little flecks of light in them. I felt myself moving closer to him and then jerked back.

'Come on, look at yourself.' He was smiling down at me, smiling just the way that he smiles at Cousin Eliza. I didn't dare look at her. I didn't dare look at anyone. I was too embarrassed to move and I knew that I had started to blush when he touched my hair.

So Henry unhooked the looking glass and brought it over to me, putting one finger under my chin and turning my head slightly so that I could see myself perfectly in the glass.

'Very nice,' said Mrs Austen drily. 'Now, girls, thank Henry and put these upstairs until Saturday night. Jane, your satin slippers definitely need cleaning before the ball, and, Jenny, you had better check yours also.'

'You do mine, will you, Jenny?' said Jane in an offhand manner. 'I must do my practising.'

She went off without saying anything else and I was a bit puzzled.

I wondered if I had offended her – or perhaps she thought the velvet bandeau was a better present than her silk ribbon.

I didn't think about it too much, though. All the way up the stairs I could feel the tingle of a beating pulse in the place where Henry had put his finger, just on the soft place under my chin.

Something very embarrassing happened later on. I was dusting the breakfast parlour after lunch while Jane was practising the piano. The boys hadn't gone back into the schoolroom yet. They were all shouting and laughing and making a great noise on the stairs.

And I overheard a conversation.

And it was about me.

And I didn't move away as I should have done.

I just stayed there with the duster in my hand, listening.

It was my aunt and my uncle in the study next to the breakfast room. They had been talking for quite some time – about vegetables and about Mr Austen's farm, I think – and I had been taking no notice.

And then I heard my name.

'Mr Austen,' my aunt had said. Her voice, as usual, was the voice of someone who is in a rush and has something of importance to say. It is a very high-pitched voice – like a corncrake, Jane says. It's the sort of voice that easily goes through walls.

'Mr Austen,' she said. 'I wish you would have a

word with Henry and tell him to stop flirting with Jenny. He'll turn that girl's head.'

Mr Austen must have said something. I just heard a murmur.

'Nonsense,' said my aunt. 'She's no child. She's sixteen years old. That's just the age when girls get all sorts of silly notions about love into their heads.'

One of the boys shouted something and then they all went running out of the hall door. I could hear the noise of their boots on the steps, and through the window I saw them running across the grass towards the field. Sometimes they played ball for a while before lessons began.

Now that they had gone, everything was quiet so I could hear Mr Austen's voice quite well.

'They would make a lovely couple, Jenny and Henry, he so tall, dark and handsome and she so small, blonde and pretty – lovely girl, lovely hair, lovely eyes, sweet-natured, too; she would make a perfect wife.' From the sound of his voice I could guess that he had a smile on his face.

'Nonsense!' Mrs Austen's voice was even more high-pitched than ever. 'Don't talk such nonsense, Mr Austen. Both of them will be as poor as church mice. How could they get married? They won't have two pennies to rub together.'

Mr Austen was saying something about how they had married without many prospects, but I didn't wait to hear any more. I slipped out of the breakfast room, replaced the duster on the shelf of the cupboard under the stairs and tiptoed up to my bedroom. I was glad that Jane was still playing the piano; if she had been in the bedroom I know she would have asked me why I was so flustered. When I got to the bedroom I leaned first one cheek and then the other against the icy coldness of the window glass.

Me marry Henry! I had never imagined that anyone would even have thought of that. I wondered whether to talk to Jane about it, but then I decided against it. I thought she was a bit short with me, a bit abrupt – perhaps she is a little jealous because Henry, her adored brother, gave me such a beautiful present and made such a fuss of me. I resolved that I wouldn't mention Henry to Jane. I didn't want her to think that I was a flirt like Eliza.

I wasn't sure whether Jane would want to go down to the village today, but she did.

George was pleased to see us. He ran up straight away, and now that I wasn't so scared of him I could hear that he was saying, 'Jane.' I tried not to look away, but to look at him. He was occupied with Jane so I could really look at him without feeling embarrassed. I began to think that he really did look like one of the Austen family. His hair is brown and curly, just like Jane's hair, and although his face was dirty and one side of it is a bit twisted, his eyes are the same green-brown colour as Jane's, and as Mr

Austen's eyes also. There was an expression in them that made me very sad. They looked as if he were trying to say something, but couldn't: almost as if he were inside a cage and trying to get out. I wondered why he couldn't talk. He seemed to be able to make noises and I suddenly thought it must be terrible if he thought he was saying words, but yet no one could understand them.

Funnily enough, he seemed to be brighter and better today. Perhaps Bet is right – perhaps having a fit is like a very severe sneeze and then feeling your head clear. Now that he has got over the fit, George feels better.

Jane had another slice of cake and we taught him the sign for the letter C with very little trouble.

On the way back I suggested to Jane that the next time we see him we should go over the three letters again and make sure that he knows them. I couldn't think of any food beginning with D so I thought we might skip that and go on to E for egg. The Austens keep their own hens so it is always easy to get hold of an egg.

Sunday, 20 March 1791

James arrived so early this morning that he was in the house before any of the family was up. He had taken the overnight coach from Oxford. Mrs Austen wanted him to go to bed after breakfast, but he wouldn't. He said that he had come on purpose to practise the play and that he wanted to have a really good practise because this was Cousin Eliza's last day.

'I want everyone there – no one going off to shoot crows,' he said, glaring at Frank.

Actually Frank was quite good at the practise today. Cassandra was being wardrobe mistress and she dressed him up as Fag, the servant, in an old, slightly ragged coat of Mr Austen's. He was very funny as the servant.

'*Rich!*' he declaimed, sounding, except for his half-broken voice, just like his father in the pulpit. '*Why, I believe she owns half the stocks! Zounds, Thomas! She could pay the national debt as easily as I could my washerwoman! She has a lapdog that eats out of gold – she feeds her parrot with small pearls – and all her curl-papers are made of banknotes!*'

James and Eliza were funny too. I thought they acted very well together. Jane couldn't stop laughing when James said, in very prim tones, after Mrs Malaprop was complaining about Lydia (Cassandra), '*It is not to be wondered at, ma'am – all this is the natural consequence of teaching girls to read. Had*

I a thousand daughters, by heaven! I'd as soon have
them taught the black art as their alphabet!'

'Time for church, everyone,' said Mrs Austen, putting
her head round the door and grinning at the way
that Mrs Malaprop was mixing up words with other
words that sounded like them, like calling *particu-*
lars 'perpendiculars'.

'Oh, Aunt dear, I have such a headache. I vow it is
a true migraine.' Eliza clasped her hand to her forehead dramatically, as if she were still in the middle
of the play. 'Oh dear, I so hate to miss church, but I
fear I cannot go.' And then she staggered off with a
quick look over her shoulder at Henry. Jane grinned
and nudged me.

Henry came with us all along the lane to the church,
but I didn't see him in church, though I turned
around a few times to see whether he was standing
at the back.

When we came back from church though, there
was no sign of Eliza, and Henry said he wanted to
practise the scene with me, and that was good. I lost
my shyness as I was determined to be as like Eliza as
I could (but without the French accent) and it was
so lovely afterwards, while Jane was playing on the
piano, when Henry whispered in my ear some words
from the play: '*Let music be the food of love.'*

* * *

After dinner, Cassandra, Jane and I went up to the guest bedroom to help Eliza to pack her clothes as she was returning to London that evening.

I said very politely to Cousin Eliza that it was a shame that she had to go back especially as she was returning a few days later, and her answer gave me a shock.

'Ah, but, *chérie*, I must go back to my poor little boy.' She pronounced the word *little* as 'leetle'.

I said that I didn't know she had a little boy – I wondered why no one had mentioned him. And then, since she had called him 'poor', I asked her politely whether her little boy was unwell.

'Poor angel! He is never well! But I have found a physician that will give a new treatment.' She was mopping her eyes with her handkerchief and Cassandra was shaking her head and frowning at me so I said no more. A minute later Eliza had gone to the window, laughing gaily and calling down to Henry. She accepted his invitation to come and see the new horse that he had bought and went clattering down the stairs on her high-heeled French shoes.

When she had gone out, Cassandra told me the story of Hastings, Eliza's son. Apparently he was now aged about four or five, but he had not been normal from the age of ten months. He suffered from fits from an early age and could not stand or walk unaided, though Eliza and her mother had managed to teach him his alphabet, according to what Eliza told her uncle.

'The trouble with Eliza is that she is so stubborn. She will not admit to herself that the child will never progress. She insists on keeping him with her and trying every cure that comes up. Last year it was sea bathing — goodness knows what it will be next year. She should find some responsible person to care for him and then just put him out of her life.' And Cassandra sighed in an elderly fashion over her cousin's obstinacy.

I said nothing, but I did not agree with Cassandra. I found myself admiring and liking Eliza more than I had done before.

I vowed to myself that if I had a child who had problems, like George or little Hastings, I would not abandon it, but would love and care for it tenderly and to me it would be the most precious child in the world.

At the end of the day, we all walked up the hill to see James and Cousin Eliza off on the stagecoach — Henry was going to stay on at Steventon for the week.

And this time I was the one that suggested to Jane that we go and see George on our way back and get on with his lessons. We didn't have any food for him, but I had my sketchbook with me and I thought he might like to see the stagecoach that I had drawn. He nodded when he saw that, but on another page I had a picture of a gun, which I had drawn for Frank in my sketchbook, like this, and George was more interested in that. As soon as he saw it, he said, 'Bang!' instantly. Jane tried to get him to make the sign for the letter *G*, but he would not do it, just kept saying, 'Bang!' and smiling as if he wanted us to be pleased with him.

'I think that is fine, Jane,' I said after a while. I could see that she was getting upset and George was beginning to look at her in a worried way. 'I think it's even better that he says "bang". That means something to him. It probably means that he can hear a little, also, if he can hear a loud sound like a shot. He's probably not completely deaf. Good boy, George, good boy,' and I patted him on the back and Jane threw her arms around him and kissed him.

Monday, 21 March 1791

When we finished our lessons this morning, Frank gave me the usual riding lesson on the donkey. I was getting on well now, and Jane could perfectly well have done it, but Frank insisted that he was the one to teach me. Cassandra is probably right about Frank. He was bored. He couldn't wait to get back to his life at sea. He and Jane kept arguing about the best way to teach me.

When we came back in, Mrs Tuckley was there and I explained to her about the new beads. She looked at them dubiously and said they would take a long time to sew on and that I should think very carefully about whether there would be time for them.

'You'll need to count them, Miss Cooper,' she said with a sigh as she slipped her thimble on to her finger. 'Then you'll have to plan where to put them. There may not be enough to arrange all over the gown.'.

I got a pewter plate from the sideboard, opened the box of glass beads and began to count them carefully, one by one, on to the plate.

Jane had promised to help me with sewing on the glass beads, but I was surprised when Cassandra joined us. The only problem was that she took charge immediately.

'Make sure that your hands are clean, Jane,' she said in a very elder-sister way. 'Now, Jenny dear, how are we going to arrange these exquisite beads?'

That was a question that didn't need an answer as Cassandra carried on almost without drawing a breath.

'I think that the best thing would be to make a triangular shape down the back and widening out to completely cover the train. I would say there aren't enough to cover the whole of the back of the gown and they need to be close together to attract the eye instantly.'

I hurriedly said I thought that was a wonderful idea, as I could see Jane opening her mouth to object. And I did really think it was a good idea. The train was my favourite part of the gown and I liked the notion of attracting attention to it – this is what it will look like.

We had quite a nice time sewing together for the next hour before Cassandra had to go and help her mother with the dinner. Jane made up a story about a young man, possessed of a good fortune, of course, who had come to the neighbourhood in order to rent Freefolk Priors, a large empty house near Steventon. Once he arrived he fell in love with the prettiest girl in the neighbourhood, Cassandra Austen. He proposed on bended knee in very flowery language (Jane was good at making up ridiculous marriage proposals) and she accepted.

'What did I say?' enquired Cassandra. She was laughing and in one of the best moods that I have ever seen her.

'Just what you ought to, of course; a lady always knows what to say.' Jane always has a smart answer for everything.

'Cassandra!' shouted Mrs Austen.

Cassandra got obediently to her feet. 'The only problem, Miss Jane,' she said, poking Jane in the shoulder with her forefinger in a friendly way, 'is that Freefolk Priors is already let — to a General Mathew.'

'A general!' Jane was impressed.

'Aged about sixty . . .'

Jane made a face at that.

'And,' continued Cassandra, 'he has no son — just one unmarried daughter — Anne — aged thirty-two and on the shelf. Mama is quite excited about this. General Mathew is the Commander-in-Chief of the Windward and Leeward Islands and Governor of Grenada. Just remember that!' And then she rushed off to the kitchen.

'Imagine!' I said to Jane. 'Thirty-two years old and on the shelf! She must feel very miserable.'

'I wouldn't care,' Jane said. She tossed her head and looked as if she would not care. 'I'd stay at home and write books and make lots of money, just like Miss Burney.'

Then her mood changed. She began to look thoughtful. 'So that's why Mama sent James to call on a General Mathew. I was wondering about that. She was very particular about brushing his coat and tying his cravat.'

We looked at each other with eyebrows raised. 'Well, well, well,' I said, but then I shook my head. 'He's too young for her; she's ten years older than him.'

'*My dear Jenny,*' said Jane, imitating her mother's voice perfectly, '*equality of age may be desirable, but money is the essential.*' She changed back to her normal voice and said, 'I bet you that this Anne Mathew has a fortune of her own. James may be the eldest and a great scholar, but he's going to be a clergyman and all he can hope for is a parish. Having a general as a father-in-law will help with that.'

After dinner it was raining so Jane and I couldn't go down to see George. We spent some time making more drawings for him. We got as far as *O* in the alphabet and I wished that we could get an orange for him to eat, but I never saw oranges at Steventon parsonage. The Austens seemed to eat only the fruit and vegetables that they grew themselves. It was a pity though, because I felt that my picture of an orange would not be understood by him unless he had tasted one once.

'Perhaps Henry would bring one from Overton,' suggested Jane. 'You ask him. He'll do it for you.'

'No, he won't.' I could feel myself going red as usual.

'Yes, he will.'

'No, he won't!'

'Yes, he will.'

'No, he won't!'

We went on like this for about five minutes, both of us getting weak with laughter, and I suppose we were getting louder and louder because Mrs Austen popped her head in to ask what on earth we were doing.

'Jenny would love an orange; she always eats oranges in Bristol, and I told her that Henry would get one for her.' Jane kept a very straight face at this and I pretended to look at something out of the window. When I turned round, Mrs Austen was looking at me with an odd expression on her face.

'Bless me, child, if you want an orange your uncle will get you one when he goes to Basingstoke tomorrow,' she said abruptly, and went out.

I was mortified that Mrs Austen would think that I was criticizing the food I get here, but Jane said it wasn't that; it was mentioning Henry. She had a thoughtful look on her face, almost as if she had just realized something.

I didn't want to hear anything more though, so I

ran out and called to Charles to come and have his drawing lesson from me. He had drawn about forty horses already on his slate and he was beginning to be quite good at shading the curves and getting expression into the horse's eye. Today, I planned, I would allow him to use a page of my sketchbook, and if it was good then we would frame it.

After supper tonight we had music and dancing as usual. Mrs Austen insisted on everyone changing partners after the first set. Cassandra, I noticed, was then paired off with Gilbert East, the baronet's son, I was paired with Tom Fowle's youngest brother, and Henry with Jane – the rest of the boys just paired up together, and there was a lot of fun about that, with Tom Fowle calling Charles a sweet maiden.

And then it was all change again – Jane took over the piano and Mrs Austen grabbed Henry while Frank firmly took my hand.

'Jenny . . .' said Frank as he twirled me expertly around. 'Jenny, tomorrow would you be able to come out for your riding lesson before breakfast, while Jane is practising?'

I told him I would without waiting to hear the reason. Frank and Jane were quite fond of each other, but they always argue, and Jane has a habit of telling Frank exactly how he should be teaching me and he doesn't like that, probably.

Tuesday, 22 March 1791

My riding lesson with Frank went very well this morning — he seemed to be pleased that Jane wasn't hanging around criticizing or making jokes. He told me all about his life at sea and his hopes of becoming a lieutenant. He said that the first lieutenant was hopeless and that he was sure he could do the job much better.

Then he seemed to get a bit embarrassed and started talking about the ball at the Assembly Rooms. He asked me if I was looking forward to it.

I just said, 'Oh yes,' and I immediately started to think about Henry, and when I next looked at Frank I thought he looked a bit sulky so I apologized quickly and asked him what a first lieutenant did on a ship.

Frank is very nice. I wish that he were my brother. He's the same age as me, of course, but I think of him as younger. Jane always says that girls are much older than boys of the same age!

After we had put the donkey away and fed her, Frank went off to see whether breakfast was ready, but I stayed outside for a while. It was windy, but not really cold. I liked the damp, fresh smell of the country air. Everything was nice and quiet except for the noise of the hens' beaks tapping their large metal dish. It was Cassandra's task every morning to let them out of their house. Jane told me that she used to help Cassandra, but in the past few weeks her sister had told her that she would prefer to do it on her own. There was no sign of Cassandra anywhere this morning, but oddly enough I heard a giggle from the hen house.

I was just going to go in for breakfast when I saw Mrs Austen come out of the kitchen. She came out very fast and hadn't stopped to put on her pattens; she still had her list slippers on. They were too big for her and just flapped around her feet. She didn't see me standing there, but headed straight for the hen house, bustling past the feeding hens, who scattered with squawks of dismay and then came running back to their dish again.

'Cassandra!' Her voice pealed out and there was an uncanny likeness to the squawk of a disturbed hen. 'Come out of there directly, the two of you.'

I should have gone indoors straight away, but I was standing just beside one of the laurel bushes and I thought it might be best to stay there in case I attracted attention to myself. I was very embarrassed though when I saw Tom Fowle follow Cassandra out of the hen house. He looked very silly, with a sheepish face and a couple of white chicken feathers sticking to his hair. (I did a sketch for Jane to show her just what he looked like – she thought it was very funny so I've stuck it into my journal here.)

172

'Go inside for your breakfast, Tom,' said Mrs Austen in a very severe tone. 'I'll get Mr Austen to deal with you later on.'

Tom gave one glance at Cassandra and then went off as quickly as he could. After a moment I heard his large feet crunching the gravel on the carriage sweep in front of the house. He probably felt relieved that it was Mr Austen who was going to deal with him. I think all of the boys were far more scared of Mrs Austen than of her husband. I heard Gilbert East say once that Mr Austen was the easiest and kindest schoolmaster that anyone could ever have.

'What have you got to say for yourself, young lady?' Mrs Austen sounded choked with rage as she faced Cassandra. Her back was towards me, but I could tell by the twitch of her head how angry she was.

'We love each other.' Cassandra was braver than I would have been. She faced her mother without going red. She wasn't crying either.

I took two steps backwards, very gently. I would try to escape while they were occupied with each other. It would be terribly awkward if one of them chanced to see me standing there listening to their private conversation.

'Nonsense!' I heard Mrs Austen say as I reached the second laurel bush.

'He wants to marry me.' I had reached the third laurel bush when Cassandra said that. Her voice was defiant and quite loud. A movement from overhead took my attention and I saw Jane up there. She was sitting on the window seat of our bedroom and the window was slightly ajar. She must have finished her piano practise and gone upstairs to air the room before breakfast. She would be listening to everything with great interest.

'Cassandra, just you listen to me,' screeched Mrs Austen. Her voice was so loud that even the hens seemed to be impressed, and they gathered around her as though she were preaching a sermon to them — or else perhaps they thought she was calling them for a second meal. I moved to the fourth laurel bush. I would go in by the front door, I planned; I would just steal along the side of the house and keep on the moss beside the wall so that my feet didn't touch the gravel.

I couldn't help overhearing though. Mrs Austen's voice was getting louder by the minute. The whole house must be hearing the words.

'No money . . . no prospects . . . What will you live on? . . . after all I have said to you . . . ashamed of yourself . . .'

Cassandra tried to say something about love, but her mother interrupted her.

'Love!' she said scornfully. 'I tell you this, Miss Cassandra, love will vanish pretty quickly when you have ten children in a couple of pokey rooms. That boy is going to be a clergyman. It's his only future. He can't marry for at least ten years, not until he makes a position for himself, finds a patron, gets a parish. And where will you be in ten years' time? Answer me that, pray. You'll be an old maid, a very poor old maid. Your father can do nothing for you; nothing, do you understand? You must marry money.'

And now I was at the kitchen door. The cook was frying eggs for breakfast; the spluttering of the hot fat had probably prevented her from hearing anything, but the parlourmaid and the kitchen maid were whispering and giggling in the corner by the scullery. I brushed past them and rinsed my hands under the tap there and then slipped into the breakfast parlour. Jane was already there, looking demure, but her hazel eyes were sparkling with excitement.

Cassandra didn't come in to breakfast. Mr Austen asked where she was and Mrs Austen told him that Cassandra had a headache. I saw the boys look at each other; Tom Fowle turned red, and Jane nudged my foot under the table. Mr Austen, I thought, was probably the only person in the house who didn't know all about the hen-house drama this morning.

'I feel sorry for Cassandra,' I said to Jane as we began our lessons. I twirled Mr Austen's globe as I thought about Mrs Austen's words. Life was hard for girls without money, I thought. Unless a rich man asked their hand in marriage, they were doomed to be old maids and that wasn't a pleasant thought!

'I wish I were a boy,' said Jane as if she had read my thoughts. 'Frank has great plans to be rich. First he is going to be the best midshipman in the navy — so good that his captain will immediately recommend that he become a lieutenant — and then he will be such a good lieutenant that he will catch the eye of some admiral, and the admiral will recommend that he become a captain and get his own ship. And then he will capture some Dutch ship and get lots of prize money and he will be very rich . . .'

I nodded, my eyes on the globe, looking at all the places where Frank would sail in his ships — the East Indies and the West Indies, the Atlantic Ocean and the Pacific Ocean. '. . . and then he will be able to marry whosoever he likes.' It would probably take about ten years for Frank to get to that position, I thought. It was just as well that I was not in love with him or I too would be an old maid by the time he came home rich and triumphant. Who would I marry though? I didn't think that Mrs Austen would like me to marry either Henry or Frank, and I didn't really know any other young man.

And then a sudden thought crossed my mind. It was more of a picture than a thought, really.

And the picture was of a very handsome young man in naval uniform, with black hair, high cheek-bones and brown eyes and a voice that was as soft and warm as chocolate.

But I didn't really want to see Captain Thomas Williams again, did I?

I couldn't see him again.

I just couldn't.

It was impossible.

Unthinkable.

If I did, I would be disgraced forever and my reputation would be in tatters.

Even if he said nothing to the Austens, what would he think of a girl who allowed herself to walk through the streets of Southampton at midnight with an unknown man? I imagined those brown eyes filled with scorn and I knew that I definitely did not want to see him again. How miserable – if only things were different. If only I had been cleverer that night, hidden myself better – not been such a coward as to stand in the middle of the pavement staring, like a frightened mouse, at that madman whirling his sword. I wish I didn't keep remembering Captain Williams. It's so stupid; I hate myself.

I'm going to turn back the pages of my journal and look at the sketch I made of him. At least I have that.

'Look at this,' said Jane. She had been scribbling on a piece of paper while I was daydreaming and now she was copying it into her notebook where she keeps her stories. I read it over her shoulder and said that she would have to change the name of Cassandra because she would be upset if she read it – everyone reads Jane's stories notebook.

'I'll change it to Rebecca then in my fair copy – you can have the one that says Cassandra, because no one reads your journal.' Jane was writing busily as she spoke.

'There you are,' she said, tossing it over to me when she had finished.

So I've put it in here. I'll have lots of Jane's written works before this journal is finished.

'Lovely and fair one,' said the noble youth, 'not withstanding your forbidding squint, your greasy curls and your swelling back, which are more frightful than imagination can paint or pen describe: I cannot refrain from expressing my raptures and asking you to marry me.'

Alas for the passionate young man, Cassandra's mama did not approve of the match on account of the tender years of the young couple, Cassandra being but 36 and the noble youth little more than 63. It was agreed that they should wait a little while till they were a good deal older before embarking on matrimony.

Wednesday, 23 March 1791

Mrs Austen is still in a bad mood today. She was very cross with Jane this morning. She says that she has no accomplishments except piano playing.

'You can't sketch, you have no interest in cooking or managing a house; you just spend all of your time making up jokes and scribbling silly stories,' scolded Mrs Austen.

'Well, I don't care,' said Jane. 'I won't want to get married to a man who would want me to be a house-keeper. I shall marry a man with a good fortune.'

'Jane . . .' said Mrs Austen. She said the words slowly and solemnly. 'Don't be silly. It won't be up to you to choose a husband. A man will choose you, and no man of fortune will choose a silly girl without any accomplishments who spends all her time making jokes and allowing boys to slide her down the stairs on a rug. I know you are not yet sixteen, but you must think of the future. Your father cannot afford to give you a dowry. If you wish to marry well, you must be willing to make yourself attractive to a young man of fortune. Why can't you be more like your cousin? Look how polite she is and how beautifully she draws. I'll tell you this, Jane: she's the sort of girl that men like. You're just a silly tomboy. The Lord forgive me, but I have no patience and no time to deal with this child!'

And then she slammed the door and went out.

'I don't care,' repeated Jane, opening the door again. And then, very loudly, she shouted after her mother, 'I don't care; so don't bother talking to me. I shall make my living by writing novels, and thousands of people will buy them, and that's that.' She slammed the door shut and scowled at me for a minute and I felt terrible. I wished that Mrs Austen hadn't said that about me.

However, Jane being Jane, after a minute she began to grin and she scribbled a few words on a piece of paper, which she crammed into her pocket. Then she jumped up and said cheerfully, 'Come on, Jenny, let's go out.'

When we had put on our bonnets and were coming down the stairs we saw Cassandra go into Mr Austen's study.

'Tom Fowle is in there, and my mother also,' whispered Jane. We looked at each other.

'I hope they don't send poor Tom away,' said Jane as we went down the avenue towards the gate. 'I like Tom.'

'And he and Cassandra are very much in love,' I said. I felt very, very sorry for them.

Mr Austen had brought an orange home for everyone. Jane had decided that she would be the one to give the orange to George as he was her brother, and I said that in that case I would share mine with her.

George was glad to see us. He was getting used to

all the strange things that we did, and I noticed that his eyes always went to the basket when we arrived.

Today I took out the picture of the orange first. I was really proud of it as I had copied it from the real fruit and blended the paints very carefully until I got the exact colour. As I had guessed, he didn't take too much interest, but I formed my fingers and thumb into a round shape and kept saying 'orange', while pointing to the letter *O*, and he made an attempt at making the sign after me.

But when Jane peeled the orange and popped a slice in his mouth, he was amazed by the taste. I don't think he had ever eaten anything so strange. For a moment he stood very still and I thought he was going to spit it out, but then he chewed and swallowed and opened his mouth for more. After every few slices we made him point to the letter and make the sign with his own fingers and thumb. By the end of the time we were sure that he knew the sign for the letter *O*, and we tested him on a few more. He remembered *A* for apple, *E* for egg and *C* for cake, but that was all.

'Still,' I said to Jane as we walked home, 'now he knows four letters of the alphabet and a month ago he didn't know any; perhaps by Christmas he will know them all.'

Mrs Austen was in a much better mood at dinner time, and what was even more surprising was that Cassandra was looking very well. She was smiling to herself and being very helpful to her mother.

'I'll help Mary with the clearing up, Mama,' she said when everyone had finished. 'You go and have a rest.'

'We'll help too,' said Jane virtuously. She carefully closed the door after the last of the boys had gone out and came back over to the table and started to pile the dirty dishes on the tray.

'Come on, Cassandra, tell us what is happening,' she coaxed.

For a minute Cassandra hesitated. I felt awkward because I thought she would tell Jane to mind her own business, but I think she was so happy that she wanted to tell someone about it.

'You mustn't say a word,' she said warningly.

'Your secret is safe with me, young maiden,' hissed Jane. I thought this would annoy Cassandra, but it didn't. She just laughed.

'Well, Papa talked to Mama last night and then he talked to Tom again this morning and then we all talked together. Papa was very nice.' Cassandra's eyes filled, though her lips curved in a smile; she was halfway between laughter and tears. She looked very pretty, I thought.

'Go on,' said Jane. She didn't normally hug her sister, but she did so now. And Cassandra hugged her back.

'We've promised to wait,' she said. 'We're going

to be engaged, but not married. Tom told Papa that he does have some prospects. He has a distant cousin who is a lord – Lord Craven.'

'He never spoke of that before!' Jane sounded impressed. Her stories were full of lords.

'Tom's not like that.' Cassandra smiled gently and blushed a little. 'He never boasts. He only mentioned it to Papa today. He said that Lord Craven has promised to get him a place as a chaplain on one of his ships going to the West Indies. When he comes back Lord Craven will do his best to get him a parish.'

Jane asked her when they would be able to get married, and Cassandra told her that it would probably not be for five or six years yet. She still looked very happy about it, but when Cassandra carried out the tray to the kitchen, Jane and I agreed that the time was far too long.

'Perhaps Lord Craven will die and leave Tom ten thousand pounds,' said Jane cheerfully.

'Shh!' I said, energetically dusting the crumbs from the tablecloth. I could hear Cassandra coming back.

'You sit by the fire and we'll do the work,' said Jane solicitously, taking the copper kettle from her sister. 'People need to rest after an emotional shock, and being proposed to is probably the greatest shock that any girl can have.'

'I must find out what he said,' she muttered to me

as we carried out the kettle and teapot to the kitchen. 'How can I write romantic novels unless I know what they say on such occasions?'

I said that it was probably private, but Jane didn't look as though she were listening.

'Cassandra,' she said when the tablecloth had been folded and put away in the drawer, the fireplace swept and new wood put on the fire.

'Yes, Jane.' Cassandra was in a happy dream, staring at the flames.

'What did Tom say when he proposed?' asked Jane pleadingly.

For a moment I thought Cassandra would tell her to mind her own business. On a normal day she certainly would, but she didn't. 'He said, "How many hens will you and I have when we are married?"'

I could see Jane opening her mouth to exclaim: *What!* So I frowned at her and said very quickly, 'And what did you say, Cassandra?'

'I said, "Oh, Tom!"' And Cassandra smiled even more at the memory.

As soon as the room was tidy we left Cassandra to her happy dreams and went upstairs to our bedroom.

'Well,' said Jane as soon as the door was closed. 'I must say that I can write a better proposal than that.' She went across to her writing desk, took out a half-sheet of paper and picked up her quill. 'I'll tell you one thing, Jenny,' she said over her shoulder, 'I'm going to make sure that all my heroines fall in love with a man who can propose properly.'

'And who are in possession of a good fortune, of course,' I said quickly. This 'possessing a good fortune' was by now quite a joke between Jane and myself.

'What do you think of this for a proposal?' Jane tossed over her piece of scrap paper when she had finished and I stuck it into my journal.

'And now, my adorable Laura,' said the amiable young man, taking my hand tenderly, 'when may I hope to aspire to receive that reward for all the painfull sufferings I have undergone in the course of my Attachment to you, to which I have ever aspired? Oh! When will you reward me with Yourself?'

'This instant, Dear and Amiable Edward,' I replied.

We were immediately united by my father who, though he wasn't a clergyman, had always intended entering the church.

I'm not sure what Mr Austen might think of the idea that he wasn't really a clergyman, but at least this time she had written Laura instead of Cassandra.

Thursday, 24 March 1791

Frank was a bit shy and embarrassed when we met in the stables this morning. Sometimes he's quite brotherly, but at other times he seems uneasy with me when I am by myself. We had a good lesson though. Frank was very encouraging about my progress as a rider. He wanted me to come with him to Deane Gate Inn for the letters, but I didn't feel confident to ride my donkey on the road.

When I went indoors, after he had gone, Jane was still practising the piano so I found Charles and suggested that he give his framed picture of the horse to his mother.

Mrs Austen was very pleased with Charles's drawing. She praised it and immediately got John Warren to knock a nail into the wall in the breakfast parlour so that it could be hung up where everyone could admire it. She's a funny woman; she can be so cold, but also so warm and friendly. She tried to kiss Charles, but he didn't want her to in case the other boys laughed at him, so she kissed me instead and told me what a good girl I was and what a comfort it was to have me. I wish she would act like that to Jane, and then Jane wouldn't be so prickly with her.

But then a minute later, when Henry came down to breakfast and jokingly kissed my hand and told me how pretty I was looking, I saw Mrs Austen look at me with quite a different expression.

The parlourmaid was just bringing in the dish of eggs when Frank arrived back. There was one letter for Henry. He took it reluctantly from Frank's outstretched hand, made a face over it and stuck it into his pocket immediately. There was also one for Mrs Austen. She left hers lying on the table while she was making the tea and then opened it while she was munching through the dry toast that was all she ever ate for breakfast.

'Who's your letter from, my dear?' Mr Austen was always very obliging. He knew that his wife loved to gossip about her letters.

'From Mrs Portal.' Mrs Austen was very thoughtful. The letter was a short one, but she read it through again. I was opposite her at the table and I thought it was probably the third time that she had reread it.

'John's mother?' Henry looked up. 'Perhaps she thinks that I didn't give enough money for his horse. He's her darling only son, you know.'

'No, it's nothing about a horse at all,' said Mrs Austen. She scrutinized Henry from his glossy hair to his well-brushed coat.

'Who is your letter from, Henry?' teased Frank, and Henry gave him an angry look. Jane had told me that Henry was living at home for a while as he had got into debt and owed money to lots of tradesmen and a lodging-house keeper in Oxford. I saw Mr Austen look at Henry in a worried way and then at his wife. She, however, was taking no notice of anyone, but had gone back to staring at her own letter as if she was planning something. When she spoke, it was still in that thoughtful manner.

'I was thinking that we would ask the Portals to drink a dish of tea with us tomorrow evening. Henry, I wish you would ride over there and take a note from me, inviting them. The young people could have a dance with all of you afterwards.'

'What young people?' asked Frank. 'There's only one – just John.'

'They have a visitor.' While Mrs Austen spoke, her eyes rested on Henry, tall and handsome, his morning coat spotless as always, his white silk stock neatly knotted around his neck, his leather boots polished (by Charles) to a high shine. When she spoke again it was directly at him and her voice was low, impressive and full of meaning. 'A Miss King.'

Jane looked at me and I looked at her. Jane's lips formed the words 'possessed of a good fortune'.

I gave her a smile, but I felt a little hurt at the way Henry so quickly got to his feet, checked himself in the looking glass at the top of the room and then waited attentively while his mother rapidly wrote the note, sealed it and handed it to him.

'Take it over to Laverstoke House yourself,' she said. 'Make sure that you give Miss King my compliments and say that I am looking forward to meeting her.'

Friday, 25 March 1791

The Portals didn't come to drink a dish of tea with us today. Henry brought back a polite note saying that Miss King was tired after her journey and wanted to reserve her energies for the ball at the Assembly Rooms in Basingstoke. Mrs Portal hoped that Mrs Austen and her charming family would be present. Henry had not met Miss King, as she had been upstairs when he called. Apparently Mrs Portal had spent some time trying to persuade her to come downstairs, but Miss King had not appeared, although Henry had spent half an hour there making polite conversation in the drawing room.

At lunchtime Mrs Austen seemed to be turning matters over in her mind.

'How did you like William Chute, Jenny?' she enquired casually.

I replied carefully that I thought him very pleasant, but I could feel my cheeks getting red.

'He danced with you, didn't he? Usually he's keener on playing cards than dancing. His mother despairs of him. He's thirty years old and no sign of a wife. And there he is, the master of such a fine property.'

'He danced with all three of the Bigg sisters too,' said Jane promptly. 'Do you think that he will make an offer for every one of them as well as for Jenny?'

'Don't be ridiculous, Jane,' said Mrs Austen automatically.

'They're going to the Assembly Rooms ball tomor-row night, you know,' said Jane warningly. 'And their little brother, Harris, is going too. That's prob-ably a plan. They think that William Chute will be fond of children and Catherine will lead Harris by the hand up to William Chute and then cast down her eyelashes, and William Chute will immediately think what a beautiful mother she will make for his children, so he will propose.'

'Harris Bigg is a confounded nuisance,' said Henry. 'He almost lamed my mare the last time I had her out. He managed to fall off his pony just in front of me. He's the clumsiest child I have ever known. I think he might be a bit simple.'

I wondered what Henry thought about his own brother, George. Jane had said that she was the only one that cared. It seemed strange to me. I had only known George a few weeks, but I was fond of him and I worried about him.

'Harris Bigg! He's younger than me!' Charles stopped eating for a moment, but then carried on again. He still looked indignant, but he liked his food.

'So?' Henry was in a sour mood this morning.

'Well, why can't I go?' Charles swallowed his mouthful.

'You'd have to wear white gloves,' said Mr Austen warningly.

'And no one would dance with you,' said Frank.

'I'll dance with Charles,' I said boldly. Mrs Austen smiled at me affectionately and Charles stuck his tongue out at Frank.

'Save me a dance, Jenny, also,' said Henry. His voice sounded very affectionate and I could feel the warm colour rushing to my cheeks. I looked down at the table and then looked up again. He was still watching me with a smile on his face. I wondered if he thought that I was pretty. I wished that it was just the two of us there in the parlour by ourselves. We had never been alone since that night after the Chutes' dinner party. What did he feel when Mrs Austen talked of William Chute dancing with me? Perhaps he was jealous and that was why he asked me to save him a dance at Basingstoke. If only he knew! William Chute would be nothing to me if only Henry cared for me. But did he? I made myself remember how he flirted with Eliza and forgot me when she was around, but I couldn't help my heart beating very quickly and I hope that nobody noticed that my breaths were short.

'You'll be wearing your new gown, will you?' asked Henry softly. His head was quite close to mine and he seemed to be trying to catch my eye.

'We're hiring a carriage, and Henry and Frank can go on the back. I suppose that Charles could fit in there with them,' said Mrs Austen.

'I don't want to go on the back; Henry and I will ride,' grumbled Frank, to my relief, as my aunt had begun to eye me in an irritable way with Henry still smiling at me, and my cheeks were hot with embarrassment. Now she turned her annoyance on Frank.

'You will do no such thing,' she said decisively. 'We don't want you arriving with mud-splashed breeches. And what about your shoes? You would have to carry them with you. You can't dance at the Assembly Rooms in riding boots.' She wasn't looking at Frank now but at Henry.

'Would you powder your hair, Henry?' she enquired, tilting her head as she surveyed him carefully. 'It would look very good.'

I had to bite my tongue to stop myself exclaiming. I liked Henry's dark hair, tied behind his neck with a plain black ribbon. Powdered hair always looked so artificial.

'Certainly not,' said Henry sternly. 'I have enough expenses without having to buy hair powder, especially now that they are talking of putting a tax on it.'

'Still' – Mrs Austen was trying to console herself – 'I dare say that many young ladies these days may think it looks old-fashioned.'

'Don't worry, Mama.' Henry stooped and gave her a kiss. 'I won't disgrace you. Charles will polish my new shoes with the buckles on them – won't you, Charles?'

'Oh yes,' said Charles eagerly. I guessed that Henry would give him sixpence for doing it. Jane told me that although Henry was in debt, he was always very generous to Charles, and Charles, like Jane, adored him.

'How's James going to get there then? He's coming too, isn't he?' asked Frank, who was still annoyed.

'James,' said Mrs Austen with a small smile, 'will be going with General Mathew and his daughter, Anne.'

'Really?' Mr Austen looked surprised but Mrs Austen distracted him by asking him had he finished with his newspaper – knowing that he hadn't, of course.

'What shall you wear, Mama?' asked Cassandra. She was very careful of her mother's feelings these days, I noticed. Poor girl – she was so relieved at being allowed to consider herself engaged to Tom Fowle.

Mrs Austen laughed. 'I think my yellow silk will have another outing,' she said. 'It's an old friend of twenty years and I wouldn't want to neglect it. Thank God I am too advanced in years for this new fashion of straight-down muslin gowns. I like a gown with a good wide skirt.'

'Jenny,' said Jane later on, 'I was thinking that we might try to dress up George one day, especially now that he has got used to having his hair combed and his face washed. There is an old suit in the theatre dressing-up box. My mother made it for Frank a couple of years ago when he was acting the part of a parson.'

I asked her if she was sure that it was worth bothering George about a small thing like clothes. She didn't reply for a moment, but when she did her answer sent goose pimples down my back.

And this is what she said:

'I'm thinking of bringing him over one day next week and showing Mama and Papa how he can read some of his letters.'

Saturday, 26 March 1791

Cousin Eliza and James arrived on the stagecoach this morning. They hadn't told their time of arrival so they drove from Deane Gate Inn by post-chaise. Jane and I were out in the garden gathering daffodils when the chaise, driven by the post boy, skidded across the gravel of the sweep and pulled up in front of the hall door. Eliza was laughing and so was James. He didn't often laugh; I realized that when I saw him now. He handed Eliza out of the chaise with quite an air of a man of the world, and Eliza dropped a splendid curtsy to him. He whispered something in her ear as she rose up gracefully and she said, 'Fie, fie, Sir Anthony!' and they were both laughing as they went up the steps.

I wondered whether Henry saw them.

Jane and I still had a last fitting for our gowns this morning and we had to help with the sewing of the hems, so we didn't join in the rehearsals in the barn. I kept wondering how they were getting on and who Eliza was flirting with – Henry or James?

Eliza was in great good humour at dinner time. Mr Austen laughed so much at one of her tales that a button flew off his waistcoat and Mrs Austen had to sew it on again.

After dinner, Cassandra, Jane and I tried on our new gowns so that Mr Austen and Cousin Eliza could see them. Jane wanted the boys called in, but neither Cassandra nor I agreed with her. I think Cassandra wants to surprise Tom Fowle tomorrow night – and I want to surprise Henry. Cousin Eliza said that she will wash and dress our hair in the latest style from Paris and that we should not let anyone see us until the transformation (she pronounced it in the French fashion) had taken place.

Cassandra took off her gown quite quickly and went back downstairs just as the boys were coming out of the schoolroom. Jane and I stayed chatting with Cousin Eliza and listening to her talk about Marie Antoinette, the Queen of France, and the things that used to go on in the court before this revolution came along.

Cousin Eliza had great plans for doing our hair. She went to her trunk and got out some trimmings for Jane and me. There was a red velvet rose for Jane and a beautiful blue velvet one for me. I explained that Henry had given us a ribbon each for our hair. I could feel myself getting red, but although the velvet rose was nice, I still wanted to wear his gift. Cousin Eliza didn't mind in the least. She helped us to trim our gowns with the roses instead. They were sewn to the left shoulder and they looked lovely there.

She said that we were two of the prettiest girls in England and that the young men would be queuing up to dance with us. I hope she is right. I really only know two young men, Henry and Frank.

Frank is very nice, though he's quite young. He probably will dance with me, but I hope that Henry dances with me also.

Eliza then gave us both a little card to record the names of our partners. It was small enough to go in the smallest reticule and it had a tiny little silver pencil attached to it.

'And you must have a fan,' she said suddenly. She went over and rummaged in her trunk and eventually she found two of the most beautiful fans, made so finely of ivory that they were no thicker than a pencil.

'There you are,' she said triumphantly. 'These come from my beloved France. The one with the little pink rosebuds on it for Jane, and the one with white and gold lilies for Jenny.'

'It's lovely, but it's just that I don't want a fan dangling from my wrist all the evening,' said Jane, handing hers back.

'But, *chérie*, you don't dangle your fan from your wrist; you use it, *mon enfant*. Don't you know the language of the fan?'

Jane and I looked at each other and we both

raised our eyebrows. 'No, we don't, Eliza,' said Jane. 'Tell us.'

'Dear, dear, dear, *ma pauvre petite*! Your poor *maman*, Jane! She is so busy with the meals and the washing she has not time to teach the young girls the things that matter.'

'Tell us, Cousin Eliza, please,' I repeated. I couldn't ever imagine Mrs Austen, with her work-worn hands and her battered features, fluttering a fan in front of her face. If we were going to learn, it would have to be from Eliza.

'There are so many things you can say with a fan!' Eliza spread her hands in a very foreign way and then took my fan from me. '*Regardez, mes enfants!* Like this' — she half folded her fan and put her head on one side — 'you say, "I'm not sure," and then, like this' — she folded up the fan and turned its left side uppermost — 'this says, "Call tomorrow," and . . .'

'Jane,' screamed Mrs Austen from the bottom of the stairs, 'where did you put my shawl? I declare to the heavens, you are the untidiest girl I have ever seen or heard of in my life! Come down at once and find it.'

'Wait till I come back — I want to hear all the rest.' Jane slammed the door behind her and went clattering down the stairs.

When she was gone I asked Eliza how men knew how to understand the language of the fan. Did someone teach them? I was thinking about Henry, and the strange thing was that I think Eliza might have been thinking about Henry too when she answered with a slight smile on her beautifully rouged lips.

'*Chérie*, a wise young man will always get an experienced lady to teach him the language of love.'

For a few minutes neither of us said anything, but then as we heard Jane's footsteps running up the stairs, Eliza said, very softly, 'Jenny, Henry is sweet and good-natured, but he is a young man, and young men love to play games. Do not get too serious. You have fun while you are young.'

And then Jane whirled back into the room and Eliza gave us more lessons on the language of the fan until we were quite perfect — though I could never imagine myself unfurling my fan in that dramatic gesture that meant: *I love you!*

'I'm going to have such fun teaching Tom Chute all about this!' said Jane in the end.

But I'm not going to have to teach Henry, I thought to myself; I think he probably knows it already. Did

I mind? I decided not to think of it any more. Cousin Eliza was just having fun with Henry. Perhaps I should do the same.

Before we left, Eliza told us both to come to her room after supper.

'Her first ball is the most exciting event in a young girl's life,' she said dramatically. 'You come here to my *chambre* after supper, and I will get you ready. You will bathe here —' She gestured theatrically towards the hip bath by the fire. It had a screen half around it, but I could see a basket full of little jars and bottles on a stool. 'And I shall shampoo your hair with my special shampoo from India. My godfather, Warren Hastings, brings me a present of some every time he visits England, so I shall shampoo and dress your hair and then you can have a little rest. One should always rest before dancing — and then you will come back in here and don your new gowns. And then the ball!'

'Thank you very much, Cousin Eliza,' I said, and Jane hugged her.

'I shall enjoy it hugely,' said Eliza. 'You must go now, *mes petites*. I shall take a little *promenade* over to the barn to run through my part again.' She slipped on her cloak and pulled the large hood over her head.

I don't know who she is going to practise with as James has already left for General Mathew's place. She and Henry don't have a scene together.

I could hardly eat any supper as I was so excited and so nervous, and Jane was almost as bad. As soon as the meal was over and the table cleared, we slipped upstairs, telling Mrs Austen that we were going to have a rest. First of all we went into our bedroom. It was still bright out of doors, but the room was dim and the two white and silver gowns hanging on the closet door gleamed with the shimmer of moonlight.

'I can't believe that it is going to happen, can you?' I asked Jane, but she just said, 'Grab your towel and wrapper before Cassandra comes along to see what we are doing.'

We tiptoed down the stairs, taking the steps cautiously one by one so that the wood did not squeak. Just as we got to the bottom of the flight, Sukey, the kitchen maid, came toiling up, carrying two heavy pails of steaming hot water, one in either hand. Jane opened the door for her and then we went in. The room was already steamy, with a huge glowing fire, and it smelt of rich and exotic scents. As we came in, Eliza was emptying a small bottle of bright red liquid into the water already in the bath. Sukey poured first one pailful and then the second one and the red liquid swirled in cloudy whirls and coils, the vivid colour changing to a dusky pink. The air was filled with a sweet fragrance and then Eliza added a handful of lavender to the water and the clean, sharp smell blended with the perfume of roses.

'Thank you, Sukey,' said Eliza gently. Sukey looked almost bewitched by the scents, but she pulled herself together and bobbed a curtsy. 'Here you are,' said Eliza, handing her a coin. 'Come back with two more pails in half an hour.' And then, Eliza being Eliza, she took a little scented muslin bag from her basket and handed it to the kitchen maid. 'Put that under your pillow tonight, Sukey, and you will have sweet dreams.'

'Thank you, ma'am.' Sukey bobbed another curtsy and went towards the door, taking one last look at the steaming bath before closing the door quietly behind her.

'Now, *mes petites*, we have to decide on a soap for you.'

'We brought our soap, Eliza,' said Jane, holding out the scummy white bar that lived on our washstand.

'*Mais non! Mais non!*' Eliza was getting more French by the moment. She took the soap from Jane, smelt it and put it down with a shudder. 'No, that coarse lye soap is *terrrrrible* for your delicate skins. How could your *maman* give you such a thing?

Voilà!' And Eliza went in behind the screen and came out with two bars of soap and held them out. Jane touched the orange one, but I only had eyes for the second piece of soap. It was a pale green, shiny and smooth and glossy. I sniffed the bar, and Eliza handed it to me with a smile. I held it up to the light from the window. It was completely translucent and it smelt wonderfully romantic and aromatic – like pine needles under a hot sun.

'Mine smells of oranges,' said Jane, sniffing hers.

'You have chosen so well, my children,' enthused Eliza. 'I knew that the green would suit Jenny's character – shy, like a little violet in the moss beside a spring – and you, my Jane, this is your scent – sharp, exotic, spicy – just like your personality.'

First Eliza washed my hair with her special Indian shampoo. She rubbed and massaged my head and then showed me in the looking glass. I had white foam like a whipped syllabub all over my head, almost like a very curly wig, and I smelt of incense.

While I bathed, Jane had her hair shampooed and then she bathed. Eliza insisted that we use her thick Turkish towels, not the thin, hard towels from our bedroom, and while we sat, wrapped in these, in front of the fire, she styled our hair.

Mine was pulled back from my face, with just one little curl hanging over my forehead. Then Eliza fastened the rest of my hair with a little ribbon of rubber on the back of the crown of the head and allowed the whole weight of it to flow down my back. While the hair was still damp, she quickly wound strands of it around spills of paper and tied them tightly with rags.

'Leave them in place until after your gown is on. I myself will brush it out and fasten the blue velvet bandeau. You will be ravishing, *ma petite*!'

And then Eliza went to work on Jane's hair. First she sprinkled it with an exotic oil that filled the room with its spicy smell and then she wound each curl around her finger, brushing it and holding it in place until it dried before going on to the next.

'I shall just take some of this back hair to form *un petit chignon*,' she cried. 'Ah, now, it starts to come together. *Voyons,* we will make you a little dark-haired rose.'

And the amazing thing was that Jane's head did look like a rose — like one of those huge French roses with hundreds of curled petals. I told her how pretty she looked — she couldn't do the same for me with my hair all screwed into corkscrew spirals, but I had complete confidence in Cousin Eliza.

'And now, *mes enfants,* go back to your room and sleep. I will wake you before the carriage comes and help you to get dressed. But sleep now.'

Jane is asleep as I write this, but I couldn't sleep. I wanted to write down everything about that extraordinary hour in *Madame la Comtesse*'s room. When I am old, I will read these pages again and I will remember what it was like.

The Assembly Rooms
at Basingstoke

Sukey taps at the door and we both wake with a start. She puts fresh wood on to the fire, lights the candles, and then goes out with a last look at the two beautiful gowns. 'Jane, help me with my stays. Lace them tighter . . . tighter. They should push the bosom up.'

I can hardly breathe, but then Jane opens the laces a little. 'You look fine,' she says. 'At least you have a bosom to show off. I wish my bosom would grow a bit. I'm going to stuff a couple of Cassandra's torn silk stockings inside my stays.'

I slip on my chemise and then my finest lawn petticoat. I wear my shortest petticoat. I don't want any of it to be seen under the gown. The gown is too beautiful.

And then Eliza appears with her hair in curling papers and wearing a very becoming wrapper of lace; she seizes the two gowns and we follow her to her chamber, which is lit by at least twenty candles. She hangs up the gowns and then shakes a little more of that spicy, aromatic oil over Jane's hair and brushes her curls once more.

Then Jane has to sit very still with a piece of old muslin over her head to absorb the extra oil while Eliza takes out my curling papers and brushes each fat ringlet over her finger and arranges Henry's bandeau carefully, pulling forward a couple of curls over my forehead. She brings over the looking glass and I think that I look years older, that my hair is blonde and beautiful, that my eyes are large and even bluer than my velvet bandeau. I don't even notice my snub nose.

Then Eliza slips our gowns over our heads very carefully, produces two pairs of superfine white elbow-length gloves from her trunk, hands us our fans and our reticules. Last of all she leads us over to a full-sized cheval looking glass – the only one in the house, I think – and we both tell each other how lovely we look.

'That gown really suits you. I think white is your best colour,' I say to Jane. 'I like you better in white than in pink.'

'I'm glad we forced Mama to agree to short sleeves, aren't you?' Jane was admiring her bare arms.

'I love them.' But I was too busy looking over my shoulder, admiring the shimmer of blue light from the beads on my train, to bother about my arms.

'Sit on the bed, *mes enfants,* while I dress,' says Eliza, and we sit and admire how swiftly she gets ready, patting her lips with a piece of damp red leather from Brazil (so she told us), brushing out her curls, dusting her face with some talc and pulling on a pair of superfine silk stockings before taking a gown of shimmering lilac from her press.

'The coach from the inn has arrived.' Charles is clattering up the stairs, his voice high with excitement.

'Let's go,' I say, opening the door and looking out.

Charles is wearing a pair of white gloves; they are far too big for him and look quite comic next to his young-boy skeleton suit.

'Don't forget you promised me a dance, Jenny,' he says. He looks so sweet with his well-brushed hair that I feel quite motherly towards him. He sounds a bit anxious so I smile reassuringly at him as I drape a lace shawl lent by Eliza over my shoulders. Mrs Austen says that I will be cold, but I don't want to spoil the effect of my lovely gown with my old blue cloak.

In the end, Mr Austen, Henry and Frank have gone to Basingstoke by stagecoach with the other boys from Mr Austen's school. It is just as well; I'm worried about my gown as Jane and I squeeze next to Eliza, while Cassandra, Charles and Mrs Austen sit opposite. I wish I didn't have to sit down; I'm worried in case I lose one of the glass beads, although Jane and I sewed them on as firmly as we could. It seems an age before we arrive at Basingstoke.

When we get out of the coach we have to walk up the stairs. Luckily they are laid with a beautiful red carpet so I allow my train to swish up behind me, though Mrs Austen, Cassandra and Jane hold theirs up.

The Assembly Rooms are grander than I could ever have imagined. The ballroom is painted in red and gold. The ceiling is embossed with curls and scrolls of stucco, all crusted in white. Four great chandeliers, their diamond-shaped crystal droplets flashing in the light of the hundreds of beeswax candles above, hang from the ceiling, and in their light, gowns – pink, white, green, blue – revolve in the dance.

I can't walk in. I can't follow the others. I just stand, looking, until Henry comes back to me.

'Come on, Jenny,' he whispers, taking my arm. 'You look lovely. They're just finishing the cotillion and then they will have a country dance. You'll be my partner, won't you?'

And then we are in the line facing each other and the music has begun. We move to and fro. Other couples are talking but we are just dancing: just dancing and looking at each other. His eyes are fixed on me.

And then we take hands and Henry swings me around and around. He is smiling and I start to smile too.

And then I see Eliza. She is dancing with a foreign-looking man. They pass down the row in front of us and they are both chattering in French. They act like old friends and he is calling her *'chérie'*.

And then Henry and I thread in and out of the line, going down to the bottom of the row and then back again. For a moment, Jane and I are briefly opposite each other. She doesn't even see me; she is too busy laughing with the Irish cousin of the Lefroys.

Now Henry takes my hand and we join with Gilbert East and a girl called Charlotte Palmer, who are the couple nearest to us, and we whirl around in a circle.

And then the music stops and everyone stands laughing and chatting.

'Henry!' It's a fine young gentleman in a red coat with gold epaulettes on the shoulders and a high gold collar. 'Henry, what's the news? What did your father say? Will he be able to come up with the money to buy you a commission?'

A commission? Suddenly I stop smiling. Does Henry really want to join the army?

'Frederick!' Henry is a bit uneasy. He looks at me and then across at his mother, sitting on a sofa by the wall.

'Come on, Jenny,' he says, 'you look a bit tired after that dance. I'll take you over to Mama so you can have a rest.'

I'm not tired, but I allow him to walk me across the room. He is the most handsome man in the room, I think proudly, admiring the glossy black of his evening coat and the snowy whiteness of his cravat.

'Jenny! Is it time for our dance?' Little Charles is jumping up and down with excitement. Quickly he takes his white gloves out from his pocket and does his best to pull them as high as possible so that his fingers can come some way near to the tips of the gloves' fingers. He is so excited that I feel ashamed. If Henry had wanted to go on dancing with me, I would have forgotten all about the poor little fellow.

'Quick,' I say. 'The music is starting. Let's take our place in the line.'

I see a few people smiling when I join the line and face my little escort. His face is pink with excitement and he bows to me in a very courtly way. Gilbert East bumps into him purposely, but Charles takes no notice. He is concentrating very hard and I see his lips counting 'one, two, three; one, two, three' as we whirl around.

'The next dance is mine, Jenny,' says Henry as we cross over. I feel his gloved palm touch my bare arm for an instant, above my elbow. Even though my gown is so light and I didn't obey Mrs Austen and wear a flannel chemise, I suddenly feel very hot.

'Do you like dancing?' asks Charles in a very grown-up manner.

'I love it,' I say. I hope he won't keep talking to me; I want to think about Henry. I needn't have worried; even those few words make him miss his step, and he goes back to counting, his lips moving silently. Jane is dancing with Tom Chute. They are having a good time; as I'm not talking I can hear them making funny remarks to each other as they stand at the end of the row, waiting their turn to go up to the top again.

'A fine sight, ma'am,' says Tom. 'It makes one proud to be a part of this great civilization where such sprightly dancing takes place.'

'Nonsense, my dear man,' says Jane, imitating her mother's voice as usual. 'Every savage can dance.'

'There's Anna Terry over there,' I say to Charles when the dance has finished. 'Why don't you go and ask her to dance?' Anna Terry is younger than Jane and she looks a bit bored, leaning up against the sofa where her mother is sitting.

Charles eyes her doubtfully for a moment; I fear that

he will want me to dance with him again, so I quickly say, 'I've promised the next one to Henry.'

He nods and saunters off towards Anna in a very 'man-of-the-world' fashion. I don't look after him though, because I am looking for Henry. This will be a beautiful dance, a dance to remember. I know that by the slow, sweet music that is coming from the violins.

And everything is perfect. Henry doesn't want to talk either, so we just move silently through all the figures of the dance, going forward, reversing, bowing, curtsying, threading our way in and out, crossing over, the skirt of Henry's frock coat brushing against my hip as we pass one another.

And then the dance is over. Henry and I are standing beside the refreshment table and I am drinking a small glass of wine. I don't like it much, but I drink it because Henry has fetched it for me. He is standing so close to me. I remember the time that he lifted me from the coach in his arms.

And then that friend of Henry's, the officer, comes up with a very fashionable lady. She is wearing a jaconet dress, and the muslin is the finest and softest that I have ever seen. It fits her like a glove and it is cut so low that I can see most of her bosom. She is the only young lady wearing a hat, and a splendid hat it is, beaded all over and crowned with some very tall ostrich feathers. It makes her look even taller than she is – she towers over me. I don't care. Tonight I don't mind being small. I don't mind not having a hat. I like the way that Jane and

I are wearing our hair. And I like the velvet ribbon and the feel of the curls falling down my back. Henry likes them too, I think. I felt him touch my curls once when he was leading me back to my place.

'Miss King,' says the officer, 'may I present my friend Mr Henry Austen.'

I know who she is now. She's the heiress from London, the one who is staying with the Portals at Laverstoke House. Jane overheard Mrs Austen yesterday, joking about her to Henry and telling him that Miss King has a fortune of thirty thousand pounds.

And now Henry is bowing over her hand. 'May I have the pleasure of the next dance, Miss King?' he enquires.

I feel my cheeks burn. I put down the glass of wine. I don't know what to do. I had assumed that Henry would dance with me next. The officer has gone back to his own party and I am left standing there feeling awkward. I have a quick look around for Jane, but she is with the Lefroy party. Perhaps I should just walk across the room and go to sit beside Mrs Austen. Perhaps that was my last dance and I shall spend the next three sitting out. I start to move away, but then Henry suddenly remembers me.

'My cousin Miss Cooper, Miss King,' he says, and we both bow stiffly at each other. I can see her looking me up and down, perhaps trying to assess what my gown cost or how old I am.

Then Henry beckons to Frank. Frank instantly comes

across. He gives Henry a glance and then turns to me.

'Dance with me, Jenny,' he says. He sounds uncomfortable and self-conscious. I wonder whether Henry has teased him about me, although we have often danced together at Steventon. Now he's awkward with embarrassment. I put my hand in his though. At least it gets me away from Henry and Miss King.

Frank is not much of a talker; he is too busy looking around the room to see if there is anyone from the navy present. He spends all of his time talking just about the navy, and he is always going to visit naval men. While we are waiting for the music to begin he tells me all about how someone he knows captured a French frigate – or perhaps it was Spanish – and all the officers got a fortune.

'When do you leave to join your ship?' I ask him politely as we meet in the centre, but he has gone, moving around Tom Fowle with a cheerful grin.

I give up trying to talk. It leaves me time to watch Henry and Miss King. He is smiling at her in just the same way as he smiled at me, bending his head and then laughing at something she says. I suppose she is very witty, not shy and quiet like me.

'Guess what,' says Jane as I move around her on my way down to the end of the row.

'What?' I slow down a little. I don't suppose Frank will miss me.

'Fanny Dashwood opened the ball with Mr Wickham and now she is dancing with William Denn. They

215

say that she is going to jilt Mr Wickham,' Jane hisses in my ear and then we part, she moving up the room still opposite the Irish cousin of the Lefroys, and me going down opposite Frank. I can see that she is using her fan energetically and he is laughing aloud as she explains it to him.

'You're looking lovely, Jenny,' says Frank, as he holds my hand and twirls me around.

I smile at him and think it is nice of him to make the effort to compliment me, but his head has twisted around almost before the words are out of his mouth.

'Who's that?' he asks. 'Look, Jenny, the chap who has just come in – the fellow in the blue coat. Who's that, I wonder?'

He doesn't expect me to know, or even to answer him.

But I do know who it is.

It is a tall, black-haired, handsome young man wearing the blue uniform of a naval officer, his coat opened at the top to show the white ruffled shirt. It is Captain Thomas Williams.

I just can't believe it. I never expected to see him again in my life. What is he doing here? Why isn't he in Southampton? Or why isn't he on his ship? I am glad that I am holding Frank's hand, otherwise I might faint. What am I going to do? What if he sees me? What if he tells someone about me?

Frank and I have danced to the end of the line and now it is our chance to talk. I look at him and he looks at me. We both begin to say something at the same time, but Frank's remark is probably more interesting than mine.

'Do you know, Jenny, a fellow told me that Captain William Parker has got forty thousand in prize money after only ten years of being in command of his own ship.'

'Really,' I say, trying to control the panic in my voice. 'That sounds a lot of money. How did he get all that?'

Frank gives an impatient sigh. 'By capturing frigates, of course! Each petty officer and midshipman gets his share. Freddie was only a midshipman on his last voyage, but he got seven hundred and ninety-one pounds as his share of the prize money . . . and eight shillings and a halfpence,' he added after a minute. At any other time this would have made me giggle, but now I am too worried about Captain Williams.

I wonder what the prize money for the captain was, but I don't ask as we have started to dance again. Is there any way of avoiding Captain Williams? He's bound to tell everyone where and how he met me. What will Mrs Austen say if she hears that I was out in the streets of a rough place like Southampton at midnight? What if Augusta gets to hear of it? I close my eyes at the terrible thought.

'Jenny?' Suddenly I realize that the music has stopped and that Frank has asked me a question.

'Sorry, Frank, what did you say?' My voice sounds as distracted as I feel.

'Would you like me to take you back to Mama?' Two

other naval officers have joined Captain Williams and I can see that Frank is itching to join their group.

'No, don't worry about me, Frank. Look, there's Jane over there. I'll join her.'

Jane has left the Irish Lefroy cousin. I rush over and seize her by the hand.

'Jane,' I whisper, 'help me. I'm in terrible trouble. I don't know what to do. He's here.'

'Who? The love of your life? The man that has your heart? Oh, Jenny, Jenny, show him to me, I pray.' Jane's eyes are sparkling with fun; obviously she has not understood the situation.

'Jane!' I hiss. Usually I find it funny when Jane talks like the characters in Mrs Radcliffe's novels, but now is not the time.

'What's the matter, Jenny? You've gone as white as a sheet.' Jane's voice changes: she knows that this is not a joke.

'It's that man,' I whisper. 'He's here.'

'What man?' Jane looks all around the crowded Assembly Rooms.

'The man at Southampton. The man I told you about. The man I met when I went to post the letter to your mother.'

'What! The one waving the sword?' Jane stares over at a crowd of scarlet-coated army officers who are laughing uproariously at some joke.

'No, not him.' Quickly I duck beneath one of the huge parlour palms. Its fronds make a dark cave from which I can peer out. I can still see the naval officers. Frank has joined them now. 'No! The other one – Captain Williams the naval officer.'

'Well, you'd better keep out of his way,' says Jane, looking all around her. 'Anyone except me would die of horror if they knew that you were out at midnight in the streets of Southampton without a chaperone.'

'Oh, Jane, what will I do?' I am in despair. I can't spend the rest of the evening hiding under a potted palm.

'I think you'd better go and sit by Mama for the next dance. He won't notice you there; young men are looking at the young ladies on the dance floor, not at the old ladies by the wall,' says Jane wisely. 'Walk on this side of me. Keep your face turned towards the wall. Here, link your arm in mine.'

'Is he looking?' I whisper.

'Which one is he?' Jane speaks in her normal tone.

'The black-haired one.'

'He's quite handsome.'

'Quite handsome!' He's as beautiful as a god, I think, but I don't say it aloud. I can see Jane smiling though, so I think she is just trying to tease me.

'Well, very handsome. I see what you mean about those cheekbones. He probably is a man of property. His breeches are very white. That shows the wool is of superfine quality,' says Jane, sounding like Cassandra in one of her instructing moods. 'No, he's not looking. He's chatting to Frank.'

I keep my head turned away and Jane links me so tightly that we are almost like one girl as we move through the room.

'My dear creature, let us keep together; let no man come between us.'

Jane is getting as much fun as she can out of the walk down the room, but I feel my legs trembling and I can't help peeping around Jane to see if the dark head and the splendid lace shirt of Captain Williams are turned in my direction.

Mrs Austen is not best pleased to see us. Mr Austen has gone to play cards in the card room and his wife is enjoying a good gossip with an old school-friend of hers, a Mrs Allen.

'Very rich indeed,' she is saying in a penetrating whisper as we draw near. 'It would be just the thing for him. He's always had a way with him, you know. Could always charm the birds out of the trees. I . . . Yes, girls?' Her tone to us is quite sharp.

'Jenny is tired,' says Jane. 'I thought she could sit the next dance out here with you.'

'Sit here, my dear.' Mrs Allen is probably getting tired of the conversation about Henry and the very rich Miss King, because she makes room for me on the sofa beside her.

'Come on, Jane.' Tom Chute comes up and takes Jane by the hand. She puts her fan into the 'maybe' position and then they both laugh uproariously. I envy her. She is having such fun at this ball and I am not. I am torn by worries and by jealousy. Henry and Miss King are taking their place in the line again and they seem to be on very good terms. I shrink back behind Mrs Allen's bulk as I see John Portal approaching. I don't want to be asked to dance now. I don't want to stand in the line. Only two more dances and then my ordeal will be over. I'm beginning to hope that I might get out without being seen. I peep cautiously at Captain Williams. He hasn't moved; nor has Frank; the three young men are talking and joking and waving their arms around.

'Jenny, could you go and bring two glasses of wine from the buffet for myself and Mrs Allen.' On the dance floor, Miss King is laughing heartily as she touches her hand to Henry's and he is laughing also. They look as if they are getting on very well indeed, and Mrs Austen probably wants to talk it over with Mrs Allen. There is no help for it. I get to my feet and walk across the room to the buffet. I take the two glasses of wine and walk back. The music pauses, everyone is still. Only one person is moving, and that one person is me.

And our eyes meet. Captain Williams sees me and he knows me. He doesn't bow, but I know that he recognizes me; I can see from the way that his tall, broad-shouldered figure suddenly becomes rigid and his head turns towards me – not moving, just looking – while all around him the other naval officers are laughing noisily and slapping each other on the back. His brown eyes are focused on me and somehow they seem darker than I

remember them – almost black. His lips are just parted –
I'd forgotten what a beautifully shaped mouth he has.
I look carefully at the two drinks and hear the first bars
of the new set strike up. In a moment the whole room
is in motion again. I keep walking; my eyes are now on
the sofa. I will not look at anything else. I carefully hand
the two glasses to Mrs Austen and her friend. I don't sit
down on the sofa again. There is no point now.

He has seen me.

I go and stand by the window and look down into the
street below. If only I had not met him that night at
Southampton. If only we were strangers, and then Frank
could introduce me and he would ask me to dance and
he would say to me, 'Tell me all about yourself.'

But that is just a fairy tale.

In another minute he's going to say to one of his
friends, 'I know that girl! I met her walking the streets
of Southampton at midnight . . .'

And Frank will say, 'But that's my cousin . . .'

And he will come across the room and talk to Mrs
Austen about me . . .

Now the music stops and the line breaks up. The laughing, talking girls and their escorts move around the
room, taking a glass of wine from the buffet, greeting
friends, curtsying to new partners.

And Captain Thomas Williams starts to walk across
the room.

222

Sunday, 27 March 1791

Jane has gone down to the village to see George. Just before she went she said to me, 'This will give you a chance to write in your journal. You must have plenty to say.' She didn't realize that I had been writing half the night already by firelight and now I am so tired that I don't know how to tell the rest of it properly.

I've done all the easy bits:
    Henry . . .
    Henry with me . . .
    Henry with Miss King . . .
    Two dances with me . . .
    Four dances with Miss King . . .
    And my dances?
    Well, one dance with Henry . . .
    One with little Charles . . .
    Another with Henry . . .
    One with Frank . . .
    One with William Chute . . .
    One with John Portal . . .
    One dance wasted, sitting on the sofa with Mrs Austen and her friend Mrs Allen . . .
    And that leaves two dances.
    And I did dance these two.
    And this is how it happened.
    It was Frank who introduced Captain Williams to

his mother. He hurried up after him and made the introductions as well as he could. My heart was thudding, but I had plenty of time to recover as no one looked at me for a few minutes. Luckily Cassandra and Tom Fowle had just joined Mrs Austen and she spent some time introducing them both to Captain Williams and explaining about their recent engagement.

'I hope you will both be very happy.' These were the first words that I heard him say. I remembered the voice though, velvet-smooth like chocolate. By this time my heart had slowed down and the strange singing in my ears had gone. Now Jane had come over. She looked at Captain Williams with an innocent expression, as if wondering who he was.

'And this is my younger daughter, Jane, and a neighbour, Tom Chute.'

I was getting the impression that Mrs Austen liked the young captain, or perhaps she was just in a good mood because Henry was still with Miss King, handing her a glass of wine and laughing uproariously at some remark she had just made.

'And this is Jenny Cooper, my niece.' Mrs Austen sounded very affectionate as she beckoned me forward.

I curtsied. I did not dare look at him, but from under my eyelashes I saw him bow.

'Miss Cooper.' He sounded as if he had never seen me before in my life. After a moment I got the courage to look at him.

He did know me though.

I knew that by the look in his eyes.

He has lovely eyes.

Lovely big, brown eyes, with long black eye-lashes . . .

'Will you do me the pleasure of dancing the next dance with me, Miss Cooper?' The words were ordinary, but he sounded as if he really did want to dance with me. He bowed with great politeness and held out his arm.

I curtsied again. I did not feel that I could be sure of my voice if I said anything.

I felt slightly light-headed as I put my gloved hand on his outstretched arm.

We took our place in the line. I wondered what to say. I almost felt as if tears would come soon. I gulped and then looked at him.

'Are you enjoying the dance, Miss Cooper?'

He sounded as though he had never met me before in his life, but I knew better. When I glanced up at him there was a look of amusement in his brown eyes. He must have thought it all very funny. I remember the great shouts of laughter that were coming from the group of naval officers. I thought they were laughing about me, that perhaps he had said to them, '*Look at that girl over there in the white gown. You'd never guess, but the last time that I saw her she was wandering around the streets, all by herself, at midnight in Southampton.*'

'Have you ever been to the Assembly Rooms here before?' He was doing his best to keep the conversation going, but I had such a lump in my throat that I could say nothing.

To my horror, I felt a tear trickle from each eye. In another moment I would be crying and I would spoil everything. I didn't care who I danced with: Frank, Charles, William Chute – anyone except this man that knew my dark secret. Mrs Austen's words – *'Men talk together in card rooms and drinking places about girls like that'* – were burning in my ears.

'Miss Cooper.' His beautiful deep voice was very soft. 'Don't look so worried. I won't tell anyone that I met you before. Let's just pretend we met for the first time tonight and then we'll both enjoy the dance.'

I looked at him doubtfully. There was still a look of amusement, but there was something else also in those brown eyes. I can't quite describe what that look was. His eyes changed colour a lot. Now they had gone very dark again and they were looking at me steadily. I remember Jane giggling about the expression *'smouldering eyes'* in a Mrs Radcliffe novel; I had giggled too, but when I looked up into those almost-black eyes, I knew what *smouldering* meant. I looked down at my fan and then at my shoes. He didn't seem to want to talk; he seemed just to want to look at me, and the few minutes that we stood together seemed almost like an hour . . .

Then I looked up at him a little fearfully and at last he smiled.

White teeth, a curve of smooth lips . . . soft brown eyes above the strong bones of his cheeks . . .

I had forgotten how broad-shouldered and tall he is, and how protected I had felt when we walked arm in arm at Southampton that night . . .

And suddenly I felt happy.

I remember laughing.

And he laughed too as we joined hands and danced down to the bottom of the set.

We were almost like old friends, quite at ease with each other.

And then we were in a group of four with Jane and Tom Chute.

'He's certainly very handsome,' whispered Jane as we linked hands and went around in a circle.

'Do you like him?' I whispered the next time we met.

Jane didn't have time to answer as Tom Chute whirled her around and around. I was looking forward to talking to her after the dance was over, but I didn't have a chance, because when it was over Captain Williams offered me his arm and escorted me over to the supper table, where I sat down.

'Have some cake,' he said, and his voice was very gentle. 'Sweet cake is always good for shock. And it was a bit of a shock for you to see me again, wasn't it?'

I smiled gratefully. Charles passed us, giggling

happily with thirteen-year-old Anna Lefroy, and gave us a merry wave. I waved back.

'Who's that? One of your admirers?' I loved his laugh. There was something about it that made me feel that we were very close to each other. My face flushed at the thought.

I told him that Charles was my cousin, and I explained how he was so keen to join the navy and how he wants to be a midshipman, just like his brother Frank.

'Well, I hope his parents don't let him join too early,' he said seriously. 'A couple of years ago, I had an eleven-year-old midshipman, called Charles also, by coincidence. He was wished on me by my uncle the admiral, who was friendly with the boy's mother. I seemed to spend all of his first year with me saving him from sudden death!'

And then he told me the story of how a Spanish ship attacked his ship and how the Spaniard fired a ball and chain from the cannon and brought down the rigging – block and tackle and all.

'And of course young Charles was standing right underneath it. He was too petrified with fear to move. I barely managed to get myself in the path to deflect it, then stupidly bungled it and took the weight of it on my left shoulder. It would have killed the boy if it had hit his head. As it was . . .' Almost automatically his hand went up and rubbed his left shoulder.

'Does it still hurt?' I had noticed that during the left swings in the dance he had seemed to hold that arm a little stiffly.

'Not much,' he said briefly. 'Now, tell me about all of your cousins. I've met Frank.'

So one by one I pointed out all the Austen family to him: Jane laughing with Tom Chute, James being very gallant with Anne Mathew, Henry still with Miss King (funnily enough I didn't care), Cousin Eliza flirting outrageously with the French gentleman, Cassandra and Tom Fowle talking quietly in a corner, Mrs Austen still on the sofa, of course, and Mr Austen coming out of the card room with a couple of his friends. I didn't mention my brother, Edward-John, or his wife, Augusta. I didn't want to think about them.

What I was thinking about was the story that Captain Williams had told – so lightly and so humorously – painting a picture of himself to be clumsy and stupid for not pushing the rigging away more quickly – rather than making himself a hero for saving a boy's life.

'Is Jane, Miss Jane . . . she's the cousin that you were trying to get help for, isn't she?'

I nod. 'She's fine now,' I said. 'Mrs Austen came immediately. She did get the letter that morning just as you said. Jane recovered once she came home again. I fell ill then, but I recovered very quickly.'

'You were ill?' He asked the question in a strange sharp voice.

'But I'm well again now.'

He said nothing, but he lifted my hand and I felt the pressure of his lips on my fingers.

That was the second time that he had kissed my hand, I thought, remembering how he had done this in Southampton as he left me at the front door of Mrs Cawley's. There was a strange look in his eyes and it seemed to me that there was almost something like fear in them . . . or perhaps it was anger . . .

But then the fiddles struck up again. It was the boulanger, the last dance of the evening. I couldn't believe it. If only it were the first!

'This is my favourite dance,' said Captain Williams when he heard the music. His lovely brown eyes smiled down at me as he took my hand. It was a lively tune and it seemed to bring a smile to every face. Perhaps it was my mood, but I thought that I had never seen everyone look so happy.

And we set out hand in hand, skipping to the tune, going right down to the bottom of the line and then back up again. Jane was dancing with the Irish cousin of the Lefroys again and they were joking about his coming from a place called Limerick.

'What shocking behaviour,' she murmured as I paused beside her, marking time with my feet while the men crossed and recrossed the central space. 'I saw you, you sly creature. I saw you sitting out with your beau and flirting with him.'

I only laughed. I wasn't embarrassed. I was feeling too happy. I felt like I haven't felt since I was about five, I think – just quite carefree and merry and without any responsibilities. But when his turn came to swing me from his left hand I was very careful not to lean outwards and put pressure on his sore shoulder.

When the dance was over he tucked my arm inside his, reminding me once more of the time we walked together in Southampton, and escorted me over to Mrs Austen. 'You will permit me to call to see you at Steventon,' he said, lifting my hand to his lips. Even through my glove I felt the warmth of his mouth.

And then he took leave of Mrs Austen. She had overheard him, I know, and she invited him very warmly to visit us at Steventon and gave him all sorts of directions so that he would not miss his way.

Six o'clock on Sunday, 27 March

And he didn't come.

And now it is probably too late.

After church, Mrs Austen reminded Henry in a sharp tone that he should go and see Miss King.

'Surely you know by now that it is etiquette to enquire after a lady that you danced with at a ball.'

'Enquire what?' yawned Henry, and put up his hands to defend himself as his mother tried to box his ears.

'Enquire whether she is rested after her exertions at the ball, you big booby.' Mrs Austen was laughing, but then she glanced at me and glanced at the clock. And a slightly worried look came over her face.

'Where is Captain Williams staying, Jenny?' she asked.

'I don't know, ma'am,' I said. I didn't dare mention the word *Southampton* in case I blushed.

'Do you know, Frank?' she asked.

'No, I don't,' said Frank. He sounded grumpy too. Perhaps everyone is out of sorts after a ball.

Jane looked at me and I looked at her.

'It's only one o'clock,' she whispered.

But then it was two o'clock . . .

Three o'clock . . .

Four o'clock . . .
And then five o'clock . . .
And then six o'clock . . .
And then I couldn't bear it any longer and I slipped
upstairs to write in my journal.

Monday, 28 March 1791

And Captain Williams didn't come today either.

Henry was in a bad mood after dinner. He kept giving short answers to his mother and father and teasing Frank, mocking his adolescent voice that occasionally went high and then very low. Eventually Frank kicked over a chair and stormed out. After a minute I went after him. I felt sorry for him. Frank has a very intense and fiery temperament and hates to be made a fool of.

There was no sign of him when I got outside so I went into the stables. Frank was there, taking down his saddle, but he was in a thoroughly bad mood, hardly answering when I spoke to him. I cast around for something to say and then told him that Captain Williams had said something about the repairs to Frank's ship, *Perseverance*.

It didn't work though; he just grunted and busied himself with the straps of his saddle. His back was towards me when he spoke.

'I'll tell you one thing, Jenny, about your wonderful Captain Williams. All the men say that he is a terrible flirt and that he has a girl in every port, so I wouldn't trust him too much, if I were you.'

And then he jumped on his horse and was riding fast down the avenue. I stayed for a few minutes to pat my donkey and then when I turned to go back Henry was behind me.

I asked him whether he was looking for Frank — I thought that perhaps he had come to apologize, but Henry shook his head.

'What would I want that overgrown hobble-dehoy for?' He said the words so scornfully that I felt even more sorry for Frank. I know what it feels like to be half grown-up and it's not a comfortable feeling. Eleven-year-old Charles was much happier than Frank. He never worried about how he looked or what he sounded like. Frank did, I know. I understand that because I am always remembering things that I said and then blushing as I think I probably sounded silly.

'Poor Frank,' I said aloud.

'You're so sweet, Jenny; it's like you to worry about everyone.' Now he was holding my hand and squeezing my fingers very gently.

Love is a funny thing. Two days ago I would almost have fainted with delight to be next to Henry in the dim light of the stables, to have him standing so very close to me, my hand in his and his other arm going around my waist.

But now . . .

But now, I felt nothing.

That's not quite true . . .

If I think back carefully, I felt embarrassed and I wanted to get away from him.

I had fallen completely out of love with Henry . . .

'You'd better go to see Miss King,' I said, taking a

step backwards as I saw him bend his head. I wasn't going to allow him to kiss me on the cheek again.

'Are you jealous, little Jenny?' Henry's voice was warm and teasing, the sort of voice that would have given me goose pimples two days ago.

'No.' I can still hear the way I said that 'no' and I think it sounded quite right. It sounded as though I didn't care for him, and that was right also. 'She's just right for you.' I said the words as if I were his mother.

He laughed then, but the laugh didn't seem natural; he sounded a bit uncomfortable.

'I'd better go; I have some tasks to do.' Again, to my surprise, the words came out smoothly and I managed to move away from him as I said it. He followed me and again tried to put his arm around me.

'Excuse me, Henry.' I stole a quick look at him when I said that and I saw that he looked quite taken aback. I know that I sounded brisk, just as if he were Charles getting in my way.

And then I didn't look at Henry any more, just went straight through the yard, in through the back door, up the stairs. Once I reached our bedroom, I took out my journal and unlocked it.

But then I thought about Frank's words. Is it really true that Captain Williams has a girl in every port? I wish I knew.

Perhaps that is why he hasn't come to see me.

Or perhaps he thought I was just boring and stupid.

Jane has just come in and I told her about what Frank said and we discussed why Captain Williams has not called on me when he said that he was going to.

'That's interesting about having a girl in every port,' said Jane thoughtfully. 'I wonder, does he get their names muddled? That would make a good story.' And then she saw my expression, I suppose, because she quickly told me that she was only joking and that she didn't think that Captain Williams looked like that sort of man at all.

'I was looking at him when he was dancing with you,' she said, 'and he wasn't looking at anyone else – just at you.'

'I wish I knew what to do now.' I felt so depressed that I think I was near to tears.

'I'll go and fetch Eliza,' said Jane, and she was gone before I could call her back. I wasn't sure that I wanted to discuss the matter with Eliza, but when she came she was very kind and very reassuring, talking about all the duties that naval captains have and the emergencies that might have arisen.

'Don't worry, Jenny,' she said. 'I saw the way that Captain Williams looked at you and I know that he was *très, très épris*.'

'Very taken by you,' translated Jane. Her French is better than mine as she often chatters in it to Eliza.

'You have captured his heart, *ma petite*,' said Eliza solemnly.

'Should she write to him, do you think?' asked Jane. 'Just something casual – ask him how he is and how his ship is – just to remind him of her.'

'*Mais non, mais non, mais non* . . .' Eliza became very agitated. 'A lady must never do that. It's for the gentleman to make the first move. A lady must wait. You have made an impression; now stand back and let him come forward!'

'I'm not sure that I made a great impression,' I said, and I probably said it rather dolefully because Eliza gave me a motherly pat on the shoulder.

'Did he pay you any compliments?' asked Jane.

I told her that he said I had lovely eyes and she immediately asked me what I said in return and shook her head reprovingly when I admitted that I said nothing.

'You should have said, "La, Captain Williams, you do me too much honour!" That's what she should have said, Eliza, isn't it?'

I said hotly that I thought that sounded ridiculous. I was embarrassed to think how I had blushed when he admired my eyes.

Eliza pursed her lips, but tactfully did not agree with either of us. She was thinking hard though, and when she spoke she was quite decisive.

'You see, Jenny, my dear,' she said briskly, 'it's very pretty to look shy, but don't be too shy. You must be ready to give the gentleman a hint of your feelings.'

'Just take one step forward, and then a step back! That's right, isn't it, Eliza?' Jane was getting excited. I half expected her to fly across the room and take out her writing desk.

'*Précisément!*' Eliza beamed fondly at Jane and then turned back to me with a serious look. 'Think of it like a dance, Jenny. A gentleman pays you a compliment, you look up at him and let him see your feelings for him — just for one moment — and then you drop your eyelashes to hide your eyes — use your fan — I showed you how. Then if a gentleman talks of his feelings, don't hold back. If you are too shy to respond, then just look up and let him read the message of love in your eyes.'

'And don't forget your fan,' advised Jane. 'But she'll have to say something if he asks her to marry him, won't she, Eliza? She can't just look at him and hope that he guesses.'

'Who says anything about marriage?' Eliza pronounced it '*marrrriaage*'. 'Jenny doesn't know him well enough for any talk about marriage. She'll have to get to know him a lot better before she agrees to marry him. She only met him for less than an hour. No young girl should be talked into marriage before she is ready!' And Eliza sighed heavily and looked into the fire with an air of tragedy.

'Oh, but she knew him before——' Jane stopped suddenly and put her hand in front of her mouth.

Eliza dropped her tragic-muse pose and swivelled around to look at me with an air of interest.

'I don't mind Cousin Eliza knowing,' I said reassuringly to Jane. I could see how horror-filled she looked and I guessed that there was no way out of telling Eliza the whole story. In any case, she was going back to London.

'But you must swear never to tell a soul,' said Jane, and then she dramatically told Eliza the whole story. Eliza listened with parted lips, and when Jane had finished she said, 'Jenny, this is a man who will love and cherish you. When this man comes back to tell you of his love for you, you will know what to do. This is a man who has shown gentleness and kindness to an unprotected girl. He will make a wonderful husband.'

'Perhaps he was still just being kind to me though.'

Eliza shook her head. 'You forget that I have studied him, *chérie*. Even across the ballroom floor I could see that he was in love with you. I know about these things. I could tell you such stories.' And Eliza heaved a sigh and smiled a world-weary smile.

'Oh, do tell us some stories of your time in Paris, before you were married, Eliza. You're going away tomorrow so this is the last opportunity,' urged Jane.

'I'll be back for the performance of the play at Easter, *chérie*,' said Eliza, 'but . . .'

So for the rest of the evening, Eliza sat by our

fireside and told so many stories and gave us so much good advice that by bedtime my head was in a whirl. Before she left she kissed me and whispered in my ear, 'Now remember, he will come, and when he does, you will know what to say to him.'

Jane is now asleep and I am still writing in my journal and hoping that Mrs Austen won't notice the light of the candle shining under our door.

I've been thinking about Eliza's words so I've fetched my journal from my trunk and am trying to sort out my feelings.

I can see where I've gone wrong. I've been too shy, too silent.

When Captain Williams told me that story of how he saved the boy, I was dying to show him how wonderful I thought he had been.

But I was just too shy – that's what I told myself at the time.

Perhaps, though, I'm getting too old to be shy . . .

Perhaps it's just a form of selfishness . . .

Perhaps Thomas (secretly in my mind I like to call him Thomas) would have been pleased to hear himself praised.

When he told me the story and I said nothing, perhaps he felt embarrassed . . .

The next time that I meet him I will know what to do . . .

If ever I meet him again . . .

Tuesday, 29 March 1791

And today he came!

And I didn't show him my feelings.

Everything went wrong.

All Jane's and Eliza's good advice seems to be thrown away on me.

This is how the day went.

Frank had got back his good humour this morning when he was giving me my riding lesson; he was very nice and complimented me on my riding and without much prompting on my part he started to tell me about the duties of a captain. It was a fine morning and we had now progressed to riding side by side down the lane towards the church. I was enjoying the morning sun and watching the brisk wind stirring and blowing the white petals of the cherry trees drifting down, looking like snow as I half listened to a long description of everything that captains did on board ship (and of course all about what a midshipman would do, as well) and eventually I managed to slip in the question that I wanted to ask.

'And when captains are on shore, is their time their own, or do they have any duties then?'

Again I had to listen to a long description of how ships had to be cleansed, refitted, all about ships' stores and chandlers.

'So a captain would have to supervise all of that?' I said thoughtfully as soon as I could get a word in.

'Of course! It's no easy life, being a captain of ship. Not like those idle dogs in the army.' Frank was very scornful of the army, where a man could buy a commission and not rise through merit, as they do in the navy.

I didn't listen to the rest of his opinions about soldiers. My heart was happy again. Thomas was probably down in Southampton seeing to his ship. He would have no time to waste calling upon young ladies. Frank didn't say any more about Thomas having a girl in every port so I hope that what he said yesterday is not true.

We went to see George this morning, and brought a piece of pork pie. He enjoyed the pie, but he had problems with making the sign for *P*. This was difficult for him as it involved – according to the book that Jane had taken from her father's library – folding his thumb and two fingers. In the end I said to Jane that we should be content with him trying to say the name. I had more hopes of teaching George to talk than to read or to spell, but Jane was of the opinion that reading and spelling would impress her mother more. On the way home I was thinking about George and I was thinking that it was strange that Jane was the only one of his seven brothers and sisters to worry about him. After all, the others – including James, who had great influence with his mother – knew that their brother was lodged with a poor family down in the village. They knew that he shambled around dirty and perhaps ill-fed – he always seemed hungry to me – and yet none of them ever took any interest in him.

After dinner it poured with rain and everyone was in the parlour. There was no opportunity for the boys to go out of doors before lessons started again so we all settled down with books or card games or chess, and Mr Austen was reading through the sermon that he had preached on Sunday. Charles was first 'broke' (and out of buttons!) in our game of pontoon so he left the table and wandered over to the window.

'There are two horses coming up the drive,' he called out.

'Is it William Chute?' Henry had been yawning in a bored sort of way, but he suddenly sounded interested and he put his book down on the table.

'No,' said Charles. 'It's Newton Portsmouth and someone in naval uniform with him.'

'Cassandra, Jane, Jenny, put this room in order,' scolded Mrs Austen, scurrying around picking up books and shaking cushions.

The Honourable Newton Wallop was the second son of the Earl of Portsmouth, and Mrs Austen was very fond of the aristocracy. She had some far-distant ancestor who was the brother of a duke.

'Who's with him, Charles?' she asked as she tipped Mr Austen's Sunday sermon into the wood scuttle beside the fire.

'Let me see,' said Frank, getting up and going to the window. 'It must be Frederick. No, it's not, it's Captain Williams. He must be staying at Hurstbourne Park or with the Portsmouths. What can he want? You remember him, Mama? I introduced him to you at the Assembly Rooms on Saturday. Do you know, Papa, Captain Williams had his own ship when he was eighteen years old?'

'Lucky him,' murmured Henry.

'He must be a very worthy young man,' said Mrs Austen warmly.

'His uncle is an admiral,' said Henry. 'That's a piece of good luck that any of us would enjoy having. Being worthy has nothing whatsoever to do with it.'

'Don't be ridiculous, Henry,' scolded Mrs Austen. 'And why are you lounging around here? You should be over at Laverstoke House paying a visit to Miss King. It will impress her if you come in this weather.'

Henry rose reluctantly to his feet, giving a look of dismay at the sight of the rain pouring down on the sodden lawn outside.

'Well, Mama,' said Jane pertly, 'if your son should have a dangerous fit of illness, if he should die, I hope that it will be a consolation to you that it was all in pursuit of your orders – and of Miss King, of course.'

'Nonsense,' said Mrs Austen. 'People don't die of a little rain. I go out in the rain every day myself.'

My heart began to beat faster. I looked across at Jane, but I had no time to make contact with her as her father had caught her by the hand.

'Jane, dear, give me back my sermon. No one listens much to my words, so this sermon will do perfectly well some Sunday next year. And who is this Captain Williams?'

'Good gracious, Mr Austen, it's the young man that I told you about, the one that was so taken by our Jenny. You must remember, Mr Austen; I told you all about him last Saturday night at bedtime. Jenny, dear, leave those cards there; Jane will attend to them. You just run upstairs, take off that brown calico and put on your blue muslin, the one that you wore to church on Sunday.'

'I'll go with her to brush her hair,' said Jane swiftly. 'Cassandra will tidy the cards away.'

Mr Austen looked as if he didn't remember too well who Captain Williams was. Probably he had heard a lot about Miss King and then fallen asleep before the bit about me and Captain Williams. However, he slipped his sermon into his waistcoat pocket, straightened his wig and sat up, resigned to losing his after-dinner doze.

Frank went out to the front door and Jane and I raced upstairs.

'What a shame that it is raining so hard,' said Jane as she brushed my curls around her finger. 'If it had been fine, then you could have taken your beau for a walk in a pretty little wilderness, just like the girl in *The Mysteries of Udolpho*.'

This made me giggle a little. I was quite excited. Lavinia at Mrs Cawley's Seminary for Young Ladies was always boasting of having a 'beau' who came calling.

'I expect that he has just come to see Frank,' I said, trying to sound offhand, but Jane wasn't fooled.

'You're not still scared that he will tell anyone about Southampton, are you?' she asked, looking at me enquiringly.

I told her that I wasn't because Captain Williams had promised faithfully not to tell anyone.

Jane's eyes narrowed. 'It sounds as though he cares for you,' she said. 'Oh la . . .' And then the door was pushed open. It was Cassandra.

'There, you look very nice, Jenny. Come on, come

downstairs. There's nothing to be afraid of. Captain Williams is just doing the civil thing, visiting neighbours of the Portsmouths.'

'I'm not scared,' I said. I wasn't going to be patronized by Cassandra — after all, she's only two years older than I am.

'Come and sit beside me, Jenny,' said my aunt in a motherly way when Jane and I went into the parlour. She was sitting next to Captain Williams on the sofa. Newton was chatting to Tom Fowle and Henry, and Mr Austen had started to doze off again. Frank was fetching one of his naval books from the bookcase and he looked a bit annoyed when Mrs Austen made room for me between herself and Captain Williams and sternly waved him away, while Captain Williams, who had jumped up from his seat, was bowing over my hand.

We sat down, side by side on the sofa. It wasn't a very big sofa, and Mrs Austen is a large, wide-hipped woman, so it ended up with us sitting very close together.

It wasn't easy to talk though. Everyone in the room was looking at us — the boys with curiosity, Cassandra with a degree of jealousy, Jane beaming enthusiastically. I didn't dare look at Mrs Austen, but I knew that she was looking at me encouragingly.

'You're well after the ball?' asked Captain Williams.

'Very well,' I said, wondering whether it was etiquette to ask him if he was well also.

'You weren't too tired?' was his next question.

'No,' I said. 'I wasn't a bit tired.' I could hear my voice sounding stilted and mechanical. I tried to remember all the things that Eliza had told me to do. But he wasn't paying me compliments or speaking of love, so none of these was of any use.

Jane and I had been practising being sophisticated and flirting in our bedroom, but all I could think of was pinning the wrapper to my shoulders. He was so near to me that I almost felt a little faint. I had a sudden longing for everyone to go out of the room and then perhaps he would hold my hand or even put it to his lips as he did at the Assembly Rooms and that night at Southampton.

'It was the first time that I have ever been to Basingstoke Assembly Rooms. I found them very pleasant.' He was doing his best, but I didn't know what to say.

'It was my first time too,' I said after a minute. I was conscious that Mrs Austen was listening to every word. She got up now and went across the room and opened the piano.

'Let's have a little music, Jane,' she said. For once Jane did not argue but sat down on the piano stool. Mrs Austen leafed through the music books on the piano and then opened one and plonked it in front of

Jane. When the music came, it was soft and gentle, ideal for conversation. Mrs Austen stayed beside her to turn the pages. It was no good though. I just couldn't talk to him. Not with everyone watching us. No matter what subject of conversation we tried, I could only answer *yes* or *no*. After a whispered suggestion from his mother, Frank had taken Newton to the stables to see a litter of pointer pups, and Tom Fowle and the other pupils had gone with them. Only Mr and Mrs Austen, Cassandra, Jane and I remained.

And Captain Thomas Williams, of course.

Eventually Newton and Frank returned. Cassandra slipped out to join her fiancé and Jane stopped playing the piano.

'We must go now,' said Newton, with a quick look at Captain Williams. 'I have to call on neighbours with a message from my mother, but let me give it to you first of all. We are holding a ball at Hurstbourne Park this Saturday and all the Austens are invited. And Miss Jenny, of course. Here is the invitation card.'

Lord & Lady Portsmouth
request the pleasure of the company of
Mr & Mrs G. Austen & Family
at a ball to be held at
Hurstbourne Park,
Saturday 2 April 1791
RSVP

'A ball!' exclaimed Jane. 'Oh, wonderful! I promise to save you a dance, Newton.'

'Jane!' exclaimed Mrs Austen, but I knew she was
not really annoyed. Jane's remark had raised a laugh
and it finished that awkward silence that had fallen
in the room. I laughed too. Suddenly I felt at ease and
I looked up at Captain Williams with a smile. 'Will
you be there?'

He smiled back. 'Only if you come,' he said, and
his brown eyes were dancing.

'You should have taken him out for a walk until you
found a pretty little wilderness — what does a little rain matter in the cause of true love?' said Jane
later when we were brushing our hair and I was telling her how stupid and embarrassed I felt and how I
couldn't think of a word to say to him when we were
sitting side by side on the sofa in the parlour.

'I'm not sure that would have been any better,' I
said doubtfully. 'I just don't think I am very good at
things like that.'

'I know what I'll do,' said Jane enthusiastically.
'I'll go through Mrs Radcliffe's novels and I'll make
a list of things that young ladies say to their young
men. Then you can learn a few sentences off by heart
every night. I'll hear you say them until you are
word-perfect.'

I couldn't help laughing. I didn't think that it would
work for me, but I didn't like to disappoint Jane.

'I'll try,' I said.

'You were all right at the ball though, weren't you? I saw you talking to him. You didn't look shy then. You'll probably be fine on Saturday,' she said, and I thought again about the look on his face just before he left when he whispered in my ear, 'Keep all your dances for me, won't you?'

Wednesday, 30 March 1791

There was great excitement at the breakfast table to-day. A letter came from Kent, saying that Edward, Jane's brother who was adopted by rich cousins, would be arriving at Bristol today. He would be stay-ing the night there and then would come by stage-coach tomorrow to spend a night here at Steventon.

'He's been on a Grand Tour,' said Mrs Austen to me. Apparently Edward spent the last couple of years going from country to country in continental Europe and seeing all that was most interesting in each country.

'Great buildings, works of art, miracles of na-ture . . . Edward has seen them all,' finished Mrs Austen before flying out to the kitchen to order the cook to kill a couple of turkeys from the yard and hang them up, ready for tomorrow's dinner.

'Does Edward look like James or like Henry?' I asked Jane when we were doing our schoolwork.

'He's like Cassandra,' said Jane briefly. 'He's got grey eyes and blond hair – at least he had when I saw him last. We don't see much of him here.'

'Don't you like him?' I asked. There was some-thing odd about the tone of her voice.

'Oh, he's all right. Quite nice really . . . nicer than James. He's the third in our family. George is between James and Edward.'

I didn't say any more then. I could understand

what she was feeling. There was James, the scholar, a Fellow at Oxford (and I gathered from Mrs Austen that you had to be a great scholar to be a 'Fellow') and then there was Edward, adopted by a couple so rich that they could send him wandering around continental Europe for two years just to complete his education. He would inherit their two estates, one in Kent and one in Hampshire, and their two grand houses. Edward would be very rich.

And then there was George, in between these two fortunate brothers.

And poor George has nothing.

Thursday, 31 March 1791

Just before dinner today we all walked up to Deane Gate Inn to meet Edward — even Mrs Austen herself came. The procession was led by Cassandra and Tom Fowle, followed by Mr Austen and the other pupils, and ended with Mrs Austen and Charles.

The sight of us caused great interest in the village and many people came to greet us or to enquire about our journey. From a distance I saw Bet trying to lead George into a field, but he broke away from her. He passed his father and brothers without a glance, but stopped opposite Jane and myself, making inarticulate noises and trying to see whether I had anything for him.

'Off home, George! Go on, off you go. Bet, don't allow him to bother the young ladies.' Mrs Austen's voice was not unkind, but it held the tone that the shepherd used to his dog, Rover.

I winced a little and I could sense how Jane was suffering. She was George's sister and I was his cousin, and yet he was ordered away from 'the young ladies'.

I felt I had to say something so I told Mrs Austen that Jane and I would walk back with George and Bet and catch them up straight away. I was surprised at myself to hear how firm and grown-up my voice sounded.

'Come on, George,' said Jane cheerfully. 'You be a good boy now and we'll bring you some cake later on.'

I think he understood the word 'cake' and he probably understood the shooing motions that Mrs Austen
was making with her hands. In any case, he turned
around and shambled off. Bet gave a rather scared and
very apologetic look at Mrs Austen, bobbed a quick
curtsy and then hurried after George. We went a little of the way with Bet and George, but once we saw
that he was happy we returned to join the others.
Mrs Austen turned her attention to me.

'So you know George, Jenny?' she asked, and cast
a quick annoyed glance at Jane.

I nodded. 'I've met him a few times in the village,'
I said carelessly. And then I turned away from my
aunt and towards Jane. 'Jane, is Edward as tall as
Henry?'

'No, he's not too tall, not much bigger than Frank.'
Jane's voice was as casual as mine, but she quickened
her pace and together we overtook John Warren and
Gilbert East.

'Slowcoaches,' I said teasingly over my shoulder as
we passed, and I was amazed at myself. And then I
thought about George.

'Jane, I think you are right about George,' I said in
a low voice. 'I think that we should try to persuade
your father and mother to have him live in the house.
We might succeed. We'll have to think of some good
arguments – like that it would save money. After all,
I suppose they have to pay for the Littleworths to
look after him.'

'When they see that he can read they will want him back home,' said Jane with conviction. Jane was very determined, and she was sure that she could teach George to read.

I hesitated a bit, but then the new grown-up me spoke out.

'Jane . . .' I said with a quick glance over my shoulder to check that we were outside Gilbert and John Warren's listening range. 'Jane, I think that you should be prepared for the possibility that it might be impossible for George to learn to read. Let's just love him for what he is.'

And then Henry dropped back to walk with us and no more was said about George.

Edward was wearing a wig and that surprised me, because although I had never seen my uncle without one, the other boys just wore their own hair tied back. He was not very tall, rather squarely made with broad shoulders. He was dressed very fashionably, wearing a pair of tightly fitting salmon-coloured breeches, with knee-length white silk stockings, a white and gold waistcoat buttoned over his ruffled shirt and over it all a magnificent coat in blue brocade with a dozen gilt buttons, each the size of a sovereign.

He seemed nice, kissing his mother and two sisters, shaking hands with his brothers and father, bowing over my hand as if I were an adult and telling me how small I was when he last saw me. He had a kind face and a sweet smile.

'And how is your brother, my Cousin Edward-John?' he asked me, raising my hand to his lips in a very courtly way. 'Still the same Edward-John, is he? Always ready for a debate.'

'He's married now,' I said. I tried to remember what my brother had been like before he married Augusta. Did he have opinions of his own then? I wondered. I couldn't remember him saying much in the last year or so. I hadn't ever heard him argue with Augusta, but she would have talked him down if he had even tried.

'So, he's married.' He sounded surprised. I was sure that his mother must have told him, but he had probably forgotten. Life had been exciting for Edward during the past few years.

'He's been landed, poor fish,' said Henry, and Mrs Austen glared at him.

Edward did not appear to notice his mother; he was now busy slapping Tom Fowle on the back and congratulating him about his engagement to Cassandra. Of course, he knew all of the older boys at the school as Edward had been a pupil there before he embarked on his Grand Tour of Europe. The Knights, his adoptive parents, had been anxious that he not lose contact with his birth parents, so that arrangement had been made for his education. I wondered whether either James or Henry were ever jealous of

Edward; he had been the least clever of the three brothers, according to Jane, and yet he was the one that was sent to all of those foreign countries and was now able to speak French and Italian like a native apparently.

'Another poor fish that has been landed,' said Henry, giving Tom Fowle a few extra slaps on the back, and this time everyone laughed, even me. Tom Fowle didn't seem to mind. That is the thing about Henry. He can say anything, do anything, and people always forgive him. I wondered whether he would marry the very rich Miss King. If he wanted to, he probably could do it, I thought. He has lots of charm.

'Shall we leave most of your luggage, Edward?' asked Mr Austen. The inn yard was piled high with heavy leather trunks and travelling bags, but Edward would be returning there next day for the coach to Kent.

'We'll take these few here.' Edward was obviously used to travelling. In a moment he had sorted out three of the bags, taken a handful of small silver coins from his purse and distributed them among the ostlers and coachmen, divided the bags among the boys and then set off strolling down the lane to Steventon, chatting to his father.

Edward had a generous nature. Two of the bags he brought to the house were stuffed with presents for the family. Mr Austen went back to his study bearing a handsome case of clay pipes, a tobacco pouch and a leather-bound volume for his library. The pupils returned to the schoolroom with small gifts of linen handkerchiefs or cravats and then the family gathered around the leather bag for the rest of the present-giving.

There was a very handsome Indian shawl for Mrs Austen, a case of pistols for Henry, a fowling gun for Frank, a leather bridle and the whispered promise of a pony for Christmas for little Charles, and lace shawls for both Jane and Cassandra. I was admiring Jane's when suddenly Edward produced one for me also. I couldn't believe it. It was not so much that he had spent money on me, as the fact that he had remembered that I was staying at Steventon and brought me a gift just as if I were one of his sisters.

Then there were more presents: boxes of French bonbons, some beautifully illustrated books, a pair of pictures for the girls' bedrooms, a painting of a waterfall for the parlour – there seemed to be no end to what was coming out of that wonderful bag. Dinner was late that afternoon, partly because Mrs Austen had been delayed with the opening of the presents, but partly because in fashionable society — so she told Jane and myself — dinner was often not eaten until darkness fell. She thought Edward might lack appetite if we had it too early.

Everything was arranged to suit Edward. Mrs Austen must have been up half the night. I had never seen the parlour look so lovely, with even an Indian rug, unearthed from a chest in her bedroom, decorating the highly polished floor.

It was funny, I thought, that two of Mrs Austen's six sons did not live at the parsonage. One, George, was barred from the house, but the other, Edward, was treated like royalty when he spent a night with his parents.

After dinner Jane disappeared, but the rest of us stayed sitting around the parlour, listening to Edward's tales of his adventures in foreign countries. Eventually he was almost hoarse with talking and Mr Austen gave him a glass of port and looked around for Jane to play the piano for everyone.

It was at that moment that the door opened.

It is ten o'clock. I have just written lots about Edward and about the presents, but I haven't written about the most important thing.

I have a new quill in my hand — it's one that Frank gave me. He gave it to me because Jane tells everyone that I am always writing. I have sharpened it to a neat point with my penknife, but now I don't know what to say.

I should be writing about what happened today after dinner. Every night I write about what happened during the day, and usually I just write and write and the words come to my mind faster than my quill can form them on the page.

Let me see if I can sort it out, minute by minute.

Dinner had finished, and the Digweeds and the Terrys, neighbours to the Austens, had come by to see Edward, so the parlour was full to bursting point with them and their children and with Mr Austen's pupils.

And Jane opened the door and stood there, holding George by the hand.

I think if I had been Jane, when I saw them all there, I would have quickly shut the door and taken George away and given him lots of cake and biscuits and talked with him and laughed with him and perhaps taught him some more of his letters, but I would have definitely taken him straight back to the village.

But Jane is not me.

She opened the door and she just stood there with everyone looking at her, and then peering past her to see, standing behind her, George, the abandoned son. A queer little stunted figure, all dressed up like a miniature parson.

And Jane said in a clear, ringing voice, 'Mama,

Papa, here is George, come to see his brother Edward. He'd like to show you all what he has learned.'

I can't remember what happened next. I suppose she must have got him into the parlour. I just remember her putting him on a chair in front of a small table. She was like a player, setting the scene. She took out the cake and the biscuits and the apple from her basket and then she arranged them on the table. George began to tremble. I came over next to him and tried to squeeze his hand so that he wouldn't feel so nervous.

He did manage to make the sign for A and also for C, but when I put the biscuits in front of him he began to shake violently.

And then Henry jumped up. 'Let go of him, Jenny,' he shouted.

I got such a shock at Henry yelling at me that I couldn't move. I still held George's hand, but now Mr Austen had his arms around George, and Mrs Austen undid my grip. Henry helped Mr Austen and they almost lifted George. He was shaking all over from head to toe and they laid him on the ground. I could see how the froth came to his lips and how his eyes rolled. I can still hear Mrs Digweed's voice proclaiming, 'He's having a fit.'

I suppose Mrs Austen managed very well. I remember her calm voice ushering everyone into the breakfast parlour, chatting to the Terry children, explaining that the boy – she called poor George *the boy* – would be fine in a moment, saying in a sort of comic tone to Mrs Terry, '*That girl* (she meant Jane) *will be the death of me one day,*' and giving quick instructions to Frank to bring the cart around.

And then Jane ran upstairs to the bedroom and I followed her.

I did my best to console her, but she was beyond consolation.

'I've made a mess of everything' was the only thing that she would say, her face streaming with tears. No matter how much I told her that she had tried and that perhaps she could talk to her parents tomorrow, she still would say no more than that one sentence.

I think I understand her. She was very upset for George, but also her pride is hurt. She thought her plan would work and it didn't. I can understand why she didn't want to discuss it, so I just sat by her bed, stroking her hair until she stopped sobbing and sat up.

'I wish I lived in a novel,' she said with an attempt at a small smile. 'I could make such a happy ending to this story. George would learn to talk, and to read, my father and mother would want him back in the house, and he would be a brother to us all.' And then she took up a book and started to read it.

* * *

Nothing I could say to Jane tonight seemed to make her feel better, but, funnily enough, writing it down has made it seem better to me.

My brother has not been a very good brother to me — I can say it now without feeling guilty and thinking it was my fault that he was no fonder of me. However, this present of the pack of three journals was the best thing that he has done for me.

And I suppose it has not been easy for him. I understand him a bit better now. Augusta would probably have been jealous and made a fuss if she thought her husband was fond of me. He was probably torn between doing what Mama begged he would do for me, and what his wife, Augusta, felt should happen.

Friday, I April 1791

I woke at dawn to hear Edward and Frank talking quietly on the sweep outside our window. I got out of bed and peeped at them as they strode up the lane towards Deane Inn. Edward had to catch the early stagecoach from there and Frank was carrying his bag. I dressed quietly and then just sat by the window thinking about everything that had happened last night.

Jane got up at her normal time and did her piano practise. Frank and I went riding for half an hour. He said nothing about George and I said nothing. And yet, I thought as we trotted along the lane, side by side, there was something very strange about this. Why weren't we discussing it? Why weren't we saying things like: 'What a shame about George'?

And Henry – why had he said nothing last night?

Or Cassandra?

Or even Edward – after all, George is his brother also.

Except for Jane, the whole family is just embarrassed by George – just wants to forget that he exists.

And yet, if Henry took an interest in George, that would influence Mr Austen greatly. Henry and Jane are his two favourite children, but he consults Henry about lots of things and seems to respect his opinion, whereas Jane is just his clever little girl – amusing but not to be taken seriously.

As soon as I had groomed and fed my donkey and washed my hands under the pump in the washroom, I went into the parlour to find Jane. She was playing, playing badly, strumming a few bars and then resting her fingers on the keys and then playing a false note.

'Jane,' I said without stopping to think for too long, 'I think you did a good thing yesterday. I think that this business about George has been a secret for too long. Why don't people talk about him? Why don't they say things like, "*What a shame about George. What can we do to make his life a little better?*" I think it's time that everyone was talking about it, that everyone acknowledged the truth. It's a bit like shutting the doors and windows of a room and never letting the air in . . .'

I stopped because I was running out of breath, but also because Jane's eyes had gone from mine and were looking at something behind me.

In my haste I had not closed the door properly, and Mr and Mrs Austen had come in behind me and were standing listening to me. Mr Austen looked deeply troubled and I was sorry about that; he is a kind and gentle man. His wife, though, looked the same as always: tough, competent and just a little amused at the silliness of young people.

It was Mrs Austen who shut the door.

'So how long has all this been going on for?' she asked drily.

'A few weeks,' said Jane defiantly.

'A few weeks . . .' repeated Mr Austen, and then he smiled, that very sweet smile that he always seemed able to produce even in a situation where another man would be angry. 'And you were teaching him his alphabet, were you?'

'He knows lots of letters now.' Jane was on her feet now, her back to the piano and facing her mother and father.

I noticed that they both looked very tired, almost as if they had spent a lot of the night awake — perhaps talking about George.

'The problem is, Jane,' scolded Mrs Austen, 'that you always think that you know best. You're only fifteen years old, so you should allow your father and mother to know what's best and do the right thing.'

I believe that if Jane had just nodded here, all might have gone quite well. I imagine that Mrs Austen didn't really want to scold, but of course Jane, being Jane, had to argue. 'So you think it's the right thing for your son to live down in the village like an animal.' Her voice was very harsh and rough. Tears came to my eyes and through my tears I could see how she glared at her mother.

'Don't talk nonsense, Jane!' snapped Mrs Austen. 'George, you deal with her. I have too much to do!' And then she was out of the room, slamming the door behind her. I had never heard her call her husband by his first name before; it was always 'Mr Austen' with her. That showed how angry and upset she was.

Jane didn't look worried though. She faced her father, cheeks blazing and eyes sparkling. 'I suppose it's nonsense to care about your brother. Well, I do, and I'm the only one in the family that cares. You must realize he's not properly looked after.'

'Jane, Jane, that's not true.' Mr Austen sounded very upset. 'You know that Dame Littleworth looks after him very well.'

I wiped my eyes with my pocket handkerchief, but Jane was not tearful. She was almost shouting at her father.

'He doesn't look like Frank or Charles or Henry or any of the other boys, does he? He's not cared for in the same way as they are cared for, is he? Would anyone guess that he is your son?'

'But, Jane,' said Mr Austen gently, 'George is not the same as the other boys.'

Jane frowned, but she didn't say anything else. She couldn't really argue with that, I thought. George was not the same as the other boys, and dressing him up and even teaching him his ABC wasn't going to make him the same.

'However, I think that in some ways you are right,' continued Mr Austen. His voice was loving, and he looked very anxiously at Jane. 'It is possible that Dame Littleworth has too much to do to care for George in the way that we would like him to be cared for.'

'I don't want to get her into trouble.' Jane sounded a bit calmer now.

'No, no, Dame Littleworth is a good woman and she does do her best, but she doesn't have a husband or a son and I think the task might be too much for her. I've heard tales that George is allowed to wander alone even up as far as Deane Gate Inn. Goodness knows what might happen to the poor lad with the coaches going at speed along that road. Something has to be done. We can easily compensate Dame Littleworth by taking her daughter, Bet, on as a kitchen maid, if we make other arrangements for the poor fellow. We want to do the best thing for George. You do believe that, don't you?' He hesitated for a moment and then said, 'There is another man with George's problem – a relative of ours – who is happy and being well cared for at Monk Sheraton. Perhaps George could join him.'

Jane frowned. I could see that she did not know what to think about that. I swallowed hard to get the lump out of my throat and forced myself to speak. I said that I thought that would be a good idea and that George would be happier if he had someone like himself for a companion. I kept on talking for a while. I was trying to give Jane time to get used to the idea. The trouble between Jane and her mother usually happens when Jane speaks too hastily. It would be best if her father could calm her down before she left the room and perhaps bumped into Mrs Austen again. I hoped that Mr Austen would not ask her what she thought.

I think that Mr Austen knew what I was doing because he started to talk also. He described George as a baby – and how he, Mr Austen, had taken comfort in the fact that he could not ever be a bad or wicked child.

And then that was that.

Jane said nothing. She loved her father very much and she would not argue with him, and I apologized for the two of us and then, somehow, we were out of the room and going into the breakfast parlour with no cross words spoken.

Edward and Henry were having fun at the breakfast table, talking nonsense French, and Frank was joining in and for once Henry treated him like an equal. Tom Fowle was calling Cassandra '*Mademoiselle*' and Charles was going around saying '*Excusezmoi*' and purposely bumping into everyone. It was the usual fun and high spirits and it was as if the tragedy of George had not come into all our lives for a few brief minutes. I could see Jane's lips quiver from time to time, but she said nothing.

Saturday, 2 April 1791

My white dress has been carefully washed in the best soap and lavender water by Mrs Austen herself. She waved me away when I wanted to iron it and she did it herself, rubbing the bottom of each iron with a piece of coarse cloth every time she took a new one from on top of the stove. Not a single one of the beautiful blue glass beads was damaged as she took such care with it.

No Eliza to get us ready this time — but she left her soaps and her bath oils and some of her special shampoo so Jane and I confided in Sukey, who was happy to light the fire in the guest bedroom, lug up the pails of hot water and allow us the use of the hip bath and the wonderful full-length cheval mir-ror. I'm going to do Jane's hair and she's going to do mine. I'm going to have one change though. I've put away Henry's bandeau and I've carefully unpicked Eliza's blue velvet rose from my gown. I will wear that at the place where my hair is gathered at the back — just as Eliza had intended.

'Wish we had the Turkish towels,' said Jane while we were getting everything ready. 'If you marry that Captain Williams, my dear Jenny, I hope you will have a guest bedroom that supplies Turkish towels.'

'And Indian bath oil,' I said.

'And shampoo and soap.'

'And a glass of wine to sip while bathing.'
'And rose petals heaped upon the bed.'
'And three dozen beeswax candles.'
'And Indian spices burning in an oil lamp.'
'And soft music in the background.'

And then our imaginations ran out. The room was looking quite lovely already. 'Lucky no one has discovered us,' said Jane. 'If Mama finds out, well, I shall just say that Eliza told us to do all of this. And she did, in a way, because she left us the soap and the shampoo and the bath oil.'

The funny thing is that I think Mrs Austen knows. She couldn't not know — she knows everything that goes on in the house.

When we were having our rest after our bath, Jane read aloud several remarks that ladies could make to gentlemen and I obediently repeated them after her until I got too sleepy so now I will blow out my candle and go to sleep — perhaps to have a happy dream about Thomas and me, whirling and dancing together at the ball.

The Portsmouths' Ball

And now I am walking under the stone portico of Hurstbourne Park. The house is huge – bigger than anything I have ever seen.

Everything is very formal here. We are invited to leave our wraps in a beautiful room downstairs and then a footman precedes us up the stairs and announces us with great formality:

'The Reverend George Austen, Mrs Austen, Miss Austen, Miss Jane Austen, Miss Cooper, Mr Henry Austen and Mr Frank Austen.'

The earl and his lady are very grand and they bow ceremoniously to us. I don't suppose that we would have been invited if Mr Austen had not tutored their three sons so well. Lady Portsmouth is saying something about knowing my sister-in-law – 'Dear Augusta'. I hardly look at her; I am too anxious to see whether Thomas is there.

And then we are through into the ballroom.

The ballroom is huge, bigger than the Assembly Rooms at Basingstoke.

I know many of the people here though: the Chutes from the Vyne, the Portals from Laverstoke House, the Biggs from Manydown House, the Digweeds from Steventon Manor.

'Big London crowd here tonight,' says Henry, and he

saunters off towards the Portal family. Mrs Austen has been impressing on him the necessity of asking Miss King to be his partner for the first dance, but he's been muttering that Miss King is too opinionated and that he is tired of her. I'm not sure that there will be a match there, no matter how much Mrs Austen tries to push Henry. I don't care one way or the other but I do think that Henry should have a chance to choose a wife that he loves.

'Do as you please,' Mrs Austen said to him before we left Steventon. 'But remember your father can't afford to buy you a commission in the militia. You'll have to find the money somewhere. Just face the facts, Henry. You must marry money.'

'Oh, Jane, Jane,' says Alethea Bigg, rushing into the suite of huge bedrooms where we took off our wraps, 'Jane, John Harwood has asked Elizabeth to give him the first two dances. He took her card and wrote his name twice and then he squeezed her hand! Shh, here she comes – don't say that I told you.'

Elizabeth and her older sister, Catherine, are walking rather apart and not looking at each other as they come in. There is a rather sour look on Catherine's face. I guess that she is jealous of Elizabeth. All these girls are so anxious to secure an offer of marriage. I don't think that their parents give them a chance to fall in love.

Neither stays long – Catherine goes off with Cassandra, Elizabeth gives her face a hasty glance in the looking glass, pinches her cheeks and bites her lips to bring the colour to them and goes after them.

'She shouldn't wear green,' observes Jane to Alethea. 'It makes her too pale.'

'Oh, Jane,' says Alethea. 'I would so like to have a beau.'

'A man of fortune, I should hope,' says Jane primly.

'Well, that would be nice,' admits Alethea, 'but to be honest, any old beau would do to practise on.'

We all giggle and then Jane says that she is thinking of setting up a school for young ladies. 'No time-wasting nonsense about globes and needlework and such things,' she says, imitating her mother's downright tone. 'I've been coaching Jenny in how to make conversation with her beau and if you like I'll take you on as a pupil too, Alethea. Teaching is in our family: my father coaches young gentlemen for Oxford; I'll coach young ladies for marriage.'

She says all this with such an air as Alethea and she go out giggling. I stay behind, pretending to fix my curls, but really I just need to have a few minutes on my own. What will I do if HE's not here, or if he has forgotten that he asked me to dance with him tonight?

And what about my midnight walk in Southampton? I ask myself as I walk out. Has he kept it to himself, as he promised? It seems so strange that he has the power to ruin me with one careless word, and yet I trust him implicitly.

The music becomes a little louder now and people are leaving the supper buffet table and starting to take their partners over towards the line that is forming down the middle of the ballroom.

Elizabeth is with John Harwood now, and Cassandra is scolding Jane and Alethea when I join them.

'Jane, don't be silly,' snaps Cassandra. 'You and Alethea are just two stupid little girls. You don't know what you are talking about.' She sees me smiling and she adds, 'And you too, Jenny. At your age you are too young to be thinking of gentlemen.'

I'm not smiling because of what she said; I'm smiling because I can see Captain Williams. He's pushing through the crowd, making his way towards me.

Jane is not taking any notice of Cassandra either. 'There's that Irish cousin of the Lefroys,' she says. 'He is rather fun. His name is Tom. Did you know that, Cassandra? I think I am fated to marry a Tom ... It used to be Tom Chute and now it is Tom Lefroy.' And then Jane is off, making her way down the ballroom, before Cassandra can say another word.

In a minute Captain Williams is bowing over my hand. He kisses it and the kiss seems to last a long time. I feel his lips on my hand. The backs of my fingers feel hot. I know that I am blushing, but I don't care.

'I've been thinking about you every day this week,' he says. 'I wanted to come to see you again, but I had to go to Southampton. We are recruiting men for a voyage to the East Indies; I'm so busy that I mostly only have the weekends to myself.'

I hardly hear him; nothing seems to matter except that he is with me and that he has missed me during the week. I don't need Jane to tell me that I am in love. My heart is beating very quickly and I want to go even closer to him; I want to feel his arms around me.

'Let's dance,' he says.

And we dance.

I don't know who is beside me, or who is opposite me when we cross over. I am conscious of only three things: a pair of brown eyes that are looking into mine, a hand that touches my waist as we walk down to the end of the line and a voice as smooth as chocolate in my ear.

And then the dance is finished. Everyone is standing in the line, breathless and laughing.

'I think Jenny is the prettiest name in the world,' says Captain Williams. In quite a natural manner he keeps his hand at the back of my waist. I don't move away from him; I don't care who is looking at us.

'I like your name too,' I say.

'Don't call me Tom, though, will you? I hate Tom. Everyone is called Tom; I much prefer Thomas.' There is laughter in his voice as he speaks. I so love his voice. I laugh too as I think of Jane and her two Toms. We are both still laughing when we reach the buffet table and he says, 'Would you like an ice?'

I nod. I have never eaten an ice, but at this moment I would agree to anything he suggests.

There is quite a crowd there; I am squeezed up against some very fat lady with a large fan and a hat full of swaying feathers. She is much taller than I am, and on my other side is Thomas, tall and broad-shouldered, towering over everyone in the room. No one can see me. Thomas glances around and for a moment he bends towards me. I think he is going to kiss me, but he just touches my cheek with his finger and then he is gone.

'Let's get out of this crowd,' he says when he comes back with two plates. So we go and sit under the palm-filled colonnade at the side of the ballroom.

'How do you like your ice?' he asks.

Anything he had brought to me would have tasted good, but the ice is especially delicious. I have never tasted anything like that. It is frozen and yet sweet.

'Sweet.' He just murmurs the word. I find myself wondering whether he is talking about me or the ice.

'Let's dance,' he says when I finish. He takes my hand and tucks it around his arm, and gently sweeps a stray curl away from my face with his other hand. I wonder whether it is improper, but no one seems to have no-ticed. We join the line that is forming and he releases me with one of his ravishing smiles – the flash of white teeth drawing attention to the smooth colour of those very high cheekbones and the softness of his brown eyes.

He is a very good dancer. He keeps perfect time with

me – all the Austens are good dancers, and so are their pupils, but Thomas is the best partner that I have ever had. Up and down the row, crossing hands, whirling around, marking time, my train with its lovely blue beads swirling behind me – I want that dance to go on forever. From time to time I remember his shoulder and am careful not to put my weight on his arm during left swings, but mostly I just enjoy myself. My busy, worrying brain has gone silent – only my body is working.

'Like another ice?' he asks when the music has finished and he has led me to a seat under the colonnade of marble pillars. And then he is gone before I can even answer. I look after him, admiring the way he makes his way so quickly and neatly through the crowd that's clustered around the laden supper table, how he smiles and nods and says a few words here and there but never allows himself to be slowed or diverted from his task. He is the most handsome man in the room, I think, as he comes back smiling with a bowl of pale pink ice in his hand.

'What about yourself?' I ask.

'I'll finish yours if it's too much for you,' he says. It sounds rather improper, I think, but there is no one near enough to hear.

And then we talk, mostly about our childhoods. He tells me that he went to a naval college when he was only twelve years old – his uncle, the admiral, paid his fees, and his mother was glad that her brother took such an interest in her son. Then, when his mother died, his uncle became guardian to both him and his sister.

'Tell me about your family,' he says then. And so I start to tell him about Augusta. I wish that I could make it sound funny, as Jane would have done, but my feelings are too strong for that, and from time to time I hear my voice wobble. I am only about halfway through telling all the things that she used to say to me, when it occurs to me that I am sounding childish and silly so I stop abruptly, take another spoonful and say, 'Tell me some more about your sister.'

'You should stand up to her, you know,' he says, ignoring me. 'People like your Augusta are just bullies. If you stand up to them, they back down, but if you give in to them they get worse and worse.'

'That's easy to say.' I surprise myself by saying that quite loudly, and he looks a little surprised too. And then he grins. 'That's the spirit,' he says with another of his devastating smiles. 'I know it's not easy.' His voice is very gentle now and the tone of it sends shivers down my back. He stretches out a hand and I place mine in his. He runs a finger of his other hand up and down the stitching on my glove, just between my own fingers. His eyes are not looking at me though, but gaze unseeing into one of the potted palms. 'I know when I was about your age I tried to stand up to the admiral and insisted that my sister should be brought home from that awful boarding school that she hated, but he just told me to leave the room, and I'll never forgive myself for going off with my tail between my legs.' His smooth voice deepens and roughens and his eyes harden. And then he says, 'That's the last time that I ever allowed anyone to push me around. Girls died in those boarding schools, you know. If my sister had died from lack of food or care, I would have killed the admiral.'

I give a little shiver and hand him the rest of my ice. I don't know whether it is the ice making me cold or the expression on his face.

For a few minutes nothing is said while he moodily spoons the rest of the ice into his mouth, but then he touches the curl that hangs down over my forehead and smiles at me.

'There's no need for you to be scared of anyone.' His voice is very gentle now, and his brown eyes are soft again. 'If Augusta scolds you, stand up to her. If she finds out about Southampton – and it doesn't really matter if she does; she or anyone else – then just say that you did the right thing and you saved your cousin. And if that doesn't work, send for me – night or day, I'll come riding to the rescue with my two pistols at the ready.'

And then he laughs, and I laugh at the thought of Augusta being threatened with two pistols.

And after that it is time to line up again. This time Jane, partnered by Tom Lefroy, is beside me. I see her looking up at Thomas as they cross hands together in the middle of the line.

'Oh heavens, my dear, what a very fine beau you have found for yourself. I do declare that he is almost as fine as Valancourt in *The Mysteries of Udolpho,*' she murmurs in my ear when she returns to my side. I am not embarrassed. I just chuckle. Suddenly I feel full of confidence. The most handsome man in the room is my partner and I feel as though I am in heaven. I see Lady Portsmouth staring at me, but I don't care. Nothing matters except Thomas.

'Jenny, let's not dance the next dance,' he says.

I have lost count; I don't know whether it is the fourth or the fifth dance, but I don't mind as long as Thomas is with me.

'Let's go and sit out in the colonnade again.' He leads me over to a small stone bench beside one of the tall marble pillars. I sit down and cool first one cheek and then the other against the cold marble of the pillar. He sits down beside me. There is barely room for the two of us.

'Are you tired?' I ask.

He shakes his head. 'I just want us to talk,' he explains.

He tells me about the East Indies, and about the tigers and elephants that he has seen and about his voyages to the other side of the world – to the West Indies. I tell him a bit more about my life in Bristol – about my brother and his wife and about my life before that. I tell him about my mama, and tears come into my eyes. He puts his arm around me and holds me very close to him for a minute. When he releases me I know I am blushing, but it doesn't matter. Here under the palms no one can see my hot cheeks.

And then, as the music slows and the dance is finishing, he says, 'Perhaps you will come and see my home one day and meet my uncle and my sister – will you do that?'

I can't say anything. He doesn't seem to want an answer. He can probably read it in my smile.

'Sitting under these palms makes me feel as if we are on one of those islands near Barbados that you were telling me about,' I say.

'I wish we were,' he answers. 'You can't imagine what the islands are like, Jenny. The sea is so blue and the sands are so white. The sun is dazzling.'

'Mama would say that is bad for the complexion,' I say, smiling. It's strange, but it is the first time since Mama died that I am able to mention her without pain.

'You would sit under the shade of the palm trees during the day,' he says, taking my hand to pull me to my feet. The master of ceremonies is calling everyone to take their places for the next dance. 'And by moonlight you could bathe in the warm sea,' he whispers in my ear as he escorts me across the ballroom so that we can join the long line of gentlemen and ladies.

I'll remember this all my life, I think: the candles flickering in the cut-glass chandelier; the sudden scent of lavender water wafted on the hot air; the pungent smell of hot wax and of buckskin gloves; the musicians playing very softly, the voices murmuring, exclaiming, laughing; the gentlemen handsome in black coats, but more dashing in the red coats of the army or in the royal blue of the navy; the pretty whites, pinks, blues and yellows of the muslin gowns as we all cross and cross back from partner to partner.

Saturday night, 2 April 1791

I'm sitting here thinking about the ball — trying to put off the moment when I must write down what happened after those first most wonderful, magical few hours . . .

Everything was going well.

And then I had to spoil it all. I think it started when he said, 'Don't stand there; that candle is drooping; you'll get hot wax all over you,' as I took my place beside Elizabeth Bigg. His hand was on my arm and he moved me down a little, just as someone would move a child.

'Don't pout,' he said. 'I wouldn't like to see the candle drip on your curls.' He was quite casual about it. A minute later he was looking with a puzzled frown on his face at someone at the top of the room, near the doorway.

I could see that Elizabeth Bigg had heard what he said and I felt very embarrassed. I felt annoyed that he was treating me like a child. I remembered all the things that Jane told me, and what Eliza told me. I wanted to behave like a sophisticated woman and I tried to flirt with him, but it didn't seem to work. He just looked amused and the frown disappeared from his forehead. He took no notice when I used my fan and cast down my eyelashes and then peeped up at him. I even tried saying, 'Oh la . . .' but he didn't seem to respond. He just danced with a faint smile on his face and a look as if his thoughts were far away.

When we sat out after this dance, it seemed as if Thomas was still thinking of that terrible night again. He started questioning me about it. In a way it was a relief to pour it all out — I often had night-mares about it still. I told him all about the sailors who shouted, 'Look at that little beauty!' and called to me to join them, about the inn full of drunken men, and the lady who stared at me with such dis-approval and then pulled down the blind. When I had finished he took my hand and kissed my fingers, but his face was very serious and his brown eyes were dark and hard.

'Promise me that you will never do a thing like that again,' he said.

I took my hand away from his and shrugged my shoulders. He was treating me like a little girl again, I thought. Men should fall at your feet — if I could believe Eliza and Jane — not order you to do things.

'I don't know,' I said, and I thought I sounded grown-up and sophisticated. 'I suppose it was rather an adventure.'

I could see a flush come to his cheekbones — it sur-prised me that I could see it as his face was so tanned and his colour so good already. His eyes were still very hard. I looked down and played with my fan, placing it into the 'maybe' position. Already I was wishing that I had not said that. It sounded silly. When I looked up he was not even looking at me. He was looking quite away from me.

'Excuse me for a moment,' he said, and then he walked away from me. I was left sitting by myself, eating my ice; after a minute I pushed it away. It had begun to melt and the taste was too sweet. What was he doing? He had gone towards the door and had now completely disappeared. There was a crowd of naval men near the door, all laughing, and I wondered whether he was among them. But no, he was so tall that he would have been head and shoulders over most of them. He must have gone out. But why? And where had he gone? Surely he wasn't so offended by my silly remark that he was going to leave me alone here.

'Are you all right, Jenny?' It was Frank passing by. He stopped, looking concerned. I smiled up at him, thinking how nice he was.

'Yes, I'm fine, Frank,' I said, trying to sound normal.

He hesitated for a moment, and then his eyes went to a tall figure approaching – two figures. Frank nodded to me and then walked away as Captain Williams and his companion drew near.

'Miss Cooper, may I introduce First Lieutenant Price?' I got up and curtsied, and Lieutenant Price gave me a splendid bow.

'It's an honour to meet you, Miss Cooper. Would you favour me with the next dance?'

But this was the last dance! I couldn't believe that Thomas would want me to be with someone else for the last dance of the evening. I looked at him and saw that the flush was still on his cheeks and his dark eyes were still hard. He hardly seemed to look at me, just bowed and took his leave as if we were almost strangers.

Lieutenant Price was a good-humoured, cheerful young man who seemed to want to earn his captain's approval by paying me lots of compliments. Funnily enough, although I was worried about why Thomas had suddenly shot off like that, I found it quite easy to respond to him. I even practised flirting with my fan and saying, 'Oh la, sir, you make me blush.' It was all a game – like playing pontoon – and I thought that I could probably get used to doing this.

Lieutenant Price was full of praise for his captain when we had reached the end of the line and were marking time. He seemed to really worship Thomas. He told a story about how once when they were in action his captain had been prepared to sacrifice his own personal prize money of at least five hundred pounds when they had an opportunity of capturing a Spanish frigate because one man had gone overboard. Thomas had ordered the boat to be lowered, but while this was being done he himself had dived into the water and rescued the drowning man by the hair of his head and held him out of the water until the boat arrived to pick them both up.

'He's the bravest man in the world and the best captain! And do you know something, Miss Cooper? He's the youngest captain in the whole British navy and yet middle-aged men are proud to serve under him!'

And this bravest man in the world, this youngest captain in the navy, this hero who was willing to sacrifice life and fortune for his men, this man handsome as a god, this kind, beautiful, exciting man had danced with me for almost the whole evening, I thought to myself as we went home in the hired coach.

But why did he suddenly leave?

If it were something to do with the ship, then surely Lieutenant Price would have told me about it. Goodness knows he talked enough about that ship.

Could it be that he thought I was too young, too silly, for him and he suddenly tired of me and handed me over to one of his junior officers?

I'm not going to think of it any more tonight or I won't sleep. I'll just think about that time when we sat under the palms and talked about the white sand of Barbados.

Sunday, 3 April 1791

When I woke up this morning I felt quite exhausted. I asked Jane to tell Frank that I was too tired for a riding lesson. Jane decided that she was too tired to do her piano practise so we both curled up on my bed and discussed the ball. I told her all my worries and fears about Thomas not dancing the last dance with me, but she brushed them aside. When I told her that Thomas had left the ballroom for a few minutes, she suggested that Lord Portsmouth probably sent for him to come to the card room to make a fourth at the whist table.

'He couldn't refuse – after all, he has been stay- ing there at Hurstbourne Place as a guest for the last week or so. My father always says that the earl lives for his card games.'

I turned that around in my mind. It did seem to make sense.

'Well, I won't expect to see him this week as he is going to the Isle of Wight tomorrow to visit his uncle and his sister.'

Then I told Jane all about how he wanted me to meet them, and Jane got very excited about this. She told me that everyone was looking at us and talking about us and speculating on whether it would be a match. All three of the Bigg girls were certain that he would propose.

'Shocking behaviour!' Jane giggled. 'Sitting out,

dancing with only one man, exposing yourself to the gossip of the county . . .'

'Did my aunt say that?' I asked the question anxiously, but Jane shook her head. 'No, no, but never mind about Mama . . . Tell me, did he make an offer?'

I told her no, that he just spoke of my visiting his sister and his uncle, the admiral, and Jane nodded wisely, as if she were at least thirty years old.

'That's the first step towards making an offer,' she said sagely.

'But what if his uncle doesn't like me?'

'It doesn't matter − he's of independent means.' Jane was always very sure of herself when it came to matters like that.

'In any case . . .' It was nice to have a best friend to talk things over with, I thought. My mind was full of worries, though I felt happier than I had ever felt before. For the first time, yesterday, I had tasted Champagne, and I felt as if the wine was still bubbling inside me. However, Jane's question made me bite my nails anxiously. Would Thomas ask me to marry him? This would be every girl's dream − that the man she loved would propose marriage. But perhaps it was just a dream. I got off the bed and walked over to the window.

'What is troubling you, my dear Miss Cooper?' enquired Jane. 'Don't you want to get married then? Perhaps you want to become a writer, to devote your life to your art. Is that it?'

I shook my head, laughing. Jane always managed to find something ridiculous to say.

'Or an artist, a painter?' Her eyebrows were raised.

'No, I'd just like to be married,' I said.

'I wonder how much a year Captain Williams possesses?' murmured Jane, sounding like a concerned mother. 'I must have a chat with Frank about this.'

'Don't,' I said. Somehow, inside all my happiness, there was a vision of Frank's young, hurt face as he stepped politely to one side when Thomas was escorting me. I don't think that Frank is really in love with me — boys are younger than girls in these matters, Jane tells me — but I think he feels something for me, and I thought that he looked a little jealous when he saw how Thomas's arm was still around my waist even though the dance had finished. 'Don't,' I said again. 'I don't mind how much Thomas has. I'd marry him if he didn't have a penny.'

'Dear, dear, dear.' Jane clicked her tongue reprovingly. 'You shouldn't be like that. Now, me, I'm determined to marry no man with under ten thousand pounds a year. So, my dear young creature, will you accept him if he asks you?'

I nodded. 'Yes, of course, but . . .'

'But?' Jane's eyebrows rose. 'Are his breeches just too white? Is that it?'

I went back and sat on the bed again.

'I'm worried that people will think I'm too young.

I'm only sixteen – perhaps I *am* too young – my brother is very particular about things. And Augusta was twenty-three when she married so I bet she will think that is the exact right age to get married.' I remembered that Thomas had asked me for Edward-John's address. Why did he want that? What was he going to write to them about? Surely he wasn't going to mention marriage before asking me?

But if he did, what would Edward-John and, more importantly, Augusta, think about a girl of sixteen getting engaged to be married? I remembered over-hearing Augusta whispering to one of her friends about how Edward-John would have problems if I ever did get married. I didn't understand it, but I guessed that perhaps the fifty pounds a year that Edward-John has now to maintain me would have to be given up if I married. How would Edward-John react to that? Augusta was extravagant and al-ways had to have the best of everything. I knew that Edward-John worried about the bills that came in from the haberdashery and furniture shops. It would be a blow to him to give up my little fortune.

'I just know that Edward-John and Augusta will say that I am too young to get married,' I said aloud. The more I thought about it, the more despairing I felt.

'Well, look at all those queens that Cassandra was trying to make me study!' Jane always had an answer to every problem. 'They got married very young. Henry VII's mother was married at twelve and she had a child at thirteen. And there was that unspeakably learned Lady Jane Grey — who only lived to annoy everyone by showing off the fact that she could speak Greek. Do you know that when she saw her husband's body being brought back from the scaffold, she sat down and wrote a sentence about it in Latin and then another one in Greek? Well, she was not only married when she was sixteen, but got her head chopped off before she was seventeen as well. Now, that was packing a lot into a short life! You'll never do as well as Lady Jane Grey, my dear. Just be content with getting married at sixteen — and keeping your head on your shoulders, of course!'

And then we both rolled on the bed giggling and I began to feel quite a bit better. I would just have to wait until I saw Thomas again and then I could see whether he really did care for me. If he did, well, he would handle Augusta and Edward-John for me.

The rest of the day was quite uninteresting: church, dinner, music, card games in the parlour . . . Frank was missing because Mrs Austen had sent him over to Lady Portsmouth with a note saying how we had all enjoyed the evening, and then Henry went off to visit the Portals. Things were dull without them.

That night before going to bed, Jane said to me

solemnly, 'Don't look so worried, Jenny. No man tells a girl that he wants his nearest relations to meet her unless he is on the point of proposing. You can take my word for that — I assure you I have made a life study of this subject.'

Monday, 4 April 1791

Jenny Williams

Mrs Thomas Williams

Mrs Thomas Williams

Mrs Thomas Williams

Tuesday, 5 April 1791

Jane and I were going out with a basket today. We had a slice of meat in it for George, and I had drawn some pictures of all kinds of meat. At the gate we met Mr Austen on his way back from church. He asked us where we were going and when Jane, who is always very courageous, told him, he looked a little embarrassed, gave a quick glance at the house to make sure that his wife wasn't watching and then said that he would come with us.

George wasn't alarmed – though I'm not sure whether he knew it was his father. He learned the sign for meat and then we put out all the pictures, made the signs, and one by one he was able to point to the pictures. Each time that he pointed, Jane dug into her basket and produced something. We didn't have an orange and he was upset at that, searching the basket himself. Eventually he found a small piece of orange peel and he ate that. I hoped it wouldn't harm him, but he seemed very happy.

'Well,' said Mr Austen as we walked home together, 'I think you two girls have done a marvellous piece of work. I wouldn't have believed it was possible. Where did you get the idea of teaching him sign language?'

'I read it in a book from your library,' explained Jane. She was glowing with excitement, her round cheeks as rosy as apples.

'I know the one,' said Mr Austen. 'I think I'll write to the man who wrote that book and consult him about George. It may be that he can recommend a teacher for him.'

He hesitated a bit, looking at Jane, and then he said, 'Jane, I want to tell you about Thomas.'

I gave a start when he said that, but it was another Thomas that he was talking about.

'Who's Thomas? I haven't got another brother hidden away, have I?' asked Jane in that ugly, harsh voice she used to her mother.

'No, no.' Mr Austen was patient where Mrs Austen would have started to scold. 'Thomas is your mother's brother and he, like George, was born disabled. He is being cared for by a very good and devoted family in the village of Monk Sheraton. It was of him that I spoke the other day. We think that it might be a good idea to take George there and lodge him with his uncle. They would be companions for each other and he would be well looked after. There is a big family there at Monk Sheraton. I've been to see Thomas there and I think that they are good to him. He helps on the farm a bit, and they are all very kind there. He was feeding the hens when I came and he looked very happy. We want to do the best thing for George. You do believe that, don't you? And we will try to get someone to continue the tuition that you have started.'

'What does Mother think about this?' Jane was

slightly unsure of what to say; I could hear that in her voice.

Mr Austen sighed and then he said very simply, 'Don't judge your mother too harshly, Jane. The trouble is that your mother and I have been short of money all our married lives. Running the school was the only way that we could manage and do the best for you all. And of course I could not have run the school without your mother's help. She has had all the hard work: looking after the pupils, their laundry, their food, their happiness even. She could not have cared for George at the same time.'

I could see that Jane was not impressed by this, but she said nothing. She was too fond of her father and she was keen to give advice on how George could be taught sign language and lay out a programme of study for him.

'The thing is that if he could learn to spell easy words like *cat* and *dog* and *gun* and other words, then he could go on to talking on his fingers. I remember Charles learning his alphabet, and when he learned his letters Cassandra and I used to put the letters together to make little words for him. It would be wonderful if George could read, wouldn't it, Papa? Even very simple books. And I'd love to be able to talk to him. If he goes over to Monk Sheraton, you will take me to see him, won't you?'

Mr Austen promised, and Jane beamed happily at him.

And for a lot of this evening Jane and I chatted about George and how wonderful it would be if he could talk to us.

Neither of us mentioned Jane's mother. I don't know what Jane felt, but I worried in case Mrs Austen would think a teacher for George a complete waste of money, with the other four boys still to be launched into the world.

And for the rest of the evening we talked about Thomas and about the ball . . . and about Tom Chute and Tom Lefroy . . .

Wednesday, 6 April 1791

Something terrible has happened today.

And to begin with it was just an ordinary, quiet, happy day.

It all started off when Frank asked me to ride up to Deane Gate Inn to collect the post. I always enjoyed that and I am very confident with my donkey now.

When we arrived at the inn, the ostler came out as soon as he saw us and said that there were five letters for the parsonage. Frank took them and scrutinized their outsides.

'One from James for my father . . . one for Jane from Cousin Eliza . . . two for Henry, probably creditors . . . this one is from Bristol.'

I immediately guessed that it would be from Augusta and then, thankfully, I noticed that it was for my Aunt Austen. 'Good,' I said to Frank. 'It's for your mother.' I remember thinking what a relief that was, and being pleased that I wouldn't have to write back. If only I had known what was in that letter I could have dropped it in the ditch and at least enjoyed a couple more happy days.

And we went back and went into breakfast.

They were all sitting around the table, the family and the pupils. I gave out the letters.

Henry pushed his two into his pocket rapidly and avoided his father's worried look.

Mrs Austen poured the tea, broke the seal on the back of her letter and then put it down without reading it as she took a bite of her usual dry toast.

Mr Austen was the first to open his letter.

'Henry, James wants to know if we will come to Oxford on Saturday to hear him speak at a debate. I think that would be quite a treat, wouldn't it? What do you think, my dear? James says that he can put us up at his lodgings on Saturday night. If we get the early mail coach on Sunday morning, we'll be back in time for morning service.'

'Mama,' said Jane, 'Cousin Eliza has some news about the king and queen of France, King Louis XVI and Marie Antoinette. Apparently they have been imprisoned in Paris by the angry mob. Eliza is worried about her husband. Mama, are you listening?'

But Mrs Austen wasn't listening to anyone. She was reading Augusta's letter. I could see the big, bold handwriting – just one page and not even crossed. It should not have taken long to read it. But Mrs Austen was now going back over it again. She frowned and then looked at me. I felt puzzled. There was an odd look in her eye. For the first time since I have known her, Mrs Austen looked as though she was unsure of what to do.

After breakfast, I rose to help Cassandra and Jane with our task of clearing the breakfast plates. Mrs Austen stopped me, however.

She put a hand on my arm and stood there

looking indecisive. Mr Austen gave her a puzzled look, but she said nothing to him and so he shuffled off to the schoolroom with his pupils. Henry and Frank followed at a slow pace. Both were studying with their father at the moment, but neither was enthusiastic. Frank had told me that he knew more of mathematics than his father did, and that Latin was useless to him; and Henry was obviously wishing himself back at Oxford with all the fun and parties and 'wild living', as Jane expressed it.

'Come with me, Jenny.' That was all that Mrs Austen said as she took my hand, but there was something in her tone that alerted Jane.

'Shall I come too?' she asked.

'No, I just need Jenny for a few minutes.' Mrs Austen sounded sure of that, at least. The brisk tone was back in her voice and she moved quickly to the door, still with my hand in hers as if she thought I might run away.

'Come upstairs into my bedroom, my dear; we'll get some privacy there,' she said as we passed the parlour where the housemaid was lighting the fire.

What could Augusta have to say to Mrs Austen that was so important? I wondered. Mrs Austen's routine normally never varied. By now she should have been out in the dairy, checking on the amount of milk brought in, inspecting the cleanliness of the churn and directing the dairymaid in loud, penetrating tones. Perhaps something had happened to Edward-

John, I suddenly thought, and although he was never very friendly to me, my heart almost stopped for a moment. My brother was the only family I had left.

'Sit here next to me, Jenny dear.' Mrs Austen plumped herself down on the window seat and I squeezed in beside her. She still held Augusta's letter in her hand. For a moment she seemed unsure as to what to do, but then she suddenly held it out to me.

'What's all this nonsense about?' I could hear her voice, but it seemed to come from a long way away. The letter was not very long; I read it in a few seconds, but suddenly my life was in ruins.

How could he?

How could Thomas have betrayed me like this?

It had to be him.

How could he, before he left Hurstbourne Park, have taken his pen and sent this letter to Edward-John and Augusta? And I had been imagining him, coming down to breakfast in Lord and Lady Portsmouth's magnificent dining room, thinking of me as he ate his buttered eggs, deciding to go to see his uncle and sister . . .

Well, I was probably right. He had thought of me, but it was not with love and understanding. He had thought of me and he had found my conduct so shocking that he had written to Edward-John as my guardian. Or else he wanted to force me to stand up to Augusta — either way, I could never forgive him.

And he had promised never to tell anyone.

Perhaps when I had refused to promise never to do it again he was so annoyed that he took revenge by telling my brother and sister-in-law.

I blinked the tears from my eyes and read Augusta's letter through again.

Dear Mrs Austen,

The most distressing and alarming communication has come to me today from Hurstbourne Park. It was lucky that my dear husband was still by my side when I opened the letter or else I would have fallen to the ground in a deep faint. I do declare that I am still suffering from such severe palpitations that the quill quivers in my hand as though it were still part of the living bird.

Madam, I hesitate to communicate to you the terrible information that I have received. I wish I could bring myself to make the usual enquiries about your health but I can send no compliments to you, your husband and your charming children. My whole heart and mind is filled with horror at the behaviour of one that I considered as a sister to me as well as to my darling husband, Edward-John.

It has been reported to us, madam, that this miserable girl has been, alone and unchaperoned, walking the streets of Southampton at midnight.

I can assure you, madam, that I have received this information from a most reliable source. There can be no doubt as to its accuracy.

Edward-John and I can see only one solution to such appalling behaviour and lack of decorum. We can no longer leave her - I cannot bring myself to say her name - we can no longer impose the care of such a wicked and abandoned creature upon your good selves. We have decided to place her in a very strict boarding school here at Bristol. The girls are locked in their bedrooms every single night - so the mistress of the school assures me. And there are no holidays so there will be no opportunities for further bad behaviour.

Edward-John and I will arrive to collect the sinful girl by the overnight stagecoach from Bristol. We should be at Deane Gate Inn by ten o'clock of the morning.

I am, etc.

Augusta Cooper

'I just came for a handkerchief.' Mr Austen slid apologetically around the door, but then he exclaimed, 'Jenny dear, what's the matter?'

I was crying too hard to say anything. Last night I felt that I was floating on a cloud of perfect happiness and now I was drowning in despair. He came across the floor and bent down and took one of my cold hands in his own. Through the blur of my tears I saw Mrs Austen pass Augusta's letter to him. He read it quickly and then handed it back.

'But, Jenny, dearest little Jenny, we don't believe this!' Now he had taken out his clean muslin handkerchief and was trying to mop the tears that slid down my face.

'Don't cry, Jenny. Neither your aunt nor I could believe such a thing of you.'

'That's all very well, Mr Austen,' said my aunt. 'But an accusation like this could ruin Jenny forever. Where on earth did that woman get that story?'

'Mama, what piano piece would you like me to practise today?' Jane was at the door. I took the handkerchief from Mr Austen and dried my eyes and face.

'Jane dear, your mother is busy.' Mr Austen looked anxiously from one to the other of us.

'What's the matter with Jenny?' Jane had closed the door and come across to the window seat.

'Oh, come in, come in,' said Mrs Austen wearily. 'Let's have the whole of Hampshire in here, why not?'

No one answered her, but I saw Mr Austen hand

the letter to Jane. I began to cry again and Mr Austen's handkerchief was soaked through in the minute it took for Jane to scan the letter. I looked at her and saw my own thoughts mirrored in her eyes.

'Of course we don't believe this, Jenny.' Mr Austen's voice was so affectionate that it made me cry even harder. 'This is some malicious person. My dear ' — he addressed his wife — 'do you think that it could be one of the young Portsmouths? That Coulson! He would do anything for a joke! Shall we send Henry over to Hurstbourne Park to make enquiries?'

'No, no.' I felt I could not bear to have everyone at Hurstbourne Park talking about me. It was bad enough to know that Thomas had betrayed me, that I had been mistaken in him. He was not really in love; he just thought of me as a silly child and, when thinking it over, decided to let my brother and my sister-in-law know all about my dreadful secret. He probably thought it would be good for me to stand up to them. He didn't realize the importance of a young girl's reputation. I had wondered why he asked me so particularly about where they lived. I wished now that I hadn't given him the address.

'Just tell us it is not true, Jenny, and your uncle and I will do everything to sort out this matter and to save you from being sent to boarding school.' Mrs Austen was herself again, decisive and practical.

'It is true.' I said the words boldly and gave my eyes a last mop. I sat up very straight.

'What?!' both husband and wife exclaimed on the one note like a well-trained pair of singers.

'Tell them,' I said to Jane.

And Jane made a wonderful dramatic story of how I had taken the letter at the risk of my life and liberty – these were her words – and how I had braved the midnight streets of Southampton and delivered the letter to the post-inn. And how I had saved her life by my courage!

When she had finished, Jane put her two arms around me and held me very close in a hug, and Mr Austen stroked my hair with a gentle hand. Then I saw him take Jane in his arms as if he suddenly realized that he might have lost her. I think that we were all crying for a minute – all except Mrs Austen, who still had a worried and slightly annoyed expression on her face.

'This is a most unfortunate affair,' she said, and her lips were compressed together in a straight line. 'If this gets out about Jenny, what on earth are we to do? Her reputation will be ruined.'

'But, Jenny, who could have told that abominable sister-in-law of yours?' Mr Austen was obviously quite upset; normally he was very careful not to say anything about Augusta.

'I met a gentleman that night in Southampton,' I said hesitantly. I buried my face in my hands. I could not look at either my aunt or my uncle while I spoke the words that had to be said. 'He was very kind to me. He escorted me to the post-inn and then he took me back to the school. He waited until I was safely inside.' I swallowed another sob as the picture of Thomas in his deep blue coat, with the gold braid flashing under the glare of the chair-men's torches, came into my mind. I had to finish my story though.

'It was Captain Thomas Williams,' I said desperately. 'The naval officer who is a guest of the Portsmouths at Hurstbourne Park.'

'Captain Williams.' Mr Austen sounded relieved. He had liked Thomas. I think he was reassured to know that he had been looking after me on that terrible night.

'Captain Williams?' Mrs Austen sounded puzzled. I knew how she felt. A horrified expression crossed her face. I could follow her thoughts; Captain Williams had shown affection to me, but then he must have thought it over and decided to have no more to do with me.

'I wonder why he felt he had to talk to your brother.' Mrs Austen's voice was still puzzled – puzzled and worried.

'And he promised that he would never tell a living soul.' I felt sick and faint and was glad of Jane's arm around me.

No one said anything for a full minute. I sensed rather than saw Mrs Austen exchange glances with her husband and with Jane. Then she got to her feet.

She crossed over to her bedside table, poured a small measure of wine and brought it over to me.

'Drink this, Jenny,' she said soothingly. 'Jane, take her back up to your bedroom. You are both excused from lessons this morning. Don't worry, Jenny. I will sort out Mrs Augusta Cooper, and young Edward-John, when they come on Saturday. That lady will find that your uncle and I have something to say about them trying to ruin your reputation and risk your life by sending you off to boarding school again. After all, I am your poor mother's elder sister. The main thing is to hush up this terrible business as much as possible. Let us hope that Captain Williams is a man of honour and he doesn't mention it to anyone else.'

Thursday, 7 April 1791

I did nothing much but cry yesterday, but this morning I got up with a resolve. I would write Thomas a letter, finish this business now and put him out of my head forever. Then I would concentrate on avoiding being sent to boarding school. Jane had great plans about the two of us running away, but I thought I would prefer to rely on Mrs Austen.

'Here's some paper.' Jane arranged the clean sheet and a new quill and the inkhorn in front of me with a very sympathetic face.

I dipped the quill into the ink, but then left it there, stroking the smooth curved shape of the horn with my fingers while I tried to think of what to say. A big tear dropped down on to the clean sheet of paper.

'Don't.' Jane was at my side, blotting the tear with the corner of her handkerchief. 'You'll spoil the paper and water down the ink. Let me write. You can dictate it.'

'*Dear Captain Williams,*' I began, getting up obediently and allowing her to sit in my place.

'Just call him "Sir",' advised Jane, carefully selecting a large goose quill and dipping it into the inkstand.

'Sir.' Then I stopped. I didn't know what to say.

I just wanted to cry, but I knew I shouldn't allow myself to start again. Soon it would be time for the bread-and-cheese lunch that the Austens always took at eleven o'clock, and I didn't want all the boys to see my blotchy face and red eyes. I went to the window and opened it, leaning out to cool my cheeks before turning back to Jane.

'I never want to see you again,' I said as steadily as I could.

Jane made a face. She stirred the ink with her quill, but did not write. I could see that she didn't think much of this, but I couldn't think of anything better to say so I bit my lip and tried not to think about Thomas and how splendid he had looked at the ball.

'What about this?!' exclaimed Jane. She opened her writing desk, took out her notebook, turned over the pages and then gave a satisfied nod.

'This will do,' she said. 'It is from *Jack and Alice*.'

She read it aloud as her quill scratched out the letters on the page.

'"*Sir, I may perhaps be expected to appear pleased at and grateful for the attention that you have paid me, but let me tell you, sir, that I consider it an affront.*" . . . What do you think of that, Jenny?'

I didn't reply; I couldn't. I was trying too hard not to sob aloud.

'I'll put in "*considering your vile and deceitful*

behaviour",,' said Jane, writing rapidly. She needed to mend her pen; I could hear the point spluttering as it moved across the page, but once Jane was composing she never allowed anything to slow her down.

I nodded, but I didn't really care what she said. Thomas had hurt me so badly by telling my terrible secret that I could never forgive him. Even if he really did love me — and now I doubted that he ever had — and even if I could have brought myself to forgive him, my brother would never have allowed me to marry a man who had walked with me in the streets of Southampton at midnight. I was ruined for life. If he had told my secret to Augusta and Edward-John, he would tell it to everyone.

'"*I look upon myself, sir, to be a perfect beauty — where would you see, sir, a finer figure or a more charming face?*"'

I stopped her. 'That's silly. Just say that after his behaviour I never want to see him again . . .'

'Don't cry,' said Jane sympathetically. 'Don't worry about the letter. I'll just finish it off and sign it "Jenny", and then I'll give it to Frank and he'll ride to the post with it straight away. I won't read out any more. You can rely on me to make a good letter out of it. You just read a book or something.'

'I'll go and walk in the fresh air,' I said, wrapping my cloak around me and then taking down my bonnet. I tried to shut my ears to the words she was muttering as I was tying my bonnet strings, but I could hear them as I went out of the door: '*my accomplishments . . . my sweet temper . . . your dastardly behaviour . . .*'

That was the thing with Jane, I thought as I escaped down the stairs. She was very fond of me; I knew that. I was her best friend, just as she was my best friend, but writing always came first with her. Although very sorry for me, she was really enjoying composing this letter. I wondered whether she would change when she fell in love. I hoped for her sake that she never did. It all hurt too much. It was never worth it.

And then I thought about Thomas and I knew that I couldn't send him a letter like that. I raced back upstairs and burst into the bedroom.

'Jane,' I said, 'I am very, very grateful to you, but I just think that I'd better write the letter myself.' I could see she looked disappointed so I said that I thought her letter was too good for Thomas and would be best kept for a novel.

And then very quickly I wrote to Thomas and said that after what had happened I would prefer not to see him again and that I hoped that he would respect my wishes. I ended it: 'Yours, etc., J. Cooper.'

I thought that sounded the right note and then very quickly, before I could change my mind, I ran downstairs and asked Frank if he would take it to the post for me. He told me that it wouldn't get to

Southampton before Friday as the mail coach had already gone, but I told him it didn't matter as long as it arrived before the weekend. I could see him looking at my red eyes and tear-stained face, but I was past caring. I had a terrible pain in my heart and I just wanted to get into bed, draw the blankets over my head and moan.

'Are you all right, Jenny?' Frank's young, slightly hoarse voice sounded so concerned that a lump came into my throat and I found it hard to answer him.

The whole Austen family are being so nice to me. Henry allowed me to win some pennies from him in a game of pontoon, Frank offered to lend me his pony whenever I wanted it and, just because I ate so little at breakfast, Cassandra made a special dish of syllabub for me, whipping up the cream and white of eggs and flavouring it with orange juice and lots of sugar. Even that wasn't enough to make me hungry though, and I shared it between Jane and little Charles when she had gone back to the kitchen.

Friday, 8 April 1791

I don't think I'll ever write in this journal again.

Saturday, 9 April 1791

The mail coach is due at ten o'clock this morning. I wish I didn't have to go to meet Augusta and Edward-John, but Mrs Austen is insistent with me. She says that Cassandra and Charles must go too, as well as Jane, of course. Mr Austen and Henry have taken an earlier coach to visit James at Oxford; Frank has gone over to join a shooting party at the Portals' place.

'We'll show them that you have a family here, and that family values you,' she says to me, pinching my cheeks to give me some colour. Then she sends me up-stairs to change my calico gown for my best blue muslin. 'Go up with her to do her hair, Cassandra,' she says. 'Do it the way she had it at the ball, just pinned on top of her head with a few stray curls around her neck. I thought she looked very grown-up with that hairstyle. Boarding school indeed . . . we'll see about that!'

I feel my feet dragging as we set out and for once Mrs Austen isn't shooing everyone along to hurry them up. 'Ten o'clock,' she says with a glance at her timepiece as we pass through the village. 'We're going to be quite late.'

'Oh dear,' says Cassandra in a worried way, but Mrs Austen just smirks.

'They invited themselves; let them wait on our

convenience.' She sounds quite pleased with herself.

When we reach Deane Gate Inn though, there is no sign of the coach, no bustling around, no changing horses, no piles of luggage on the ground – just the innkeeper's wife peering anxiously down the road.

'Oh, Mrs Austen, ma'am, I'm that worried; I don't know what to do,' she says. She looks at Mrs Austen. Everyone in the neighbourhood relies on Mrs Austen to tell them what to do, so now the innkeeper's wife comes back to the gate and joins us. 'The coach is overdue, ma'am. I'm feared that there might have been an accident. Do you think that I should send the man out to look for them? The trouble is that my husband isn't back from Basingstoke.'

'We'll walk down the road to see whether it is coming.' As always, Mrs Austen makes up her mind immediately. 'They can give us a lift back if we meet them.' She's in a good mood, relishing the prospect of the battle ahead, but I'm worried. I know what Augusta is like. I always have a feeling that she hates me. I know that she resents that my mother left me fifty pounds in order to give me a dowry when I marry or when I reach the age of twenty-one – whichever happens first.

Mrs Austen glances at me a few times but says nothing. Cassandra is silent because Tom Fowle has gone home for the weekend, Charles is looking into the little stream that runs along the side of the road to see if there are any sticklebacks in it, and Jane, I reckon, judging by her glowing cheeks and sparkling eyes, is making up a story where Augusta would be defeated by some splendidly funny device – last night she was suggesting things like steel traps set all around Steventon!

So we are silent when we come around the corner. There are poplar trees belonging to the Ashe family's woodlands on either side of the road, making it almost a tunnel of green, but the sun shines down through the tunnel and we can see plainly the scene ahead of us.

The coach is there in front of us. It has not over-turned or anything like that. The four horses are still harnessed to it. However, the doors are widely ajar and the six passengers, including Edward-John and Augusta, are out on the road. Their luggage has been taken off the coach. One masked highwayman is ran-sacking the bags and trunks, while the other keeps two pistols aimed at the huddled group, the coachman and guard included.

The highwaymen haven't seen us. The early-morning sun will be shining directly in their eyes if they look at us, but their whole attention is on their prisoners. Mrs Austen puts a finger to her lips and edges over to touch Charles on the shoulder. She makes urgent beckoning signs, and we all step cautiously across the ditch and into the woodland. None of us makes a sound, and in another moment we might creep away through the trees and make our way back.

But then everything changes.

Further up the road, on the left-hand side, there is a large juniper bush. As I give one glance backwards

it seems to move. I stop. Jane bumps into me and she stops also. Mrs Austen looks around impatiently.

And then a loud, hoarse sound . . . A word . . . But a word only to someone who knows the speaker . . .

'Bang!'

And George, with his unsteady gait, lurches out from behind the bush, pointing his finger at the gun and repeating proudly, 'Bang!'

'Get over there!' The armed highwayman points one gun at George while keeping the other pointed at the group by the coach. His head swivels nervously between the two.

'Bang!' says George, advancing with what passes for a smile on his poor face. He stretches out his hand, saying, 'Bang!' again. It's obvious to me that he expects the highwayman to give him the gun as a reward for saying the word.

'Halt, or I fire,' says the highwayman in shrill, nervous tones. He doesn't know what to do about George.

I hold my breath. I hear Jane give a nervous gasp beside me, but Mrs Austen doesn't hesitate; she steps out on to the road. The highwayman's gun swivels.

'You fellow! Don't point that gun at the boy – you'll frighten him into a fit.' Mrs Austen is marching resolutely over to George.

'What's it to you, lady?' The highwayman has a gruff, hoarse voice, the voice of someone who has a perpetual sore throat. 'Get back, or you'll have a bullet in the stomach.'

'He's my son, and I'm not going to allow you to terrify him,' says Mrs Austen calmly. 'Come along, George, let's take you back to Nanny Littleworth.'

And then she puts her arm around George's shoulders and turns him around gently, almost tenderly, until he is facing back towards Deane Gate and Steventon beyond. Slowly, steadily, the two figures come back down the road, while the highwayman continues to point his pistol at their backs, his whole attention now on the two moving figures. His partner takes his head out of a trunk and also stares incredulously at George and Mrs Austen.

It might have worked. In the bright, clear early-morning sunshine, I can see the faces of the highwaymen. They are puzzled, hesitant. It's obvious that George is retarded, and Mrs Austen looks just like any old countrywoman. They want money and jewels, not unnecessary bloodshed.

But then the guard of the coach, who is watching them as closely as I, makes a move. He slowly passes his arm behind Augusta, reaches for the blunderbuss in its place by the roof, grabs it by its short barrel and tries to reverse it.

And the highwayman whirls around and fires straight at the guard.

Then everything happens at once.

A roar of pain from the guard, a high-pitched neigh from the rearing horses, a hysterical screech from Augusta, shouts from the other passengers and blood everywhere.

And then a voice from the trees beyond the coach, a voice filled with authority but as velvet-smooth as chocolate: 'Drop those pistols and put your hands up, my men. I've got you both covered.'

They look at each other and hesitate, but less than a second later a warning shot explodes – fired over their heads, but near enough to be convincing. A second scream from Augusta, more neighing from the horses, and then the two pistols are flung hastily in the direction of the hedge.

'Very wise.' Thomas, the gold braid on his coat

glowing, strolls down the road, an ornate silver-mounted pistol in each hand. Without taking his eyes from the highwaymen, he addresses Edward-John, the only male passenger.

'Could I trouble you, sir, to pick up the blackguards' pistols and keep them trained on both men? Coachman, could you bind up your guard's arm? He's losing blood rapidly. Ladies, you follow behind us. Charles, would you untie my horse from the tree back there? Good lad! He shouldn't give you any trouble. He's had a long, hard gallop this morning.

'We'll lock these highwaymen in the stables at the inn,' he says decisively to Edward-John, and then rather sharply, 'Careful with that gun, sir, it's loaded.'

'Here's the innkeeper,' calls back Mrs Austen. She still has an arm around George, who is trembling violently, but he has not had a fit.

Even after the innkeeper arrives Thomas is still in charge, giving directions for the summoning of a magistrate and the safe custody of the prisoners, brushing aside the thanks of the passengers, praising and thanking Charles, reassuring the women passengers – but never once does he speak to me, or even glance at me.

And now the men are gone to the stables to see to the prisoners. Cassandra is fetching a glass of wine for Augusta, while Edward-John dithers between following Thomas and hanging anxiously over his wife . . .

Mrs Austen is in great good humour. 'What do you

think of this boy of mine, Mrs Deane?' she says to the innkeeper's wife. 'You wouldn't believe it, but he was telling the highwayman to hand over his gun.' She squeezes George's shoulder and he looks up at her in a wondering sort of way.

'You want something to eat now, don't you, George? And something to drink?' Mrs Austen chats to George in a perfectly natural manner, making motions with her hands to indicate eating and drinking, even rubbing her stomach to indicate food. A big smile lights up George's face.

'You go with Mrs Deane – she'll find some nice hot sausages for you and a glass of ale, won't you, Mrs Deane? Off you go with her now, George.' And all the time that she is saying the words, she is making signs in quite a natural manner – rather like how you would to a baby, I think. Much easier, I realize now, than trying to teach him his alphabet.

And George understands her perfectly. He rubs his own stomach and grins from ear to ear. He follows Mrs Deane and then he turns back, making a great effort until a word comes out. It's easy to understand the word. It's 'Mama'.

And when he's gone, Mrs Austen – tough, unsentimental Mrs Austen – has tears in her eyes.

This is almost like a play, I think.

First everyone is onstage in the coach yard in front of Deane Gate Inn. Then the men go off to the stables, followed by Charles, while Augusta retires to faint on a sofa in the comfort of the inn parlour, attended by Cassandra.

Then it's the scene between Mrs Austen and George, where she seems able to chat to him in an easy, natural way before he trundles happily off with Mrs Deane.

Now just Jane and I are left with Mrs Austen.

And Jane throws herself into her mother's arms and starts to cry.

It is so unlike Jane that I feel completely bewildered.

But Mrs Austen just pats her on the back and says, 'Come, come, Jane. Were you so very frightened of those highwaymen? That's not like my brave girl!' Her tone is light and amused, but loving.

I hold my breath. It just needs a few words from Jane now and perhaps they will be friends evermore.

But Jane says nothing and, after a moment's silence, I hear my own voice.

'Jane wasn't frightened for herself, Aunt,' I find myself saying. 'She was frightened for you.'

Mrs Austen draws back, bends down, looks into Jane's face and presses a quick kiss on one round cheek. I notice how their bonnets meet with a slight click.

'Come on, my pet,' she says. 'Let's go and thank Captain Williams properly. What a hero he's been! You could get a good novel out of this, Jane. I declare I feel like commemorating it in verse myself.' And, laughing cheerfully, she sweeps out with her arm around Jane.

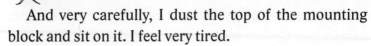

And very carefully, I dust the top of the mounting block and sit on it. I feel very tired.

And very lonely.

'We'll send the post boy down to Steventon with you, ma'am,' says the innkeeper's wife. 'This lady' – she means Augusta – 'is not strong enough to walk, and Miss Jenny looks very white too. The captain has got his horse, and the other passengers will wait for the stagecoach to go on when we get another man to act as guard.'

'You should have fainted on the sofa too,' whispers Jane as we walk towards the post-chaise. 'I'd have made Augusta give you a turn. You could have fainted alternately.' Jane sounds like her old self again, grinning as her mother issues orders to everyone.

'Cassandra, you sit over there with Edward-John and his wife; Charles, you get up on the seat beside the post boy; Jenny, you sit beside me; and, Jane, you go on the other side of her. We'll follow you down to the parsonage, Captain Williams. You'll come in and have breakfast with us, won't you? Then we can all thank you properly.'

'Oh yes, indeed.' Augusta has given up fainting, though she still speaks in a small, slightly squeaky voice, like a six-year-old. 'Do come and ride on my side of the chaise, Captain Williams. How lucky for us all that you were passing by.'

'I'll ride behind you all, ma'am, so that my horse does

not kick up the dirt on to you,' says Thomas with a bow, and then to Mrs Austen, 'I was taking the liberty of paying a call to you, ma'am. My ship is stocked and ready to go; I've a few days' leave and you were kind enough to invite me to stay for a night or so on my next visit.'

'What a charming man,' enthuses Augusta once Thomas has fallen to the rear. 'I do declare that I have not heard of him, but I am sure that he is a real hero at sea. Where is his ship docked?'

'At Southampton.' Cassandra obviously does not know the full story of Augusta's letter.

'Southampton! I can't bear the word!' Augusta shudders and then looks at me crossly. 'Oh, Jenny, you sad, sad girl! What are we to do with you? I do declare, ma'am' – now she addresses herself to Mrs Austen – 'that I have not had a single night's sleep – Edward-John will tell you – since that letter came from Lady Portsmouth.'

'Lady Portsmouth?!' exclaims Jane, and she turns and looks at me, her eyes wide with amazement.

'Lady Portsmouth?' echoes Mrs Austen.

'Was your letter from Lady Portsmouth, Augusta?' I say. Suddenly I lose all fear of her. Only one thing matters now, and that is Thomas. 'Are you sure it was from Lady Portsmouth, Augusta?'

'Yes, of course.' Augusta sounds intensely annoyed. She turns away from me and towards my aunt. 'I told you, ma'am, did I not? Lady Portsmouth wrote to me that when Jenny came to a ball at her house she recognized her. She saw her last February when she was staying with a friend in Southampton. They were all listening to the young lady of the house perform on the piano when Lady Portsmouth saw a young girl, all alone and unprotected, look in through the window. She imagined her to be some sort of streetwalker and went to close the shutters. What was her astonishment to see her at her own ball at Hurstbourne Park and to learn that she is related to *me*?! Of course, she wrote to me. After all, my mama is one of her close friends.'

I look at Jane and she looks at me. She moves very close to me and squeezes my hand. Augusta looks at us with dislike.

'You two seem very thick,' she says disapprovingly.

'Yes, we are,' says Jane demurely. And then she can't resist adding, 'But I'm the thinner of the two . . .' and smiling sweetly when Augusta looks puzzled.

'Well, here we are in Steventon,' interrupts Mrs Austen. 'In another few minutes we will be at the parsonage and you will have a good cup of tea. That will restore your nerves. Charles,' she says as the chaise goes through the gates, 'you jump down and find the stable-man for Captain Williams's horse.'

'No,' says Jane. In her hurry to get out, she almost stumbles. 'No, Mama, let Charles ride back up to Deane Gate Inn with the post boy to find out how the guard is. The surgeon should be there by now. He can bring us news; I'll see to Captain Williams and his horse.'

'Go straight into the house, Jane,' says Mrs Austen

sternly. 'Tell Susan that we have arrived. Charles, you do what I told you.'

Jane rolls her eyes at me, but she dares not disobey her mother. I stay sitting in the post-chaise until Thomas has gone into the stable.

He still has not once looked at me.

'You sit here opposite Jenny, Captain Williams; Cassandra, make room for your Cousin Augusta next to you; Edward-John, could you take the bottom of the table, please?' Mrs Austen is back in control, beaming at me and adding in a loud whisper to Augusta: 'Jenny and Captain Williams are great friends.'

I feel as if I want to be sick, but reluctantly I take the indicated seat.

Luckily Thomas doesn't notice. He is busy chatting to Charles and promising him the first vacancy for a midshipman when he reaches fifteen years old.

'There are just a few words that I would like to say first, dear Aunt.' Edward-John is standing stiffly at the bottom of the table with a large black book in his hand, almost as if he is about to read prayers. 'Captain Williams, sir,' he continues, 'your conduct, your gallantry, your courage, your quickness of thinking, your—'

At this point Charles yawns and stretches out his hand towards the dish of buttered eggs. Cassandra gives him a sharp tap and an angry look, but Edward-John is too discomfited to go on for much longer. 'But I weary my young cousin,' he says, trying to get his dignity back. 'May I just present to you, Captain William, this humble volume of my collected sermons?' And then he bows ceremoniously. Thomas jumps up, but hardly seems to know what to do with the book once he has it in his hand.

'Well, well, well,' he says, 'this is—'

'Very weighty,' interrupts Jane, picking up the dish of eggs and the serving spoon and walking around the back of the table.

'Perhaps grace first?' suggests Edward-John.

Normally Mr Austen mutters a perfunctory, one-sentence grace before meals, so Jane does not sit down again, but holds the spoonful of eggs poised over Augusta's plate. I am embarrassed and worried about Thomas, but I have to choke back a giggle at the expression on Jane's face as Edward-John's grace wanders on and on, going from giving thanks to God for the food that not one of us has yet touched to giving thanks to God who sent an angel to help us in our hour of peril this morning. Charles gives a great snort and then covers his face rapidly with a grubby handkerchief when Edward-John mentions the 'angel', and I can't help glancing at Thomas. His brown eyes are dancing with amusement, and I feel myself getting very red when I realize that he has seen me looking at him.

Mrs Austen, I see with satisfaction, when we are all eating our buttered eggs – and consoling ourselves, as Jane whispers in my ear, with the thought that Augusta has the coldest eggs of all – Mrs Austen does not like either of them. Augusta is very haughty and condescending, and Edward-John sounds a false flattering note, admiring all the battered out-of-fashion furniture in the parlour, but giving an occasional sly glance at his wife that shows that he does not mean his praise.

I keep wondering what will happen after breakfast. The meal is an agony to me. I have no appetite for the food and every time I look up I can see Augusta looking at me with her pale eyes which are so like boiled gooseberries that I will never again eat that fruit without thinking of her.

After breakfast will come the moment, I keep thinking to myself, and I wish that Charles will go on eating for a long time. However, he has stopped eating now and is telling Thomas all about his ambitions. Even in the middle of my misery I think that Thomas is being very nice to him. Mrs Austen rises to her feet and starts loading dishes rapidly on to a tray, obviously making sure that Edward-John doesn't start on another long prayer.

And then Augusta clears her throat.

'Ahem!' It is so loud that everyone stops and looks at her with interest.

She smiles around, enjoying the moment, and then looks at me, her eyes as hard as glass.

She has left it too long though. Before she can speak, Thomas gets to his feet with easy grace and bows to Mrs Austen.

'I wonder, ma'am, if I might invite your niece to take a short walk with me. It's such a fine day—'

'It's raining,' Charles tells him bluntly.

'Just a mizzle! My favourite weather! When you're a sailor on my ship and you've spent as much time in the East Indies as I,' he tells the delighted Charles, 'then you'll love our English mists.' Thomas gives a half-glance towards the window and then holds out his arm to me. I take it. I am still very embarrassed about that letter, but anything is better than staying and having Augusta tell me that no matter what anyone says, she and Edward-John, as my guardian, are determined to send me to that boarding school, which has no holidays and where the girls are locked in their dormitories every night.

'I'll run and get your cloak and your bonnet.' Jane thrusts the dish she is holding at Charles, who, with a quick glance at the back of his mother's head, proceeds to lick the remains of the eggs from its sides.

And then we are outside and the hall door is closed on the rest of the family.

But still I can say nothing.

I know that I am on the verge of tears and think it is better not to risk making any polite remarks about the weather or enquiries about his journey.

'What's the matter, Jenny? Don't you like the rain? Let's walk under the trees here. Your bonnet will remain quite dry.'

I tell him that the rain is nothing and I try to make my voice ordinary, but even I can hear how it shakes.

'Take my arm,' he says after a minute. 'It's slippery here with the wet moss on these paths.'

I take his arm and begin to feel better. The damp air is fresh and clean and perfumed by the brilliantly white lilies of the valley that edge the path.

'I got your letter. Why were you so angry with me?' His face is gentle but puzzled. 'Did you think it was terribly rude of me to go away from the ball without telling you where I was going? I should have really, but I was so angry and so ashamed of my men. I don't know whether you saw my sergeant come into the ballroom, looking for me. I was puzzled when I noticed him talking to Lieutenant Price and then I thought I'd better see what he wanted. He came to tell me that the boat crew were turning my ship into a drinking shop, with all sorts of terrible behaviour going on. I just wanted to sort it out straight away before anyone heard of the disgrace to the *Bonaventure*.'

'What?!' I'm sure I shriek the word before telling him the whole story of how I thought he was angry with me and had written to Augusta with the story of me in the midnight streets of Southampton.

'What!' His exclamation is even louder than mine, so I tell him quickly that now I know that it was Lady Portsmouth who wrote to Augusta. I tell him all about Augusta's letter and about the boarding school in Bristol where there are no holidays and the girls are all locked into their dormitories at night.

His eyes become very black and he begins to get so angry with Augusta that to distract him I say, 'I wish I had asked Lieutenant Price. He could have told me where you'd gone, and then I would not have suspected you of writing that letter.' (At least, I think that I might not have, though I don't think I could have guessed that Lady Portsmouth knew my secret.)

Thomas smiles then and he looks a little less angry.

'Lieutenant Price,' he says, 'bless him – he would never have told you. This was a disgraceful thing to happen to our ship. He wanted to go himself, but I wouldn't permit that. It was the business of the captain to sort this matter out.'

I ask him what he did to the boat crew, and no sooner is the question out of my mouth than I'm sorry that I asked it. I had to shut my ears to Frank's tales of floggings, but Thomas just says casually, 'I stood over them for three days while they were on their hands and knees scrubbing everything that could be scrubbed and polishing everything that could be polished. I don't think they'll try that again in a hurry. Of course it was very boring for me, but it gave me a lot of time for thinking . . .'

He pauses for a moment and then adds, 'For thinking of you.'

I say nothing – just fix my eyes on the raindrops glistening on the glossy green of a harts-tongue fern under the rhododendron bush. In the distance a cuckoo calls, and seconds later another replies.

'Don't you want to know what I was thinking?' His voice is very low and very soft, but I feel it vibrate within me.

'Yes,' I say at last. He has stopped walking and I stop

too. Just above our heads a tiny wren begins a piercingly sweet song. I lift my head to see it, and look straight into Thomas's face. The air of calm authority seems to have gone from it, and his eyes are gentle and pleading. I remember Eliza's words of advice. I cannot fail him now. Quickly I take off my bonnet. I feel that the deep rim of it forms a barrier between us. Now our faces are quite close, his bending over mine. I no longer hear the birdsong, just the sound of us both breathing in unison.

'What I was thinking was that I was in love with you,' he says in a voice that is barely audible to me. 'I've been in love with you, I think, ever since that night when I met you at Southampton. There you were, a timid young girl, out by yourself at midnight in streets where no man would go without a sword or a pistol. You were terrified, and yet you kept going because you were determined to get help for your cousin. All the time that I was at sea I could not get you out of my head. I loved you then, and when we met again I loved you even more. When you told me how you nearly died, it frightened me. I realized then that I could not live without you. I felt that I would never be happy unless you were with me.'

Thomas holds out his hand and I put my damp, cold one in his and am glad that this time no glove comes between us and that I can feel his warmth.

'And what about you?' He is smiling now. Even in the dim light under the trees I feel that he can, indeed, read my answer in my eyes.

'I love you too.' I'm pleased to hear how steady my

voice sounds. 'I love you and I think I too have loved you since we met in Southampton and you rescued me.'

I force myself to go on. 'And I love you because you are kind and gentle and noble and brave, and I would like to spend the rest of my life with you.'

I bend down and pick a small pale primrose and before I straighten up I put it to my lips, and then I hand it to him. He puts it to his own lips and sticks it in his buttonhole. And then he takes me in his arms.

'Will you marry me, Jenny?' he says, and his lips are almost touching my ear.

I turn my head so that my lips are at his ear, but when I speak the words 'I will marry you', they come out clear and confident.

And then his lips come down on mine and our kiss lasts for a long time.

Eventually we walk on and everything is even more exciting than a ball, because it is just the two of us and we are talking about our future.

We will get married in June – that's the plan. A June wedding, and I will wear roses in my hair.

And I will visit his uncle and his sister.

They will love me, Thomas says. He has told them all about me, and they are looking forward to my visit.

And he will show me his ship at Southampton. He tells me all about it and about the new sails that he has ordered.

And by the time we come back indoors, it is almost

time for dinner. Frank and John Portal are there, talking to Edward-John about the sport that they had in the woods at Laverstoke House. Augusta gives me a long look, but I just look at Thomas. Suddenly I have lost all fear of my sister-in-law.

Mrs Austen and Cassandra are looking at me too – perhaps waiting for something to be said.

We have it all planned though. Thomas is going to ask my uncle for my hand. That is the way it is going to be done. We have discussed it – Thomas and I – and we feel that will be best. Edward-John will be a little in awe of his uncle, who has been a clergyman for so long.

Although I want everyone to know about us, to know that Thomas and I will be getting married, and it seems a long time to wait until tomorrow morning when Mr Austen and Henry will arrive, still we have our whole lives ahead of us.

'Ahem! Jenny,' says Augusta.

But at the same moment Mrs Austen says, 'Jenny dear, run upstairs and change your shoes and stockings. We don't want you to catch cold.'

'I'll go with her,' says Jane quickly.

We both escape and run up the stairs.

'Well?' says Jane as soon as the door is safely closed behind us.

'Yes!' I say.

Sunday, 10 April 1791

It is six o'clock of the morning. I am still dressed in my nightcap and wrapper, but I have got out of bed and put some more wood on our fire. There is just enough light from the flames for me to see the words that I write.

These are the last pages in my journal. They will be happy pages. I'm glad of that, because it began sadly and I want it to end joyfully.

Thomas loves me.

He loves me and he wants to marry me.

And no one except Jane knows about it yet.

But soon after breakfast everyone will know about the splendid future in front of me.

'Don't worry about anything. Everything will be fine. I have a very high opinion of your uncle and your aunt is a woman of great common sense – I like the way she got Augusta and Edward-John out of our way for the whole evening by proposing a visit to the Lefroys.' Thomas said this to me last night before going up to share Frank's bedroom for the night. The guest room had to be given over to Augusta and Edward-John, but Frank was very pleased to be able to offer Henry's bed to a naval officer. He and Charles had even disappeared upstairs to make sure that everything was 'shipshape', as he put it, so there was no one on the stairs at the time when Thomas kissed me goodnight.

'I've an idea,' said Jane when we were talking in bed last night. 'Your Thomas has to go on his voyage to the East Indies and you will miss him, so you will need diversion. When the pupils are on their holidays, we'll ask Mama to take us both to Bath for a little break. We can stay with her rich brother, my Uncle Leigh-Perrot. Bath is full of romance. And of course, since you'll be a betrothed young lady, you'll be able to find me a fine young beau so that I can become engaged also. We'll have a great time at Bath, going to balls and private parties and even perhaps getting some new gowns made.'

I assured her that she would be the heroine of the next story about Jane and Jenny and she remarked: 'If I am to be the heroine, something will throw a hero in my way. I'm sure I'll get plenty of material for a new novel out of it all.'

'I think secretly you are more interested in writing novels than in finding a young man, Jane.' I smiled fondly at my cousin.

Jane wasn't listening. She had a thoughtful look on her face. She took her writing desk out of the drawer, set it on the table, and then she dipped her quill in the inkhorn.

'What are you writing now?' I asked, going across

to look over her shoulder. Jane is not like me: her writing is never private.

'I'm writing a happy ending,' said Jane with great seriousness. 'I have decided what every good novel needs is a happy ending and this one will probably come in useful for me one day. I thought it up while you were talking about Thomas and about how happy you are feeling. I want to put it down before I forget it.' She wrote for a moment and then said, 'Listen to this.'

She picked up her paper and dramatically read aloud:

'The joy, the gratitude, the exquisite delight may be imagined. Her doubts and worries had all disappeared; she was really in danger of becoming too happy for security. What had she left to wish for? Nothing! In the gayest and happiest spirits, she looked forward to spending the rest of her days by the side of the man whom she had loved for so long.'

'Loved for so long?' I queried.

'Well, for at least three weeks,' said Jane, and after we had finished laughing we stayed awake for a long time, planning what we would do at Bath.

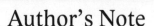

Author's Note

Whenever I finish reading a novel about a person who really existed, one of the first questions in my mind, before I close the book, is always: *How much of this is true?*

Although a lot is known about Jane Austen as a woman, not much is known about her as a teenager so I had to use my imagination to portray her. However, luckily her family did keep a number of the stories that she scribbled in her notebooks between the ages of thirteen and eighteen so I could get an impression from them of what she was like. I thought she seemed very clever, very witty, but above all I felt that she was enormous fun – quite wild – and would be someone who was great to have as a friend.

Very little indeed is known about Jenny – and I must confess here I am guilty of changing two things. One is that her name was really Jane Cooper, but because I couldn't have two Janes I changed her name to Jenny, a common pet-name form of Jane at the time. As well as that, I made her younger than she really was so that she and Jane were nearer in age, and I changed the year that both she and Jane were at Mrs Cawley's school in Southampton.

What we do know about Jenny (Jane Cooper) is that she was an orphan (with no family other than one brother) who lived with the Austen family at Steventon in the year in which she met Captain Thomas Williams (later Sir Thomas Williams, which turned Jenny into Lady Williams). They fell instantly in love with each other, were engaged three weeks after their first meeting (a real whirlwind romance!) and were married at Steventon later in the year. Jane and Cassandra were her bridesmaids.

When Mr Austen retired, his furniture was put up for sale at an auction, and one of the items in the barn at Steventon was 'a set of theatrical screens'. We know from a letter sent by Eliza to a cousin in Kent that Jenny was very pretty and acted opposite Henry in one of the plays put on in the barn.

We also know that Jenny is the one who was brave enough, against

CORA HARRISON fell in love with Jane Austen when she first read *Pride and Prejudice* at the age of twelve. She has published many novels for children and adults. She and her husband live on a small farm in the west of Ireland with a very large and rather lunatic German shepherd dog called Oscar and a very small white cat called Polly.

Mrs Cawley's orders, to smuggle out a letter from the school informing Mrs Austen that Jane was terribly ill and that by doing this, she is considered to have saved Jane's life.

All the neighbours, friends and relations and people in the village — and Mr Austen's pupils — that I mention in the book, like the Chutes at the Vyne, the Biggs at Manydown House, and the Portsmouths, were real people. Jane did have a handicapped brother, called George, who did not live with the family but was boarded out with a villager. Later in life she spoke of being able 'to talk on her fingers' — in other words, she had learned sign language. And as far as can be ascertained, Nanny Littleworth was foster-mother to all the young Austens.

For the story and the characters of the people, I suppose my imagination was triggered by the six novels that Jane Austen wrote. I love the balls and the snippets of conversation as they move down the sets in the dances as described in those books, and I am a great fan of the gowns they wore then — so much more elegant and flattering than the later Victorian dresses. When I wrote the description of Jenny's first ball, I was remembering Catherine at the Assembly Rooms in Bath in *Northanger Abbey* and how she met a young man there, fell in love, and by the end of the book he had proposed marriage to her. Captain Williams is like some of Jane Austen's heroes — a bit of a Mr Darcy from *Pride and Prejudice*, or perhaps a Captain Wentworth from *Persuasion*. Jenny's preaching brother (loathed by Jane Austen) is a bit like Mr Collins in *Pride and Prejudice*, and his wife is rather modelled on Mrs Elton in *Emma*.

Mrs Austen and Eliza were both prolific letter-writers, and it is from their letters that I got an impression of their characters. They are both great favourites of mine. No letters from Jenny (Jane Cooper) survive, and in some ways perhaps that is good because now she is mine — my own creation, and I can imagine her emerging from a sad time of her life after the death of both parents into the fun and glamour of balls and cousinly chats and then falling madly in love and being loved in return by the handsome Captain Williams.

The sort of wonderful year that people remember for the rest of their lives!